Cases and Readings

for use with

Cost Management

A Strategic Emphasis

Third Edition

Edward J. Blocher
University of North Carolina – Chapel Hill

Kung H. Chen
University of Nebraska

Gary Cokins, CPIM
SAS / Worldwide Strategy

Thomas W. Lin
University of Southern California

w/D

McGraw-Hill Irwin

Boston Burr Ridge, IL Dubuque, IA Madison, WI New York San Francisco St. Louis Bangkok Bogotá Caracas Kuala Lumpur Lisbon London Madrid Mexico City Milan Montreal New Delhi Santiago Seoul Singapore Sydney Taipei Toronto

McGraw-Hill Irwin

Cases and Readings for use with
COST MANAGEMENT: A STRATEGIC EMPHASIS
Blocher / Chen / Cokins / Lin

Published by McGraw-Hill/Irwin, an imprint of The McGraw-Hill Companies, Inc., 1221 Avenue of the Americas, New York, NY 10020.

1 2 3 4 5 6 7 8 9 0 QPD/QPD 0 9 8 7 6 5 4

ISBN 0-07-283569-9

www.mhhe.com

The McGraw-Hill Companies

Preface

To extend the teaching materials of *Cost Management: A Strategic Emphasis*, this *Cases and Readings Manual* provides additional cases and articles for each chapter. The cases and articles are an important part of the text and have the same teaching objectives. The problem material in the text includes short cases and exercises, while this casebook provides longer cases and articles to facilitate more extensive discussion and analysis.

Of special note in the 3rd edition is the inclusion of two new cases that utilize the ABC costing system (Oros Quick ® Software) from SAS Institute. One of the cases is an extension of a case used in prior editions, Blue Ridge Manufacturing Company Case, and another is specially written for the 3rd edition—The Sunny View Diary Farm Case. Both of the cases can be found in Chapter 5 and the Oros Quick ® software is available for student download at www.mhhe.com/blocher3e. Instuctors: Please see the Instructor's Resource Guide for guidance on how to utilize these cases.

We feel that cases serve a very important role in the cost management course. We know of many faculty who use cases from a variety of sources to supplement the text they are using. We have provided case materials in this manual for easier access, greater convenience, and lower overall cost to the instructor and student.

Using cases has two important benefits. First, the use of a case requires the student to develop analytical skills by organizing the unstructured information in the case, devising appropriate analyses, and drawing appropriate conclusions. Second, the cases permit a more thorough strategic analysis of a given firm than would be possible with a problem or exercise. With a richer amount of information about the case firm and its environment, the student can more effectively apply the concepts of strategy and competitive advantage explained in chapter 2: Strategic Analysis and Strategic Cost Management.

Each of the cases can be used as an exercise in competitive analysis to set the stage for the decision problem in the case, whatever that might be. A firm facing a lease-or-buy decision will want to assess the strategic, competitive situation of the firm before making the decision. Similarly, a firm considering the outsourcing of a department or activity will want to begin the analysis with an assessment of the strategic issues facing the firm, and then make their decision with these issues in mind. In this way, the cases can be used to effectively put each decision problem in a strategic context. Rather than to make a cost calculation and then "consider the qualitative factors," which can be done with problems and exercises, the case more readily allows an approach in which the strategic issues are considered first and are an integral part of the solution of the case.

Additionally, one or two articles are included for each chapter to provide an opportunity for more in-depth coverage. We have included discussion questions for each article. Some of the articles are examples of how actual firms have implemented the cost management methods explained in the chapter. These scenarios show some of the implementation issues that arise in practical situations. Other articles report the results of surveys, which provide perspective for how the cost management methods are used in practice. Others have a technical focus, and provide an opportunity to look more closely at the methods explained in the chapter and on the effects of using these methods.

We hope you will find these cases and readings helpful. We welcome feedback from students and instructors.

Edward J. Blocher
Kung H. Chen
Gary Cokins
Thomas W. Lin

Acknowledgments

The following materials have been reprinted with permission from the **Institute of Management Accountants** (© Copyright by Institute of Management Accountants, Montvale, NJ):

Management Accounting

Robin Cooper and Regine Slagmulder, "Integrating Activity-Based Costing and the Theory of "Constraints," February 1999

Jack Bailes, James Nielsen, Stephen Lawton, "How Forest Product Companies Analyze Capital Budgets," October 1998.

Chee W. Chow, Kamal M. Haddad, James E. Williamson, "Applying the Balanced Scorecard to Small Companies," August 1997.

Steve Coburn, Hugh Grove, Tom Cook, "How ABC was Used in Capital Budgeting," May 1997. Priscilla

Nick Fera, "Using Shareholder Value to Evaluate Strategic Choice," November 1997.

Robert S. Kaplan, Dan Weiss, Eyal Desheh, "Transfer Pricing with ABC," May 1997.

Gerald H. Lander, Mohamed E. Bayou, "Does ROI Apply to Robotic Factories?".

Peter J. Leitner, "Beyond the Numbers," May 1998.

Kenneth A. Merchant, "How Challenging Should Profit Budget Targets Be?"

Adel M. Novin, "How to Find the Right Bases and Rates," March 1992.

George Schmelze, Rolf Geier, Thomas El Buttross, "Target Costing at ITT Automotive," December 1996.

Bonnie P. Stivers, Teresa Joyce Covin, Nancy Green Hall, Steve W. Smalt, "How Nonfinancial Performance Measures are Used," February 1998.

Dan W. Swenson, "Managing Costs Through Complexity Reduction at Carrier Corporation," April 1998.

Robert N. West, Amy N. Snyder, "How to Set Up a Budgeting and Planning System," January 1997.

Management Accounting Quarterly

Thomas L. Burton and John D MacArthur, "Activity Based Costing and Predatory Pricing: The Case of the Petroleum Retail Industry," Spring 2003

Russell F. Briner, Mark Alford, and JoAnne Noble, "Activity Based Costing for State and Local Governments," Spring 2003

Bea Chiang, "Activity Based Benchmarking and Process Management – Managing the Case of Cardiac Surgery," Fall 2002

Anthony J. Hayzen, James M. Reeve, "Examining the Relationships in Productivity Accounting," Summer 2000.

David Johnsen, Parvez Sopariwala, "Standard Costing is Alive and Well at Parker Brass," Winter 2000.

Priscilla O'Clock and Kevin Devine, "The Role of Strategy and Culture in the Performance Evaluation of International Strategic Business Units," Winter 2003

Harper A. Roehm, Larry Weinstein, Joseph F. Castellano, "Management Control Systems: How SPC Enhances Budgeting and Standard Costing," Fall 2000.

William W. Stammerjohan, "Better Information Through the Marriage of ABC and Traditional Standard Costing Techniques," Fall 2001

Audrey G. Taylor and Savya Rafai, "Strategic Budgeting: A Case Study and Proposed Framework," Fall 2003

Lakshmi U. Tatikonda, and Rao J. Tatikonda, "Activity Based Costing for Higher Education Institutions," Fall 2001

Kennard T. Wing, "Using Enhanced Cost Models in Variance Analysis for Better Control and Decision Making," Winter 2000.

Strategic Finance

Terrell L. Carter, Ali Ml Sedghat, Thomas D. Williams, "How ABC Changed the Post Office," February 1998.

C.S. Kulesza, Keith Russell, Gary H. Siegel, "Counting More, Counting Less," September 1999.

Gregory T. Lucier, Sridhar Seshadri, "GE Takes Six Sigma Beyond the Bottom Line," May 2001.

Joseph A. Ness, Michael J. Schroeck, Rick A. Letendre, Willmar J. Douglas, "The Role of ABM in Measuring Customer Value: Parts I and II," March and April 2001.

Jon Scheumann, "Why Isn't the Controller Having More Impact?" April 1999.

Gary Siegel, James E. Sorensen, and Sandra b. Richtermeyer, "Are You a Business Partner?" Parts 1 and 2, September and October 2003

Richard H. Snyder, "How I Reengineered a Small Business," May 1999.

Nancy Thurley Hill, Kevin T. Stevens, "Structuring Compensation to Achieve Better Financial Results," March 2001.

Ann Triplett, Jon Scheumann, "Managing Shared Services with ABM," February 2000.

Paul B. Weiss, "Buy or Lease" November 2003

Cases from Management Accounting in Practice

Volume 1 (1985): The Pump Division

Volume 2 (1986): The Atlantic City Casino , Analysis of the Accounting Function; Polymer Products Company

Volume 4 (1987): Industrial Chemical Company

Volume 5 (1989): The Rossford Plant, The United L/N Plant

Volume 6 (1992): Superior Valve Company

Volume 7 (1992): Toll Revenue Sharing

Volume 8 (1992): California Illini Manufacturing

Volumes 10/11 (1997): East River Manufacturing

Volume 12 (1998): Brookwood Medical Center, Precision System Inc.

Volume 14 (1998): OutSource, Inc., Wellesley Paint

Volume 15 (2000): Mercedes-Benz All Activity Vehicle (AAV)

The following materials have been reprinted with permission from the **American Accounting Association**:

Horizons

Wilton L. Accola, "Assessing Risk and Uncertainty in New Technology Investments," September 1994.

Carole B. Cheatham, Leo R. Cheatham, "Redesigning Cost Systems: Is Standard Costing Obsolete?" December 1996.

Robert S. Kaplan, David P. Norton, "Transforming the Balanced Scorecard from Performance Measurement to Strategic Management: Part 1," March 2001.

Robert E. Malcolm, "Overhead Control Implications of Activity Costing," December 1991.

Issues in Accounting Education

Ramji Balakrishnan, Utpal Bhattacharya, "Ace Company (B): The Option Value of Waiting and Capital Budgeting," Fall 1997.

Linda Smith Bamber and K. E. Hughes II, "Activity Based Costing in the Service Sector: The Buckeye National Bank," August 2001

Peter C. Brewer, Robert J. Campbell, and Richard H. McClure, "Wilson Electronics (A) and (B): An ABC Capstone Experience," August 2000

Robert Capettini, C.W. Chow, J.E. Williamson, "Instructional Case: The Proper Use of Feedback Information," Spring 1992.

Chee W. Chow, "Instructional Case: Vincent's Cappuccino Express – A Teaching Case to Help Students Master Basic Cost Terms and Concepts Through Interactive Learning," Spring 1995.

Chee W. Chow, Yuhchang, Dennis F. Togo, "Ace Company: A Case for Incorporating Competitive Consideration into Teaching of Capital Budgeting," Fall 1995.

Dean Crawford, Eleanor G. Henry, "Budgeting and Performance Evaluation at the Berkshire Toy Company," May 2000.

Vijay Govindarajan, John K. Shank, "Profit Variance Analysis: A Strategic Focus," Fall 1989.

Julie H. Hertenstein, "Component Technologies, Inc.: Adding Flexconnex Capacity," May 2000.

Alison Hubbard Ashton, Robert H. Ashton, Laureen Maines, "Instructional Case: General Medical Center -- Evaluation of Diagnostic Imaging Equipment," November 1998.

Jack M. Ruhl, Jerry G. Kreuze, "Startup, Inc.: Linking Financial Accounting, Managerial Accounting, and Strategic Management," Fall 1997.

George J. Staubus, "The Case of the Almost Identical Twins," Spring 1993.

Additional Acknowledgements:

Robert J. Bowlby, "How Boeing Tracks Costs A to Z," *The Financial Executive*. Reprinted with permission.

David A. Kunz, Keith A. Russell, "Midwest Petro-Chemical Company," Institute of Management Accountants, 1996. Used with permission.

Joseph San Miguel, "Target Costing," "Emerson Electric Company," "Dallas Consulting Group" . Reprinted with permission.

Table of Contents

Chapter 1
Cost Management and Strategy: An Overview

Cases

1-1 Critical Success Factors
1-2 Contemporary Management Techniques
1-3 Pricing
1-4 Selected Ethics Cases

Readings

"Are You a Business Partner?"
This article is based on a interviews of 100 accountants who have made the transition to business partner. For firms such as McDonalds, Trane, and Boeing, they explain the transition from traditional accountant to accountant as business partner. The study is a follow-up to the 1995-1999 research by the same authors, shown below in "Counting More, Counting Less."

Discussion Questions
1. What are the key findings of the recent research of 100 accountants, now business partners?
2. What are the implications of these findings for the education and training of management accountants?

"Counting More, Counting Less"
This article is a survey to update the 1995 Practice Analysis of Management Accounting. The highlights of the survey include an improved image of management accounting, a continued focus to forward-looking, strategic types of tasks, and more of a shift to business partnership in contrast to financial reporting only.

Discussion Questions:
1. What are the key findings of the Practice Analysis of Management Accounting?
2. What are the implications of these findings for the education and training of management accountants?

"Practice Analysis: Skills Needed for Entry-Level Management Accounting Positions"
This article is based on the research cited in the above to readings. It sets out the implications for education of entry level management accountants.

Discussion Questions:
1. What are the key skills needed for entry-level management accountants?
2. How do you think these skills are best obtained?

Cases

Cost Management and Strategy: An Overview

1-1. Critical Success Factors

Kirsten Malon has found a way to profitably exploit her computer know-how. She has started a firm that offers consulting services for computer and software repair and analysis. Most of her customers have purchased computers or software systems with little vendor support and need help in installing and using the systems effectively. Kirsten has expanded her business recently to include 25 technicians besides herself, and her client base has grown to over 1,900. Many of these clients are on a retainer arrangement (a fixed fee per month which guarantees access to a certain number of hours of technician time) to stabilize her cash flow. With the success of the business, Kirsten is now thinking about beginning a related business which would publish books and newsletters on computer and software issues.

REQUIRED:

What are the critical success factors likely to be for Kirsten's business, now and into the future? What cost management information is she likely to need: management planning and decision making, management and operational control, or product and service costing, and why?

1-2. Contemporary Management Techniques

DeLight Inc., is a large manufacturer of lighting fixtures for both wholesalers and electrical contractors. An important aspect of the business with electrical contractors is Delight's ability to develop product leadership through innovation, quality, and service. In contrast, in the wholesale business, Delight competes primarily on the basis of lowest price. DeLight has prospered in the recent five years because of its careful attention to developing and maintaining a sustainable competitive advantage in each of its markets.

REQUIRED:

Which of the ten types of contemporary management techniques does DeLight probably use? Explain your answer.

1-3. Ethics, Pricing

AeroSpace Inc. is a manufacturer of airplane parts and engines for a variety of military as well as civilian aircraft. Though there are many commercial customers for most of the company's products, the U.S. government is the only buyer of the firm's rocket engines. Because AeroSpace is the sole provider of the engines, the government buys the engines at a price equal to cost plus a percent markup.

The cost system in place at AeroSpace is under review by top management, with the objective of developing a system which will provide more accurate and more timely cost management information.

At the current phase of the study of the cost system, it is now apparent that the new system, while more accurate and timely, will result in lower costs being assigned to the rocket engines and higher costs being assigned to the firm's other products. Apparently, the current (less accurate) cost system has over-costed the engines and under-costed the other products. On hearing of this, top management has decided to scrap the plans for the new cost system, because the rocket engine business with the government is a significant part of AeroSpace's business, and the reduced cost will reduce the price and thus the profits for this part of AeroSpace's business.

REQUIRED:

As a staff cost analyst on the cost review project, how do you see your responsibility when you hear of the decision of top management to cancel the plans for the new cost system?

1-4. Selected Ethics Cases

After his first two years at Bronson Beverages (BB), a publicly held wholesaler of beers and wines, Jim Best has advanced to a senior cost analyst position with a very good salary.

REQUIRED:

For each of the following situations Jim will face in the coming year, indicate how you see his responsibility, and how he should respond.

1. Jim learns that a significant portion of the firm's beer inventory has passed its shelf life and by local ordinance and company policy, should be destroyed. Because of concern about the effect on profits and his bonus, the chief operating officer decides that the beer should be sold anyway.
2. As part of his regular duties, Jim reviews BB's financial statements for inconsistencies and errors. While reviewing the recent report, Jim notices that non-trade accounts receivable (note: non-trade receivables arise from non-operating events, such as a loan to an employee, customer, etc; trade receivables arise from sales on credit) have increased sharply over the prior year. Upon inquiry, Jim finds out that the firm is lending money to one of its customers so that it can make purchases from BB. Jim knows that in his state, beer and wine purchases must be paid for in cash, by state law. Jim wonders if the treatment of the loan as a non-trade receivable is OK, or if it should be classified as a trade receivable?
3. Jim learns that BB has just been granted the franchise to sell a popular new line of custom-brewed beers. The franchise will improve BB's sales and profits substantially, and should mean a significant boost to BB's share price. Jim knows that, until the news of the franchise is made public, he is restricted by the SEC from using this insider information to trade in BB's shares and make unfair profits as a result. That evening, Jim and his wife have dinner with some friends, and one of them says she has heard there are some good things going on at BB, and asks Jim to comment. What should Jim say?
4. Jim is analyzing the sales and cost of sales in specialty wines when he discovers that one of the firm's customers has greatly increased purchases in this, the last month of the firm's fiscal year. Jim goes to talk to the salesperson for this customer to offer his congratulations. The salesperson says that he has simply shipped in advance the customer's order for the following month, so that it would appear on the current year's financial report. This tactic would help the salesperson meet his sales target and would also improve BB's sales and profits for the current year. The salesperson says there is a small chance that the

customer will reject the shipment and send it back, but then says, "We will worry about that if it happens."

5. Working late one night, Jim notices that one of the top marketing executives has come into the office and is removing a box full of office supplies. He says in a joking manner to Jim as he leaves, "BB won't miss this stuff, and I really need it for my other business."

Readings

ARE YOU A BUSINESS PARTNER?

By Gary Siegel, James E. Sorensen, and Sandra B. Richtermeyer

PART I

Business partners help run businesses. They are consulted on all major decisions. They are proactive with information, are focused on improving business processes, and are team leaders.

Their work is exciting, and they are enthusiastic about what they do. The financial professionals who have become business partners say they are thriving since they added this dimension to their work.

What is a business partner? It's difficult to define a business partner in two or three sentences because the work they do requires a variety of skills, encompasses several disciplines, and impacts the organization in various ways. Are they accountants? In one sense, you could say that business partners are accountants. They still hold fiduciary responsibility and carry out all of the traditional accounting functions. They just do it a lot faster and with a lot fewer people than they used to. But they definitely do more than accounting. They are involved in strategic planning, process improvement, team building, and a host of other activities.

Textbooks tell us that management accountants do scorekeeping, attention directing (for example, alerting management to problems with the management control system and established policies and procedures), and problem solving. Business partners do very little scorekeeping and a lot more problem solving. But they also do more than solve problems.

Business partners have transformed themselves from accountants to superaccountants—from accounting specialists to business generalists. Their perspective has changed. They still do the accounting work but don't see it as their mission. Their mission is business success and performance excellence. They focus on running the business, and accounting is a vehicle to improve performance and help people make better decisions.

So are these superaccountants still accountants? They'll tell you, no. They call themselves business partners. Their titles don't include the "A" word. Sure, if we point out to them that they are a CMA, CFM, or CPA, they will say, "Yes, we earned those credentials, but we don't do accounting." And, yes, they still have to know their debits and credits. But as a business partner at UPS told us, "Our business is delivering packages, not debits and credits."

Making the transition. They have transformed into business partners. They perceive themselves differently, and the people they work with see them differently. But do their colleagues refer to them as business partners? A controller at McDonald's explains:

We probably get called everything in the book—I hope all of it good. I don't know if they call us business partners or not. I hope they would. If you asked them a question about me or some of the other folks in accounting, I would hope they would say, "He is much more than just an accountant." If you asked them, "What types of things does this person do?," they will talk about strategic plans, they will talk about evaluations, they will talk about impact on the business, having an influence on—in my case—individual brands, striving for better business results. All these things are driven around the business, not debits and credits, not anything that is in a traditional accounting realm. Whether they call us a business partner or not, we are doing a lot more than traditional accounting.

Again, are they accountants? Technically, yes. But substantively, no. These financial professionals do much more than traditional accounting. They do decision support, but they are beyond decision support. They are business analysts, but they do more than simply analyze. They are valued for their business savvy and financial insight. They are focused on improving business processes. Their work is light years away from the work traditional accountants did as recently as 15-20 years ago.

Scope of change. Accountants' work had been pretty constant from the development of double entry bookkeeping in 1492, but it took a dramatic turn with the development of high-speed computers in the 1960s and again with the widespread diffusion of electronic spreadsheets in the early 1980s. The old accountant is dead or dying. Long live the new accountant! We aren't the same as we were in 1985 or even 1995, which should be a wakeup call to leaders in the profession, business school educators, and corporate executives.

Traditional accountants. To appreciate what a business partner does, let's contrast their role with the role of traditional accountants. Historically, accountants collected and manipulated data, manually worked spreadsheets, checked expense reports, produced inventory reports and standardized financial statements, complied with federal and local tax laws, prepared and maintained the budget, handled the treasury function, worked with outside auditors, held fiduciary responsibility for the company's assets,

"Yes, I'm a Business Partner. You have to know the business. You have to have some credibility, and you have to push your way into things. I have always done that. You have to get some understanding. This is a strongly engineering- and operations oriented company. You have to get to know the business and understand it and not be afraid to push outside of your sphere and then show the link. You just have to push that."— A controller at Trane

made sure that bills were paid and receivables collected, and were available to answer accounting- or tax-related questions. They were the keepers of financial records, preparers of financial reports, treasury officers, internal auditors, and compliance and fiduciary agents. They provided a vital service to their organizations, but they weren't central to running the business. In organization charts, accounting was off to the side—it was a staff function that supported line managers.

Accountants worked mainly with other accountants on accounting projects, such as cost reports, payables, yearend closings, and inventory. They worked in their own world, physically and psychologically isolated from the people who were running the business. In the actual work environment, there were "departments." Accountants worked in the accounting department, but the people running the business worked in other departments. This doesn't imply that accountants had no interaction with other people in the organization. They did. But the accountant's focus was on "doing the accounting": getting the report out on time, doing the payroll, working on the budget. The focus of the line people was on "running the business." Accountants weren't expected to be participants in this.

Accountants were psychologically distant as well. They were seen as numbers crunchers, bookkeepers, and bean counters. Because they prepared and enforced the budgets, they were the corporate cops, the people who could make a line manager's life miserable. They were the naysayers. They were seen as obstacles, not enablers. In the course of interviewing dozens of accountants over the past several years, we have heard many stories about their purposely being kept out of the decision making process. They simply weren't consulted about upcoming decisions involving expenditures. They learned about decisions only after they were made. Why? A frequent explanation is that they were seen as protectors of the budget—the guys (there were few women accountants in the old days) who always said no. So why bother asking?

Accountants were valued for the information system they maintained and the reports they provided. But they weren't valued for their interpretation of the information or the advice they could give on a business question. This implies that accountants weren't considered "big picture" people. They were seen as too focused on the numbers. The implication is that they really didn't sufficiently understand the complexities and nuances of the business, so few people sought their opinions.

Business partners. Then the business world changed. Manual spreadsheets disappeared, and management accountants no longer had to spend hours calculating and checking calculations. Bureaucracies were flattened. Company precedents were questioned. Shared services emerged. Technology made a quantum leap. Continuous improvement became a reality.

As accountants were liberated from the time-consuming, mechanical aspects of accounting, they had to move from the operational level in organizations to the strategic level for the profession to survive and remain relevant. Their knowledge of basic financial tools wasn't sufficient to keep them relevant; they had to enhance their knowledge and acquire advanced financial tools. In many companies, financial professionals used their freed-up time to create a new role for themselves as business partners, which required them to become generalists. Those who have successfully made the switch tell us that there are some lingering jokes about "bean counters" in their organizations, but that isn't how they are perceived anymore. Now they are considered proactive and available and are sought-after participants in the decision making process. They are seen as valued team members and enablers. As another business partner at McDonald's said, "We are not asked when the project is almost done to come out here and run some numbers; we are invited early on."

The physical and psychological isolation has broken down. Physically, those who have become business partners have moved out of the accounting department. Many work with the groups they support. This means their desk could be in the marketing department, on the factory floor, or in an office adjacent to the president's. Most of their day is spent sharing information with others. Shared objectives and shared perspectives have erased the psychological isolation. The term "business partner" is itself very telling of a new identity. Partners have an equal voice and an equal vote on decisions. They have the right to challenge faulty logic or faulty assumptions, regardless of who makes a statement. Indeed, it is expected that a partner do this. A partner is actively involved in business decisions. Before accountants became business partners they "serviced their internal customers." Their mission was to satisfy their customers' needs. A principle of quality service is that the customer is always right. In practice, this meant that if a marketing vice president asked for a particular report, the accountant was expected to deliver it as ordered. It didn't matter if the requested information wasn't the most relevant to the decision or if interpreted in a particular way could result in a dysfunctional decision. "The customer was king," and it wasn't accounting's prerogative to second-guess the decision maker.

Not so with business partners. They have to understand what the business problem is and work with the team to determine which information is most relevant. Then they interpret the information and work with the team to make the decision. They have to understand how accounting information and practices impact behavior and, ultimately, performance. They have to foresee how company decisions and practices will impact accounting reports. And they educate their teams about the tax and financial implications of company actions.

A corporate controller from a large, publicly traded company describes the business partner philosophy: *"I just made a presentation to a group of 20-30 of our assistant regional controllers from around the country, and I told them that the most important thing they can do is move the business, which really doesn't have much to do with numbers. It has to do with understanding that you have fiduciary duty, but you can never fulfill your fiduciary duty and get the business moving in the right direction unless you have the right kind of relationships with your management. You start with your regional manager. You should be the first person the regional manager goes to when they want to ask a question. I don't think accountants can do their job unless they know almost as much about the business as everybody around them because we are supposed to assess the answers we get. If you are able to understand the various parts of the business, you are the best person for senior management to go to for advice and guidance. This doesn't just happen because you are an accountant or are good analytically. It happens because you go out of your way to create relationships that allow you to do that when the time comes. I think that's the biggest thing we are talking about nowadays—customer satisfaction at a very high level. It's very much about having the confidence of the people that you need to do this interpretation for to help run the business.*

> *"Yes, I'm a Business Partner. ...it was an open dialogue and they [accountants] were treated as an equal at the table, and they were at the front end making the decision, not given the answer and go figure it out. "—A controller at Boeing*

In many organizations, business partners have taken leadership roles on teams. Unlike team members in marketing or engineering, accountants aren't seen as having their own agenda. As corporate insiders explained to us, the marketing person is focused on market share, and the engineer is focused on design issues. But the business partner is perceived as having an overview of the organization as a whole and an understanding of the financial implications of actions. They can point out to the marketing person or the engineer whether a proposed action will enhance the company's well being. In this way, business partners are perceived as committed to the organization's goals.

Skill set. What skills do business partners need to do all of this? They need excellent communication and interpersonal skills, team-building skills, and analytical skills.

> "Yes, I'm a Business Partner. I see an overall trend that has been going on for some time of more empowerment at lower levels of the organization. More and more individual work teams and work groups are trying to make decisions that have a large financial component to them in managing their daily work, whereas they might not have been thinking about it in that way before. I think it is going to increase. There is more demand for financial support at a lower level—more demand for accountants to help. In wing manufacturing, [the staff focuses] on particular parts of the process in building the airplane. The demand for financial support is insatiable. They want to know, and they need to know: What is the consequence of doing this? If we streamline this, how does it impact us financially? What does that do to us? Does it impact the value stream? They need accountants to help them with that kind of information. I see a continued growth in that kind of activity and the need for accountants as the trusted business advisor. That is one aspect that I really think will continue to expand and grow."—A financial director from Boeing

They need a thorough understanding of the business they work in. This is critical because, without that understanding, they can't add value. They should be familiar with the quality literature (cost of quality, Six Sigma, ISO 9000-2000, Criteria for Performance Excellence, and the like) and know how to use quality tools (affinity diagrams, interrelationship digraphs, cause-and-effect diagrams). And an understanding of psychology and social psychology will help them learn how to resolve conflicts and motivate people. What about accounting skills? This is a given. Any business partner is expected to have a comprehensive knowledge of accounting and tax laws.

Their work encompasses the disciplines of accounting, some finance, some systems, and some decision support. To be effective in their roles, they have to be familiar with all of the business functions (marketing, purchasing, engineering), the processes that run their organization, and how the processes, functions, and people work together. As another McDonald's controller observed regarding decision support: *When voice recognition becomes even more prevalent, the chief executive is just going to scream at a computer, and it is going to tell him the answers to the question. So the fundamental basics of scorekeeping will be done by machines, all of it, and also much of the analytical work. Accountants are basically interpreters. That doesn't mean that they just interpret numbers. They tell people what to do with them.*

The future. For accountants who have made the transition to business partner, or would like to make the transition, the way to remain relevant is perseverance, stamina, and a commitment to lifelong learning. For educators, the challenge is to prepare their students to become business partners, not "accountants." Accounting programs still have to teach students the intricacies of the accounting information system, cash flows, data flows, the relationships between the financial statements, and the like. But there has to be more emphasis on decision support and understanding a business—more emphasis on using the information. Students must learn how to handle qualitative data because they will be attending meetings and will have to make sense out of hours of back-and forth discussion. They should be introduced to the Baldrige Criteria for Performance Excellence. They should learn how to use some quality tools. But step one is that they need to be informed that there's a new occupation called business partner to which they can aspire.

For leaders in the profession, many issues have to be addressed. Do we continue to call ourselves accountants, or do we select a new name? How can the most appropriate continuing professional education (CPE) be developed and delivered? How should professional associations respond to the ongoing changes in work roles and responsibilities? The answers to these questions will determine the future of our profession. ■

"Yes, I'm a Business Partner. ... once we went to business units, people started acting like [they were] their independent businesses. So suddenly it was more important for them to have broader business knowledge. At that point, I think in almost every profit center the senior accounting person became the righthand person to business unit managers because they were the person they turned to with, 'Help me understand the financial data I'm getting. Help me understand what levers I can move to make the financial data to be what I want it to be.'"—A corporate accounting manager from Caterpillar.

PART II

There are many paths you can take to become a business partner. And it's up to you to select the path. Don't expect someone in your company to suddenly declare that you are a business partner; you're the only one who can make it happen. You have to want the role, and you have to work for it. As a controller at McDonald's put it *The accounting department proved itself. It wasn't that all of a sudden we said we wanted to be business partners and everybody applauded. It was a process. We made sure we hired the best and the brightest. They are well rounded in technical skills and analytical skills, and one of the key competencies they had was the ability to communicate financial information. We set the tone by our higher-level financial organization...and, over time, the financial organization proved its value in projects, in identifying certain business opportunities, and the like.*

There are other necessary factors also. To become a business partner, it's a given that you know your accounting cold. You're expected to know the tax implications of proposed courses of action. You need to understand cost flows and information flows. You have to be very comfortable with technology and be an expert in the company's business and accounting software. You have to be a generalist. You need a working knowledge of what people do in marketing, engineering, human resources, and other departments. You need to understand how the processes, departments, and functions work together to run the business. You'll be expected to contribute ideas at planning meetings, so you have to see the big picture, keep a focus on the bottom line, and think strategically. Most important, you must understand the business. You have to know how the company makes money and how the industry is structured. Another controller from McDonald's explained:

> *McDonald's is very heavily operations oriented, which means that the operations guys are first, second, third, fourth, and fifth. We managed to create a situation in the U.K. where accounting was first and operations was second. The way we did that was understanding the business, building relationships, and showing we were willing to participate in the day-to-day operation of the business. For instance, in 1996, before I came to the U.S., I spent seven months going through full-time operations training in a restaurant, starting as a crew member and ending up as an assistant manager, so that I understood what the operations folks had to do on a day-to-day basis. Once I got to that level, the rest of it was just normal management practice. So it was a willingness to go well beyond just thinking about accounting to thinking about the business as a whole that generated that kind of reputation.*

MAKING THE TRANSITION

The transformation to business partner requires vision, hard work, and perseverance. It occurred differently in each of the six companies we interviewed, so we thought it would be beneficial to concentrate on one company at a time. In this article we focus on Caterpillar, where changes were driven by a corporate reorganization. We'll tell Caterpillar's story in the words of the accountants who experienced the changes—a controller, a vice president, a financial reporting manager, and several business managers of product lines (business managers are at the same level as product managers). Accounting at Caterpillar has always been held at a pretty high plane, partially because in the 1950s and 1960s, two of the Caterpillar chairmen were former controllers at Caterpillar. They and the whole organization realized the importance of accounting. Also, they were instrumental in creating Caterpillar's cost system, which we are very proud of and which is seen as a world-class cost system. Accounting wasn't just a function at Caterpillar—it was a vital function.

Changes started about 1986 when Caterpillar initiated a $2 billion worldwide modernization program, a large sum for any company. And Caterpillar is conservative. We run things by the numbers a lot, and this modernization program was such a big commitment that people really looked to the accounting organization for the objective and financial perspective on how things were going. They wanted to make sure that we got the returns we expected in terms of working capital improvements, labor efficiencies, and so on. They looked to the numbers to help support the direction in which we were going. This really created the partnership or cemented the partnership relationship. By 1989, I felt we were partners with the manufacturing people, the planning people, and the executive officers. Then in 1990, Caterpillar reorganized itself into profit centers. Before the reorganization, we were an extremely centralized, bureaucratic company, with decisions being made at the top. Then we changed from a functional organization to one that was organized on a profit-center basis with about 26 profit centers or business units. The person in charge of running a business unit was evaluated on return on investment and the unit's profitability. Each vice president had to run his business with a P&L. Each unit had a business manager reporting to the profit center in that organization. These business managers were accountants. With the creation of business units, obviously, you become a business manager rather than an accountant. As a business manager, you get involved in all aspects of the business, in finding ways and solutions to help the business achieve strategic objectives.

In the old days, you had a plant accountant who worked at the plant and didn't have much responsibility other than to cost the product. But after the reorganization we had an entrepreneurial relationship within that plant. Caterpillar created, for the first time, high-level managers at the plant level who had total responsibility for the product, for the design, manufacturing, pricing, and all those functions that used to be in a central location in the functional organization. Then the business manager was created at the business-unit level who was at as high a level as the product managers who ran the company.

What helped make the accountants partners and a big part of the management community is that each vice president relied on us to help run his business. We analyzed the results, answered questions about why things were better, and, maybe even more important, why things were worse. This is critical.

ORGANIZATIONAL EDUCATORS

The organizational change was advanced by a companywide educational program initiated by the accounting leadership. Caterpillar business partners describe that effort.

To get people to really understand what we were doing, we spent a large amount of time training this new organization that we split into business units. The accountants took on the burden of educating the various divisions about what the numbers meant and how they could impact them. We had a program called "Understanding the Business 101" that we presented to all 1,100 salaried people and all 2,000 hourly people. Everybody was interested because they knew it was going to impact their incentive plan. We taught them what financial results are, how we get the information, and how we measure it. We showed them how a welder impacts our business, how a purchasing person impacts our business. This put us in something like a counseling position because we were the teachers. One of the great things that the reorganization did in unbundling the corporation and developing 26 different business units was to create 1,000 businesspeople. Now, the best engineer is a general manager, and the best planning person is running a new business.

We accountants took the leadership role, became counselors, and helped cultivate a real business sense within Caterpillar. We would have floundered had we not done that. These businesspeople we created came back to us and involved us in running their business, which was a major transformation for the company.

LINES OF RESPONSIBILITY ARE IMPORTANT

The following vignette reveals the thought that went into building a new organization and the importance of clear lines of responsibility. Some of us were concerned about the control aspects of the new organization—we weren't very familiar with it.There was some thought given to the idea that maybe the business managers ought to report to the corporate controller rather than up through the profit-center chain. While that might have made us feel better from a control standpoint, it wouldn't have cemented the partnership relationship. So our business managers report to the profit center. That was a big decision. As it turns out, control issues haven't been a problem over the years.

Coupled with the reorganization of the profit centers was a change in the function of the corporate offices, which were once accounting general offices that told people what to do. In our new organization, we had to charge for our services, which also makes for a partnership point of view. We had to become very customer friendly, and, rather than tell people what to do, we had to jointly agree on things, and we had to get them to agree to take charges for our services.

CHANGING ACCOUNTANTS' SELF-IMAGE

What effect did the change to business partner have on accountants' self-image? What were some of the challenges encountered in the process of change? Caterpillar business partners describe the events: First and foremost is the mental attitude—accepting the fact that you have a different role to play other than just reporting the results. That was the first thing the accountants had to learn.

Our purpose now was to help guide the different business units and profit centers—help them achieve their strategic goals and objectives. Accountants had to say: "We have a different role to play. We are no longer going to be people who just present data or monitor activities to ensure that people perform according to certain guidelines. We are here to identify opportunities that we could capture and lock in."

Everything started from defining our role. Was it simply to collect and present the data, or was it to analyze the data and look at opportunities outside the accounting functions and say, "How do we leverage that to make this more of a successful approach to doing the business?" We became involved in different aspects of the business. We got involved in marketing strategies, in acquisitions, in designing strategic directions. It became important that we were viewed as a partner with the different business units rather than their just viewing us as presenting information or monitoring.

ORGANIZATIONAL CULTURE

The change in self-image coincided with a change in the organizational culture at Caterpillar.

It used to be, "I'm an engineer; I design. I'm an accountant; I will keep track of the cost." The culture evolved to where everybody's role was broadened in that they became part of a business and became better businesspeople. Engineers had to think: "How much does it cost to produce a part if I design it this way or that way?" They didn't think this way before. They used to design a part, give it to a manufacturing guy who had to provide it, and then down the road the accountant had to cost it. But now, as a result of the reorganization and the fact that every business unit has their own P&L responsibilities, everybody is more aware of the commercial aspects of what they are doing. Everybody's level was raised, and the accountant became a higher species in the food chain. They were looked to for guidance as things were thought about in a P&L commercial aspect, which wasn't the case before.

OBSTACLES

Common obstacles in making the transition to business partner are lack of time, expertise, top-management support, and operational support. In addition, difficulty changing the corporate culture, obtaining trust, and gaining access to information may also create roadblocks. Here's what the Caterpillar financial professionals say: The biggest obstacle on the path to becoming a business partner was the cultural change in getting people to think more broadly. Another challenge was having to come up with a balanced set of measures to measure the new organization—a set of measures that could be used for incentive pay to motivate the behavior the company wanted.

That was probably our biggest challenge. Some people found the change to be difficult. But the majority saw it as an opportunity to grow and contribute. In any kind of activity, there are those who are locked into the way they think and behave, but those who were open minded and had a broader perspective succeeded. As accountants and younger people saw the successes of some of the original participants, they tried to emulate that. They wanted to get outside the accounting pigeonhole they had been identified with. The more they did differently and the more they participated, the more the enterprise valued them and the more in demand they became. The more they were in demand, the more activities they became involved in. The more activities they were involved in, the more attractive it became for the other managers to ask for their help.

EFFECT ON NONACCOUNTANTS

We also asked the Caterpillar accountants how the change to business partner affected non-accountants.

They told us: Many leaders in the business units were not accountants, not finance people. They were marketing people, manufacturing people, and others, so they tended to depend more and more heavily on the accountants for their success. As the rest of the organization began to recognize that the accountants not only talked about numbers but talked about strategies and approaches to business, they began to listen to them. It started at the top. It definitely didn't bubble from the bottom up. It started at the top by the business-unit managers and profit-center vice presidents depending more and more on the accountants and using the accountant as a right-hand man or woman in helping them guide their businesses. The organization, having seen that, was willing to listen to the accountants.

WILL YOU MAKE THE LEAP?

Once more, becoming a business partner takes a great deal of hard work, perseverance, vision, and spirit. Most of the financial professionals we interviewed who have made the transition say the effort was worth it and that they are thriving in their new roles. They say they feel more valued, more a part of the business, and more challenged to do excellent work.Will you make the leap and join them?

This article is based on interviews with more than 100 accountants who have made the transition to business partner. The interviews were part of the research project, "How to Become a Business Partner," the fourth in a series of applied IMA research studies that focus on the changes in accountants' work and work roles. The authors are the research team. Previous IMA projects are "What Corporate America Wants in Entry-Level Accountants" (1994), "The Practice Analysis of Management Accountants" (1996), and "Counting More, Counting Less: Transformations in the Management Accounting Profession" (1999). Executive summaries of the previous research are available on IMA's website at www.imanet.org. Click on Resources, then IMA Studies. Results of "How to Become a Business Partner" will be available this fall in hard copy form and also on the IMA website.

COUNTING MORE, COUNTING LESS

Transformations in the Management Accounting Profession

By Keith A. Russell, CMA; Gary H. Siegel, CPA; and C.S. "Bud" Kulesza, CMA, CFMA

From bean counter, corporate cop, and financial historian to valued business partner, the role of management accountants in many firms in the last decade has evolved into the center of strategic activity. Escalating change in an increasingly competitive international business environment has provided management accountants with the opportunity to reinvent the profession and increase their value to the organization.

These changes are among the major findings of the largest continuing analysis of the management accounting and finance profession. The 1999 Practice Analysis of Management Accounting, titled *Counting More, Counting Less: Transformations in the Management Accounting Profession*, provides a snapshot of the current state of the management accounting profession in the U.S., how the profession has changed, and where the profession is headed. The key events leading to this latest report are described in the sidebar, "Why Research Was Needed."

HIGHLIGHTS OF THE 1999 PRACTICE ANALYSIS

The 1999 Practice Analysis focuses a lens on the accounting function and offers insight into the broad changes under way in American firms in the new information economy. The 1995 Practice Analysis described a profession in transition. The 1999 Practice Analysis documents the transformation of corporate accountants from financial historians to business partners. Increasing numbers of management accountants spend most of their time as internal consultants or business analysts. Many have moved from the accounting department to be physically located in the operating departments they service. They work on cross-functional teams and are actively involved in decision making.

As firms adopted a customer focus as the key component to their quality improvement programs, management accountants focused on serving their "internal customers." Accepting the adage, "the customer is always right," management accountants work closely with their "customers" to provide the right information and help use the information to make better decisions.

The 1999 Practice Analysis results reflect the current state of the management accounting profession in the U.S. and indicate where the profession is heading.

IMPROVED IMAGE

When compared to the baseline measures of the 1995 Practice Analysis, the 1999 results show ongoing and escalating change in the work performed by management accountants, in their role in the organization, and in the value they bring to decision making. Clear winners in the technological revolution that fostered the new information economy, management accountants are in increased demand within their organizations for their advice, expertise, and involvement. About 70% of the respondents in all size firms say that compared to five years ago people outside the finance function believe that management accountants bring more value to the company.

COMMUNICATION WITH NONACCOUNTANTS INCREASING

In 1995, 48% of management accountants worked on cross-functional teams. In 1999, that has increased to 56%. Management accountants spend more time communicating with people in their firm than five years ago. Universally, respondents agree that good interpersonal skills are essential for success.

SHIFTS IN WORK LOCATION

Traditionally, accountants worked in accounting departments that were physically removed from the operating departments of their companies. In 1999, however, 20% of all respondents report that at least half the management accountants in their company have moved out of the centrally located accounting area and are located with the operating departments they serve as part of the business team. In larger companies, 45% of respondents indicate that at least half are now located with the operating departments they service.

HOW MANAGEMENT ACCOUNTANTS DEFINE THEMSELVES

When asked which term they used to describe their work, 39% of respondents said finance, 33% said accounting, and 28% use a different term. Finance appears to be a more inclusive and acceptable term for describing all the varied activities the respondents perform. The most common reasons given for using the term finance have to do with the positive connotations associated with finance and the negative connotations connected with accounting. Interestingly, none of the respondents used the term "management accountant" to describe themselves.

- Finance is forward-looking, while accounting looks backward.
- Finance is more all-inclusive.
- Accounting refers to debits and credits.
- Accountants are "number crunchers."

Skills needed for success. The 1995 Practice Analysis includes a database with information about 162 knowledge, skills, and abilities (KSAs) necessary for success in the accounting profession. The 1999 Practice Analysis respondents were asked to describe, for the benefit of undergraduate accounting majors, the most important KSAs necessary for success. They are:

- Communication (oral, written, and presentation) skills.
- Ability to work on a team.
- Analytical skills.
- Solid understanding of accounting.
- An understanding of how a business functions.

Respondents also were asked to identify the most important new KSAs they learned over the past five years. See Table 1 for their answers. It shouldn't be surprising that computer skills topped the list.

QUALITY OF LIFE

Due to the increased demand for their services, finance function personnel work long hours. As a result, there is increasing concern on the part of respondents about the balance between work and personal life. Two comments from the survey reflect this concern:

"In the last couple of years especially, we have just been burning people out. They've been working incredible hours trying to get information out faster than they've ever gotten information out before."

"I think one of the real issues is work/life balance. I don't think you find work/life balance in most finance jobs ... Frankly, I think people are feeling that they are running and they are giving up family life. We are recognizing it; we are concerned."

THE PACE OF CHANGE

Change in the profession is ongoing and accelerating. The overwhelming majority of respondents interviewed stated that the rate of change in their organizational role has been more rapid over the 1995-99 period than the 1990-95 period.

Not one respondent expects the rate of change to decrease! In fact, respondents expect the rate of change to increase over the next three years. Management accountants say that change is driven by technology, the need for more rapid information, globalization, and the increasingly competitive environment. Management accountants aren't just managing change: They are initiating change.

WHERE THE PROFESSION IS GOING

Financial professionals report a shift over the past five years from traditional accounting work activities to newer, more value-added activities. Compared to five years ago, respondents spend more time performing the following work activities:

- Internal consulting.
- Long-term, strategic planning.
- Computer systems and operations.
- Managing the accounting/finance function.
- Process improvement.
- Performing financial and economic analysis.

Looking ahead three years, they expect to spend more time on the same work activities. Compared with five years ago, respondents say that they spend less time performing the following work activities:

- Accounting systems and financial reporting.
- Consolidations.
- Managing the accounting/finance function.
- Accounting policy.
- Short-term budgeting process.
- Project accounting.
- Compliance reporting.
- Cost accounting systems.
- Tax compliance.

Looking ahead three years, they expect to spend less time on these same critical work activities. Interestingly, these are traditional accounting work activities. Respondents were asked to identify the single most critical work activity for their firm's success in 1999. See Table 2 for their responses.

Long-term strategic planning, process improvement, and customer and product profitability were recently introduced to the profession. Indeed, these functions weren't part of the traditional accounting vocabulary 10 years ago.

CHANGES IN THE ROLE OF THE FINANCE FUNCTION

Many respondents believe the changes taking place in their work are driven by changes in the finance function. Leading changes include:

- Partner/consultant in management decisions.
- Finance is more involved with other aspects of business.
- More planning/strategy.
- More computerized technology.
- More involved in team building/decision making.
- More involved in evaluating company efficiency.

Management accountants also believe the current trend toward business partnering will continue. Changes expected over the next three years are:

- Less reporting of information; more planning and analysis.
- More computerized/technology/software.
- More partnering and consulting in management decisions.
- More involvement with operations.
- More analysis of profitability and performance evaluation.

IMPLICATIONS AND RECOMMENDATIONS FOR ACCOUNTING EDUCATORS

The two most critical work activities for the success of respondents' companies in 1999 are strategic planning and process improvement; neither is taught in most accounting curricula. To better meet the needs of their students and corporate customers, college and university educators should obtain a better understanding of the work performed in modern firms. The insights gained from the 1999 Practice Analysis should be used to address needed curriculum changes.

FOR CORPORATIONS

Corporations should become more involved in the academic community through advisory boards, participation in job fairs, faculty internships, guest speaker activities, plant visits, etc. This involvement will help ensure that the changes occurring in corporate America are shared with the academic community. Such interaction is necessary to enable students and faculty to remain abreast of the changes taking place in the profession and to identify the KSAs needed for success.

FOR PROFESSIONAL ASSOCIATIONS

Professional associations need to maintain their leadership role of identifying, supporting, and perpetuating the positive changes taking place in the profession. Specifically, they should:

- Continue the development of CPE courses and benchmarks for finance function organizations.
- Continue to encourage and support the interaction between accounting educators and practitioners.
- Compare professional certification examinations contents and specifications with the results of this research.
- Develop a universally accepted title for the new organizational role of management accountants.
- Inform accounting educators about the changes that occurred in the profession and where the profession is headed.
- Work closely with accounting educators to develop changes in the accounting curriculum consistent with the future of the profession.

BEYOND STRATEGIC PARTNERING

In a November 1990 article in Management Accounting, Gerald Ross, managing director of Change Lab, Toronto, Canada, predicted the changes under way for management accountants. Ross stated that the 1990 management accountant was using traditional tools at the operational level. He felt that to survive and flourish in the new technological world, management accountants would need to begin using more sophisticated tools and move from the operational level into the strategic level in their firms.

Events over the past decade have proven Ross to be prescient. Where does the profession go from here? The 1999 Practice Analysis predicts that management accountants go beyond business partnering and broaden their role to strategic partnering. Management accountants will become more involved in running the business. They will become more proactive.

Clearly, change will be the constant into the new millennium for finance function professionals.

WHY THIS RESEARCH WAS NEEDED

IMA, in an ongoing effort to meet member needs, formed an alliance with the Financial Executives Institute (FEI) to complete a research project to determine the skills corporate executives expected from entry-level accountants and the skills entry-level accountants brought to the job. *What Corporate America Wants in Entry-Level Accountants* (IMA, 1994) revealed a significant gap between corporate expectations and entry-level skills. The gap had developed because the curricula of many accounting and business programs weren't focused on the changes occurring in corporate accounting or on the needs of the corporations that hired accounting and business graduates. (This gap was later confirmed by the AACSB in *A Report of the AACSB Faculty Leadership Task Force,* 1995-96).

The obvious question raised by *What Corporate America Wants* was, "What knowledge, skills, and abilities (KSAs) were necessary for entry-level professionals?"

To answer this question, the IMA completed its first study of work, *The Practice Analysis of Management Accounting* (IMA, 1995). This study documented in unprecedented detail the work activities performed in U.S. companies and the KSAs necessary for competent performance of those work activities. Respondents for the study were drawn from membership rosters of the AICPA, IMA, FEI, and IIA and included management accountants at all organizational levels, entry-level to CFO. Many colleges and universities used the Practice Analysis database to revise curricula, and businesses used it to develop skill-based training.

The 1995 Practice Analysis also revealed the emerging contours of the new management accountant: one who was working on cross-functional teams and becoming more heavily involved in strategic planning and business decision making. Less time was being spent in traditional roles because technology automated many time-consuming tasks. Instead, management accountants were spending increasing amounts of time in new roles as an internal consultant, analyst, and valued business partner.

In 1999, IMA heard from members that change in the profession was accelerating. Accordingly, the Institute, with participation and cooperation from the AICPA, undertook the 1999 Practice Analysis to focus on change in the profession. The Gary Siegel Organization completed the research on this follow-up research study as well as the two earlier studies. *Focus on the Horizon: CPA Vision Project* (AICPA, 1998), identified forces that were impacting, and provided visioning for, their members.

Using information provided from respondents drawn from members of the IMA and AICPA, researchers set out to determine:

1. How the work of management accountants and their role in their companies have changed over the past five years, and
2. How the work will change in the next three years.

Table 1.
MOST IMPORTANT KSAs
ACQUIRED OVER THE PAST 5 YEARS

	Number	Percent
Computer skills/technology/networks	146	49.70%
Accounting software	60	20.40%
Teaching/speaking/communication	44	15.00%
Project management/leadership	40	13.60%
New laws/accounting rules/SEC requirements	33	11.20%
Interpersonal skills	28	9.50%
Learn about operations, i.e., HR/marketing	25	8.50%
Evaluation of profitability/financial analysis	22	7.50%
Other	20	6.80%
Process evaluation skills in own or other business	19	6.50%
Auditing/tax laws	18	6.10%
Internet skills	16	5.40%
Long-range planning	16	5.40%
Mergers and acquisitions	15	5.10%
New degree/certificate	9	3.10%
Cash management	7	2.40%
Risk management	4	1.40%
TOTAL CASES	294	100.00%

Table 2.
SINGLE MOST CRITICAL
WORK ACTIVITY IN 1999

	Number	Percent
Long-term, strategic planning	75	25.30%
Process improvement	30	10.10%
Customer and product profitability	27	9.10%
Accounting systems and financial reporting	16	5.40%
Short-term budgeting process	15	5.10%
Mergers, acquisitions, and divestments	15	5.10%
Perform financial and economic analysis	14	4.70%
External financing	14	4.70%
Computer systems and operations	13	4.40%
Performance evaluation	9	3.00%
Project accounting	7	2.40%
Internal consulting	7	2.40%
Tax planning and strategy	7	2.40%
Capital budgeting	6	2.00%
Cost accounting systems	5	1.70%
Quality systems and control	5	1.70%
Risk management	5	1.70%
Investment of funds	5	1.70%
Credit and collection	4	1.30%
Educating the organization	4	1.30%
Managing the accounting/finance function	4	1.30%
Compliance reporting for government or regulatory agencies	3	1.00%
Resource management	3	1.00%
Consolidations	1	0.30%
Internal auditing	1	0.30%
Tax compliance	1	0.30%
Human resources and personnel	1	0.30%

PRACTICE ANALYSIS:

Skills Needed for Entry Level Management Accounting Positions

By Gary Siegel

What do management accountants look for in recruits for entry level positions? Here are some hiring criteria from the leading-edge companies interviewed for IMA's Practice Analysis. Companies can benchmark, and accounting educators and students can evaluate how well their curriculum prepares people for work in the new world of management accounting.

Grades. For many companies, grades come first. "Typically, we've got a grade point cutoff," a Caterpillar accountant explained. "When we start flipping through resumes, we will look at only the best because we want people who could be a business manager some day."

But according to a US West financial executive, being a good student isn't enough. You must be able to express yourself and understand areas outside accounting, especially those that relate to your business, such as engineering or manufacturing.

Self-Confidence and Self-Assurance. Several management accountants mentioned the confidence factor. "The entry level people are not very assertive. They are so timid and scared," observed a Hewlett-Packard accountant. An accountant at a Caterpillar production facility cited universities as the problem. "I think schools could better prepare people for the work environment ...they have to teach students how to talk to people and not step on their feet."

One solution is to do things that generate self-confidence, such as getting a broader education or becoming involved in sports. Nevertheless, as time passes, confidence will increase. "Once they've been around for a couple of years they find out they were really pretty assertive all along," said the Hewlett Packard accountant. "The few who become real stars are the ones that have that assertiveness to disagree with their manager."

Accounting Skills/the Basics. It may seem obvious, but management accountants should be grounded in both managerial and financial accounting. They also should take a few management courses to appreciate and relate to leaders. "The first piece of advice I would give them is to learn the basics," another HP accountant said. "Be very competent in spreadsheets and decision tools, plus other things like OLAP and reporting products."

The same view was expressed at Abbott Labs. An accountant there advised students to ground themselves in their technical skills: cost accounting, general accounting, and financial statement analysis. He also urged students to take audit, cost accounting, and, if possible, operations classes. He noted the value of classes with teamwork and unstructured assignments. Those skills and the ability to find information will be handy in the business world.

Communication, Initiative, and Leadership. As fundamental accounting skills are, they aren't sufficient for success. "Leadership, initiative, communication skills. These are our top three. If you don't have these, you don't have a place here at Caterpillar," said one accountant. Indeed, at the company headquarters, some entry-level employees give presentations to group presidents after only three to six months.

At the core of communication skills is the ability to take a complex subject, boil it down into easily understood language, and explain it to non-accountants. Interpersonal skills are critical—you should be able to influence people and must be comfortable dealing with coworkers at different levels. After all you aren't always talking to a peer.

To succeed, you need initiative. This means taking that extra step, asking a coworker or supervisor if they need help, making recommendations after you do the analysis on a problem, or finding alternatives and making recommendations to management. It means following through to complete the picture.

Critical Thinking. For many companies, critical thinking and its corollary, creative problem solving, are key. You should be able to step back and look at something "out of the box." "the skills that I find the hardest to get in people are analytical thought processes and critical thinking," said a Caterpillar management accountant. "Nine out of 10 people that I see coming here can be wizards at spreadsheets, can manipulate data effectively, but they aren't very good at figuring out whether the information in front of them is reasonable or realistic. When you ask, 'Is that reasonable?'...the critical thinking aspect is just not there."

Accuracy. Accuracy is crucial. An error in a calculation could amount to millions of dollars, which in turn could lead to an erroneous decision. A Boeing executive highlighted the difference between school and the work world: The real world "is not like a test where you turn it in and get 10 points off because you screwed up a on a number. ...When you get into business and mess up your numbers, the ramifications are a whole lot bigger. It's part of your job and your responsibility to check every number or to set up a system where you know that the numbers are correct."

OTHER ADVICE TO STUDENTS AND ENTRY-LEVEL ACCOUNTANTS

- Accept the idea that training and education are a lifelong process.
- Be more IT/database savvy.
- Have a passion for the business. Don't work for a company if you have no interest in what it does because you're going to be required to strategically influence that business.
- Understand that business is different overseas. Cultures are different, the way you do business is different, and markets are different.
- Understand relationships between data and how systems work.
- Be able to think logically. If you can do that, then you can learn almost anything fairly quickly because you wont be memorizing.
- Have a good business understanding. Be able to look at a business and really understand what drives it and what the key factors are that make it go well or not go well.
- Be able to do projections, set goals, and determine a path to get to that goal.
- Be able to work in a team environment.
- Be able to apply what you learn.
- Be mature. I don't know if you can teach that, but with business comes a higher level of responsibility.
- Develop computer skills.
- Develop writing skills
- Be patient enough to work in a bureaucracy and impatient enough to be willing to change it.
- Be willing to take risk—it's the only way to grow.
- Be willing to make mistakes, and don't let them devastate you. Be smart enough not to make the same mistake twice.
- Have a good idea of how a company runs.
- Continually educate yourself, whether it's formal or informal, taking additional courses or keeping current.
- Have a process view, be very process focused, and look at things not just where finance starts and ends but as a whole.
- Have high energy and a positive attitude. Be very proactive.
- Have integrity. If you are going to become the confidant of the top management people, if you are going to be the advisor, they've got to trust you implicitly.

Chapter 2
Implementing Strategy: The Balanced Scorecard and the Value Chain

Cases

2-1 Atlantic City Casino (Value Chain Analysis)
2-2 Strategic Analysis
2-3 Business Strategy
2-4 Strategic Analysis

Readings

"Strategy Focused Performance Measures"

This article looks at the execution of strategy from the point of view of the need to identify the performance evaluation measures that are highly aligned with the firm's strategy.

Discussion Questions:

1. Why is it so important to align performance measures with the firm's strategy?
2. What is the role of the firm's value chain in the determination of strategic performance measures?

"Applying the Balanced Scorecard to Small Companies"

This article reports the findings of a case study of four small firms to identify the potential use of the balanced scorecard in these firms and to determine the differences in the use of the scorecard across industries. The industries include a food ingredients company, a commercial bank, a biotechnology firm, and an electronics firm.

Discussion Questions:

1. Did these four firms adopt the balanced scorecard? Why or why not?
2. For each of the firms, examine the scorecard presented in the article and use it to determine what you think is likely to be or should be the competitive strategy of the firm. Does it seem that the balanced scorecard is consistent with the nature of the firm's business and strategy?
3. How do the scorecards differ across firms? Can you explain why?

Cases

2-1. Atlantic City Casino

Several years ago the management of a large hotel chain, Hotel Corporation of American (HCA) purchased a casino in Las Vegas. Pleased with the results HCA constructed another casino in Atlantic City shortly after casino gaming was legalized in that city. At the time the proposal in this case arose (see below) there were 9 other casinos operating and 2 additional casinos under construction.

The casino is an independent operating unit within the hotel chain. For example, all financial and accounting services are provided in-house. The casino has been profitable since the day it opened. However, the level of profits has not been satisfactory. Corporate management is well aware that HCA would have been better off if the huge sums involved in the construction of the casino had been invested in certificates of deposit.

THE PROPOSAL

Management of the Atlantic City Casino has employed several consulting services to study the market and the casino's position in the market. Consumer surveys have shown that the casino is viewed as an average casino, with no distinguishing characteristics. Coupled with its location (several blocks from where most of the casinos are located) this perception of blandness seems to explain the casino's relatively small walk-in trade (most visitors to Atlantic City visit more than one casino; people staying at one casino who visit a second are considered walk-ins at the second casino).

A proposal has been made to expand the casino and hotel (state law prescribes a fixed number of hotel rooms per square feet of casino space). As part of this expansion, the proposal includes the construction of a theme entertainment center. The center would be separate from, but attached to, the casino. The showpiece of the center would be a large Ferris wheel designed to look like a giant wheel of fortune. It would be visible from a large portion of the boardwalk. Additionally, the area would include a unique water slide, bumper cars, a space capsule ride and a fun house. Throughout the area would be a number of small souvenir and snack shops, push carts, tent shows and midway-type games to provide an old-fashioned style carnival atmosphere. An admission fee would be charged to enter the theme center and most of the rides and entertainment would be included in the admission fee. Management expects to be able to use free admission tickets to the center as a promotional item. There would be easy access from the center to the casino floor. It is anticipated that a large number of the visitors to the center would also visit the casino.

Although management is impressed by the plan and has already had detailed architectural plans prepared for the expansion, they are cautious. When the casino was first built, everyone was enthusiastic about the casino's potential, but the results have been disappointing. Management wants a thorough study made of the financial prospects for this expansion before committing funds to it.

Detailed financial data for every casino in Atlantic City are public information and are routinely exchanged. Thus, data such as that given in Tables A and B are readily available.

REQUIRED:

1. Complete a value chain analysis. Describe your understanding of the competitive position of the Atlantic City Casino. Identify areas for potential cost reduction and/or value added for customers.
2. Should HCA make the investment in the theme entertainment center? Why?
3. HCA is considering a balanced scorecard for the Atlantic City Casino. For each of the four areas within the balanced scorecard, list two or three examples of measurable critical success factors which should be included.

(IMA adapted)

TABLE A
Selected Annual Financial Data
(000s omitted)

Property	Revenues			
	Casino	Rooms	Food and Beverage	Net Income
Atlantic City Casino	$220,183	$14,862	$36,833	$23,921
Competitors				
1	254,753	17,604	36,457	40,979
2	224,077	14,836	34,493	18,834
3	237,700	15,787	35,168	47,146
4	158,602	9,897	18,788	1,574
5	210,848	13,870	35,265	64,765
6	251,675	17,665	33,867	17,904
7	147,037	10,191	35,020	(9,075)
8	121,581	13,469	21,863	2,246
9*	123,947	12,157	22,643	(1,176)

* In operation in 19X4 for only 6.5 months

TABLE B
Selected Statistics

Property	Casino Space (square feet)	Number of Rooms	Number of Restaurants
Atlantic City Casino	50,850	521	7
Competitors			
1	59,857	727	9
2	59,296	645	9
3	59,439	512	9
4	49,639	501	14
5	52,083	750	7
6	40,814	504	8
7	50,516	500	5
8	34,408	504	6
9	60,000	612	8

2-2. Sovera Enterprises (Strategic Analysis)

Sovera Enterprises, an expanding conglomerate, was founded 35 years ago by Emil Sovera. The company's policy has been to acquire businesses that show significant profit potential; if a business fails to attain projected profits, it is usually sold. Currently, the company consists of eight businesses acquired throughout the years; three of those businesses are described here.

LaBue Videodiscs produces a line of videodisc players. The sale of videodisc players has not met expectations, but LaBue's management believes that the company will succeed in being the first to develop a moderately priced videodisc recorder/player. Market research predicts that the first company to develop this product will be a star.

Ulysses Travel Agencies also showed potential, and the travel industry is growing. However, Ulysses' market share has declined for the last two years even though Sovera has contributed a lot of money to Ulysses' operations. The travel agencies located in the Midwestern and eastern sections of the country have been the biggest drain on resources.

Reddy Self-Storage was one of the first self-storage companies to open. For the last three years, Reddy has maintained a large market share while growth in the self-storage market has slowed considerably.

Ron Ebert, chairman of Sovera, prepared the agenda for the company's annual planning meeting where the present businesses were evaluated and strategies for future acquisitions were formulated. The following statements of strategy for each of the subsidiary companies discussed were formulated on the basis of the master plan:

LaBue Videodiscs. Sovera's discretionary resources are to be employed to support the growth of this business. The future officers of Sovera are to be developed here.

Ulysses Travel Agencies. An orderly disposal of the least profitable locations is the initial objective. Once the disposals are complete, an acceptable profit and growth strategy for the remaining locations will be formulated.

Reddy Self-Storage. The strategy for this company is to maintain efficient operations and maximize the generation of cash for use in the further development of Sovera's other businesses.

These strategy statements were part of the strategic plan presented to Sovera's board of directors. The directors' only debate was whether Sovera should sell the entire Ulysses organization rather than parts of it. However, the board approved all three statements as presented and circulated them to managers throughout the three units as the corporation's "new marching orders."

REQUIRED:

1. Identify at least four general characteristics that differentiate the three businesses described above, and explain how these characteristics influenced the formulation of a different strategy for each business.
2. Discuss the likely effects of the three strategy statements on the behavior of top management and middle management of each of the three businesses.
(CMA adapted)

2-3. Accounting and Tax Practices (Strategic Analysis)[1]

Terry Merton, CPA, hardly noticed the bright sunshine as she drove down the freeway in late October, 20X0 on her way to her job as controller for a small manufacturing company in her hometown of Brightside, California. She was contemplating the prospect of starting an accounting and tax practice. Although quite satisfied with her present employment, she was very excited about the possibility of owning her own business. Prior to her present position, Terry had worked for four years in the small business division of a Big 5 public accounting firm's Brightside office and had dreamed of opening her own practice. Terry had decided that 20X1 is the year her dream will become a reality.

Arriving at her office early, Terry began to think about the possible market segments she might serve and the types of tax and accounting problems these potential clients might have. For instance, Terry might simply establish a tax practice which would focus on serving individuals who typically require only simple return preparation. Serving this target market segment would mean preparing simple tax returns, such as form 1040 and other schedules commonly completed for individuals along with the 1040.

On the other hand, Terry could establish both a tax and accounting practice. This would mean she would serve both individuals and small businesses, although her primary target market would be small businesses. Pursuing this alternative would mean that she would render tax services for individuals, small businesses, estates, trusts and pension plans. Further, she would provide compilation, review and audit services for small businesses, as well as advice on designing accounting information systems. Terry knew that her first step would be to identify the market segment she wished to serve. To be successful, she would have to serve the selected target market very well.

Once she identified her target market segment, Terry could then make a decision about her competitive strategy -- whether to implement a cost leadership of differentiation strategy.

Pursuing a cost leadership strategy meant that she would attract clients by keeping her prices (and her costs) low. At the same time, Terry would still be attentive to providing quality service on a timely basis. She would compete on the basis of price and monitor costs to be sure they were kept low.

Pursuing the differentiation strategy meant providing services which are considered to be unique. Differentiating her product probably meant that Terry would provide above-average service and develop a more personal relationship with clients. With the differentiation strategy, Terry would be able to charge above-average prices for the services provided to clients and would not have to be as attentive to cost control as she would under the cost leadership strategy.

In considering which strategy to pursue, Terry thought about a nationally known provider of tax preparation services for individuals, which had offices located throughout the U.S. This national firm used television, radio and billboard advertising to present 17 reasons why taxpayers should do business with their firm. Terry was certain that the national firm had a costly centralized administrative structure. The firm's tax preparers were typically not CPA's, but were graduates of a training program conducted by the firm. Terry felt that this nationally-known firm was pursuing a differentiation strategy, since it emphasized the 17 reasons but did not emphasize low price.

If Terry selected the individual tax market, she could employ the cost leadership strategy. The limited tax expertise required would allow Terry to remain at her present employment. She would hire Jim Wallace, an experienced semi-retired preparer of uncomplicated tax returns. Terry would locate her tax practice in a storefront in a nearby shopping mall. Rent was very low there, and there was a high volume of pedestrian traffic past the location. Given this heavy pedestrian traffic, Terry reasoned that she

---

[1] Prepared by Jack M. Ruhl and Jerry G. Kreuze, © American Accounting Association, 1997. Used with permission.

would incur little advertising cost. Terry expected that her costs could be kept low compared with the nationally-known firm for two reasons: (1) she would provide minimal training for Jim and (2) she would have minimal administrative and advertising costs.

Now, Terry thought about the small business market. Here, Terry thought about using the differentiation strategy. With the differentiation strategy, the services she would provide would be significantly different from the services provided by competitors. Terry would differentiate herself along a number of dimensions, many of which related to her extensive experience with the Brightside business community. First from her experience working in a Big 5 firm's small business division, Terry is acquainted with all the bankers in town. She knows how to prepare financial presentations for clients seeking loans in such a way that the loan applications are almost always approved. She also is familiar with virtually all the small business rental property in town, and can direct clients to the most reasonably priced locations. Finally, she is thoroughly familiar with the operation of a small business and can provide extremely useful insights to small business owners. Terry would provide small businesses with many reasons to patronize her new firm. If the small business strategy is pursued, Terry will leave her $40,000/year controller position to become the principal employee of Startup, Inc.

Terry would like to finance her new business start-up costs entirely from her personal savings. This is not possible, however, since she just recently purchased a new automobile for cash, which left her with a savings account balance of only $2,400. She will need a business loan to cover start-up costs including the purchase of a computer and software. Prior to contacting Bill Andersen, the loan officer at a nearby bank, Terry prepares some preliminary profit estimates. Terry's estimates of the revenues and costs associated with each strategy for the first year of operation, 20X1, are presented in exhibit 1.

Terry projects revenues of $67,500 (450 Clients at $150/client) and $91,350 (203 clients at $450/client) under the cost leadership and differentiation strategies, respectively (see exhibit 1). Supplies average $10 per client and constitute the only variable costs for Startup, Inc. The fixed expenses vary between the strategies in several respects:

1. If she pursues the small business strategy, Terry will incur significantly higher liability insurance costs each year than she would under the cost leadership strategy. This is due to the fact that she has much more liability exposure since she will be doing attest work (reviews and audits).
2. Annual computer software costs will be greater under the small business strategy. This is because each year Terry will purchase specialized CD-ROM tax preparation disks needed to properly prepare the estate and trust returns. Additional software is also needed if she wishes to advise clients with regard to pensions.
3. If she pursues the small business strategy, Terry will incur additional expense for club membership dues and entertainment expenses compared with the cost leadership strategy. This is due to the fact that Terry knows that she can develop the estate and trust work through social contacts with bankers and attorneys.
4. Under the individual tax strategy, Terry will continue in her present employment position. She will hire Jim Wallace for $500/week. Although not a CPA, Jim is approaching retirement at the public accounting firm where Terry had been employed. Jim would be happy to work part-time at Startup, Inc. Terry is impressed with Jim's qualifications and is confident he could prepare uncomplicated tax returns. The differentiation strategy, however, will entail more complicated tax return preparations, which are beyond Jim's capabilities. Under the small business strategy, Terry would resign from her controller position and work full-time for Startup, Inc., drawing a salary of $600 per week.
5. Terry's home has a very large attached apartment which she presently leases to two college students at a rent of $500 per month. The students' lease expires on December 31, 20X0. Under the small business strategy, she will not renew the lease. Instead, she will set up the offices of Startup, Inc. in the apartment. Under the cost leadership provider strategy, the students would continue to occupy the

apartment, since space in a nearby strip mall will be leased for Startup's offices. The strip mall space would provide needed pedestrian traffic and high visibility for Startup, Inc., and avoid traffic congestion in Terry's residential neighborhood.

6. Anticipating the complexity of clients under the small business strategy and considering the fact that she has been out of public accounting for three years, Terry estimates $8,000 in annual training costs. Minimal training costs are projected with the individual tax strategy since Jim Wallace already possesses the necessary experience, and the level of tax expertise required is minimal.

OBTAINING A BUSINESS LOAN

Terry faxed the financial projections in Exhibit 1 to Bill Andersen in early November 20X0. As a loan officer, Bill must follow a set of specific guidelines in making his loan approval decisions. If Bill approves too many loans which ultimately are "bad," he will be dismissed from his job. For all loan applications, he must be able to justify after-the-fact his decision to the bank's board of directors, based largely on the loan applicant's financial statements. In assessing the credit worthiness of Terry's loan application, Bill plans to use operating income before depreciation and working capital as surrogates for cash-paying ability. Terry will offer her nearly new automobile as collateral. The bank's policy is to approve loans only if the annual payments are less than the beginning working capital balance and the projected before depreciation operating income for the next 12 months. The bank has also instituted a policy to have all loans due and payable on demand at the end of any calendar year if the payee is not in compliance with the original loan requirements.

Bill's bank has a maximum loan period for startup companies of five years. At an interest rate of ten percent per annum, Startup, Inc. qualifies for an $8,000 maximum loan requiring a $2,110 annual payment. Consequently Startup's December 31 working capital balance and annual operating income (before depreciation expense) must not fall below $2,110, or the bank loan becomes due and payable.

REQUIRED:

1. From Bill Andersen's perspective, which practice strategy is better? Why?

2. From a managerial and strategic planning perspective, which practice strategy should Terry pursue? Why?

EXHIBIT 1
Startup, Inc.
Projected Income Statements Under Two Competitive Strategies
For the Twelve Months Ended December 31, 20X1

		Strategies for Practice	
		Cost Leadership	Differentiation
Revenues	(450 clients at $150)	$67,500	
	(203 clients at $450)		$91,350
Variable Expenses			
	Supplies ($10 per client)	4,500	2,030
Contribution Margin		63,000	89,320
Fixed Expenses:			
	Depreciation—Computer	1,600	1,600
	Software	500	4,000
	Liability Insurance	2,400	11,680
	Rental—Furniture	5,660	5,660
	Club Membership & Entertainment	—	1,200
	Preparer Salary	26,000	31,200
	Secretarial Salary	16,000	16,000
	Advertising	200	1,180
	Rent—office	8,400	—
	Training	—	8,000
	Total Fixed Expenses	60,760	80,520
Operating Income		$ 2,240	$ 8,800

2-4. Strategy, International

Barry McDonald, CFO for Recreational Products, Inc (RPI), is convinced it would be profitable for his firm to invest in a manufacturing operation in Singapore. RPI makes a variety of recreational products, including sporting goods, sportware, and camping equipment. RPI is known as a very high quality producer, with features and prices greater than most in the industry. One of the largest divisions in RPI is the boating division, which makes a variety of sailboats and fishing boats from 16 feet up to large sailboats of 40+ feet in length. These boats are now manufactured in two US plants. Barry's idea is to utilize the available low cost labor, materials resources and the favorable business climate in Singapore to build a manufacturing plant there for producing the larger sailboats. The finished boats would be sold to existing customers (boat dealers) in the United States and Canada, and a new effort would be made to sell some of the product in Asia and Australia. Barry forecasts sales of US$50 million, cost of sales (manufacturing in the Singapore plant) of $34 million, and other expenses of approximately $10 million. The government of Singapore would provide a tax holiday for the project, but the return of profits to the United States would be taxed in the US at the US rate of 34%.

Barry's research showed that the cost of the plant in Singapore would be $20 million. Funds for the investment could come from the firm's own resources at a cost of approximately 12%, or through a subsidized loan from the government of Singapore at a 5% rate. With these figures and other estimates, Barry figured the after-tax cash flow of the plant would be a positive $4 million per year for the next 15 years, the expected life of the plant.

REQUIRED:

1. What does RPI's competitive position appear to be for the entire firm, and for the boating division? What are some of the likely critical success factors for the boating division?
2. Does Barry's plan for the Singapore plant fit the strategic competitive position you developed in (1) above?
3. What do you think are some of the key international issues that are relevant for Barry's proposal?

Readings

STRATEGY FOCUSED PERFORMANCE MEASURES

By Mark L. Frigo

Performance measures that are highly aligned with and linked to an organization's business strategy are critical for communicating and executing strategy. But how can an organization develop performance measures that are truly strategic? This article presents a few guidelines based on detailed, ongoing research with the IMA as well as in-depth applications of strategic performance measurement systems in North American and Europe. These guidelines can be considered by any organization in its quest to improve the way it measures and manages strategy.

Strategy and Performance Measures are Inseparable: At many companies, there are gaps between strategy and performance measures. In fact, the IMA survey on Performance Measurement found that more than half the survey respondents considered their company's performance measures inadequate in communicating strategy. This is often the result of the separation between strategy development processes and performance measurement (strategy-execution) processes. Instead, organizations should treat strategy development and strategy execution as parallel, interrelated processes. Strategy-focused performance measures must be driven by a process encompassing the ongoing reevaluation and redesign of business strategy as well as a fervent attention to making strategy execution through performance measurement part and parcel of the strategy design itself. This approach would lead naturally to the types of performance measures the balanced scorecard and other strategic performance measurement systems would encourage.

Strategy First, Then Performance Measures: Ignoring this guideline is a common problem. The first questions some managers ask when embarking on a performance measurement initiative are "What should we measure?" or "How should we measure performance in a given area?" In fact, these are the last questions management should focus on. Strategic performance measurement systems, like the balanced scorecard, are first and foremost about strategy. This requires the development of a business strategy with execution in mind. Once the strategy is well developed, then performance metrics can be identified.

Metrics Should Change as Strategy Changes: Too often organizations are using performance measures that are no longer relevant to their business strategy. Over time, existing strategy can become outdated because products and services are less needed by the marketplace, the market segment may be shrinking in size, or the way the company creates or delivers the product or service offerings may become outmoded as new technologies become available or laws and regulations that restrict or allow activities change. You must consider how forces of change affect the entire value chain of an organization and how those changes can affect the interrelationships of activities within that value chain. All of this affects performance measures.

During the late 1990s, technology took center stage, reshaping the way companies conducted business and the demands consumers place on the goods and services they receive—as companies like Dell have proven. Dell's initial strategy and performance metrics differed from competitors like Compaq. Dell initially focused on operating effectively and efficiently, which, in part, involved shortening its cash conversion cycle by managing days' sales outstanding, days in inventory, and days' payables outstanding. But when the market demanded more innovation of offerings in product and post-sales service, Dell needed to adjust its strategy and performance metrics accordingly.

Align Strategy and Performance Measures with the Right Goal: The highest tenet of Return Driven Strategy is to ethically manage for maximum financial value of creation. This goal provides the anchor that will help management make the right decisions as they develop and execute business strategy. Strategic performance measures must be focused on maximizing financial value creation, something many companies fail to do because of misaligned compensation plans and/or misdirected motivations. Are the performance measures used in your organization truly leading to managing for maximum financial value creation? Or are flawed financial metrics leading in the wrong direction? Increases in revenue and earning per share (EPS) are still widely reported as primary metrics of determining value creation, but when business decisions are based on those metrics, terrible activities can result. These activities can range from value-destroying mergers and acquisitions, growth at the expense of return on investment, and harvesting of assets—which may increase accounting profits but actually destroy value. In fact, in one study, Hewitt Associates found evidence that companies highly aligned with traditional metrics tend to be the worst performers in shareholder returns.

Use Performance Measures That Help Synchronize Strategic Activities: How well do existing performance measures enable your organization to synchronize the combination of strategic competencies and supporting activities to fulfill unmet needs in large, growing market segments? For successful companies, all strategic activities must be highly aligned and synchronized to create the right kinds of offerings. In my research on Return Driven Strategy with Joel Litman, we found that the most successful companies were vigilant in detecting changing or unmet customer needs in large and high-growth market segments. They constantly made innovations in their product and service offerings, leveraged economies of scale and scope, and branded the offerings in a manner that met those needs. These companies included great companies like General Electric and a broad range of industries involving retailers like Walgreen and Home Depot, consumer products companies like Gillette, services companies like ADP and Cintas, manufactures like ITW, and pharmaceutical companies like Abbott and Pfizer. But underlying the consistent and disciplined execution of strategy was a myriad of performance metrics that encompassed the right financial measures, customer and value proposition measures, internal processes, and other measures that uniquely reflected the company's strategy and helped in its execution.

Strategic performance measures should be closely focused around a line of sight, driven from the strategy. Michael Porter of Harvard Business School puts it this way: "Measure how various parts of your value chain actually fit together to lead to an overarching advantage, rather than using process-by-process metrics." ("The Importance of Being Strategic" *Balanced Scorecard Report,* March-April 2002) Are your performance measures truly unique and relevant to the strategy of the organization?

Strategic Performance Measurement: The guidelines of strategic performance measurement can provide a refreshing alternative to the endless performance metric debates that have so plagued corporate management over the last decade. Strategic performance measurement begins with a sound philosophy pertaining to and a sound judgment surrounding how strategic decisions will be made and how performance measurement will be used to make decision and execute the strategy. Management must be vigilant in aligning performance measures with the strategy of the organization and in ensuring the strategy itself is executable.

APPLYING THE BALANCED SCORECARD TO SMALL COMPANIES

Companies are designing their performance goals—and keeping score—based on their unique needs and perceived critical success factors.

By Chee W. Chow, Kamal M. Haddad, and James E. Williamson, CPA

On October 30, 1996, Pacific Inland Bank of Anaheim, Calif., announced that it had changed its vision and strategy to such an extent that it was also changing its name to Security First Bank in a complete restructuring to transform it into "a true community bank, one that serves small businesses, professionals, and consumers."[1]

The restructuring at Security First is only one example of how American companies are making major changes in responding to an increasingly competitive global economy. Indeed, the need for fundamental change is so strong that some leading authorities from academia and industry have called for a complete rethinking and reengineering of Corporate America. For example, in their book, *Reengineering the Corporation*,[2] authors Hammer and Champy emphasize that it no longer is enough to do traditional tasks better. Rather, the realities of the current competitive environment require that the old "individual-based task-oriented" management concept be discarded completely and replaced with a "team-based process-oriented" management concept.

The current emphasis on restructuring has created a new problem for management because traditional measures of financial performance no longer are adequate to fully assess how the newly restructured organization is doing. Not only will successful restructuring require innovation in the way organizations view and measure performance, but developing, implementing, and evaluating such measures may be the greatest challenge that companies will have to face. In fact, a recent survey has found that "80% of large American companies want to change their performance measurement systems."[3] The "Balanced Scorecard" may be just what organizations need to help them restructure successfully to meet the demands of the 21st Century.

WHAT IS THE BALANCED SCORECARD?

Essentially, the Balanced Scorecard is a set of financial and nonfinancial measures relating to a company's critical success factors. What is innovative about the concept is that the components of the scorecard are designed in an integrative fashion such that they reinforce each other in indicating both the current and future prospects of the company. More than others, Kaplan and Norton probably deserve much of the credit for elucidating and increasing the awareness of this concept.[4]

When Kaplan and Norton introduced the concept of the Balanced Scorecard they were looking for ways to concentrate corporate focus on performance measurement innovation. This focus was considered necessary because traditional management reporting systems have been found to be not much help in measuring performance in the new manufacturing environment. While these backward-looking "task" or "cost object" oriented measurement systems generated financial results for numerous organizational units—including results by entity, lines of business, cost centers, and profit centers—they failed to supply the information necessary to pull strong future performance out of the organization.

Today's managers know that yesterday's accounting results tell little about what actually can help grow market share and profits—things like employee development and turnover, innovative services that enhance customer values, the quality of vendor services, and benefits from advancements in research and development. A key advantage of the Balanced Scorecard is that it puts strategy, structure, and vision at the center of management's focus.

Another advantage is that because the Balanced Scorecard emphasizes an integrated combination of traditional and nontraditional performance measures, it keeps management focused on the entire business process and helps ensure that actual current operating performance is in line with long-term strategy and customer values. In so doing, the Balanced Scorecard helps maintain a balance

Figure 1. TRANSLATING STRATEGY INTO OPERATIONAL TERMS*

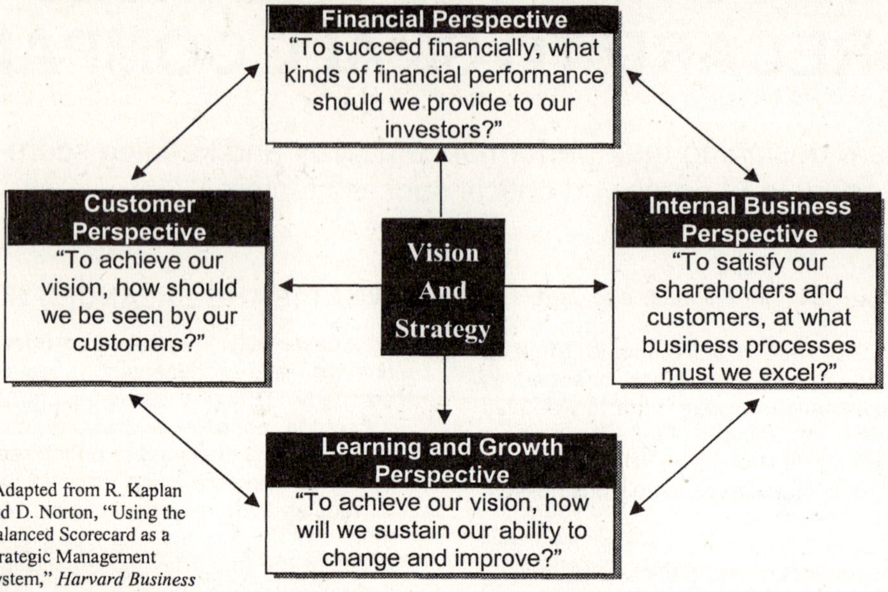

*Adapted from R. Kaplan and D. Norton, "Using the Balanced Scorecard as a Strategic Management System," *Harvard Business Review*, January-February 1996, p.76.

between building long-range competitive abilities and recognizing investors' attention to financial reports. To this extent the Balanced Scorecard does retain traditional financial measures. But these financial measures are viewed in the larger context of the company's competitive strategies for creating "future value through investment in customers, suppliers, employees, processes, technology, and innovation."[5]

Because of the way the Balanced Scorecard aids in successful restructuring by linking together all subunits and members in a concerted effort to enhance the overall goals and objectives of the organization, many leading-edge companies have begun to adopt this new approach. For example, in late 1989, Bank of Montreal's "corporate performance was heading downhill fast." Chairman and Chief Executive Officer Mathew Barrett and his team, deciding that "a successful turn-around strategy had to include a new approach to performance measurement," used the Balanced Scorecard to help solve the company's problems. A partial list of other adopters includes KPMG Peat Marwick, Tenneco, Allstate, AT&T, and Elf Atochem.[6]

MAJOR COMPONENTS OF A BALANCED SCORECARD

A well designed Balanced Scorecard combines financial measures of past performance with measures of the firm's' drivers of future performance. The specific objectives and measures of an organization's Balanced Scorecard are derived from the firm's vision and strategy. As such, the relevance perspectives and their relative importance can be expected to vary among firms. There is some agreement, however, that the framework for a Balanced Scorecard will include at least four major perspectives: financial, customer, internal business process, and learning and growth (Figure 1).

The financial perspective serves as the focus for the objects and measures in the other scorecard perspectives. This perspective reflects the concern in for-profit enterprises that every action should be part of a network of cause-and-effect relationships that culminate in improving short- and long-run financial performance. In the process of identifying goals and measures, different financial metrics may be appropriate for different units within the organization, linking that unit's financial objectives to the overall business unit strategy.

But how is a company to achieve its financial goals? Current wisdom is that every company needs to pay attention to the needs and desires of its customers because customers pay for the company's costs and provide for its profit. Companies need to identify the customer and market segments in which they choose to compete. This customer perspective allows companies to align their measures of customer values (i.e., satisfaction, loyalty, retention, acquisition, and profitability) with targeted customers and market segments.

Table 1. RESPONSE FROM AN ELECTRONICS FIRM

Goals	Measures
Customer Perspective	
Quality	Own quality relative to industry standards; number of defects; first pass yields; delivered product quality; number of visits to customers to calibrate quality; number of returns; number and quality of customers.
Price	Own price relative to competitive market price; sales volume; customer willingness to pay.
Delivery	Actual versus planned; number of ontime deliveries; number of days early/late; current backlog; aging of past due orders.
Shipments	Sales growth; number of customers that make up 90% of shipments; % military sales; number of new-to-us part numbers shipped.
New products	Number of new products to support new semiconductors; rate of technology improvements; % of sales from products introduced in last two years.
Support	Response time; customer satisfaction surveys.
Internal Capabilities	
Efficiency of manufacturing process	Cycle time; lead time; manufacturing overhead cost/quarter; rate of increase in use of automation each quarter; days' sales in WIP; yield.
New product introduction	Rate of new product introduction/quarter
New product success	New products quarterly sales; number of orders.
Sales penetration	Actual sales versus plan; increases in number of $1 million customers each quarter.
New businesses	Number of new businesses each year.
Innovation	
Technology leadership	Product performance compared to competition; number of new products with patented technology in them; annual rate of increase in number of new products per engineer.
Cost leadership	Manufacturing overhead per quarter as a percent of sales; rate of decrease in cost of quality per quarter.
Market leadership	Market share in all major markets; number of systems developed to meet customer requests and requirements.
Research and development	Number of new products; number of patents.
Financial Perspective	
Sales	Annual growth in sales and profits.
Cost of sales	Extent it remains flat or decreases each year.
Profitability	Return on total capital employed.
Prosperity	Cash flows.
Employees and Community Perspective	
Competitive salaries and benefits	Salaries compared to norm in local area.
Opportunity	Individual contribution, personal satisfaction in job; opportunity to share in company financial success.
Citizenship	Company contributions to community and the institutions that generate the environment; extent to which employees are encouraged to contribute to the community.

Another component of the scorecard focuses on those internal business processes that will deliver the objectives that the financial and customer perspectives have established for customers and shareholders. This component expands the focus beyond improving existing operating processes to defining a complete internal process value chain that includes identifying current and future customer needs and developing solutions for those needs. This perspective will be unique to each company as it identifies the complete chain of processes that add to the value customers receive from its products and services.

Based on the objectives established in the financial, customer, and internal business process perspectives, a company needs to identify objectives and measures to drive continuous organizational learning and growth. The objectives in the learning and growth perspective should be the drivers of successful outcomes in the first three perspectives.

Because the Balanced Scorecard expands the company's set of objectives beyond traditional financial measures, managers will be able to measure how their business units create value for current and future customers. The Balanced Scorecard also helps to measure the need to enhance internal capabilities and the firm's investment in people, systems, and those procedures necessary to improve future performance. In other words, the Balanced Scorecard is an attempt to capture the essence of the organization's critical value-creating activities. The Balanced Scorecard also aids in communicating the company's goals and rewarding those employees whose efforts enhance those goals. Because of the financial perspective, the Balanced Scorecard retains an interest in short-term performance but, at the same time, clearly reveals those drivers leading to long-term financial and competitive performance.

FITTING THE BALANCED SCORECARD TO THE ORGANIZATION

Developing a Balanced Scorecard involves a process of custom designing a strategic management measurement system for a specific organization. The process is begun by making a preliminary assessment of the overall business strategy of the organization. The focus is on integration of the entire business process but not overly emphasizing the individual tasks. Once the overall business process is identified, along with its goals and objectives, it should be possible to identify and rank the measures believed to capture the essence of the organization's progress toward those goals and objectives.

To date, reported applications of the Balanced Scorecard mostly have been confined to large, international companies. These companies tend to face more turbulent and competitive environments, have more dispersed and varied products and processes that they to coordinate and monitor, and also have more resources for undertaking change initiatives. In comparison, small or local companies may have different needs such that what works for large companies may be ineffective or unnecessary for them. To gain some insights into the potential applicability of the Balanced Scorecard in small or local companies, we undertook a dialogue with four such companies operating in Southern California whose size ranged from 100 to 1,200 employees. This dialogue with a top-level manager, either the CEO or a senior vice president from each company, was loosely structured in the form of a question and response survey asking to what extent the company had considered developing a Balanced Scorecard to fir its particular needs. Each company was asked to identify up to five major components, along with the goals and associated performance measures, that might form the basis for an effective Balanced Scorecard for it.

Another objective of our study was to explore how the Balanced Scorecard might vary across industries, so we looked at four companies from different industries: electronics manufacturing, food ingredients, banking, and biotechnology. The Balanced Scorecards suggested by these companies are shown in Tables 1-4. Because of space limitations, however, we will discuss only the responses from the electronics firm, as shown in Table 1, in any detail.

We also asked each of the top managers to what extent their company had implemented a performance monitoring system similar to the Balanced Scorecard and if they thought such a system could be beneficial to their company. Only one of the responding companies said it had totally implemented such a system, with the other companies reporting that their current implementation status ranged from 3 to 7 on a scale of 1 to 10. All responding companies, however, said they thought such a system would be extremely beneficial, with the lowest score being 8 on a scale of 1 to 10, and half of the companies gave the value of the concept a perfect 10 rating.

The electronics firm selected the customer perspective, emphasizing the goals of quality, price,

Table 2. RESPONSE FROM A FOOD INGREDIENTS COMPANY

Goals	Measures
Financial Perspective	
Capture an increasing share of industry growth.	Company growth versus industry growth.
Secure the base business while remaining the preferred supplier to our customers.	Volume trend by line of business; revenue trend by line of business; gross margin.
Expand aggressively in global markets.	Ratio of North American sales to international sales.
Commercialize a continuous stream of profitable new ingredients and services.	Percent of sales from products launched within the past five years; gross profit from new products.
Customer Perspective	
Become the lowest-cost supplier.	Total cost of using our products and services relative to total cost of using competitive products and services.
Tailor products and services to meet local needs.	Cross-sell ratio.
Expand those products and services that meet customers' needs better than competitors.	Percent of products in R&D pipeline that are being test-marketed by out customers (percent of pipeline value).
Customer satisfaction.	Customer surveys.
Internal Perspective	
Maintain lowest cost base in the industry.	Our total costs relative to number one competitor; inventory turns; plant utilization.
Maintain consistent predictable production processes.	First pass success rate.
Continue to improve distribution efficiency.	Percent of perfect orders.
Build capability to screen and identify profitable products and services.	Change in pipeline economic value (risk-adjusted decision tree approach similar to option pricing methodology).
Integrate acquisitions and alliances efficiently.	Revenues per salary dollar.
Learning and Growth Perspective	
Link the overall strategy to the reward and recognition system.	Net income per dollar of variable pay.
Foster a culture that supports innovation and growth.	Annual preparedness assessment; quarterly reports (done by VP-MGR).
Develop those competencies critical to the overall critical gaps to be filled.	Percent competency deployment matrix filled.

delivery, and development of new products as of primary importance. This selection probably is typical of the contemporary world view that customers and their values must come first if the company is going to maintain long-term financial stability and growth.

The second component selected is internal capabilities. But analysis of the goals and measures attached to this component indicates that customer values and market penetration are still on the minds of the company's management. There definitely is a linkage here that the management clearly recognizes.

Third, the company values innovation which, again, clearly reflects the linkage with customer values and market penetration. In this area, we also see that they are very concerned with quality, the cost of quality, and its cause and effect on competitive market prices.

Fourth, the company indicates, but with little discussion, that there is a need to provide shareholders some relatively short-run traditional financial results. That the company places this component fourth is an indication that it sees customer values, product development and innovation, and market penetration as drivers of financial performance.

Finally, the company management's explicit identification of an employee perspective reflects its belief that a well-paid and satisfied workforce is key to attaining the company's overall goals and objectives.

DIFFERENT GOALS AND SCORECARDS

As we mentioned earlier, an important consideration in applying the Balanced Scorecard approach is to recognize that each organization is unique and, therefore, requires a different set of goals, objectives, and strategies to attain its mission. This fact is evident when we look at the items selected by some of the other companies for their scorecard.

A company in the food ingredients industry (Table 2) says it is first interested in the financial perspective but then proceeds to identify many goals and measures in the other perspectives that will enhance the financial goals along with the goals of perspective.

The responses from a commercial bank are illustrated in Table 3. An interesting observation about this scorecard is that it sets out a separate community perspective. This viewpoint probably reflects the traditional community role that bank managers think may be expected of them.

Finally, a biotechnology firm in its Balanced Scorecard (Table 4) selected the customer perspective as of primary importance. The financial perspective comes after customers and technological leadership. Thus, across the four types of companies considered there is a clear indication that management is designing the goals and measures to fit the company's unique needs and perceived role. Further, these responses suggest that the Balanced Scorecard can be an effective management tool for small companies as well.

FOUR NEW MANAGEMENT PROCESSES

Kaplan and Norton show how the Balanced Scorecard will let managers introduce "four new management processes that, separately and in combination, contribute to linking long-term strategic objectives with short-term actions."[7] Figure 2 shows how the integration of the four processes lead to the Balanced Scorecard.

The first process—translating the vision—helps managers build a consensus of opinion about the organization's vision and strategy. Because it is very important to translate vision and strategy into operational terms that employees can understand and use to guide actions at their local level, the vision and strategy statements must be expressed as an agreed-upon integrated set of objectives and measures that describe the long-term drivers of success.

The second process—communicating and linking—helps management tie overall objectives and strategies to department and individual objectives. This process replaces the traditional way departments are evaluated by financial performance and individual incentives. The advantages of this new approach is the way it ensures that all levels of the organization are made aware of and understand the company's long-term strategy. The scorecard also ensures that individual and departmental objectives are in agreement with the long-term strategy.

The third process—business planning—helps organizations integrate their business and financial plans. Kaplan and Norton explain that most organizations today are trying to implement a variety of change programs that are competing with each other for time, energy, and resources.[8] This competition can be so intense and inner focused that it is difficult to integrate these diverse initiatives to achieve the firm's overall strategic goals. The Balanced Scorecard can be used to set goals that provide a basis for allocating resources and setting priorities. The scorecard also can aid in eliminating some initiatives and selecting others that are more effective for moving the organization toward its long-term strategic objectives.

The fourth process—feedback and learning—helps management direct the organization toward strategic learning. This process is different from traditional feedback and review models that focus on whether the company, departments, or individuals have met their budgeted financial objectives. An advantage of the Balanced Scorecard approach over traditional models is that it focuses management's attention on managing results from the perspective of customers, internal business processes, and learning and growth. This real-time learning perspective can increase organizations' nimbleness in modifying strategies in response to changing circumstances.

THE PERSONAL SCORECARD

Because achieving a company's goals requires a concerted effort on the part of everyone, there is a need to translate the goals and objectives down to the individual level. Translating the company scorecard into specific goals and measures at the individual level is important for motivating and focusing the individuals and teams performing the work. There is no reason why all the individual scorecards should be identical because each member may have a unique role in the

Table 3. RESPONSE FROM A COMMERCIAL BANK

Goals	Measures
Shareholders — Financial Perspective	
Return on assets of 1% or more and return on equity of 15% or more.	Net interest margin; noninterest income; noninterest expense.
Efficiency ratio of 68% or less.	Overhead expenses.
Growth in assets of 15% or more.	Asset growth.
Loan losses of .5% or less.	Number of problem loans; early detection rate.
Loan delinquencies over 30 days of 2% or less.	Number of bad loan underwriting; number of loan delinquencies.
Customer Perspective	
Personalized quality service	Number of complaints; amount spent on training; number of rewards and recognitions; customer satisfaction.
Competitive products	Sales volume; number of customers; number of products offered a year; extent products are "user friendly" compared to competition; degree of use of technology (where appropriate).
Pricing	Cost of doing business; own price relative to competition; extent service is better than competition.
Customer satisfaction	Customer surveys.
Employee Perspective	
Competitive wages and benefits.	Annual market review.
Participation in success of the organization.	Bonuses based on corporate and personal performance; sales incentives; recognition.
Enhanced job skills.	Training/schooling; coaching.
Objective evaluation of performance.	Performance standards; job descriptions.
Enhance upward career movement.	Number of promotions from within; posting of most open positions.
Community Perspective	
Support worthwhile community activities	Extent of employee participation, extent of financial support.
Act as good corporate citizens.	Extent employees are encouraged to vote; extent of support and activities that foster this attitude.

organization. The goals and needs of any organization are many and varied, and skills, talents, and interests also vary across individuals. To attain the greatest success as a whole requires organizations to exploit these individual differences and to seek and create synergies among its members. Thus, unlike a golf team, where the team score is simply the sum of individual team members' scores, most organizations are more like a football team, where the team outcome depends on coordination and cooperation in addition to specialization among team members. Accordingly, while the individual personal scorecards need to be consistent with the organization's overall strategies, goals, and measures, there also needs to be flexibility in accommodating individual strengths and weaknesses.

A question that remains is whether an organization's compensation system should be linked to its Balance Scorecard measures. Some companies believe that tying financial reward to performance is a powerfully motivating incentive and have done so.[9] If an organization is considering using such a linkage in its compensation scheme, however, it is important to realize that there also are risks involved with this approach. Does the organization have the right measures on the scorecard? Does the organization have valid and reliable data for the selected measures of performance? Are there undesirable consequences that could arise from actions aimed at achieving the

Table 4. RESPONSE FROM A BIOTECHNOLOGY FIRM	
Goals	**Measures**
Customer Perspective (How can we improve customer perceptions and relationships?)	
New products	Percent of sales from new products.
Early purchase of seasonal products	Percent of sales recorded by early purchase date.
Accurate invoices	Percent error-free invoices.
Early payment	Percent of customers who pay early.
Product quality	Product performance vs. industry quality standards.
Customer satisfaction	Customer satisfaction surveys.
Internal Business Perspective (Efficiency; how can we be more cost-effective?)	
Low-cost producer	Unit cost vs. competitors.
Reduce inventory	Inventory as percent of sales.
New products	Number of actual introductions vs. target.
Innovation Perspective (How can we establish and maintain technological leadership?)	
New active ingredients	Number of new ingredients identified by internal discovery program.
Proprietary positions	Number of patents that create exclusive marketing rights.
Financial Perspective (How do we build shareowner value?)	
Growth	Percent increase in top line revenue.
Profitability	Return on equity; earnings per share.
Industry leadership	Market share.

established targets? Those types of questions need to be explored before an organization adopts an incentive strategy based on achieving certain targeted goals.

We do know that if the current trend of shifting emphasis from individual achievement to cooperation and teamwork continues, companies will need to reexamine their short-term formula-based incentive compensation systems. Moreover, when companies adopt the Balanced Scorecard approach, they move to a longer-term viewpoint and may need to set incentive rewards more subjectively. According to Kaplan and Norton, the longer-term subjective evaluation process appears to have the advantage of being less susceptible to the game playing and distortions associated with explicit, formula-based rules.[10] There is little doubt that the Balanced Scorecard has a role to play in incentive compensation systems. Exactly what that role will be will become clear as companies experiment with various ways to link rewards to scorecard measures.

IMPLEMENTING THE BALANCED SCORECARD

If the experience of other companies is any guide,[11] the design and implementation process for installing a Balanced Scorecard may take two years or more. A typical schedule may contain all or some of the following component stages.

Stage 1. A strategic planning retreat involving all levels of management is held to identify strategic issues and discuss possible solutions. A major purpose of this meeting is to achieve a consensus among the individual members concerning the company's overall vision and strategic goals and objectives. This step should lead to identifying the critical perspectives in the company's Balanced Scorecard.

Stage 2. A strategic planning committee is formed to formulate objectives for each previously identified perspective in the firm's Balanced Scorecard.

Stage 3. Using the Balanced Scorecard as a communication tool, the strategic planning committee seeks comments on and acceptance of the company's Balanced Scorecard from all members of the organization.

Stage 4. Based on feedback from the dialogue with the individual members, the strategic planning committee revises the company's Balanced Scorecard.

Figure 2. MANAGING STRATEGY: FOUR PROCESSES*

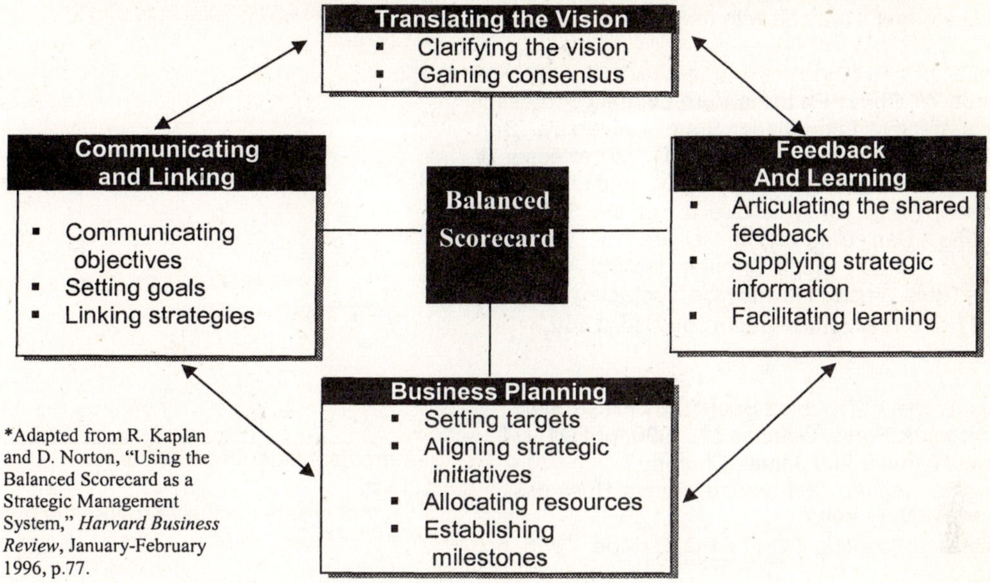

*Adapted from R. Kaplan and D. Norton, "Using the Balanced Scorecard as a Strategic Management System," *Harvard Business Review*, January-February 1996, p.77.

Stage 5. The revised balanced Scorecard is communicated to the individual members. Thereupon, each individual member is required to develop a personal Balanced Scorecard that supports the company's overall goals and objectives described in its Balanced Scorecard.

Stage 6. The strategic planning committee reviews the individual Balanced Scorecards and may revise not only the personal scorecards but also the company's Balanced Scorecard.

Stage 7. Based on final Balanced Scorecards, management formulates a five-year strategic plan for the overall organization. The first-year plan is expanded into the annual operating plan for the following year.

Stage 8. Individual and company progress is reviewed quarterly to identify areas that need immediate attention and additional work.

Stage 9. Based on the individual personal Balanced Scorecards, the company's personnel committee in conjunction with each individual's supervisor evaluates each member's performance for the past year and makes recommendations relating to retention promotion, salary increases, or other rewards.

Stage 10. The strategic planning committee revises the company's Balanced Scorecard and the five-year strategic plan based on external and internal scanning of the company's current condition and changes in the economic environment.

Because the process is so lengthy, managers should lose no time in evaluating the Balanced Scorecard concept to see if they want to implement it or other methods that will promote and support change to better measurement and reward systems.

A SCORECARD FOR THE 21ST CENTURY

Maybe it is time to try something new. The Balanced Scorecard appears to be an exciting new idea that may help firms restructure to survive in difficult times. The scorecard also appears to be a concept that helps management direct its attention to those goals and objectives and the measures that drive the company toward achieving those goals and objectives that will allow the company to reengineer or restructure to meet the needs of the 21st Century.

The Balanced Scorecard is not so structured that it can serve all organizations uniformly. But, instead, its strength really lies in providing for management the ability to design a unique scorecard that specifically firs the needs of that company, subunit, or individual employee.

Perhaps most important, while the Balanced Scorecard is relatively new on the performance measurement scene, its perceived advantages at this time indicate that it may be with us for quite awhile.

Chee W. Chow, Ph.D., is Vern Odmark Professor of Accountancy, San Diego State University, San Diego, Calif. Kamal M. Haddad, Ph.D., is professor of finance, San Diego State University, and James E. Williamson, Ph.D., CPA, is director of the School of Accounting, San Diego State University. He is a member of the San Diego Chapter, through which he submitted this article. He may be contacted at (619) 594-6021 or e-mail jameswilliamson@sdsu.edu.

[1] James Granelli, "Troubled Bank Tries Fresh Start," *Los Angeles Times*, October 31, 1996, pp. D1, D4
[2] Michael Hammer and James Champy, *Reengineering the Corporation*, Harper Business, New York, N.Y., 1993.
[3] Bill Birchard, "Making it Go," *CFO*, October 1995, pp. 42-51.
[4] Robert Kaplan and David Norton, "The Balanced Scorecard—Measures That Drive Performance," *Harvard Business Review*, January-February 1992, pp. 71-79.
[5] Robert S. Kaplan and David P. Norton, *Translating Strategy Into Action: The Balanced Scorecard,* Harvard Business School Press, Boston, Mass., 1996, p.7.
[6] Birchard, pp. 49-51.
[7] Robert Kaplan and David Norton, "Using the Balanced Scorecard as a Strategic Management System," *Harvard Business Review*, January-February 1996, p. 75.
[8] Kaplan and Norton, p. 75.
[9] Kaplan and Norton, p. 81.
[10] Kaplan and Norton, p. 82.
[11] Kaplan and Norton, p. 78-79.

Chapter 3
Basic Cost Concepts

Cases

3-1 Strategy, CSFs, Cost Objects, and Performance Measures
3-2 Cost Drivers and Strategy

Readings

"Managing Costs Through Complexity Reduction at Carrier Corporation"
This article, based on the experience of Carrier Corporation, a United Technologies company, and one of the world's largest manufacturers of heating and air conditioning products, explains how product complexity is a key driver of total costs. The article also explains how product complexity can be measured and some techniques for reducing complexity.

Discussion Questions:
1. Why does product complexity lead to increased costs?
2. Explain 3-4 useful measures of product complexity.
3. Identify and explain 2-3 techniques for reducing product complexity and cost.

Cases

3-1. Strategy, CSFs, Cost Objects, and Performance Measures[1]

Three years ago, Vincent Chow completed his degree in accounting. The economy was in a depressed state at the time, and Vincent managed to get an offer of only $20,000 per year as a bookkeeper. In addition to its relatively low pay, this job had limited advancement potential.

Since Vincent was an enterprising and ambitious young man, he declined this offer and started a business of his own. He was convinced that because of changing lifestyles, a drive-through coffee establishment would be profitable. He was able to obtain backing from his parents to open such an establishment close to the industrial park area in town. Vincent named his business The Cappuccino Express and decided to sell only two type types of coffee; cappuccino and decaffeinated.

As Vincent had expected, the Cappuccino Express was very well received. Within three years, Vincent had added another outlet north of town. He left the day-to-day management of each site to a manager and focused his own attention on overseeing the entire enterprise. He also hired an assistant to do the record keeping and to perform selected other shores.

REQUIRED:

1. What is the competitive strategy of Vincent's business – cost leadership, differentiation, or focus?
2. What are the critical success factors of The Cappuccino Express? Which of these are controllable by Vincent?
3. What major tasks does Vincent have to undertake in managing The Cappuccino Express?
4. What are the costs of operating The Cappuccino Express? Choose a cost object and classify each of these costs as direct or indirect, fixed or variable, controllable or uncontrollable, product cost or period cost, or opportunity cost.
5. Vincent would like to monitor the performance of each site manager. What measure, or measures, should he use?
6. If you had suggested more than one measure, which of these should Vincent select if he could use only one?

---

[1] Prepared by Chee W. Chow, © American Accounting Association, 1997. Used with permission.

3-2. Cost Drivers, Strategy.

Joe Costanzo is owner of a growing chain of grocery stores in the Richmond, Virginia and the Washington, D.C. area. Joe's stores specialize in organic and other specialty foods and other specialty products, which have attracted a strong following. As his business matures, Joe is now more interested in understanding how he can better manage the profitability of his stores. In particular, he is interested in understanding what drives the costs in his business.

REQUIRED:

As a potential consultant to Joe, develop a proposal for a consulting engagement which would focus on the profitability and cost driver issues Joe is concerned about. The proposal should address which types of cost drivers should be studied and why. Also, the proposal should identify what are likely to be the important cost drivers in this business.

Readings

MANAGING COSTS THROUGH COMPLEXITY REDUCTION AT CARRIER CORPORATION

By Dan W. Swenson, CMA

Carrier, a United Technologies' Company, is the world's largest manufacturer of air conditioning and heating products. Competition is intense, however, and among its six largest competitors, Carrier is the only one that is not Japanese owned. The director of cost improvement for Carrier's worldwide operations notes that Carrier's customers demand "a wide range of products that have unquestionable quality and include state-of-the-art features. Further, they expect these products to be delivered when needed, at a competitive price."

As the industry leader, Carrier strives to maintain its dominant position through innovative product design (product differentiation), high-quality low-cost manufacturing (zero defects and cost leadership), and time-based competition. (See Figure 1.) To achieve these objectives, Carrier implemented a series of improvement initiatives, including just-in-time, product and process standardization, strategic out-sourcing, supply chain management, target costing, and performance measurement. Complexity reduction is a common goal among each of these initiatives.

While Carrier's manufacturing environment was changing dramatically at the plant level, its parent company, United Technologies, continued to emphasize financial reporting and control at the corporate level and placed relatively little emphasis on developing modern cost management systems for its manufacturing plants. Therefore, the manufacturing plants lacked the cost management information that was needed to support the above improvement initiatives adequately, and profitability suffered. "The intense competition, coupled with ever increasing customer demands, have made it difficult to maintain adequate profit margins on many products. Accordingly, NAO's (Carrier's North American Operations) profitability had dropped significantly below historical levels."

Carrier needed what it describes as a set of "enablers" to support the development of cost effective product designs and manufacturing processes. Activity-based cost management was selected as the enabler, or tool, that provides the necessary financial and activity information. Following its implementation, ABCM has been used by Carrier to quantify the benefits of redesigning plant layouts, using common parts, outsourcing, strengthening supplier and customer relationships, and developing alternative product designs. In some cases, even though management knows intuitively how to improve its operations, until the improvements are quantified they are not acted upon.

COMPLEXITY REDUCTION PROGRAM

Carrier embarked upon its complexity reduction program to reduce the amount of complexity in both the design and manufacture of its products. In many ways the term complexity is analogous to variety. A company's complexity increases as the breadth of its product line expands, as each product uses more unique components, and as more process options are available to manufacture the product. The costs associated with this complexity fall as manufacturing processes are simplified and standardized and as companies offer fewer product options. At Carrier, a strategy to reduce complexity is the common thread that runs through each of its improvement initiatives (see Figure 1). Excessive product and process complexity drives costs up, increases lead time, and makes quality more difficult to control. According to Gonsalves and Eiler,[1] "Complexity factors are the biggest single driver of cost. They are also the single biggest inhibitors of throughput."

To measure its progress at reducing complexity costs, Carrier classifies manufacturing costs as being either unit-related, batch-related, product-sustaining, or structural. Unit-related costs fluctuate with the number of units produced. Direct material and direct labor are examples of unit-related costs. Batch-related costs vary according to the number of batches produced, and examples include material handling and first-part inspection costs. Product-sustaining costs change based on the number of different types of products produced. Designing new products and maintaining part numbers in the information system are examples of product-sustaining costs. Finally, structural costs tend to be fixed and are not related to the number of units, batches, or products produced.[2]

For most companies, batch and product-sustaining costs are closely associated with manufacturing complexity. These costs increase as product lines expand, as more component parts are developed, and as batch production is utilized. For measurement and control purposes, Carrier classifies all batch and product-sustaining costs as "costs of complexity." Furthermore, Carrier has developed financial and nonfinancial performance measures to benchmark its progress at removing complexity from its value chain. Financial performance measures include complexity costs as a percentage of overhead, complexity costs as a percentage of total product costs, and complexity costs as a percent of revenue. Nonfinancial performance measures include the number of common components and manufacturing process options available (which it tries to minimize) and the extent to which certified suppliers and strategic outsourcing are used (which it tries to encourage). Complexity reduction targets are in place for Carrier's current product line, and they also are used during the development of new products. Some of its complexity measures are illustrated in Table 1.[3]

Carrier's complexity reduction process has evolved into a formal, systematic program with corporate-wide visibility. The cost of complexity (COC) programs are administered at the plant level by COC teams. COC teams are formed by recruiting mid-level managers from each functional area including manufacturing, engineering, accounting, and materials management. Once a team is formed, it documents its goals, objectives, and deliverables. It then agrees to a methodology for financially evaluating complexity costs and potential cost reduction opportunities. The team also develops a process to target products and processes for standardization (a primary means of complexity reduction). The COC teams receive top management support from a steering committee that oversees and monitors the success of the COC program. Carrier considers this program to be one of its critical success factors.

STEPS TO COMPLEXITY REDUCTION

The complexity reduction process begins when someone (the originator) proposes an idea for complexity reduction, completes a Complexity Reduction Form, and marks up the product's prints, specification sheets, and other applicable documents. The originator also can use the Complexity Reduction Form to suggest changes in parts, processes, or procedures. For example, the originator might see an opportunity to eliminate the use of single-application unique parts and replace them with common parts that have multiple applications. Originators also might propose process cost reductions, such as replacing a batch process with a point-of-use process.

The Complexity Reduction Form is forwarded to the plant coordinator who records the proposal in the Complexity Reduction Log. The coordinator also records a description of the proposal, the date it was received, its status, and potential outcomes.

The proposal then moves on to one of the area coordinators who evaluates its feasibility and uses an activity-based costing methodology to perform a financial analysis. (See Table 2.)

If the area coordinator rejects the complexity reduction proposal, he or she will provide the originator with a written explanation of reasons for the rejection within two weeks of receiving the proposal. (The originator can appeal a negative decision by resubmitting his or her proposal to the steering committee that oversees the COC program.)

Figure 1. LINKING STRATEGIES TO ENABLERS AND OBJECTIVES

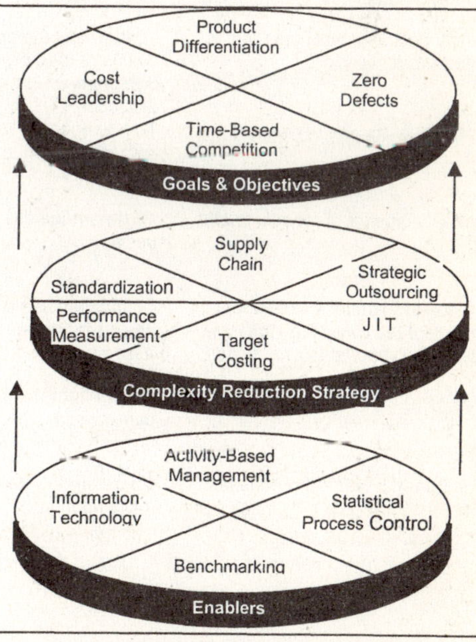

Table 1. SUGGESTED COMPLEXITY MEASURES

Measures	Purpose	Objective	Benchmark
% of components that are standard—parts that are readily available and can be purchased in very short lead times (off the shelf).	To determine if we are taking advantage of opportunities to purchase components at low prices due to market pressures on suppliers.	To generate cost reductions by using standard components for noncore competency parts.	To be determined.
% of components that are unique—used in less than 50% of the models.	To determine the degree we use common components in our products.	To promote the use of common components.	To be determined.
% of purchased parts that are certified.	To determine the confidence level we have in our suppliers.	To encourage actions to eliminate incoming inspection of material.	100%.
# of suppliers by commodity code.	To determine progress made in establishing long-term strategic relationships with suppliers.	To promote actions to reduce the number of suppliers and development of long-term supplier relationships.	To be determined.
% of suppliers up on EDI.	To determine percent of supplier base that we use EDI technology to obtain material for production requirements.	To use EDI technology to reduce lead times and manufacturing material coordination cost.	To be determined.
Number of processes in plant (assembly 1,2 press, coil, paint, weld, etc.).	To determine degree of vertical integration.	To encourage focus on just a few key capabilities in each plant.	To be determined.
Number of process types (number of machines, i.e., brake presses, turrets).	To determine degree of process proliferation.	To reduce process-sustaining cost.	To be determined.
Capacity utilization by process type.	To identify the degree of excess capacity by process type.	To obtain the benefits of process rationalization.	80-85% utilization on a two-shift basis.
Complexity cost batch cost + product sustaining cost.	To highlight the overhead cost associated with manufacturing complexity.	To establish targets and plans for reducing these costs. To track progress against plans.	To be determined.
Complexity cost % batch + product cost/total overhead.	To highlight the percent of overhead cost associated with manufacturing complexity.	To establish targets and plans for reducing these costs. To track progress against plans.	To be determined.
Complexity cost as a % of cost of completed production.	To highlight the percent complexity cost is of total product cost. To demonstrate impact of capacity utilization.	To encourage actions to increase capacity utilization of resources.	To be determined.
Complexity cost as a % of revenue.	To highlight the percent complexity cost is of revenue.	To ensure an adequate return is obtained in complexity cost.	To be determined.
Commonality index # of models/total # part.	To determine the degree modularity is used.	To encourage use of modularity in product designs.	To be determined.
Proliferation index/total # of different components used divided by the average # of components in a model.	To highlight the attention given to design for manufacturability and assembly.	To encourage the use of common components.	To be determined.
Total # of components.	To highlight the total number of components managed in the operation.	To encourage design for manufacturability and assembly actions to reduce the number of components.	To be determined.
% of components that are purchased.	To determine degree of vertical integration.	To encourage more strategic outsourcing.	To be determined.

Table 2. STANDARDIZATION SAVING WORKSHEET — ABC BURDEN ANALYSIS									
Nonstandardized *									
Part Number	Unit Volume	WIP	Prime Costs		ABC Burden				
			Material	Labor	Unit	Batch	Product-Sustaining Cost	Structural	
40RM500061	10,000		80.11	16.50	17.7665	2.1080	2.8693	2.4638	
40RM500071	500		80.11	20.90	22.4731	4.5135	3.9245	3.0897	
40RM500081	250		80.11	20.90	22.4731	6.4042	4.3440	3.1927	
TOTAL EXTENSION BY VOLUME	10,750		$861,182.50	$180,675.00	$184,519.83	$24,937.80	$31,741.25	$26,981.03	
Standardized									
Part Number	Unit Volume	WIP	Prime Costs		ABC Burden				
			Material	Labor	Unit	Batch	Product-Sustaining Cost	Structural	
40RM500061	10,750								
TOTAL EXTENSION BY VOLUME	10,750		$861,182.50	$177,375.00	$190,989.88	$22,633.05	$30,829.93	$26,981.03	
Savings			$0.00	$3,300.00	$3,529.95	$2,304.75	$911.32	$0.00	
Total Savings			$10,046.03						

* Note that in this example the nonstandardized costs represent the current costs (using ABC) for making the three component parts. The proposal is to eliminate the three components and replace them with one common component. This analysis illustrates how the proposed change would produce savings of $10,046 due to reductions in labor, unit, batch, and product-sustaining costs.

If the area coordinator approves the complexity reduction proposal, it is prioritized and scheduled for implementation by the production engineering coordinator.

Once the project is under way, its progress is monitored through a Complexity Reduction Project Status Report. This report identifies the responsible individuals, the planned implementation dates, and projected cost savings.

The Complexity Reduction Log and Project Status Reports are maintained in an online computer network. All projects are updated at least once a month. Hard copies of the log and status reports also are posted monthly on the plant bulletin boards.

LINKAGE TO OTHER INITIATIVES

Carrier implemented ABCM to support its complexity reduction programs.[4] The financial analysis in the previous example illustrates how ABCM information is used to compare the costs and benefits of changing to a standardized part. In addition to the cost/benefit analysis for complexity reduction proposals, ABCM also is used to support other improvment initiatives as illustrated at Carrier's McMinville manufacturing plant.

Just-in-time. The McMinville plant began its complexity reduction journey by simplifying and streamlining manufacturing processes. Just-in-time (JIT) production methods were adopted, and modular work cells were set up for equipment in the factory. These changes were supported by an activity analysis that pointed to material handling as a major cost driver. Furthermore, ABCM was used to calculate the financial benefits of reducing cycle times, raw material, work-in process inventories, and storage space requirements. After implementing JIT, savings occurred through reduced material handling costs, lower inventory investments, and by avoiding a physical expansion of the plant (even though new products were transferred to McMinville from other Carrier factories).

In the early stages of the complexity reduction program, management realized that production workers were an untapped resource for productivity improvement ideas. Therefore, these workers were placed on work cell teams, and each team became responsible for workflow, quality, and throughput. Prior to these changes, the production supervisors spent most of their time troubleshooting problems and expediting work orders. These problems currently are being handled by the line worker teams, and the supervisors now have enough time to plan their workloads and monitor the financial results of their work cells.

CARRIER CORPORATION: A BEST PRACTICE COMPANY

The American Productivity and Quality Center (APQC) and the Consortium for Advanced Manufacturing-International (CAM-I) recently sponsored a study to benchmark best practices in the installation and use of activity-based cost management (ABCM) systems. Seven hundred and fifty manufacturing and service organizations were invited to participate in the study, and 166 responded by completing a 20-page survey instrument. Approximately 50% of the 750 companies that were invited to participate in the study had either not yet adopted ABCM or were in the early stages of implementation and thus could not complete the survey.

The survey results and telephone- interviews then were used to select 15 "best practice" companies. The best practice companies were selected based on their ABCM system's maturity, the breadth of their ABCM applications, the extent of their systems integration, and their level o success with ABCM.

Carrier Corporation participated in the survey and was selected as one of the best practice companies. Carrier currently has more than a dozen manufacturing sites located throughout the world, and it was Carrier's McMinville, Tenn., manufacturing plant (located near Nashville) that was identified as the best practice site. Carrier uses ABCM to support its complexity reduction program.

Standardization. Standardizing parts and manufacturing processes is another way in which the McMinville plant has achieved complexity reduction. The standardization process is divided into two different programs—one targets new product designs, and the other one targets existing products. The objective for both programs is to encourage the use of common components and manufacturing processes. For example, the plant has a preferred parts list for new products to minimize the proliferation of new component parts and thus control product-sustaining costs.

McMinville also has financial incentives (lower product costs) to reduce the number of components used in existing products. The plant currently maintains 280 different circuit breakers and 580 different fasteners to support its product lines. Its goal is to eliminate well over 50% of the circuit breakers and fasteners by promoting the use of common components. Maintaining an extensive parts list causes complexity whether the parts are components or finished goods. The high costs of unique components now are reflected in McMinville's product costs.

As a specific example of complexity reduction, product and process complexity was reduced at the McMinville plant when it developed common sizes for some of the sheet metal components that go into subassemblies. Each subassembly has a minimum size requirement for its sheet metal components. Therefore, if a sheet metal component will be used for multiple subassembly sizes, it must be cut large enough to fit the largest subassembly. The decision maker is now confronted with a cost-benefit tradeoff—he or she must balance the savings associated with using common components against the scrap produced by trimming the oversized sheet metal components to fit small subassemblies. The power of ABCM is its ability to compare the savings from lower batch-related and product sustaining costs with the additional cost of producing sheet metal scrap.

If common components are not practical, the next best alternative to reduce complexity is to use common manufacturing processes. In fact, some manufacturing processes become more cost effective when flexible, but expensive, computerized equipment is replaced with inexpensive dedicated equipment. The McMinville plant used dedicated equipment to achieve fewer and less expensive changeovers, to lower work-in-process, and to reduce cycle times. For this manufacturing process, JIT sparked the interest in dedicated equipment, but ABCM supported the financial analysis that justified the changes. Change occurs much more quickly at McMinville when the financial impact is highly visible.

Strategic outsourcing. As McMinville's complexity reduction program evolved, management considered many change proposals to reduce complexity and improve productivity. One such proposal was to outsource the sheet metal painting operation. Intuitively, managers at the plant were confident that outsourcing the painting operation would be cost effective and improve productivity. At a higher level, however, management would not approve the change. These managers relied upon a traditional

Figure 2. NEED TO REDUCE COMPLEXITY

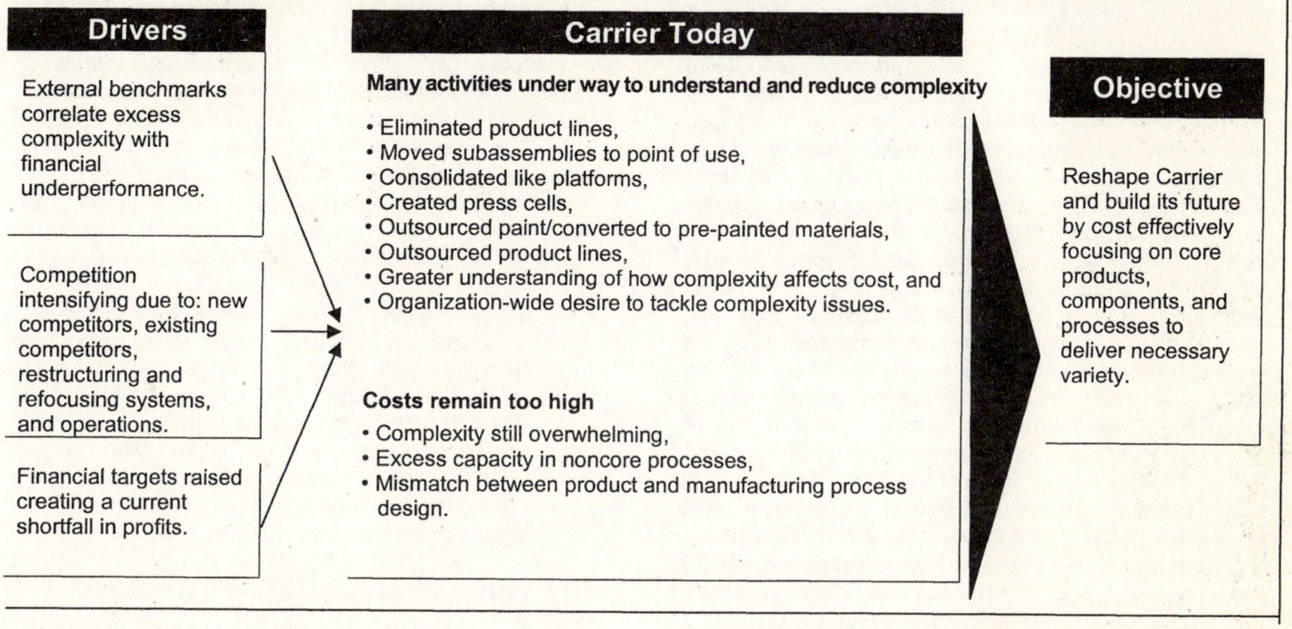

financial analysis that only considered the cost of direct materials, direct labor, and an overhead allocation. Using this analysis, outsourcing the painting operation appeared to have a negative payback.

Once ABCM data were available, however, an analysis produced results that were quite different from the traditional financial analysis. ABCM quantified the cost of many support activities that had not been considered previously, such as material handling, inspection, inventory holding, and environmental costs. After including the cost of these activities, managers at the plant found the cost of in-house painting to be considerably higher than the cost of outsourcing the painting operation. Furthermore, by purchasing pre-painted sheet metal, quality improved and in-plant cycle time fell by five days. In the final analysis, outsourcing the painting operation proved to be very cost effective, and it also supported the goals of JIT and complexity reduction.

Supply chain management. To further improve its competitiveness, Carrier has been strengthening its supplier relationships. Actions taken by its suppliers greatly influence the price, quality, and delivery speed of Carrier's products. For example, the McMinville plant has developed a partnership with a supplier of nonproduction service parts. This supplier now staffs McMinville's service parts warehouse and is fully responsible for purchasing, stocking, and scheduling service parts. McMinville's ABCM model illustrates how the supplier can source service parts and actually run the warehouse more cost effectively than McMinville can with its own employees.

The McMinville plant currently is considering a partnership with a supplier of copper tubing. This supplier would be responsible for managing the copper tubing portion of McMinville's raw materials warehouse. Through this partnership, the copper tubing supplier would exploit certain of its core competencies. It has detailed knowledge of material flow from its own plants, where the tubing is formed, to its customers. Many of the copper tubing suppliers also have the latest technology for copper tubing fabrication. Therefore, the partnership might be expanded to include some fabrication of copper tubing parts. (The vendor may choose to perform some operations at its own facility and others at McMinville.) As the vendor becomes directly involved in McMinville's production process, it can (or might be required to) propose improvement programs. These improvements might be in product functionality, the production process, or quality. And, finally, vendor management of this activity also will reduce cycle time. Once again, ABCM helps Carrier make better decisions by considering the entire cost of an activity and not just the "out-of-pocket" costs such as the cost of the raw materials.

Target costing. In the current competitive marketplace, customers often dictate the price they will pay for a given set of product features. Therefore, Carrier has eliminated "cost plus" pricing for its products and now uses a target costing approach. The target costing process begins when Carrier estimates the price customers will pay for a new product offering (the target selling price). After subtracting a desired profit margin from the target selling price, a target cost is established. The new product's target cost then is compared with its estimated cost. (Cost estimates are based on the new product's initial design and current manufacturing processes.) If the product's estimated cost is higher than its target cost, engineers will attempt to either design costs out of the product or improve the manufacturing process. In the end, if the target cost cannot be met, the product will not go into production.

Both the complexity reduction program and ABCM are linked to target costing at Carrier. These initiatives encourage engineers to control costs by designing products that use common components and standard manufacturing processes. Gone are the days when engineers prided themselves in developing unique, elegant parts.[5] When the new products do require new component designs, the engineers try to use existing manufacturing processes to build the components. To facilitate this new directive, product designers are now part of an engineering team that includes manufacturing engineers. The team uses a "design for manufacturability" philosophy in which the design team works with manufacturing to introduce product designs that use cost effective manufacturing processes.

Performance measures. An activity dictionary with common process definitions supports performance measurement among the Carrier plants. Managers at the plants use the dictionary to develop internal benchmarks for activity-based process costs. The managers also share information to learn from the low-cost producers. At the McMinville plant, the first line production supervisors also receive monthly reports with financial (labor, material usage, and scrap) and nonfinancial (production schedule targets) information. The supervisors are accountable for budgeted process costs in their areas, and the results influence their performance evaluation.

At the product level, Carrier uses ABCM to support product mix decisions. Its product mix at each site is based on a product profitability analysis. For example, unprofitable products are either dropped or moved to another Carrier location, and profitable products are emphasized. Essentially, this system encourages competition among the plants—the most efficient plants win bids for new products and take over production contracts from less efficient plants.

Even though the McMinville plant appropriately has dropped some product lines and added others, it has taken some missteps along the way. Some products that appeared to be unprofitable mistakenly were dropped (existing products) or avoided (new business). This scenario occurred because management did not conduct the following analysis:

- Before rejecting an unprofitable product, management should make every effort to remove costs from the product's design or production process.
- When the plant has excess capacity in the short run and sales revenue more than covers variable cost, new products should be considered for production (and existing products should not necessarily be dropped).

STAYING COMPETITIVE WITH HARD DATA

Carrier's complexity reduction program along with its other improvement initiatives have combined to produce quantifiable results (Figure 2). But more work needs to be done for Carrier to maintain its competitive edge. In the current competitive environment, Carrier is striving to better understand cost behavior and the steps it can take to maintain its position as the world's largest manufacturer of air conditioning and heating products. Even though Carrier's management believes that product and process complexity hurts profitability, it needs hard financial data. ABCM provides the information managers need to make difficult decisions.

Dan Swenson, CMA, Ph.D., is assistant professor of accounting, College of Business and Economics, University of Idaho, Moscow, Idaho. He submitted this article through the Washington Tri-Cities Chapter, of which he is a member. He can be reached at (208) 885-7367.
The support of the American Productivity and Quality Center (APQC), the Consortium for Advanced Manufacturing-International (CAM-I), the sponsor companies, and the other members of the research team (Richard Brown, John Campi, George Foster, Larry Maisel, and John Miller) is gratefully acknowledged.

[1]F.A. Gonsalves and R. G. Eiler, "Managing Complexity Through Performance Measurement," MANAGEMENT ACCOUNTING, August 1996, p. 35.

[2]For an in-depth discussion of this classification scheme, see Robin Cooper, "Cost Classification in Unit-Based and Activity-Based Manufacturing Cost Systems," *Journal of Cost Management,* Fall 1990, pp. 1-14.

[3]In their article, "Managing complexity Through Performance Measurement," Gonsalves and Eiler provide additional examples of complexity performance measures.

[4]As part of the ABCM best practices study, sponsored by the APQC and CAM-I, the research team searched for characteristics that were common among the best practice companies. One finding was that each of the 15 best practice companies had linked ABCM to another improvement initiative. Total quality management (TQM). Just-in-time (JIT) manufacturing, and business process reengineering (IBPR) were some of the other initiatives that were linked to ABCM. This linkage provides direction for the ABCM implementation and a ready application for the ABCM information once it becomes available.

[5]A new product at the McMinville plant recently required three design attempts before its target cost was achieved. It was obtained only after the design team brought the part count down from 160 to 60 parts.

Chapter 4
Job Order Costing

Cases

4-1 Constructo Inc. (Under or Over-Applied Overhead)
4-2 East River Manufacturing (A) (Problems of Traditional Job Costing)

Readings

"How I Reengineered a Small Business"

This article describes both the old and new job costing systems at James Street Fashions (also called Latt-Greene), a small textile knitting and converting operation in Vernon, California. The author is the controller of Latt-Greene. He instituted a spreadsheet-based job costing system that helped to reverse a $5 million loss on $65 million in sales revenue to a $3 million profit on just $32 million in sales revenue. He also eliminated unnecessary overtime and increased the overall quality of the company's product line.

Discussion Questions:

1. Briefly describe the company, its products and customers.
2. What problems did the author discover when he conducted his initial interviews with the company in early 1990.
3. Describe the company's old financial costing system, and identify its weaknesses as well as business operating and profit consequences cause by its poor costing system.
4. What are major impacts of the company's new computerized costing system on its business operations, product prices and quality, and company's profit?
5. What are general principles learned by the author for changing or reengineering a company's costing system?

Cases

4-1. Under or Overapplied Overhead

Constructo Inc. is a manufacturer of furnishings for infants and children. The company uses a job cost system and employs a full absorption accounting method for cost accumulation. Constructo's work-in-process inventory at April 30, 2001 consisted of the following jobs.

Job No.	Items	Units	Accumulated Cost
CBS102	Cribs	20,000	$ 900,000
PLP086	Playpens	25,000	420,000
DRS114	Dressers	25,000	250,000
			$1,570,000

The company's finished goods inventory, which Constructo evaluates using the FIFO (First-in, first-out) method, consisted of five items.

Item	Quantity and Unit Cost	Accumulated Cost
Cribs	7,500 units @ $ 64 each	$ 480,000
Strollers	13,000 units @ $ 23 each	299,000
Carriages	11,200 units @ $102 each	1,142,400
Dressers	21,000 units @ $ 55 each	1,155,000
Playpens	19,400 units @ $ 35 each	679,999
		$3,755,400

Constructo applies factory overhead on the basis of direct labor hours. The company's factory overhead budget for the fiscal year ending May 31, 2001, totals $4,500,000, and the company plans to expend 600,000 direct labor hours during this period. Through the first eleven months of the year, a total of 555,000 direct labor hours were worked, and total factory overhead amounted to $4,273,500.

At the end of April, the balance in Constructo's Materials Inventory account, which includes both raw materials and purchased parts, was $668,000. Additions to and requisitions from the materials inventory during the month of May included the following.

	Raw Materials	Purchased Parts
Additions	$242,000	$396,000
Requisitions:		
Job CBS102	51,000	104,000
Job PLP086	3,000	10,800
Job DRS114	124,000	87,000
Job STR077		
(10,000 strollers)	62,000	81,000
Job CRG098		
(5,000 carriages)	65,000	187,000

During the month of May, Constructo's factory payroll consisted of the following.

Account	Hours	Cost
CBS102	12,000	$122,400
PLP086	4,400	43,200
DRS114	19,500	200,500
STR077	3,500	30,000
CRG098	14,000	138,000
Indirect	3,000	29,400
Supervision		57,600
		$621,100

Listed below are the jobs that were completed and the unit sales for the month of May.

Job No.	Items	Quantity Complete
CBS102	Cribs	20,000
PLP086	Playpens	15,000
STR077	Strollers	10,000
CRG098	Carriages	5,000

Items	Quantity Shipped
Cribs	17,500
Playpens	21,000
Strollers	14,000
Dressers	18,000
Carriages	6,000

REQUIRED

1. Describe when it is appropriate for a company to use a job cost system.
2. Calculate the dollar balance in Constructo's work-in-process inventory account as of May 31, 2001.
3. Calculate the dollar amount related to the playpens in Constructo's finished goods inventory as of May 31, 2001.
4. Explain the proper accounting treatment for overapplied or underapplied overhead balances when using a job cost system.

(CMA Adapted)

4-2. East River Manufacturing (A)

Power Services Industries has been in business since 1907. PSI's principal business is the design, manufacture, and erection of steam generation equipment for utility and industrial customers. PSI also serves the after-parts market, which includes individual boiler components and loose tubes for repair and replacement. Their primary product, coal-fired boilers, burns fossil fuels to heat water, which turns to steam, and is used either for electrical generation or industrial process. Boilers are highly engineered products which can take anywhere from six months to five years to complete from the design stage through manufacturing and erection phases.

The East River, Illinois plant is one of three manufacturing facilities of the Services Division of the Energy Group. The East River plant has over 503,000 square feet of fabrication area, nine fabrication bays, and a practical capacity load of 1,345,000 manhours. There are over 500 hourly and salaried employees at the East River plant.

MARKET AND COMPETITIVE ENVIRONMENT

Throughout the post-World War II period and up until the mid-1970s, the demand for power-generating capacity increased steadily. PSI was a prime beneficiary of this growth in demand for electricity. They were awash in orders for original equipment. Backlogs of orders for forty or more radiant boilers were common, and when measured in manhours, were equivalent to over five years of work. The typical order for original equipment boilers averaged $30 million. Prior to the eighties, the original-equipment market (OEM) made up more than 60 percent of East River's revenues. Throughout this period, PSI earned a very respectable return on its investment.

As a sideline to the OEM, East River also serviced the replacement-parts (known as loose tubes) market. Tubes wear out in the hostile environment (e.g., coal-fired boilers generate fly ash which is very corrosive when it continually beats against a tube wall) and need to be replaced. However, demand for service work (replacement parts and components or subassemblies) is extremely difficult to project. Replacement-parts business requires short lead times, on-time shipments, and competitive prices. Service work is made more demanding because customers want made-to-order replacement tubes in small quantities. The typical replacement-parts order was $50,000 and usually had to be delivered in less than ten days, although the need to expedite an order overnight was not unusual. Replacement orders made up about 40 percent of revenues. And while the reported gross profit margins on individual loose tubes were high, the absolute size of and total returns on OEM projects made that market more attractive.

In the early eighties, a combination of fuel price increases, high interest rates, and a global recession hit and the bottom fell out of the OEM. In the past, this was normally a temporary setback and orders always picked up once the economy recovered. But this time it was different. The steady growth in electricity consumption, which had been predictable for so long, leveled off and OEM orders plunged. A number of factors led to a permanent drop in demand by the OEM, including the sharp increase in the cost of energy, unsympathetic utility regulatory agencies, uncertainty related to deregulation, environmental concerns about acid-rain, and improved capabilities to transmit excess energy across markets.

This new environment was marked by wide swings in business and fluctuating manning requirements. OEM business picked up again in the mid-eighties, but total OEM business and profits never returned to their former high levels and the total workload at the East River facility continued to drop. The inevitable profit squeeze caused by excess capacity and by ever-rising costs led PSI to look to the replacement-parts business to offset the declining OEM business.

Demand for replacement parts expanded as orders for original equipment declined. The principal reason was that utility and industrial customers wanted to maintain and prolong the useful life of power-generating equipment by replacing worn out parts rather than build new capacity. In addition, PSI engineers worked closely with customers to achieve greater efficiencies and enhance the power output of existing power sources by redesigning components or adding additional parts.

The determinants of successful management of large and complex OEM projects are very different from the key success factors in the replacement-parts market. Critical market drivers in the loose-tube replacement market are:

- Increased flexibility
- Reduced lead time
- Low price
- On-time delivery
- High Quality

Except for high quality, these factors did not carry the same weight in the OEM. As a result, PSI had to quickly adapt. For example, fast turnaround of worn or damaged parts is crucial once a boiler is in operation. Replacement parts availability is critical to a pulp and paper customer like Weyerhaeuser. Customers can suffer losses in the tens of thousands of dollars daily if their boilers are shut down as a result of part failure. East River always tried to accommodate customers' needs for replacement parts. But East River was structured to capitalize on the returns to be made on large-scale OEM projects. Primary considerations on OEM projects were to complete the boiler on time, within budget, and according to contract specifications.

The urgency of meeting contract lead times and completion dates on new equipment was not as critical as it was for replacement parts. But now, replacement parts were the primary source of revenues. And while new boilers were still being sold, replacement parts for existing boilers now made up 70 percent of East River's workload. Since PSI's major competitors (e.g., Asea, Brown, Bovari/Combustion Engineering; Babcock & Wilcox; Riley, Foster, & Wheeler; and Zurn) were suffering from the same drop in OEM orders, they too started to compete aggressively for the growing replacement-parts business. The field was crowded with competitors. But the expanding replacement-parts business was not large enough to offset the lost OEM orders. By the early nineties, total OEM and replacement-parts business was significantly less than it was in the early eighties (Refer to Exhibit 1). There was now a glut of industry-wide capacity. By 1989, the industry was overcapitalized and demand from the OEM and replacement-parts markets was running at a level which utilized only 45-50 percent of East River's capacity. The inevitable outcome was constant pressure on prices, margins, and market share.

MAJOR PRODUCTS

The East River plant manufactures a wide variety of components for boilers including wall panels— a collection of steel tubes (carbon steel, stainless, or composites) which are welded together with membrane bars in between them; loose tubes that have a number of bends in them or studs applied to them for heat transfer capability; burners which can burn coal, oil, or gas; structural members which contain the tubes that make up the walls of the boiler; expansion joints; dampers; economizers; risers and supplies tubes.

The Bay 7 facility was configured and equipped to process straight lengths of loose tubes into various shapes and lengths, suitable for the repair and replacement-parts market or needed as component parts of other assemblies completed at East River. Replacement parts and components are custom-made from unique materials compositions and configurations so that the parts can function reliably in a power-generation environment where steam may be generated by burning any one of hundreds of different kinds of coal or other fossil fuels.

Exhibit 1
East River Plant (A)

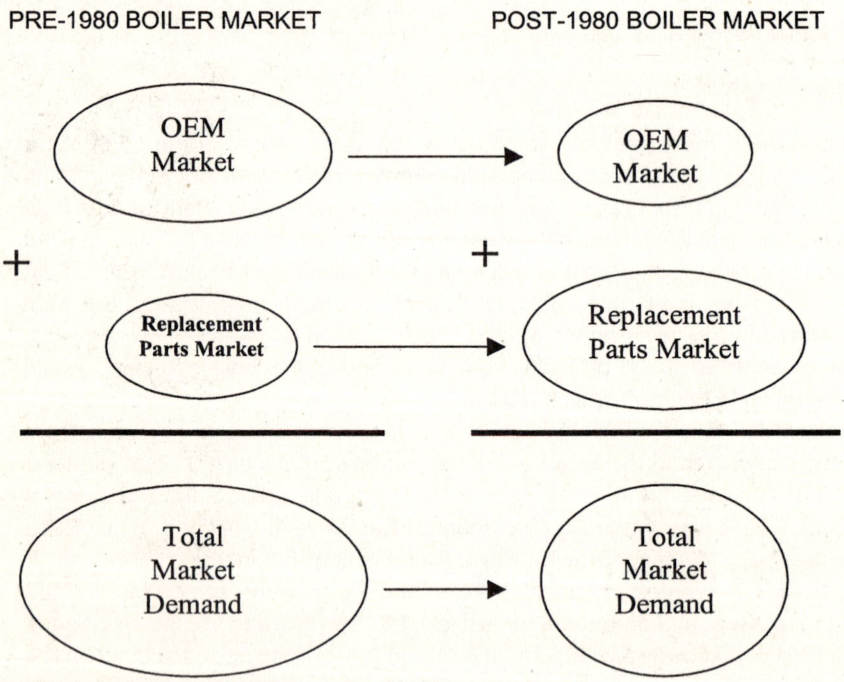

Many of the tubes manufactured have difficult welds and intricate bends in several different planes. All of these bends are engineered to a certain size, dimension, and location on the tube. Quality has to be right the first time. Once parts are in the field, they have to fit exactly. There is no reworking on the line.

ENGINEERING AND PRODUCTION PROCESS

Customer orders for individual boiler components and loose tubes to be fabricated in Bay 7 are initially processed at PSI's Dallas, Texas headquarters. Since there are no off-the-shelf parts, preliminary tube designs are prepared by product design engineers from historical data. Cost estimators use these preliminary tube designs to prepare estimates of the tube's manufacturing and material cost. The base estimating data used by cost estimators was developed from industrial engineering time studies completed in the early seventies. There are enough similarities to previously-fabricated tube variations that customer requested quotes can be developed on a timely basis by querying the parts database. If the proposal is accepted and becomes a contract, the proposal becomes the base-line or "as-sold" estimate (i.e., the budgeted cost) for cost monitoring and measuring actual performance.

Once a proposal is accepted, product design engineers "start from scratch" and prepare detailed part and component designs on computer-aided design (CAD) systems. They also determine the materials composition for all tubes. This product structure and tube geometry, which describes the physical characteristics of the tube, is then transferred to draftsmen who transform the product structure into detailed graphics (blueprints). Draftsmen manually load information on the tube's geometry into three different computer systems: (1) the Bill of Material system; (2) the CAD drawing system; and (3) the Tube Detail file which converts tube geometry along with design, process, machine, and tooling constraints data into process plans. This information is downloaded to East River's mainframe computers.

Purchasing places orders for all stock and non-stock items, many of which have long leadtimes. The process engineering group uses the Tube Detail file to generate the route sheet generation program or RSGP. RSGP creates a routing for each part with specific work centers, operations descriptions, and estimated process times. Customer order information is entered into MAPICS II (Manufacturing Accounting Production Inventory Control System), an IBM MRP II system. MAPICS generates bill of materials, routing sheets, order quantities, and required delivery dates. Manufacturing orders released by MAPICS were hand delivered to their respective work centers. Exhibit 2 shows the sequential flow of a contract from the preliminary proposal through shipment to the customer.

The East River plant has nine manufacturing bays. By 1990, the average age of equipment in Bay 7 was greater than 29 years. Bay 7 has practical capacity of 160,000 manhours. Tubes were received by truck and unloaded by a radio controlled overhead crane with the assistance of two workers. Tubes moved through the shops by a series of overhead cranes, jib cranes hung from building supports, forklifts, and transfer cars.

Tubes were shotblasted, cut to length, and machined as required. Tubes may be welded together prior to moving to the stencil/layout table, where the tubes were paint marked for a variety of studding and bending patterns. Tubes were then moved to a staging area near the stud welders and benders. Tubes were processed through a series of stud welding and bending stations, which were machine-assisted but still highly labor-intensive. Exhibit 3 displays certain tube features. Bending dies were stored outside Bay 7 and, when needed, transported by forklift to the proper bending station. Tube bundles were moved from station to station through Bay 7 by a series of pendant operated overhead cranes. Tubes were then checked, inspected, finished, and cleaned prior to shipment to the customer or transferred to another bay where they were assembled into boiler components. Average throughput time in the bay was approximately 3-4 weeks with high work-in-process. About 40 percent of the manhours in Bay 7 were attributable to material handling at the work stations or movement between work stations. Exhibit 4 shows the process flow for Bay 7, including machine count and headcount.

Exhibit 2
East River Plant (A)
Proposal-to-Shipment Process

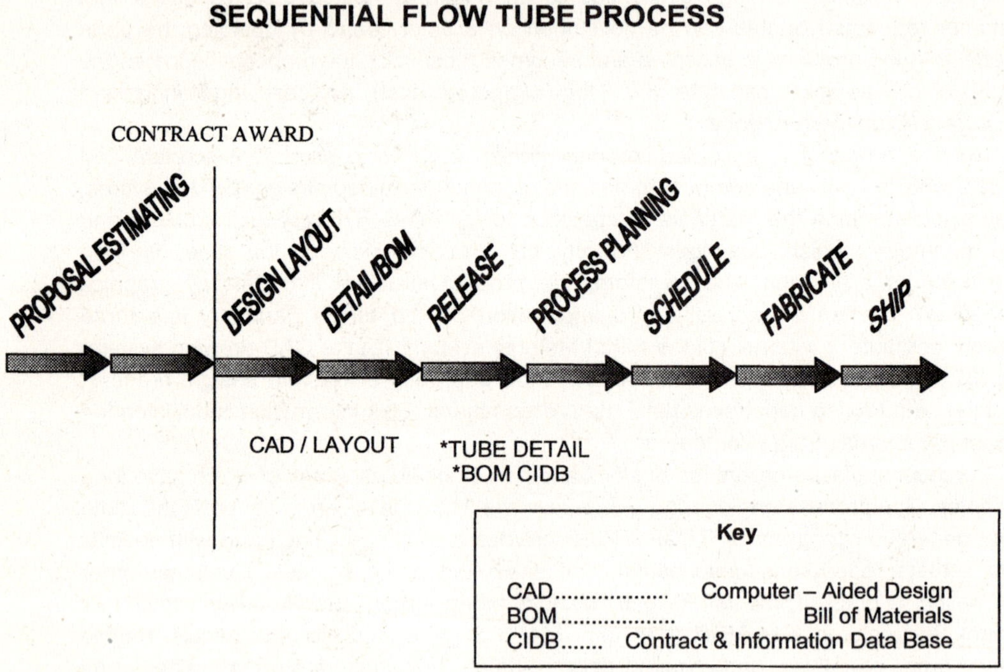

It was not unusual for bottlenecks and scheduling difficulties to arise during processing. Work-in-process was stored adjacent to work stations to alleviate any disruptions which might occur in upstream operations. There was approximately $7 million worth of inventory at East River at any given time.

Over the years, maintenance expenditures were kept at levels sufficient to sustain current operations. Competing on cost meant that operations management focused on high levels of equipment utilization. However, machine downtime and costs to repair equipment were now rising rapidly. In addition, depreciation expenditures were not reinvested in new equipment.

Furthermore, the collective bargaining agreement with the union did not allow workers to be cross-trained to run multiple machines and perform a variety of functions. Part of the difficulty was that over the years the collective bargaining unit negotiated fifteen different job levels along with several classes within each level. But now competition was placing a premium on flexible work rules and East River was saddled with a labor agreement which made it difficult to respond quickly. With so much to disrupt shop floor control, it was hard to consistently maintain contract work schedules and meet customers' requested shipping dates.

Exhibit 3
East River Plant (A)

TUBE FEATURES

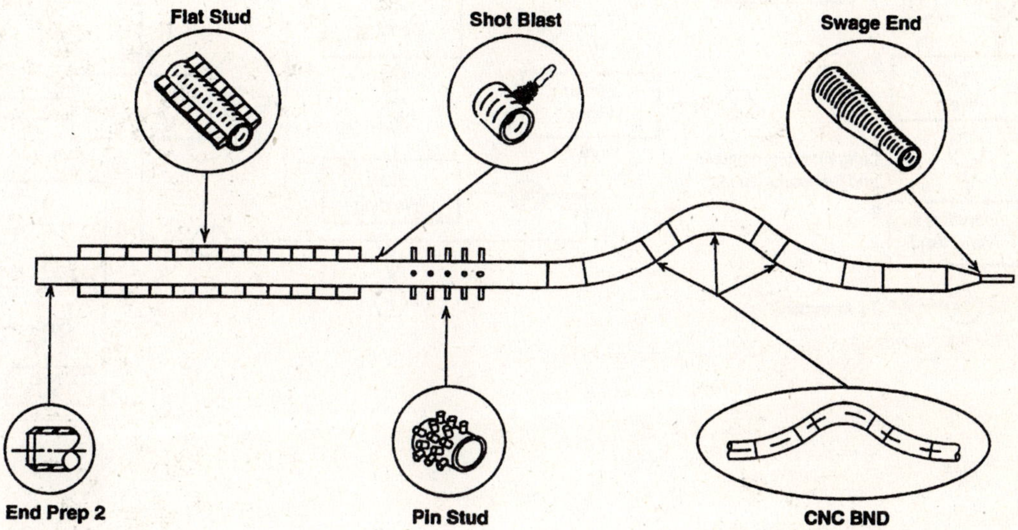

Exhibit 4
East River Plant (A)
Tube Shop Manual Line

EXISTING PROCESS FLOW/MACHINE COUNT/HEADCOUNT

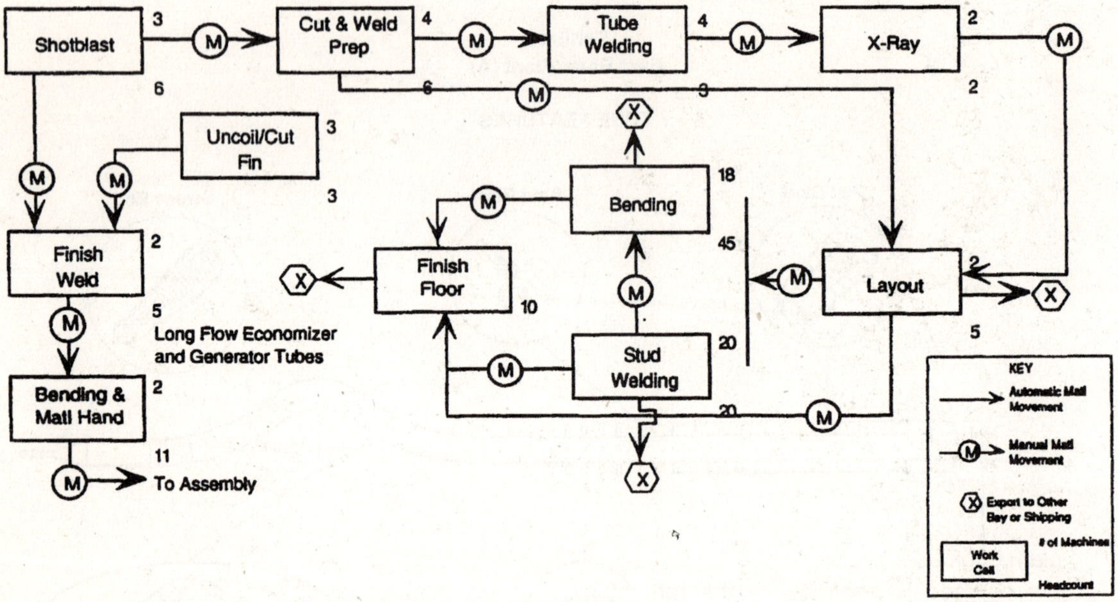

EXISTING COST SYSTEM

Traditionally, throughput in East River's labor-intensive shops was measured by manhours. The East River facility is on a job cost system. The same job cost system was installed in all plants built during the 1950s. In the case of East River, the job cost system was installed in 1951 and remained virtually unchanged until 1992, with two exceptions: (1) practical capacity replaced a three-year average of expected actual capacity for determining burden rates in 1982; and (2) a material burden rate was developed in the late 1980s. A job or contract cost system is necessary since PSI doesn't make a standard product. End products are manufactured to customer's specifications. The entire project is designed and engineered at PSI's Dallas, Texas headquarters. Materials composition and product structure are based upon the type of fossil fuel that will be used by the power generator and other environmental variables.

The contract is the primary cost object. Orders are grouped by contract, and costs are accumulated for purchase orders as well as manufacturing orders. The cost system charges materials and labor costs directly to the contract and to the part. Product design engineering, drafting or graphics, machine setup, and material handling costs are also directly charged to contracts. Burden rates are based upon practical capacity. A material burden rate of 5 percent of material cost covers the cost of purchasing and material control costs. Pressure Shop 415's overhead for three bays includes indirect labor and fringes, equipment-related costs, maintenance and repairs, and supplies. Shop 415 overhead was charged to contracts and other cost objects at 150 percent of direct labor cost. Plant support services, known as works-general costs, consist of production control, plant engineering, quality assurance, payroll, accounting, and other support services and are charged to contracts at the rate of 40 percent of direct labor cost. In addition, operating-all-works (OAW) costs associated with Dallas support services are charged to contracts at the rate of 15 percent of direct labor cost. OAW consists of manufacturing engineering support and the resource allocation group which plans and monitors plant loads, product mix, and production volume. These costing procedures were more than adequate given market conditions and the focus on large OEM projects throughout most of the post-war period.

In addition to costing the contract at practical capacity, the cost system was also capable of providing operating personnel with contract-related performance information. One of the most critical performance indicators was the monthly ratio of Estimated Man Hours to Actual Man Hours (E/A). Given that contracts could easily extend over a period of years, operating management could not wait until the project was completed to determine whether the contract was coming in over budget. It was essential to have some basis for monitoring progress on each project on an on-going Percentage-of-Completion basis. Using information supplied by process engineering, accounting staff estimated time for every task that had to be performed. As tasks were completed, comparisons of estimated manhours with actual manhours resulted in an E/A performance percentage. If performance was at 100 percent or better, the contract was going well and the plant would earn a respectable profit. If performance was below 100 percent, say 75 percent, contract performance was not going very well.

The relationship between equipment age and equipment tolerances is an example of how E/A could gradually worsen over long periods of time even when no changes were made in the tube design. One study of studding machines revealed that time and cost overruns were occurring with increasing frequency. Studding machines spot weld studs to the tubes. These machines were some of the oldest equipment in the Tube Bay. Therefore, controls on the stud welders were old and not as effective as they were when the equipment was newer. The welds did not always achieve the degree of penetration on a weld necessary to pass quality specifications. Studs which were not welded correctly could break off. These studs had to be manually rewelded because the number of studs on the tube precluded it from being rewelded on the studding machine.

Periodic monitoring of actual contract costs against the original bid or as-sold estimate assisted plant management in managing costs on a contract. The contract cost accounting system provides reports which show actual costs incurred for the contract to date, as well as reports which show the actual costs incurred for a contract during a specific period. All reports provide variances between actual costs and as-sold estimated costs and the engineered standards. This information was reviewed informally on a weekly basis and underwent a thorough, formal review each quarter (Exhibit 5).

Exhibit 5
Project / Contract Cost Monitoring

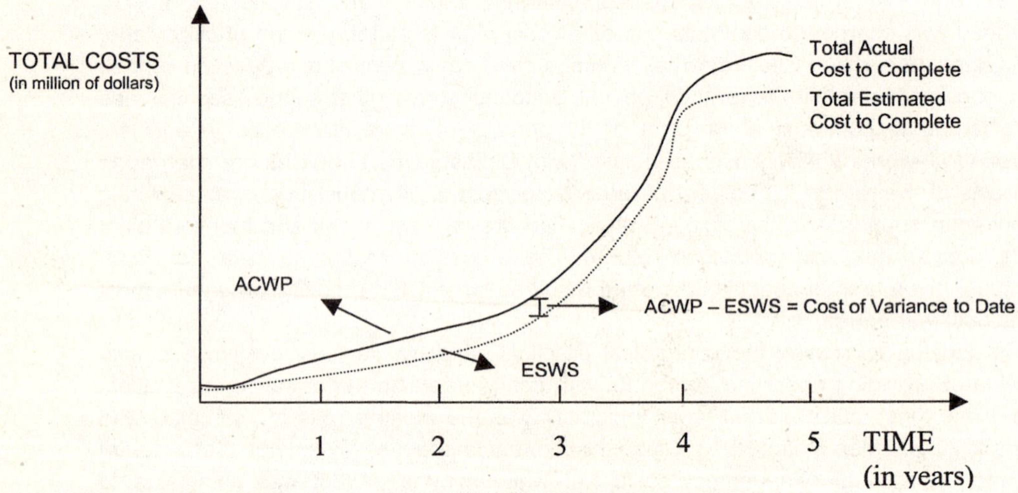

ACWP = Actual Costs for Work Performed
ESWS = As-Sold Estimated Costs for Work Scheduled on Percentage-of-Completion Basis

From a customer's perspective, there are two other critical performance indicators: (l) on-time delivery—meeting the customer-requested delivery schedule; and (2) quality. Often, customers have planned outages and want replacement parts delivered during a certain outage window—a specific date and time. If this window is missed, at the very least, customers lose confidence in suppliers. In some cases, there are substantial liquidating damages associated with a missed delivery date.

Quality Assurance reports defects. If a defect will cost more than $1,000 to repair, a separate sub-account is established for the contract, called a C-order, and all costs of reworking the part(s) is charged to this account. Accounting supplies the cost information to QA, which then identifies what the problem was, where it occurred, what the root cause was, and who had primary responsibility for correcting it. Some defects are due to a design errors, referred to as a D-orders. Design flaws can be identified when parts don't assemble properly. It is important to determine the cause of design errors so that they do not repeat these mistakes on future contracts of a similar nature or, if the error is the result of a flaw in the manufacturing process, the process gets corrected. Guarantee-orders or G-orders accumulate the cost of corrective work on a unit in the field that doesn't meet its warranted performance. Reserves are set up for C-, D-, and G-orders to cover the estimated cost or liability. These costs are built into the base estimating data used for proposals and establish allowances for contract cost.

(IMA Case)

REQUIRED:

1. Briefly summarize and contrast the competitive environment in the pre-1980 era with that of the early nineties.
2. What are the problems that plant management has to resolve?
3. What potential problems may occur between the as-sold cost estimates and the actual contract cost?
4. Diagram the structure of the existing cost system and explain how cost information is used for decision-making, cost control, and performance evaluation purposes.
5. Is the labor-based cost system appropriate for this facility? Should activity-based costing be implemented to analyze product costs?
6. Prepare a set of recommendations for changes in the cost system. Describe a general framework for costing products in an automated facility.

Readings

HOW I REENGINEERED A SMALL BUSINESS

BY RICHARD H. SNYDER, CPA

Reengineering is not just for large businesses. It's true that only giant corporations can afford to pay the fees for high-powered consultants to come in and turn the organization upside down. But for those brave souls in small businesses willing to think the unthinkable, reengineering can be managed without huge money outlays.

The major stumbling block in reengineering a small business is the staff who has worked at the business for years and tends to develop an ownership in the current process and, as a result, may be unable or unwilling to consider a revolutionary change in the process. What is required is knowledge of the system that exists and a willingness to consider radical new processes that would dramatically improve the system. In such circumstances an outsider may he necessary in order to produce dramatic change.

Take as an example the case of James Street Fashions dba Latt-Greene, a knitting and converting operation in Vernon, Calif. I became controller of the company on January 2, 1990, at the request of the owner in order to introduce control into the activities of the company. I had a prior knowledge of the textile industry, having been in public accounting for many years and having had some textile companies as clients (not Latt-Greene). I also had controllership, internal auditing, and cost accounting experience and had guided businesses though bankruptcy.

Latt-Greene knits textiles for the women's and children's apparel market, dyes and prints designs on the textiles according to customer instructions, and delivers the product to the customer ready for cutting and sewing into clothing. The customers of the company consist of clothing manufacturers who sell to clothing retailers.

In the initial interviews at this family-owned and operated company, I discovered some of the concerns: severe negative cash flow, a belief that not all sales to customers were being billed or collected, a paper-heavy system that was being crushed by its own weight. In my initial walk-through, I was astonished to see that the accountant was still keeping records on a "one-write" system. There wasn't a single computer to be found on the premises. I told the owners that if I were hired I would be making some dramatic changes including introducing data processing.

Table 1

YEAR ENDED 05/31	NET SALES	ROI
1985	16.5	11.3%
1986	19.8	(46%)
1987	24.8	(18%)
1988	33.6	33%
1989	39.2	11%
1990	54.8	(6%)
SEVEN MONTHS ENDED 12/31		
1990	31.3	63%
YEAR ENDED 12/31		
1991	54	61%
1992	30	7%
1993	32	41%
1994	38	53%
1995	31	28%
1996	30	30%
1997	36	43%
1998	30	24%

UNRAVELING THE OLD

The first thing I did upon being hired was to purchase a personal computer. I purchased one without any networking software because at that moment I had no one to network with. But I did look forward to that day in the future and purchased a computer with the capability of being turned into a central server at a future date. The only software that I installed at that time was a powerful spreadsheet, Quattro Pro. In order to gain insight and perspective into the problems of the system, I loaded into a spreadsheet all the invoices billed to customers during the month of November 1989, the most current period available at that time. I then began filling in columns with dyeing and printing costs from the subcontracting companies who did this work for Latt-Greene. I also calculated and added yarn costs and added a knitting cost, a tricky and inaccurate process because such costs had never been accumulated or calculated. The only financial records being prepared at this time were the general ledger, cash receipts journal and customer ledgers, and a cash disbursement journal. As yarn was knitted into unfinished textiles (called greige goods), sheets were manually prepared showing what pieces were assigned to what lot and what the lot weighed. But no attempt was made to cost the greige goods. When the finished goods were delivered to customers, they were billed as per the purchase order, but again no attempt was made to cost the product. The owners believed they knew what their knitting costs should be, and so I used that number as a starting point.

As I developed the cost sheet, several problems began to surface. One, I couldn't locate dyeing and printing invoices that could be matched up against the sales invoices. There was no controlling order number that followed the job through all its steps before the finished product was delivered to the customer. The dye house assigned its own number to the orders, and the print plant did the same. In some cases it was virtually impossible to determine to which order the costs applied. Two, I found purchase orders for which no shipment to the customer could be located. Three, I found many orders being delivered late. The person who placed orders into work kept the orders in an alphabetical file on her desk and each day rummaged through the file, pulled some orders from it, and told her assistant to put them into work. Many orders were delivered very late simply because they didn't get pulled from the file, and there was no control over the orders that were in process.

As I completed input for the month of November, I began seeing that a large number of the orders either had a too low gross margin to generate a profit on the sale, or even incurred a gross loss. I began analyzing these orders, and several problems came to the surface. First, like a conscientious baker who regularly gives his customers a "baker's dozen' Latt-Greene was producing textiles that were heavier than required. If an order called for goods that weighed eight ounces to the running yard, we were filling it with goods that weighed nine ounces. This extra weight made for a nice finished product, but it also often meant the difference between a profit and a loss. Second, in many cases, while the weight was okay, and all other factors in the production were correct, the order didn't produce a profit. We came to the conclusion that in many cases the product was simply being sold for too low a price. No wonder the company's sales increased from $16 million to over $54 million in five short years.

During the time that I was developing this spreadsheet, the solutions to the problems being uncovered were becoming clearer. I developed a manual costing system whereby every new order coming in was costed as it progressed through the stages of production. When it was delivered to the customer we knew immediately whether we made or lost money and the reasons for an unsatisfactory result. But this manual costing system required a tremendous amount of time to maintain and keep current.

KNITTING THE NEW TOGETHER

While searching for computer software that would take the place of the manual system, I looked at several programs, but each had some faults or shortcomings that disqualified them. Finally, I was introduced to a company that had produced a textile conversion system for a business which was smaller than Latt-Greene, and which did no knitting. But I liked what I saw because it had many fine features and controls. Talking with the developer convinced me that the knitting operation could be added to produce a system that met our needs.

In October 1990, we installed a computer system using my old personal computer as the central server and added 10 stations using the Novell system. After installation, I had to train the employees to use the new system. For some who resisted abandoning "the way we had always done it' I had to warn them to either do it my way or I would get someone who would. Over several months they learned to become computer operators, and the old system was forgotten.

As better and better cost data was developed using the new system, we refined our sales prices. In some cases major customers were lost because we raised our prices. But most customers were retained because we improved our service to them in several ways. Delivery schedules were met on a more consistent basis, and product consistency and quality improved as the employees were able to spend more time on those aspects of the product and less time on paperwork and trying to track down product location.

The system developer and I were able to develop a system that works very well for us because we took the time to thoroughly understand the business of Latt-Greene and the problems that occur in the textile industry. I took the time to talk to everyone involved in the process of converting yarn into a dyed and printed textile. I looked at every piece of paper being produced and traced an entire month's orders through to the final invoicing of the finished product. This thorough analysis uncovered the problems. All that was left was the development of the systems necessary to fix the problems. I involved as many of the employees of Latt-Greene as possible in identifying the problems and in suggesting solutions. Then, when the final system was installed, many of the people who would be working with it already felt ownership of the system. The few who felt threatened by it and resisted it subsequently left the company.

How successful were we in turning the company around? The table on page 28 displays sales and return on owners investment (ROI) for the years 1985 to 1998.

The big ROI fluctuations up to the year ended May 31, 1990, represent the agonies the company was experiencing because of its rapid growth without corresponding improvements in the systems. The marked decline in ROI in 1992 was due to the upheavals introduced when the recession hit the clothing industry with a vengeance that year. But the important thing here is that even in the deep recession into which the clothing industry sank that year, Latt-Greene continued to be profitable. The 1998 numbers reflect the fact that tremendous quantities of Asian textiles were "dumped" in the United States at prices that we cannot compete against. Several of our clothing customers closed up because of this situation. Even during this "textile depression" however, Latt-Greene continued to be profitable.

The lesson here is that reengineering can have a dramatic impact upon a business. Huge costs to implement change aren't necessary. The entire cost of our new system was approximately $150,000. Turnaround was swift and dramatic. Downsizing did *not* take place. We have about the same size office staff as we did in 1990 (eight people). The difference is that now we know what our costs are, we bill all our sales, and collect all our receivables. We are able to plan and to develop strategy. While marketing mistakes still occur (for example, when we miss a season because of incorrect designs), the cost of these mistakes is minimized because we can measure them and identify exactly what the nature of the mistake was and make corrections before the mistake becomes a catastrophe.

AN UPDATE

Nine years after inception, the system has changed considerably from the initial setup, but we have never had to do another reengineering. The staff today is still about the same size as it was in 1990. All the personnel that I hired in 1990 to assist in administering the system are still with us. The only office staff to leave were those who refused to work with the new system and had left by the end of 1990.

Some general principles that I learned from this reengineering and which may be helpful to others who would like to upgrade their operation:

- Be open with all employees regarding the process.
- Solicit input from all employees.
- Involve everyone in the implementation of the new system.
- Understand the system yourself because this understanding is more important than bringing in consultants and helps to ensure that costs are kept under control.

Richard H. Snyder, CPA, is controller of Latt-Greene in Vernon, Calif

Chapter 5
Activity-Based Costing and Management

Cases

5-1 Blue Ridge Manufacturing (Activity-Based Costing for Marketing Channels)
5-2 Blue Ridge Manufacturing (Using SAS Activity-Based Costing Software)
5-3 Implementation of Activity Based Costing for Sunny View Dairy Farm Using SAS Activity-Based Costing Software
5-4 Wilson Electronics (A)
5-5 Wilson Electronics (B)
5-6 Pecos Products (Complexity into the Study of Activity-Based Costing)
5-7 The Buckeye National Bank (Activity-Based Costing in the Service Sector)

Readings

"Activity-Based Costing and Predatory Pricing: The Case of the Petroleum Retail Industry"

The assignment of indirect costs in a volume-based costing system can lead to product-cost subsidization—overcost high-volume products and undercost low-volume products. Undercosted products can lead to the appearance of predatory pricing where it actually does not exist. This article focuses on a lawsuit brought against a major chain of retail motor fuel (gasoline) service centers for allegedly selling regular-grade gasoline below cost, as defined by state statutes. The defendant employed ABC analysis to support its position that it was not selling its regular gasoline below cost. After the ABC analysis was presented, the case was settled, and the judge lifted the initial injunction.

Discussion Questions:
1. What are product-cost subsidizations?
2. What are possible consequences of product-cost subsidizations?
3. List alternative approaches to assign costs in a gasoline service center.
4. Identify cost hierarchy level groups in classifying activities at the retail level of a gasoline service center and give at least one example each.
5. What are overheads activity-cost pools pertaining to selling gasoline in a retail gasoline service center and what is the activity level for each of the cost pools?
6. Identify the activity drivers for overheads activity-cost pools identified in this study and explain the reasons for the selection?
7. List examples of gasoline-dispensing facilities for a gasoline service center and identify whether each of the facilities is a common or a gasoline grade-specific asset.

"Activity-Based Benchmarking and Process Management—Managing the Case of Cardiac Surgery "

Through a study of resource consumption, hospitals can get a more accurate picture of how practices are linked to cost.

Discussion Questions:
1. Describe briefly hospital's costing system.
2. Describe steps in activity-based benchmarking for medical-care processes.

"Activity-Based Costing for Higher Education Institutions"

Using tools and techniques such as activity-based costing (ABC), business process reengineering, concurrent engineering, and total quality management, universities can gain a better understanding of costs, simplified products and procedures, eliminated waste, cut costs, added value, and gained customer satisfaction. ABC helped several universities in Great Britain with tighter financial management and better resource allocation.

Discussion Questions:

1. Give two examples each of activities at unit, batch, and product levels in higher education institution and their cost drivers.
2. What are some of the benefits ABC might provide to academic institutions?

"Activity-Based Costing for State and Local Governments"

This article explains the ABC system and shows its applications to state and local governmental entities. The authors identified nine distinct activities at the livestock inspection facilities of the TDA and accounted for the costs via four primary categories and one indirect cost category. These costs are assigned to the activities followed by a pooling of activities and their costs, and five pools resulted. Three of the pools contained batch-level activities, while the activities of the others occurred at the facility level. Finally, the total costs of each pool were expressed on a per-unit basis according to the appropriate driver for the particular activity. The result is a much more meaningful analysis of costs that allow the TDA to become much more effective in cost management and cost control.

Discussion Questions:

1. Describe the steps in the ABC system for Texas Department of Agriculture's livestock facilities.
2. What are activities during the livestock inspection process?
3. Of the activities occurred during the livestock inspection process, which are batch-level activities and what are their cost drivers?

Cases

5-1 Blue Ridge Manufacturing

BACKGROUND:

Blue Ridge Manufacturing is one of a dozen companies that produces and sells towels for the U.S. "sports towel" market. A "sports towel" is a towel that has the promotion of an event or a logo printed on it. They're called sports towels because their most popular use is for distribution in connection with major sporting events such as the Super Bowl, NCAA Final Four, Augusta National Golf Tournament and the U.S. Open Tennis Tournament. Towels with college, NBA and NFL team logos, and promotions for commercial products such as soft drinks, beer, fast food chains, etc., are also big sellers.

The firm designs, knits, prints and embroiders towels. The firm knits all the towels it sells and tracks costs for towel production separately from the cost to customize the towels. Seventy-five percent of its orders include logo design, while the balance are print only and require the payment of a license fee for the logo used. However, about 15% of its orders include embroidery. Towels are made in three sizes: regular (18" x 30"), hand (12" x 20") and mid-range (15"x 24"). The normal production cycle for an order of white towels is three days. If a customer wants a colored towel, the basic white towel made by Blue Ridge is sent to a dyeing firm, which extends the production cycle of an order by three days. Also, occasionally, customers order towels in sizes other than the three standard sizes. These towels are called "special".

The firm now produces a "medium" quality towel. They have had some difficulty with the "staying power" of the material printed on these towels, which is attributed to the towel quality, the ink and the printing process. Customers have complained that the ink "lays on the surface" and it cracks and peels off.

Blue Ridge recently made a break-through in developing an ink that soaks into the towel, won't wash out and is non-toxic. A big advantage of this ink is that it avoids EPA disposal requirements because is can be "washed down the drain". Due to these characteristics of its new ink, Blue Ridge is considering upgrading the quality of the basic towel it produces because it will "take" the ink better, both the towel and the ink will last longer and the product will sell at a higher price. If it takes this step, the company will evaluate expanding its marketing and sales area with the objective of "going national".

CUSTOMERS:

Except for a few non-regional chains, Blue Ridge's sales are predominantly in the southeastern states. The company sells its products to 986 different customers. These customers differ primarily in the volume of their purchases, so management classifies each customer in one of three groups: large (8 customers), medium (154 customers) and small (824 customers). Large customers are primarily national chains, small customers are single store operations (including pro shops at golf courses) and medium-sized customers are small chains, large single stores or licensing agents for professional sports teams and manufacturers of consumer products. Table 1 gives the product and customer size statistics for 2001.

Blue Ridge has a different approach to customers in each of its three categories. A small group of in-house sales people sell directly to buyers in the large customer category. Independent manufacturer representatives, on commission, call on the license holder or the manager of a store in the medium customer category. Ads placed in regional and national magazines and newspapers target customers primarily in the small-customer segment, who call or mail in their orders.

Blue Ridge does not give discounts and it ships all order free on board (FOB) point of origin, i.e., customers pay their freight costs.

MANUFACTURING:

Blue Ridge has a modern knitting and printing plant in the foothills of North Carolina's Blue Ridge Mountains. Upgrading the facilities over recent years was accompanied by the introduction of an activity-based costing (ABC) system to determine product costs. The cost accounting system is fairly sophisticated and management has confidence in the accuracy of the manufacturing cost figures for each product line. Table 2 shows the firm's unit costs for various items.

Company management is committed to adopting advanced manufacturing techniques such as benchmarking and just-in-time (JIT). The corporate culture necessary for the success of such techniques is evolving and worker empowerment is already a major program. In addition, workers are allowed several hours away from regular work assignments each week for training programs conferring on budgets and work improvements and applying the ABC system.

PERFORMANCE:

The company is profitable. However, management has become concerned about the profitability of the customers in its three customer-size categories—large, medium and small. Different customers demand different levels of support. Management has no basis for identifying customers that generate high profits or to drop those that do not generate enough revenues to cover the expenses to support them. Under the previous accounting system, it wasn't possible to determine the costs of supporting individual customers.

With the introduction of ABC, it now may be possible to determine customer profitability. Table 3 shows how the administrative and selling costs are assigned and re-assigned between various functions within the selling and marketing areas and to sub-activities in the selling and marketing areas. Table 4 provides a list of selling and marketing activities and the activity base to use in assigning costs to each.

REQUIRED:

The managers of Blue Ridge Manufacturing have hired your consulting firm to advise them on the potential of using strategic cost analysis in assessing the profitability of their customer accounts.
Your analysis should include:

1. What is Blue Ridge's competitive strategy?
2. What type of cost system does Blue Ridge use, and is it consistent with their strategy?
3. Develop a spreadsheet analysis which can be used to assess the profitability of the three customer groups of Blue Ridge—large, medium and small customer account sizes. Use the information in Tables 1-4 to trace and allocate the costs necessary for the analysis.

TABLE 1
BLUE RIDGE MANUFACTURING
Sales Information

Product and Customer Size Statistics		Sales in Units by Customer Account Size			
		Large	Medium	Small	Total
Towel:	Regular	27,250	16,600	10,550	54,400
	Mid-Size	36,640	18,552	10,308	65,500
	Hand	35,880	19,966	95,954	151,800
	Special	480	3,426	594	4,500
Number of Units Sold		100,250	58,544	117,406	276,200
Number of Units Embroidered		5,959	6,490	29,394	41,842
Number of Units Dyed		20,536	9,935	12,328	42,798
Sales Volume Revenue		$308,762	$183,744	$318,024	$810,530
Number of Orders Received		133	845	5,130	6,108
Number of Shipments Made		147	923	5,431	6,501
Number of Invoices Sent		112	754	4,737	5,603
Accounts with Balance >60 Days		1	11	122	134

TABLE 2
BLUE RIDGE MANUFACTURING
Unit Cost Information

Line 1 Direct Manufacturing Costs Per Unit

		Quantity	Sales Price	Material	Labor	Overhead	Unit Cost
Towels:	Regular	54,400	$3.60	$0.60	$0.37	$0.22	$1.19
	Mid-Size	65,500	3.20	0.50	0.33	0.20	1.03
	Hand	151,800	2.55	0.39	0.31	0.19	0.89
	Special	4,500	4.00	0.67	0.48	0.29	1.44

Line 2 Direct Costs of Customizing Per Unit

	Quantity	Cost	Material	Labor	Overhead	Total
Inking (based on passes)	552,400	—	$0.0030	$0.0045	$0.0742	$0.0817
Dyeing	42,798	$0.11	—	—	0.0000	0.1100
Embroidery	41,842	—	0.0026	0.1750	1.0994	1.2770

Direct Labor Wage Rate: $9.00 (Including Fringes)
Inking requires one pass for each color used; average two colors per towel (i.e., 2 per unit), and is used on all towels.

TABLE 3
BLUE RIDGE MANUFACTURING
Selling and Administrative Costs and Activities

Costs Incurred in Each Function (Shipping, Sales, Marketing)

Directly Assigned To:

	Total	**Shipping**	**Sales**	**Marketing**	**Other**	**Total Assigned**	**Unassigned**
Administration	$170,000	$ 17,000	$ 37,400	$20,400	$56,100	$130,900	$39,100*
Selling	155,000	15,500	117,800	9,300	12,400	155,000	
	$325,000	$ 32,500	$155,200	$29,700	$68,500	$285,900	$39,100

Each function is used for the Following Activities

Selling and Administrative Activities:	Percentage of: **Shipping**	**Sales**	**Marketing**	**Other**
Entering Purchase Orders		55		10
Commissions		10		
Shipping Activities	65			15
Invoicing				20
Cost to Make Sales Calls		30		10
Checking Credit				10
Samples, Catalog Info.	5		10	
Special Handling Charges	5			5
Distribution Management	10		10	
Marketing, by Customer Type		5		
Advertising/Promotion			30	
Marketing	15		50	5
Administrative Office Support				20
Licenses, Fees				5
	100	100	100	100

* Note that $39,100 of the SG&A cost was not directly assigned. This amount represents the facility-sustaining activity cost.

TABLE 4
BLUE RIDGE MANUFACTURING
Activities and Cost drivers

Cost Drivers for Allocating Costs of Activities to Customer Groups (Large, Medium, Small)

Activity	Cost Driver
Entering Purchase Orders	Number of Orders
Commissions	Sales Dollars with Medium Customers
Shipping Activities	Number of Shipments
Invoicing	Number of Invoices
Cost to Make Sales Calls	Sales Dollars with Large Customers
Checking Credit	Percent Accounts >60 Days
Samples, Catalog Info.	Sales Dollars
Special Handling Charges	Management Estimate[1]
Distribution Management	Sales Dollars
Marketing, by Customer Type	Sales Dollars
Advertising/Promotion	Management Estimate[2]
Marketing	Number of Units Sold[3]
Administrative Office Support	Number of Units Sold[4]
Licenses, Fees	Sales Dollars with Medium Customers

[1]20% to medium-sized customers; 80% to small-sized customers.
[2]25% to medium-sized customers; 75% to small-sized customers.
[3]Excluding Specials
[4]Excluding Specials

5-2 Implementation of Activity Based Costing for Blue Ridge Manufacturing Company Using SAS Activity-Based Costing Software

REQUIRED:

Use the data for Blue Ridge Manufacturing Company in 5-1 to complete the following requirements:

1. Download and install the Oros Quick® ABC/M program from the textbook website: www.mhhe.com/blocher3e under Premium Content. (It's a WinZip file).
2. Download the Oros Quick® Tutorial from the text website: www.mhhe.com/blocher3e under Premium Content (It's an Adobe Acrobat file)
3. Work through the Oros tutorial (you can skip the sections on attributes and on the balanced scorecard)
4. Create a folder labeled "Blue Ridge." You will save the ABC model you create within that folder.
5. Use the information in the Blue Ridge Manufacturing Company Case (Case Number 5-1) and in the Tutorial to complete an ABC costing application using Oros; determine the ABC-based unit costs for Blue Ridge's three customer groups
6. Create and print a unit cost report for Blue Ridge, using the Oros system.

Case 5- 3 Implementation of Activity Based Costing for Sunny View Dairy Farm Using SAS Activity-Based Costing Software

Sunny View Dairy Farm is a small, family-owned and run business that started its operations in Hillsborough, North Carolina in 1996 with the goal of using all natural processes to create high quality dairy products. These products are sold in health food stores and supermarkets in the area as well as in the Sunny View Country Store. Sunny Views' products are well known and have gained a strong brand-loyalty throughout the region it operates.

Since Sunny View's production is currently limited by the facilities on site that can only accommodate 300 animals (of which 130 cows are part of the milking herd). It is considering expanding its operations to allow a wider distribution area for its products. In order to expand, Sunny View would have to build more barns and enlarge the milking facility. Sunny View's management is concerned about the large investment that would be necessary with expansion and feels that it should examine whether or not its current operations are efficient and cost effective before expanding. Sunny View has asked you to build an activity-based costing model to determine the cost of its products (the five varieties of milk: whole milk, low-fat milk, skim milk, chocolate milk, and eggnog) and aid in its decision-making process.

Production Process

The main processes involved in milk production are as follows:

1. Milking: An employee begins by sanitizing the cows. Once this is done, the employee attaches the cows to an electronic milking machine. The machine automatically provides information on the number of gallons produced by each cow and pumps the milk into a holding tank before the next process begins. This is a very time-consuming and labor-intensive process because the milking pen currently only accommodates 12 cows at a time. The rest of the cows are kept in the milking barn until it is their turn to be milked. Milking the entire milking herd takes between three and four hours.
2. Separating: In this process, a machine sorts the cream from the milk. The cream is then stored in a vat until it is added back to the milk to create either low-fat, chocolate, whole milk or eggnog.
3. Pasteurizing: Pasteurizing is the process by which any bacteria in the milk is killed. Milk runs through hot plates, bringing it to a temperature of 175 degrees. Then, the milk is run through cold plates to bring it to the optimal storage temperature of 38 degrees.
4. Homogenizing: After pasteurization, the milk is homogenized by breaking up fat molecules in the milk by running it through a high pressure system. This process is done for cosmetic purposes to create a rich, creamy finished product. The whole milk, low-fat milk, and skim milk are then stored in separate holding tanks until the bottling process begins.
5. Mixing: This process is only completed for chocolate milk and eggnog. In this process, sugar and other ingredients are added and mixed into the milk.
6. Bottling: Bottling is a very costly process. Sunny View only uses glass bottles to package its milk products. Before the bottles can be filled, employees must sterilize and sanitize the glass bottles. The clean bottles are then placed on a conveyer belt to be filled. The filling of the bottles is completed through an automatic filler machine. The machine also places plastic caps on the bottles. An employee removes the filled bottles from the conveyor belt and places them into crates.
7. Warehousing: When the crates are filled, an employee moves them to the refrigeration room in the warehouse. They are stored in the room until they are shipped. In addition to the refrigeration room, the warehouse also holds new and returned glass bottles as well as ingredients that are added to the milk in the mixing process.

Other, minor processes include general and administrative costs (keeping track of customer orders and invoices, etc.), repair and maintenance of farm equipment, and receiving & inspecting bottles and materials.

Sunny View's accounting system keeps track of overhead costs in four accounts: bottling equipment, facilities, processing, and general and administrative. There are sub-accounts in each of these accounts except for bottling equipment.

Accounts	**Sub accounts**	**Actual Costs**
Bottling Equipment		$1,528,620
Other Facilities Costs	Utilities	72,395
	Depreciation	22,976
	Property Tax	10,014
Total Other Facilities Cost		$105,385
Other Processing Costs	Labor and materials	428,800
	Supplies	4,278
	Equipment repairs and maint.	21,565
	Depreciation	13,688
Total Other Processing Cost		$ 468,331
General and Administrative	Administration	105,522
	Interest Expense	23,471
Total General and Administrative		$ 128,993
Total		**$ 2,231,329**

The following is a list of activities used by the farm in producing and bottling its products, as well as information to be used to assign overhead costs from the overhead accounts to the eight different activities:

	Overhead Accounts			
Activities	**Bottling Equip.**	**Facilities**	**Processing**	**G&A**
Milking		10,000	30%	
Separating/Pasteurizing/Homogenizing		2,000	15%	
Mixing		1,000	15%	
Bottling	90%	1,500	25%	
Warehousing		12,500	10%	
General and Administrative (G&A)		2,000		100%
Receiving and Inspecting	10%			
Cleaning and Repairs		1,000	5%	
Total	100%	30,000	100%	100%
Resource Driver for Overhead Account	Percentage above	Sq. Feet	Percentage	Percentage

The following information shows the use of activities by the cost objects, the different products:

Activities	Whole Milk	Low-Fat Milk	Skim Milk	Chocolate Milk	Eggnog	Activity Driver
Milking	373	933	653	280	280	Number of purchase orders
Separating/ Pasteurizing...	162	406	284	122	122	Machine Hours, Separating..
Mixing	0	0	0	365	365	Machine Hours, Mixing
Bottling	189	473	331	142	142	Machine Hours, Bottling
Warehousing	135	338	237	101	101	Labor Hours, Warehousing
G&A	270	676	473	203	203	Number of Invoices
Receive and Inspect	0	0	0	65,700	76,650	Ounces
Cleaning and Repairs	108	270	189	81	81	Labor Hours, Clean and Repair

In addition to the costs of these activities, Sunny View has direct costs for bottles and other materials. These materials are purchased from a variety of suppliers. Each glass bottle costs Sunny View $.75, including both purchase and recycling cost. Other ingredients include cocoa, sugar, and spices. Cocoa, used in the production of chocolate milk, costs $.05 per bottle. Sugar, used in both chocolate milk and eggnog, costs $.05 per bottle. Spices, used to make eggnog, cost $.08 per bottle.

The number of bottles produced by Sunny View per year (all quart bottles):

Product	Bottles Produced
Whole Milk	292,000
Low-Fat Milk	730,000
Skim Milk	511,000
Chocolate Milk	219,000
Eggnog	219,000

Required

1. Download and install the Oros Quick® ABC/M program from the text website: www.mhhe.com/blocher3e, under Premium Content (It's a WinZip file).
2. Download the Oros Quick® Tutorial from the text website: www.mhhe.com/blocher3e, under Premium Content (It's an Adobe Acrobat file)
3. Work through the Oros tutorial (you can skip the sections on attributes and on the balanced scorecard)
4. Create a folder on your computer labeled "Sunny View." You will save the ABC model you create within that folder.
5. Use the information in the case above and in the tutorial to complete an ABC costing application using Oros; determine the ABC-based unit costs for Sunny View's products.
6. Create and print a unit cost report for Sunny View, using the Oros system.

5-4 Wilson Electronics (A)*

CASE OVERVIEW

During the afternoon of August 30th, a meeting was convened of the senior finance managers and the industrial engineering manager of Wilson Electronics Company. The meeting had been called by Alice Johnson, controller, following her disturbing conversation with the president, Bill Simms. Johnson had approached Simms to discuss the idea of committing the resources necessary to update Wilson's activity-based costing (ABC) model. This idea seemed reasonable, given that the previously designed ABC model relied upon information that was more than one year old. Much to Alice's surprise, Simms responded to her inquiry by questioning the value of ABC altogether. Simms commented that he was well aware of the time and money spent designing the ABC model; however, he was not comfortable that a game plan existed for starting to actually use the ABC system to help make business decisions. In fact, Simms was concerned that even though the ABC model-building process had been completed, the idea of educating the management team on the potential applications of ABC had completely stagnated since the recent departure of the former controller and ABC champion, Mike Foster.

Simms explained to Johnson that simply re-arranging the company's general ledger expenses into an activity-based format was not beneficial enough to justify the continued support and maintenance of the ABC system. Instead, the ABC system needed to help Wilson's management team make better decisions that would improve overall company profitability. He informed Johnson that the ABC system was on the agenda for the next management team meeting to be held in three weeks. Her task for this meeting would be to substantiate the potential value of ABC to Wilson's management team. Simms knew that if Johnson could not demonstrate the potential applications of ABC to his company, he would halt the finance department's intentions of committing additional resources to updating an offline ABC system that had yet to be used within his organization to support decision making.

Johnson concluded that for ABC to survive the upcoming management team meeting, she would have to demonstrate its value in terms of cost reduction rather than just cost reporting. In particular, she thought it would make sense to narrow the scope of her presentation to focus on a recent cost cutting proposal that called for a reduction in the number of different types of parts contained in the A12 junction box. This product line had recently been threatened by a major competitor's announcement to reduce its price by $0.40 per unit. Wilson's management team felt that it must find a way to meet the price cut without causing a decline in the company's profits. Johnson believed that the ABC system would survive Simms's scrutiny if she could use ABC data to help Wilson effectively respond to the A12 price reduction.

COMPANY BACKGROUND

Wilson, located in Middletown, Ohio, builds components, such as ducts, connectors, and junction boxes, which are used in the installation of power cable and data communication cable management systems. These systems are typically installed within concrete floors in office buildings and shopping malls. Wilson employs 300 people who are responsible for engineering, fabricating, and assembling these products for resale through its two primary regional customer channels-large contractors and wholesale electrical supply houses. The firm's strategy is to "offer superior quality products and customer service at competitive prices."

*Peter C. Brewer, Robert J. Campbell, and Richard H. McClure, *Issues in Accounting Education*, 15 (3), pp. 415-429.

Wilson's 1999 revenues were $60 million. The company's sales growth has been steady over the past several years; however, profit margins have shrunk as the company has experienced an increase in expenses that cannot be passed on to its customers in the form of higher prices. In 1999, Wilson's average cost structure across all product lines was as follows: 59¢ of each sales dollar was material cost, 14.7¢ was conversion cost, 13¢ was fixed selling and administrative expenses, and 6¢ was sales commissions. This provided financial results in 1999 of a 7.3 percent before-tax profit margin and (given a 40 percent tax rate) an after tax return on sales of 4.4 percent, which compared unfavorably with industry norms of 10 percent and 6 percent, respectively. (See Exhibit 1 for summary financial information, by major product line.)

Wilson sells more than 100 different product types and models across four major product lines. It is currently operating at or near its practical capacity. Most of Wilson's products are commodity-type products that have standard designs and applications. The technology of these products does not change rapidly; therefore, each competitor offers similar functionality and design. However, a growing source of revenue for Wilson during the past five years has been customized production of orders with unique size and feature requirements for customers outside of Wilson's normal distribution channels. In 1999, Wilson secured record highs in its growing custom business in terms of number of orders received (740) and total number of units produced (68,500). Even though the volume is lower, Wilson's management team considers the custom business to be attractive because it utilizes previously idle plant capacity, earns reportedly high profit margins, and offers some pricing flexibility. Furthermore, Wilson has been able to adapt its existing manufacturing equipment to handle most of the custom business with minimal additional capital investment.

THE COST ACCOUNTING SYSTEM

In 1998, Wilson, with the support of Mike Foster, the controller at that time, decided to develop an ABC model that would encompass the materials acquisition and manufacturing departments. After this model gained acceptance within the company, Foster's long-term goal was to expand the ABC model's scope to include all of Wilson's departments. The model-building process included: (1) gathering activity definition, resource driver, and activity driver data; (2) creating an ABC cost model that had the ability to model the effect of changes in product design on activity frequencies; and (3) inputting data into the model. The ambitious goal of creating "what-if" activity-cost modeling capability was understood by Foster to be more time-consuming because of the need to create activity time standards, but he also viewed this capability as essential to managing the business from an activity-oriented perspective.

At the outset of the ABC project, Foster expressed the desire that the ABC model rely on activity charge rates that represented the cost of creating activity capacity. For example, a rate such as $100 per material move should reflect the investment in resources necessary to provide the capacity to make material moves. Therefore, unlike many ABC systems that use annual estimates of activity driver counts needed to satisfy demand, Wilson developed measures of activity driver capacities that were used as the denominators in its ABC rate calculations.

Foster decided that Wilson would state its activity driver capacities in terms of employee capacity. Accordingly, he worked with Wilson's Industrial Engineering group to develop activity time standards that could be used to determine activity capacity estimates. (See both Exhibit 2 for a summary of the estimates of employee capacity in each department and Exhibit 3 for a summary of the activity time standards and activity driver capacities established for each activity in the ABC model.) For example, the first activity, "analyze purchase decision reports," has a time standard of 50 minutes per batch. Purchase orders are prepared for specific customer orders produced in batches. The average time to review the order requirements and make the purchase decision represents a general range of time from 35 minutes to 70 minutes. Over many orders, the average time of 50 minutes was fairly representative and deemed adequate for the ABC project.

Foster's ABC philosophy was that periodic drops in activity frequency should be viewed as evidence that temporary levels of idle activity capacity existed, rather than as evidence that ABC rates should be raised. The ABC model was designed to isolate idle capacity as a cost to the company, rather than treating it as an expense to be borne by customers. This approach was intended to put pressure on management either to fully utilize existing activity capacity or to adjust that capacity downward when lower levels of activity frequency became permanent.

THE TRANSITION

After completing the ABC model (see Exhibit 4 for a summary of the model), Foster spent a month experimenting with activity-based report formatting. The primary type of report format that he designed for analyzing annual product-line profitability was called a "bill of activities," which Foster referred to as the activity-based alternative to a conventional "bill of materials." Foster was beginning the process of organizing a presentation for Wilson's management team that explained the full range of the ABC model's potential applications when he received an outstanding job opportunity to be the chief financial officer of a manufacturing firm near his hometown of Athens, Georgia. While Foster opted to take the job in Georgia, he agreed to remain at Wilson for six weeks to oversee the hiring and transition of his successor. Unfortunately, during his last six weeks, Foster was unable to complete his ABC presentation.

Once the new controller, Alice Johnson, was hired and briefly oriented to Wilson's operations, Foster departed for Georgia. His departure struck a blow to the momentum of Wilson's ABC system. Although a bright young prospect with ample financial accounting experience, Johnson did not have any prior ABC experience. Furthermore, none of Wilson's functional managers had familiarity with how to use output from the ABC model, given that they were merely asked to provide some data inputs during the model-building process. In short, the core of Wilson's ABC knowledge base walked out the door with Foster's departure. Not surprisingly, after Foster's exit, the ABC model ended up sitting on the shelf for the next year as efforts to apply the data to real decisions took a back seat to the day-to-day tasks that demanded everyone's attention. During this time, the direct-labor-hour-based standard cost system continued to support all financial reporting and decision making at Wilson, while the ABC system and its offline computer terminal sat untouched in the finance department.

Aware that the ABC project had stagnated, and intrigued by thoughts of the system's potential, Alice Johnson contemplated the idea of dedicating resources within her department to update the ABC model. Since the original ABC project was started almost two years ago and finalized over one year ago, Johnson felt that refreshing the data in the ABC model made sense. In all likelihood, some changes within the organization and its manufacturing methods had likely occurred, thus calling into question certain assumptions built into the initial ABC model. Updating the model would require performing interviews again within each department and reassigning organizational expenses to activities. Of course, Johnson's unexpected conversation with Simms shifted her focus from refreshing the ABC model to defending its continued existence.

THE A12 JUNCTION BOX AND ITS COST-REDUCTION PROPOSAL

The A12 junction box product line accounted for approximately 18.5 percent of Wilson's sales in 1999. It has generated approximately 300 customer orders per year and an annual volume of 100,000 units that is expected to continue for the next several years. Wilson maintains a 20 percent market share in this product line, while its five major competitors each possess market shares ranging from 8 percent to 25 percent. Wilson offers little product differentiation on the junction box line; therefore, it must be price-competitive in this commodity business or risk loss of substantial market share.

Junction boxes are installed at intersections of tubes or ducts containing cables, allowing for turns and connections to other ducts. When installed in concrete floors, they provide limited access to the cable management system for additions or changes in the type and quantity of cable used. The outer shell of the junction box is assembled from a steel housing comprising a separately fabricated top and bottom. Assembly workers assemble and mount electronic components inside the junction box. The current model A12 junction box contains ten different types of parts and 26 total parts.

The A12 cost-reduction proposal was predicated on the belief that the number of different types of parts used in each model is an important cost driver, along with the total volume of parts used annually in production. Therefore, the product engineering group wanted to redesign the A12 model of the junction box so that it would require only 21 total parts (instead of 26) and eight different types of parts (instead of ten different types) with virtually no loss in quality or functionality. The group's expectation was that the primary savings would come through improving operational efficiencies.

Exhibit 5 provides an overview of the material cost impact of the redesign. Three old parts, labeled part numbers #3, #5, and #7, would be replaced by a single new part. The cost for the new part is $12.85. Since two of these new parts would be required per unit, the added product cost would be $25.70 per junction box. The three deleted parts have a cumulative cost per junction box of $24.70; therefore, the total increase in material costs based on 100,000 units of production would be $100,000 or $1.00 per unit.

As part of the cost-reduction proposal, the product-engineering group solicited numerous bids from potential suppliers of the new part. Applied Technologies was identified as the preferred supplier of the new part because of its competitive price ($12.85), reputation for high quality, and commitment to customer service. Wilson's engineers believe that, since Applied Technologies is ISO 9000 certified, incoming inspection of the parts would not be necessary. If this turns out not to be the case, three other potential suppliers (all ISO 9000 certified) could be called upon to source the new part at price and quality levels comparable to Applied Technologies, with slightly inferior customer service.

The estimates of the project's upfront costs include $10,000 for product engineering work and $9,500 for process engineering work. In the event the proposal resulted in any layoffs, Wilson would have to cover severance pay of approximately $5,000 per employee. Any future cash flows associated with the proposal would be evaluated using a 14 percent discount rate.

The product engineering group believes that the extra up-front costs and material costs associated with the A12 redesign would be more than offset by future savings created by activity reductions in procurement, material handling, and manufacturing. The product engineering group's problem has been trying to use existing information databases, such as the standard cost system, to estimate the potential savings associated with the A12 redesign. Data provided by the standard cost system, with its labor-based factory burden rate, makes it difficult for the group to predict credible changes in operating costs for the A12 product line.

THE AUGUST 30TH MEETING

Alice Johnson (Controller), Ed Branson (Head of the Industrial Engineering group), Phil Markley (Assistant Controller), and Sally Jones (Cost Accounting Manager) were all in attendance at the August 30th meeting. Alice began the meeting by saying:

> As you know, Mr. Simms has put the ABC system on the agenda for the management team meeting in two weeks. My task at the meeting is to substantiate the potential value of our ABC system to this company. If my presentation bombs out, Simms may permanently revoke any additional support for maintaining the offline ABC system. I believe that to save the ABC system we need to shift our focus from cost reporting to cost reduction. More specifically, I believe that we have to prove ABC's worth by demonstrating how it can help management quantify the costs and benefits associated with the cost-reduction and profit-improvement proposals that have become more prevalent in recent months. Right now, the standard cost data that our managers look at to help make business decisions is misleading. I have reviewed the design of the ABC system and believe that the cost pools created and activity drivers chosen are reasonably accurate; therefore, I feel confident that the ABC system can do a much better job of supporting decision making than the standard cost system.
>
> The A12 junction box proposal is our opportunity to show how ABC can make a difference. It can provide the "proof of concept" that we need to sustain the system. With the impending price reduction on the A12 product line, our target cost reduction is $0.40 per unit. The initial report on the re-design is not very encouraging. The re-engineering plan, while achieving a reduction in the number of different types of parts per unit from 10 to 8, projects that material costs will increase by $1.00 per unit. (See Exhibit 5.)

Ed Branson interrupted, saying:

> So, the key to our analysis is determining if the potential cost savings associated with the reduction in number of different types of parts exceeds the $1.00 per unit increase in material costs by more than the $0.40 per unit market-driven price reduction. Given the annual product volume of 100,000 units, this means a total parts reduction of 500,000 parts per year, which should generate significant savings in employee time from the standpoint of buying, storing, moving, and assembling these parts into products. We know the savings are there; it is just a matter of properly quantifying them. Clearly, the standard cost system cannot do it, so this presents a good opportunity to show the value of the ABC system.

Alice interjected:

> To that end, I asked Sally [cost accounting manager] and Ed [industrial engineering head] to use the "what-if" capability of the ABC model to estimate the impact of the parts reduction on the workload of the departments directly affected-Purchasing, Stores, Material Handling, and Assembly. I have further asked Sally to quantify the cost savings using our existing activity driver charge rates.

Sally Jones offered:

> Ed and I began by reviewing the available ABC data on the A12 junction box as shown in the bill of activities (Exhibit 6). The current unit cost is $82.72, composed of $64.00 in direct materials, $13.51 in ABC costs, and $5.21 in overhead charges from departments that were not included in the ABC project. Of course, these costs are based upon the ten-parts version of A12.
>
> We then used the ABC model to adjust the activity driver counts affected by the change in parts. The model assumes the same size and contents of parts containers. It also assumes that the distance traveled and carrying capacity of the forklift trucks would be unchanged. The projection of activity driver count changes is shown in the report that I prepared on "Estimated Cost Savings Using ABC" (Exhibit 7). For example, activity #5b (unload materials and put in stores-assembly) uses the activity driver "# parts containers." Notice the proposal calls for reducing the total number of parts used by 19 percent, from 26 to 21. However, adjusting for parts volume changes as well as parts size changes, the ABC model estimates that the number of parts containers will be reduced by 16 percent. This works out to be a reduction of 3,200 containers, from 20,000 to 16,800.

My report (Exhibit 7) shows how the ABC model estimated the related cost savings by taking the activity driver count reductions and multiplying them by their corresponding ABC rates. For example, activity #5b (unload materials and put in stores-assembly) has a potential cost savings of $6,016, determined by multiplying the ABC rate of $1.88 per parts container times the projected reduction of 3,200 parts containers. As you can see, whenever we reduce activity counts, we achieve cost savings. Looking at the eight activities that are affected by the A12 redesign (#3, #4, #5b, #6b, #8, #13, #15, and #16), we can see that the total annual cost savings due to activity reductions will be $147,231, as shown in the Exhibit. This translates to a $0.47 per unit savings net of the increase in material costs.

The redesign proposal prepared by the product-engineering group relies upon the standard cost system to estimate the savings associated with the A12 redesign. The standard cost system is based on the assumption that direct labor is the only relevant cost driver and, therefore, reductions in direct labor will result in proportional reductions in overhead. Obviously, that assumption is flawed! We could never have identified all of these cost savings using the traditional labor-based overhead allocation method, because the plant-wide overhead rate effectively hides any specific changes in resource costs that might result from mix and volume changes. Thanks to the ABC model and its "what-if" capability, we can estimate with much greater certainty what our cost savings will be in each one of these support departments.

Ed Branson interrupted at this point:

Sally, that brings up an interesting point. You just used the term "cost savings." What does cost savings really mean to us? What does it mean to the line managers and to our company's top management? What does it mean to our stockholders?

I think that the estimates generated by the ABC model are flawed because they do not account for the fact that this type of proposal essentially boils down to quantifying cash savings-"cash" being the key word. Tangible reductions in cash outflows most often will be found by making specific reductions in employee headcount and payroll. Estimating these potential reductions in spending, particularly with respect to payroll, depends upon two factors: the aggregate change in activity demand within each department and the amount of idle capacity that may now be available within each department. For example, if eliminating 800 forklift moves freed up 333 hours of labor time, this would not necessarily save us any money. In other words, since each forklift operator provides 1,571 hours of productive capacity (see Exhibit 2), a reduction in demand of 333 hours does not allow us to let one forklift driver go without becoming shorthanded. On the other hand, if we knew that we had idle capacity in this activity area, say 1,250 hours of unused forklift driver time, we could now be confident that letting one driver go would still leave us with sufficient capacity among the remaining drivers to handle all workload needs. So, it is not a matter of how much we reduce activity levels and release employee time, but whether we can reduce our capacity by one or more workers. So, it seems to me the value of ABC for evaluating this type of proposal rests upon whether it can help us assess short-run changes in spending.

I propose that we consider the impact of the activity reductions identified by the ABC model on departmental workloads and savings in employee hours. As we know, no employee performs just one activity. Rather, within a departmental structure, employees are trained to perform a set of activities. Whether enough time can be saved to release an employee is dependent on what is happening to all the activities within a department. For example, within Purchasing we want to determine how much time is saved by the impact of the A12 proposal on two activities-#3, issuing purchase orders for parts, and #4, expediting open parts orders-and whether that time savings is sufficient to allow us to reduce the number of people we employ in that department. The cost savings materialize only if we can reduce our payroll expense.

Based on discussions with department heads, I have developed an estimate of idle employee time within each department. Believe me, they were not very happy about providing these estimates because our department heads are very protective of their staffing levels. Nonetheless, almost every manager did admit to having some idle capacity within his or her respective departments, as shown below:

Department	Estimate of Total Idle Capacity
Purchasing	0.75 full time equivalents
Stores	0.25 full time equivalents
Crane Operators	0.25 full time equivalents
Forklift Operators	0.50 full time equivalents
Fabrication	0.50 full time equivalents
Assembly	0.00 full time equivalents

For example, the Purchasing manager admitted to having three fourths of a person idle or 0.75 fulltime equivalents (FTEs). By using the practical capacity estimate of one purchasing agent (1,537 hours), we can determine that the parts reduction proposal needs only to produce a time savings of approximately 385 hours (0.25 x 1,537 hours) to generate the opportunity for real cost savings. Assembly was the only department that would not concede any idle time. Of course, that probably makes sense, given how backed up they have been lately, coupled with Mr. Simms' reservations about increasing payroll expense by hiring more people.

Alice Johnson interrupted with several questions:

Why are you bringing up the issue of existing idle time in the departments? Don't these crude estimates change from week-to-week? It seems that the inclusion, or exclusion, of existing idle time can have a significant impact on cost savings according to your point of view. Yet, the parts-reduction proposal on the table is not in any way responsible for the current level of idle capacity within each department. How can you justify linking these idle-capacity estimates to the analysis of this proposal? If I were seeking approval of a cost-reduction proposal, using your mode of thinking, I would wait for a down period in our business when capacity utilization drops and then make my pitch to the management team.

Phil Markley spoke up at this point:

I think an important point that we have yet to mention is the notion of time frame. What time horizon should we consider when trying to estimate the economic benefits of these types of cost-reduction proposals? Sally's approach to estimating cost savings seems to be more long-term oriented, while Ed's point of view is more short-term in nature. There is no doubt that Mr. Simms is pretty focused on getting short-run results to appease our creditors and investors. Yet, the rhetoric suggests that we are supposed to be managing for long-run success. Should our perspective of cost savings be focused on a 6-12 month time horizon, or something more long-term?

As the meeting progressed, little consensus emerged regarding how to measure the cost savings associated with the A12 proposal. Alice was becoming somewhat concerned. The management meeting was less than two weeks away and she was not confident about what to say regarding the A12 proposal.

SUGGESTED CASE DISCUSSION QUESTIONS

1. Describe the position taken by Sally Jones. Prepare a new bill of activities for the revised version of the A12 junction box, based on the old bill of activities provided in Exhibit 3. How much cost savings per unit will be realized? How does the capacity-based approach to designing an ABC system enable the measurement of changes in resource usage?
2. Describe the position taken by Ed Branson on what is meant by cost savings. Prepare a schedule of employee time savings and a schedule of cost savings according to this viewpoint. How much cost savings will be realized in the next year-in total and per unit for the A12 junction box-according to this viewpoint? Decide if you should recognize available idle time estimates in your analysis.
3. With which point of view (Question 1 or 2) do you agree? Why? What net dollar amount of savings, per unit and in total, would you use to analyze this proposal?
4. Does this proposal meet the strategic needs of the company, with respect to competition on the A12 junction box product line? What other advice would you give Alice Johnson to help her prepare for the management team meeting? What do you think the response of President Simms will be to Alice Johnson's presentation? Assuming Simms takes Alice Johnson's recommendation and commits the resources necessary to update Wilson's ABC model, do you think this overall ABC initiative will be successful?

EXHIBIT 1
Wilson's Financial Performance vs. the Industry Average
(in thousands of dollars)

1997	Ducts (Segments)	Connectors (Segments)	Junction Boxes (Segments)	Custom[a] (Segments)	Total	(%)	Industry Average
Sales $17,515	$13,560	$20,905	$4,520	$56,500	100.0	100.0%	
Direct materials	10,118	8,040	12,125	2,600	32,883	58.2	58.0
Direct labor	650	450	750	150	2,000	3.5	4.0
Overhead	2,145	1,485	2,475	495	6,600	11.7	10.5
Gross margin	$ 4,602	$ 3,585	$ 5,555	$1,275	$15,017	26.6	27.5
S, G & A	2,978	2,305	3,554	768	9,605	17.0	17.0
Profit before tax	$ 1,624	$ 1,280	$ 2,001	$ 507	$ 5,412	9.6	10.5
Tax expense	650	512	800	203	2,165	3.8	4.2
Profit after tax	$ 975	$ 768	$ 1,201	$ 304	$ 3,247		
Profit margin	5.6%	5.7%	5.7%	6.7%	5.7%	5.7%	6.3%
1998							
Sales $16,820	$13,920	$20,880	$6,380	$58,000	100.0	100.0%	
Direct materials	10,183	8,213	12,110	3,365	33,871	58.4	58.0
Direct labor	442	394	734	230	1,800	3.1	4.0
Overhead	1,729	1,541	2,871	900	7,040	12.1	10.0
Gross Margin	$ 4,466	$ 3,772	$ 5,165	$1,885	$15,289	26.4	27.5
S, G & A	2,994	2,478	3,717	1,136	10,324	17.8	17.5
Profit before tax	$ 1,472	$ 1,294	$ 1,449	$ 750	$ 4,965	8.6	10.0
Tax expense	589	518	579	300	1,986	3.4	4.0
Profit after tax	$ 883	$ 777	$ 869	$ 450	$ 2,979		
Profit margin	5.3%	5.6%	4.2%	7.1%	5.1%	5.1%	6.0%
1999							
Sales $16,800	$14,200	$21,000	$8,000	$60,000	100.0	100.0%	
Direct materials	10,550	8,430	12,320	4,100	35,400	59.0	58.0
Direct labor	392	368	680	260	1,700	2.8	4.0
Overhead	1,646	1,546	2,856	1,092	7,140	11.9	10.0
Gross margin	$ 4,212	$ 3,856	$ 5,144	$2,548	$15,760	26.3	28.0
S, G & A	3,192	2,698	3,990	1,520	11,400	19.0	18.0
Profit before tax	$ 1,020	$ 1,158	$ 1,154	$1,028	$ 4,360	7.3	10.0
Tax expense	408	463	462	411	1,744	2.9	4.0
Profit after tax	$ 612	$ 695	$ 692	$ 617	$ 2,616		
Profit margin	3.6%	4.9%	3.3%	7.7%	4.4%	4.4%	6.0%

[a] The "Custom" segment represents the Ducts, Connectors, and Junction Boxes that were uniquely designed to meet specific customer requirements. The other three segments represent the standard versions of those products made for the customers in Wilson's normal distribution channels.

EXHIBIT 2
Employee Annual Capacity in Labor Hours
(excludes supervisory labor)

Employee Classification	Employee Headcount	Theoretical Capacity[a]	Practical Capacity[b]	Average Employee Practical Capacity	Average Wage + Fringe[c] per Employee	Average Hourly Wage per Employee
Purchasing Agents	15	30,000	23,050	1,537	$30,373.33	$12.66
Stores Employees	12	24,000	17,880	1,490	29,066.67	12.11
Crane Operators	2	4,000	3,230	1,615	31,100.00	12.96
Forklift Operators	13	26,000	20,420	1,571	29,509.54	12.30
Fabrication Workers	32	64,000	50,880	1,590	30,510.94	12.71
Assemblers	103	206,000	157,220	1,526	29,800.00	12.42

[a] Theoretical capacity is defined as 50 weeks/year multiplied by 40 hours/week, or 2,000 hours/employee/year.

[b] Practical capacity equals theoretical capacity less nonproductive times, such as vacation and sick time, planned idle time, scheduling, and other downtime. Idle capacity estimates were obtained from departmental managers in the form of FTEs.

[c] Fringe benefits are 20 percent of employee wages.

EXHIBIT 3
Activity Capacity Estimates in Hours

Activities	Allocation of Hours of Employee Capacity		Activity Driver	Activity Time Standards	Activity Capacity by Activity Driver Count
Purchasing Department					
1. Analyze purchase decision reports	2,080	9%	# production batches	50 min./batch	2,496 batches
2. Issue purchase orders for sheets	1,850	8%	# production batches	45 min./batch	2,467 batches
3. Issue purchase orders for parts	,600	33%	# unique parts/batch	20 min./count	22,800 count
4. Expedite open parts orders	11,520	50%	# unique parts/batch	30 min./count	23,040 count
	23,050	100%			
Stores					
5. Unload materials and put in stores					
a. Fabrication-steel sheets	2,330	13%	# sheet bundles	16 min./bundle	8,738 bundles
b. Assembly-parts	10,190	57%	# parts containers	5 min./container	122,280 containers
6. Process material requisitions					
a. Fabrication-steel sheets	890	5%	# sheet bundles	5 min./bundle	10,680 bundles
b. Assembly-parts	4,470	25%	# parts containers	2 min./container	134,100 containers
	17,880	100%			
Material Handling					
7. Move sheets to Fabrication by crane	3,230	100%	# crane moves	60 min./crane move	3,230 crane moves
8. Move parts to Assembly	11,640	57%	# forklift moves	25 min./forklift move	27,936 forklift moves
9. Move steel housing to Assembly	5,100	25%	# forklift moves	45 min./forklift move	6,800 forklift moves
10. Move finished goods to warehouse	3,680	18%	# forklift moves	30 min./forklift move	7,360 forklift moves
	20,420	100%			
Fabrication					
11. Setup equipment	5,090	10%	# setups	150 min./setup	2,036 setups
12. Fabricate steel housing units	40,702	80%	# housing units	6 min./unit	407,020 units
13. Rework defective units	5,088	10%	# of rework hours	10 min./unit	30,528 hours
	50,880	100%			
Assembly					
14. Unload steel housing units	12,580	8%	# housing units	1.5 min./housing	503,200 units
15. Unload parts and hold	18,870	12%	# parts used	0.10 min./part	11,322,000 parts
16. Assemble finished products	94,330	60%	# parts used	see note below	11,322,000 parts
17. Inspect finished goods	17,290	11%	# finished units	2 min./unit	518,700 units
18. Package finished goods	14,150	9%	# finished units	1.5 min./unit	566,000 units
	157,220	100%			

Total assembly times (in minutes and hours) for the original A12 and the revised A12 are provided in Exhibit 5.

EXHIBIT 4 Activity Cost Pools

Process 1: Materials Procurement	Wage and Fringes	Supervision	Supplies and Utilities	Equipment	ABC Cost Pools	Activity Driver	Activity Cost Rate	Activity Driver Capacity
1. Analyze purchase decision reports	$ 41,004	$ 5,000	$ 3,000	$ 2,181	$ 51,185	# production batches	$20.51	2,496
2. Issue purchase orders for sheets	36,448	6,000	4,000	1,938	48,386	# production batches	19.61	2,467
3. Issue purchase orders for parts	150,348	10,000	8,000	6,481	174,829	# unique parts/batch	7.67	22,800
4. Expedite open parts orders	227,800	31,000	6,380	5,380	270,560	# unique parts/batch	11.74	23,040
Subtotal	$455,600	$52,000	$21,380	$10,600	$544,960			
Stores Personnel								
5. Unload material and put in stores								
a. Fabrication-steel sheets	$ 45,344	$ 8,160	$ 5,200	$ 4,440	$ 63,144	# sheet bundles	7.23	8,738
b. Assembly-parts	198,816	18,000	6,300	6,290	229,906	# parts containers	1.88	122,280
6. Process material requisitions								
a. Fabrication-steel sheets	17,440	5,780	8,500	3,145	34,865	# sheet bundles	3.26	10,680
b. Assembly-parts	87,200	16,860	7,000	4,625	115,685	# parts containers	0.86	134,100
Subtotal	$348,800	$48,800	$27,500	$18,500	$443,600			
Process 2: Manufacturing								
Material Handlers								
7. Move sheets to Fabrication by crane	$ 62,200	$11,200	$ 9,600	$42,800	$125,800	# crane moves	38.95	3,230
8. Move parts to Assembly	218,666	24,350	17,200	38,600	$298,816	# forklift moves	10.70	27,936
9. Move steel housing to Assembly	95,906	7,525	10,600	32,250	146,281	# forklift moves	21.51	6,800
10. Move finished goods to warehouse	69,052	6,063	8,500	26,930	110,545	# forklift moves	15.02	7,360
Subtotal	$383,624	$37,938	$36,300	$97,780	$555,642			
Fabrication Workers								
11. Setup equipment	$ 97,635	$ 22,000	$14,400	$ 38,450	$ 172,485	# setups	84.72	2,036
12. Fabricate steel housing units	781,080	78,800	15,000	126,500	1,001,380	# housing units	2.46	407,020
13. Rework defective units	97,635	11,200	10,000	100,000	218,835	# of rework hours	7.17	30,528
Subtotal	$976,350	$112,000	$39,400	$264,950	$1,392,700			
Assembly Workers								
14. Unload steel housing units	$ 245,552	$ 52,600	$ 3,000	$ 17,200	$ 318,352	# housing units	0.63	503,200
15. Unload parts and hold	368,328	72,000	3,900	33,700	477,928	# parts used	0.04	11,322,000
16. Assemble finished products	1,841,640	36,000	18,100	66,500	2,012,240	# parts used	0.18	11,322,000
17. Inspect finished goods	337,634	94,200	11,300	23,000	466,134	# finished units	0.90	518,700
18. Package finished goods	276,246	66,000	6,500	33,000	381,746	# finished units	0.67	566,000
Subtotal	$3,069,400	$370,800	$42,300	$173,400	$3,656,400			
Total Activity Costs					$6,719,102			

EXHIBIT 5
Junction Box-Model A12
Summary of Direct Material Cost and Assembly Time per Unit

Direct Material Cost per Unit

Unique Part Number	Vendor Cost per Part	Original Number of Parts per Unit Model A12	Original Materials Cost Model A12	Model A12 Revised Parts List	Revised Materials Cost Model A12
1	$ 0.50	4	$ 2.00	4	$ 2.00
2	2.80	3	8.40	3	8.40
3	4.00	2	8.00 0 -		
4	2.50	1	2.50	1	2.50
5	3.50	3	10.50	0	-
6	2.75	2	5.50	2	5.50
7	3.10	2	6.20	0	-
8	2.40	4	9.60	4	9.60
9	2.00	3	6.00	3	6.00
10	2.65	2	5.30	2	5.30
New part	12.85	0	-	2	25.70
		26	**$64.00**	21	**$65.00**

1997 Production Volume (units)	100,000	100,000
1997 Direct Materials Estimate	**$6,400,000**	**$6,500,000**

Assembly Time per Unit

Unique Part Number	Assembly Time in Minutes	Original Number of Parts per Unit Model A12	Assembly Time/Unit (Original A12)	Model A12 Revised Parts List	Assembly Time/Unit (Revised A12)
1	0.25	4	1.00	4	1.00
2	0.50	3	1.50	3	1.50
3	0.75	2	1.50	0	0.00
4	1.00	1	1.00	1	1.00
5	0.50	3	1.50	0	0.00
6	0.75	2	1.50	2	1.50
7	1.00	2	2.00	0	0.00
8	0.25	4	1.00	4	1.00
9	0.50	3	1.50	3	1.50
10	0.75	2	1.50	2	1.50
New part	1.71	0	0.00	2	3.42
Total		26	14.00	21	12.42

Production volume (units)	100,000	100,000
Total Assembly minutes	1,400,000	1,242,000
Minutes per hour	60	60
Total Assembly hours	**23,333**	**20,700**

EXHIBIT 6
Bill of Activities for Current Version of A12 Junction Box

Activity#	Quantity of Activity Driver	Activity Rate	Total Activity Charge	Volume of Production	Activity Charge/unit
1	300 batches	$20.51	$ 6,153	100,000 units	$ 0.06
2	300 batches	19.61	5,883	100,000 units	0.06
3	3,000 unique parts	7.67	23,010	100,000 units	0.23
4	3,000 unique parts	11.74	35,220	100,000 units	0.35
5a	1,500 bundles	7.23	10,845	100,000 units	0.11
5b	20,000 containers	1.88	37,600	100,000 units	0.38
6a	1,500 bundles	3.26	4,890	100,000 units	0.05
6b	20,000 containers	0.86	17,200	100,000 units	0.17
7	600 crane moves	38.95	23,370	100,000 units	0.23
8	3,333 forklift moves	10.70	35,663	100,000 units	0.36
9	1,500 forklift moves	21.51	32,265	100,000 units	0.32
10	1,500 forklift moves	15.02	22,530	100,000 units	0.23
11	300 setups	84.72	25,416	100,000 units	0.25
12	100,000 housing units	2.46	246,000	100,000 units	2.46
13	4,550 hours	7.17	32,624	100,000 units	0.33
14	100,000 housing units	0.63	63,000	100,000 units	0.63
15	2,600,000 parts	0.04	104,000	100,000 units	1.04
16	2,600,000 parts	0.18	468,000	100,000 units	4.68
17	100,000 finished units	0.90	90,000	100,000 units	0.90
18	100,000 finished units	0.67	67,000	100,000 units	0.67
Total Activity Charges			$1,350,669		$13.51
Overhead from departments not included in ABC study[a]			520,661		5.21
Total Material Costs			6,400,000		64.00
Total Product Cost			$8,271,330		$82.72

[a] The overhead charged from the departments not included in the ABC study continues to be the same amount as would be charged from these departments using the direct-labor-based standard cost system.

EXHIBIT 7

Estimated Cost Savings Using ABC (assumed annual volume = 100,000 units)

Activity	Activity Driver	Original Activity Frequency	Revised Activity Frequency	Change in Activity Frequency	ABC Rates	ABC Cost Savings
Purchasing Department						
1. Analyze purchase decision reports	# production batches	300	300	0	$20.51	
2. Issue purchase orders for sheets	# production batches	300	300	0	19.61	
3. Issue purchase orders for parts	# unique parts/batch	3,000	2,400	-600	7.67	($ 4,602)
4. Expedite open parts orders	# unique parts/batch	3,000	2,400	-600	11.74	(7,044)
Stores						
5. Unload materials and put in stores						
a. Fabrication-steel sheets	# sheet bundles	1,500	1,500	0	7.23	
b. Assembly-parts	# parts containers	20,000	16,800	-3,200	1.88	(6,016)[a]
6. Process material requisitions						
a. Fabrication-steel sheets	# sheet bundles	1,500	1,500	0	3.26	
b. Assembly-parts	# parts containers	20,000	16,800	-3,200	0.86	(2,752)[a]
Material Handling						
7. Move sheets to Fabrication by crane	# crane moves	600	600	0	38.95	
8. Move parts to Assembly	# forklift moves	3,333	2,800	-533	10.70	(5,703)[b]
9. Move steel housing to Assembly	# forklift moves	1,500	1,500	0	21.51	
10. Move finished goods to warehouse	# forklift moves	1,500	1,500	0	15.02	
Fabrication						
11. Setup equipment	# setups	300	300	0	84.72	
12. Fabricate steel housing units	# housing units	100,000	100,000	0	2.46	
13. Rework defective units	# of rework hours	4,550	3,000	-1,550	7.17	(11,114)[c]
Assembly						
14. Unload steel housing units	# housing units	100,000	100,000	0	0.63	
15. Unload parts and hold	# parts used	2,600,000	2,100,000	-500,000	0.04	(20,000)
16. Assemble finished products	# parts used	2,600,000	2,100,000	-500,000	0.18	(90,000)
17. Inspect finished goods	# finished units	100,000	100,000	0	0.90	
18. Package finished goods	# finished units	100,000	100,000	0	0.67	
Total savings						**($147,231)**

[a] The original activity frequency for activities #5b and #6b assumed an average of 130 units per container. The revised frequency is based on fewer although larger parts, which average 125 parts per container.

[b] For activity #8, each forklift move is assumed to carry 6 parts containers. Thus, 3,333 moves would be required to move 20,000 containers.

[c] For activity #13, the revised number is an estimate based on the presumption that the change in unique parts will reduce rework by approximately 1/3.

5-5 Wilson Electronics (B)

As the date of the management team meeting approached, Alice Johnson was gaining confidence that her presentation concerning the A12 junction box would have a positive effect on her colleagues. The $0.47 per unit resource-usage-based savings associated with the A12 redesign provided her with the means to illustrate ABC's value to the company. However, a few days before the management team meeting, another one of Wilson's major competitors announced a $2.50 per unit price reduction on its version of the A12 junction box. Johnson is now convinced that her demonstration of a meager $0.47 per unit savings for the A12 junction box will have little influence on the management team; therefore, the credibility of her presentation is doomed. At a loss as to how to respond to this recent development, Alice decided to contact Mike Foster, the former corporate controller of Wilson Electronics. When Foster departed to pursue another job opportunity, he encouraged Alice to use him as a "sounding board" if any questions or concerns arose. Alice decided to take him up on his offer with a phone call.

Alice Johnson (AJ): Hello, Mike. This is Alice Johnson. How are you doing?

Mike Foster (MF): Good to hear from you. I'm doing fine, thanks. Things are a little hectic down here, but I'm hanging in. How are you doing at Wilson? Are you becoming comfortable with their systems and procedures?

AJ: Well, I'm fine, but I'm not so sure about our ABC system.

MF: What do you mean?

AJ: After you left, ABC ground to a screeching halt. In an effort to jump-start things again, I suggested to Mr. Simms that we update the model. He not only put that thought on hold, but he questioned the value of the ABC system altogether. To make a long story short, I have to make a presentation to the management team in a couple of days that explains how ABC can add value to the decision-making process within our company. If I fail to deliver a convincing argument, it's possible that Mr. Simms will essentially "pull the plug" on the ABC system entirely.

MF: Dumping ABC would be a mistake. It doesn't surprise me that, subsequent to my departure, the ABC system is on the chopping block. It was tough enough getting support for the initiative while I was there. Well anyway, what do you have up your sleeve for this presentation?

AJ: I decided that it probably makes sense to focus on a cost-reduction proposal as a way to demonstrate that ABC is capable of aiding the decision-making process. Therefore, I selected a cost-cutting proposal that relates to the redesign of the A12 junction box.

MF: Tell me a little bit about that particular proposal.

AJ: The proposal is designed to reduce the total number of parts in the A12 junction box from 26 to 21. Also, the number of different types of parts used in each junction box is being reduced from ten to eight. What is interesting about the proposal is that the revised bill of materials projects that raw material costs will increase $100,000 as a result of the product redesign. Since the standard cost system is unable to link the reduction in the number of parts to activity reductions and cost savings, this proposal provides a good opportunity to demonstrate the value of ABC.

MF: Sounds like an interesting proposal. So, how is your presentation to the management team shaping up?

AJ: Well, this is where the problem starts. A few months ago one of our major competitors announced a $0.40 per unit price reduction on its version of the A12 junction box. I concluded that if we could use ABC to document a net savings in excess of $0.40 per unit, then my presentation to the management team would be a success. I met with Sally and Phil from Accounting and Ed from Industrial Engineering to see if we could use the data from the ABC system to estimate the cost savings potential of the A12 redesign proposal.

---

*Peter C. Brewer, Robert J. Campbell, and Richard H. McClure, *Issues in Accounting Education*, 15 (3), pp. 415-429.

MF: So, what did your cost savings estimates turn out to be?

AJ: We didn't exactly reach a consensus on this point. Sally applied what I now understand to be the resource-usage viewpoint to calculate an estimated cost savings of $0.47 per unit, net of the material cost increase. However, Ed took a more short-run-oriented perspective that focused on spending reduction. According to Ed's viewpoint, the A12 redesign doesn't generate enough savings to offset the increase in material cost.

MF: What was your reaction to these two sets of cost savings estimates?

AJ: I tend to agree with the long-run-oriented resource-usage-based perspective that Sally used to calculate her numbers. Therefore, I was going to build my presentation around the $0.47 per unit savings figure that she derived. I was intending to make the argument that ABC could enable us to make a data-driven decision to match the $0.40 per unit price reduction while maintaining profitability.

MF: You just said that you "were intending" to make this point, but it sounds like you've changed your mind.

AJ: Actually, I was forced to change my mind because yesterday another one of our primary competitors announced a $2.50 per unit price reduction on this product. So, if I go into the management team meeting bragging about a $0.47 savings on a product in need of a $2.50 per unit price cut, I'm going to look foolish! It's the proverbial "eleventh hour" and I'm feeling a little stressed out! So, I decided to call you to see if you could offer any advice as to where I should go from here.

MF: First of all, the work that you have done regarding the A12 redesign was not wasted time. The information that you've conveyed to me regarding your analysis is interesting and it should comprise a portion of your presentation. However, you're correct in assuming that the A12 proposal can't be the basis for your entire presentation.

AJ: But, should I use Sally's numbers or Ed's? I'm inclined to use Sally's, but what do you think?

MF: Personally, I prefer the usage model because I believe that it puts the focus on redeploying freed-up capacity as opposed to the spending model that tends to focus on headcount reduction. Nonetheless, I would present both modes of analysis as potentially useful sources of information 432 Issues in Accounting Education depending upon the decision context. Furthermore, I think that both modes of analysis are an improvement over the existing standard cost system.

AJ: Okay, what else can I build into the presentation beyond the usage-vs.-spending analysis of the A12 proposal?

MF: My suggestion is that you use the ABC cross model as a way to broaden the scope of your presentation to include some "big picture" issues that you're currently overlooking if your focus is exclusively on the cost-reduction potential of the A12 proposal. I'll have my assistant send you a copy of an article describing the ABC cross model, but for now, here is a thumbnail sketch. The ABC cross model will not only give you a platform for talking about applications of ABC from a "what-if" cost-modeling perspective, which you're already touching upon with the A12 proposal, but it will also enable you to discuss ABC applications from both a product-mix-strategy perspective and a process-cost-management perspective. Right now, your presentation game plan is overlooking these two potential applications of ABC that I've always felt are critical to Wilson. I think it's important for you to consider why the product-engineering group picked the A12 product line over other product lines as the focal point of its product redesign cost reduction efforts.

AJ: Probably it was a "knee-jerk" reaction to our competitor's announced price reduction of $0.40 per unit coupled with the already low 2.2 percent profit margin on this product reported by the standard cost system. Of course, you and I know that the 2.2 percent margin is probably distorted, but....

MF: So, in other words, management's perception was that the A12 junction box was marginally profitable before any price reduction, and a further reduction in price without taking any type of management action would drop this product into the "red." So, a response was necessary and cost reduction seemed to be the most likely option.

A "big picture" question that you should ask is: Should Wilson be focusing its attention on products such as A12? Is A12 really a loser even before the price cut? Products such as A12 are the perceived reason that overall company profits have been shrinking, but what about all those low-volume, custom products that look so great according to the standard cost system? Right now, nobody outside your finance department has a clue about the true relationship between the revenue being generated by the growing custom business and the costs being driven by that segment of Wilson's business.

AJ: Wow, I guess in the back of my mind I was aware of this issue, but I allowed myself to get caught up in the detail of A12 proposal, while turning a blind eye to the product-mix-strategy issue.

MF: Keep in mind that there's nothing wrong with the details of the A12 proposal that you've been wrestling with. After all, if Wilson reduces its price on the A12 junction box by $2.50 without any true accompanying cost reduction, your company will see its profits decline regardless of what the ABC system indicates about A12's profit margin. So the usage-vs.-spending issue is worth thinking over and incorporating into your presentation, but it's not the whole ABC story. While we're talking, here's another issue to think about.

Let's assume for a minute that your focus is the A12 junction box. You just told me moments ago that Sally's projected cost savings were well short of the market-driven $2.50 price cut. Look at the activity costs that are being charged to the A12 line and are being passed on to Wilson's customers. How many of those activities in the ABC model are value-added from the customer's perspective?

AJ: You're right-moving, storing, setting-up equipment, expediting-none of those activities adds any value. We could be spending time analyzing these non-value-added costs to find ways to reduce support costs without sacrificing product quality or customer service.

MF: Given the volume of sales associated with A12, it may make more sense to talk about cost reduction from a process-redesign perspective instead of a product redesign perspective. There is probably a big savings opportunity associated with creating a manufacturing cell for A12. I think the big dollars are there instead of the proposed product redesign. Obviously, Wilson cannot snap its fingers and have a manufacturing cell up and running, but the purpose of your presentation should be simply to create an awareness of this application of ABC data. In other words, how on earth would you quantify the resources being consumed in non-value-added work using the standard cost system? Furthermore, how would you use the standard cost system to estimate the cost savings associated with a process redesign initiative?

AJ: Good point. These process cost management issues definitely need to be included in my presentation.

MF: Listen, I have an appointment coming up, but I want to mention one last thing for you to think about for your presentation. Spend some time contemplating the tone of your message. If your sole focus is on cutting-cutting product lines and cutting nonvalue-added workers-your fellow managers may begin to get resentful and see you only in the role of the proverbial "bean counter." I know the people out on the manufacturing floor are going to want to talk about revenue growth, not just cost reduction. You probably should be prepared to offer some comments regarding ABC from a resource redeployment and revenue growth perspective. Make the point that once ABC has helped identify freed-up resources in support as well as production departments, those valuable resources do not necessarily need to be eliminated; rather, they can be channeled to growing revenue and contributions from other product lines. In that way, total profitability can be increased without sacrificing people. That will appease the manufacturing managers.

AJ: Good advice. I'll need to consider that point. Perhaps the theory of constraints [TOC] could come into play here since we are talking about revenue growth, and we have recently been operating at practical capacity. I know the Assembly Department has been particularly backed up in recent months.

MF: You're right. I never really thought about that, but perhaps TOC could somehow work in a complementary fashion with ABC.

AJ: All right, I've taken up enough of your time. I know that you're busy and must go. You've given me a ton of great ideas to think about. Thanks a million!

MF: It was my pleasure to help. Give me a call after the meeting to let me know how it worked out.

AJ: Will do. Talk to you later and thanks again.

As Alice hung up the phone, she continued to fill her note pad with a summary of the insights provided by Mike Foster. Alice had become well aware that her original game plan for the management team presentation would probably have failed. Thanks to Mike's advice, Alice was beginning to crystallize in her mind a presentation that she felt was sure to impress Simms, thereby saving the ABC system from discontinuation.

DISCUSSION QUESTIONS:

Assuming that you hold the position of corporate controller (that of Alice Johnson), organize a written presentation to the Wilson management team attempting to sell the virtues of ABC. To help organize your thoughts and presentation, consider the following questions:

1. What is the ABC cross model? Define what is meant by the product costing, process costing, and the "what-if" cost-modeling perspectives of ABC.

2. Estimate an income statement for the current version of the A12 junction box using the direct-labor-based standard cost system. Compare the profitability of the current version of the A12 junction box as reported by the direct-labor-based system to the ABC system and relate these cost numbers to the competitor's announced price reduction of $2.50 per unit. What conclusions may be inferred from this information?

3. Estimate the average overhead charge per unit for the custom product lines using the direct-labor-based standard cost system. How do these charges compare to the per unit charges assessed against the A12 junction box using the standard cost system? What conclusions may be inferred from this information?

4. Estimate an income statement for the A12 junction box, assuming that Wilson implemented a manufacturing cell for the A12 line and was able to eliminate all non-value-added resource costs associated with producing A12. What other information could you present that would highlight the dollar value of resources that Wilson is channeling to non-value-added activities?

5. What role would the data from the resource usage vs. resource spending analysis play in your presentation? How could net present value analysis be incorporated into the usage-vs.-spending analysis?

6. How would you use data from Wilson's activity model to estimate the throughput growth potential associated with the A12 redesign?

5-6 Pecos Products

CASE OVERVIEW

Hannah Evans, Manager, Panther product line: "You have to give me some flexibility on pricing! Our sleeping bags are already priced higher than the market, and now Renegade is lowering their prices even more. We can't compete at our current pricing level."

Henry Norman, Vice President, Camping Products Division: "I understand, but we have to maintain profitability, and we're barely breaking even on our sleeping bags right now. If we lower the price, we'll be losing money on every sleeping bag we sell."

Evans: "I don't believe it. I know we're getting our fabric cheaper than Renegade. There's no way it's costing more for us to make our bags. It's just the accounting system. Have you seen how much overhead we're carrying on the Panther? It's killing our profitability! Where is all that overhead coming from, and why are our sleeping bags getting hit with so much of it?"

Norman: "Good question!"

THE COMPANY

Pecos Products is a manufacturer of outdoor recreation equipment, selling its high-quality/high-price products to outdoor specialty retailers such as REI (a national chain), Campmor (a mail-order house), and Whole Earth (a small regional retailer). The company was started over 30 years ago by two friends who had an idea for an innovative backpacking tent design. The product was an immediate success, and later generations of this tent, as well as newer tent designs, still serve as Pecos' flagship product line.

Over the years, the company has gone through three strategic phases. The market for tents, especially highend tents like those produced by Pecos, has shown slow but steady growth. But after its first decade as a "tent company" (Phase 1), Pecos' founders decided to grow the company faster by repositioning it strategically as a "camping goods company" (Phase 2). This change allowed the company to establish relationships with larger retailers who wanted to deal with a full-line supplier. With the strategic change came an expansion of its product lines into backpacks and sleeping bags, and its expanded retail prowess helped Pecos become a nationally known and respected supplier of camping goods. The third and current strategy for Pecos was adopted eight years ago, with its repositioning as an "outdoor recreational equipment" company.

This project considers the operations at Pecos' original camping goods manufacturing plant, known within the company as CAMP-1. This plant was built at the beginning of Pecos' second strategic period to allow them to produce a complete line of camping goods in one ocation. (They have since added a second camping goods production facility, CAMP-2, as well as other production sites for other product lines). CAMP-1 is a 75,000-sq.-ft. manufacturing facility where four basic products are sequenced through one or more of three production departments: Cutting, Sewing, and Assembly. The manufacture of the products is supported by three service departments: Receiving, Logistics, and Shipping. These six departments are referred to as Cost Centers for accounting purposes.

Each of the products produced at CAMP-1 and each CAMP-1 cost center is discussed in greater detail below.

THE CAMP-1 PRODUCTS

The process required to produce each of the four products is described in the paragraphs below, and is summarized in Exhibit 1, the Product/Process Matrix. Exhibit 2 lists the competitive advantages and disadvantages of each product.[1]

Tents

As the original Pecos product, tents have long been an important product for the company. The CAMP-1 plant produces only one tent model, the high-volume Maverick, which is a descendant of the original backpacking tent design on which

---

1 As context for thinking about Pecos and its products and opportunities, you may find it helpful to study the web sites of similar manufacturers (for example, http://www.slumberjack.com or http://www.johnsonoutdoors.com) or distributors (for example, http://www.rei.com or http:// www.campmor.com).

Source: David E, Platt and Kristy L. Towry. 2001. *Issues in Accounting Education*. 16 (1), 99-110.

EXHIBIT 2
Pecos Products—CAMP-1
Product Market Attributes

Maverick Tents
Competitive Advantages:
    Pecos identity and retail network
    "Maverick" brand identity and loyalty
    Quality reputation
Competitive Disadvantages:
    Price

Bandito Backpacks
Competitive Advantages:
    Pecos identity and retail network
    Strong niche market share
    Quality reputation
    Price
Competitive Disadvantages:
    None

Panther Sleeping Bags
Competitive Advantages:
    Pecos identity and retail network
    Quality reputation
Competitive Disadvantages:
    Price
    Narrow product line

Saguaro Sleeping Pads
Competitive Advantages:
    Pecos identity and retail network
    Competitive Disadvantages:
Late to market
    Narrow product line

the company was founded. (Several other tent products are produced at the CAMP-2 manufacturing site using somewhat more modern, automated sewing machinery.) The tent production process consists of the following steps:

a. Cutting nylon "canvas" fabric (a heavy-weight nylon) and mesh (windows, doors);
b. Sewing together fabric, mesh, and zippers;
c. Sealing all seams (waterproofing);
d. Kitting the finished product (i.e., doing minor assembly and packaging).

Production of the tent poles, stakes, and storage bag is outsourced. These items are combined with the manufactured tent and placed in a box in the Kitting step.[2]

Backpacks
The second of the original camping products, also manufactured at the CAMP-1 facility, is the Bandito backpack. The Bandito backpack is assembled from two grades of nylon and is mounted on a titanium frame that is produced to Pecos' specifications by a metal fabricator. The backpack production process consists of the following steps:

[2] Kitting and Seam Sealing for all products requiring these activities are performed in the assembly cost center.

a. Cutting and sewing together the two grades of nylon fabric;
b. Attaching (sewing in) zippers;
c. Sealing all seams (waterproofing);
d. Kitting the finished product.

The manufactured backpack is combined with the purchased frame and various other accessories (straps, for the most part) and placed in a box in the Kitting step.

Sleeping Bags
Another product manufactured at the CAMP-1 facility is the Panther premium sleeping bag, made of a nylon shell filled with a synthetic fiber insulation. Dramatically changed in design since its introduction as the third of the "camping goods company" products, the Panther sleeping bag has been a huge success for Pecos and is produced in very large quantities. The sleeping bag production process consists of the following steps:

a. Cutting nylon fabric and synthetic fiber insulation;
b. Sewing insulation to the inside layer of fabric so it won't shift and bunch up, and sewing together fabric with insulation inserted;
c. Sewing in the zipper;
d. Kitting the finished product.

Production of the storage bag and tie cord is outsourced. These are combined with the manufactured sleeping bag and placed in a box in the Kitting step.

Sleeping Pads
The most recent addition to the Pecos camping goods product line is the Saguaro, a self-inflating sleeping pad. A single model of this new product is being produced in the CAMP-1 facility. The product, introduced to the camping goods market by a competitor four years ago, consists of a baffle assembly (a honeycomb-like system for evenly distributing air) sandwiched between two layers of coated, heavy-duty ("canvas" grade) nylon. When the pad's valve is opened, the compressed baffles expand, drawing air into the pad. The valve is then closed, and the trapped air provides an air-mattress-like barrier between the sleeping bag and the tent floor and ground. At present, Pecos purchases the baffle assembly from an outside supplier. The sleeping pad production process consists of the following steps:

a. Cutting nylon "canvas" fabric;
b. Pad Pressing: sandwiching the baffle assembly between two sheets of fabric, and heat-sealing the fabric's edges;
c. Kitting the finished product.

The storage bag, whose production is outsourced, is combined with the manufactured sleeping pad and placed in a box in the Kitting step.

The CAMP-1 Production Facility
CAMP-1 is Pecos' "high-variety" camping goods plant: as described above, several diverse products share CAMP-1's production resources.

Workers at the CAMP-1 plant oversee their entire production operation, including online quality inspection, setting up their own machines, performing their own preventive maintenance, and suggesting process improvements. As a result, considerable worker time is spent on indirect cost activities. Based in part on their ability to master these indirect cost activities, workers are promoted through a limited number of skill classes (here simplified to two, Low-Skilled and High-Skilled). Production supervisors in each production department are responsible for assisting and supervising workers, and also providing training and participating in scheduling departmental production.

The work of each cost center is described in the paragraphs below:

Cutting
All of Pecos' manufactured products begin their production flow in the Cutting department, which operates two shifts each day, five days per week. The department consists primarily of several very-high-speed cutting machines. Each machine is operated by two workers, one to load the rolls of fabric and oversee the machine's cutting operation, the

second to handle the machine's output, organizing and inspecting it in preparation for passing the cut pieces on to the next department.

Sewing
In the Sewing department, pieces of fabric are stitched to one another and to zippers. The sewing machines are semi-automated, allowing a high-speed sewing rate, but each machine does require a dedicated operator to set up the pattern, load in the cut fabric, stack the output, and clear jams. The department operates two shifts per day, five days a week.

Assembly
Operating one shift per day five days a week, the Assembly department performs three different tasks. First, seams on tents and backpacks are sealed (waterproofed) by operators carrying portable seam-sealing machines. Second, pads are assembled on the new, highly automated pad-assembly machine that requires only one operator. This process is known as "Pad Pressing." Third, all products are matched with their purchased components and placed into boxes. This process, called "Kitting," sometimes includes minor assembly, such as attaching the backpack to its purchased metal frame. The boxes of completed products are stacked onto pallets, where they wait for Logistics to pick them up.

Receiving
The Receiving department is where raw materials and purchased components arrive at CAMP-1. Receiving's work consists primarily of tracking and controlling inventory and moving inventory from the receiving dock into the staging area, where it is picked up by Logistics.

Logistics
This department consists of the equipment (forklifts, handcarts, overhead cranes) and operators required to move inventory throughout the plant. Workers transport (1) fabric rolls from Receiving to Cutting, (2) zippers and other miscellaneous items from Receiving to Sewing, (3) cut fabric from Cutting to Sewing, (4) purchased components from Receiving to Assembly, (5) work-in-process from Sewing to Assembly, and (6) pallets of boxed units from Assembly to Shipping.

Shipping
The Shipping department tags and wraps pallets of products for shipment to customers. Full pallets of a single product are often shipped to the distribution centers of high-volume retailers. For smaller retailers, Shipping takes boxed units off pallets and combines them into retailer orders, packages the orders for shipment, and records the completed units and orders into the materials control system.

The Problem
Renegade Designs, Pecos' key competitor, has recently announced price reductions on its sleeping bag lines, and Pecos' top management is considering possible responses to the price cuts. The Marketing department believes that Pecos will lose significant market share if it does not respond with price cuts, but other members of the management team are concerned that if prices are cut, the profitability of the sleeping bag line will be compromised. The Finance group has dedicated significant resources to analyzing the implications of price cuts. Most of this analysis has focused on Pecos' highest volume sleeping bag, the Panther, which is manufactured at CAMP-1. The projections (not included here) indicate that if Pecos cuts the price of the Panther, the company will actually be selling sleeping bags at a loss for the first time in its 30-year history.

Hannah Evans, the Panther product line manager, argues that the Panther is actually more profitable than the accounting numbers indicate. She notes that over half the cost of the Panther comes from overhead, and she contends that sleeping bags are being assigned more than their "fair share" of these indirect costs. Evans has discussed her concerns with many of Pecos' top managers, and it is increasingly clear that the management team does not have confidence in the product costs produced by the current accounting system. Competition is increasing in the market for outdoor recreation equipment, and management believes that accurate product costs are essential if Pecos is to formulate a successful strategy for dealing with this competition.

Planning Data
The data in Exhibit 3 summarize Pecos' *planning* figures for future short-term production and sales of the four products produced at CAMP-1. The price shown for the Panther sleeping bag represents an increase of almost 4 percent over the current quarter, although, as noted above, management is considering revising this pricing plan significantly downward.

Because the CAMP-1 facility is successful at maintaining an extremely low level of inventory, it is reasonable to make the simplifying assumption that production and sales (in units) are approximately equal.

ASSIGNMENTS

The project is composed of several assignments, detailed below. Today, Pecos Products operates a "traditional" single-pool, volume-based product-costing system. All costs are assigned to products at pre-determined rates based on machine hours. Nancy Cherry, the controller of the CAMP-1 plant, recognizes that upper management is not confident about the costs from the current system, and she thinks that one reason is her plant's fairly high degree of product diversity. She has asked you to help develop plans for a pilot study of an ABC system, with a goal of understanding the structure, economic consequences, and cost-benefit of such a system relative to the present "traditional" system.

Assignment 1: Download and Exploration

Assignment 1 does not include any "deliverables." Instead, it provides you with the opportunity to download and explore the data related to this case. Using your favorite web browser, go to:

http://www.bus.utexas.edu/~platt/pecos/

and download the following three workbooks:

GENINFO: Pecos Products General Information File (geninfo.xls)
PRODINFO: Pecos Products Product Information File (prodinfo.xls)
CCINFO: Pecos Products Cost Center Information File (ccinfo.xls)

EXHIBIT 3
Pecos Products Campus Planning Data

	Next Quarter Production (units)	Selling Price ($/unit)	Planned Revenues
Maverick Tents	42,982	115	$ 4,942,913
Bandito Backpacks	34,116	60	2,046,938
Panther Sleeping Bags	98,107	55	5,395,861
Saguaro Sleeping Pads	17,540	25	438,492
Total			$12,824,204

These workbooks will provide you with extensive data regarding Pecos' products and operations. It will make your life much easier if you start getting to know these workbooks now! The workbooks are very large, and two of them contain several worksheets each (look for the tabs at the bottom of the page).[3] The following discussion provides a summary of the data in each workbook (follow along in the workbooks as you read this):

GENINFO

This workbook has only one worksheet, which provides the quarterly production figures for the four products over the last five years. *Year 5 is the most recent year just ended.*

PRODINFO

This workbook contains one worksheet for each of the four products. The worksheets provide quarterly processing data over the last five years. You will notice that much of the data do not change much from quarter to quarter. In a real company, this would not likely be the case, but your calculations (in later assignments) will be more manageable with this simplified set of data.

---

[3] These are Microsoft Excel workbook files. If you prefer to use another spreadsheet rogram, go to http://www.bus.utexas.edu/~platt/pecos/txt/ and download the files found there. These are tab-delimited text files that should be readable by virtually all spreadsheet programs; however each spreadsheet is a separate file and no formatting (such as underscores before totals) is preserved. Download pecos_nonXL.txt, which will tell you how to match each Excel workbook with its corresponding text file.

CCINFO

This is the most complicated of the three workbooks. It contains one worksheet for each of the six cost centers. The first item on each worksheet is a list of the general ledger categories. To the right of the list, you will see headings, but no data are included under the headings. Disregard this part of the worksheet for now (we will return to it in Assignment 3).

Below the list of general ledger categories, you will see a second listing of the general ledger categories along with the quarterly costs associated with each category over the last five years. Below this, other quarterly data are also displayed. You will notice that, as with the case of PRODINFO, much of these data do not change quarter to quarter.

Finally, two sections of data ("How Indirect Labor Time is Spent" and "Primary Materials and Supplies") are presented. Note that these data are *not* quarterly. These numbers reflect the *averages* for the year, but the actual quarterly numbers (which you do not
see) do vary somewhat. (For example, training is likely to be higher in high-volume quarters, whereas set-up time is likely to be lower.)

Assignment 2: Volume-Based Costing Systems

Perform an analysis of product costs and profitability, following the steps outlined below.

- Calculate the full-absorption product cost for each product during Year 5 using a traditional single-pool, volume-based approach. (Calculate the full-year average costs, not separate costs for each of the four quarters.) You should go through this exercise *twice*, once using *machine hours* as your allocation base (as in Pecos' present cost system) and once using a *direct-labor-based volume measure* (direct labor hours or direct labor cost).

	Selling Price ($/unit)
Maverick Tents	112
Bandito Backpacks	58
Panther Sleeping Bags	53
Saguaro Sleeping Pads	25

- Calculate the per-unit and total profitability for each product, using the Year 5 (average) prices shown above, for each of the two versions of costs calculated above.

- Write a two to three page paper describing your cost-allocation process and summarizing the results of your calculations. Be sure to answer the following questions, including how the answers would differ depending on which volume measure you use:
  2(a) Under volume-based costing, which products seem to be most important to CAMP-1's overall profitability?
  2(b) How is top management likely to react to the suggestion of a price reduction for sleeping bags?
  2(c) Based solely on this limited financial analysis, what actions can the controller recommend to make the plant more profitable?

Assignment 3: ABC System

Design an ABC system for the CAMP-1 plant, following the steps outlined below. You will find it necessary to make many difficult decisions in the design process. Use the data provided in the project workbook files to help you make these decisions. Where it is necessary to make an assumption, do so, but be prepared to defend both the need for the assumption and its reasonableness.

The following steps will guide you through the process of designing your proposed ABC system for CAMP-1:

- In the *CCINFO* workbook, use the information provided about each cost center to make your best estimate of how the costs of resources, as listed in the General Ledger Summary Accounts in the top half of each worksheet, should be assigned to the plant's activities (i.e., to cutting, sewing, packing, etc.). Note that the appropriate activities have been chosen for you; these are the headings we told you to ignore earlier, and there is a column for each activity. If you were designing a system in the real world, you would have to identify the appropriate list of activities yourself, a process requiring significant effort. There are many possible choices of activities, and these can be combined at various levels of aggregation. The list provided in the CCINFO workbook reflects an effort to balance the benefits of precisely defined activities with the costs of measuring and maintaining a high volume of data. As you work with this list of activities, you may identify improvements that could be made to the choices. If so, please suggest these improvements in your case write-up, but use the list provided for calculating your ABC solution. Specify your chosen distribution of resource costs by typing a percentage in the appropriate cells of the top portion of the spreadsheet (each row should total 100 percent). Document the reasons for your chosen distributions. You will need to do this for each of the six cost centers.

- Add a worksheet to the *CCINFO* workbook and call it "Activity Cost Summary." Use your spreadsheet skills to summarize on this worksheet the costs assigned to each activity (in total, across all cost centers) based on the percentages you recorded in the cost center worksheets. In this assignment, you are required to report the costs for the most recent year (Year 5) only. You do not need to calculate the costs for each quarter of Year 5, but instead you can calculate a full-year average. However, for analysis purposes, you will probably want to calculate the totals for each *activity* for each quarter of all five years.
  Check: Does the total indirect cost assigned to activities equal the total of all cost center general ledger accounts for Year 5? If not, you have made a mistake in your allocations.

- Consider the activities and their costs that you have summarized on the new "Activity Cost Summary" worksheet. Group these activities into cost pools to create a cost-effective ABC cost system.

  Guidance: When your cost system design is reviewed, the evaluation will include your system's success at balancing the trade-off between system cost and quality, where quality means its ability to realistically represent products' consumption of resources. Reporting distorted costs can cause bad decisions, but measuring and maintaining a great many cost components can be expensive. For example, treating each activity as a separate cost pool would make it easier to choose the best possible cost driver for each pool, but would also make for a very expensive system to design, run, and maintain. As you are considering this step (how to pool activities) and the next (choosing cost drivers), keep the following in mind:

  - Does the cost driver have a logical relationship with the costs in the pool, and would we expect this relationship to persist into the future?
  - Cost drivers should vary with the level of costs captured in a pool and be able to be measured reliably and with as little random noise as possible. When you look at the historical data provided, do you see a consistent relationship between the costs in your pool and the level of the units of the cost driver? For a statistical look at this relationship, try Excel's regression function.[4]
  - Some cost drivers are readily available in existing accounting systems; others are not. Thus, you might have to use a cost driver that is less than ideal, because the ideal cost driver is not easily measured.
  - Fewer cost pools are less expensive to maintain than more cost pools: when you add a cost pool to your working solution, how much do reported costs for each product change?

- Choose a cost driver for each cost pool by reviewing the information provided in the case and in the workbooks. Using the volumes of your chosen cost drivers, calculate the Year 5 cost-driver rates for each cost pool.

- Calculate the Year 5 full-absorption product cost for each product under your ABC design. Calculate product profitability based on these costs (using the prices given in Assignment 2).

- Write an eight- to ten-page paper discussing your proposed CAMP-1 ABC cost system. Attach exhibits as necessary. The first part of the paper should address issues of cost system design and the choices you made in implementing the steps above. The second part of the paper should deal with the effects of your proposed system on managers, their decision making at Pecos CAMP-1, and the pricing problem regarding the Panther sleeping bag. On the day the paper is due, submit via email one copy of *CCINFO* containing the percentages from your final solution. Also, be sure to create and include the following two exhibits in your write-up:

  In the course of your eight- to ten-page discussion, you should be sure to address the following issues:

[4] Recall, however, that some information (how indirect labor time was spent and indirect materials/supplies used) was provided as a yearly average instead of on a quarterly basis. This introduces some inaccuracy into your quarterly data. For this reason, it may be more appropriate to run the regressions only on full-year (totaled) data.

Cost and Profit Comparisons: Current Year (Year 5)

		Per Unit			Total		
		DL-Based Allocation	MH-Based Allocation	ABC-Based Allocation	DL-Based Allocation	MH-Based Allocation	ABC-Based Allocation
Maverick Tents	DM						
	DL						
	Overhead						
	Total Cost						
	Profit						
Bandito Backpacks	DM						
	DL						
	Overhead						
	Total Cost						
	Profit						
Panther Sleeping Bags	DM						
	DL						
	Overhead						
	Total Cost						
	Profit						
Saguaro Sleeping Pads	DM						
	DL						
	Overhead						
	Total Cost						
	Profit						

Cost Pools

Cost Pool Name	Activities Included	Cost Driver

3(a) Compare the product costs from the ABC system with those you calculated in your team's two versions of the "traditional" system.

3(b) Look again at the questions asked in Assignment 2 above. In what ways are your answers different using the ABC system?

3(c) Discuss ways in which management's view of the Panther sleeping bag and its competitive challenges might be different if product costs were provided by your ABC system. What would you recommend and why? Be specific.

3(d) Given the company's present strategy, discuss two additional examples of ways in which the revised (ABC) view of product costs may affect managerial decisions.

3(e) Provide an assessment of Pecos' business health in its camping goods product line. Is your view different using an ABC system?

3(f) In what ways might your results affect management's view of the company's strategy?

To conclude your analysis, please address the following design and implementation issues:

3(g) Earlier, you used percentages to assign resource costs from the general ledger to the activities they support. How else might this assignment be accomplished? What advantages and disadvantages would your alternative method present?

3(h) Should this system be integrated into the general ledger system, or should it be operated as a stand-alone system? What are the advantages and disadvantages of your recommended approach? Relate your answer to the Panther sleeping bag issue.

3(i) The controller has decided to use your design for the ABC pilot project. What other implementation issues should she be thinking about?

5-7 The Buckeye National Bank

INTRODUCTION

The Buckeye National Bank began operations in the mid-1980s. The bank quickly grew by providing checking account services to many small businesses that preferred to do business with a "local" bank. Although Buckeye initially offered checking account services for individual accounts (retail customers), the bank primarily focused on serving its business customers. During the economic slowdown of the early 1990s that weakened the local economy, growth in business customer accounts began to decline. In response, Buckeye's senior management adopted a new strategy, focusing on increasing the number of retail customer accounts. By aggressively marketing individual retail accounts, Buckeye continued to grow. Today, the Buckeye National Bank strives to maintain a stable base of business customers, while actively competing for an increased market share of retail customers.

Recent income statements (Exhibit A) reveal a decline in the bank's profits. The bank's primary (noninterest) expense consists of salaries and employee benefits. Most full-time employees' first priority is providing services to customers; these employees conduct their administrative responsibilities during slack times. The Bank schedules additional part-time employees to work during peak demand times, from 11 AM–2 PM and Friday afternoons. Flexibility in scheduling part-time employees means that the bank's staff is lean and fully utilized. Buckeye's CEO, Rob Garrison, believes that this staffing arrangement allows the bank to provide speedy customer service, while operating at practical capacity. (That is, the bank's staff is fully utilized in efficient operations, after allowing for bank holidays and other scheduled staff activities such as training.)

To counter falling profits, Buckeye's directors took two actions last year, both aimed at increasing the bank's retail customer base. First, Buckeye established a service call center to respond to customer inquiries about account balances, checks cleared, fees charged, and other banking concerns. Second, Buckeye's directors authorized year-end bonuses to branch managers who met their branch's target increase in the number of customers. However, even though 80 percent of the branch managers met the targeted increase in customer accounts, the Bank's profits continued to decline. CEO Rob Garrison does not understand why profits are declining, given that the Bank is serving more customers. Buckeye's southeast regional manager, Erik Larsen, has also noticed that while small retail customers flock to the bank, the number of business customers is barely stable.

Erik Larsen suspects that Buckeye's costing system may be part of the problem. Buckeye developed its simple costing system when the bank began operations in 1985. The bank does not trace any costs directly to individual customers. It simply treats all (noninterest expense) operating costs identified in the Income Statement in Exhibit A as indirect with respect to the customer line. The bank allocates these indirect costs to either the retail customer line or the business customer line, based on the total dollar value of checks processed (which is readily available because each branch must provide the dollar values of daily transactions for internal control). For the current period, Buckeye processed a total of $95 million in checks, of which $9.5 million was written by retail customers, and $85.5 million was written by business customers. This costing approach was fairly typical of banks and other financial institutions at the time Buckeye developed its cost system.

In college, Erik learned about an alternative costing approach called activity-based costing (ABC). However, the examples he remembered involved manufacturing firms. He wondered whether Buckeye could develop an ABC system, with the business account customer line and the retail account customer line as the two primary cost objects. Erik approached Rob Garrison with this suggestion. Rob was skeptical, exclaiming, "Our profits are going down the tubes and you want me to spend money developing a new *accounting* system?" However, Erik persisted, and Rob eventually authorized a pilot ABC study using three local branches of the bank.

The ABC implementation team included Erik, the managers of each of the three bank branches, a bank teller, and a representative from the customer service call center. The team began by identifying the activities Buckeye National Bank performed. To start a simple pilot study, the team identified the three most important activities:

Source: Linda Smith Bamber and K. E. Hughes II, Activity-Based Costing in the Service Sector: The Buckeye National Bank. *Issues in Accounting Education, 16 (3) 381-87.*

EXHIBIT A
Buckeye National Bank
Consolidated Income Statement
For the three years ending December 31, 20x5

	20x5 ($000)	20x4 ($000)	20x3 ($000)
Net interest income[a]	$3,486	$3,417	$3,349
Provision for credit losses	484	475	465
Net interest income after provision for credit losses	3,002	2,942	2,884
Noninterest income	1,207	1,199	1,190
Income prior to noninterest expenses and income tax	4,209	4,141	4,074
Noninterest expenses	3,805	3,539	3,362
Income before income taxes	404	602	712
Income tax expense	130	194	230
Net income	$ 274	$408	$ 482

[a] Net interest income equals interest income less interest expense. The bank's primary income is from interest-bearing checking accounts. Noninterest income includes fees charged for various services, such as checking account fees charged if the account balance falls below the required minimum level. Noninterest expenses are all of the bank's operating costs, including those associated with paying checks, providing teller services, and responding to customer account inquires.

1. Paying checks
2. Providing teller services
3. Responding to customer account inquiries at the customer service call center

If this pilot study turned out to be successful, then the team planned to refine the system by conducting a more detailed activity analysis the following year. The ABC team began by determining the costs that are associated with each of the three activities. The team quickly discovered that, as is typical in service industries like banking, labor (personnel) costs dominate. The ABC team asked each employee to fill out a short questionnaire to find out how the employee spends his or her time. The team then followed up with an in-depth personal interview with each employee. The ABC team used this combined information to estimate the percentage of time each employee spent on each of the three activities: (1) paying checks, (2) providing teller services, and (3) responding to customer account inquiries.

The team then estimated the other (nonlabor) resources that each of the three activities consumed. For example, they traced to the "responding to customer account inquiry" activity: (1) the cost of toll-free telephone lines at the customer service call center, and (2) depreciation on other equipment and facilities the call center personnel use. Similarly, the ABC team estimated the percentage of time the bank's information system was used for check processing and providing teller services (vs. other uses such as compiling periodic financial statements), to determine how much of the equipment's depreciation to assign to the activities "paying checks" and "providing teller services."

To complete the pilot study in a timely fashion, the ABC team based their estimated activity costs on last year's actual data, which were already available. If the pilot study succeeded, then the ABC team planned to develop *budgeted indirect cost rates* for each activity the following year. The advantage of budgeted rates over actual rates based on the prior year's data is that budgeted rates (budgeted cost associated with the activity divided by the budgeted quantity of the activity's cost driver) can incorporate expected changes in costs and operations.

After examining the three branch banks' indirect costs (that is, the cost items making up the branch banks' noninterest operating expenses), the ABC team classified the annual costs in each activity's cost pool (hereafter, all numbers are in thousands)[1] as shown in Exhibit B.

The team identified the following cost drivers[2] for each activity cost pool:

---

[1] An activity's cost pool is simply a grouping, or aggregation, of all the individual costs associated with that activity. The bank's ABC team created separate activity cost pools for the costs associated with each of the three activities: (1) paying checks, (2) providing teller services, and (3) responding to customer account inquiries.

EXHIBIT B
Assignment of Indirect (Noninterest Expense) Costs to Activity Cost Pools[a]

Indirect Cost	Activity Cost Pool to which Indirect Cost is Assigned	Estimated Annual Total Costs (in $1,000s)
Salaries of check-processing personnel	Paying checks	$ 700
Depreciation of equipment and facilities used in check processing	Paying checks	440
Teller salaries	Providing teller services	1,000
Depreciation of equipment and facilities used in teller operations	Providing teller services	200
Salaries of customer representatives at call center	Responding to customer account inquiries	450
Toll-free phone lines plus depreciation of equipment and facilities in customer call center	Responding to customer account inquiries	60
Total indirect costs		$2,850

[a] These indirect costs are part of the $3,805 "noninterest expenses" in the bank's 20x5 Income Statement in Exhibit A. The rest of the noninterest expenses in the Income Statement shown in Exhibit A pertain to other operating costs that are excluded from the pilot ABC study, such as the CEO's salary. (The costs listed in Exhibit B are indirect with respect to the retail customers and business account customers.)

EXHIBIT C Activity Cost Drivers by Customer Line

Activity Cost Driver	Annual Number of Units of Activity-Cost Driver Used by Retail Customers (in 1,000s)	Annual Number of Units of Activity-Cost Driver Used by Business Customers (in 1,000s)	Total
Checks processed	570	2,280	2,850
Teller transactions	160	40	200
Account inquiry calls to customer service call center	95	5	100

Activity Cost Pool	Activity Cost Driver
Paying checks	Number of checks processed
Providing teller services	Number of teller transactions
Responding to customer account inquiries	Number of account inquiry calls to customer service call center

The ABC team estimated that for the three pilot-test bank branches, the retail and business customer lines experienced the annual activity levels (in thousands) as shown in Exhibit C. For example, Exhibit C reveals that retail customers had 160,000 teller transactions and made 95,000 account inquiry calls to the customer service call center.

Buckeye National Bank currently services 150,000 retail customer checking accounts and 50,000 business customer checking accounts. The bank earns net interest revenue on the balances that customers keep in their checking accounts.[3] On average, the bank earns the following annual revenue from each type of account:

Average annual revenue per retail customer account	$10
Average annual revenue per business customer account	$40

[2] A cost driver is a factor, such as the number of checks processed, that causally affects costs. For example, the costs associated with the activity "paying checks" rise and fall as the quantity of the cost driver (the number of checks processed) rises and falls.

[3] The bank earns net interest revenue by managing the "interest rate spread." This spread is the difference between the interest rate the bank earns on customer deposits (say 8 percent), less the interest rate the bank pays the customer on the average checking account balance (say 4 percent).

Required:

Your task is to assist Erik Larsen and his ABC team by providing the following information:

1) Under the *original* (old) cost system:
   A) Compute the *single* indirect cost allocation rate that the bank would use to allocate the total indirect costs presented in Exhibit B.
   B) Use your answer to part A to determine the total annual indirect cost assigned to:
      (i) the retail customer line, and
      (ii) the business customer line. What drives these allocations?
   C) What proportion of the total indirect cost is assigned to:
      (i) the retail customer line, and
      (ii) the business customer line? Why? That is, what is the underlying rationale for indirect cost allocation under the old system? What assumption must hold approximately true for the original cost allocation procedure to generate "accurate" customer cost information?
   D) Use your answer to part B and data on the number of retail and business accounts to determine:
      (i) the indirect cost per retail account, and
      (ii) the indirect cost per business account.
   E) Assuming there are no direct costs or other indirect costs, compute the average contribution to profit per account for retail customers and for business customers. What business strategy would a manager using the original cost allocation system likely adopt? Why?
2) What are the signs that Buckeye's original cost system is "broken," such that it needs refinement or improvement?
3) Under the new activity-based costing (ABC) system, compute the indirect cost allocation rates for each of the three activities:
   A) Paying checks
   B) Providing teller services
   C) Responding to customer account inquiries
4) Use the following schedule to compute the total indirect cost allocated to each customer line (show your computations beside the activity description):

Activity	Total Indirect Cost Assigned to Retail Customer Line	Total Indirect Cost Assigned to Business Customer Line
Paying checks		
Providing teller services		
Responding to customer account inquiries		
Total Indirect Costs		

5) What proportion of each activity is attributable to:
   (i) the retail customer line, and
   (ii) the business customer line?
6) Using the ABC data from Requirement 4, compute
   (i) the indirect cost per retail customer account and
   (ii) the indirect cost per business customer account.
7) Explain why the results in Requirement 1, Part D, and Requirement 6 differ. Be specific.
8) Using the ABC data, compute the average contribution to profit per account for both retail and business customers. What business strategy would a manager using the ABC cost system likely adopt? How does this result compare to your response to Requirement 1, Part E?
9) Recall Buckeye National Bank's bonus-based incentive plan to increase the number of customers. Do you believe this strategy is wise? Would you suggest any change in strategy based on the ABC analysis?
10) Activity-based management (ABM) refers to managers' use of ABC data in making business decisions. How can Buckeye's managers use the ABC data to plan more profitable marketing strategies? How can Buckeye's managers use ABC information to identify opportunities to trim costs while still satisfying customers' needs?
11) Why might Erik Larsen have suspected that the benefits of ABC would likely outweigh the costs of implementation at Buckeye National Bank?
12) Why do you think it is important for a CEO or a bank branch manager to understand ABC?

Readings

Activity-Based Costing and Predatory Pricing: The Case of the Petroleum Retail Industry

By Thomas L. Bar Ton And John B. Macar Thur

ABC ANALYSIS HELPED SETTLE A LAWSUIT AGAINST A GASOLINE RETAILER, PROVING THE COMPANY HAD NOT COMMITTED PREDATORY PRICING.

EXECUTIVE SUMMARY: The assignment of indirect costs in a traditional costing system can lead to product-cost subsidization. This is where excessive costs are charged to high-volume products and insufficient costs are charged to low-volume products. The result can lead to increased consumer demand for the undercosted—and underpriced—products and reduced customer demand for the overcosted—and thus overpriced—high-volume product. One way to deal with this problem is to employ activity-based costing (ABC). Product-cost subsidization also may have legal consequences, which ABC can help address. Undercosted products can lead to the appearance of predatory pricing where it actually does not exist. This article focuses on a lawsuit brought against a major chain of retail motor fuel (gasoline) service centers for allegedly selling regular-grade gasoline below cost, as defined by state statutes. The defendant employed ABC analysis to support its position that it was not selling its regular gasoline below cost. After the ABC analysis was presented, the case was settled, and the judge lifted the initial injunction.

Activity-based costing (ABC) was originally developed by companies to deal with the problem of product-cost subsidization in traditional costing systems.[1] This is where the assignment of indirect costs leads to excessive costs being charged to high-volume products and insufficient costs being charged to low-volume products. The result can lead to increased consumer demand for the undercosted—and underpriced—products and reduced customer demand for the overcosted—and thus overpriced—high-volume product.[2] Subsequently, ABC has been found useful for several other purposes, such as costing nonvalue-added activities, long-term pricing, and capacity management[3]

When prices are based on cost, product-cost subsidization can lead to increased demand for undercosted and underpriced low-volume products, which are probably being sold at unprofitable prices. Conversely, companies experience reduced customer demand for overcosted, overpriced high-volume products and services. These are unwanted economic consequences from product-cost subsidization that ABC seeks to correct by assigning indirect costs to products and services using appropriate unit-level and nonunit-level activity drivers that reflect resource consumption by the cost objects. ABC can also help address any legal consequences of the product-cost subsidization problem.

LEGAL CONSEQUENCES FROM PRODUCT-COST SUBSIDIZATION

State and federal laws have been enacted against predatory pricing, which is the selling of products below cost as a deliberate action to drive out the competition.[4] Alternatively, products may appear to be priced below cost because of the use of unrealistic, unit-based traditional costing systems, which results in the appearance of predatory pricing where it does not exist. This occurred in a case brought under the "Motor Fuel Marketing Practices Act" of Florida.

COST ASSIGNMENT USING ABC IN A RETAIL GASOLINE SERVICE CENTER

The lawsuit was brought against a major chain of retail motor fuel (gasoline) service centers, alleging that the chain was selling regular-grade gasoline below cost, as defined under state statutes. The plaintiff's expert used a unit-based approach to assign the gasoline service center's average monthly costs (as defined by statute) to the three grades of gasoline: regular (87 octane), plus (89 octane), and premium (93 octane). When these monthly costs were added to the purchase costs of the gasoline, this approach supported the allegation of predatory pricing. See Table 1A for the results.

On the other hand, the defendant's original expert used a simple average-cost approach to assign the average monthly gasoline service center costs equally to the three grades of gasoline (see Table 1B), which supported the defendant's position that regular gasoline was not being sold below cost. The judge in the case made a preliminary ruling that rejected the defendant's analysis and accepted the plaintiff's. The judge then issued an injunction prohibiting the defendant from selling regular gasoline below cost as determined in the plaintiff's analysis.

The defendant engaged an accounting professor as an expert witness to review the cost-assignment process and make his own recommendation as to the most reasonable determination of cost in applying state statutes. The expert witness used ABC as a third approach to cost assignment (see Table 1C), which involved performing activity analysis and selecting activity drivers.

ACTIVITY ANALYSIS

The purchase, storage, dispensing, and sale of gasoline at the retail level can be divided into activities grouped according to their cost hierarchy level:

- *Unit-level activities* are undertaken for each gallon of gasoline sold (such as electricity to power pumps when dispensing gasoline);
- *Batch-level activities* are the same for each gasoline transaction irrespective of the volume of gasoline purchased (for example, transactions to process customer payments for gasoline by cash, check, or debit/credit card);
- *Product-level activities* are conducted for specific gasoline products such as regular, plus, and premium gasoline and motor oil (for instance, gasoline tanks that are dedicated to specific gasoline grades); (Customer-level activities are conducted for specific gasoline customers (such as using billboard advertisements to promote the benefits of premium gasoline); and (Organizational-supporting activities are for the gasoline dispensing organization as a whole and cannot be causally identified with units, batches, or individual products (including payroll and many other centralized activities).

Activities at the same hierarchy level that share a common activity driver could further be grouped into homogeneous activity cost pools.

The defendant's retail stores consisted of two main activities: the sale of gasoline and the sale of convenience store merchandise, such as bread and milk. With limited data, the expert witness developed a straightforward ABC model that identified three distinct overhead activities involved in selling gasoline in a retail outlet. First, it is necessary to have at least one attendant to receive payments for the gasoline sales transactions. Second, it is necessary to have a facility to house the gasoline attendant(s). This does not require a space the size of a convenience store, so the expert assumed that a small kiosk would be used if there were no store. Third, it is necessary to have gasoline storage and dispensing assets.

Activity Cost Pool 1: Gasoline Sales Attendants (Labor).

Attendants are needed to receive payments from customers who do not pay electronically at the gasoline pump. Attendants also can deal with malfunctioning gasoline pumps, security issues, and other problems as they arise. This is a batch-level activity because payment transactions occur only once for each purchase of gasoline, regardless of the volume of gasoline purchased.

Each service center has a convenience store with attendants who handle payments from the customers for gasoline and for any purchase of food, drink, and other products sold in the store. For the purpose of the case, it was necessary to estimate the labor cost including fringe benefits) of attendants, assuming that gasoline was the only product sold. It was decided that only one attendant would be required for the gasoline sales activity in the absence of a convenience store. Multiple regression analysis results confirmed that convenience store sales, not gasoline sales, were the major cost driver of labor cost above the base salary and benefits of one sales attendant.

Activity Cost Pool 2: Kiosk Facility and Activity Cost Pool 3: Gasoline-Dispensing Facility. Under state statutes, it was necessary to determine a "reasonable rental value" for the retail gasoline facility.5 In the absence of a separate convenience store, it would be the rental value of the kiosk. It can be argued that this is a batch-level activity, following labor, as it facilitates the payment transactions that occur once per gasoline purchase.

Also, it was necessary to determine a "reasonable rental value" for the gasoline-dispensing facility, which, in general, can be classified as a product-level activity.6 This activity cost pool includes assets that are specific to a particular gasoline grade and common gasoline dispensing assets. In a more comprehensive activity analysis, this cost pool could be divided into two or more activity cost pools that would be more homogeneous in nature.

In determining a reasonable rental value, lease information was obtained for the assumed rental of a kiosk and gasoline-dispensing assets in comparable gasoline retail outlets in the surrounding geographical market area.[7] The actual cost of insurance and average cost of repairs and maintenance, utilities, and real/property taxes was added to the reasonable rental value.[8] The total cost was divided between the kiosk facility and gasoline-dispensing facility in proportion to the estimated kiosk and actual gasoline-delivery assets

Table 1: Comparative Cost Assignment Bases in a Gasoline Service Center1

FACILITY-WIDE COST	TOTAL	ACTIVITY DRIVER	REGULAR	PLUS	PREMIUM
A. Unit-Based Approach:					
Average Monthly Cost	$26,300	Gas Sold2	$16,674	$5,129	$4,497
Cost Per Gallon Sold			$ 0.058	$0.058	$0.058
B. Simple Average Approach:					
Average Monthly Cost	$26,300	1/3 each	$8,766	$8,767	$8,767
Cost Per Gallon Sold			$0.030	$0.099	$0.113
C. ABC Approach:					
Pool 1-Labor	$ 9,300	Gas Sold[2]	$ 5,896	$1,814	$1,590
Pool 2-Kiosk	2,737	Gas Sold[2]	1,735	534	468
Pool 3-Gas Dispensing	14,263	1/3 each	4,754	4,754	4,755
Total Cost	$26,300		$12,385	$7,102	$6,813
Cost Per Gallon Sold			$ 0.043	$0.080	$0.088

[1] The original information has been disguised.
[2] Gasoline Sold Proxy Transactional Cost Assignment Base Calculations:

	TOTAL	REGULAR	PLUS	PREMIUM
Average gallons of gas sold per month	454,000	288,000	88,500	77,500
	(100.0%)	(63.4%)	(19.5%)	(17.1%)

Table 2: Estimated Cost of Kiosk and Gasoline Dispensing[1]

Description			**Percent**
Cost of Gasoline-Dispensing Facilities[2]		$422,000	83.9%
Cost of the Convenience Store Building[2]	$506,250		
Kiosk Cost Estimate versus Existing Convenience Store	16%		
Imputed Kiosk Cost[3]		81,000	16.1%
Total Imputed Cost of Facility without Convenience Store (Excluding Land)		$503,000	100.0%
Rental[4] and Other Costs[5] Assigned to Gasoline Sales		$17,000	
Rental and Other Costs Assigned to Activity Cost Pool 2, Kiosk		2,737	16.1%
Rental and Other Costs Assigned to Activity Cost Pool 3, Gasoline Dispensing		14,263	83.9%
		$17,000	100.0%

[1] The original information has been disguised.
[2] Asset values were obtained from the company's fixed-asset master listing.
[3] If the location had mainly gasoline sales with no large, separate convenience store, this is the imputed cost of a "kiosk" to house an attendant to ring up gasoline sales.
[4] See endnote 7 for details of the sources of rental cost data.
[5] The actual cost of insurance and average cost of repairs and maintenance, utilities, and real/property taxes was added to the reasonable rental value of the kiosk and gasoline-dispensing facilities.

total value obtained from the company's fixed-asset master listing (see Table 2).

ACTIVITY DRIVERS

The volume of gasoline sold was readily available and was selected as the proxy activity driver for both the labor and kiosk activity cost pools. The average quantities of the three grades of gasoline sold over a 14-month period (October 1996-November 1997) were used to assign the activity costs. This was basically the same approach used by the plaintiff. The gasoline-dispensing activity cost pool was assigned equally to the three grades of gasoline because each grade of gasoline had exactly the same dispensing infrastructure.

Labor Activity Cost Pool. The volume of gasoline sold is a unit-level activity driver but can be justified for assigning labor activity costs to the gasoline grades as follows:

Table 3: Gasoline-Dispensing Facilities

Facilities	Type of Asset
Gasoline Sign	Common Fixed Asset
Canopy	Common Fixed Asset
Cooler Vault	Common Fixed Asset
Gasoline Tanks	Gasoline Grade-Specific Fixed Asset
Pump & Tank Equipment	Common and Gasoline Grade-Specific Fixed Assets
Multi-Product Dispensers (MPDs)	Common Fixed Asset
Plumbing	Common and Gasoline Grade-Specific Fixed Assets
Electrical—Equipment	Common and Gasoline Grade-Specific Fixed Assets
Electrical—Canopy/MPDs	Common Fixed Asset
Lighting Fixtures	Common Fixed Asset
Area Lighting	Common Fixed Asset
Islands	Common Fixed Asset
Tank Excavation	Gasoline Grade-Specific Fixed Asset
Piping	Common and Gasoline Grade-Specific Fixed Assets

- The principal responsibility of a kiosk attendant would be to receive payments from customers for gasoline purchases, which is a batch-level activity. The volume of gasoline sold can be used as a proxy activity driver for these payment transactions if the average volume of gasoline sold to each customer is about the same, regardless of the gasoline grade, which appeared to be true in this case. The volume of gasoline sold is a better transaction proxy cost driver than the dollar sales because receiving payment from customers is not driven by the dollar amount of the purchases. In the case of credit/debit card payments made directly at the pump, an attendant is necessary to monitor these transactions, especially if the pump malfunctions, such as not printing a receipt. In any case, it can reasonably be assumed that sales transactions of each grade of gasoline that involve an attendant directly in processing customer payments are proportionate to the total gallons sold of each grade of gasoline.
- The number of gasoline sales transactions will be a major factor in determining the number of kiosk attendants and the hours a gasoline station is open, which directly affect the level of salary and benefits payments.

Kiosk Facility Activity Cost Pool. The volume of gasoline sold can be justified as an activity driver for the kiosk activity cost pool in the following ways:

- The entire purpose of the kiosk facility is to house the attendants who receive payments from customers for gasoline purchases. It is logical to use the same activity driver to assign both the labor and kiosk facility activity cost pools.
- The expected volume of gasoline sales will help determine the size of the kiosk necessary to house the number of attendants, which directly impacts the imputed rental payments.
- The volume of gasoline sales will determine the hours a gasoline station is open, which directly affects the level of repairs and maintenance, utilities costs, and so on.

Gasoline-Dispensing Activity Cost Pool. The facilities used for dispensing the three grades of gasoline are either common fixed assets (like the gasoline sign) or fixed assets that are identical in size and cost for each grade of gasoline irrespective of the volume of gasoline sold (for example, the gasoline tanks). Note that the gasoline tanks are identical in size and cost even though the demand is considerably higher for regular gasoline versus the other two grades. Table 3 identifies the major gasoline-dispensing fixed assets and whether they are common and/or gasoline grade-specific fixed assets.

This commonality of some gasoline-dispensing fixed assets with the cost equality of other, grade-specific gasoline-dispensing fixed assets means, for example, that if two grades of gasoline were sold instead of three, the reasonable rental and other long-run variable costs of the gasoline-dispensing facility would likely be one third less than is the case when three grades are sold. For example, one less tank excavation and gasoline tank would be required. Also, one-third fewer pump and tank equipment items would be needed, assuming each pump serves one grade of gasoline only. In terms of common assets, this would likely result in one-third fewer islands, a smaller canopy, and so on. In the case of multipurpose pumps that provide each grade of gasoline, the complexity and cost should be lower for pumps that serve two versus three grades of gasoline. Therefore, an equal assignment of the gasoline dispensing activity costs among the three grades of gasoline is a reasonable activity cost-driver measure.

ABC ANALYSIS RESULTS

The results from this straightforward ABC analysis can be considered from both the legal and cost management points of view.

Legal Outcome. According to the ABC analysis, the cost per gallon sold actually fell in between the amounts derived from the plaintiff's unit-level approach and the defendant's equal split of labor and overhead costs. In essence, the ABC approach split the difference between the costs per gallon sold obtained from the two extreme approaches. After this analysis was presented, the case was settled and the injunction lifted.

Cost Management Outcome. From a cost management perspective, the ABC model obtained a result that helped to correct the problem of product-cost subsidization of low-volume products by high-volume products, which often occurs when a pure unit-level cost assignment base is used. In this case, the low-volume products (plus and premium gasoline) were undercosted by the volume-based approach, whereas the high-volume product (regular gasoline) was overcosted. Thus the regular gasoline appeared to be more costly and priced under cost because of the use of the inappropriate unit based cost assignment method.

FURTHER REFINEMENT

Clearly, an ABC approach improves costing in a gasoline dispensing retail facility, but this model could be further refined. The use of practical capacity rather than expected or budgeted capacity may avoid charging the grades of gasoline for the costs of unused capacity.[9] A likely refinement would be the identification and measurement of nonunit-based activity drivers for the labor and kiosk facility costs. It is important to realize that more driver refinement away from unit-based activity drivers would only continue to strengthen the defendant's case by further lowering the cost of regular gasoline per gallon. Also, greater costing refinement usually entails greater information processing costs. It is important to ensure that the costs of ABC models are justified by the benefits obtained.

[1] See "John Deere Component Works (A)," *Harvard Business School Case Series 9-187-107* (Rev. November 1987).

[2]For a numerical example of overcosting and undercosting products, see John B. MacArthur, "Activity-Based Costing and Activity-Based Management: An Introduction," in *Guide to Cost Management*, Barry J. Brinker, editor, John Wiley & Sons, New York, N.Y., 2000, pp. 397-410.

[3] For discussion on ABC and capacity management, see Robin Cooper and Robert S. Kaplan, "Activity-Based Systems: Measuring the Costs of Resource Usage," *Accounting Horizons*, September 1992, pp. 1-13.

[4] For example, in Florida, the "Motor Fuel Marketing Practices Act" (526.302) states that: "Predatory practices and, under certain conditions, discriminatory practices, are unfair trade practices and restraints which adversely affect motor fuel competition." This legislation, in section 526.304, stipulates that: "(1)(a) It is unlawful for any refiner engaged in commerce in this state to sell any grade or quality of motor fuel at a retail outlet below refiner cost, where the effect is to injure competition" and "(b) It is unlawful for any nonrefiner engaged in commerce in this state to sell any grade or quality of motor fuel at a retail outlet below nonrefiner cost, where the effect is to injure competition."

[5] In Florida, the "Motor Fuel Marketing Practices Act" (526.303) states: "(9) 'Reasonable rental value' means the bona fide amount of rent which would reasonably be paid in an arm's length transaction for the use of the specific individual retail outlet, including land and improvements, utilized for the sale of motor fuel. The value of the land and improvements shall include the costs of equipment; signage; utilities, property taxes, and insurance, if paid by the owner; and environmental compliance, such as testing, detection, and containment systems; but does not include the costs of environmental cleanup and remediation. In determining the reasonable rental value of the specific retail outlet, the rental amount of comparable retail outlets in the relevant geographic market shall be considered. When motor fuel is sold at the retail level along with other products, the reasonable rental value attributable to the sale of motor fuel at the retail outlet shall be allocated by the percentage of gross sales attributable to motor fuel sales."

[6] *Ibid.*

[7] Comparable lease information was obtained from an outside appraisal service. This allowed the conversion of asset value into a reasonable rental value.

[8] The current actual cost of insurance was obtained from the defendant company, and the average cost of repairs and maintenance, utilities, and real/property taxes was calculated from monthly company data.

[9] See Cooper and Kaplan, September 1992.

Activity-Based Benchmarking and Process Management—Managing the Case of Cardiac Surgery

By Bea Chiang, Ph.D., CPA

THESE TECHNIQUES FOCUS ON IN-DEPTH IDENTIFICATION OF BEST PROCESSES AND PRACTICES THROUGH A STUDY OF RESOURCE CONSUMPTION. FROM THEM, HOSPITALS CAN GET A MORE ACCURATE PICTURE OF HOW PRACTICES ARE LINKED TO COST.

The increasingly competitive nature of the healthcare market and the managed care system have put tremendous pressure on hospitals to control costs, manage service processes, improve quality of care, and market services competitively. Healthcare providers are now expected to manage economic resources prudently and need to be on top of their costs to ensure that revenues are sufficient for them to survive. Benchmarking is a strategic approach used widely in the manufacturing sector to monitor costs. It is a continuous process of measuring products, services, and activities against the best levels of performance.[1] This approach can also benefit healthcare organizations where the close monitoring of resources is critical to ensure the organization's effectiveness.

COSTING PROCESSES AND ACTIVITY-BASED BENCHMARKING

Healthcare organizations are increasingly sharing cost data on a per patient and per case basis for benchmarking the performance of individual units. There are several external industry benchmarks that a hospital can use to compare its operation to other healthcare providers. Examples include total margin, occupancy, cost per certain medical procedure, total cost per case, and cost per inpatient day. Some of these external benchmarks, however, confound direct cost comparisons, as costs may be aggregated in different ways by different hospitals. For instance, the selection of direct cost centers and the methods chosen to spread the indirect costs to other departments are hospital environment specific and affect the cost accumulation process for services delivered.

Generally, the hospital's costing system begins with the division of each general ledger account into cost types: variable direct cost, fixed direct cost, and fixed indirect cost. At the cost center or department level, each indirect cost center is assigned an allocation base (such as total cost, square feet, or gross revenue) to be used to spread the indirect costs to the direct cost centers. The departmental direct costs and allocated indirect costs become departmental total costs. The direct cost center or department is defined as a primary product/service unit. An example of a primary product/ service is a prescription, an injection, or a bed bath.

The next step is to calculate the standard unit cost of the primary product/service. This is done by first allocating the departmental total cost based on the relative value units (RVUs) multiplied by the budgeted volumes of each individual product/service to obtain the budgeted total cost of each basic product/service.[2]

Finally, the standard unit cost is calculated by dividing the total cost of the individual product/service by its budgeted volume. Once standard unit costs are established for primary products/services, they can be summed up into intermediate products, such as a surgical procedure. These, in turn, can be rolled up into final product/service, such as inpatient days or admissions. The hospital costing process is presented in Figure 1.

From the hospital's costing procedure, the unit cost of a product actually includes allocated indirect costs that are beyond the control of physicians and other medical personnel. Indirect cost is the cost that does not relate directly to the provision of medical services to patients. Examples include the salary of the administrative staff, the cost of the laundry department, cafeteria, and so forth. For pricing purposes, the accounting system needs to allocate these indirect costs to direct cost centers to account for each unit of product/service. The physicians or medical personnel, however, do not have control over the method or the amount of the indirect cost to be allocated to the department. Total unit cost, which includes both direct and indirect costs, does not reflect the efficiency of activities performed in the medical processes. Therefore, instead of total cost, activity-related measurements such as equipment setup time or surgery time tie in more to the resources consumption in the process and are more appropriate for benchmarking.

IMPROVING CARDIAC CARE PROCESSES BY ACTIVITY-BASED BENCHMARKING

In an economic sense, macro-level costs (like cost per certain diagnosis) are driven by numerous and complex micro-level decisions, such as procedures taken or equipment used by physicians and specialties. Macro cost control can be achieved only through reference to micro-level analysis.[3] Therefore, the benchmarking process should also use internal procedures data. This type of data is more activity specific and task related. It facilitates direct benchmark comparisons among physicians or staff so that these groups can see clearly how their practices need to be improved. The internal procedure level of performance may be identified in an organization through internal benchmarking. The internal benchmarks help the hospital ask why its costs differ from other hospitals, why costs differ among patients with the same diagnosis within the same hospital, and identify which practices can be transferred from less cost-effective to more cost-effective methods.

Studies have found that physicians do respond to benchmarking.[4] They also are more likely to be persuaded to change their practices if they see how they can use such data to improve their processes.[5] Activity-based benchmarking for medical-care processes involves three steps: (1) analyzing process flow and identifying major activities, (2) choosing the appropriate measurement of resource consumption for benchmarking, and (3) identifying the best process and practice as benchmarks.

ANALYZING PROCESS FLOW AND IDENTIFYING MAJOR ACTIVITIES

The first step in the benchmarking process is to perform an analysis of the activity across all operations and processes required to move the patient from admission to discharge. The case of a cardiac patient can be used to illustrate the benchmarking process. The patient is admitted on the scheduled date for an open-heart surgery. After going through the administration process, the patient will undergo many tests. Immediately before surgery, the patient will be given specific preoperative medications and will then be "prepped" for surgery. An intravenous (IV) line will be administered. The patient will then be given a sleep-inducing medication through the IV and anesthetic gas to breathe (general anesthesia). After the patient is asleep, the cardiac surgery procedure begins.

There are a variety of different types of open-heart surgeries, depending upon the condition being treated and the overall health of the patient. The surgery itself takes an average of five hours. After surgery, the patient is moved to a hospital bed in the cardiac surgical intensive care unit. The patient is carefully monitored in the cardiac intensive care unit for 12-24 hours and then on the general floor (step-down units). Throughout the process, from admission to discharge, major activities include general administration and patient education, lab procedure/test, medical equipment and supplies administration, setup, operation, nursing, and general services. The summary presented in Figure 2 details the process flow and activities engaged in providing the services. Costs incurred at each stage depend upon types of personnel, equipment, and supplies involved in the process. They are listed as cost inputs.

CHOOSING THE APPROPRIATE MEASUREMENT FOR BENCHMARKING

For different costs, there are different activity characteristics that drive the costs. For example, nursing costs are different when comparing the operating room to the cardiac intensive care unit because different types and numbers of nurses engage in different activities. To better capture cost incurrence in the case of a cardiac surgery patient, an activity-related measurement must be selected to measure the resource consumption.

Pre-Surgery

At the admission stage, the number of patients per registration staff or number of documents generated per staff hour can be used to measure the efficiency of the registration process. During the preparation for surgery (ambulatory care unit), medical staff explain the operation process to the patient, perform additional tests, and prepare the patient for surgery. At this stage, the preparation time, patient education time, number of tests performed by type, and the amount of medical supplies used can be drawn on to measure the performance.

Operating Room

The number of specialists and medical staff assigned to the operating room are defined by the hospital's surgery policy and remain consistent from patient to patient. Resource consumption among physicians and other medical personnel varies, however, in three significant ways: surgery time, operating room setup time, and medical supplies usage.

Surgery time is a critical indicator of cost. It relates to costs associated with the time for the operation, anesthesia, perfusion service, and nursing staff. Setup time is the time required to prepare equipment, tools, and medical supplies for the surgery. It is considered a major indicator of efficiency.[6] Reducing setup time shortens the lead-time of service delivery and helps to keep it at a reasonable level. Medical supplies and equipment represent a significant part of hospital expenditures and are one of the major factors that drive healthcare costs.[7] Finding the best practices in using the facilities and supplies will help healthcare providers manage their costs. Benchmarks can be established to measure the performance of an operating room in terms of operation time, setup time, and medical supplies usage.

Post-Surgery

After the surgery, most of the resources and time are spent on monitoring surgery results, providing patient education, performing additional tests, taking vital signs,

FIGURE 1

Costs of Primary Products/Services

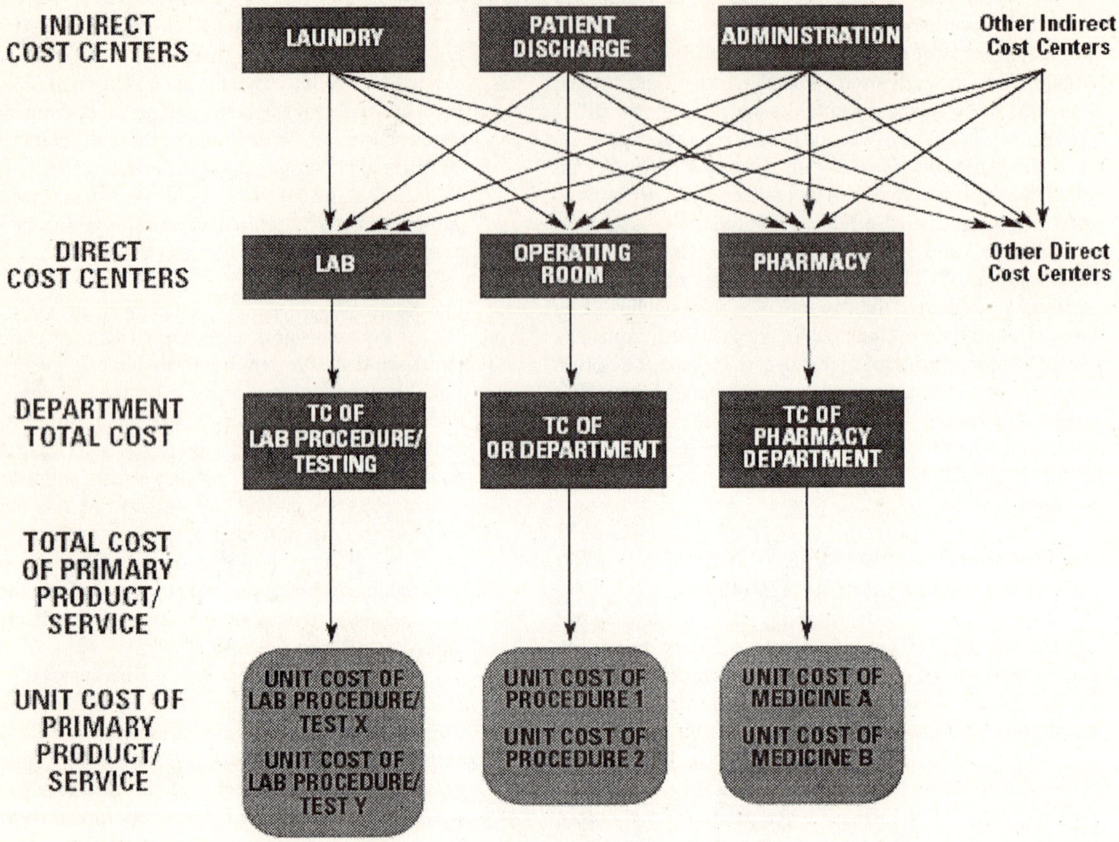

Costs of Intermediate and Final Products/Services

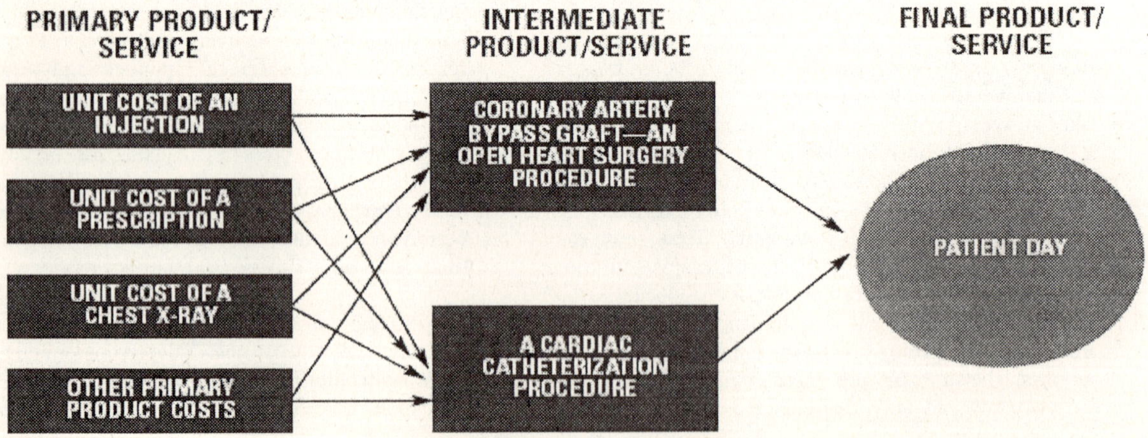

FIGURE 2: Process Flow, Activities, and Cost Inputs for Cardiac Surgery Patient

Process	Activities
ADMISSION	**Administration and Patient Education** ◆ Registration ◆ Provide complete medical records of surgery ◆ Provide patient education ◆ Patient screening interview ◆ Collect and record pre-surgery information **Cost inputs:** Administration personnel
AMBULATORY CARE UNIT	**Surgery Preparation** ◆ Perform pre-surgery tests: urine and blood tests, electrocardiogram, chest x-ray ◆ Prepare equipment, supplies, and medication for surgery ◆ Swab patient, surgical area, and create sterile environment ◆ Insert IV **Cost Inputs:** Lab technician, nurses, cardiologist, and medical equipment and supplies
OPERATING ROOM	**Setup** ◆ Set up surgical equipment, supplies, and monitoring devices **Cost Inputs:** Medical staff and medical equipment and supplies
	Pre-surgery Anesthesia ◆ Provide sleep-inducing medication through IV: mixture of oxygen and anesthetic gas **Cost Inputs:** Anesthesiologist, nurses, and medical equipment and supplies
	Cardiac Surgery ◆ Perform surgical procedures **Cost Inputs:** Specially trained OR personnel, 2 cardiac surgeons, 1 resident, 1 cardiologist, 2 cardiac intensive care nurses, 2 scrub nurses, 2 circulation nurses, 1 CRNA, 2 pump technicians, medical equipment and supplies
CARDIAC SURGICAL INTENSIVE CARE UNIT	**Closely Monitoring** ◆ Provide nursing care ◆ Perform post-surgery diagnostics and report results ◆ Collect post-surgery data such as recovery scores and vital signs ◆ Assess post-surgery outcome **Cost Inputs:** Nurses, staff cardiologist, lab technician, and medical equipment and supplies
STEP-DOWN UNIT	**Monitoring and Testing** ◆ Perform more tests to assess and report results ◆ Provide general and dietary services ◆ Provide patient education ◆ Measure post-surgery outcome **Cost Inputs:** Nurses, staff cardiologist, lab technician, and medical equipment and supplies
DISCHARGE	**Discharge Instruction** ◆ Patient education and discharge instruction **Cost Inputs:** Nurse, medical personnel

FIGURE 3: Activity-Based Benchmarking

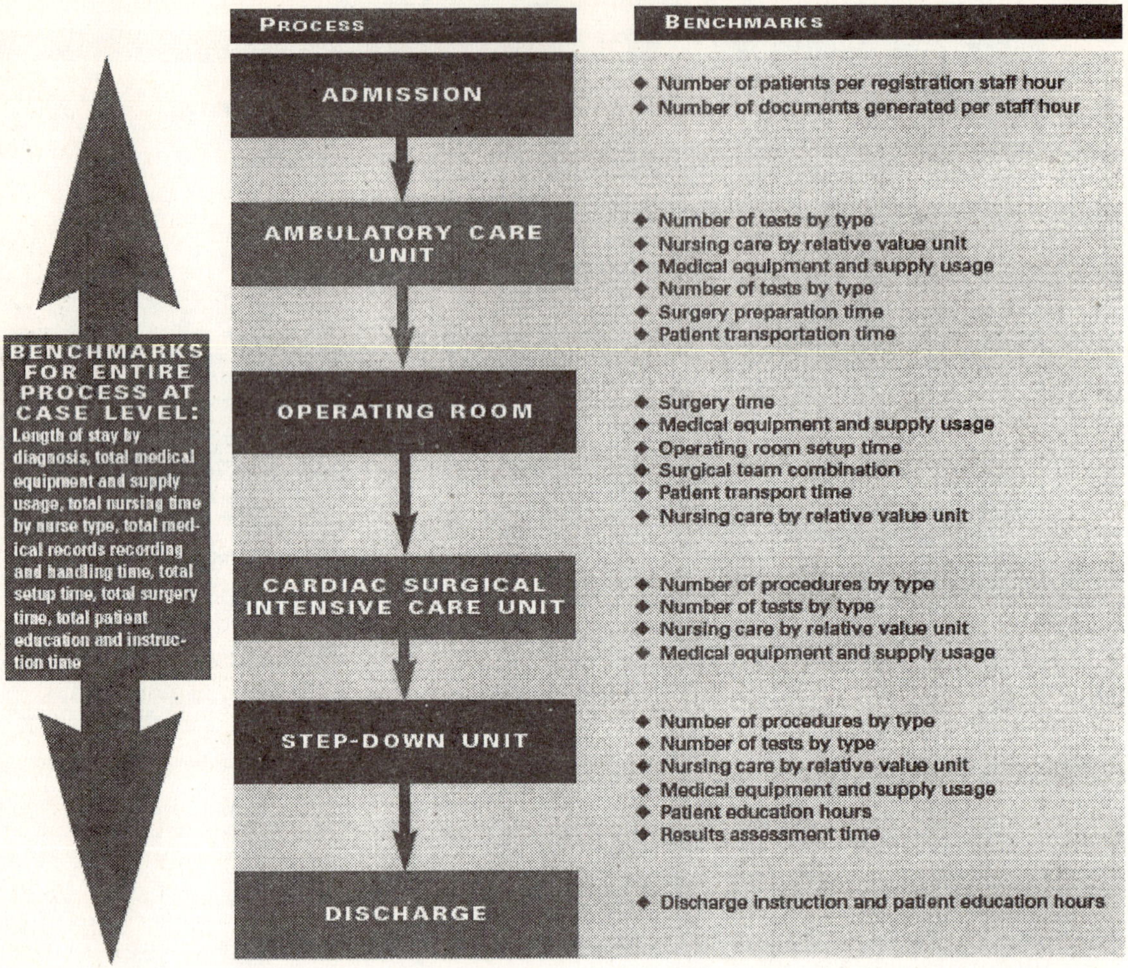

assessing post-surgery outcome, and providing general and dietary services. Major cost inputs in this stage include nursing staff, cardiologist, lab technician, general service staff, and medical supplies. Benchmarks such as results-assessment time, nursing care time by nurse type, medical supply usage, and patient education hours can be established to measure the performance.

NURSING-CARE SERVICES

Nursing services count as a significant part of activities in every stage of the process. The essence of the problem with nursing services is that the costs usually are averaged into room and board in most hospitals. As a result, all patients in a given unit of the hospital will receive the same daily charge for nursing-care services. It is presumed that all patients consume exactly the same amount of nursing resources. The fact that different patients have different nursing needs does not enter into consideration. For the purpose of improving the process through benchmarking, this approach provides very poor information. The most accurate method would be to measure the time each nurse spent with each patient. This, however, is an impractical, costly, and time-consuming way to account for the cost. One alternative, suggested by B. Dieter and J. Moorhead, is assigning each nursing procedure a predetermined relative value unit (RVU) based on the time taken to perform that task.[8] Initially, the relative value might be determined according to prior experience or by polling full-time staff nurses on the amount of time it takes them to complete each procedure. Thus, instead of counting nursing time spent

TABLE 1: Benchmarking Report—A Case of Cardiac Surgery

1. BENCHMARKING DATA: CARDIAC OPERATING ROOM (ACTIVITY LEVEL)

DRG: 107—Coronary Bypass with Cardiac Catheterization
Principal Procedure Code: 36.11 **Severity Level: 2**
Attending MD: # 11111

SEVERITY LEVEL:	PATIENT ENCOUNTER NO.: 00000100 SEVERITY LEVEL 2			PATIENT ENCOUNTER NO.: 00000500 SEVERITY LEVEL 3		
	PHYSICIAN #11111	AVERAGE	BEST PRACTICE	PHYSICIAN #11111	AVERAGE	BEST PRACTICE
1. Cardiac Surgery Time (*minutes per surgery*)	300	281.35	225	345	300.63	228
Perfusion Service (*minutes*)	300	281.35	225	345	300.63	228
Anesthesia (*minutes*)	300	281.35	225	345	300.63	228
2. Operating Room Total Setup Time (*minutes per surgery*)	65	53.2	38	66	49.72	40
Anesthesia Setup Time (*minutes*)	31	26.01	22	35	27.21	25
3. Equipment and Medical Supplies (*number of units used*)						
Aortic Punch	1	1	1	1	1	1
Bovie Pencil	3	2.74	2	2	2.57	2
Bulb Syringe	1	1	0	1	1.11	0
Bifur Blood Infusion Set	0	0.31	0	0	0.1	0
Breathing Circuits	1	1	1	1	1	1
Cable Ven	2	1.95	1	2	1.95	1
Cautery Electro Unit	1	1.62	1	1	1.48	1
Chest Tube	2	2	2	2	2	2
CO_2 Coupling	1	1	1	1	1	1
CVP Tray Arrow	1	0.8	0	1	1	0
Ioban Drape	2	1.19	1	1	1.15	0
Mayo Cover	2	1.24	0	1	1.22	0
Scapel Blade	6	5.19	4	4	4.86	4
Saphenous Vein Adaptor	2	2.19	1	2	2.38	2
Stopcocks 3 Ways	1	1	0	1	1	0
Sutures Cabg Pack	2	1.05	1	1	1	1
Y-Adaptor	0	0.2	0	2	0	0
Temp Sensing Foley	1	1	1	1	1	1
Blood Warmer Set	1	1	1	1	1	1
Imed Cassette	3	3.62	3	4	4.5	2
Hemaclip	4	3.2	2	3	3.2	2
Skin Prep	3	2.81	2	1	1.5	1
Transducer	1	0.4	0	3	2.77	0
Transducer Triple	1	1	1	1	1	1
Disposable Gown	3	3.43	2	3	3.9	2
Clip Applier	9	3.52	2	7	3.75	2
Extra Pressure Transducer	0	0.4	0	1	1	0

TABLE 1 (*continued*): Benchmarking Report—A Case of Cardiac Surgery

2. BENCHMARKING DATA: PRE- AND POST-SURGERY (ACTIVITY LEVEL)

	PATIENT 00000100	AVERAGE	BEST PRACTICE
1. NURSING CARE[1] (RVU)[2]			
Vital Signs (*Registered nurse, Licensed nurse, Unlicensed assistant*)			
Registered nurses	40	38.44	32
Licensed nurses	25	30.12	32
Unlicensed assistants	18	18.20	17
Patient Education and General Service (*Registered nurse, Licensed nurse, Unlicensed assistant*)	40	40.51	35
Medical Records Assessment (*Registered nurse*)	62	60.21	60
Administration of Medications (*Registered or Licensed nurse*)	81	70.21	60
Surgery Preparation (*Unlicensed assistant or Apprentice nurse*)	22	30.21	25
IV, Diagnostic Tests (*Registered nurse*)	75	70.21	66
2. LAB (RVU)			
Blood Tests	98	78.21	75
Pathological Tests	45	50.30	38
Other Tests and Procedures[3]	39	36.12	34
Radiology Films	40	42.69	39
3. CARDIAC CATHETERIZATION			
Cardiac Catheterization Time (*minutes*)	45	35.78	30
Cardiac Catheterization Setup Time (*minutes*)	20	18.23	16
4. RESPIRATORY THERAPY			
Setup Time (*minutes*)	17	18.20	15
Cont Oxygen Therapy (*units*)	114	96.25	88
Pause Oximeter (*units*)	3	4.55	3
5. TOTAL PATIENT TRANSPORTATION AND PREPARATION (*minutes*)	55	47.33	45

3. BENCHMARKING DATA: CASE LEVEL[4]

	PATIENT 00000100	AVERAGE	BEST PRACTICE
1. Length of Stay (*days*)	7	8.20	5
2. Total Actual Costs	$24,188	$22,521.20	$19,888
3. Total Surgery Time (*minutes*)	630	561.25	450
4. Total Cardiac Catheterization Time (*minutes*)	890	897.30	750
5. Total Nursing Costs[5]	1,419	1,410.42	952
6. Total RVU of Lab Test	1,418	1,082.52	899
7. Total RVU of Radiology	101	81.33	67
8. Total Medical Records Handling and Assessment Time (*RVU*)	772	630.55	521
9. Total Medical Supplies and Sterile (*units*)	250	225.17	155
10. Total Respiratory Therapy Time (*minutes*)	387	301.22	280

1 To simplify the illustration, only vital signs are reported by nurse type. Total RVUs are shown for the rest of the activities.

2 In the lab-testing and nursing-care areas, RVU represents the amount of time to complete a certain task or procedure.

3 A detailed benchmarking report will be sorted by test types.

4 The average and benchmarking data are based on patients with the same diagnosis and level of severity.

5 Total nursing costs are determined as follows: (nursing hours) x (nurse-patient ratio) x (hour rate). The hour rate will depend on the type of nurse.

on each activity with each patient, nursing care will be benchmarked based on RVU for procedures or tasks performed.

Figure 3 summarizes a set of benchmarks established to measure the performance of major activities in the care process. Benchmarks can be established at a detailed activity level as well as at the case level.

IDENTIFYING BEST PROCESS AND BEST PRACTICE AS BENCHMARKS

Table 1 shows an internal benchmarking report of a hospital. The hospital combined clinical records, nursing logs, and surgery logs with the financial accounting records to benchmark performance. The data were sorted by Diagnosis Related Group (DRG), primary procedure code, and severity level.[9] Benchmarks are the cases that have the lowest-quantity usage in terms of surgery time, setup time, nursing-care time, lab tests/procedures time, and consumption of medical equipment and supplies. The benchmarks were determined by data collected from 259 patients admitted to the hospital for heart surgery in 1998 and 1999. The benchmarking report compares individual information to the overall average of the 259 cases and to the best practice. The first part of the report presents the comparative benchmarking data of two cardiac surgeries in the operating room (cardiac primary procedure code 36.12), performed by physician #11111, one at severity level 2 and the other at level 3 (Note: The report is shown as a subset of the results, so it does not include all benchmarking items).

The report shows that the surgery time taken by physician #11111 for a principal procedure code 36.11 at severity level 2 was 300 minutes, compared to an average time of 281 minutes and 225 minutes for the best practice. The same comparisons are made for anesthesia and perfusion service. The benchmarking also shows medical equipment and supply usage. It reveals that some equipment items were required for the surgery, such as a blood warmer set (individual, average, and best practice all show one unit). Some items, such as clip applier, however, could be used in a more cost effective way: Nine units of clip appliers were actually used, compared to an average of 3.52 units in all cases and two units for the best practice. Some items, such as transducers, were used on average in 104 cases out of 260 (an average of 0.4 usage) but were not used at all by the best practice. This raises the question of whether or not this procedure can be performed without the use of transducers.

The report provides a general internal profile of practices in the operating room. Physicians could review such a report to determine exactly how their consumption of supplies compares to the average consumption level in all cases and to the consumption level of the best performer. The report also is useful to physicians and other clinical personnel because it highlights the usage differences in a principal cardiac procedure and shows what supplies were not used in the best practices.

The second part of the benchmarking report shows pre- and post-surgery data. In the interest of providing a simple illustration, the report only shows a subset of benchmarking data. For nursing care, different types of nurses and nursing assistants, such as registered nurses, licensed nurses, unlicensed assistants, and apprentice nurses, are employed to provide services. Each of them has a different hour rate and skill set. Some tasks require a specific type of nurse for a specific task; for example, the operating room requires cardiac registered nurses for assistance. In the step-down unit, only registered nurses can perform certain tasks, such as an IV or any injection. Others, such as a bed bath, however, can be performed by licensed nurses. The benchmark report shows the time (measured by RVU) spent on each type of nursing activity. Detailed nursing activities can be reported by nurse type. For example, vital signs took 40 RVUs of a registered nurse's time, 25 RVUs of a licensed nurse's time, and 18 RVUs of an unlicensed assistant's time. In the best practice, 32 RVUs of a registered nurse's time, 32 RVUs of a licensed nurse's time, and 17 RVUs of an unlicensed assistant's time were devoted to taking vital signs. In this instance, the best practice utilizes more licensed nurses instead of registered nurses to take vital signs. Having licensed nurses take vital signs instead of registered nurses, therefore, can lower costs. The use of unlicensed assistants is about the same because of restrictions on the use of unlicensed assistants for quality considerations. These benchmarking data help the hospital monitor nursing services to ensure the quality of nursing care. In addition, the nursing department manager is able to assign the lowest-cost combination of nursing staff to provide the required services at the desired level of quality care.

The lab tests are also measured and benchmarked by RVU. The performance of the cardiac catheterization lab and respiratory therapy are benchmarked by setup time, procedure time, and medical supplies usage. Section three of the report presents the benchmarking data at case level. This information facilitates comparisons of cardiac surgery cases at a broader level. If the case and benchmarks show significant differences (for example, total RVUs of lab tests are 1,418 compared to 899 of the best practice), the case can be traced down to the activity level in order to explore the factors responsible for the high cost.

FOCUSING ON PROCESS IMPROVEMENT

Activity-based benchmarking focuses on in-depth identification of best processes and practices. The best practices can be found through the use of internal benchmarking. One of the benefits is that we can obtain specific and detailed information with which to facilitate process improvement. Hospitals can use benchmarking data to identify critical success factors and appropriate measures in the service process. Benchmarking also enables us to use both clinical and accounting information more effectively. When applied along with external benchmarking measures, internal procedure benchmarking helps the organization to determine major areas for improvement.

Information provided by the internal activity benchmarking process benefits hospitals by highlighting the resource consumption of particular procedures in the process flow so that physicians and staff have a more accurate picture of how practices are linked to cost. More important, activity benchmarking provides specific direction for the continual improvement of the care process and provides an explicit means of communication among various departments.

[1] Charles T. Horngren, George Foster, and Srikant M. Datar, *Cost Accounting: A Managerial Emphasis*, Prentice Hall, 2000, pp. 236.

[2] The relative value unit (RVU) is a measure of resource consumption in the healthcare organization. It is defined as the amount of time to complete one unit or the amount of supplies for one unit.

[3] Ron Eden and Colin Lay, "Benchmarking on costs in healthcare," *Management Accounting*, March 1998, pp. 28-31.

[4] J. Evans, III, Y. Hwang, and N. Nagarajan, "Physicians' response to length-of-stay profiling," *Medical Care*, Vol. 33, No. 11, 1995, p. 1106.5 Girard Senn, "Clinical buy-in is key to benchmarking success," *Healthcare Financial Management*, Vol. 52, No. 5, May 1998, p. 46.

[6] Horngren, Foster, *et al.*, p. 726.

[7] *Material Management in Healthcare*, April 2000, Vol. 9, No. 4, pp. 6-9.

[8] B. Dieter, "Determining the Cost of Emergency Department Services," *Hospital Cost Accounting Advisor*, Vol. 2, No. 1, February 1987, pp.1, 5-7; J. Moorhead, "Costing Accounting for Emergency Services," *Hospital Cost Management and Accounting*, Vol. 1, No. 2, May 1999, pp. 1-7.

[9] DRG is a system used for classification of inpatient hospital services based on principal diagnosis, secondary diagnosis, surgical procedures, age, sex, and presence of complications. This system of classification is used as a financing mechanism to reimburse hospitals and selected other providers for services rendered.

Activity-Based Costing for Higher Education Institutions

By Lakshmi U. Taikonda,CMA, CPA, Ph.D., And Rao J. Taikonda, CFPIM, Ph.D

EXECUTIVE SUMMARY

Higher Education Institutions (HEIs) are in a state of turmoil and fiscal crisis. Escalating costs, diminishing resources, increased competition, unhappy customers (students, parents), and state legislators demanding accountability are reassuring them to manage their costs better. These pressures are not much different from those experienced by the manufacturing industry of yesterday. Using tools and techniques such as activity-based costing (ABC), business process reengineering, concurrent engineering, and total quality management, manufacturers gained a better understanding of costs, simplified products and procedures, eliminated waste, cut costs, reduced lead times, improved quality, added value, and gained customer satisfaction and loyalty. Though activity-based costing is used successfully by a variety of manufacturing and service industries, educational institutions are lagging. Only a few colleges and universities in the United States apply ABC. In Great Britain several universities have recently introduced ABC accounting. These universities found that ABC helped them with tighter financial management and better resource allocation.

IMAGINE A COMPANY that produces a variety of products, yet, within the company, autonomous departments make almost all decisions regarding product mix, batch sizes, and scheduling. Duplication of products among departments is common. New products are added continually, but managers rarely close product lines despite their lack of usefulness or marketability. Outdated and bureaucratic procedures plague the business, as do inefficiency and waste. The time to complete a single unit, which once took four years, now takes five or more years.

In this company, managers have little knowledge of the company's product costs. They treat all products as if they cost the same to produce and sell all products at the same price. Departmental budgets are based on the number of units they produce, and, despite lip service to quality, administrators are more concerned with quantity of units produced. Departments that fall short of production quotas are expected to pay part of their budget back to the company. Cost increases surpass inflation and are passed on to customers. Customers complain about rising prices and declining quality, but no one takes them seriously. Despite all this, the company stays in business. What company is this? It is a higher education institution (HEI).

HEIs are in a state of turmoil and fiscal crisis.[1] Average tuition costs increased from $624 in 1976 to $3,151 in 1996, far exceeding inflation and average wage gains. A variety of forces—diminishing resources, increased competition, unhappy students, parents, and state legislators—are pressuring HEIs to manage their costs better.[2] These pressures differ little from those experienced by the manufacturing industry of yesterday. The manufacturing industry responded by reinventing itself through activity based costing, business process reengineering, concurrent engineering, and total quality management. It gained a better understanding of costs, simplified products and procedures, eliminated waste, cut costs, reduced lead times, improved quality, added value, and gained customer satisfaction and loyalty. In coming years, the higher education industry will have to do the same.

Among these techniques for reinvention, activity based costing (ABC) has been the most widely adopted throughout other industries. The healthcare, banking, and insurance industries have all adopted ABC, but higher education lags far behind. Studies indicate it takes 25 years or more for at least half of HEIs to adopt a standard innovation after it was adopted by the first one.[3] Only a few higher education institutions in the United States apply ABC, and these applications are limited to allocation of overhead costs such as libraries and admissions. In Great Britain, however, several universities have adopted ABC, resulting in tighter financial management and better resource allocation.[4]

Understanding activities is the first step in reducing costs. Costs of activities needed to support a course vary significantly from subject to subject and from course to course within the same subject. Yet administrators rarely know enough about activities and costs to make appropriate cost management and cost containment decisions. Volume and complexity add to the cost of courses and degree programs just as they increase product costs in manufacturing companies. After applying ABC, one university found that some graduate programs cost more than three times the revenue received from student fees and student work activities in the school.[5] Another university suddenly found itself with surplus space: Before ABC was applied, academic departments wanted to control as much space as possible because space was considered a free good. Under ABC, however, overhead cost for space was allocated to

Figure 1: Activity-Based Costing: Generic Application
(Resources, Activity Centers, and Cost Objects)

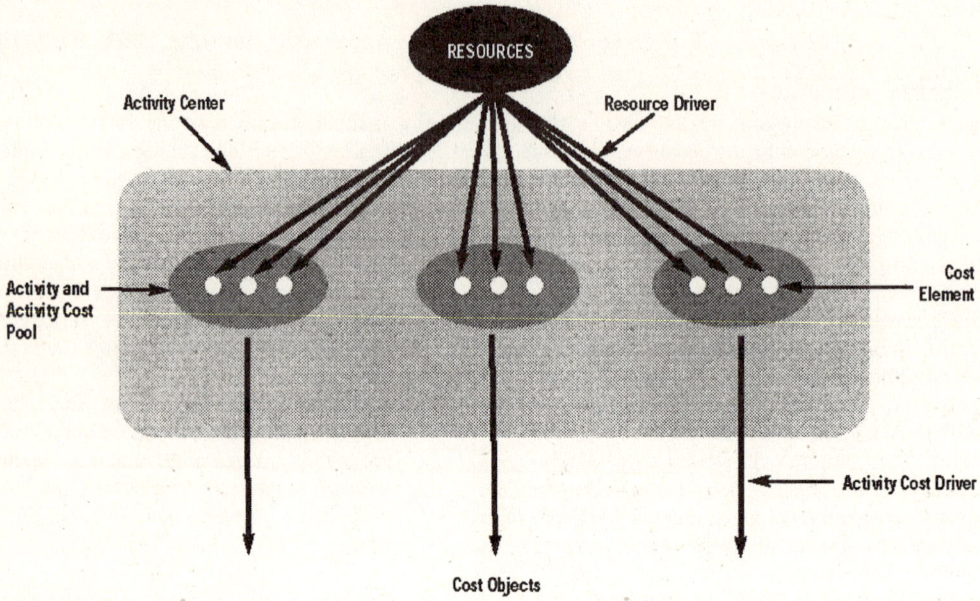

departments, and the departments began releasing unused space to avoid overhead charges.[6]

Achieving excellence in higher education requires the critical evaluation of academic and support activities. HEIs need to figure out ways of performing work more effectively and efficiently without sacrificing quality. In this article, we question conventional wisdom, challenge the status quo, and describe how ABC principles can be applied to the country's more than 3,000 colleges and universities.

ABC METHODOLOGY

Activity-based costing is an accounting methodology that links the following elements:

♦ **Costs**—Expenditures are classified as product costs—costs that are related to manufacturing the product—and period costs—costs that are expended in the period they were incurred. Product costs are further classified as direct (traceable) and indirect (shared) costs, which are allocated to products using a selected basis such as labor hours. University costs can be classified as instruction costs—costs that are directly or indirectly related to instruction—and noninstruction costs, which are allocated on a selected basis such as number of students or number of student credit hours.

♦ **Activities**—An activity is a unit of work performed within an organization or a work process, such as processing invoices or grading papers.

(Resources—Expenditures incurred by the organization, such as salaries, utilities, and depreciation.

(Cost Object—The reason for computing the cost. Product costs are an example.

As shown in Figure 1, ABC assigns resources to cost objects in two stages.7 In the first stage, resource costs are assigned to two areas. The first area is activity cost pools, the basic unit in an organization for which costs are accumulated, such as purchasing, academic unit, a single course. The second area is resource drivers, the various factors that determine where resources will be allocated, such as square feet of space, number of students. In the second stage of ABC, costs accumulated in the activity cost pools are assigned to cost objects according to activity cost drivers, a measure of the demand placed on activities by the cost object, such as the number of material moves, number of papers graded.

STEPS IN APPLYING ABC

ABC application involves the following six steps:

1. Identifying cost objects—Put simply, cost objects are what ABC seeks to measure: the cost of delivering a single course, for example. Cost objects are a sum of

Table 1: Activity Hierarchy in Manufacturing and University

Activity Level	Manufacturing Activity	Manufacturing Driver	University Activity	University Driver
Unit Level	Assembling	# of units	Grading papers	# of papers
	Machining	# of machine hours	Office hours	# of students
Batch Level	Purchasing	# of purchase orders	Orientation to group of students	# of groups
	Billing	# of bills	Lecturing to class	# of courses
Product Level	Product design	# of products	Course design	# of courses
	Parts support	# of parts	Selecting course materials	# of courses

individual cost units. If the cost of a single course is the cost object, the cost unit is the cost per student.

2. Identifying output—The desired end results are called output. Courses and programs are examples of output in HEIs.
3. Identifying activities—These are the activities that are needed to deliver the outputs.
4. Allocating resources and making cost pools—Resource costs are allocated to cost pools based on direct or indirect costs.
5. Linking activity costs to output—Once the cost pools are made and cost drivers identified, costs from these pools are assigned to cost objects according to activity levels.
6. Analysis and cost reporting—The final step is to analyze the cost information generated by the ABC applications and make relevant conclusions such as whether to keep, modify, or remove a specific course.

ACTIVITY CLASSIFICATION

While the first two steps are fairly straightforward, identifying activities is somewhat more complex. ABC systems identify and classify major activities into four levels: unit, batch, product, and facility.8 Table 1 gives examples of these activities in industry and in education.

(Unit-Level Activities—Activities that are performed each time a unit is produced. Unit-level activities assume that inputs are consumed in direct proportion to the number of units produced, such as assembling a widget or grading papers.

(Batch-Level Activities—Activities that are performed each time a batch of units is produced. Batch-level activities assume that inputs are consumed in direct proportion to the number of batches of each product produced, regardless of the size of the batch, such as processing purchase orders, lecturing to a class, or holding orientation for a group of students.

(Product-Level Activities—Activities that are performed as needed to support the production of each type of product. Product-level activities assume that inputs are consumed to develop or permit production of individual products, such as promoting a product, designing a product, preparing for a course, or designing a course.

(Facility-Level Activities—Activities that are needed to sustain the facility's overall functioning. These costs are either allocated on an arbitrary basis or not allocated at all, such as corporate headquarters cost or salary of the university president.

ABC APPLICATIONS IN HIGHER EDUCATION INSTITUTIONS

Degree programs, the primary output of HEIs, are a collection of courses. Core activities of HEIs— teaching, research, service, and outreach—are supported by functions such as administration, facilities maintenance, security, library and learning resources, and labs. College and university department budgets are typically based on several factors: credit hours produced, sections offered, number of students, and size of the teaching staff. Traditional costing at HEIs assumes that all courses are the same, and cost accounting usually tracks only budget compliance.

There are several problems with these simple models. First, costs are allocated on a single volume basis, with no distinction between fixed costs and variable costs. Second, the methods fail to account for students who take courses outside their college or major. Third, the models assume that all courses consume the same activities in the same proportions, when, in fact, some programs maybe subsidizing others.

Activity-based costing allocates differently. Take a hypothetical university called Degrees R Us University (DRU). Let's say that DRU offers courses in two different academic units. For purposes of illustration, let's assume the units have equivalent numbers of faculty, courses, and students. These similarities will help highlight differences between courses among units and courses within units. Figure 2 shows how ABC can help determine the cost of a course.

Figure 2: Activity-Based Costing: Application to Higher Education
(Resources, Activity Centers, and Cost Objects)

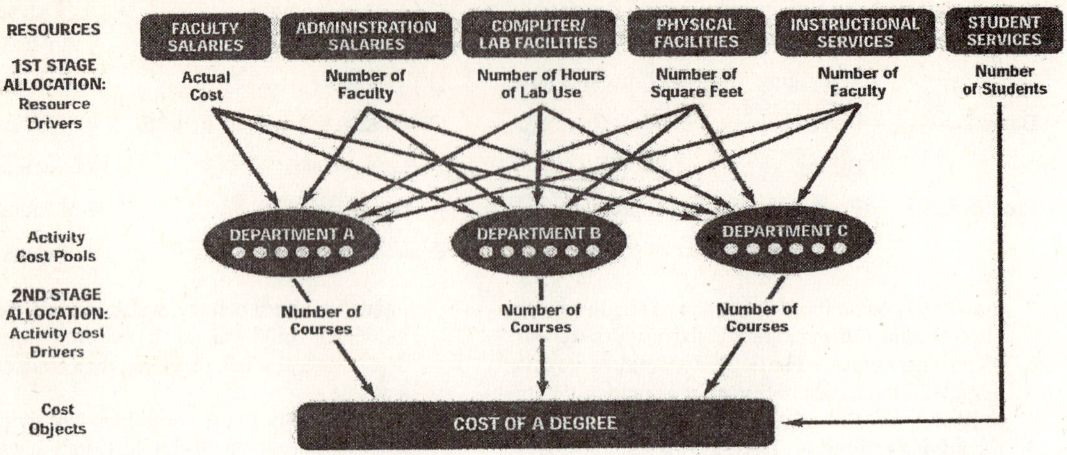

Example 1: Estimating the Cost of a Course—Varying Resource Consumption Between Academic Units

Different academic units consume resources—teacher salaries, computers, facilities, and student support services—in different proportions. Table 2, for example, shows proportional costs between two academic units. Table 3, on the other hand, uses ABC to show the cost of a single course. Table 4 shows the distortions caused by traditional costing by contrasting the two accounting methods in Tables 2 and 3. Using the traditional single volume based allocations, the cost of a course is total cost ($3,660,000) divided by total number of courses (122): $30,000. From the numbers shown in Table 3, it is obvious that costs of courses in different academic units are not the same. Courses of academic unit # 1 are over cost by 24%, whereas courses in academic unit # 2 are under cost by 55%.

Example 2: Estimating the Cost of a Course—Varying Resource Consumption Within Academic Units

What does it take to deliver a course? What activities occur before, during, and after a class meeting? University budgets rarely capture the full scope of activities needed to teach a class. The true cost of a course includes pre-class activities, such as course design and outline preparation, and post-class activities, such as grading to estimate the cost of a course. These activities—and hence the relative cost of a single course—vary from department to department and from course to course within the same department.

In this example, a bill of activities is developed using time spent byte instructor as a surrogate for the cost of instruction and related activities. These activities and the time they consume vary from course to course. We made the following assumptions to illustrate how a bill of activities can be developed for a course. The following data and assumptions constitute the bill of activities shown in Table 5:

Assumptions

1. Average faculty salary including fringe benefits: $115,200.
2. Average distribution of faculty time: 50% teaching, 30% research, and 20% service.
3. Average number of working hours = 9 months x 4 weeks x 40 hours = 1,440 hours.
4. Average cost per hour = $15,200/1,440 = $80/hour.
5. Average duration of a course: 3 hours per week over 15 weeks.
6. Normal teaching load: 18 credits per year (6 classes @ 3 credit hours each).
7. Average number of different courses per year: 3.
8. Average class size: 30 students per class.
9. Average noninstructional cost: $96 per student credit hour.

Table 2: Degrees R Us University—Activity and Cost Data

Costs	Academic Unit # 1	Academic Unit # 2	Total Activity Units	Total Cost	Cost per Activity Unit
Direct Costs					
# of Faculty	20	10	30		
Avg. Salary	$30,000	$60,000			
Total Direct Costs	**$600,000**	**$600,000**		**$1,200,000**	
Indirect Costs					
Computer Use	400 hours	1,600 hours	2,000 hours	$800,000	$400/hr.
Facility Use	600,000 sq. ft.	400,000 sq. ft.	1,000,000 sq. ft.	$400,000	$0.40/sq. ft.
Instructional Service Use	20 faculty	10 faculty	30 faculty	$600,000	$20,000/faculty
Student Service Use	2,700 students	600 students	3,300 students	$660,000	$200/student
Total Indirect Costs				**$2,460,000**	
Total Costs				**$3,660,000**	
# of Courses	**85**	**37**	**122**		

Table 3: Degrees R Us University—Cost Per Course—Activity-Based Costing

Cost Element	Cost/Activity Unit	Academic Unit # 1		Academic Unit # 2	
		Activity Consumed	Total Cost	Activity Consumed	Total Cost
Computer Use	$400/Hr.	400	$160,000	1,600	$640,000
Facility	$0.4/Sq.Ft.	600,000	$240,000	400,000	$160,000
Instructional Services	$20,000/faculty	20	$400,000	10	$200,000
Student Services	$200/student	2,700	$540,000	600	$120,000
Salaries		$600,000	$600,000		
Total Costs		$1,940,000	$1,720,000		
# of Courses		85	37		
Cost/Course		$22,824	$46,486		

Table 4: Degrees R Us University—Comparison of Cost Per Course

Course	Traditional Costing	Activity-Based Costing	Distortion in $	Distortion as %
Academic Unit # 1	$30,000	$22,824	($7,176)	24% over
Academic Unit # 2	$30,000	$46,486	$16,486	55% under

Table 5: Degrees R Us University—Bill of Activities for a Course

Activity	Activity Level	Activity Driver	Activity Quantity	Proportion of Usage	Activity Quantity per Section in Hours
Designing Course	Course	# of courses	64 hours	1/16	4 hours
Initial Preparation	Course	# of courses	96 hours	1/16	6 hours
Preparing Course Outline etc.	Batch offering	# of preparations	10 hours	1/2	5 hours
Updating and Preparation	Batch offering	# of preparations	45 hours	1/2	22.5 hours
Meeting Class	Batch separation	# of class hours	45 hours	1 45 hours	
Grading Exams, etc.	Unit	# of students	1/2 hour	30	15 hours
Office Hours	Unit	# of students	1/2 hour	30	15 hours
Grading Assignments, etc.	Unit	# of assignments	1/3 hour	30	10
Total Hours					122.5 hours

Activities that support a course can be classified as unit (student), batch (section), product (course), and facility (room):

Product (Course)-Level Activities—These are the activities that are undertaken before a course is actually taught. They include:

♦ **Course Design**. Assume design consumes 64 hours, including activities such as developing objectives and material selection. Courses are usually offered eight times over four years, with two sections at each offering—a total of 16 sections. Design time per section = 64 hours/16 sections = 4 hours.

♦ Initial Preparation. Say this takes 96 hours, including learning new topics, organizing topics, preparing class notes, and the like. Initial preparation time per section = 96 hours/16 sections = 6 hours.

Batch-Level Activities—These are the activities that are undertaken each time a course is offered, regardless of the number of sections offered. They are similar to set-up costs in a manufacturing environment. Some of these activities include:

♦ Prep Time. This includes creating course outlines, homework assignments, quizzes, exams, and the like. Estimated at 10 hours per course, prep time per section = 10 hours/2 sections = 5 hours.

♦ Getting Ready. This includes the time spent updating notes, reviewing notes, preparing and getting ready for class, which is 45 hours per course. Time to get ready per section = 45/2 = 22 hours.

Unit-Level Activities—These are activities undertaken each time a section is taught or a student's paper is graded. Some examples are:

♦ Lecturing/class meeting time = 45 hours/section (15 weeks @ 3 hours/week).

♦ Grading exams/assignments: Half hour per student or 15 hours per a class size of 30.

♦ Office hours: Meeting with students, 1/2 hour per student or 15 hours per a class size of 30.

(Grading assignments: 1/3 hour per student, or 10 hours per a class size of 30.

The total amount of time required for teaching a section is the sum of the time per each activity multiplied by the quantity of activities consumed per class. In this example, the total time is 122.5 hours.

The cost of a course instruction per section equals the instructor's time, measured in hours, multiplied by the cost per instructor hour. The instructional cost of a course per student is the total cost of instruction per section divided by the average number of students in each section. A course's cost per student will be the total cost divided by the number of students. The cost of noninstruction per section per student is noninstructional cost per credit hour multiplied by number of hours:

Instructional cost of a course per section = 122.5 hours x $80.00 = $9,800.00

Instructional cost of a course per student = $9,800.00/30 students = $326.67

Noninstructional costs per a course per student = $96.00 x 3 = $288.00

Total cost per course per student = $326.67 + $288.00 = $614.67.

Example 3: Estimating the Cost of a Degree

The cost of a degree is the sum of both the costs of courses and costs of services. As illustrated by the

Table 6: Degrees R Us University
Bill of Activities—Degree X and Degree Y

Course	Cost/Course	Degree X # of Courses	Degree X Total Cost	Degree Y # of Courses	Degree Y Total Cost
Type A	$300	4	$1,200	24	$7,200
Type B	$600	6	$3,600	6	$3,600
Type C	$900	10	$9,000	6	$5,400
Type D	$1,200	20	$24,000	4	$4,800
Total		40	$37,800	40	$21,000
Noninstructional Cost @ $500 per Semester			$4,000		$4,000
Total Cost per Degree			$41,800		$25,000

above examples, different courses consume different activities and hence have different costs. This example assumes all courses offered by DRU can be classified into four groups—A, B, C, and D—according to the activities consumed by each course. We assume the following:

(Costs per course in groups A, B, C, and D are $300.00, $600.00, $900.00, and $1,200.00, respectively;

(Student services such as healthcare total $500.00 per semester per student;

(DRU offers two different degree programs: X and Y; and

(The average student takes 15 credits, or five three-credit courses per semester, and will complete the degree (120 credits or 40 courses of three credits each) in eight semesters.

Traditional costing would calculate a degree's cost by adding the average cost per course ($750.00, the simple average of four groups) and the noninstructional costs of $500.00 per semester per student. Accordingly: 40 courses @ $750.00 (academic costs) + 8 @ $500.00 (noninstructional costs) = $30,000 + 4,000 = $34,000 for degrees X and Y.

Using ABC, however, a degree program that requires a larger number of courses in an expensive group will cost more than a degree that requires fewer expensive courses. Using the bill of activities (see Table 6), the cost of degree X and degree Y differ significantly. As shown in Table 7, the cost of degree X is 23% under cost, whereas the cost of degree Y is 26% over cost.

Cost of Degree X = 4 x $300 + 6 x $600 + 10 x $900 + 20 x $1,200 + 8x $500 = $1,200 + 3,600 + 9,000 + 24,000 + 4,000 = $41,800.

Cost of Degree Y = 24 x $300 + 6 x $600 + 6x $900 + 4x $1,200 + 8x $500 = $ 7,200 + 3,600 + 5,400 + 4,800 + 4,000 = $25,000.

IS ABC THE RIGHT WAY TO GO?

Unhappy customers (parents and students), legislators, and granting institutions are pressuring colleges and universities to find ways to cut costs without reducing quality. Across-the-board cuts, which is the most common approach, fail to consider the varied activities needed to support different programs. Developing accurate and relevant costs of courses and programs helps universities to determine which courses and programs to keep, which to promote, and which to do away with. Activity-based costing gives a much more accurate picture of true costs and can help academic institutions allocate resources better. Knowledge of true costs of courses/programs helps HEIs to manage their course/program mix better and helps eliminate course proliferation and obsolete courses/programs.

Here are some of the benefits ABC might provide to academic institutions:

Better Cost Information: ABC cost information provides educational institutions and legislators a better picture of true costs of different programs.

Better Identification of Resource Needs: Across-the-board volume-based allocations distort the true needs of departments and programs. Using ABC, academic institutions can better identify areas that need more resources and areas that need fewer resources.

Better Distribution of Scarce Resources: At present, tax money is allocated on the basis of the number of students, the number of semester credit hours, or incremental budgets. Identifying true costs of supporting different programs can lead to better distribution of scarce resources.

Better Course and Program Mix: Knowledge of true costs of courses/programs helps HEIs manage their course/program mix better and helps eliminate course proliferation and obsolete courses/programs.

Better Cost Control: Identifying activities associated with different courses/programs helps HEIs

Table 7: Degrees R Us University

Cost Comparison of Degree Programs: Traditional and Activity-Based Costing

Degree	Traditional Costing	Activity-Based Costing	Difference in $	Difference as %
X	$34,000	$41,800	$7,800 under	23% under
Y	$34,000	$25,000	$9,000 over	26% over

determine which activities are value adding (help students learn) and which are nonvalue adding (require a dozen approvals for a new course or frequent changes in teaching schedules) and can be eliminated/simplified.

Better Public Relations Tool: ABC can be seen as an essential public relations tool. As more and more HEIs are assessed based on performance, they need to explain how they effectively and efficiently deliver their services and fulfill their mission. The ABC approach provides a reasonably reliable and valuable tool to capture and report how resources are used and how they contribute to the overall mission and performance of an HEI.

Despite the seemingly obvious benefits, implementing ABC raises many questions. What costs should be included? What if the same course is taught in different buildings? What are the opportunity costs? What about part-time vs. full-time faculty? Should universities charge different tuition fees for different degree programs? Will different tuition fees discourage students from taking expensive courses? There are two ways to deal with these issues: Administrators can ignore these issues and maintain the status quo, or they can develop roughly relevant cost assignments. Using roughly relevant estimates is preferable to waiting for precision and accuracy, which may be impossible to achieve.

ABC is not just an allocation method. It is also an estimation process. ABC attempts to estimate the cost of performing an activity. It is theoretically possible to install elaborate tracking and monitoring mechanisms that measure precisely all costs and quantities of resources required in performing each activity. But these mechanisms rarely are cost justified. One should be aware of the costs and the benefits of selecting a number of cost drivers. There are tradeoffs between the costs of measurements and the costs of errors from inaccurate data. ABC is labor intensive, and users must weigh the cost of detailed measurement against the benefits of such accuracy. Good cost systems do not have to be elaborate to be useful, and they should try to minimize the total cost while maintaining relevancy and cost effectiveness. Data needed for ABC can be obtained through many sources such as faculty interviews and operating data that are readily available. Though not 100% precise, these estimates usually are accurate enough for most managerial decisions.

Education is a public good, and because taxpayers directly subsidize many higher education institutions, cost effectiveness is a legitimate public concern. Many critics complain that only the rich can attend colleges, but accurate costing could potentially free up public resources, allowing resources to flow into scholarships and grants for needy students rather than into inefficient programs and curriculum. Selective grants based on need beat across the board cost subsidization. By focusing on activities, ABC exposes long-standing shortcomings in academic planning and could potentially challenge the status quo by systematically addressing the issues of cost, productivity, efficiency, and effectiveness. □

1 Council for Aid to Education, "Breaking the Social Contract: The Fiscal Crisis in Higher Education," Commission on National Investment in Higher Education, New York, 1997, pp. 16-17.

2 Mike Mitchell, "Activity-Based Costing in UK Universities," Public Money & Management, Vol. 16, No. 1, pp. 51-57.

3 J. J. Siegfried, M. Getz, and K. H. Anderson, "The Snail's Pace of Innovation in Higher Education," Chronicle of Higher Education, Vol. 41, No. 6, 1995, p. A56.

4 See S. Cox Kelline, Ronald Downey, and Laurinda G. Smith, "ABCs of Higher Education—Getting Back to Basics: An Activity-Based Costing Approach to Planning and Financial Decision Making," paper presented at the Association of Institutional Research 39th Annual Forum, Seattle, Wash., May30 -June 2, 1999; and Mike Mitchell, "Activity-Based Costing in UK Universities," Public Money & Management, Vol. 16, No. 1, pp. 51-57.

5 Daniel W. DeHayes and Joseph G. Loverinic, "Activity-Based Costing for Assessing Economic Performance," New Directions for Institutional Research, No. 82, Summer 1994, pp. 81-93.

6 Gus Gordon and Maria Charles, "Unraveling Higher Education's Costs," Planning for Higher Education, Vol. 26, No. 2, pp. 24-26.

7 Robin Cooper, "The Rise of Activity-Based Costing: Part One: What Is an Activity-Based Cost System?" Journal of Cost Management, Summer 1988, pp. 45-54.

8 Ibid.

Activity-Based Costing for State and Local Governments

By Russell F. Briner, Ph.D., CMA, CPA; Mark Alford, Ph.D.; And Jo Anne Noble

State and local governments have a common goal: to provide products and services to their taxpaying constituents at the lowest possible cost. Many governments, however, are not perceived to be particularly efficient in realizing this goal. To illustrate, Jonathan Walters quoted Anne Kinney, who was director of the budget office for the city of Milwaukee: "...there is pressure on virtually all governments to cut costs and hold the line or even cut taxes. To do that in the best way, you have to develop good cost information. Otherwise you might just decide to cut services rather than figure out a way to deliver those services more efficiently."[1]

Traditionally, state and local governments have practiced cost control by simply aggregating costs for the units within a governmental body and comparing the total costs of these units from period to period. Overhead costs that applied to multiple units were normally allocated to the units based on arbitrary measurements that are common to all units, such as square feet occupied or direct labor costs. A more sophisticated costing system, called activity-based costing (ABC), has emerged in for-profit business environments but has been used little in government accounting.

In this article, we explain the ABC system and advance its application to state and local governmental entities. We also highlight the benefits of using ABC for state and local governments.

ACTIVITY-BA SED COS TING

The primary objective of an ABC system is to improve the accuracy of product and service costs. The result is that more meaningful input for management decision models is available. In ABC, costs of activities are connected to the primary drivers of those activities. To clarify, in an ABC system where the objective is to assign overhead to units of products or services, the "activities" that cause resources to be consumed (overhead costs to be incurred) are identified first. Next, overhead costs are assigned to each of the activities in accordance with the resources consumed by each. Then, overhead rates are determined for each activity or group of activities when activities and their costs can be pooled. These rates ultimately are used to assign the activity costs (overhead) to the products or services that consume the activities.

ABC addresses the real possibility that a portion of overhead is not driven by volume or a volume-related variable. Volume-based measurements are used predominately in traditional, non-ABC systems to determine overhead rates and to assign overhead costs to products and services. ABC recognizes that activities and their costs can be driven by either volume-related or nonvolume-related variables. As a result, both types of drivers are used, as appropriate, to determine overhead rates. The expectation is that the overhead costs assigned to products and services will be more representative of the actual overhead consumed. The benefits of ABC for product and service costing are certainly applicable in determining the costs of the departments or other units within an entity when enhanced accuracy is desired. This and other aspects of ABC that provide costing advantages for state and local governments are discussed and illustrated below.

ABC IN STATE AND LOCAL GOVERNMENTS

Katherine Barrett and Richard Greene indicated that "Governments are finally beginning to figure out how to develop solid figures for the cost of the services they provide."[2] They say that cities like Washington, D.C., and Dallas have taken strides to improve cost information. For example, Washington, D.C., determined the cost of issuing individual checks, while Dallas "has been a leader in the use of cost accounting in areas where it charges fees for services or considers outsourcing." Also, state governments in Utah and Iowa have demonstrated the usefulness of activity-based costing. In Texas, a number of state agencies have embarked on pilot projects involving ABC, including the General Services Commission, the Water Development Board, the Workforce Commission, the Office of the State Comptroller, and the Departments of Economic Development and Transportation.

As in private-sector businesses, ABC can be a valuable tool used to better understand costs and provide more accurate costs of services offered by state and local governments. Because ABC traces costs to the activities that cause the costs to be incurred, these costs can be understood better and reported more accurately.

Mark D. Abrahams and Mary Noss Reavely detailed an application of activity-based costing at the Iowa Department of Transportation.[3] The example outlined ABC procedures for paint crews on Iowa highways. Their presentation indicated that the implementation of an ABC system involves the following four steps:

1. Identification of costs and resources,
2. Identification of the direct and indirect costs of activities,

3. Assignment of costs to activities, and
4. Calculation of unit costs.

Abrahams and Reavely proposed two methods to assign indirect costs to activities.[4] The first, called the Keep It Simple (KIS) approach, is used when precision is not overwhelmingly important. According to the authors, "It is in keeping with the American Institute of Certified Public Accountants' spirit of: It is much better to be approximately right than precisely wrong." Basically, the KIS method uses a single, sometimes seemingly unrelated basis to allocate indirect costs. The alternative is the full costing approach. This latter approach places a premium on accuracy by using individual activity bases to assign various components of indirect cost. No doubt the full costing method requires a more significant commitment of time and labor. Regardless of the approach employed, the authors concluded, through the use of ABC, governments are poised "to redesign processes or to apply process improvement techniques to reduce cost, improve customer value, enhance accuracy, reduce response time, or otherwise improve efficiency and effectiveness."

We can't overemphasize enough the importance of ABC in providing meaningful cost information. The following section illustrates the benefits of employing ABC in a state agency.

ACTIVITY-BASED COSTING AT A TEXAS STATE AGENCY

The Texas Department of Agriculture (TDA) operates six livestock facilities primarily along the South Texas border with Mexico for inspecting animals prior to exporting them to Mexico. Livestock inspections are necessary to discern whether or not the animals being prepared for export are in compliance with Mexico's health regulations. We will review operations at three of the inspection stations. While the facilities are real, the financial data used in the illustration are fictitious but based on fact. The stations selected for the ABC example are located in Brownsville, Laredo, and Del Rio, Texas. State employees at these stations coordinate the inspection of a variety of animals including cattle, sheep, goats, hogs, horses, poultry, and exotic animals not native to the United States. Licensed veterinarians perform the actual inspections.

The Texas Department of Agriculture establishes fees for the inspections. In one recent year, the three stations mentioned above reported a combined net loss of more than $40,000. While this loss is small, the objective of any governmental agency should be to operate effectively and efficiently and not lose money. The TDA's past reluctance to raise inspection fees creates an added incentive to contain costs. The inspection stations currently accumulate costs in the following categories: personnel, administration, livestock handling, and pen operations. The TDA is not currently aware of segments of their inspection facility operations that are cost effective. The establishment of an ABC system for the inspection facilities should help the TDA determine actual cost effectiveness and enable the agency to cut costs where inefficiencies exist.

The Inspection Process. Animals inspected are identified as breeding or slaughter animals. The fee structure differs because the charge for inspecting breeding animals is higher. When trucks carrying livestock arrive at one of the TDA export pens, the driver presents the required paperwork to the pen manager. If the driver's documents are in order, the pen manager authorizes facility workers to unload the truck. All animals (breeding and slaughter), with the exception of poultry, are offloaded from trucks and placed in pens where they rest and are provided water. Poultry is inspected on the truck. The unloading activity consumes about one hour.

In the meantime, the veterinarian who will perform the necessary inspections is summoned. If any of the required paperwork is missing, the load is rejected, and no unloading occurs.

Once the veterinarian arrives, the livestock is moved to an inspection area. If any of the animals do not pass the inspection, the livestock is reloaded, fees are collected, and export into Mexico is denied. If all the animals do pass inspection, they are either immediately reloaded or returned to the initial pen to await a truck. The inspection/reloading process takes about one hour. Once the truck has been reloaded and cleared for export, required fees are collected, documentation is returned to the driver, and the truck is sealed for departure to Mexico.

THE ABC SYSTEM

Step 1: Identification of Costs and Resources. We use four primary resource categories in the TDA Inspection Station ABC System. They are personnel, administration, livestock handling, and pen operations, which correspond to the categories currently used. Personnel costs include the compensation of the pen manager and any additional employees (the Brownsville site has only one employee, the pen manager, while the other sites employ additional workers). Administration costs consist primarily of office supplies, utilities, and rent. Operations costs include costs of maintaining the pens and pen-related supplies. Included in livestock handling are veterinarian fees and costs of equipment required to accommodate the livestock. We include a fifth category for indirect expenditures. This category will include costs incurred at TDA that are allocated to the individual inspection sites (see discussion of indirect cost allocations below).

The costs in each of the above categories for each location are:

	Brownsville	Laredo	Del Rio
Personnel	$22,399	$65,813	$82,796
Administration	10,181	16,324	13,967
Operations	36,395	19,767	13,566
Livestock handling	68,935	3,145	24,086
Indirect expenditures	13,671	13,671	13,671
Total Costs	$151,581	$138,720	$148,086

The indirect expenditures are assigned based upon an allocation of Division Headquarters expenditures. We determine this allocation by dividing the total indirect expenditures incurred at Division Headquarters by the number of export pens (six). Then we multiply this result by 40% because interviews with Division staff indicated that export pen issues consumed roughly 40% of their time. The indirect expense for the year for each of three locations is $13,671, for a total of $41,013.

Step 2: Identification of the Direct and Indirect Costs of Activities. Costs incurred in the primary resource categories are considered direct costs of activities, while the costs of Division indirect expenditures are considered indirect. Specific activities that occur during the inspection process include:

1. Processing transfer paperwork,
2. Completing paperwork and collecting fees,
3. Preparing reports for TDA,
4. Unloading livestock (poultry is not unloaded),
5. Reloading livestock,
6. Cleaning pens after each load,
7. General pen operations,
8. Facility maintenance, and
9. Daily disinfecting of pens.

Step 3: Assignment of Costs to Activities. The time each employee spends in each of the activities identified above has been determined and provides a basis for linking personnel costs to activities. Table 1 presents data regarding time spent for both the pen manager and the additional workers.

Now the four categories of costs can be allocated to one of the nine activities. The fifth category, indirect expenditures of $13,671, is allocated equally to the activities by dividing by nine (the number of activities). Thus, $1,519 is assigned to each activity.

In an ABC system, the linking of costs and activities can be simplified if pools of activities and their related costs are formed. This can occur when the activities are logically related in some way. In order for pooling to occur, activities must first be incurred as part of the same process. Don R. Hansen and Maryanne M. Mowen define a process, for purposes of activity-based costing, as "a series of activities that are linked to perform a specific objective."[5] We identify three processes at the TDA livestock inspection facilities: administration, livestock handling, and pen operations.

Table 1: Employees' Time Allocated

Employee	Duties/ Responsibilities	Estimated Amount Of Time Spent
Manager	Process transfer paperwork	20%
	Perform/account for Financial transactions and collect fees	20%
	Prepare daily, weekly, and monthly reports for TDA	10%
	Unload livestock	25%
	Load livestock	25%
	Total	100%
Workers	Unload livestock	30%
	Load livestock	30%
	Clean pens after each load	10%
	Disinfect pens at the end of each day	10%
	General pen operations	10%
	Maintenance of facilities	10%
	Total	100%

Once processes have been identified, the pooling effort continues by identifying the "level" at which activities occur. This step takes place within each process. Again, according to Hansen and Mowen, activities can occur at one of four levels.[6] Unit-level activities are those that occur repetitively for each unit produced or, in this example, head of livestock inspected. Batch level activities occur for each batch produced or, in this case, inspected. The volume of a particular batch does not affect batch-level activities. Product-level activities are those that support a particular product or product line. Facility-level activities are those that support the overall operations of the entity. In a manufacturing environment, for example, facility-level activities "sustain a factory's general manufacturing processes."[7] At this point, activities and their costs that are part of the same process and occur at the same level can be pooled if they share the same activity driver. Activity drivers cause activities to occur and, thus, cause the costs of activities to be incurred.

Here is a summary of the pooling of activities and their costs:

ACTIVITY	PROCESS	LEVEL	DRIVER
1. Processing transfer paperwork	Admin.	Batch	Number of loads
2. Completing paper-work and collecting fees	Admin.	Batch	Number of loads
3. Preparing reports for TDA	Admin.	Facility	
4. Unloading livestock	Livestock handling	Batch	Number of loads
5. Reloading livestock	Livestock handling	Batch	Number of loads
6. Cleaning pens after each load	Pen operations	Batch	Number of loads
7. General pen operations	Pen operations	Facility	
8. Facility maintenance	Pen operations	Facility	
9. Daily disinfecting of pens	Pen operations	Facility	

Note that no driver has been identified for the activities that occur at the facility level. This is because the output of the facilities—inspected livestock—does not consume facility-level activities. Put another way, facility-level activities occur to sustain the existence of the pens. As a result, the assignment of the costs of facility-level activities to the various types of livestock will be somewhat arbitrary.

Given the data above about activities and their costs, we could logically pool the costs of "processing transfer paperwork" and "completing paperwork and collecting fees." Note that these two activities are part of the same process (administration), occur at the same level (batch), and share the same driver (number of loads). We will call these activities and their costs Pool 1. The costs of Activity 3, preparing reports for TDA, cannot be pooled with others because no other facility-level activities occur in the administration process. The costs of this activity will form Pool 2. Activities 4 and 5, however, can be grouped together because both are part of the livestock handling process, occur at the batch level, and are driven by the number of loads. These activities and their costs will form Pool 3. The costs of Activity 6, cleaning pens after each load, must be kept separate from others because Activity 6 is the only activity that is part of the pen operations process that occurs at the batch level. This activity and its cost will be Pool 4. Finally, the facility-level activities that are a part of the pen operations process (Activities 7-9) will form the final pool, Pool 5.

From the information above, we will express the cost of the activities in Pools 1, 3, and 4 on a per-load basis because the number of loads in each case is the activity driver. The costs of the other two pools (2 and 5) that represent the costs of facility-level activities should be expressed on some logical "per-unit" basis. Recall that there is no measure of activity that drives the activities in these pools and, thus, expressing these costs on a per-unit basis is somewhat arbitrary. One choice would be to express the cost of these pools on a per-head basis or even a per-hour basis. Our decision was to use the latter choice, the number of hours, to express the costs of Pools 2 and 5.

Step 4: Calculation of Unit Costs. The final step in the activity-based costing system for the TDA inspection facilities is to calculate the unit cost. We illustrate these calculations for the Laredo station. Recall that the costs of the Laredo facility totaled $138,720 incurred in the areas of: (1) personnel, (2) administration, (3) operations, (4) livestock handling, and (5) indirect expenditures. These costs, when assigned to activity-based pools, result in the following:

Pool 1	$ 28,842.40
Pool 2	7,975.10
Pool 3	62,418.50
Pool 4	9,871.00
Pool 5	29,613.00
	$138,720.00

To illustrate the allocation of costs to the pools, we assign the costs of $28,842.40 to Pool 1. Recall that Pool 1 is made up of Activities 1 and 2 (processing transfer paperwork and completing paperwork and collecting fees). In Table 1, note that 20% of the pen manager's time is spent in Activity 1, and another 20% is spent is Activity 2. Therefore, 40% of the manager's salary of $31,813 is assigned to Pool 1. Note also from Table 1 that the facility manager is the only individual who performs administrative duties. Of the total time spent performing these functions, 80% is consumed in the first two activities (40% in each). As a result, 80% of the costs of administration at the Laredo site ($16,324) is assigned to Pool 1. There are no costs of either livestock handling or pen operations included in Pool 1. The final cost component of Pool 1 is the share of indirect expenditures allocated to each activity discussed above. The costs of Pool 1 are:

Pool 1 Costs (Include Activities 1 And 2)

Cost Category	Cost Assigned
Personnel manager's salary (.40 * $31,813)	$12,725.20
Administration (.80 * $16,324)	13,059.20
Livestock handling	0.00
Pen operations	0.00
Indirect expenditures (2 * $1,529)	3,058.00
Total	$28,842.40

The costs of the remaining four pools are allocated in a similar fashion. Note that Pool 1 did not include costs of either livestock handling or pen operations. Instead, Pool 3—composed of loading and unloading livestock—includes all of the livestock handling activity. As a result, we assigned 100% of livestock handling costs ($23,145) to Pool 3. In addition, 50% of the manager's salary is assigned to this pool, as is 60% of the workers' compensation (see Table 1). Additional details of costs assignments to pools are omitted.

Once we complete cost assignments to pools, costs per unit of the activity driver can be calculated. For example, the unit cost of Pool 1 is determined by dividing its costs by the number of loads processed during the period (in Laredo the number was 1,612). Thus the cost per load for Pool 1 is $17.89 ($28,842.40/1,612). Recall that the number of loads will also be used as the basis for determining unit costs for Pools 3 and 4. Meanwhile, we use labor hours worked for the period (11,745) as the cost assignment basis for Pools 2 and 5.

Unit Costs In Pools

Pool	Pool Costs	Activity Driver		Cost Per Unit Of Driver	
1	$ 28,842.40	1,612	loads	$17.89	per load
2	7,975.10	11,745	hours	.68	per hour
3	62,418.50	1,612	loads	38.72	per load
4	9,871.00	1,612	loads	6.12	per load
5	29,613.00	11,745	hours	2.52	per hour
Total	$138,720.00				

We made similar cost assignments to pools for the inspection stations at Brownsville and Del Rio. Here are the resulting unit costs (with Laredo figures from above):

Pool	Laredo	Brownsville	Del Rio
1	$17.89/load	$16.42/load	$19.70/load
2	.68/hour	.33/hour	.61/hour
3	38.72/load	26.95/load	14.65/load
4	6.12/load	13.47/load	7.32/load
5	2.52/hour	2.08/hour	2.29/hour

Comparisons of unit costs provide some interesting data. TDA may be curious to learn why Pool 1 per-load costs (those primarily related to processing paperwork) are slightly higher in Del Rio relative to the other two facilities. In addition, they may be intrigued by the low per-hour costs of Pool 2 (costs associated with preparing paperwork for TDA) in Brownsville compared to the other two locations. Another point of interest is Pool 3 per-load costs that are significantly lower in Del Rio (Pool 3 costs are related to livestock handling), particularly when compared to Laredo. Finally, the results indicate much higher per-load costs in Pool 4 (related to cleaning pens after each load) in Brownsville when compared to Laredo and Del Rio. Interestingly, there is not a large variance in costs per hour in Pool 5 (the pen operations costs incurred at the facility level).

ADOPTING ABC

Our illustration will ideally encourage state and local governmental units to examine the possibility of adopting an ABC system. An ABC approach is designed to assist in linking the costs of activities to the activities themselves. At the livestock inspection facilities of the TDA, we identified nine distinct activities. Then, we accounted for the costs via four primary categories and one indirect cost category. Next, we assigned costs to the activities followed by a pooling of activities and their costs, and five pools resulted. Three of the pools contained batch-level activities, while the activities of the others occurred at the facility level. Although the TDA example was replete with unit-level and product level activities, these activities could certainly occur in different environments. Finally, the total costs of each pool were expressed on a per-unit basis according to the appropriate driver for the particular activity. The result is a much more meaningful analysis of costs that should allow the TDA to become much more effective in cost management and cost control.

[1] Jonathan Walters, "A Dollar's Worth of Government," *Governing,* vol. 9, no. 10, July 1996, pp. 45-47.

[2] Katherine Barrett and Richard Greene, "The Rise of Cost Accounting," *Governing,* vol. 13, no. 6, March 2000, p. 80.

[3] Mark D. Abrahams and Mary *Noss Reavely, "Activity-Based Costing: Illustrations from the State of Iowa," Government* Finance Review, vol. 14, no. 2, April 1998, pp. 15-20.

[4] *Ibid.*

[5] Don R. Hansen and Maryanne M. Mowen, *Cost Management: Accounting and Control,* Third Edition, South-Western College Publishing, Mason, Ohio, 2000.

[6] *Ibid.*

[7] *Ibid.*

Chapter 6
Cost Estimation

Cases

6-1 The High-Low Method and Regression Analysis
6-2 The Pump Division (Cost Estimation)
6-3 Laurent Products (Cost Estimation, Activity-Based Costing)
6-4 Custom Photography (Regression Analysis)

Readings

"Applying Overhead: How to Find the Right Bases and Rates"

This article shows an actual application of regression analysis for determining multiple overhead rates using spreadsheet software. The steps and the results are very similar to EXCEL which has regression under TOOLS/ADD-INS/DATA ANALYSIS. The article explains the interpretation of the R-squared and t-values and provides a good discussion of when regression analysis is useful.

Discussion Questions:

1. What is regression analysis used to accomplish in this article?
2. What are the steps to perform a simple regression analysis?
3. What does Table 7 tell you? Which cost driver would you pick for each cost type—maintenance, packaging, materials handling, storage, and production scheduling?

Cases

6-1. The High-Low Method and Regression Analysis

The Brenham General Hospital was approached by Health Food, Inc. (HFI) which specializes in the preparation of meals for institutional patients. HFI stated that it would prepare all inpatient meals to provider specifications and deliver them on time for $11.50 per meal. The hospital was facing a steady decline in bed occupancy and was determined to hold the line on costs wherever possible.

Hospital management did not have a clear idea what the present system of providing meals to patients was costing. Hospital staff gathered the information below, which covered expenses for the dietary department for the past year.

The hospital has 120 beds. It is open year-round and has a 33% percent occupancy rate. Patients are served an average of 2.8 meals per occupancy day.

It was determined that the dietitian provided valuable counseling and advising services. Should the hospital eliminate in house meal preparation, it would want to retain her services. Also, the administration wanted to keep and maintain the kitchen and equipment.

REQUIRED:

1. Using the high-low method and regression analysis, determine the variable and fixed costs of the in-house meal service.
2. Which cost estimation method would you choose and why?
3. Should the hospital administration accept the offer of the outside company? Why or why not?

	Dietitian	Other staff	Food Costs	Maintenance	Patient Equipment	Days
January	$2,875	$ 3,122	$ 9,674	$ 1,401	$ 1,649	1,382
February	$2,875	$ 2,908	$ 9,184	$ 1,322	$ 1,415	1,312
March	$2,875	$ 2,655	$ 8,302	$ 1,322	$ 1,313	1,186
April	$2,875	$ 2,600	$ 7,084	$ 1,288	$ 1,105	1,012
May	$2,875	$ 2,433	$ 6,398	$ 1,200	$ 1,089	914
June	$2,875	$ 2,083	$ 4,338	$ 1,133	$ 1,011	604
July	$2,875	$ 1,809	$ 3,612	$ 1,093	$ 900	516
August	$2,875	$ 2,322	$ 6,275	$ 1,122	$ 1,112	896
September	$2,875	$ 1,434	$ 6,734	$ 1,235	$ 1,103	962
October	$2,875	$ 2,700	$ 9,002	$ 1,302	$ 1,300	1,286
November	$2,875	$ 2,798	$ 8,456	$ 1,300	$ 1,442	1,208
December	$2,875	$ 2,600	$ 7,798	$ 1,322	$ 1,396	1,114
TOTAL	$34,500	$29,464	$86,857	$15,040	$14,835	12,392

6-2. The Pump Division

The Pump Division has one plant dedicated to the design and manufacture of large, highly technical, customized pumps. Typically the contract life (production cycle) is one to three years. Most original equipment (OE) orders are obtained by preparing and submitting a bid proposal from a cost estimate analysis and conducting negotiating sessions with the customer. Sometimes orders are accepted as loss leaders in order to establish a position in the more profitable aftermarket business.

The contracts generally are fixed price. When coupled with the highly technical specifications and the length of the "in process" time, there is a high risk of job cost overruns. Company policy is to record revenue and costs on a completed contract basis, rather than as a percent of completion.

After a major decline in profitability, combined with several unfavorable year-end surprise inventory adjustments, new plant management decided to undertake a review of the operation to identify the key factors that affect inventory control. Management analysis revealed the following:

- The cost estimating function reported to the sales department.
- Final job costs varied significantly from original cost estimates. It was difficult to determine the source of variances until analyses were made upon completion of the jobs.
- The negotiated pricing of a contract was almost always on the basis of "whatever it takes to get the order," particularly when there was excess productive capacity in the industry.
- Progress payments/advanced payments were secured on some contracts, but such payments often were dropped if pricing competition was severe.
- When inflation was at double-digit levels, the company attempted to insert escalation clauses into contracts based on government indexes. However, most often, this resulted in fixed-price contracts with some estimate of inflation included.
- During the audit at the end of each year, a lower-of-cost-or-market analysis was made on major jobs in process. It was this exercise that revealed unfavorable inventory adjustments in recent years. Two examples are shown below:

(In Thousands)	Job 1	Job 2
Original cost Estimate	$2,113	$1,800
Costs Incurred to Date:		
Manufacturing	2,100	—
Engineering	373	100
Estimate to Complete	367	2,500
Total Current Estimate	2,840	2,600
Lower-of-cost-or-market: Contract Sales Price	2,520	2,000
Less 10% Allowance for Normal Profit Margin	(252)	(200)
Inventory Value	2,268	1,800
Inventory Reserve Adjustment (loss)	$ (572)	$ (800)

On job 2, the engineering department determined that the pump would not meet specifications in accordance with the original cost estimate and re-engineered the pump. This led to an increased estimate before the job entered the manufacturing stage.

REQUIRED:

1. What courses of action might be appropriate for the plant manager and his controller relating to (a) estimating costs, and (b) application of the lower of cost or market rule?
2. What is the significance of progress payments/advanced payments and escalation clauses on the performance of the operation?

(IMA, 1986)

6-3. Laurent Products

Laurent Products is a manufacturer of plastic packaging products with plants located throughout Europe and customers worldwide. "There is no doubt that the need to continue to grow sales is an important corporate objective and one which we need to always have in mind," remarked Arnoud Baynard, managing director. "Not only is this important in terms of continuing to increase sales revenue overall but it is an essential part of our commitment for next year's budget. Resisting group pressure and allowing ourselves this time to test the market for other new segments has brought some order into this phase of our development. The segment penetration achieved so far and the opportunity to build on this most successful initiative augers well for the future. Thank you, George, for a comprehensive summary of the market result to date" concluded Arnoud. "It seems as though this initiative is one which will help us meet out short and longer-term objectives." Arnoud Baynard's summary concerned a strategy overview provided by George St. Marc, marketing director of the company.

MARKETING STRATEGY

During the past ten years Laurent Products has successfully developed a line of packaging materials and a unique bagging system which present an important opportunity to increase the productivity of checkout counters in grocery stores. The plastic bags manufactured by Laurent are produced in several sizes, different plastic film colors, and may have attractive multi-color printed designs on one or both sides to meet the specification of a particular grocery store. The company concentrated its efforts in selling to the top twenty grocery market chains in Europe. By limiting its marketing efforts to a relatively few, very large multi-outlet grocery chains (which have centralized purchasing groups), the company achieved low marketing and selling costs but high market penetration. Last year the company reached a market share of 65% in the large grocery chain market and, in turn, relatively large customer order sizes. Two market segments are evident in the large grocery chain market. In the first (called the value added segment) customers buy the company's product primarily because of its advantage in reducing operating costs at checkout counters. The advantages provided by the Laurent bagging system include the lower cost of bags and labor costs of running the checkout counter as well as improved customer service. Frequently, the store operations personnel in this segment are active in making the buying decision. The second segment is referred to as being price sensitive as the customers purchase these products primarily on the basis of price. For these customers, purchasing managers are the key decision-makers in the buying decision.

RECENT COMPETITION

Laurent's success in the grocery chain market has attracted an increasing number of competitors into the market. While the company had been very successful in bringing out a series of new product types with innovative labor-saving features for the grocery stores, the competitors have eventually been able to develop quite similar products. The result has been increased competition with a substantial reduction in Laurent's prices (dropping 26% last year), and a major decline in the firms' profit margin. The size of the price sensitive segment is growing rapidly while the value added market segment is shrinking in size. The company faces an increasingly competitive market situation characterized by significant excess producer capacity.

WHOLESALE MARKET INITIATIVE

As a result of the increased competition in the grocery chain market, George has proposed to begin to a focus on the small independent grocery stores who purchase bags from large wholesale distributors. The potential sales for this wholesaler segment is about the same size as the grocery chain market (20 billion bags per year versus 25 billion bags per year), but includes a much larger number of independent store customers. At this time less than 15% of the bags sold in the wholesaler market are made of plastic. The independent grocery stores differ from the large grocery chains in that they purchase their grocery bags from wholesalers and distributors. Compared to the grocery chains, there are many more independent grocery store outlets widely dispersed over a large geographical area. The pilot marketing studies run last year by Laurent indicate that the customer order sizes for the wholesaler segment tend to be relatively small, and that the number of different product variations (in terms for example of print color, film color, and print type) tend to be relatively large in comparison with the grocery chain market. These studies also indicate that prices (and corresponding profit margins) are much higher than in the price sensitive segment currently served by the company.

MANUFACTURING

To support domestic and export sales, the company has located a number of plants throughout Europe to best support the geographical spread of the supermarket and hypermarket outlets of its various customers. "In the early years," explained Marcel Ray, manufacturing director, "capacity had, by necessity, always chased demand. The rapid growth in sales during the past few years and the need to make major decisions concerning new plant locations and process investments had understandably contributed to this capacity following the demand situation. However, with sales starting to level off this problem of capacity has now corrected itself."

Investments in manufacturing had been to support two principal objectives; to increase capacity and to reduce costs. The cost reduction initiatives principally concerned material costs and reduced processing times. "Current initiatives," explained Marcel "are continuing these themes. Our capacity uplifts will take the form of equipment similar to our existing machines. Over the years we have deliberately chosen to invest in machines which are similar to existing equipment in order to capitalize on the fact that the process is relatively simple and that products can, with relatively few exceptions, be processed on any machine in the plant. The only major restriction is the number of colors which a machine can accommodate on a single pass. Future investment proposals now being considered are based on this rationale."

In order to make best use of total capacity at all sites, customer orders are collated at the head office site in Lyon. They are then allocated to plants to take account of current plant loading, available capacity, customer lead times, and transport distances between the plant and a customer's required delivery location. As a result, forward loading on a plant is only two or, at most three days ahead. Plants then schedule these orders into their production processes in order to meet customer call-offs and individual equipment loading rules.

Once the printing details are agreed with a customer, a plate is produced and checked. In line with a call-off schedule, the plates are allocated to machines. Color changes (where necessary) are also part of the setup details. Table 1 provides an actual schedule of orders for four different bagging lines which is representative of the operations in the Paris Plant (and also for the company's other plants).

CONCLUDING REMARKS

In reviewing the proposed marketing initiatives regarding the wholesaler market, Arnoud Baynard, commented, "Since sales in our traditional markets are leveling off, the new marketing initiative appears to be an important step in giving us a fresh impetus to sales volume growth. We have now reached a point in our company where we do not have to endure capacity shortage problems. In fact, with the drop in sales last year, the company currently has excess capacity with which to pursue the wholesaler market. So, our main concern is to improve the decline in the profit performance that has occurred during the past year, and the new marketing initiatives should help to restore the profit margins and hence to secure this necessary, overall improvement."

REQUIRED

1. Discuss briefly Laurent's competitive position and strategy.
2. What are the implications of the marketing and manufacturing initiatives undertaken by Laurent?
3. How does Laurent's strategy deal effectively with global competition in its business. How should it?
4. Using the data in Table 1 and appropriate methods of analysis such as regression, analyze the effect of order size and product variety on the productivity and cost structure of the Paris plant.

TABLE 1

Machine Number	Prod. Order Quantity	Print Type Complexity	Per unit Downtime & Setup	Per Unit Runtime	Total Setup & Downtime	Total Runtime	Total Variable Cost/Unit
2	480	1	0.0023	0.0423	1.10	20.30	7.04
2	489	1	0.0001	0.0434	0.07	21.20	6.99
2	480	1	0.0054	0.0419	2.60	20.10	6.99
4	180	1	0.0039	0.0400	0.70	7.20	6.97
4	2160	2	0.0022	0.0355	4.70	76.60	6.94
4	1377	2	0.0023	0.0405	3.10	55.70	6.95
4	120	2	0.0042	0.0400	0.50	4.80	6.97
4	540	2	0.0026	0.0413	1.40	22.30	6.97
4	360	2	0.0142	0.0411	5.10	14.80	6.98
4	1080	2	0.0111	0.0376	12.00	40.60	7.01
4	300	2	0.0037	0.0430	1.10	12.90	7.03
4	2400	2	0.0046	0.0345	11.00	82.90	7.05
4	81	2	0.0457	0.0407	3.70	3.30	7.09
8	360	1	0.0022	0.0425	0.80	15.30	7.82
8	120	1	0.0017	0.0433	0.20	5.20	7.83
8	120	1	0.0067	0.0417	0.80	5.00	8.17
8	60	1	0.0083	0.0417	0.50	2.50	8.83
8	240	1	0.0079	0.0425	1.90	10.20	7.94
8	60	1	0.0050	0.0467	0.30	2.80	7.97
8	240	1	0.0008	0.0583	0.20	14.00	8.2
8	120	1	0.0183	0.0433	2.20	5.20	8.09
8	60	1	0.0183	0.0433	1.10	2.60	7.93
8	480	1	0.0106	0.0435	5.10	20.90	8.23
8	240	2	0.0054	0.0413	1.30	9.90	7.91
8	537	2	0.0047	0.0423	2.50	22.70	7.87
8	420	2	0.0060	0.0421	2.50	17.70	7.89
8	1182	2	0.0150	0.0416	17.70	49.20	7.89
8	60	2	0.0550	0.0483	3.30	2.90	8.83
8	180	2	0.0122	0.0422	2.20	7.60	7.9
8	60	2	0.0417	0.0400	2.50	2.40	7.9
8	240	2	0.0067	0.0429	1.60	10.30	7.86
8	60	2	0.0083	0.0417	0.50	2.50	7.93
8	41	2	0.0293	0.0463	1.20	1.90	7.96
8	60	2	0.0417	0.0467	2.50	2.80	8
8	120	2	0.0117	0.0467	1.40	5.60	8.08
8	60	2	0.0617	0.0417	3.70	2.50	7.9
8	60	2	0.0433	0.0433	2.60	2.60	8
8	360	2	0.0108	0.0428	3.90	15.40	8.01
8	120	2	0.0200	0.0467	2.40	5.60	7.97
8	180	2	0.0144	0.0494	2.60	8.90	8.15
8	60	2	0.0233	0.0433	1.40	2.60	8.27
8	60	2	0.0400	0.0400	2.40	2.40	8.55
8	60	2	0.0417	0.0433	2.50	2.60	8.66
8	60	2	0.0467	0.0467	2.80	2.80	8.17
8	60	4	0.0483	0.0417	2.90	2.50	8.06
8	60	4	0.0150	0.0417	0.90	2.50	8.55
8	60	4	0.0583	0.0417	3.50	2.50	8.11
8	120	4	0.0167	0.0450	2.00	5.40	8.17
8	60	4	0.0567	0.0400	3.40	2.40	8.06
13	120	1	0.0050	0.0392	0.60	4.70	6.98
13	717	1	0.0043	0.0411	3.10	29.50	7
13	1500	1	0.0063	0.0427	9.50	64.10	7.08
13	2475	1	0.0091	0.0335	22.50	83.00	7.2
13	240	1	0.0100	0.0475	2.40	11.40	7.25
13	882	2	0.0178	0.0302	15.70	26.60	6.47
13	1677	2	0.0111	0.0361	18.60	60.50	7.04
13	243	2	0.0021	0.0457	0.50	11.10	7.05

6-4 Regression Analysis

Custom Photography is a small company that provides photography services primarily for medium to large size local businesses. Most of the work is special assignments involving professional models, displays, and sets. At the end of 2001, Janice Glass, the owner of Custom Photography is interested in predicting the average hourly payroll cost of the professional models and others who work in the set-up and design of the photo sessions in 2002. In order to do this, she has taken the payroll costs for each of the prior 20 quarters and the approximate number of hours devoted to these photo sessions during the quarter.

The independent variable in this application is the number of hours for the sessions and the dependent variable is the payroll expense.

QU/YR	Hours	Payroll Expense
1/1997	145	5,122
2	90	3,011
3	25	1,203
4	175	5,188
1/1998	112	3,877
2	267	8,712
3	212	7,355
4	132	4,123
1/1999	289	9,938
2	235	7,327
3	156	5,592
4	277	9,387
1/2000	302	10,993
2	72	2,761
3	88	2,766
4	212	8,246
1/2001	155	5,499
2	222	7,729
3	116	3,892
4	250	8,473
Projected Data for hours:		
1/2002	188	?
2	233	?
3	145	?
4	298	?

REQUIRED:

1. Develop a regression analysis to predict payroll costs, using Excel or equivalent regression software and the first 20 quarters of data. Evaluate the precision and reliability of the regression.
2. Predict payroll expense for each quarter of 2002.

Readings

APPLYING OVERHEAD: HOW TO FIND THE RIGHT BASES AND RATES

Determine the relationship between overhead costs and various cost drivers with the help of regression analysis.

By Adel M. Novin

Direct labor no longer may be the most effective base for applying factory overhead costs to various jobs and products. With today's highly automated systems, labor-related costs constitute only a small portion of total manufacturing costs, and overhead costs now correlate more with factors such as machine hours and material quantities. Accordingly, many companies are beginning to identify application bases that better reflect the causes of overhead costs in their unique manufacturing environments.

Selection of proper application bases also has received a boost from the recent growth in activity-based costing (ABC), ABC applies accumulated costs for each activity to products and jobs using a separate base for each activity. Thus, it is crucial to select the right bases (cost drivers) for applying the costs of various activities to products and jobs.

SEARCHING FOR A PROPER BASE

Theoretically, the factory overhead cost application base should be a principal cost driver—an activity (or activities) that causes factory overhead costs to be incurred. In other words, there should be a strong cause-and-effect relationship between the factory overhead costs incurred and the base chosen for their application. Selecting the proper base requires knowledge of the relationships between the overhead costs and various cost drivers such as machine hours, direct labor hours, direct labor costs, space occupied, pounds handled, invoices processed, number of component parts, number of setups, units produced, and material costs or material quantities.

Using an objective technique, regression analysis, rather than experience or observation of activities can be helpful in ascertaining the relationship between the overhead costs and various cost drivers. Regression analysis has not been explored fully in practice, possibly due to its computational complexities coupled with a lack of easily accessible computer software. With the widespread use of spreadsheet programs, however, regression analysis now can be performed rather easily. The regression analysis described below was done using a computer spreadsheet.

Regression analysis is one of the few quantitative techniques available for: (1) determining and analyzing the extent of the relationship between overhead costs and various cost drivers and (2) estimating the linear or curvilinear relationship between overhead costs and cost drivers. One of the values provided by regression analysis, the coefficient of determination or R Squared, measures the extent of the relationship between the two variables. More specifically, the value of R Squared indicates the percentage of variation in the dependent variable (overhead costs in this case) that is explained by variation in the independent variable (the cost driver). The value of R Squared is always between zero and 100%. The closer its value is to 100%, the stronger the relationship between the two variables.

Regression analysis can help us investigate the strength of the relationship between the overhead cost and various cost drivers. In simple terms, the cost driver that receives an R-Squared value closest to 100% will be the most accurate predictor of overhead costs. The following section will illustrate this concept.

To find the proper application base, the first step is to identify the various cost drivers that might explain changes in overhead costs. Suppose that in searching for an application base for overhead costs, we have found three possible cost drivers—direct labor hours, machine hours, and number of production setups.

Regression analysis requires actual data on selected variables for several periods. Suppose we have data from 12 consecutive months (with outliers excluded) on overhead costs, direct labor hours, machine hours, and number of production setups, as shown in Table 1.

With three possible cost drivers, three different regression analyses should be performed. Of course, a different output-range should be selected for each variable.

Table 2 presents the regression output obtained for the three regression analyses. According to the R-Squared values, machine hours explain about 77% of changes in variable overhead costs, while the number of set-ups and direct labor hours explain 39% and 29%, respectively. Thus, it appears that the most proper base for application of overhead costs in our example is machine hours because it has the strongest relationship with overhead costs.

CONSTRUCTION OF A SINGLE OVERHEAD RATE

Referring to the regression results in Table 2, "Constant" represents an estimate of the fixed portion of the overhead cost, while "X Coefficient(s)" represents an estimate of the variable rate of the overhead costs. For example, based on the regression results for machine hours, the estimated linear relationship between monthly overhead costs (OH) and machine hours (MH) can be presented by the following simple regression line: OH = $72,794 + $74.72 MH, where $72,794 is an estimate of total monthly fixed overhead costs and $74.72 is the rate for the application of variable overhead costs (i.e., $74.72 per machine hour).

We then come to the question of how to assign the fixed portion of overhead costs to products and jobs. Often, a separate base that reflects the demands made by products and jobs on a firm's fixed resources is used to apply fixed costs to products and jobs. This base may be determined by engineering methods such as time and motion studies. In this case, there would be two rates based on two different bases for the application of overhead costs, one for fixed overhead and one for variable overhead costs.

TABLE 1
DATA FOR REGRESSION ANALYSIS

	A	B	C	D
1	FOH	DIR LABOR	MACHINE	NO. OF
2	COSTS	HOURS	HOURS	SETUPS
3	155,000	985	1,060	200
4	160,000	1,068	1,080	225
5	170,000	1,095	1,100	250
6	165,000	1,105	1,200	202
7	185,000	1,200	1,600	210
8	135,000	1,160	1,100	150
9	145,000	1,145	1,080	165
10	150,000	1,025	1,090	180
11	180,000	1,115	1,300	204
12	175,000	1,136	1,400	206
13	190,000	1,185	1,500	208
14	200,000	1,220	1,700	212

TABLE 2 REGRESSION OUTPUT		
REGRESSION RESULTS FOR OVERHEAD COSTS WITH DL HOURS		
Regression Output:		
Constant		919.02
Std Err of Y Est		17,267.60
R Squared		0.29
No. of Observations		12
Degrees of Freedom		10
X Coefficient(s)	148.74	
Std Err of Coef.	74.35	
REGRESSION RESULTS FOR OVERHEAD COSTS WITH MACHINE HOURS		
Regression Output:		
Constant		72,793.81
Std Err of Y Est		9,799.08
R Squared		0.77
No. of Observations		12
Degrees of Freedom		10
X Coefficient(s)	74.72	
Std Err of Coef.	12.91	
REGRESSION RESULTS FOR OVERHEAD COSTS WITH NUMBER OF SETUPS		
Regression Output:		
Constant		74,033.14
Std Err of Y Est		15,909.72
R Squared		0.39
No. of Observations		12
Degrees of Freedom		10
X Coefficient(s)	465.00	
Std Err of Coef.	182.47	

CONSTRUCTION OF MULTIPLE OVERHEAD RATES

In a complex manufacturing environment, variable overhead costs may be driven by several equally important factors. Under such circumstances, the use of more than one base for the application of variable overhead costs to products and jobs results in a more accurate cost estimate. For example, the cost of one activity, material handling, may be applied to products based upon both the number of material requisitions and the number of parts per material requisition. To accommodate the use of more than one independent variable, we would need to perform a multiple regression. Thus, we can construct more than one overhead rate.

Continuing our prior example, suppose that we want to apply overhead costs based on the two cost drivers with the strongest relationship to overhead cost—machine hours and number of setups. To perform multiple regression analysis, follow the same steps as for performance of simple regression, except that the "X-Range" will consist of the range of observations for both machine hours and number of setups.

Table 3 presents the results for the multiple regression. "Constant" represents an estimate of the fixed overhead cost, while "X Coefficients" represent an estimate of the variable rates of the overhead costs. For example, the estimated relationship between the overhead costs (OH) and the two driving factors, machine hours (MH) and number of setups (NS), can be expressed by the following multiple regression line: OH = $19,796.43 + $65.44 MH + $322.21 NS, where $19,796.43 is an estimate of the total monthly fixed overhead costs, and $65.44 and $322.21 are the estimated variable overhead costs per machine hour and per setup, respectively. The value of R Squared for the multiple regression line is 95%, which is greater than that of the simple regression line based solely on machine hours (77%). This fact implies that the application of variable overhead costs based on both machine hours and number of setups would result in more accurate cost estimates.

TABLE 3 MULTIPLE REGRESSION RESULTS FOR OVERHEAD COSTS WITH MACHINE HOURS AND NUMBER OF SETUPS			
Regression Output:			
Constant			19,796.43
Std Err of Y Est			4,951.11
R Squared			0.95
No. of Observations			12
Degrees of Freedom			9
X Coefficient(s)	65.44	322.21	
Std Err of Coef.	6.74	58.66	

Here, again, total fixed overhead costs may be applied to jobs and products either using a different base determined by engineering methods such as time and motion studies or using the same base as for variable overhead (machine hours and number of setups). Use of a separate base for the application of fixed costs would result in a total of three overhead rates, one for fixed overhead and two for variable overheads.

It is important to remember that the variable overhead rates computed by regression analysis (the "X Coefficients") are estimates derived from our 12 observations. The reliability of the estimated variable overhead rates can and should be determined by computing the t-test value for each rate. The t-test value equals the "X Coefficients" over the "Std Err of Coef." As a general rule, if the absolute value of the t-test for any variable rate is greater than two, then the estimated overhead rate is considered highly reliable. Referring to Table 3, for example, the value of the t-test for the variable overhead based on machine hours is about 5.8 (74.72/12.91), which tells us that the rate can be relied upon. The overhead sites determined from regression analysis, after adjusting for expected future inflation, would be usable as long as no major change in the cost structure and manufacturing process has occurred.

RATES FOR ACTIVITY-BASED COSTING

For more accurate product costing, firms are beginning to use activity-based costing for computing overhead costs. under this system, accumulated costs for each activity are applied to products and jobs using a separate base for each activity. in a manner similar to that described above, regression analysis can be used to investigate the strength of the relationship between various activities and cost drivers in order to determine the proper base(s) and rate(s) for applying the cost of each activity to products and jobs.

We also may use regression analysis to classify a large number of activities into a few groups (cost pools) based on common bases. Suppose that through use of simple regression analysis, we have computed the R-Squared values for the pairs of activities and cost drivers shown in Table 4. Based on the R-Squared values, we may group the five activities into two cost pools. It appears that the principal cause of the packaging, materials handling and storage activities costs is pounds of materials. a few groups (cost pools) based on common bases. Suppose that through use of simple regression analysis, we have computed the R-Squared values for the pairs of activities and cost drivers shown in Thus, the cost pool consisting of the accumulated costs of these three activities can be applied to products and jobs based on number of pounds of materials used. Similarly, the accumulated costs of maintenance and production scheduling, which have a high correlation with machine hours, can be applied to products and jobs based on machine hours. In this way, all costs included in each cost pool will have the same cause-and-effect relationship with the chosen cost allocation base.

As business becomes increasingly more competitive, decision makers are demanding more accurate cost figures from cost accounting systems. For accurate costing, it is crucial that factory overhead and activity costs be applied to various products and jobs using bases that reflect principal causes of the overhead costs. Regression analysis has proved to be a practical, effective, and objective method for selecting proper cost application bases.

In addition to its usefulness for determining proper application bases, regression analysis is a practical method for developing single or multiple overhead rates for the application of overhead costs to products and jobs. With the widespread use of spreadsheet programs, regression analysis can be performed easily.

Note: The article was edited with the author's permission to remove references to Lotus 1-2-3 and replace them with generic spreadsheet references.

TABLE 4
R-SQUARED VALUES FOR VARIOUS PAIRS OF ACTIVITIES AND COST DRIVERS

	Maintenance	Packaging	Materials Handling	Storage	Production Scheduling
Machine Hours	.85	.46	.68	.45	.82
Pounds of Material	.38	.88	.90	.75	.43
Labor Hours	.30	.28	.38	.22	.43

Chapter 7
Cost-Volume-Profit Analysis

Cases

7-1 Cost-Volume-Profit Analysis and Strategy
7-2 Cost-Volume-Profit Analysis and Cost Estimation
7-3 Cost-Volume-Profit Analysis and Strategy
7-4 Cost-Volume-Profit Analysis and Strategy: The ALLTEL Pavilion
7-5 Sensitivity Analysis; Regression Analysis

Readings

"Tools for Dealing with Uncertainty"

This article explains how to use simulation methods within a spreadsheet program such as Excel to perform sensitivity analysis for a given decision context. The available spreadsheet simulation software systems include the programs Crystal Ball and @Risk, among others. These software systems allow the user to analyze the effect of uncertainty on the potential outcomes of a decision. These tools can be applied directly to CVP analysis. The tools allow the user to see the potential effect on the breakeven level or total profit of potential variations in the key uncertain factors in the analysis. The uncertain factors affecting breakeven might be the unknown level of unit variable cost, price or fixed cost. Also, in determining total profit, the unknown level of demand might be a key uncertain factor.

Exercise: Use a spreadsheet simulation tool such as Crystal Ball or @Risk to analyze the uncertain factors in given case situation. Cases 7-1,2 and 3 could be used for this exercise.

Cases

7-1. Cost-Volume-Profit Analysis and Strategy

Mr. Carter is the manager of Simmons Farm and Seed Company, a wholesaler of fertilizer, seed, and other farm supplies. The company has been successful in recent years primarily because of great customer service—flexible credit terms, customized orders (quantities, seed mix, etc), and on-time delivery, among others. Global Agricultural Products, Inc., Simmons' parent corporation, has informed Mr. Carter that his budgeted net income for 19x7 will be $120,000. The budget was based on data for the prior year and Mr. Carter's belief that there would be no significant changes in revenues and expenses for the coming period.

After the determination of the budget, Carter received notice from Simmons' principal shipping agent that it was about to increase its rates by 10%. This carrier handles 90% of Simmons' total shipping volume. Paying the increased rate will result in failure to meet the budgeted income level, and Mr. Carter is understandably reluctant to allow that to happen. He is considering two alternatives. First, it is possible to use another carrier whose rates are 5% less than the old carrier's original rate. The old carrier, however, is a subsidiary of a major customer; shifting to a new carrier will almost certainly result in loss of that customer and sales amounting to $70,000.

Assume that prior to the recent rate increase, the shipping costs of the principal carrier and the other carriers were the same, and that costs of the other carriers are not expected to change.

As a second alternative, Simmons can purchase its own trucks thereby reducing its shipping costs to 85% of the original rate. The new trucks would have an expected life of 10 years, no salvage value and would be depreciated on a straight line basis. Related fixed costs excluding depreciation would be $2,000. Assume that if Simmons purchases the trucks, Simmons will replace the principal shipper and the other shippers.

Following are data from the prior year:

Sales	$1,500,000
Variable costs (excluding shipping)	1,095,000
Shipping costs	135,000
Fixed costs	150,000

REQUIRED:

1. Using cost-volume-profit analysis and the data provided, determine the maximum amount that Mr. Carter can pay for the trucks and still expect to attain budgeted net income.
2. At what price for the truck would Mr. Carter be indifferent between purchasing the new trucks and using a new carrier?
3. Mr. Carter has decided to use a new carrier, but now is worried its apparent lack of reliability may adversely affect sales volume. Determine the dollar amount of sales that Simmons can lose because of lack of reliability before any benefit from switching carriers is lost completely.
4. Describe what you think is the competitive strategy of Simmons Farm and Seed Company. What should be the strategy? How would the use of a new carrier affect the strategy?
5. Can Mr. Carter use value chain analysis to improve the profits of Simmons Farm and Seed Company? If so, explain how briefly.

7-2. Cost-Volume-Profit Analysis and Cost Estimation

The following requirement is based on information in the Atlantic City Casino case, case 2-33 at the end of Chapter 2. Re-read the case and complete the requirements below.

REQUIRED:

1. Using the data provided in the case, build a cost estimation model to predict net income based on total revenues. Then, use this model to determine an estimate of the industry-wide breakeven point in sales revenue. Evaluate the reliability and precision of the estimation method you have chosen.
2. Develop a cost estimation model to predict casino revenues based on square feet of casino floor space. Use this model to determine the expected full-year revenue for casino number nine. Evaluate the precision and reliability of the method you have chosen.
3. Repeat part (2) above, using number of rooms to predict room revenues, and number of restaurants to predict food and beverage revenues for the full year for casino number nine.

7-3. Cost-Volume-Profit Analysis and Strategy

Melford Hospital operates a general hospital, but rents space and beds to separately-owned entities rendering specialized services such as pediatrics and psychiatric care. Melford charges each separate entity for common services such as patients' meals and laundry, and for administrative services such as billings and collections. Space and bed rentals are fixed charges for the year, based on bed capacity rented to each entity.

Melford charged the following costs to pediatrics for the year ended June 30, 2002:

	Patient Days (variable)	Bed Capacity (fixed)
Dietary	$ 600,000	—
Janitorial	—	$ 70,000
Laundry	300,000	—
Laboratory	450,000	—
Pharmacy	350,000	—
Repairs and maintenance	—	30,000
General and administrative	—	1,300,000
Rent	—	1,500,000
Billings and collections	300,000	—
Total	$2,000,000	$2,900,000

During the year ended June 30, 2002, pediatrics charged each patient an average of $300 per day, had a capacity of 60 beds, and had revenue of $6,000,000 for 365 days. In addition, pediatrics directly employed the following personnel:

	Annual Salaries
Supervising nurses	$25,000
Nurses	20,000
Aides	9,000

Melford has the following minimum departmental personnel requirements based on total annual patients days:

Annual Patient Days	Aides	Nurses	Supervising Nurses
Up to 21,900	20	10	4
21,900 to 26,000	26	13	4
26,001 to 29,200	30	15	4

These staffing levels represent full-time equivalents. Pediatrics always employs only the minimum number of required full-time personnel. Salaries of supervising nurses, nurses, and aides are therefor fixed within ranges of annual patient days.

Pediatrics operated at 100% capacity on 90 days during the year ended June 30, 2002. It is estimated that during these 90 days the demand exceeded 20 patients more than capacity. Melford has an additional 20 beds available for rent for the year ending June 30, 2003. Such additional rental would increase pediatrics' fixed charges based on bed capacity.

REQUIRED:

1. What is the strategic role of CVP analysis for the pediatrics unit of Melford hospital?
2. Determine the minimum number of patient days required for pediatrics to breakeven for the year ending June 30, 2003, if the additional 20 beds are not rented. Patient demand is unknown, but assume that revenue per patient day, cost per patient day, cost per bed, and salary rates will remain the same as for the year ended June 30, 2002.
3. Assume that patient demand, revenue, revenue per patient day, cost per patient day, cost per bed, and salary rates for the year ending June 30, 2003 remain the same as for the year ended June 30, 2002. Prepare a schedule of increase in revenue and increase in costs for the year ending June 30, 2003, in order to determine the net increase or decrease in earnings from the additional 20 beds if pediatrics rents this extra capacity from Melford.

7-4. Cost Volume Profit Analysis and Strategy: The ALLTEL Pavilion

The ALLTEL Pavilion in Raleigh, North Carolina is an outdoor amphitheater that provides live concerts to the public from April through October each year. The seven-month season usually hosts an average of 40 concerts with 12 year-round staff planning and managing each season. SFX Entertainment Inc. operates the pavilion. SFX is the largest diversified promoter, producer, and venue operator for live entertainment events in the United States. Upon completion of pending acquisitions, it will have 71 venues either directly owned or operated under lease or exclusive booking arrangements in 29 of the top 50 U.S. markets, including 14 amphitheaters in nine of top 10 markets.

History/Development

The ALLTEL pavilion was built in 1991 by the City of Raleigh and Pace Entertainment Company of Houston, Texas. The management of the pavilion was contracted to Pace Entertainment and Cellar Door Inc. of Raleigh, NC. Hardee's Food Systems, Inc. of Rocky Mount, NC, the original sponsor of the amphitheater, paid an annual fee to carry their name and logo on all signs and ads regarding the amphitheater. On February 3, 1999 the title sponsor for the amphitheater became ALLTEL Corp.

The demand for the outdoor facility came about because the rapidly growing city of Raleigh lacked a major entertainment complex. So, in the mid to late 80's and early 90's Pace Entertainment and the City of Raleigh came to an agreement to build the facility. The City of Raleigh would own the land while Pace Entertainment would assume sole operations of the facility and Cellar Door would do the booking for all the concerts.

In 1998, SFX Entertainment Inc. acquired Pace Entertainment Inc. The amphitheater facility and its employees became part of SFX Entertainment Inc. Also, in 1999 SFX Entertainment Inc. acquired Cellar Door Inc. and merged with Clear Channel Communications Inc., the largest owner of radio stations in the country. This move brought together both worlds of the entertainment business. While the company has diverse holdings, the philosophy of SFX is "*One Company, One Mission.*" Many companies that are now owned by SFX were at one time hard-nosed bitter rivals in the concert promoting business. These companies now maintain good working relationships within SFX.

Personnel

When the marketing department plans a promotion for an up-coming event, it coordinates with sales to see if there is a conflict in sponsorship. Marketing also coordinates with operations to effectively manage the activities in preparation for and on show days. Finally, the budgets of each department (sales, marketing, and operations) are reviewed by the accounting department and head of finance for the overall financial management of the project.

Bringing Concerts to Reality

A concert becomes reality in many steps. First, a group or performer with an interest in performing at ALLTEL will discuss with Cellar Door, Inc the possibility of performing at the pavilion, and look at the open dates. When agreement is reached, Cellar Door and the booking agent for the performer sign a contract. A time is specified for gate openings and once the gate is opened the show is underway. The job of the staff during a concert is to make sure every patron of the ALLTEL Pavilion has a pleasant experience and that the mission of the company is clearly seen by everyone that "a concert...*it's better live.*" After a show, Clean Sweep Inc. of Raleigh handles the clean up.

Key Business Issues

Marketing has an important role in the success of ALLTEL Pavilion, but marketing expenditures are carefully watched. For every show, the marketing budget is limited to $20,000. For many shows it is difficult to stay within the budget, since the Pavilion serves a 5-market region consisting of Raleigh-Durham, Fayetteville, Wilmington, Greensboro, and the Carolina Coast. Most of the marketing budget is spent on advertising with radio, TV, and print media in the designated regions. Prior to developing advertising plans, the marketing staff analyzes ticket sales geographically over the five-market region. It is important to know the demographics of the five regions and compare them with the profile for each performer. The more ALLTEL Pavilion can know about the fans, the more they know about where to spend the $20,000.

While the different advertising media were viewed initially as cost-based strategic business units, SFX now considers them to be profit-based SBUs and develops measures of performance and profitability for each advertising media, by region. This type of analysis is important to the ALLTEL Pavilion because increased ticket sales, through effective advertising, not only affects ticket revenues but also revenue from parking, merchandise, and concessions. It is also important because of the increased cost of advertising. The advertising rates in the Raleigh-Durham region are comparable to the rates in Washington, D.C. The rates are up two hundred percent over the last five years while the budgets per show are only up fifteen percent over this time.

Other areas where costs have increased dramatically include the cost of the performing artist. The average cost for an artist is approximately $160,000. Some of the artists are paid on a fixed-fee basis, and others are paid on a per capita basis. Generally, the most popular artists seek a per capita contract because they are confident of a high level of attendance. In contrast, the artist paid on fixed base is guaranteed the same fee whether 100 or 20,000 people attend (the capacity of the Pavilion is approximately 20,000 attendance). The fixed-fee shows often have a projected attendance under 10,000. These artists do not have the "draw' of the other artists. In these types of shows, the role of marketing is especially important, as the Pavilion must work hard to attract attendance for the artist. As noted above, lower ticket sales also mean less money spent on parking, concessions, and merchandise, so effective marketing is critical. One method the Pavilion uses in addition to advertising is to distribute "comp" tickets (comp tickets are free tickets distributed throughout the community) to build interest in the Pavilion that will later be realized in paying customers, and because the comp customers will spend on parking, concessions, and merchandise.

This cost of the performing artists grows annually, so that it is very important for the ALLTEL Pavilion to reduce non-artist costs. There are a number of operating costs at ALLTEL Pavilion, including expenses for parking, security, concessions, and merchandise. Also, there are a number of other methods used to make the concerts more profitable. For example, the parking service passes out flyers for upcoming events. Also, the pavilion trades "comp" tickets for online spots in the radio industry and gives local businesses tickets in exchange for advertising on their premises.

Funding and Flash Report

The sources of funding for the Pavilion are ticket revenues , concession (food) revenues, merchandising revenues, parking revenues, sponsorship revenues, and other. Exhibit A is a mock flash report for an example show, the KFBS Allstars. A flash report is a projection of what a concert will cost and what revenues will be received. The guaranteed talent costs ($160,635) is the amount the KFBS Allstars are guaranteed for the show. Attendance is the number of projected **paying** ticket holders, while the "drop count" is total attendance, both for paid tickets and comp tickets. The drop count is usually projected to be about 125% of paying attendance. The Flash Report then projects total revenues including parking, food, and merchandise based on per capita (drop count) rates. Also, other revenues include per capita facility charges and service charges paid by the performer. The parking, food concession, and merchandise operations are outsourced to other service providers, so the direct costs for parking, merchandise and concessions are determined based on contracts with the service providers which include both a percentage (10%) of applicable (parking, merchandise or concession) revenues and a fixed fee. Operating expenses include an allocation of the total of fixed production and operations costs for the season, the advertising expenses for the KFBS Allstars event, and other variable expenses. These are then added to the direct costs for concessions, merchandise, parking, and insurance to determine total operating expenses.

Required:

1) How would you describe the competitive strategy of the ALLTEL Pavilion? What do you think it should be?
2) For the show illustrated in Exhibit A, the KFBS Allstars, how many tickets must ALLTEL Pavilion sell to break even?
3) For which type of performer (fixed fee or per capita) is breakeven analysis particularly important, and why?
   Which type of performer is preferred by the Pavilion, and why?
4) Explain how sensitivity analysis could be used to better understand the uncertainty surrounding the KFBS Allstars event.

Exhibit A – Flash Report for The KFBS Allstars

ARTIST NAME	The KFBS Allstars
ACTIVITY/EVENT NUMBER	10310001
EVENT MONTH	7
EVENT DATE	7/31/00
Projected Sales (Number of Seats)	
A Seats	2,778
B Seats	2,845
C Seats	1,747
D Seats	881
TOTAL Number of Seats	8,251
Projected Ticket Price (net of 3% tax)	
A Seats	$36.29
B Seats	$22.22
C Seats	$11.31
D Seats	$ 4.92
PROJECTED NET AFTER TAX ADMISSIONS	$182,479
AVG TIX PRICE NET OF TAX PER PAYING PATRON	$22.12
TALENT %	88.03%
GUARANTEE/TALENT COSTS	$160,635
NUMBER OF PERFORMANCES	1
DROP COUNT (includes comp tickets)	10,349
Other Ticket-Related Revenue	
FACILITY CHARGE	$24,010
Per-capita	$2.91
S/C REBATES	$16,172
Per-capita	$1.96
REVENUE FROM TICKETING	$222,673
Per-capita	$26.99
ANCILLARY REVENUES	
PARKING	$19,767
Per-capita	$1.91
FOOD CONCESSION	$79,273
Per-capita	$7.66
MERCHANDISE	$36,428
Per-capita	$3.52
RENTALS	$0.00
REVENUE FROM ANCILLARIES	$135,468
Per-capita	$13.09
TOTAL REVENUE	$358,141
Per-capita	$34.61
Other Direct Costs	
PARKING CONTRACT	$4,448
CONCESSION CONTRACT	$43,356
MERCHANDISE CONTRACT	$17,826
TOTAL DIRECT COSTS	$226,265
Per-capita	$21.86
PERCENT OF SALES	63.2%

Flash Report (continued)

TOTAL REVENUE (from above)	$358,141
TOTAL DIRECT COSTS (from above)	$226,265
GROSS PROFIT	$131,876

OPERATING EXPENSES:	
TOTAL PRODUCTION EXPENSE	$15,506
TOTAL OPERATIONS EXPENSE	$14,991
TOTAL OTHER VAR. EXPENSE	$14,323
TOTAL ADVERTISING EXPENSE	$20,030
TOTAL OPERATING EXP	$64,850
Per-capita	$6.27
PERCENT OF SALES	18.1%
OPERATING INCOME	**$67,026**
Per-capita	$6.48
PERCENT OF SALES	18.7%

DETAIL: OTHER CONCERT VARIABLE EXPENSE (per person in attendance):

Insurance Expense per person	$0.17
COGS – Concession per person	$0.35
COGS – Merchandise Inventory per person	$1.12
COGS – Parking per person	$0.08
Other Variable Concert Expense per person	$0.02
TOTAL OTHER VARIABLE EXPENSE	$14,323

7-5. Sensitivity Analysis; Regression Analysis

Fast Shop, Inc is a chain of 10 convenience stores located in and around Houston, Texas. Selected operating data for the 10 stores for the most recent month is shown below. All but two of Fast Shop's stores sell gasoline as well as convenience items, primarily food, beverage, and household products. Because of zoning and other restrictions, the other stores sell only convenience items. Jim Sacco, the chief financial officer for Fast Shop, plans to utilize multiple regression analysis to determine which stores are most effective in generating sales, given differences in size (square feet) among the stores, differences in advertising and promotion costs for the stores, and whether or not the store sells gasoline. Jim knows that stores which sell gasoline typically have better than average sales because gasoline sales bring in sales for other convenience items.

Jim also knows that if regression analysis can be used to develop a sensitivity analysis of the effect of advertising and store size on sales. If he prepares a multiple regression analysis in which all the numerical variables are transformed by their natural logarithm, then the coefficients for each independent variable in the resulting regression equation will represent the percentage effect on sales for a given percentage change in the independent variable.

Selected Operating Information for the 10 Locations of Fast Shop Inc

Store	**Sales**	**Advertising**	**Square Feet**	**Gas Sales**
1	$ 56,034	$ 5,540	2,200	No
2	23,045	3,310	1,200	Yes
3	89,337	8,837	2,800	No
4	66,073	11,200	2,000	No
5	18,993	1,879	1,500	No
6	64,926	6,648	2,300	No
7	28,773	3,756	1,500	No
8	46,294	5,899	1,800	No
9	73,546	6,899	2,400	Yes
10	36,968	5,100	1,600	No
	$ 503,989	$ 59,068		

REQUIRED:

1. Using regression analysis, determine which store(s) seem to be operating below their potential, given advertising expenses, gasoline sales, and size?
2. Using regression analysis and log transforms, determine the sensitivity of sales to advertising and store size.

Readings

TOOLS FOR DEALING WITH UNCERTAINTY

Sophisticated spreadsheet software incorporating probability functions can help you forecast more accurately.

BY DAVID R. FORDHAM, CMA, AND S. BROOKS MARSHALL

Aside from the proverbial death and taxes, there is little in life that is certain. As management accountants, we recognize that one of our most crucial uncertainties involves capital investments. Why, then, are so many of us still using analysis tools designed for fixed numbers?

Let's take a simple example. Your company is considering a $1 million capital investment. The project is expected to return 12% per year, with the annual profits reinvested annually. What will be your final compounded return at the end of 20 years?

If you are like most management accountants, you will use the traditional compounding formula (multiplying your initial investment times one plus the rate of return raised to the 20th power). This time-honored analysis approach tells you that your final compounded return should be $9,646,293. But is this the best answer?

Unfortunately, it is not—at least for most capital investment projects. The compounding formula works well for investments in which the annual rate of return is fixed. But this is not the situation with most capital investments. While the initial outlay may be a fairly

Figure 1. FORMULA ESTIMATE

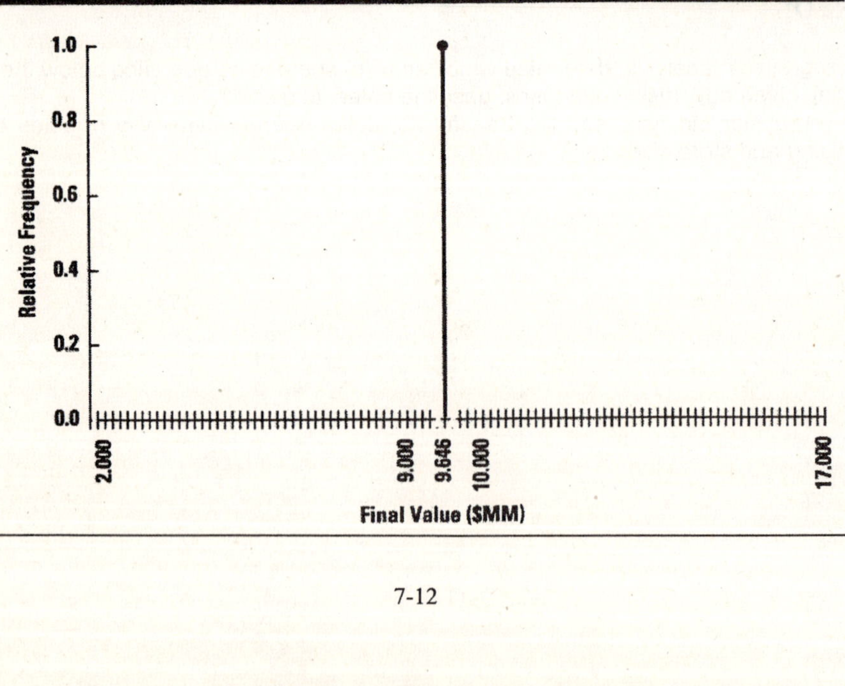

firm number, the annual rate of return most likely will vary from year to year. Thus, this project might yield a 25% (or higher) return in a good year and a 0% return (or even a loss) in another year. Even a relatively safe capital investment (say, a market-rate financial instrument) can involve variable rates of return.

But the compounding formula operates as though the rate of return is exactly 12% for all 20 years, with no variability. Because the formula has no way of recognizing the uncertainty in the annual rates of return, it may not be providing the best answer.

The most popular capital budgeting tools (the compounding formula, the internal rate of return, and net present value calculations) are simple to use and can be handled with little more than a pocket calculator. But they all suffer from a major drawback: They provide a single-number answer by assuming that their input is a set of fixed or known numbers, with no provision for variability.

A POPULAR WAY OF DEALING WITH UNCERTAINTY: SENSITIVITY ANALYSIS

One way of providing for uncertainty is to rerun the calculations several times using different fixed values. Today's computerized spreadsheets make it easy to play "what-if"" games. By changing the numbers and re-performing the calculations, we can generate various possible outcomes. Comparing these different outcomes generally provides a better analysis than merely looking at a single point estimate.

Continuing our example above, a modern analyst would use the compounding formula to arrive at the $9,646,293 figure and also to provide alternative possibilities from the what-if analyses, showing the effect of changing the estimated rate of return from 12% to, say, 10% or 14%. By reporting multiple possible final values, the analyst is providing more and better information than by reporting a single point estimate. The name for this technique is "sensitivity analysis."

This approach provides a much more realistic means of analyzing uncertain situations than simply using the compounding formula alone, but it still uses analysis tools that operate on only one set of numbers at a time. The fact remains that no matter how many times we rerun the calculations, the formula still operates as though the rate of return is constant throughout all 20 years of the project's life. Ideally, our analysis should employ a tool that incorporates the possible changes from year to year in the annual rate of return. Even more important, we need to know the probability of earning different amounts from our project, not just a list of some possible amounts.

A BETTER WAY: PROBABILITY DISTRIBUTION

Statisticians tell us that the law of large numbers applies to most situations involving uncertainty and

Figure 2. NORMAL DISTRIBUTION

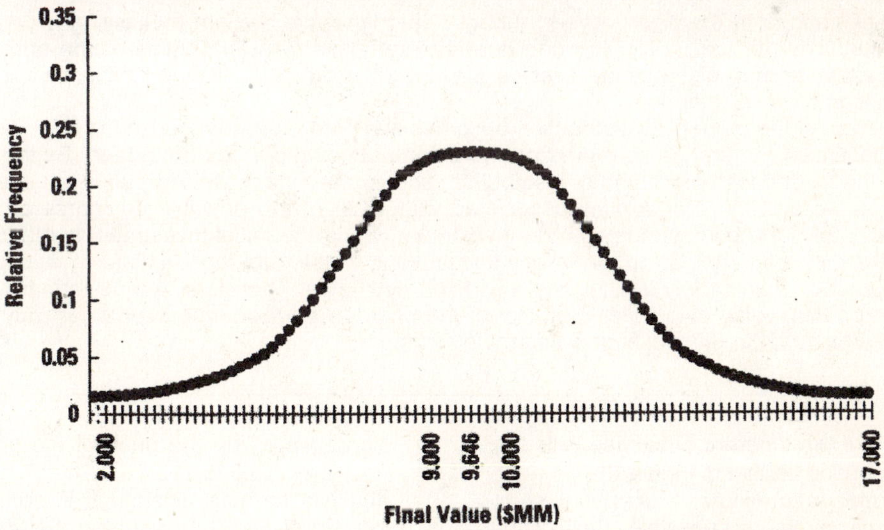

that variable numbers tend to cluster around a central value or mean. Financial research has shown that annual rates of return on most modern investments do indeed form a "normal distribution" around a mean. Values close to the mean occur with greater frequency than values farther away from the mean. If you can establish a reasonable estimate of the mean and have some idea of the range of possible realistic values, you generally can get by with handling your uncertainty as a probability distribution.

Traditional analysis tools (the compounding formula in our example) yield a single point estimate of the project's final value (see Figure 1). If we were to use the formula by itself, our analysis would show that the project will return exactly $9,646,293. Most management accountants, however, recognize the uncertainty and report several different possible outcomes, assuming that the most likely final values will center around $9,646,293. Values far away from this figure will be unlikely, while values close to it will be more likely. The analyst even may illustrate the relative likelihood of the different outcomes with such a probability distribution as that in Figure 2.

Figure 2 is superior to Figure 1 in that it shows relative likelihoods of many possible final values ranging from a very unlikely $2 million figure all the way up to an equally unlikely $17 million. The most likely values, however, are close to $9,646,293. And most analysts assume that the probability curve is symmetric, as shown in Figure 2. In other words, they assume the chances of earning slightly less than the projected amount are about the same as the chances of earning slightly more than the projected amount.

But is this the case? Assuming the rate of return does average 12% over the life of the project, are the chances of slightly underperforming the estimate the same as the chances of slightly outperforming it? It might surprise you to learn that Figure 3 is actually a more accurate illustration of the likely final values of our project!

SURPRISES FROM MODERN ANALYSIS TOOLS

Figure 3 reveals some startling new information about our project. First, the most probable final value (represented by the peak of the probability curve) is not the $9,646,293 predicted by the traditional analysis formula! Rather, it is somewhat less. From looking at Figure 3, you see that it is more likely that

Some Surprising Statistics

When using analysis models that approximate reality surprising results sometimes emerge. Take the probability distribution of our compound investment's final value. Most people, including many financial analysts, would assume that if the annual rate of return varies in a normal (and symmetric) fashion across the 20-year life of the project, then the possible final values also should vary in a symmetric pattern. This makes intuitive sense. But it isn't what actually happens.

Consider closely the value of the investment at the end of the first year. The exact rate of return during that year is unknown, but it will vary around a 12% expected value. If we expect the rate of return to vary in a normal fashion, at the end of the first year we will have a range of possible final values that will be centered around $1.12 million (for our $1 million original investment). This probability distribution is symmetric because it is the product of a fixed amount (the original investment) multiplied by a normal probability distribution (the rate of return).

Most things change in the second year, though. This time, we are not multiplying a constant by a normal distribution. We are multiplying one normal distribution (the final value at the end of the first year) by another normal distribution. It yields a skewed, asymmetric distribution known in statistical circles as a log-normal distribution.

The skewness of the probability distribution becomes even more pronounced in the third year, and the symmetry continues to degrade as more and more compounding periods are added. By the 20th year, you have the noticeably asymmetric distribution shown in Figure 3. The unusual shape of the distribution curve and the probabilities associated with each of the possible outcomes of the project derive directly from the compounding of the investment. Once the initial investment is made, all future values are unknown figures. Using probability distributions to illustrate these unknown values is a more accurate approach than simply treating them as fixed estimates. Therefore, the asymmetric probability of the project's final value is a better predictor of the project's performance than a perfectly symmetric curve fitted around the traditional financial formula's output.

our project's final value will be approximately $9 million rather than the approximately $9.6 million reported by the traditional analysis approach.

Management accountants and financial analysts who have for years relied on the formulas are astounded to see this increase in the likelihood of underperforming the formula estimate. But even more surprising is the fact that the probability distribution is not symmetric. For example, the chances of the project yielding half a million dollars less than the $9,646,293 are actually much greater (perhaps two or three times as great) than the chances of earning half a million dollars more than that amount. In other words, while the chance of slightly underperforming the formula's prediction has increased, the chance of outperforming the formula's prediction by the same amount has gone down quite dramatically. Also, the probability of "losing one's shirt" has diminished somewhat, while the probability of making much more than the formula estimate has increased.

What causes these surprising results? The answer lies in the fact that the rate of return can vary from year to year. Each year's earnings are dependent not only on that single year's rate of return, but also on all previous years' rates, because the project involves compounding reinvestment. Thus, if you assume that the rate of return averages 12% annually over the course of the 20-year project, and you assume that the changes occur in accordance with the law of large numbers (specifically, in accordance with a normal probability distribution from year to year), you still come up with the skewed probability curve for the final value of the project shown in Figure 3 because of the changing rates of return. (For an explanation of this phenomenon, see the sidebar, "Some Surprising Statistics.")

SOPHISTICATED TOOLS, BUT EASY TO USE

Probability curves such as Figure 3 can give a much more accurate picture of the likely outcome of projects under uncertainty. These analyses can be generated by a little-used analysis tool that is included in most of today's modern spreadsheet software. This tool enables us to create mathematical models that more closely approximate real-life situations involving uncertainty.

As our capital budgeting problem involves an uncertain annual rate of return that varies from year to year, we must develop an analysis model with a rate of return that varies from year to year. In addition, we need to analyze many different combinations of these varying annual rates of return.

Until a few years ago, creating such a model required extensive computer programming, weeks of effort, and significant time on a large mainframe or minicomputer. Today, though, with the recent advances in personal computers, including larger memory capacities, faster and more powerful

Figure 3. MONTE CARLO DISTRIBUTION

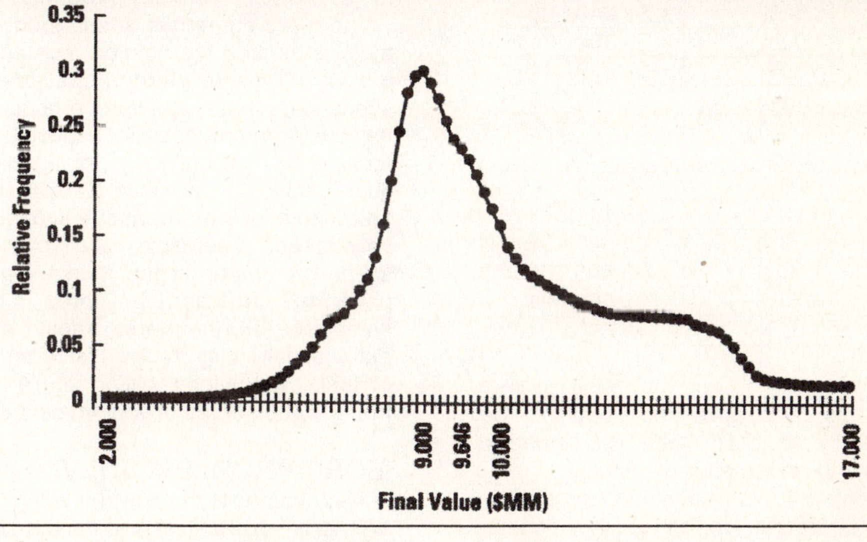

Figure 4

Year	Rate of Return	Final Value
1	12.00%	$1,120,000
2	12.00%	$1,254,400
3	12.00%	$1,404,928
4	12.00%	$1,573,519
5	12.00%	$1,762,342
6	12.00%	$1,973,823
7	12.00%	$2,210,681
8	12.00%	$2,475,963
9	12.00%	$2,773,079
10	12.00%	$3,105,848
11	12.00%	$3,478,550
12	12.00%	$3,895,976
13	12.00%	$4,363,493
14	12.00%	$4,887,112
15	12.00%	$5,473,566
16	12.00%	$6,130,394
17	12.00%	$6,866,041
18	12.00%	$7,689,966
19	12.00%	$8,612,762
20	12.00%	$9,646,293

Figure 5

Year	Rate of Return	Final Value
1	11.30%	$1,113,000
2	12.10%	$1,247,673
3	13.30%	$1,413,614
4	14.10%	$1,612,933
5	9.00%	$1,758,097
6	10.00%	$1,933,907
7	13.00%	$2,185,315
8	15.50%	$2,524,038
9	16.50%	$2,940,505
10	14.00%	$3,352,175
11	14.50%	$3,838,241
12	8.00%	$4,145,300
13	11.00%	$4,601,283
14	7.00%	$4,923,373
15	10.30%	$5,430,480
16	13.10%	$6,141,873
17	11.50%	$6,848,188
18	9.50%	$7,498,766
19	14.20%	$8,563,591
20	12.05%	$9,595,504

numerical processors, and advanced software, we now have the ability to build such mathematical models on our desktops in a matter of minutes.

The tools necessary to construct probability distributions can be found on all of the popular Windows-based spread-sheets—Lotus 1-2-3, Excel, Supercalc, and Quattro-Pro. Specific instructions vary from package to package, but they are contained in the On-Line Help features. Look for Help topics involving random number generators, probability distributions, and statistical tools.

To analyze our sample problem properly, we begin by constructing a spreadsheet showing how the project's returns will be reinvested (Figure 4). But instead of the 12% annual rate of return for all 20 years, we want to substitute a variable rate of return, one that is expected to average 12% over the 20 years.

Because we assume the rates of return will average 12% and might vary between 0% and 25%, we can say that, in any one year, the rate of return will come from a normal distribution with a mean of 12% and a standard deviation of about 6%. We use the computer's random number generator to draw 20 values from a distribution with a mean of 12 and a standard deviation of 6. Then we incorporate these values as the assumed rate of return for each of our 20 years. This approach gives us one possible outcome of our capital project. In other words, if it just so happens that the annual rates of return come out as shown in Figure 5, then our project's final value will be $9,595,504.[1]

The particular combination of annual rates of return shown in Figure 5 is only one of many possible combinations. We also must look at others. In fact, we need to duplicate the scenario many times (a technique known as Monte Carlo analysis) to represent the many different combinations of annual rates of return. By constructing hundreds, or even thousands, of possible combinations and then displaying a histogram of the final outcomes, we begin to get a feel for the likely performance of our project.

There are numerous add-in products on the market that enhance the major spreadsheet packages, making it easy to perform thousands of Monte Carlo scenarios. These software products are surprisingly easy to learn and operate, especially for users already familiar with the Windows point-and-click system. One such package, known as @RISK, is able to perform 1,000 iterations of the above scenario with only a few keystrokes. Therefore, the calculation of 2,000 scenarios of our capital budgeting problem can be performed in less than three minutes on a 486 computer. Furthermore, most of the packages automatically display the histogram upon completion of their calculations, giving you an instant picture of the likely outcomes of your investment.

MORE PROBLEM SOLVING

This same technique (drawing numbers from a probability distribution and constructing a histogram of the final outcomes) can be used to simulate the uncertainty of discount rates for net present value analysis. It also can be used to simulate the uncertainty surrounding cash flow amounts, future

Good News, Bad News: What the Picture Tells Us

Figure 3 is a much more accurate portrayal of our project's expected performance. Most important, it presents some new information that might make a difference in the decision as to whether to accept or reject the project. Let's take a close look at exactly what this new tool is telling us that we didn't know before. To make the comparison, we will use the compounding formula's predicted value ($9,646,293) as a base because it is the figure that most analysts would have presented to management.

First, as mentioned in the text, the probability of the project's value coming in slightly under the base is much higher than the probability of hitting the base or of hitting any other possible value. Some managers may consider it misleading to say that the project likely will return $9,646,293 when, in fact, the most probable return is less than this amount.

More significant, the chance of slightly outperforming the base by a given amount is much less than the probability of slightly underperforming the base by the same amount. Again, managers may consider it misleading to quote the $9,646,293 figure when the chances of making a million less than this figure may be two or three times the likelihood of making a million more than the figure.

The bad news, then, is that the project probably will slightly underperform the base estimate and probably will not slightly overperform the base estimate. But wait! There is some good news, too.

Look at the ends of the curve. The possibility of losing your shirt on the investment has almost disappeared compared with the chance of making a killing. In other words, the possibility of coming out far under the base prediction is extremely low, compared with the chance of outperforming the base by the same large amount. Managers who don't mind the risk of slightly underperforming the base prediction but who want to avoid an extremely low final value—especially if it means a chance at yielding an extremely high final value—might be more inclined to accept the project if they had access to this probability distribution. In short, decision makers find the probability distribution analysis a much richer source of information than the traditional sensitivity analysis using common capital budgeting techniques.

revenues, and expenses. Yet another use for it might involve modeling possible changes in tax rates or inflation rates—or almost any uncertain figure. All that is needed is some idea (or assumption) about the possible behavior of the uncertain value, such as its expected average and likely variability. Often the assumption can be simply the one that would have been used in the formula analysis, coupled with the estimated rate of variability over time.

By constructing a model that resembles the real situation more closely, you can see that the likely outcome of a capital project may be very different from what you normally would expect, based on the traditional analysis output. The likelihood of doing very poorly, fairly well, or extremely well on a given project may surprise you and other decision makers. A realistic probability distribution requires additional information, which cannot be provided by the traditional analysis tools. This information even may affect management's decision in some situations (see the sidebar, "Good News, Bad News.") Regardless, it always is better to provide management with the best information possible.

THERE IS STILL UNCERTAINTY

Of course, any time we try to predict the future, we are dealing with unknown information. Modem analysis tools are only as good as the input with which they are provided. We will continue to encounter problems trying to estimate future returns' means and their variability. But for a given set of input information, these sophisticated tools can greatly expand the richness of information provided as output.

Remember: The traditional capital budgeting tools may be providing your decision makers with misleading figures regarding the likely performance of your investment projects. A much better tool would be one that enables you to construct a mathematical model that depicts the actual situation more accurately, including year-to-year variations. With the advent of powerful spreadsheet software incorporating statistical probability functions, it now is feasible to perform analyses that portray the real situation more accurately. By using these more sophisticated models, you can do a much better job of forecasting the likelihood of possible outcomes, which can lead to your making better decisions for your company.

Chapter 8
Strategy and the Master Budget

Cases

8-1 Emerson Electric company

Readings

"How to Set Up a Budgeting and Planning System"

This article demonstrates the setting up of a budgeting and planning system for Penn Fuel Gas Inc., a public utility holding company that provides natural gas storage and transportation services. It stresses the need to review the chart of accounts, account classification and the reporting system of the firm. The discussion includes factors to be considered in the budgeting process and moves to update its current accounting information system.

Discussion Questions:

1. What motivates PFG to install a budgeting and planning system?
2. Why is flexibility very important for PFG's budgeting system to be effective?
3. What problems that the budget manager at PFG had to resolve before setting up a budgeting system? Do you find these problems unique to PFG?
4. Why the authors suggest that a thorough review of the firm's chart of accounts, account classifications, and reporting systems is a must before initiating a budgeting and planning system?
5. Describe budgetary games that people play. What are the reasons for PFG to experience minimal budgetary gamesmanship?

"Strategic Budgeting: A Case Study and Proposed Framework"

Applying the Critical Chain technique proposed by Eliyahu Goldratt to budget preparations. All department budgets are reduced by 50%. The savings are grouped in a Group Budget Buffer. Department heads can request additional funds from the buffer but the request would be discussed openly with other department heads. This reduction method allows costs to be cut where the cuts will not negatively impact performance of the service departments. At the same time, it identifies areas of bloat where cost reduction can be significant increases communication between departments, lowers overall spending levels, and assures output integrity.

Discussion Questions:

1. What is the lawnmower method of cost reduction?
2. What will be the size of a division's total budgeted amount after 4-year if the division includes 10% slack each year? after 10-year?
3. What is the strategic budgeting model?
4. What are the strengths of strategic budgeting?

"How Challenging Should Profit Budget Targets Be?"

The article argues for using highly achievable budget targets, and explains six key advantages for doing so, including the favorable effect on the managers' commitment and confidence. The article also explains some of the risks of using highly achievable budget targets. The concept of risk is illustrated with probability distributions and with a relatively low-risk environment having a probability distribution with lower variance.

Discussion Questions:

1. Explain each of the six advantages of highly achievable budget targets mentioned in the article. Can you think of any in addition?
2. What are the risks of highly achievable budget targets mentioned in the article? Can you think of any in addition?

Cases

8-1 Emerson Electric Company

Emerson Electric Company was founded in 1890 as a manufacturer of motors and fans. In 1993, Emerson marked its thirty-sixth consecutive year of improved earnings per share. On $8.2 billion sales, the diversified St. Louis based company reported a 1993 profit of $708 million. In addition, the company had $2 billion in unconsolidated sales in international joint ventures. It manufactures a broad range of electric, electromechanical, and electronic products for industry and consumers. Brand names include Fisher Control Valves, Skil, Dremel, and Craftsman power tools, In-Sink-Erator waste disposals, Copeland compressors, Rosemount instruments, Automatic Switch valves, and U.S. Electric Motors in the power transmission market. Since 1956, Emerson's annual return to shareholders averaged 18 percent. Sales, earnings per share, and dividends per share grew at a compound rate of 9 percent, 8 percent, and 7 percent, respectively, over the 1983-93 period. Inter-national sales have grown to 40 percent of total sales and present a growth area for the company.

Emerson is a major domestic electrical manufacturer. Its U.S. based competitors include companies such as General Electric, Westinghouse, and Honeywell. Its foreign competitors include companies such as Siemens and Hitachi. Emerson has had the narrowest focus as a broadly diversified manufacturing company among its primary competitors. Other manufacturers, such as GE and Westinghouse, are diversified into financial services, broadcasting, aircraft engines, plastics, furniture, etc. Emerson follows a growth-through-acquisition strategy, but no one acquisition has been very large. There are periodic divestitures as management seeks the appropriate or complementary mix of products.

In 1973, Charles F. Knight was elected Chief Executive Officer, after joining the company the prior year. Under Knight's leadership, Emerson analyzed historical records as well as data on a set of "peer companies" the investment community valued highly over time. From this analysis, top management concluded that Emerson needed to achieve growth and strong financial results on a consistent basis reflecting constant improvements. The company set growth rate targets based on revenue growth above and beyond economy-driven expectations.

During the 1980s, the company maintained a very conservative balance sheet rather than using leverage. Top management felt that this was a competitive weapon because it permitted flexibility to borrow when an attractive business investment became available. In the economic downtown of the 1990s, Emerson, unlike a number of companies, was not burdened by heavy debt and interest payments.

ORGANIZATION

Historically, Emerson was organized into 40 decentralized divisions consisting of separate product lines. A president ran each division. The goal was to be number one or two in the market for each product line. The company resisted forming groups, sectors, or other combinations of divisions as found in other large companies until 1990, when Emerson organized its divisions into eight business segments: fractional horsepower electric motors; industrial motors; tools; industrial machinery and components; components for heating and air conditioning; process control equipment; appliance components; and electronics and computer support products and systems. This new structure exploits common distribution channels, organizational capabilities, and technologies.

The Office of the Chief Executive (OCE), which consists of the Chief Executive Officer, the President, two Vice Chairmen, seven business leaders, and three other corporate officers, directs management of the company. The OCE meets 10 to 12 times a year to review division performance; and discuss issues facing individual divisions or the corporation as a whole.

Each division also has a board of directors, which consists of a member of the OCE who serves as chairman, the division president, and the division's key managers. The division boards meet monthly to review and monitor performance.

Corporate staff in 1993 consisted of 311 people, the same number as in 1975, when the company was one-sixth its current size in terms of sales. Staff is kept to a minimum because top management believes that a large staff creates more work for the divisions. To encourage open communication and interaction among all levels of employees, Emerson does not publish an organization chart.

BEST-COST PRODUCER STRATEGY

In the early 1980s, the company was not globally competitive in all of its major product lines, and recognized that its quality levels in some product areas did not match levels available from some non-U.S. competitors, particularly the Japanese. Therefore, top management changed its twenty-year strategy of being the "low cost producer" to being the "best cost producer." There were six elements to this strategy:

1. Commitment to total quality and customer satisfaction.
2. Knowledge of the competition and the basis on which they compete.
3. Focused manufacturing strategy, competing on process as well as product design.
4. Effective employee communications and involvement.
5. Formalized cost-reduction programs, in good times and bad.
6. Commitment to support the strategy through capital expenditures.

Since the 1950s, the low cost producer strategy required the divisions to set cost-reduction goals at every level and required plant personnel to identify specific actions to achieve those goals. Improvements of 6 percent to 7 percent a year, in terms of cost of goods sold, were targeted. With the best-cost producer strategy, Emerson now aims for higher levels of cost reduction through its planning process. For example, machine tools were used to streamline a process to save labor costs, and design changes saved five ounces of aluminum per unit. Sometimes a competitor's products were disassembled and studied for cost improvements. Products and cost structures of competitors were used to assess Emerson's performance. Factors such as regional labor rates and freight costs were also included in the analyses. For example, before investing millions of dollars in a new plant to make circular saws, top management wanted to know what competitors, domestic and global, were planning.

In the period 1983 to 1993, capital investments of $1.8 billion were made to improve process technology, increase productivity, gain product leadership, and achieve critical mass in support of the best-cost producer strategy. Division and plant management report every quarter on progress against detailed cost reduction targets.

Quality was an important factor in Emerson's best-cost producer strategy. Improvements were such that Emerson was counting defects in parts per million. For example, in one electric motor line, employees consistently reached less than 100 rejects per one million motors.

PLANNING PROCESS

CEO Knight made the following comments on Emerson's planning process:

> Once we fix our goals, we do not consider it acceptable to miss them. These targets drive our strategy and determine what we have to do: the kinds of businesses we are in, how we organize and manage them, and how we pay management. At Emerson this means planning. In the process of planning, we focus on specific opportunities that will meet our criteria for growth and returns and create value for our stockholders. In other words, we "identify business investment opportunities."[1]

Emerson's fiscal year starts October 1. To initiate the planning process, top management sets sales growth and return on total capital targets for the divisions. Each fiscal year, from November to July, the CEO and several corporate officers meet with the management of each division at a one or two day division planning conference. Knight spends 60 percent of his time at these division-planning conferences. The meetings are designed to be confrontational in order to challenge assumptions and conventional thinking. Top management wants the division to stretch to reach its goals. It also wants to review the detailed actions that division management believes will lead to improved results.

Prior to its division planning conference, the division president submits four standard exhibits to top management. Developing these four exhibits requires months of teamwork and discipline among each division's operating managers.

The "Value Measurement Chart" compares the division's actual performance five years ago (1989), the current year's expected results (1994), and the long-range forecast for the fifth year (1999). See Exhibit 1 (Note: the numbers in all exhibits are disguised). The Value Measurement Chart contains the type, amount, and growth rates of capital investment,

---

[1] Knight, C. F., "Emerson Electric: Consistent Profits, Consistently," *Harvard Business Review,* January-February 1992, p. 59.

net operating profit after tax (NOPAT), return on average operating capital, and "economic profit" (NOPAT less a capital charge based on the cost of capital). To create shareholder value, the goal is to determine the extent to which a division's return on total capital (ROTC) exceeds Emerson's cost of capital. Use of the cost of capital rate (Line 3000 on Exhibit 1) is required in all division plans.

The next two exhibits contain sales data. The "Sales Gap Chart" and "Sales Gap Line Chart" show the current year's expected sales (1994) and five-year sales projections (1995-1999). See Exhibits 2 and 3. These are based on an analysis of sources of growth, the market's natural growth rate, market penetration, price changes, new products, product line extensions, and international growth. The "gap" represents the difference between the division's long-range sales forecast and top management's target rate for sales growth (Line 19 in Exhibit 2). Exhibit 2 shows the five-year sources of sales growth in Column H. These are illustrated in the Sales Gap Line Chart in Exhibit 3 for one of the divisions for the 1995-99 periods. The division president must explain what specific steps are being taken to close the gap.

The "5-Back by 5-Forward P&L in Exhibit 4 contrasts detailed division data for the current year (1994) with five prior years of historical data and five years of forecast data (1995-99). This comprises 11 years of profit statements including sales; cost of sales; selling, general and administrative expenses; interest; taxes; and return on total capital (ROTC). This statement is used to detect trends. Division management must be prepared with actions to reverse unfavorable movements or trends.

Beyond the review and discussion of the four required exhibits, the division planning conference belongs to the division president. Top management listens to division management's view of customers, markets, plans for new products, analyses of competition, and reviews of cost reductions, quality, capacity, productivity, inventory levels, and compensation. Any resulting changes in the division plan must be submitted for approval by top management. The logic and underlying assumptions of the plan are challenged so that managers who are confident of their strategies can defend their proposals. CEO Knight views the test of a good planning conference is whether it results in manager actions that significantly impact the business. According to Knight:

> Since operating managers carry out the planning, we effectively establish ownership and eliminate the artificial distinction between strategic and operating decisions. Managers on the line do not-and must never-delegate the understanding of the business. To develop a plan, operating managers work together for months. They often tell me that the greatest value of the planning cycle lies in the teamwork and discipline that the preparation phase requires.[2]

Late in the fiscal year, the division president and appropriate division staff meet with top management to present a detailed forecast for the coming year and conduct a financial review of the current year's actual performance versus forecast. The forecast is expected to match the data in the plan resulting from the division planning conference, but top management also requests contingency plans for several lower levels of activity. A thorough set of actions to protect profitability at lower sales levels is presented. These are known as contingency plans. Changes to the division's forecast are not likely unless significant changes occurred in the environment or in the underlying assumptions. Top management must approve changes in the forecast. It is not Emerson's practice to aggregate financial reports for planning and controlling profits between the division and corporation as a whole.

In August, the information generated for and during the division planning conferences and financial reviews is consolidated and reviewed at corporate headquarters by top management. The objective is to examine the total data and prepare for a corporate wide planning conference. In September, before the start of the next fiscal year, top management and top officers of each division attend an annual corporate planning conference. At this meeting, top management presents the corporate and division forecasts for the next year as well as the strategic plan for the next five years. The conference is viewed as a vehicle for communication. There is open and frank discussion of success stories, missed opportunities, and future challenges.

REPORTING

At its meetings the CEO uses the President's Operating Report (POR) to review division performance. Each division president submits the POR (see Exhibit 5), on a monthly basis. This reporting system is different from budget reports found in other companies.

---

[2] Knight, p. 63.

First, the POR contains three columns of data for the "current year." The third column of data (Forecast) reflects the plan agreed to by the division president and top corporate management at the beginning of the fiscal year. The forecast data is not changed during the fiscal year and the division president's performance is measured using the fiscal year's forecast. The first column reports the actual results for completed quarters or expected amounts for the current and future quarters. The division president may update expected quarterly results each month. The second column reports the "prior expected" results so that each month's updated expectations can be compared with data submitted in the prior month's POR. Updated expectations are also compared with the forecast data.

Second, in addition to current year data, the POR lists the prior year's actual results. This permits a comparison with the current year's actual results for completed quarters (or expected results for subsequent quarters) and over (0) or under (U) percentages are reported. Midway through the fiscal year, expected data for the first quarter of the next fiscal year is added to the POR.

Corporate top management meets quarterly with each division president and his or her chief financial officer to review the most recent POR and monitor overall division performance. The meetings are taken very seriously by all concerned and any deviations from forecast get close attention. When a division's reported results and expectations are weak, a shift to contingency plans is sometimes ordered by top management, Emerson does not allocate corporate overhead to the divisions but does allocate interest and taxes to divisions at the end of the fiscal year.

COMPENSATION

During the year, each division assesses all department heads and higher-level managers against specific performance criteria. Those with high potential are offered a series of assignments to develop their skills. Human resources are identified as part of the strategy implementation. In addition, personnel charts on management team are kept at corporate headquarters. The charts include each manager's photo, function, experience, and career path. About 85 percent of promotions involve internal managers.

Each executive in a division earns a base salary and is eligible for "extra salary," based on division performance according to measurable objectives (primarily sales, profits, and return on capital). An extra salary amount, established at the beginning of the year, is multiplied by "1" if the division hits targeted performance. The multiplier ranges from .35 to 2.0. Doing better than target increases the multiplier. In recent years, sales and profit margin, as identified in the POR forecast column, have had a 50 percent weighting in computing compensation targets. Other factors include inventory turnover, international sales, new product introductions, and an accounts receivable factor. In addition, stock options and a five-year performance share plan are available to top executives.

COMMUNICATION

Top management strongly encourages open communication. Division presidents and plant managers meet regularly with all employees to discuss the specifics of the business and the competition. As a measure of communication, top management feels that each employee should be able to answer four essential questions about his or her job:

1. What cost reduction are you currently working on?
2. Who is the competition?
3. Have you met with your management in the past six months?
4. Do you understand the economics of your job?

The company also conducts opinion surveys of every employee. The analysis uncovers trends. Some plants have survey data for the prior twenty years. The CEO receives a summary of every opinion survey from every plant.

RECENT EVENTS

As a result of a $2 billion investment in technology during the past 10 years, new products as a percent of sales increased from 13 percent in 1983 to 24 percent in 1993. A new product is defined as a product introduced within the past five years. About 87 percent of total U.S. sales are generated from products that are either first or second in domestic position. Still, some in the investment community do not view Emerson as a technology leader, but as a very efficient world-class manufacturer. Although internally generated new products are part of the planning process, Emerson is sometimes a late entrant in the marketplace. For example, in 1989, a competitor introduced a low-cost, hand-held ultrasonic gauge. Within 72 days, Emerson introduced its own version at 20 percent less cost than its competitor's gauge. Emerson's gauge was also easier to use and more reliable. It was a bestseller within a year.

To some Wall Street observers, it seems that Emerson is attempting to reduce its dependence on supplying commodity-type products, such as motors and valves, to U.S. based appliance and other consumer-durables manufacturers by moving into faster growing global markets, such as process controls. As the economy recovers, Emerson is likely to continue its acquisition strategy, with an emphasis on foreign acquisitions, and international joint ventures.

The impact of the recent business segment organization structure on the planning and control process is not clear. The added layer of management between the division managers and top management might change the previous relationship between them.

QUESTIONS

1. Evaluate Chief Executive Officer Knight's strategy for the Emerson Electric Company. In view of the strategy, evaluate the planning and control system described in the case. What are its strong and weak points?
2. What changes, if any, would you recommend to the CEO?
3. What role should the eight business segment managers have in Emerson's planning and control system?

Exhibit 1 The Value Measurement Chart Assesses Value Creation at a Glance*

		5th Prior Year		Current Year		5th Year		5-Year Increment				10-Year Increment	
		Actual FY 1989		Expected FY 1994		Forecast FY 1999		Historical CY vs 5th PY		Forecast 5th Yr vs. CY		5th Yr vs. 5th PY	
		Amt.	*% Sales*	*Amt.*	*% Sales*	*Amt.*	*% Sales*	*Amt.*	*% Sales*	*Amt.*	*% Sales*	*Amt.*	*% Sales*
Growth Rate and Capital Requirements	*Line No.*	*A*	*B*	*C*	*D*	*E*	*F*	*G*	*H*	*I*	*J*	*K*	*L*
Working capital operating-Y/E	1127	117.1	29.8%	120.2	21.8%	153.3	18.5%	3.1	1.9%	33.1	12.0%	36.2	8.3%
Net noncurrent assets-Y/E	1128	92.9	23.6%	150.0	27.2%	221.6	26.8%	57.1	35.9%	71.6	26.0%	128.7	29.6%
Total operating capital-Y/E	1129	210.0	53.4%	270.2	48.9%	374.9	45.3%	60.2	37.9%	104.7	38.0%	164.9	37.9%
Average operating capital	1130	201.1	51.1%	267.1	48.4%	370.4	44.7%						
Incremental investment	1584							66.0		103.3		169.3	
Net oper. prof. aft. tax (NOPAT)	1119	33.4		49.5		79.0		16.1		29.5		45.6	
Return on incremental investment								24.4%		28.6%		26.9%	
NOPAT growth rate								8.2%		9.8%		9.0%	
Capital growth rate								5.8%		6.8%		6.3%	
Rate of Return													
Return on total capital = NOPAT / Avg. oper. cap.		16.6%		18.5%		21.3%							
Net sales	0001	393.2		552.2		827.9		159.0		275.7		434.7	
Sales growth rate								7.0%		8.4%		7.7%	
NOPAT margin		8.5%		9.0%		9.5%		10.1%		10.7%		10.5%	
Operating capital turnover (T/O)		1.96		2.07		2.24		2.41		2.67		2.57	
Cost of capital	3000	12.0%		12.0%		12.0%							
Capital charge (L1130 X L3000)	3001	24.1		32.1		44.4		8.0		12.3		20.3	
Economic profit (L1119-L3001)		9.3		17.4		34.6		8.1		17.2		25.3	

*In millions of dollars (all numbers in the exhibit are disguised).

Source: Charles F. Knight, "Emerson Electric: Consistent Profits, Consistently," *Harvard Business Review*, January–February 1992, p. 63. Used with permission of the Emerson Electric Company. All numbers are disguised.

EXHIBIT 2 The Sales Gap Chart Forecasts Five-Year Plans*

				Forecast						
		Prior Year Actual FY 93	*Current Year Expected FY 94*	*FY 95*	*FY 96*	*FY 97*	*FY 98*	*FY 99*	*5-Year Source of Growth (%)*	*5-Year Company Annual Growth (%)*
	Line No.	*A*	*B*	*C*	*D*	*E*	*F*	*G*	*H*	*I*
Domestic Excluding Exports										
Current year domestic sales base @ 10/1 prices	1		305.7	305.7	305.7	305.7	305.7	305.7		
Served industry-growth/(decline)	2			3.0	24.6	39.0	49.6	58.3	21.1%	3.6%
Penetration-increase/(decrease) (Including-new line extension/ buyouts)	3			6.3	14.1	21.0	29.8	37.6	13.6	2.0
Price increases-current year through 5th year	4		3.3	7.6	14.7	21.6	29.5	38.0	12.6	1.7
Incremental new products:										
Prior 5 year introduction	5		16.1	16.4	17.7	17.4	17.5	19.0	1.1	
Current year through 5th year	6		1.4	5.6	11.6	18.5	25.9	34.2	11.9	
Other	7		3.1	1.4	1.6	2.3	2.5	2.8	–0.1	
Total Domestic	8	363.7	329.6	346.0	390.0	425.5	460.5	495.6		8.5
International Excluding Sales to U.S.										
Current year international sales base @ 10/1 prices	9		202.9	202.9	202.9	202.9	202.9	202.9		
Served industry-growth/(decline)	10			(0.1)	8.8	17.0	24.8	35.4	12.9	3.3
Penetration-increase/(decrease) (Including-new line extensions/buyouts)	11			(0.5)	18.8	27.2	36.2	45.1	16.4	3.6
Price increases-current year through 5th year	12		2.0	4.9	8.5	12.5	16.9	21.7	7.1	1.4
Incremental new products:										
Prior 5 year introduction	13		6.9	7.1	6.7	7.1	8.0	9.2	0.8	
Current year through 5th year	14		1.1	4.5	6.3	10.1	14.3	16.9	5.7	

EXHIBIT 2 The Sales Gap Chart Forecasts Five-Year Plans* (continued)

				Forecast						
		Prior Year Actual FY 93	*Current Year Expected FY 94*	*FY 95*	*FY 96*	*FY 97*	*FY 98*	*FY 99*	*5-Year Source of Growth (%)*	*5-Year Company Annual Growth (%)*
	Line No.	A	B	C	D	E	F	G	H	I
Currency	15		9.3	–	–	–	–	–	– 3.4	
Other	16		0.4	0.8	0.7	0.9	1.0	1.1	0.3	
Total international	17	204.3	222.6	219.6	252.7	277.7	304.1	332.3		8.3
Total consolidated	18	568.0	552.2	565.6	642.7	703.2	764.6	827.9	100.0	8.4
Annual growth %—nominal			–2.8%	2.4%	13.6%	9.4%	8.7%	8.3%		
Gap:										
15% Target—nominal	19			635.0	730.2	839.8	965.7	1,110.6		15.0
Sales gap—over(under)	20			(69.4)	(87.5)	(136.6)	(201.1)	(282.7)		
U.S. exports (excluding to foreign subsidiaries)	21	35.3	31.3	33.7	35.9	39.9	43.9	47.6		8.7
Foreign subsidiaries (excluding sales to U.S.)	22	169.1	191.4	185.8	216.8	237.8	260.3	284.7		8.3

*In millions of dollars (all numbers in the exhibit are disguised).

Source: Charles F. Knight, "Emerson Electric: Consistent Profits, Consistently," *Harvard Business Review*, January–February 1992, p. 64. Used with permission of the Emerson Electric Company.

Exhibit 3

The sales gap line chart projects sales growth against other targets

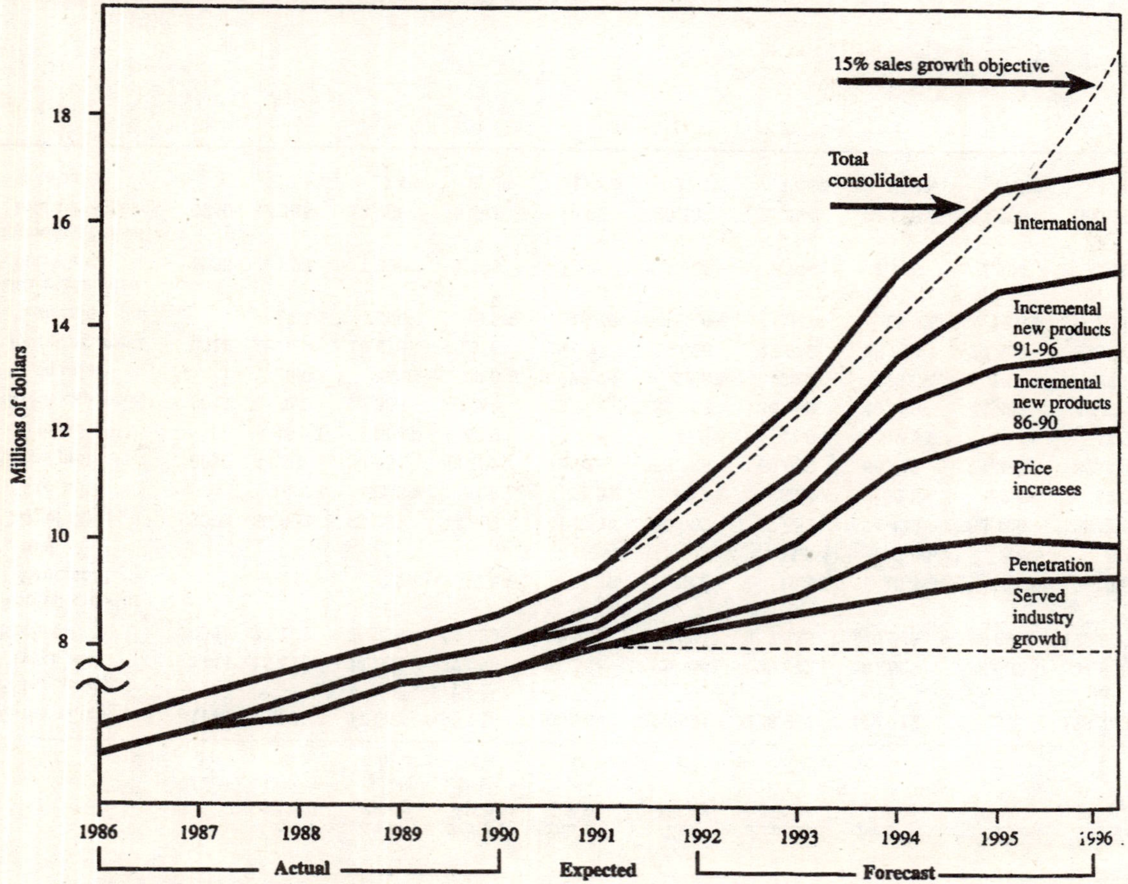

Note: All numbers in the exhibit are disguised.

Source: Charles F. Knight, "Emerson Electric: Consistent Profits, Consistently," *Harvard Business Review*, January–February 199?, p. 65. Used with permission of the Emerson Electric Company.

1992, p.

Exhibit 4 The 5-Back-by-5-Forward Chart Provides 11 Years of P&L Measures*

		Actual/Restated					Current Year	Forecast				
	Line No.	5th PY FY 89 A	4th PY FY 90 B	3rd PY FY 91 C	2nd PY FY 92 D	Prior Year FY 93 E	Expected FY 94 F	Next Yr FY 95 G	2nd Yr FY 96 H	3rd Yr FY 97 I	4th Yr FY 98 J	5th Yr FY 99 K
Order entries	1143	71,363	77,057	92,716	100,164	126,591	128,247	142,612	157,972	173,743	189,856	207,133
Sales backlog (year end)	1144	13,310	14,051	17,098	16,534	29,334	29,842	31,509	33,082	34,805	36,591	38,363
Net sales	0001	71,163	76,316	89,669	100,728	113,791	127,739	140,945	156,399	172,020	188,070	205,361
Annual growth %-nominal			7.2%	17.5%	12.3%	13.0%	12.3%	10.3%	11.0%	10.0%	9.3%	9.2%
-real							11.3%	7.8%	8.4%	6.7%	6.8%	6.1%
Cost of sales	0009	36,802	39,382	46,487	51,593	60,003	67,651	74,432	82,109	89,966	98,173	106,997
% to sales		51.7%	51.6%	51.8%	51.2%	52.7%	53.0%	52.8%	52.5%	52.3%	52.2%	52.1%
Gross profit	0010	34,361	36,934	43,182	49,135	53,788	60,088	66,513	74,290	82,054	89,897	98,364
% to sales		48.3%	48.4%	48.2%	48.8%	47.3%	47.0%	47.2%	47.5%	47.7%	47.8%	47.9%
SG&A expenses	0011	21,773	22,558	26,246	29,941	32,163	36,150	40,169	44,887	49,714	54,366	59,555
% to sales		30.6%	29.6%	29.3%	29.7%	28.3%	28.3%	28.5%	28.7%	28.9%	28.9%	29.0%
Operating profit	0012	12,588	14,376	16,936	19,194	21,625	23,938	26,344	29,403	32,340	35,531	38,809
% to sales		17.7%	18.8%	18.9%	19.1%	19.0%	18.7%	18.7%	18.8%	18.8%	18.9%	18.9%
Other (inc.)/ded. (excl. int.)	0235	423	1,090	1,395	1,232	1,488	1,764	1,766	1,794	1,530	1,438	1,423
Earnings before interest & taxes	0240	12,165	13,286	15,541	17,962	20,137	22,174	24,578	27,609	30,810	34,093	37,386
% to sales		17.1%	17.4%	17.3%	17.8%	17.7%	17.4%	17.4%	17.7%	17.9%	18.1%	18.2%

Exhibit 4 **The 5-Back-by-5-Forward Chart Provides 11 Years of P&L Measures* (continued)**

		Actual/Restated					Current Year	Forecast				
	Line No.	*5th PY FY 89*	*4th PY FY 90*	*3rd PY FY 91*	*2nd PY FY 92*	*Prior Year FY 93*	*Expected FY 94*	*Next Yr FY 95*	*2nd Yr FY 96*	*3rd Yr FY 97*	*4th Yr FY 98*	*5th Yr FY 99*
		A	*B*	*C*	*D*	*E*	*F*	*G*	*H*	*I*	*J*	*K*
Interest (income)/ expense, net	0230	(771)	(1,041)	(1,127)	(1,326)	(1,781)	(2,224)	(2,330)	(2,576)	(2,734)	(2,903)	(3,070)
Pretax earnings	0015	12,936	14,327	16,668	19,288	21,918	24,398	26,908	30,185	33,544	36,996	40,456
% to sales		18.2%	18.8%	18.6%	19.1%	19.3%	19.1%	19.1%	19.3%	19.5%	19.7%	19.7%
Income taxes	0016	5,445	6,785	7 788	8,447	9,668	10,551	11,753	13,101	14,497	15,948	17,387
Effective tax rate		42.1%	47.4%	46.7%	43.8%	44.1%	43.2%	43.7%	43.4%	43.2%	43.1%	43.0%
Net earnings	0017	7,491	7,542	8,880	10,841	12,250	13,847	15,155	17,084	19,047	21,048	23,069
% to sales		10.5%	9.9%	9.9%	10.8%	10.8%	10.8%	10.8%	10.9%	11.1%	11.2%	11.2%
Return on total capital	1324	20.4%	19.7%	20.3%	23.6%	23.8%	25.1%	26.1%	28.0%	30.1%	32.0%	33.9%
ROTC excluding goodwill	1323	27.3%	28.0%	27.2%	30.6%	31.5%	32.5%	32.9%	34.7%	36.6%	38.3%	40.2%

*In thousands of dollars (all numbers in the exhibit are disguised).

Source: Charles F. Knight, "Emerson Electric: Consistent Profits, Consistently," *Harvard Business Review*, January–February 1992, p. 66. Used with permission of the Emerson Electric Company.

EXHIBIT 5 President's Operating Report Division—Fiscal Year by Quarters/Actual and Expected

(Thousands of Dollars)

Line No.		Current Year						Prior Year		% Act/Exp O/(U) PY
		Actual/ Expected	*% Sales*	*Prior Expected*	*% Sales*	*Forecast*	*% Sales*	*Actual*	*% Sales*	
1st Quarter Ending December 31										
1	Intercompany Sales	36		36		34		37		-2.7%
2	Net Sales	29,613		29,613		29,463		25,932		14.2%
3	Gross Profit	14,065	47.5%	14,065	47.5%	13,790	46.8%	12,384	47.8%	13.6%
4	SG&A Expenses	8,312	28.1%	8,312	28.1%	8,281	28.1%	7,650	29.5%	8.7%
5	Operating Profit	5,753	19.4%	5,753	19.4%	5,509	18.7%	4,734	18.3%	21.5%
6	Earnings Before Interest & Tax	5,280	17.8%	5,280	17.8%	5,048	17.1%	4,343	16.7%	21.6%
2nd Quarter Ending March 31										
7	Intercompany Sales	5		5		9		56		-91.1%
8	Net Sales	33,324		33,324		31,765		22,661		25.0%
9	Gross Profit	15,283	45.9%	15,283	45.9%	14,812	46.6%	12,518	47.0%	22.1%
10	SG&A Expenses	9,301	27.9%	9,301	27.9%	8,937	28.1%	7,395	27.8%	25.8%
11	Operating Profit	5,982	18.0%	5,982	18.0%	5,875	18.5%	5,123	19.2%	16.8%
12	Earnings Before Interest & Tax	5,785	17.4%	5,785	17.4%	5,612	17.7%	4,918	18.4%	17.6%
3rd Quarter Ending June 30										
13	Intercompany Sales	25		25		39		146		-82.9%
14	Net Sales	32,845		32,845		33,424		30,678		7.1%
15	Gross Profit	15,353	46.7%	15,353	46.7%	15,664	46.9%	14,310	46.6%	7.3%
16	SG&A Expenses	8,916	27.1%	8,916	27.1%	9,399	28.2%	8,424	27.4%	5.8%
17	Operating Profit	6,437	19.6%	6,437	19.6%	6,265	18.7%	5,886	19.2%	9.4%
18	Earnings Before Interest & Tax	6,126	18.7%	6,126	18.7%	5,645	16.9%	5,378	17.5%	13.9%
4th Quarter Ending September 30										
19	Intercompany Sales	94		94		94		25		276.0%
20	Net Sales	36,611		36,611		35,722		30,521		20.0%
21	Gross Profit	17,109	46.7%	17,109	46.7%	16,832	47.1%	14,576	47.8%	17.4%

EXHIBIT 5 President's Operating Report Division—Fiscal Year by Quarters/Actual and Expected (continued)

(Thousands of Dollars)

		Current Year						Prior Year		
Line No.		*Actual / Expected*	*% Sales*	*Prior Expected*	*% Sales*	*Forecast*	*% Sales*	*Actual*	*% Sales*	*% Act / Exp O/(U) PY*
22	SG&A Expenses	10,537	28.7%	10,537	28.7%	10,029	28.1%	8,695	28.5%	21.2%
23	Operating Profit	6,572	18.0%	6,572	18.0%	6,803	19.0%	5,881	19.3%	11.7%
24	Earnings Before Interest & Tax	6,122	16.7%	6,122	16.7%	8,146	22.8%	5,498	18.0%	11.3%
Fiscal Year Ending September 30										
25	Intercompany Sales	160		160		176		264		–39.4%
26	Net Sales	132,393		132,393		130,374		113,792		16.3%
27	Gross Profit	61,810	46.7%	61,810	46.7%	61,098	46.9%	53,788	47.3%	14.9%
28	SG&A Expenses	37,066	28.0%	37,066	28.0%	36,646	28.1%	32,164	28.3%	15.2%
29	Operating Profit	24,744	18.7%	24,744	18.7%	24,452	18.8%	21,624	19.0%	14.4%
30	Earnings Before Interest & Tax	23,313	17.6%	23,313	17.6%	24,451	18.8%	20,137	17.7%	15.8%
31	Pre-Tax Earnings	25,154	19.0%	25,154	19.0%	24,771	19.0%	21,918	19.3%	14.8%
32	Net Earnings	14,361	10.8%	14,361	10.8%	14,024	10.8%	12,250	10.8%	17.2%
Expected First Quarter Next Fiscal Year										
33	Intercompany Sales	67		65				36		86.1%
34	Net Sales	32,830		32,311				29,613		10.9%
35	Gross Profit	15,142	46.1%	15,143	46.9%			14,065	47.5%	7.7%
36	SG&A Expenses	9,179	27.9%	9,217	28.6%			8,312	28.1%	10.4%
37	Operating Profit	5,963	18.2%	5,925	18.3%			5,753	19.4%	3.7%
38	Earnings Before Interest & Tax	5,628	17.1%	5,619	17.4%			5,280	17.8%	6.6%

Used with permission of the Emerson Electric Company. All numbers are disguised

Readings

HOW TO SET UP A BUDGETING AND PLANNING SYSTEM

BY ROBERT N. WEST, CPA, AND AMY M. SNYDER CPA
Certificate of &Merit

Two years ago, Penn Fuel Gas, Inc. (PFG) initiated its first annual and long-range operating budget process. PFG is a public utility holding company with consolidated revenues of $125 million and 550 employees. In addition to selling natural gas, the company provides natural gas storage and transportation services, provides merchandise services, and has a propane business. PFG's utility operations are split between two subsidiaries, each with a number of locations.

The motivation for budgeting came jointly from PFG's bankers, its board of directors, and its management. The information needs of all three users were fairly similar. All three were interested in cash flow projections and future earnings potential. The board was interested in improving PFG's return on equity (ROE), and it wanted to analyze the prospects of reinstituting a common stock dividend. In addition. management wanted segment P&Ls and improved departmental (cost center) expense and cash flow tracking. PFGs segments are regions, lines of business (utility, propane, and merchandise, and type of customer commercial, industrial, residential).

WHERE TO START?

The first decision was whether to use existing in-house personnel, hire consultants, or hire a full-time budget manager. Consultants or a new hire would offer the benefit of an independent, fresh perspective with no biases. The disadvantage is that they wouldn't know the business as well as an insider. Penn Fuel Gas used consultants to set up its first budget and then hired a full-time, experienced professional to handle its budgeting. PFG wisely gave the position a manager title to assign appropriate status to the position. Once the staffing decision was resolved, the new budget director faced three primary tasks.

Learn the business. PFG hired a self-directed person (co-author Amy Snyder) who could understand the business quickly and get both long-range and operating budget processes up and running. Although the operations of PFGs business are relatively straightforward, the rules and regulations of the public utility industry are complex. PFG did two things to bring the budget manager up to speed. It sent her to a week-long technical program to learn the regulatory side of the business, and it extended her an open invitation to important meetings of operations vice presidents and top management so she could learn the operating side of the business.

Budgeting for natural gas and propane operations is difficult because a significant amount of demand for these products is dependent upon Mother Nature. Penn Fuel experienced two abnormal winters in its first two years of budgeting. In 1994, Pennsylvania had its coldest, iciest winter in history In 1995, it had one of its warmest. But forecasting is difficult for many rapidly growing companies (one group for whom this article is intended). They must be flexible. For example, PFG budgets using the normal weather forecast, but it also provides sensitivity analyses and budget reprojections at least quarterly. Company and budget personnel realize that capital spending is partially a function of the winter season's revenues, which won't be known until the first quarter is over. The first quarter is particularly important in the utility and propane business as it represents 40% of total annual product delivered.

Determine the users' information needs. Different users have different information needs, and users don't always know what information they "need." If managers or board members are not financially oriented, as is the case with many small businesses, they may need a little guidance. PFG's directors included several financially astute individuals who had a clear idea of what information they wanted. Costs were budgeted on both an accrual basis (for P&L reports) and cash basis (for cash flow reports).

Review and update the information system. All accounting information systems (AIS) face the daunting task of trying to provide the appropriate output for multiple sets of users. The reports needed from Penn Fuel's MS included:

1. External financial reports (GAAP),
2. Tax reporting,

3. Internal management segment reports,
4. Cash flow reports, and
5. Reports for regulators.

The budget manager analyzed the AI to determine whether data were classified and summarized in a manner useful for internal business plans and budget reports. Most accounting systems are geared toward external financial reports, and, in the case of regulated industries, for reports to regulators as well. Internal managers usually prefer information provided in a different format, such as results by division, product line, region, or customer group.

DECISIONS TO MAKE

PFG's budget manager faced some interesting information systems setups on which she had to make decisions when she started her work.

Different internal reporting systems. The Northern division, acquired several years ago, reported its results in different formats from the Southern division. Eventually a common reporting system will be attained, but the immediate task was to rearrange the data to assist with the consolidation and make the division data comparable. The underlying information systems differed as well. The two divisions used different accounting software, adding another challenge to the eventual merging of information systems.

Treatment of a different business segment. PFG's propane business segment seems similar to the natural gas business, but it has several key differences. Because it is unregulated. it has direct control over the pricing of its product. The utility's chart of accounts was not a perfect fit. PFG had to decide whether to maintain a uniform chart of accounts or create a separate general ledger account structure for its propane business segment. PFG adapted the propane business unit's account structure to the utility account structure. The tradeoff was ease of corporate reporting versus the individual business unit's desired view of the data. A slight edge was given to corporate reporting.

Management and the board of directors wanted segment information that was difficult to obtain. Total spending and spending by operating unit were easy to retrieve, but other views of the information had not been developed. For example, segregating operating expenses by business segment was pro-vided partially by existing reports, but aggregation of all segments was tedious to reconcile to the general ledger due to corporate staff allocations. Most corporate personnel, from the president down to the fixed asset accountants, do not keep formal track of their time. Allocations were made to the various business segments on spreadsheets, requiring an audit trail and explanations to reconcile back to the results per the accounting records.

Review expense classifications. As a company grows, its chart of accounts should be reviewed periodically to determine if information is being captured in the most meaningful way. Introducing a budget system is an ideal time to modify the accounting system with a view toward future information needs. PFG's new budget manager reviewed the utility's accounting system with a fresh perspective and came up with a couple of suggestions to improve the precision of the accounting information system.

The first suggestion was to get rid of miscellaneous expense accounts with large balances. Most businesses prefer that almost nothing be recorded in miscellaneous accounts. PFG's state-mandated chart of accounts lent itself to this practice as the chart of accounts included many miscellaneous expense accounts. The challenge here was twofold:

1. Perform an account analysis to reclassify some of the charges to the miscellaneous expense account, and
2. Change the accounting system (add accounts and subaccounts) to ensure that future transactions are put into more descriptive accounts.

Lack of sufficient detail, such as the overuse of miscellaneous expense, is a common small business practice, so many new budget managers will face a housekeeping task similar to PFG's.

The next suggestion was to change the expense classification system. For example, the training & education account included charges for the training course fee, hotel, travel, meals, the salary charge for the time at the training session, and so on. This system actually was an activity-based costing system in which training included all costs driven by the decision to send an employee to a training program. While this classification of costs is perfectly acceptable, some accountants would record these items in separate accounts to maintain more detail. PFG has several hundred active general ledger accounts, so transaction classification is not a trivial task.

Most companies initiating a budgeting and planning function should review thoroughly the chart of accounts, account classification (particularly expenses), and the reporting system. In many cases, the accounting system will not have kept pace with the changes in the company (for example, expanded product lines or changes in customers and geographical regions served. It is best if the budget manager resolves information classification and reporting issues up front so that future budgets are comparable. It is difficult to change a system once it has been developed, and budget systems are no different from any other information system in that respect.

Difficulty reconciling amounts back to the ledger. Using the example of training costs cited above, some salary costs were included in accounts other than salary expense. Reconciling accounts such as salaries between the ledger and the payroll register can be difficult. Other accounts are difficult to reconcile as well. The budget manager decided to reclassify some data, but verifying the accuracy of reclassified data was, and still is, a challenge.

Information timeliness/availability. Budgeting brought the desire for better and faster information. PFG uses a minicomputer-based accounting package for general ledger, human resources, and payables. Yet portions of the accounting system still are manual, and monthly closings can take up to three weeks. PFG responded to some of its information needs by installing a new billing system that computerizes cash receipts and provides excellent summary information. PFG also is looking into a computerized project tracking system (for its many construction projects) and improving the computerized fixed assets system by adding a budget feature.

DELIVERABLES

Management wanted a one-year business plan prior to year-end as well as monthly updates (for example, budget vs. actual results). In addition, the board of directors wanted a long-range (three-year) plan each year. To meet these needs, the budget manager developed packets for the directors and management. The board wanted the financial and operational data reported by segment—some reports segmented geographically, some by product line, and others by customer type.

The monthly financial packet. The monthly financial packet includes the following schedules:

A. P&L and cash flow (by region and in total)
   1. Current month
      a. Actual vs. budget
      b. Actual vs. same month in prior year
   2. Year-to-date (YTD)
      a. YTD actual vs. YTD budget
      b. Budget projections for remainder of year
      c. YTD actual vs. prior YTD actual
   3. Two full-year monthly bar charts
      a. Actual vs. budgeted cash flow
      b. Actual vs. budgeted net income
   4. Capital structure and ROE

B. Selected five-year comparative data
   1. Current month and YTD units of product delivered
      a. Residential
      b. Commercial
      c. Industrial
      d. Resale
      e. Detail provided for 10 largest customers
   2. Gas and propane stored
   3. Comparative YTD income statements

The annual business plan. The annual business plan contains data similar to the monthly package by region and in total. Full-year budget data are compared with the current year estimated (10 months' actual plus estimates for November and December) results and prior year actual results. These data are shown in tabular and graphical form. The annual plan also contains:

A. Budgeted income statements for all 12 months.
B. Budgeted cash flow statements for all 12 months.
C. Budgeted ROE schedule for all 12 months.
D. Capital expenditures forecasts, including brief written descriptions of the projects, by segment.
   1. New business (line extensions)
   2. Replacements/betterments
   3. Meters
   4. Tools & equipment
F. Personnel data including projected new hiring, replacement hiring, and workforce reductions.

Explanations of significant variances from prior year actual results are provided in both the annual and monthly packages. Second-stage variance analysis (breaking the variance into its price and quantity components) is provided as needed.

Formatting tips. After completing the first budgeting exercises, the budget manager came to the conclusion that some formatting tips might help those persons who were not familiar with the budgeting process. First, she suggests using graphs. Whoever is preparing a budget should consider displaying the information in graphical form rather than tables of numbers so it will appeal to all levels of readers.

Second, she suggests that a company consider the direct method for cash flow reports. PFG uses the direct method for its cash flow statement because it is more informative and is easier for readers to understand. The adjustments to net income with the indirect method are confusing and do not tell the reader where the money is coming from and to whom it is going. Reports for external parties still can use the indirect method if companies prefer. Table 1 contains a sample direct method cash flow statement.

THE BUDGET CALENDAR

What does the budget group do throughout the year? Table 2 shows the other functions performed by the budget manager each month. Notice that the annual budget data collection process begins five months before the packet is due to the board of directors. A four- to six-month lead time is fairly standard.

PFG decided to prepare its three-year forecast before doing the annual budget because the board wanted information on ROE and cash flow to analyze future earnings potential, for financing requirements, and for general business planning purposes. Once the three-year plan was reviewed, the first year's data were used as a guideline for the current year annual budget's operational and segment detail.

ONGOING CHALLENGES

We already highlighted the initial challenges faced by a new budget manager. Now let's look at some ongoing challenges.

Evolving mission. The budget function is formed with planning as its primary mission. In the early stages of its existence, however, it is expected to analyze company and segment performance. Variance analysis can be both interesting and challenging, challenging because no two years are ever the same. One obvious difference in the natural gas and propane business is the weather, which rarely is the same two years in a row. But other changes such as geographical growth, changes in product mix, and restructuring of divisions increase the challenge of reconciling operating results of two consecutive periods.

Gamesmanship. Budgeting also brings behavioral challenges such as lowballing revenues or padding expenses. PFG has experienced minimal budgeting gamesmanship for two reasons that are described next.

1. Budgets are developed with management, arriving at agreed-upon, reasonable expectations.
2. PFG has not used the budget as a "hammer" at year-end for employees or divisions who did not make budget.

Get people up to speed. The behavioral challenge at PFG has been to get people up to speed with budgeting. The budget manager came from a large company where budgeting was part of the culture. At PFG, she sent out schedules and written instructions on completing the budget requests the first time through. But not everyone understood how to complete the budget forms. Her goal the next year was to sit down with people and work through the forms with those who were unaccustomed to the budget process.

When formal budgeting is new to a company, the budget manager may end up doing the bulk of the budget preparation because people are new to the process. One unfortunate byproduct that can occur is that managers then think it's the budget manager's budget. The budget manager has to impress upon them that it is their department and their budget. It is important to determine up front who is responsible and accountable.

Top management support. All new systems require top management's support. To make budgeting effective, management must communicate the importance of well-thought-out input from departments and operating units. If preparing a well-thought-out budget is not included in managers' goals and objectives for the year, employees may not make the time for the process. Resistance may result, not because employees feel threatened by the new budget system, but, rather, because they lack time.

BENEFITS FROM BUDGETING

Budgeting has improved communication throughout Penn Fuel Gas, Inc., and has improved teamwork toward a common goal. It has helped the board of directors to represent shareholders better and has provided support to management on major decisions. PFG expects even better planning in the future to result in operational improvements, improved management of resources, better cost control, earnings growth, and improved responsibility resulting from managers' active participation in the planning process.

Robert N. West, CPA, Ph.D., is an assistant professor at Villanova University. He is the author of several articles and the text, *Microcomputer Accounting Systems*. He is a member of the Valley Forge Chapter, through which this article was submitted, and can be reached at (610) 519-4359.

Amy M. Snyder, CPA, was manager of budgeting and planning at Penn Fuel Gas, Inc., when this article was written. Now she is controller of Espe America, Inc. She is a member of the Valley Forge Chapter and can be reached at (610) 277-3800.

Table 1. DIRECT METHOD CASH FLOW STATEMENT						
	Current Month			Year-to-Date		
	Actual	Budget	Variance	Actual	Budget	Variance
Cash Inflows						
Utility						
Propane						
Merchandise						
Total Cash Inflow						
Cash Outflow's						
Gas purchases						
Propane purchases						
Merchandise purchases						
Operating and maintenance expenses						
Labor and benefits						
Insurance						
Outside services						
Leases						
Storage						
Other						
Rate case preparation						
Other taxes						
Income taxes						
Interest on LTD						
Other interest						
Principal payments						
Common dividends						
Preferred dividends						
Total Cash Outflow						
Available funds						
Capital expenditures						
Net Change in Cash						

Table 2. THE BUDGET CALENDAR
PROCEDURES AND REPORTS DUE

December

Annual budget for coming year. Presentation to board of directors. Present current year results; 10 months of actual and projections for remaining two months (November's results would not be available at this point).

January

Issue approved budgets to managers and vice presidents. Set up monthly financial report for the new year.

February

Prepare actual P&Ls and cash flow by month for the prior year.

March

Clean-up work after year-end closing and audit.

April

1st quarter actual vs. budget to board of directors. Nine-month projections. Send out requests for long-range forecast.

May

Prepare long-range forecast.

June

Present long-range forecast to board of directors.

July

Requests for the upcoming year's capital spending, operating revenues, expenses, and cash flows sent to operating units and corporate departments. 2nd quarter actual vs. budget to board of directors. Six-month projections.

August

Follow up on July requests. Help employees unfamiliar with budget requests.

September

July budget requests due. Input, analyze, and summarize the data.

October

Top management reviews budgets. Have meetings, and negotiate final amounts with various vice presidents and managers. 3rd quarter actual vs. budget to board of directors. Three-month projections.

November

Prepare final budget.

Strategic Budgeting: A Case Study and Proposed Framework

By Audrey G. Taylor, Ph.D., And Savya Rafai

In 1999, a manager at one of the "Big 3" automotive companies in the Detroit area implemented a new budgeting process called strategic budgeting (SB) that reduced costs in his area by 37.6% without compromising the delivery of services or causing the layoff of personnel.

The budgeting method was based on the assumptions behind a project management technique developed by Eliyahu Goldratt in his 1997 book, Critical Chain. The technique was applied to a service department where the linkages between the "optimal level" of inputs for the outputs provided were unknown. As a project, by definition, embodies the development of a new product or process, the time needed for each task in the project is unknown. To deal with the uncertainty of each step within a project, estimates are made to ensure that milestones can be met. In a similar fashion, budgets are developed to ensure that targets can be met without going over the planned budget.

Traditionally, companies trying to reduce costs use "the lawnmower method" for cost reduction. In the lawnmower method, cost cutting does not discriminate on the basis of need or capacity. All departments are simply required to reduce costs by a given percentage. The assumption of many managers is that all budgets contain slack.[1] In his study of budgetary slack, Mohammed Onsi documented that 80% of the managers he interviewed admitted that they "bargain for slack."[2] Onsi also discovered that slack is created to ensure managers meet budget targets and to protect them from uncertainty. The problem for the upper-level manager is to identify how much slack exists in the budgets for the departments under his or her control and to remove it without jeopardizing the amount or the quality of the services provided.

In Critical Chain, Goldratt introduced a technique for removing unnecessary padding from time estimates for tasks in a project. Goldratt built his model on several observations. First, he recognized that forecasts for the timing of tasks or for cost estimation are relatively accurate in the aggregate but are much less accurate when used to estimate tasks and costs of subunits. Second, Goldratt states that managers tend to overestimate the time needed for individual tasks by a minimum of 100% (see Figure 1).

Overestimation protects managers from missing "milestones" in projects. Finally, Goldratt states that

Figure 1: Developing Time Estimates for Project Completion

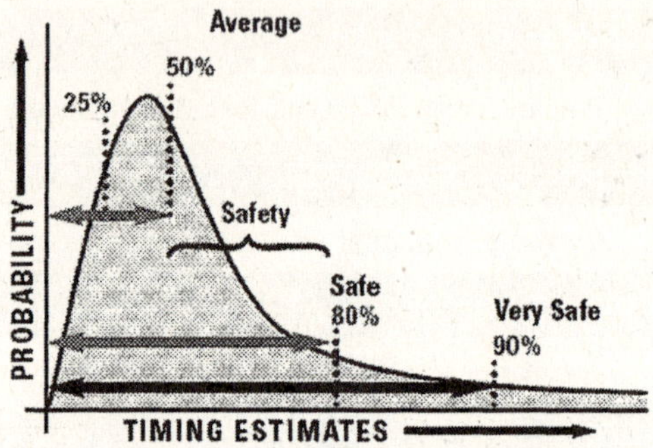

procrastination, labeled the Student Syndrome, causes estimates to be overrun and due dates to be missed.

In order to counteract the unnecessary padding of steps in a project, Goldratt recommended cutting time estimates for each project task in half and then grouping all of the time saved from individual tasks into one "project buffer" placed at the end of the project's estimated time sequence. The "project buffer" was hen reduced by one half in order to reduce the overall project time allowed by one third of its original estimate (Figure 2).

By following these simple steps, many companies experienced dramatic reductions in the time necessary to complete projects. Among those using the Critical Chain technique are DaimlerChrysler, Lucent Technologies, Israel Aircraft Industries, and Harris Semiconductor.

What Is The Strategic Budgeting Model?

Strategic budgeting bases cost reduction on the same assumptions and on the same techniques used in the Critical Chain method of reducing project time. The first assumption of SB is that service department budgets contain a great deal of slack. The slack multiples exponentially over time.

In the example in Table 1, the amount of slack buildup after just four years in a budget with 10% slack added at each level is over 100% of the original budget. By year 10 the slack has increased to almost five times the original amount. With so much potential for slack in even a modest increase of 10% over estimated needs,

Figure 2: Step 1 (Identify), Step 2 (Halve Time), and Step 3 (Create the Project Buffer)

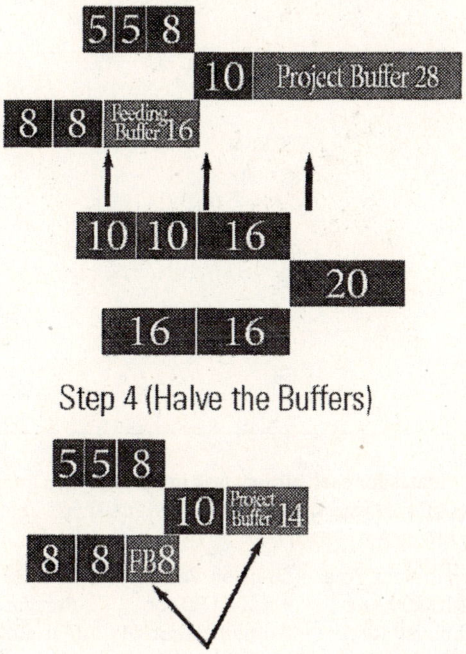

there is probably room to reduce most budgets in most service departments by significant amounts.

Even though, on average, budgets have large levels of slack, we cannot say that every budget has tremendous amounts of slack built into it. Therefore, SB allows departments to receive more funds when necessary. Kenton Walker and Eric Johnson discovered in their study of budgetary slack building in a sales division that lower-level managers built slack into their budgets in order to secure bonuses.[3] The authors also noted, however, that upper-level managers eliminated slack due to their knowledge of historical patterns of sales. It is worth mentioning that building slack is more difficult in areas with defined relationships between inputs and outputs. The department studied in this case is not a production or sales department and does not have a well-defined relationship between given inputs for a specific level of outputs.

SB also recognizes that forecasting in the aggregate is much more accurate than forecasting at the task level, an observation documented by David Otley in 1985.[4] SB allows for slack in one place only—the group budget buffer. Any department may draw funds from the group budget buffer if those funds are needed during the year. Providing the safety net of extra funds allows budgets to be drastically slashed at the lower levels without compromising performance of needed services.

A Specific Implementation Of Strategic Budgeting

In this case study, SB was implemented at a major manufacturing firm using the following process:

1. Gathered budget estimates from department heads.
2. Reduced all department budgets by 50%.
3. Grouped all "savings" from department budgets in a Group Budget Buffer.
4. Told each department head that if he or she needed further funds, the funds would be available but the request would be discussed openly with other department heads.

The Implementation Process

In 1999, shortly after a new manager took over the Testing Department of 42 employees in three functional divisions (Service, Application Development, and System Integration), the edict came to reduce operating expenses by 10%. The operating expenses under review involved the cost of purchasing services for equipment repair and calibration, hardware and software for testing services, overtime payments, and miscellaneous supplies. Each manager adamantly fought against any reductions, stating that all of the funds were needed.

In order to achieve the required reduction, another approach was taken. The first step was to develop a holistic goal for the entire department. The consensus goal was, "*To offer superior-quality products and services to our customer with a focus on speed and flexibility*." The process of using the team to develop the goal follows Joshua Ronen and J.L. Livingstone's premise that intrinsic rewards are achieved through the process of participation in goal setting.[5] Once the goal was agreed upon, the measurements for the department had to be changed to align with the new goal of working as one unit rather than as three functions. Employees were now measured on their ability to find synergies between the three functions and cross-functional team-based ideas for improvement opportunities.

Next, training started on the new Critical Chain method of reducing cost by grouping the cost reductions taken from each department together in one departmental buffer while reducing each function's

Table 1a: Budget Year 1 without Slack

Department	Lowest Tier	Second Tier	Department Total + $200,000 for Administration of Department	Division Total + $200,000 for Administration of Division	Slack as a Percent of Original Budget
RESEARCH AND DEVELOPMENT				$5,600,000	0%
Design			$1,700,000		
Feature Engineering		$500,000			
Overall Manufacturing Engineering		$500,000			
Prototype Build		$500,000			
Testing			$3,700,000		
Prototype Testing		$500,000			
Advanced Prototype Testing		$500,000			
Individual Labs		$500,000			
Lab 1	$200,000				
Lab 2	$200,000				
Lab 3	$200,000				
Lab 4	$200,000				
Lab 5	$200,000				
Lab 6	$200,000				
Lab 7	$200,000				
Lab 8	$200,000				
Lab 9	$200,000				
Lab 10	$200,000				

Table 1b: Budget Year 1 with 10% Slack

Department	Lowest Tier	Second Tier	Department Total + $200,000 for Administration of Department	Division Total + $200,000 for Administration of Division	Slack as a Percent of Original Budget
RESEARCH AND DEVELOPMENT				$7,359,000	31%
Design			$2,035,000		
Feature Engineering		$550,000			
Overall Manufacturing Engineering		$550,000			
Prototype Build		$550,000			
Testing			$4,455,000		
Prototype Testing		$550,000			
Advanced Prototype Testing		$550,000			
Individual Labs		$550,000			
Lab 1	$220,000				
Lab 2	$220,000				
Lab 3	$220,000				
Lab 4	$220,000				
Lab 5	$220,000				
Lab 6	$220,000				
Lab 7	$220,000				
Lab 8	$220,000				
Lab 9	$220,000				
Lab 10	$220,000				

Table 1c: Budget Year 4 with 10% Slack

Department	Lowest Tier	Second Tier	Department Total + $200,000 for Administration of Department	Division Total + $200,000 for Administration of Division	Slack as a Percent of Original Budget
RESEARCH AND DEVELOPMENT				$11,880,978	112%
Design			$2,708,585		
Feature Engineering		$732,050			
Overall Manufacturing Engineering		$732,050			
Prototype Build		$732,050			
Testing			$5,929,605		
Prototype Testing		$732,050			
Advanced Prototype Testing		$732,050			
Individual Labs		$732,050			
Lab 1	$292,820				
Lab 2	$292,820				
Lab 3	$292,820				
Lab 4	$292,820				
Lab 5	$292,820				
Lab 6	$292,820				
Lab 7	$292,820				
Lab 8	$292,820				
Lab 9	$292,820				
Lab 10	$292,820				

Table 1d: Budget Year 10 with 10% Slack

Department	Lowest Tier	Second Tier	Department Total + $200,000 for Administration of Department	Division Total + $200,000 for Administration of Division	Slack as a Percent of Original Budget
RESEARCH AND DEVELOPMENT				$32,744,641	485%
Design			$4,798,424		
Feature Engineering		$1,296,871			
Overall Manufacturing Engineering		$1,296,871			
Prototype Build		$1,296,871			
Testing			$10,504,657		
Prototype Testing		$1,296,871			
Advanced Prototype Testing		$1,296,871			
Individual Labs		$1,296,871			
Lab 1	$518,748				
Lab 2	$518,748				
Lab 3	$518,748				
Lab 4	$518,748				
Lab 5	$518,748				
Lab 6	$518,748				
Lab 7	$518,748				
Lab 8	$518,748				
Lab 9	$518,748				
Lab 10	$518,748				

Table 1e: Budget Increases Using 10% Slack Compounded Annually

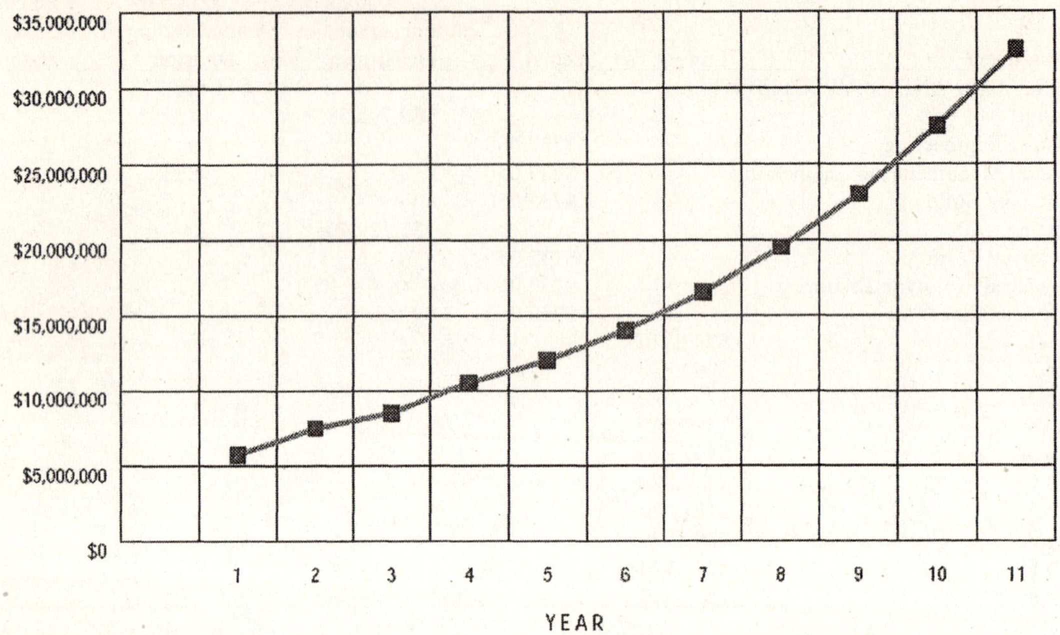

budget by one half. The departmental buffer functioned to reduce the risk of the group having insufficient funds for vital tasks. Any funds needed over the approved amount had to be explained to the other function managers and to the departmental manager. Justification for extra funds from the buffer was presented in a business case using the Theory of Constraints Thinking Process Tools, including the Current Reality Tree, CRT, and the Evaporating Cloud.[6] The CRT documented current ripple effects from current processes including, especially, any negative effects of the loss of funds on other departments' products or services.

The manager and the supervisors created a priority-spending matrix (Figure 3), which was used by the entire organization to evaluate the importance of the extra spending. The spending matrix was inspired by Steven R. Covey's book, *The Seven Habits of Highly Effective People: Restoring the Character Ethic.*

Once a month, at a departmental meeting called the Town Hall Meeting, all 42 departmental employees were briefed on the state of the departmental buffer. Any collaborative cross-functional accomplishments and any customer compliments for the department's services and products were highlighted.

During one meeting of the function managers, the Service Department manager requested buffer funds to purchase the services of an outside company to track the expenses of the Service Department. Fortunately, the Application Group's manager volunteered to develop the database for the Services Department at no charge. Through this synergy, the company avoided dipping into the departmental buffer and fostered collaboration. The event was described in an article circulated to all of the 42 departmental employees and reviewed in a Town Hall Meeting.

The Results

1. Budget Depletion for Important Tasks

After the first year, almost the entire departmental pool was intact. Of the original $6,250,000 buffer, $1,550,000 was reallocated to the System Integration function, reducing the buffer to $4,700,000. System Integration requested the extra funds for the purchase of data acquisition equipment to be used to solve warranty related problems. The managers of the other two functions agreed that the purchase of the equipment served a compelling function and furthered the goals of the department as a whole. Due to the added funds from the budget buffer, the System Integration Department ended up with almost twice the level of its original funding prior to the reductions at the start of the SB process (see Figure 4).

Figure 3: Priorities Guideline: Project and Activities

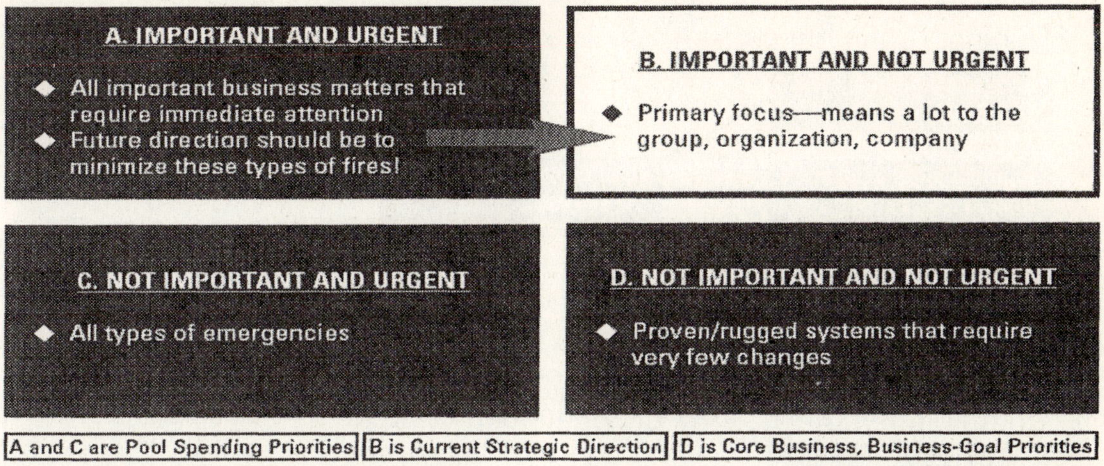

2. Utilizing Synergies to Maintain the Budget Buffer

In order to maintain the buffer, the service manager reviewed his purchases of thermocouples. He observed that, in the past, the department had stockpiled the wire without regard for the utilization patterns. After researching the historical usage patterns, he discovered that the thermocouples were only heavily used in the summer months during "In-Vehicle Testing." In addition, management discovered that several times the inventoried thermocouples were not needed because the vehicle department requesting the testing had already purchased the parts. Eventually, the purchase of thermocouples was eliminated.

Probably the largest savings came from the change in the buying patterns for data acquisition equipment. The Testing Department would traditionally purchase this equipment for customer departments requesting specific tests. The equipment was then transferred to the customer department and maintained there. The equipment generally was used only once for specific testing needs. The customer department also would calibrate the equipment, but the calibration frequently was not accurate, so testing results were suspect.

To reduce the waste of a one-time equipment purchase, the departmental manager created a library of data acquisition equipment. As a result, the equipment now is used repetitively instead of just once. Another major benefit of the library was that the Testing Department also maintained the equipment, so the calibrations were more accurate. This step not only saved costs but also improved overall quality of the services provided.

3. Removing Redundancies

In the process of reviewing spending patterns, managers discovered that one costly function performed by the department also was being handled by another department. Once the double tasking was identified, the work was returned to the department originally assigned the task and was no longer also performed by the Testing Department.

Over the next two years, the department was thrice asked to reduce expenditures by 10%. The cuts were made from the departmental buffer without any loss of headcount or product or with any project termination. During this period, employee morale was very high.

4. An Unforeseen Negative Consequence of Success

Unfortunately, the divisional manager retired at the end of the first year's implementation. The new divisional manager immediately requested another 10% reduction. Due to the projected $6,250,000 in the budget buffer, the Testing Department manager was able to immediately comply with the request. Every other departmental manager fought the reduction.

Later on in the same year, the divisional manager again requested another 10% reduction in the budgets of all departments in the division. Again, the Testing manager easily complied. Due to the alacrity of the response, the divisional manager assumed that there must be high levels of excess capacity in Testing. Therefore, she dramatically downsized the department, eliminating personnel and reassigning them to other areas within the corporation. The successful team was split up, their success rewarded with dismissal from the project.

Although the initial response of upper management was devastating to the employees of the Testing Department, eventually, after seeing the innovation of the manager in this one department, the company asked the manager to spread the Theory of Constraints innovations corporate-wide.

Figure 4:

Original Group Budget — Year 1

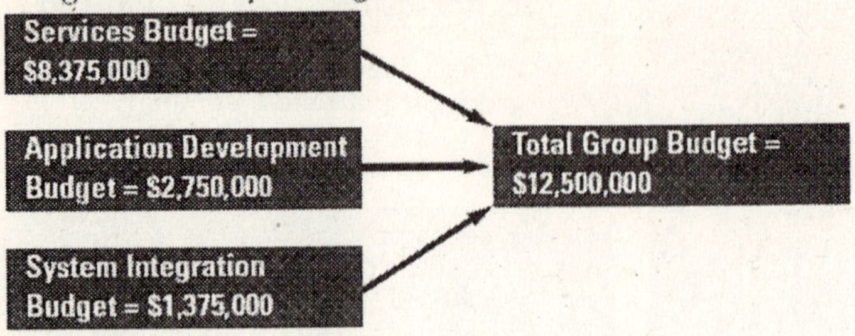

Group Budget Using Strategic Budgeting — Year 1

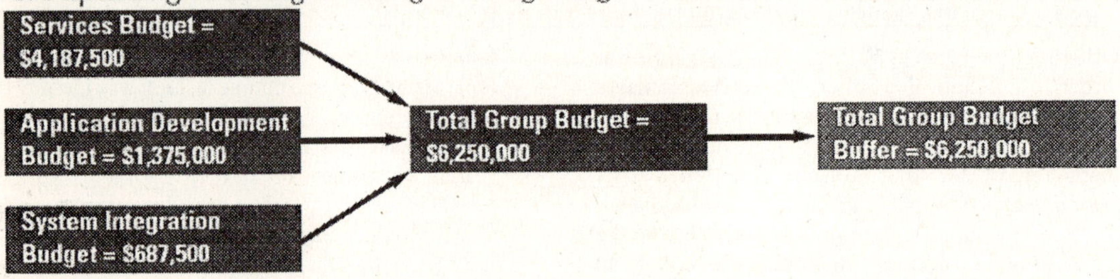

Group Budget Using Strategic Budgeting
After Group Budget Buffer Was Partially Depleted — Year 1

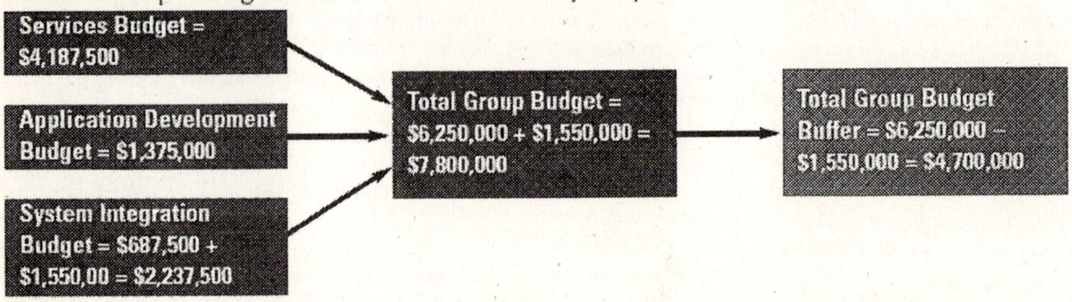

Group Budget Using Strategic Budgeting — Year 2 After Merger

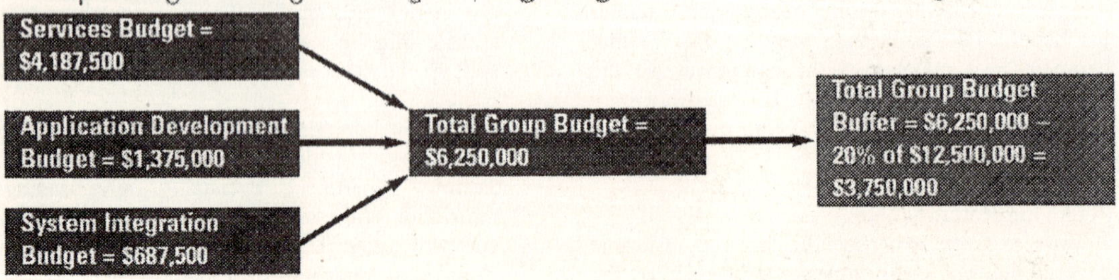

The Strengths Of Strategic Budgeting

1. Ease of Implementation

In contrast to zero based budgeting (ZBB), strategic budgeting does not require managers to rank tasks or to justify current expenditures in order to ferret out the slack within the budget.[7] Instead, strategic budgeting assumes that most budgets contain significant amounts of slack and can be cut in half without jeopardizing the output of any department. For those few departments with little or no slack, the safety provided is in the budget buffer for the entire company. Departments requiring extra expenditures can draw from the budget buffer once they have shared the need with the other affected departments.

In addition, SB can be implemented relatively quickly once the manager is determined to make the change. ZBB, on the other hand, takes a great deal of time to implement.[8] With SB, estimates of the amount of slack in each budget are not needed because all budgets are simply cut in half.

2. Increased Communication Between Departments

According to the findings of Joseph Fisher, James Frederickson, and Sean Peffer, managers are more willing to accommodate the needs of other departments when information is readily available about the other departments.[9] Requiring department heads to share their needs for buffer spending with the other department heads ensures cooperation. In addition, this practice transmits a subtle message that any buffer expenditures must be valid.

3. Lower Overall Spending Levels

In many corporations, managers are held responsible for overspending the budget. Therefore, managers tend to overstate their needs[10] and to spend the entire budgeted amount, even if excesses are available to refund to the company at year-end.[11] Budgetary slack is also difficult if not impossible to detect. In strategic budgeting, however, managers are encouraged to spend half of their original budget and to spend more only if the expenditure is valid and can stand up to the scrutiny of the managers competing for the same buffer of dollars. Through the use of this technique, true slack is identified without penalizing those areas with minimum or no slack. In fact, in this case, one department ended up with almost twice the amount of its original allotment of funds before the 50% reduction.

4. Assurance of Output Integrity

The danger of many cost-cutting initiatives is the loss of quality and quantity in the pursuit of reduced expenditures. What SB seems capable of delivering is reduced expenditures only in areas of increased slack while providing sufficient resources for those areas needing additional dollars in order to meet the corporation's stated goals. Because any expenditure of the budget buffer requires communication with other department heads, managers are reminded of the overall goal of any subunit when requesting extra funding. Those seeking unnecessary funds should be reluctant to ask for them, given the scrutiny of the other department heads. Those needing funds for legitimate corporate purposes, however, should feel totally justified in appealing for the extra funding. In fact, after using SB, some departments may end up with extra funding while others end up with significantly less.

5. Intrinsic Rewards through Goal Achievement

By eliminating significant amounts of slack, the upper level manager has created a situation where achieving the budget is something that can be valued by the lower-level manager.[13] It is difficult to meet previous output levels with half of the original funds. Therefore, the achievement of the target-spending levels is something of which to be proud. In addition, the agreement on a departmental goal and the continual realignment of departmental actions in light of the goal provide the structure and motivation mentioned by Ronen and Livingstone.[14]

Concerns And Cautions

Budget reductions of 50% in the first year of implementing strategic budgeting are relatively straightforward, but trying to continue such dramatic reductions in budgets year after year should be avoided. Once SB is implemented in the first year, managers will "know the game" and adjust their projections for needed funding accordingly. In addition, reductions beyond the original 50% would most likely be excessive and harmful to the delivery of the final product or service.

Implementation in just one lower-level area without coordinating with upper-level managers and "educating" the upper-level managers on the new technique could be suicidal. Upper-level managers who see large unspent budget amounts at year-end could assume many harmful things about the performance of the department and/or of the departmental manager. It is critical, therefore, to win the approval of the upper-level managers for the "experiment" with SB before its implementation. This case study should help in soliciting and winning such approval.

Current performance measurements reward spending the entire amount of budgeted funds and penalize underspending the budgeted amounts. Any unspent funding is likely to be lost to the department in the next budgeting cycle. Unless the performance measurement system rewards managers for spending less, they will continue to spend as much as is allowed. Therefore, the performance measurement system must be modified to encourage the creation and maintenance of a budget buffer for the protection of the overall performance of the firm. Rather than focusing on a detailed budget, employees should be focusing on the overall strategy of the corporation. To foster this team effort, management should consider rewards or bonuses that encourage team behavior and high levels of cooperation among departments.

[1] Kari Lukka, "Budgetary Biasing in Organizations: Theoretical Framework and Empirical *Evidence," Accounting*, Organizations and Society, Oxford, England, 1988, vol. 13, no. 3, pp. 281-301.
Kenneth Merchant and Jean-Francois Manzoni, "Achievability of Budget Targets in Profit Centers: A Field Study, *The Accounting Review*, July 1989, pp. 539-558.

[2] Mohammed Onsi, "Factor Analysis of Behavioral Variables Affecting Budgetary Slack," *The Accounting Review*, July 1973, pp. 535-548.

[3] Kenton B. Walker and Eric N. Johnson, "The Effects of a Budget-Based Incentive Compensation Scheme on the Budgeting Behavior of Managers and Subordinates," *Journal of Management Accounting Research*, vol. 11, 1999, pp. 1-28.

[4] David T. Otley,"The Accuracy of Budget Estimates: Some Statistical Evidence," *Journal of Business, Finance and Accounting*, 1985, vol. 12, pp. 415-428.

[5] Joshua Ronen and J. L. Livingstone, "An Expectancy Theory Approach to the Motivational Impacts of Budgets," *The Accounting Review*, October 1975, pp. 671-685.

[6] Eliyahu M. Goldratt, *It's Not Luck*, North River Press, Great Barrington, Mass., 1994.

[7] Allen Schick, "The Road from ZBB," *Public Administration Review*, March/April 1978, pp. 177-180.

[8] Norton S. Beckerman, "The Missing Link: The Planning Portion of the Zero Base Approach," *The Government Accountants Journal*, Winter 1978-1979, vol. 27, no. 4, pp. 24-31.

[9] Joseph G. Fisher, James R. Frederickson, and Sean A. Peffer, "Budgeting: An Experimental Investigation of the Effects of Negotiation," *The Accounting Review*, January 2000, pp. 93-114.

[10] Merchant and Manzoni, 1989.

[11] David T. Otley, "Budget Use and Managerial Performance," *Journal of Accounting Research*, Spring 1978, pp. 122-149.

[12] Onsi, 1973.

[13] Alan S. Dunk, "Budgetary Participation, Agreement on Evaluation Criteria and Managerial Performance: A Research Note," *Accounting, Organizations and Society*, vol. 15, no. 3, 1990, pp. 171-178.

[14] Ronen and Livingstone, 1975.

FURTHER READING

Christopher K. Bart, "Budgeting Gamesmanship," *The Academy of Management Executive*, November 1988, vol. 2, no. 4, pp. 285-294.

S. R. Covey, *The Seven Habits of Highly Effective People: Restoring the Character Ethic*, Simon and Schuster, New York, N.Y., 1989.

Joseph G. Fisher, L.A. Maines, S.A. Peffer, G.B. Sprinkle, "Using Budgets for Performance Evaluation: Effects of Resource Allocation and Horizontal Information Asymmetry on Budget Proposals, Budget Slack, and Performance," *The Accounting Review*, October 2002, pp. 847-865.

Eliyahu M. Goldratt, *Critical Chain*, North River Press, Great Barrington, Mass., 1997.

Floyd G. Lawrence, "*Zero Base Budgeting: Cure or Curse?", Industry Week*, March 20, 1978, pp. 94-98.

William C. Letzkus, "Zero-Base Budgeting: Some Implications of Measuring Accomplishments," *The Government Accountants Journal*, Summer 1978, vol. 27, no. 2, pp. 34-42.

HOW CHALLENGING SHOULD PROFIT BUDGET TARGETS BE?

By Kenneth A. Merchant
Certificate of Merit, 1989-90

It is a basic axiom of management that budget targets should be set to be challenging but achievable. But to establish that target, managers must first determine what "challenging but achievable" really means. Should profits be targeted at some easily obtainable goal, a realistic middle ground, or at a point so high that hope of attainment is slim?

There is no one right answer, given the number of purposes for which budgets are used: planning, coordination, control, motivation, and performance evaluation. Some may argue that planning purposes are served best with a best-guess budget, one that is as likely to be exceeded as missed.[1] Others may propose that, for optimum motivation, budget targets should be highly challenging, with only a 25% to 40% chance of achievement.[2]

There is one target-level choice, however, that serves the combination of purposes for which budgets are used quite well in the vast majority of organizational situations. Therefore, it provides an effective compromise. That choice is to set budget targets with a high probability of achievement—achievable by most managers 80% to 90% of the time—and then to supplement these targets with promises of extra incentives for performance exceeding the target level.[3] This prescription for the optimal budget target level, which is nearest point A in Figure 1, is made assuming that Figure 1 represents the probability distribution of forthcoming profits for an effective management team working at a consistently high level of effort.

These targets with an 80% to 90% probability of achievement are labeled properly "highly achievable" for most managers, but because of the assumption described in the preceding paragraph, the targets are at least somewhat challenging. They are not "easy." Even talented, experienced profit center managers must work hard and effectively to give themselves a good chance of achieving these targets.

THE ADVANTAGES OF USING HIGHLY ACHIEVABLE BUDGET TARGETS

Choosing budget targets with such a high probability of achievement provides many advantages to corporation, including the following:

1. *Managers commitment to achieve the budget targets is increased.* When targets are set to be highly achievable, the corporation can assess profit center managers high penalties for failing to achieve the targets at least many more years than not. These penalties can include loss of reputation, loss of autonomy, inability to get funding proposals approved, and sometimes even loss of job. Corporations can allow managers few or no excuses for not achieving the targets because the high achievability is designed to protect the managers to a considerable circumstances that were unforeseen at the time performance targets were set.

Because profit center managers face the risk of high penalties for performance shortfalls and do not have the safety net of excuses, they become highly committed to achieve their targets. This commitment causes them to prepare their budget forecasts more carefully and to spend more of their time managing rather than inventing excuses to explain their failures.

Firms that switch their budgeting philosophy to using highly achievable targets instead of "stretch" or "best guess" targets note the increase in commitment quite quickly. Comments a profit center manager in a large U.S. chemical corporation which made the switch:

> "Two years ago, our budgets were just best-effort forecasts. Today they are commitments. There is a vast difference. It's better to run this way. We have discipline. People used to make projections, but they forgot about them until they had to make another projection. Nobody ever came back and slapped their hand. Now people are challenged to put the things in place that are required to make the projections happen. The plans have begun to have credibility. Our spending plans are based on realistic projections."

Conversely, when budget targets are set at highly challenging levels, the danger exists that managers will not be committed to try to achieve their targets. For example, in a small publicly held electronics firm, which until recently had used a stretch target budgeting philosophy, profit center managers had started earning bonuses when their division's reported profit exceeded 60% of the budgeted level. But all too often, the profit center and corporate budgets were not achieved. In the words of the chief financial officer: "The system had some fudge in it. The managers were still in bonus territory, so they didn't have to worry about meeting the budget. It was like a wish, too easily blown off."

The corporation now has changed to what is known as "minimum performance standard" budget targets and its managers' commitment to these new targets has increased sharply. Since the change, the profit centers have achieved virtually all their budget targets every quarter.

The danger of lack of commitment to achieve targets is particularly acute if something goes wrong early in the year and loss of commitment leads to lower motivation. In the words of a manager whose entity had not achieved its budget targets for several years, "After the first few months of the year, we began to look at our goals as 'pie in the sky.' [The goals] didn't inspire us to do different things. They were just demoralizing."

2. *Managers' confidence remains high.* Regardless of the level of budget achievability, in the minds of most managers budget achievement defines the line between success and failure. Budget targets are the most specific and tangible goals managers are given, and most people define personal success in terms of their high degree of achievement of predetermined targets. As one manager put it, "If I were to miss my budget, I would feel like a failure. When I exceed my budget, I feel proud."

It is to the corporation's advantage to have its managers feel like winners. Managers who feel good about themselves and their abilities are more likely to work harder and to take prudent risks.

3. *Organizational control costs decrease.* Most corporations use a management-by-exception control philosophy where negative variances from budget signal the need for investigation and perhaps intervention in the affairs of the operating units. If budget targets are set to be highly achievable, negative variances are relatively rare, and top management or staff attention is directed to the few situations where the operating problems are most likely and most serious.

This point is illustrated in Figure 1. The probability distribution of profit outcomes shifts to the left (lower profit) for a lazy or ineffective manager. What was a highly achievable target for an effective, hardworking manager (point A) is not as highly achievable for an ineffective or lazy manager. Budget misses of two or three years send a strong signal that something is wrong and that top management intervention is necessary. Budget misses also provide objective rationales for relieving poor managers of their jobs.

4. *The risk of managers engaging in harmful earnings management practices is reduced.* Managers who are likely to achieve their budget targets are less likely to engage in costly actions designed to boost earnings in the short term. These actions include making potentially risky operating decisions (such as delaying preventative maintenance) and engaging in deceptive accounting practices (such as altering judgments about reserves).

FIGURE 1
PROBABILITY DISTRIBUTIONS OF FORTHCOMING PROFIT FOR EFFECTIVE AND INEFFECTIVE MANAGERS

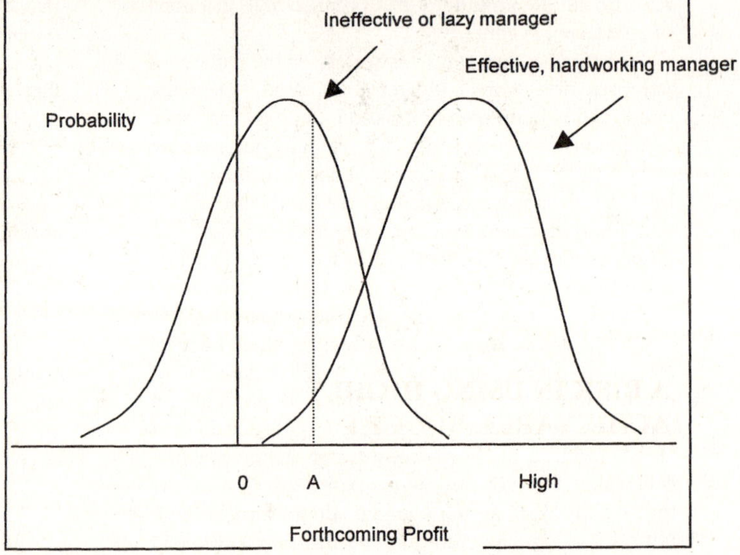

Highly achievable budget targets also lessen the incentives some managers have to reduce current period income. Those individuals who are facing stretch targets they consider nearly impossible to achieve may "take a bath"; they may take costly actions to position their entities for the subsequent accounting period. For example, they may defer sales and incur as many discretionary expenses as possible in the current period.

5. *Effective managers are allowed greater operating flexibility.* Highly achievable budget targets allow managers whose entities are performing well to accumulate some slack resources. Most managers will use this slack so that they do not have to respond to unforeseen, unfavorable short-term contingencies in costly ways, such as a suspension of productive long-term investments or a layoff. Some managers also will use the slack in productive, creative ways to fund "skunkworks" that may have high payoffs.

6. *The corporation is somewhat protected against the costs of optimistic revenue projections*. Budgets with optimistic revenue projections often induce managers to acquire resources in anticipation of activity levels that may not be forthcoming. Some of these resources, particularly people, can be difficult to eliminate when reality sets in. As one corporate president expressed it: "I think we ought to have a semiaggressive plan, but one that is achievable. We want to make it every year. It's too hard to adjust on the downside, to slough off commitments of expenses or not launch something you're psychologically committed to."

7. *The predictability of corporate earnings is increased.* When budget targets are likely to be achieved, the consolidated budget provides a highly probably lower bound of forthcoming corporate profits. This earnings predictability is valuable, particularly to managers of publicly held corporations. Earnings are usually less predictable in corporations whose business units face similar business risks, so this earnings-predictability advantage of highly achievable budget targets is higher in undiversified rather than diversified, firms.

A RISK IN USING HIGHLY ACHIEVABLE BUDGET TARGETS

The primary risk in using highly achievable budget targets is that managers may not be challenged to perform at their maximum. They may be satisfied with mediocrity—their levels of aspiration may be too low—and their motivation may slack off after the budgeted profit targets are achieved.

This problem of lack of challenge is potentially more serious when planning uncertainty is relatively high (and the inability to make adjustments for the effects of factors over which the managers had little or no control is relatively low). This is because the distance between the highly achievable target levels and the best-guess (or even higher) target levels is much greater than when planning uncertainty is low. This is shown in Figure 2. The tall curve shows a profit probability distribution in a relatively low uncertainty environment. The highly achievable budget level (B1) is not far from the most likely performance level (P). The shorter, flatter curve shows a distribution in a relatively uncertain environment. In this case, the highly achievable budget level (B2) is far below the most likely performance level.

Even in environments of high uncertainty, however, this lack-of-challenge problem is not inevitable. Most profit center managers have risen through the ranks because they are good performers with strong internal drives for competition and self-satisfaction. Furthermore, the "winning" feeling generated from budget achievement in prior periods is likely to increase, not decrease, the managers' levels of aspiration.

FIGURE 2
EFFECT OF PLANNING UNCERTAINTY ON PROBABILITY DISTRIBUTION OF FORTHCOMING PROFIT

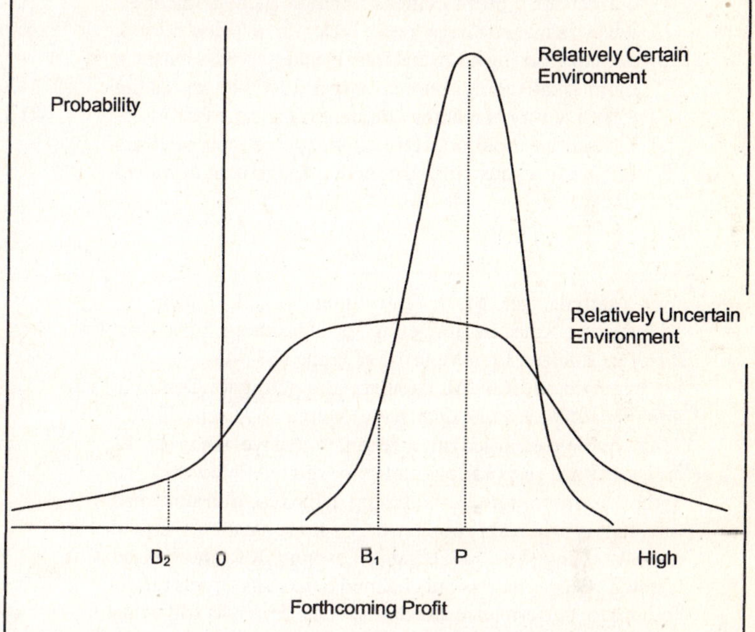

Furthermore, even when the risk of less than optimal challenge does exist, it can be minimized by giving managers incentives to strive for and to produce profits in excess of their budget targets. These incentives can be provided in combinations of many forms of rewards, including extra bonuses, recognition, autonomy, command over resources, and increased prospects for career advancement.

Profit center managers also can be asked to turn in more profit than originally was budgeted. This is a common occurrence in U.S. corporations.[4] These orders, combined with the highly achievable original targets, make the budget somewhat flexible. The highly achievable targets protect the profit center managers from the effects of unfavorable influences not explicitly expounded in the budget forecasts. The requests for profits above budgeted levels can be used to adjust for the effects of unforeseen good fortune on the measures of operating results. They can protect the corporation from the negative effects of excessive easy performance targets, such as managers' lagging ambition and the creation of excessive slack.

Only in a few organizational situations is it not desirable to set highly achievable profit budget targets. One exception is caused by organizational need. A company in grave difficulty may want to set less achievable budget targets as a signal to its managers that a certain higher level of performance is necessary for the corporation to survive or for the profit center to stave off divestment.

A second exception occurs when it is desirable to correct for a profit center's windfall gain. Sometimes when managers have been lucky in a prior period, perhaps earning large and mostly undeserved bonuses, a more challenging budget target can be set as an effective way of making compensation more fair across the multiyear period. Here, though, care must be taken to guard against unwarranted management turnover because current period expected compensation probably will fall below competitive market levels.

In virtually all other situations, it is desirable to set highly achievable profit budget targets while allowing the managers few excuses for not achieving the targets. Setting targets that are highly achievable, but not too easy takes considerable managerial skill. Upper-level managers must know enough about the profit centers capabilities and business prospects to be able to judge the probability of budget success reasonably well in order to make this budget philosophy work properly. But when they implement this combination of mechanisms effectively, they will ensure that all the purposes for which budgets are used—planning, coordination, control, motivation, and performance evaluation—are served well.

Kenneth Merchant is professor of accounting at the University of Southern California.

---

[1] For example, see M. E. Barrett and L. B. Fraser III, "Conflicting Roles in Budgeting for Operations," *Harvard Business Review*, July-August 1977, pp. 137-146.

[2] For example, see R. L. M. Dunbar, "Budgeting for Control," *Administrative Science Quarterly*, March 1971, pp. 88-96.

[3] This finding emerged in a recent intensive study of 12 divisionalized corporations and some related fieldwork. Ten of the 12 corporations participating in the research study had used highly achievable budget targets for some time. One had recently changed its budgeting philosophy. It formerly used "stretch" budget targets but changed to have its targets reflect "minimum performance standards." One firm was still using stretch budget targets, but most of the managers in the firm were recommending that this philosophy of budgeting be changed. (For a detailed report of the findings of this study, see K Merchant, *Rewarding Results: Motivating Profit Center Managers*, Harvard Business School Press, 1989.)

[4] For example, Merchant (1989) found that profit center managers in seven of the 12 firms studied were sometimes given direct orders from upper management to turn in greater profits than were budgeted. In some of these firms, the orders were given virtually every quarter.

Chapter 9
Decision Making with Relevant Costs and a Strategic Emphasis

Cases

9-1 Decision Making Under Uncertainty
9-2 Profitability Analysis
9-3 The Superior Valve Division
9-4 OmniSports Inc.
9-5 Wellesley Paint

Readings

"Buy or Lease"
This article explains a number of important considerations in choosing to lease or to buy. The article deals with a wide range of issues, including the financial statement effects and the taxation effects of the decision. In this context the article considers some of what chapter 9 points out as strategic issues in the decision to buy or lease.

Discussion Questions:
1. How does the decision to buy or lease affect the firm's balance sheet?
2. How does the decision to buy or lease affect the firm's income statement?
3. How does the decision to buy or lease affect the firm's income tax liability?
4. What strategic issues regarding a firm's operations are affected by the decision to lease or to buy a key asset?

Cases

9-1. Decision Making Under Uncertainty

Exquisite Foods Incorporated (EFI) sells premium foods. Three independent strategies are being considered to promote a new product, *Soufflés for Microwaves*, to dual-career families. Currently the contribution margin ratio on EFI's foods is 65%, which is expected to apply to the new product. EFI's policy for promoting new products permits only one type of advertising campaign until the product has been established.

STRATEGY ONE

The first strategy concentrates on television and magazine advertising. EFI would hire a marketing consultant to prepare a 30-second video commercial and a magazine advertisement. The commercial would air during the evening to address the working market, while the magazine advertisement would be place in magazines read by career-minded individuals. This advertising campaign would provide EFI $230,000 expected contribution from sales.

STRATEGY TWO

The second strategy promotes the product by offering 25% off coupons in the Sunday newspaper supplements, with a projected 15 percent redemption rate on sales revenue. EFI would hire a marketing consultant for $5,000 to design a one-quarter page, two-color coupon advertisement. The coupon would be distributed in the Sunday newspaper supplements at a cost of $195,000. Based on prior experience, EFI expects the following additional sales from this form of advertisement.

Expected sales	Probability
$500,000	10%
600,000	25
700,000	35
800,000	20
900,000	10

STRATEGY THREE

The third strategy offers a $.50 mail-in rebate coupon attached to each box of *Soufflés for Microwaves*. EFI would hire a marketing consultant for $5,000 to create a one-sixth page, one-color rebate coupon. Printing and attaching costs for the rebate coupon are $.07 per package, and EFI is planning to include the rebate offer on 500,000 packages. Although 500,000 packages may be sold, only a 10 percent redemption rate is expected. EFI expects the following additional sales from this type of promotion:

Expected sales	Probability
$400,000	10%
450,000	30
500,000	35
550,000	20
600,000	5

REQUIRED:

1. Exquisite Foods Incorporated (EFI) wishes to select the most profitable marketing alternative to promote *Soufflés for Microwaves*. Recommend which of the three strategies presented above should be adopted by EFI. Support your recommendation with appropriate calculations and analysis.
2. What selection criteria, other than profitability, should be considered in arriving at a decision on the choice of promotion alternatives?

9-2. Profitability Analysis

Sportway, Inc. is a wholesale distributor supplying a wide range of moderately priced sporting equipment to large chain stores. About 60 percent of Sportway's products are purchased from other companies while the remainder are manufactured by Sportway. The company has a Plastics Department that is currently manufacturing molded fishing tackle boxes. Sportway is able to manufacture and sell 8,000 tackle boxes annually, making full use of its direct labor capacity at available work stations. Presented below are the selling price and costs associated with Sportway's tackle boxes.

Selling price per box		$86.00
Costs per box		
Molded plastic	$ 8.00	
Hinges, latches, handle	9.00	
Direct labor ($15.00/hr.)	18.75	
Manufacturing overhead............	12.50	
Selling and administrative cost...	17.00	65.25
Profit per box		$20.75

Because Sportway believes it could sell 12,000 tackle boxes if it had sufficient manufacturing capacity, the company has looked into the possibility of purchasing the tackle boxes for distribution. Maple Products, a steady supplier of quality products, would be able to provide up to 9,000 tackle boxes per year at a price of $68.00 per box delivered to Sportway's facility.

Bart Johnson, Sportway's product manager, has suggested that the company could make better use of its Plastics Department by manufacturing skateboards. To support his position, Johnson has a market study that indicates an expanding market for skateboards and a need for additional suppliers. Johnson believes that Sportway could expect to sell 17,500 skateboards annually at a price of $45.00 per skateboard. Johnson's estimate of the costs to manufacture the skateboards is presented below.

Selling price per skateboard		$45.00
Costs per box		
Molded plastic	$5.50	
Wheels, hardware	7.00	
Direct labor ($15.00/hr.)	7.50	
Manufacturing overhead..............	5.00	
Selling and administrative cost.....	9.00	34.00
Profit per box		$11.00

In the Plastics Department, Sportway uses direct labor hours as the application base for manufacturing overhead. Included in total manufacturing overhead for the current year is $50,000 of factory-wide, fixed manufacturing overhead that has been allocated to the Plastics Department, and would not change irrespective of the option chosen. For each unit of product that Sportway sells, regardless of whether the product has been purchased or is manufactured by Sportway, there is an allocated $6.00 fixed overhead cost per unit for distribution that is included in the selling and administrative cost for all products. Total selling and administrative costs for the purchased tackle boxes would be $10.00 per unit.

REQUIRED:

1. Prepare an analysis based on the data presented that will show which product or products Sportway Inc. should manufacture and/or purchase to maximize profitability and show the associated financial impact. Support your answer with appropriate calculations.
2. Identify the strategic factors Sportway should consider in its product decisions.

(CMA adapted)

9-3 The Superior Valve Division

In 2001, the Superior Valve Division of the Able Corporation found itself in a position typical of fast-growing companies. Although sales revenues were increasing rapidly, capital equipment allocations from Able were less than desired, and profits were variable. Jerry Conrad, the general manager of the division, enrolled that year in a seminar on contribution margin income sponsored by the American Management Association (AMA). According to Conrad, "Before I went to that seminar, my knowledge of contribution margin income was limited to casual comments that I overheard at group general managers' meetings. A large acquisition in the automotive aftermarket industry had always used a contribution margin approach in its accounting systems. All other segments of the Able Corporation used the full costing method, but this company was allowed to keep its contribution margin cost system because a forced change of systems at the time of acquisition would have been too disruptive."

Jerry believed that the full cost reports used in his division were accurate. He and Frances Kardell, the Division Controller, were confident they knew the total manufacturing cost of each of their products. However, Jerry did not have the same confidence in his staff's ability to determine how volume changes would affect profits. He was convinced that better utilization of plant and equipment and a more effective pricing structure would lead to substantially improved earnings. The division was not as profitable as others in the industry or other similar-size divisions in the corporation that had comparable manufacturing processes.

A main point of the AMA seminar was that product lines do not produce profits; they produce contribution margin (sales revenue minus variable costs), which can become profits only after fixed costs are covered. The seminar also underscored not only the importance of cost behavior analysis but also the arbitrariness of many fixed cost allocations. Jerry immediately saw in contribution margin a new approach to solving Superior Valve's problems with both product mix and pricing decisions.

Jerry discussed the subject of contribution margin with Todd Talbott, the Group Controller. After hearing the advantages and disadvantages of the approach, Jerry recommended that his division's product costing system be overhauled for the third time since Able Corporation acquired Superior Valve 20 years ago. Todd agreed to support a change in the management reporting system, but he pointed out that the contribution margin approach was contrary to the reporting philosophy of the corporation and, for external purposes, did not comply with GAAP, S.E.C. reporting requirements, and Internal Revenue Service directives on inventory valuation.

When the decision to proceed was made, Frances and her accounting staff used regression analysis to classify manufacturing costs, other operating costs, and selling and general administration costs as either variable, fixed, or mixed. Mixed costs were separated into their variable and fixed components. Fixed costs then were identified as either discretionary (amounts to be expended based on decisions made annually or at shorter intervals) or committed (usually not subject to change in the short-run). A booklet on contribution margin which Jerry gave to his staff stated that fixed expenses are a function of time, and variable expenses (1) vary directly with changes in volume and (2) are usually expressed as a percentage of sales dollars or direct labor dollars.

SPECIAL ORDER

The Wadsworth Company, which was experimenting with various components of its product line, offered to purchase 6,000 Hydro-Con multi-function control valves from Superior for $160 each. Wadsworth would need 500 units per month with delivery commencing at the start of the new year. The special order would be in addition to the 80,000 units that Ralph Darwin, the division's Marketing Manager, expected to sell at the regular $200 price. Ralph considered the order to represent an excellent opportunity to increase long-term sales volume because it would be a new application for the product. He negotiated a flat $48,000 commission with the selling distributor.

Jerry was concerned that cutting the price of the valve would set an undesirable precedent. He pondered the special deal for several days before going to see Ralph. "The price is below our full cost of $175 per unit," he said. "If we accept the Wadsworth proposal, the firm can always expect favored treatment."

Jerry asked Daria Good, the Manufacturing Manager, and Frances to join this discussion in Darwin's office. When they arrived, he asked, "What is the division's capacity for making Hydro-Con Control?" Good's reply was "One hundred thousand (100,000) units per year, if we don't retool any machines dedicated to another product line."

Frances presented the following standard cost data for Hydro-Con valves:

Raw material	$ 35
Purchased components	30
Direct labor	12
Manufacturing overhead	44
Total standard cost	$121

After distributing copies of the budgeted income statement for the upcoming fiscal year (Table A), Frances revealed the variable overhead for the 80,000 unit Hydro-Con budget was $2,400,000. Of the budgeted fixed manufacturing costs, $400,000 was discretionary, with the remainder committed to basic capacity charges. Variable "other operating expenses" totaled $4 per unit; a 10% distributor commission ($20 per unit) comprised the variable portion of selling and general administration expenses. The Controller further indicated that manufacturing adjustments represented production variances and scrap, which she expected to vary with the number of valves produced. At the budgeted volume level, fixed other operating expenses would add an average of $16 to unit cost. Basic service costs such a production control, engineering administration, and accounting totaling $880,000 were allocated to Hydro-Con; the remaining fixed other operating expenses were directly related to the product line and were discretionary in nature.

As the discussion continued, Ralph reviewed next year's budget. Of the total fixed selling, general, and administrative expense, $160,000 was earmarked for future advertising space in several trade publications and an upcoming trade show. The remainder of the budget related to salaries and other firm commitments.

The Hydro-Con budget was designed to fully recover all costs at the 80,000 unit production level. The other product line budgets also were designed to fully recover costs at budgeted volume levels, and all fixed costs were expected to remain unchanged until the current maximum capacities were surpassed (Table B). Jerry asked his Division Controller what effect the Wadsworth offer would have on profits. But Daria had not yet studied the effects volume changes would have on division operations.

PRODUCT LINE ELIMINATION

Superior Valve's Marketing Department prepared a sales order plan by product line for each new year in both units and dollars. The Production Control Department then used the order plan to develop a sales shipment plan for each of the division's three plants. Ralph Darwin had very little marketing information to use in developing the Made to Order (MTO) Hydraulic Control product line plan. However, he knew that the line's compound growth pattern over the last three years had been quite disappointing, and he saw little prospect for substantial sales growth in the short-term future.

Ralph recommended the division consider eliminating the Made to Order line. Daria had assured him that the MTO-dedicated machinery could be retooled to produce either of the standard lines. Darwin was convinced he could develop a market for the additional standard product in a relatively short time, and he strongly believed the division should concentrate on its two basic product lines. "After all," he commented, "that's where we're most successful." However, until the additional market for the standard product was developed, the elimination of MTO would mean the elimination of 30 manufacturing jobs.

At the last staff meeting of the year, Jerry Conrad told Ralph he would study the product line elimination proposal after he made a decision on the Hydro-Con special order. He assigned the proposal top priority for the new year.

REQUIRED:

1. Assume that inventories will not change during the year. Prepare budgeted contribution approach product line income statements for the year ending 6/30/19X3. Categorize fixed costs as either discretionary or committed.
2. Should Jerry Conrad decide to accept the Wadsworth Company special order? If so, what will be the new Hydro-Con return on sales?
3. Should the Superior Valve Division eliminate the Made to Order product line if there were no alternative uses for its production capacity?
4. If all resulting standard products could be sold, how should the MTO capacity be allocated? (Assume only the capacity currently being used to produce 20,000 MTO units would be used to produce additional standard products.)
5. Identify the strategic factors that Superior Valve should consider.
6. What changes, if any, should be made to the division's cost system? Why?
7. What ethical issues, if any, should the division consider in connection with the decision to eliminate MTO?

TABLE A

Superior Valve Division
Budgeted Income Statement for the Year Ending 6/30/2002
($000)

	Hydro-Con	Pneu-trol	Made to Order	Total Division
Revenue	$16,000	$13,000	$ 5,000	$34,000
Material	5,200	3,900	1,300	10,400
Direct Labor	960	1,235	1,000	3,195
Overhead	3,520	2,990	1,531	8,041
Total Cost of Sales @ Standard	9,680	8,125	3,831	21,636
Gross Margin	6,320	4,875	1,169	12,364
Adjustments	800	520	554	1,874
Net Manufacturing Margin	5,520	4,355	615	10,490
Other Oper. Exp. Expenses	1,600	1,560	750	3,910
Selling & General Administration	1,920	1,560	600	4,080
Operating Income	$ 2,000	$ 1,235	$ (735)	$ 2,500

TABLE B

Superior Valve Division
Product Line Data

	Pneu-trol	MTO
Unit selling price	$ 50.00	$ 250.00
Variable overhead per unit	$ 6.50	$ 50.55
Total discretionary fixed overhead	$225,000	$100,000
Variable other operating cost per unit	$ 1.50	$ 5.00
Variable selling and general admin. per unit	$ 5.00	$ 25.00
Committed fixed other operating costs	$970,000	$550,000
Committed fixed selling & general admin.	$160,000	$ 75,000

Product Line	Present Max. Capacity in Units	Machine Hrs./Unit
Hydro-Con	100,000	6
Pneu-trol	350,000	2
MTO	50,000	5

9-4 OmniSport Inc.

OmniSport Inc. is a wholesale distributor supplying a wide range of moderately priced sporting equipment to large chain stores. OmniSport has an enviable reputation for quality of its products. In fact, the demand for its products is so great that at times OmniSport cannot satisfy the demand and must delay or refuse some orders, in order to maintain its production quality. Additionally, OmniSport purchases some of its products from outside suppliers in order to meet the demand. These suppliers are carefully chosen so that their products maintain the quality image that OmniSport has attained. About 60 percent of OmniSport's products are purchased from other companies while the remainder of the products are manufactured by OmniSport. The company has a Plastics Department that is currently manufacturing the boot for in-line skates. OmniSport is able to manufacture and sell 5,000 pairs of skates annually, making full use of its machine capacity at available workstations. Presented below are the selling price and costs associated with OmniSport's skates.

Selling price per pair of skates		$98
Costs per pair		
Molded plastic	$8	
Other direct materials	12	
Machine time ($16 per hour)	24	
Manufacturing overhead	18	
Selling and administrative cost	15	77
Profit per pair		$21

Because OmniSport believes it could sell 8,000 pairs of skates annually if it had sufficient manufacturing capacity, the company has looked into the possibility of purchasing the skates for distribution. Colcott Inc., a steady supplier of quality products, would be able to provide 6.000 pairs of skates per year at a price of $75 per pair delivered to OmniSport's facility.

Jack Petrone, OmniSport's product manager, has suggested that the company could make better use of its Plastics Department by manufacturing snowboard bindings. To support his position, Petrone has a market study that indicates an expanding market for snowboards and a need for additional suppliers. Petrone believes that OmniSport could expect to sell 12,000 snowboard bindings annually at a price of $60 per binding. Petrone's estimate of the costs to manufacture the bindings is presented below.

Selling price per snowboard binding		$60
Costs per binding		
Molded plastic	$16	
Other direct materials	4	
Machine time ($16 per hour)	8	
Manufacturing overhead	6	
Selling and administrative cost	14	48
Profit per binding		$12

Other information pertinent to OmniSport's operations is presented below.

An allocated $6 fixed overhead cost per unit is included in the selling and administrative cost for all of the purchased and manufactured products. Total fixed and variable selling and administrative costs for the purchased skates would be $10 per pair.

In the Plastics Department, OmniSport uses machine hours as the application base for manufacturing overhead. Included in the manufacturing overhead for the current year is $30,000 of fixed, factory-wide manufacturing overhead that has been allocated to the Plastics Department.

REQUIRED:

In order to maximize OmniSport Inc.'s profitability, recommend which product or products should be manufactured and/ or purchased. Prepare an analysis based on the data presented that will show the associated financial impact. Support your answer with appropriate calculations and strategic considerations.

(CMA adapted)

9-5 Wellesley Paint Company

"I'm not looking forward to breaking the news," groaned Charlie Oliver, the controller of Wellesley Paint Company. He and Don Smith, state liaison for the firm, were returning from a meeting with representatives of the Virginia General Services Administration (GSA), the agency that administers bidding on state contracts. Charlie and Don had expected to get the specifications to bid on the traffic paint contract, soon to be renewed. Instead of picking up the bid sheets and renewing old friendships at the GSA, however, they were stunned to learn that Wellesley's paint samples had performed poorly on the road test and the firm was not eligible to bid on the contract.

Wellesley's two main product lines are traffic paint, used for painting yellow and white lines on highways, and commercial paints, sold through local retail outlets. The paint production process is fairly simple. Raw materials are kept in the storage area that occupies approximately half of the plant space. Large tanks that resemble silos are used to store the latex that is the main ingredient in their paint. These tanks are located on the loading dock just outside the plant so that when a shipment of latex arrives, it can be pumped directly from the tank truck into these storage tanks. Latex is extremely sensitive to cold. It cannot be stored outside or even shipped in the winter without heated trucks, which are prohibitively expensive for a small firm such as Wellesley.

Currently, Wellesley has the traffic paint contracts for the states of Pennsylvania, North Carolina, Delaware, and Virginia. Of last year's total production of 380,000 gallons, 90% was traffic paint. Of this amount, 88,000 gallons were for the Virginia contract. Each state has unique specifications for color, thickness, texture, drying time, and other characteristics of the paint. For example, paint sold to Pennsylvania must withstand heavy use of salt on roads during the winter. Paint for North Carolina highways must tolerate extended periods of intense heat during summer months.

Due to the high cost of shipping paint, most paint producers can be competitive on price only in locations fairly close to their production facilities. Accordingly, Wellesley has enjoyed an advantage in bidding on contracts in the eastern states close to Virginia. However, one of their biggest competitors, Heron Paint Company of Houston, Texas, is building a new plant in North Carolina. With lower costs due to their efficient new facility and their proximity, Heron will become a major competitive threat.

Wellesley's commercial paint line includes interior and exterior house paints in a wide range of colors formulated to approximate authentic colonial colors. Because of the historical association, the line has been well received in Virginia. Most of these paints are sold through paint and hardware stores as the stores' second or third line of paint. The large national firms such as Benjamin Moore or Sherwin Williams provide extensive services to paint retailers such as computerized color matching equipment. Partly because they lack the resources to provide such amenities and partly because they have always considered the commercial paint a sideline, Wellesley has never tried to market their commercial line aggressively. Wellesley sells 38,000 gallons of commercial paint per year.

Charlie is worried about the future of the company. The firm's strategic goal is to provide a quality product at the lowest possible cost and in a timely fashion. After absorbing the shock of losing the Virginia contract, Charlie wondered whether the firm should consider increasing production of commercial paints to lessen the company's dependence on traffic paint contracts. Carl Bunch, who manages the day-to-day operation of the firm, believes they can double their sales of commercial paint if they undertake a promotional campaign estimated to cost $15,000. The average price of traffic paint sold last year was $9 per gallon. For commercial paint, the average price was $11.

Charlie Oliver has assembled the following data to evaluate the financial performance of the two lines of paint. The primary raw material used in paint production is latex. The list price for latex is $13.50 per pound; 450 pounds of latex are needed to produce 1,000 gallons of traffic paint. Commercial paint requires 325 pounds of latex per 1,000 gallons of paint. In addition to the cost of the latex, other variable costs are as shown below.

Raw materials cost per gallon of paint:	**Traffic**	**Commercial**
Camelcarb (limestone)	0.38	0.54
Silica	0.37	0.52
Pigment	0.12	0.38
Other ingredients	0.06	0.03
Direct labor cost per gallon	0.46	0.85
Freight cost per gallon	0.78	0.43

Last year, fixed overhead costs attributable to the traffic paint totaled $85,000, including an estimated $25,000 of costs directly associated with the Virginia contract; the $25,000 can now be eliminated. Fixed overhead costs attributable to the commercial paint are $13,000. Other manufacturing overhead costs total $110,000. Charlie estimates that $9,000 of this amount is inventory handling costs that will be avoided due to the loss of the Virginia contract. Both the remaining manufacturing overhead and the general and administrative costs of $140,000 are allocated equally to all gallons of paint produced.

Required

1. The firm's strategic goal is to provide a high-quality product to customers at a reasonable cost and in a timely fashion. What specific quality, cost, and time issues are relevant to traffic paint? To commercial paint? What information does the firm need to assess the performance of each product line on the three strategic dimensions of quality, cost, and time?

2. Calculate the contribution margin for each type of paint and total firm-wide contribution under each of the following scenarios:

Scenario A	Current production, including the Virginia contract
Scenario B	Without either the Virginia contract or the promotion to expand sales of commercial paint
Scenario C:	Without the Virginia Contract but with the promotion to expand sales of commercial paint

3. Determine whether scenario B or C (per part 1 above) should be chosen by Wellesley, and explain why, including a consideration of the strategic context.

Readings

BUY OR LEASE?

By Paul B. Weiss

Is your company's current overriding goal to make its balance sheet look better, polish its income statement, or improve its tax situation? These issues will influence its next equipment investment: whether to buy outright with cash, buy through debt financing, or lease. To help you with your decision, let's examine some advantages and disadvantages of equipment ownership vs. equipment leasing and look at current trends and recent developments in accounting, taxation, and asset management.

For more than two years, investment in new equipment has been weak in the U.S. because businesses of all sizes have deferred upgrading in favor of "making do" with existing infrastructure. Similarly, U.S. businesses have curtailed expansion plans, seeking instead to preserve profitability or protect their financial position in the face of weak demand for products and services.

There are signs of change. The National Bureau of Economic Research recently noted that Gross Domestic Product had generally been expanding since the fourth quarter of 2001. *The Wall Street Journal* commented, "The U.S. economy continues to experience growth in income and output, but employment continues to decline....The main reason for the more favorable performance of income and production...is the continuation of rapid productivity growth." The Journal attributes this to "squeezing more out of their existing workers and equipment."

This has the obvious effect of additional wear and tear on existing equipment, hastening its ultimate demise. When combined with the effort to postpone new equipment purchases, it makes it highly likely that the U.S. economy is in a condition of pent-up demand for equipment for both replacement and expansion needs.

The renewed increase in equipment investment has favorable ramifications for an economic recovery. But how will American businesses pay for the needed gear? In an outright purchase—using cash on hand or borrowing— the business will have all of the rights and privileges of ownership. But there are advantages and disadvantages to owning equipment compared to leasing it.

CONSIDERATION 1: THE BALANCE SHEET

When a company buys equipment with cash, the asset side of the balance sheet exhibits a reduction in cash and an increase in "property, plant and equipment." The money disappears from the balance sheet contemporaneously with the purchase. A purchase in which debt is incurred to buy the item of equipment leaves some of that cash on the balance sheet, but the debt balance, of course, is recorded as an increase in liabilities. In either example, there may be adverse consequences resulting from diminished liquidity ratios or increased leveraged ratios.

But if a company leases the same piece of equipment and the lease passes all the required "GAAP" tests, the equipment acquisition isn't reflected on the balance sheet. Under generally accepted accounting principles (GAAP), Statement of Financial Accounting Standards (SFAS) No. 13, "Accounting for Leases," addresses a number of underlying issues covering a wide range of facts and circumstances. Although it was issued in 1976 and later modified, the core concept of SFAS No. 13 survives and can be stated simply: If an equipment lease genuinely leaves "substantially all of the benefits and risks incident to ownership of property" with a third-party leasing company, the equipment lease transaction should qualify to be off balance sheet.

There are several empirical tests that will have to be applied to ensure compliance with the off-balance-sheet rules. The first and foremost test asks: Is the present value of the minimum contractual lease payment less than 90% of the equipment cost? In other words, let's assume that a business has only committed to pay $1,000 per year for four years and that the item of equipment being leased costs $5,000. Because the present value of the payments is less than 90% of $5,000, the leasing company still has significant risk—when the lease expires, $1,000 of investment is unrecovered. Hence, the transaction isn't an installment sale to the user nor is it a lending scheme. The leasing company hasn't passed on the "benefits and risks incident to ownership" because it must find a way to recover its "naked" 10% investment (20% in this case—$1,000) later in the life of the equipment plus whatever additional amounts it can to make it a profitable transaction.

In another example, say a piece of equipment costs $5 million. In a lease for a term of four years with monthly payments at the end of each month, the lessee is making 48 payments of $83,333.33 per month. The present value of these payments is calculated using an interest rate that reflects the lessee's cost of capital. So, using 6% interest for the calculation, the present value of the lease payment obligation is approximately $3,500,000, which is 70% of the equipment cost of $5 million. If the rent were higher, perhaps $105,000 or more per month, the present value of the payment obligation would exceed $4,500,000 (depending on the interest rate used in the calculation). Once the present value of the lease payment obligation approaches 90% of the cost of the equipment, the lease may be deemed to be a purchase and not qualify for off-balance-sheet treatment.

If a lease transaction successfully passes this 90% rule and other GAAP tests, neither the equipment (asset) nor the payment obligation (liability) appears on the corporate balance sheet. For certain companies, then, acquiring equipment through off-balance-sheet lease financing can help with their broader corporate goals of limiting leverage and maximizing cash (inasmuch as cash was not used to buy the equipment).

In today's tougher credit environments, many companies are operating under restrictive covenants put forth by their lenders or bondholders, and, in many cases, these covenants are expressed in terms of conventional working capital, debt to worth, and cash flow coverage ratios. In other words, a company with $150 million of debt and $100 million of equity may be up against its borrowing limit if its lenders have imposed a 1.5:1 debt-to-equity ratio maximum. This company might be unable to buy a $10 million item of equipment if it doesn't have cash on hand. Leasing the $10 million item with off-balance-sheet treatment leaves its leverage ratio at 1.5:1. Consequently, off-balance-sheet leasing may be a very useful tool for those companies needing the additional "legroom" in managing their financial position.

CONSIDERATION 2: THE INCOME STATEMENT

A company's income statement is also affected as a result of leasing vs. outright purchase. Cash-rich buyers will, in all likelihood, want to buy equipment in order to avoid rental expense and/or interest expense. In a cash purchase, the income statement will reflect depreciation expense but won't have any rental expense item (attributable to a lease) or any Interest expense item (attributable to borrowing to purchase). In comparison, borrowing money to buy equipment will result in higher total expenses because the company will incur depreciation expense and interest expense associated with the debt-financed purchase. This will likely reduce pre-tax income. In general, a lease transaction will result in a new expense item—rental expense—that will be less than the combined interest and depreciation expense resulting from a leveraged purchase. As a consequence, it's quite likely that in the early years of equipment use/ownership, the income statement will benefit from leasing as opposed to borrowing.

CONSIDERATION 3: TAX ISSUES

Under many circumstances, accelerated depreciation can significantly benefit companies that want to reduce taxes. But for some companies the impact can be of little value. Understanding the variables will help ensure that your business assesses the true economic opportunity and costs of leasing.

For many years, domestic fiscal policy has generously rewarded investments in equipment slated to be located within the U.S. because of the potential to improve domestic economic output resulting from high levels of domestic capital investment. This view, shared by most economists, recognizes the "multiplier effect" from an equipment purchase, which puts dollars in the pockets of equipment manufacturers, suppliers, and their employees, and the dollars are then employed again at (for example) the local grocery store, etc. Hence, "accelerated depreciation" policy provides an incentive for capital spending by allowing equipment investors to enjoy considerable cost savings from the actual expenditure. Taxes, which would have been paid in the years of and after the purchase, are postponed with Uncle Sam's blessing.

At least two types of companies, however, don't benefit from accelerated depreciation: companies in capital intensive industries that may be subject to the Alternative Minimum Tax (which limits depreciation benefits) and companies in the red that don't need the tax reduction. In the latter case, companies that have zero taxable income have no economic reason to further reduce their taxes because they were already $0. In either case, these "valuable" accelerated depreciation benefits can't be applied to effectively reduce the cost of equipment to these companies.

President Bush's tax bill provides additional tax incentives for equipment acquisition, which may increase the tax benefits for a company buying equipment. Through the end of 2004 and primarily for property to be delivered before the end of 2005, equipment buyers can claim a 30%-50% bonus during the first year of depreciation, deferring the applicable taxes. At this writing, it's unclear to what extent these fiscal initiatives will encourage capital expenditures. It is clear, though, that the generous tax deferral available for the upcoming year should be considered in a lease vs. purchase decision.

CONSIDERATION 4: FLEET FLEXIBILITY

Under most circumstances, a business seeking to acquire mission critical equipment with certainty about its permanent usefulness to the business will be better off owning rather than leasing equipment. Examples of such mission critical equipment include critical components of an assembly line or production facility, equipment necessary for power generation, oil rigs for petroleum companies, aircraft for airline companies, and other items generally inseparable from business operations. If the company is acquiring equipment that is vital to its operations, it might leave itself vulnerable if the "costs and benefits incident to ownership" were in the hands of a third party, outside of its control, as follows:

When a lease expires, the user/lessee usually has several stated options under the lease. Typically, equipment can be returned (which may not be practical for mission critical equipment) or purchased for its fair market value. "Fair market value" is a defined term in leases that utilize this concept and varies widely as to its precise definition. For critically important equipment, which has a high replacement cost, some leases define "fair market value" in a way that makes it very dear for the company to acquire the equipment. If an item of machinery cost $10 million when new—and the replacement machinery Therefore, the tax savings from ownership slightly favor buying over leasing, all the more so if the savings are viewed on a present value basis and leverage is used to buy the equipment. Whether this example holds up in the real world will depend on the precise economics of the lease and the company's tax position. A more sophisticated analysis considers the other variables as well as the opportunity cost (how the company might have benefited from keeping the $10 of equipment investment and using the cash to grow the business). is being sold for, say, $13 million brand new—an argument could be made that fair market value is $10-$12 million for the old equipment.

Normally, a user could elect to return the equipment if the fair market value seemed too high...but in a scenario where the company has no real option other than to buy the in-place asset because it's difficult or time consuming to replace it...the result can often be expensive. Leasing of business-critical components may have seemed like a good idea several years ago, and undoubtedly achieved numerous objectives at the time, but proved to be expensive in hindsight. But the majority of business equipment leasing deals don't involve business-critical equipment. Most nonessential gear, such as office equipment, can be an appropriate candidate for leasing. Other asset categories like trucks and forklifts are easily replaced by other units. We use the term "fleet flexibility" to describe the general benefit to a business of leasing equipment of "temporary utility" that can be returned easily. "Temporary" utility may mean two to 10 years in capital-intensive industries where equipment might have 12-50 years of useful life.

By not committing to pay for the equipment in full, a business retains the ability to more easily shed surplus equipment that it may not need because the business grew, shrank, or changed its plans. New technologies encourage businesses to shed obsolete equipment, and this can be achieved more easily on leased equipment because the "risk" of obsolescence is borne by the leasing company. For those companies unable or unwilling to make long-term plans for equipment in the face of rapid change, the lease alternative may be particularly suitable.

CONSIDERATION 5: THE "TRUE CASH COST" OF LEASING VS. OWNING

What makes economic sense? All other things being equal, in a perfect world the most cost-effective option for many businesses is to buy equipment with cash unless they have compelling investment opportunities for that cash. But since many businesses are operating in a world where cash is a constraint on their growth, the more frequently faced decision is often between borrowing and leasing.

In their well-regarded reference book, *Equipment Leasing*, Peter Nevitt and Frank Fabozzi stated, "Financial economists have demonstrated that if it were not for the different tax treatment for owning and leasing an asset, the costs would be identical in an efficient capital market."

Though this makes sense when applied at a macro level, the specific terms and conditions of a lease, as well as the future market for the equipment, must be quantified to the greatest extent possible and compared to the company's borrowing costs. Common sense dictates that, if a business is paying for less than 90% of the equipment value, the periodic cash payments will often be lower than if the equipment were paid for in full by means of a loan. But the lower periodic payments are only part of the economic cost comparison.

In a typical lease, the user will have the option when the lease expires to return the equipment or purchase it, and they frequently can opt to renew. If the equipment has retained value, a company may have lost a resale profit opportunity on resale because it leased (and doesn't own) an item of equipment. Conversely, equipment may prove to have disappointing value, which is a risk borne by the leasing company. After all, it's the leasing company that will take the loss on such a sale, not your company. As an example, airlines leasing commercial aircraft prior to September 11, 2001, benefited by avoiding the brunt of a sharp decline in equipment values since that date, and many leasing companies suffered severe losses.

IT'S YOUR CHOICE

For decades, the lease vs. purchase decision has been among the most complex analyses in modern finance. The net effect of balance sheet and income statement management, tax results, "fleet flexibility," and cash cost considerations is difficult to assess. Yet recent accounting and tax law interpretations highlight some near-term opportunities for companies deciding how to acquire equipment. Companies today consider all of the above factors and methods when assessing equipment expenditures. For large companies, most often the decision to lease or buy is driven by balance sheet considerations, not only by cash on hand. Those that are also public companies are sensitive to heavy emphasis on reported profitability, which affects stock prices and perceptions. For private companies, tax considerations, fleet flexibility, and the true "cash cost" often carry stronger weight than earnings management.

Chapter 10
Cost Planning for the Product Life Cycle: Target Costing, Theory of Constraints, and Long Term Pricing

Cases

10-1 California-Illini Manufacturing (The Theory of Constraints)
10-2 Blue Ridge Manufacturing (B)
10-3 Nebraska Toaster Company (Target Costing)
10-4 Mercedes-Benz All Activity Vehicle (Target Costing)

Readings

"Target Costing at ITT Automotive"

This article provides a good example of an actual application of target costing. The example is of the production and sale of brake systems, an intensely competitive industry. The article explains how value engineering is used. Two important concepts of the article are (1) target costing is a moving target, and as prices fall in the industry, target costs and manufacturing costs are required to fall as well, and (2) target costing is a bottom-up, team-oriented process that requires cross-functional teams. Also, the article explains how ITT uses "tracking sheets" to manage the life cycle costs of the product.

Discussion Questions:

1. How are prices set at ITT Automotive?
2. How does ITT Automotive obtain information about a competitor's costs?
3. What are the target costing tools used at ITT Automotive?
4. How is the tracking sheet used in ITT Automotive's target costing system?

"Integrating Activity-Based Costing and The Theory of Constraints"

The authors of this article show how ABC costing and the Theory of Constraints (TOC) methods can be compared and used in a complementary fashion.

Discussion Question: Explain how ABC and TOC can be viewed as complementary methods.

Cases

10-1. California-Illini Manufacturing

The California-Illini Manufacturing Company's (CI) plant operates in the rural central valley of California. It is family-owned and run. CI's plant manager, a grandson of the founder, went to school with many of the employees. Despite this family atmosphere, CI is the largest producer of plain and hard-faced replacement tillage tools in the United States. It averages annual sales of $13 million. Farmers use tillage tools to cultivate the land. Hard-facing, the application of brazed chromium carbide to leading edges, increases a tool's durability.

THE PRODUCTION PROCESS

Historically, CI grew from the founders' original blacksmith shop, and today the production process is still relatively simple. The plant manager described the process as "You simply take a piece of metal. And then you bang, heat, and shape it until it's a finished product. It really isn't a sophisticated process. We just do it better than anyone else." The production process is like a flow following a routing from one cost center to another in a sequence of move, wait, setup, and runtime for each process. Work-in-process inventories in the move and wait stage litter the plant. Economic lot size rules determine the size of each batch while production schedules push jobs onto the floor.

THE COST SYSTEM: MEASURING PERFORMANCE

CI uses standard unit costs to measure performance and profit potential. In this cost system, each materials and labor input is given a standard usage, and production managers are evaluated on their ability to meet or improve upon these standards. Differences from the standard were called "variances." For example, if a certain manufacturing operation required at standard 5 minutes, the operator would be expected to complete a lot of 100 parts in 500 minutes. If actually 550 minutes were required, there would be a 50 minute unfavorable variance. Also, using the operator's wage rate, the cost of the variance could be calculated.

CI'S IMPROVEMENT STRATEGY

The depressed market in the mid-1980s caused a 1986 net loss of close to $1.8 million. Inventory turns were down to one and a half, and cash flow was poor. Facing these conditions, management adopted a new strategy stressing improvements in accounting performance and reduction of inventories. Their strategies for improvement included: increasing productivity, cost cutting (overhead control), improving technology, and increasing prices.

1. **Productivity**. Productivity improvements centered on direct labor productivity measures. Output per direct labor hour was the crucial factor. Accordingly, improving efficiency, by definition, consisted of keeping direct labor busy producing as much product as possible during regular working hours. Actions supporting this strategy were 1) reducing idle manhours between jobs, 2) increasing batch sizes to maximize runtime, and 3) reducing setup times.

   The operational control system measured the "earned labor hours" for each department daily. While the plant manager only received these reports weekly, he was still aware of the daily figures. Budget reports, including variances, while processed monthly, were often two to three weeks late! Thus, they had little direct impact on day-to-day decisions. However, the plant manager knew what the accounting reports should be like from his daily earned labor hours information.

The short-term results of these efforts were impressive because plant efficiency measures rose about 15%. There were, however, some negative, unanticipated side effects in work-in-process levels, scheduling, and overtime.

First, work-in-process levels increased. In order to improve efficiency measures, departments kept processing large lots regardless of current demand. Once a machine had been set up, to economically justify large batches, the rationale was to provide for both current and future inventory needs. Consequently, finished goods grew from two to six-months' supply.

Second, the large batch sizes made scheduling difficult. They reduced plant flexibility by keeping machines on single jobs for long periods. Therefore, it was difficult to adjust for normal production problems and still maintain the production schedule. Machines were not readily available for special situations and expediting.

Finally, these large batches, while increasing productivity, created the need for overtime to maintain the schedule. Overtime in the finishing department, for example, increased by 15-20%, thus raising operating expenses. The larger lots reduced the variety of products produced each production period. This increased the lead time for custom orders could get stuck behind jobs with long runtimes. Overtime, then, became necessary to expedite out-of-stock orders. These factors combined with low sales volumes to create losses and more cash flow problems.

2. **Overhead.** Overhead improvement focused on two strategies. The first was direct cost reduction. The second concentrated on reducing unit costs by increasing volume. The higher volumes allowed overhead to be absorbed over more units. However, because CI's cost structure had large fixed obligations (like union contracted pension fund contribution), potential overhead savings were minimal.

   The results of these strategies were unimpressive. The union didn't make many concessions, and few overhead savings occurred. Production volumes did increase, but the plant was producing to cover overhead rather than to satisfy immediate demand. Management hoped that increasing sales would eventually take care of the excess production. Unfortunately, this didn't happen. By 1989 inventories were 24% higher than in 1986. And, once again, there were cash flow and earnings problems.

3. **Technology.** CI considered the technology focus to be particularly troublesome. Concentrating on reducing unit costs through technology improvement often blocked out other aspects of the decision. Management's assumptions were that the savings from each decision flowed directly to the bottom line. However for CI this myopic view of unit costs encouraged mistakes.

   Management's use of robots provided a vivid example of the problems. Robots were investigated as a means of decreasing the unit costs for the application knife. The anhydrous ammonia applicator knife was popular worldwide, to revitalize the soil with ammonia fertilizer after each harvest. Although CI led the industry in product quality, it was a high-cost producer. The primary reason was determined to be hand welding, using expensive piece rates, with manual electric arc welders.

   After a unit-cost analysis, the savings in labor and applied overhead seemed to justify the introduction of welding robots (Tables 1,2,3). Subsequent price reductions increased sales from 20,000 to more than 60,000 units in the first. At the new, lower, price the company seemed to still realize savings of $1.25 per unit.

   Unfortunately, these savings were illusory. During the second year, other manufacturers became price competitive and sales volume dropped to 40,000 units; however, management still believed the robots saved the company money. At a 10% discount rate the three-year net present value was $63,730. A major problem was that labor savings disappeared as manual welders found work in other areas of the plant. In fact, the robots required additional new hires and caused increases in utilities and maintenance costs. New operating expenses were greater than the increased throughput. Thus, management was misled by its focus on standard unit costs.

4. **Selling Prices.** Unfortunately, the market for the firm's products was very competitive. Due to such macroeconomic factors as government programs and foreign grain production, the domestic market was shrinking. Internationally, CI's high unit costs made foreign markets difficult to enter. Consequently, management perceived the marketplace to be mostly out of their control. Their main focus was on improving plant performance. Nonetheless, CI still tried to increase the sales volume in domestic markets and to find new foreign markets. As for the foreign markets they experienced some success and some failures.

    In an attempt to find new international markets, the company successfully set up a working relationship with a John Deere distributor in Mexico and, unsuccessfully pursued a contract in Saudi Arabia. This failure was very revealing because Saudi Arabian soils were made to order for CI's product. The Saudi's cultivation process was particularly abrasive for tillage tools. Because of frequent breakdowns, crews with replacement parts had to constantly follow the field workers. But with CI's parts this practice wasn't necessary. Consequently, the Saudis were very enthusiastic about the company's products. Unfortunately, CI did not believe the 10% profit margins to be large enough. CI rejected the Saudi Arabia offer. This happened while at the same time the plant was having difficulty with operating expenses, overhead, and inventories. Thus, the accounting cost standards influenced market decisions as well as leading to questionable, limited improvements in manufacturing. All was not harmonious among management as well.

    During this time, marketing and production meetings were frequent. Marketing pointed out that while quality was good, prices were too high and lead times were too inaccurate. On the other hand, production complained that marketing was constantly messing up their production schedules.

    Using this combination of efficiency improvement, overhead reduction, unit-cost reductions and sales margins, management proceeded, over an 18-month period, to reduce domestic volume by 11.5% and to turn away significant foreign opportunities. Overall, decisions to improve the performance of the company using standard cost measurement failed. By February 1989, operating expenses were 20% greater than the disastrous 1986 figures. During the same period, inventories increased by 24%, and net profits continued to deteriorate.

    At year-end CI hired a new Production Control/Inventory Control (PCIC) manager. However, the plant manager was suspicious when the PCIC manager came to him with revised schedules. The PCIC manager suggested processing job lots of 100 to 150 part rather than the current 6,000. The plant manager questioned the PCIC manager's ability. "Clearly he isn't very knowledgeable. How can we make any money running only small lots? The setup costs will kill us!

    Finally the PCIC manager gave the plant manager a copy of The Goal by E. Goldratt and J. Cox. After reading the first few pages, the plant manager recognized many similarities between his plant and the one described in this book.

REQUIRED:

1. What is the firm's competitive strategy? Does the strategy seem appropriate?
2. What motivated the cost reduction strategy? Did the cost reduction strategy work? Why?
3. How did CI's standard cost system affect the cost reduction strategy?
4. What is the role of work-in-process in the cost reduction strategy?
5. Is the new Production control/Inventory Control (PCIC) manager on the right track with the smaller lot sizes?
6. What steps is the PCIC likely to take now?
7. What type of cost system should be used at CI?

(IMA adapted)

TABLE 1
IMPACT OF ROBOTICS ON STANDARD COST
ANHYDROUS AMMONIA KNIVES

Department	Material: Before	After	Labor: Before	After	Overhead: Before	After	Total: Before	After
Cold Shear	$2.000	$2.000	$0.068	$0.068	$0.238	$0.238	$2.306	$2.306
Hot Forge			$0.127	$0.127	$0.445	$0.445	$0.572	$0.572
Heat Treat			$0.025	$0.025	$0.088	$0.088	$0.113	$0.113
Shot Blast			$0.025	$0.025	$0.088	$0.088	$0.113	$0.113
Arc Weld	$6.500	$6.500	$1.380	$0.250	$4.830	$0.875	$12.710	$7.625
Paint/Pack			$0.076	$0.076	$0.266	$0.266	$0.342	$0.342
Total	$8.500	$8.500	$1.701	$0.571	$5.954	$1.999	$16.155	$11.070
Selling Price							$18.150	$14.310
Gross Margin							12.353%	29.274%
Unit Profit							$1.995	$3.241
Note – OH/DL = 3.5/1								

TABLE 2
IMPACT OF ROBOTICS ON STANDARD COST
ANHYDROUS AMMONIA KNIVES

Year	Unit Savings	Unit Sales	+(–) Profits	Present Value (10%)
1	$1.245	6,000	$ 74,700	$ 67,909
2	$1.245	4,000	49,800	41,157
3	$1.245	4,000	49,800	37,415
Total			$174,300	$146,482
Initial investment				$ (60,000)
Net present value				$ 86,482

TABLE 3
IMPACT OF ROBOTICS ON STANDARD COST
ANHYDROUS AMMONIA KNIVES

Actual Results:

Year	Net Additional: Labor	Maintenance	Utilities	Total Additional: Expenses	Net Additional: Throughput	+(-) Profits	Present Value (10%)
1	$52,000	$2,000	$4,000	$ 58,000	$155,600	$97,600	$88,727
2	$92,000	$2,000	$4,000	$ 98,000	$ 39,400	($58,600)	($48,430)
3	$92,000	$2,000	$4,000	$ 98,000	$ 39,400	($58,600)	($44,027)
Total				$254,000	$234,400	($19,600)	($3,730)
Initial Investment							($60,000)
Net Present Value							($63,730)

10-2. Blue Ridge Manufacturing (B)

Note: For the background information on this case, see Case 5-1. Case (B) is a continuation of Case 5-1

UPDATE OF RECENT DEVELOPMENTS

Blue Ridge Manufacturing (BRM) has found that the new non-toxic ink has stimulated sales substantially, so the firm has extended its markets both nationally and internationally. It has upgraded the quality of all its products and developed new products including bathrobes and bath towels for upscale hotels and resorts, bed and breakfasts, and some corporate clients. The majority of the new products also involve imprinting a logo or some form of embroidery.

At the same time BRM has been expanding its product line, significant new competition has developed, especially from non-U.S.-based manufacturers, particularly in Asian counties. These new competitors have caused BRM to lower its prices in some markets, and has reduced BRM's market share in many markets.

An important aspect of the new products for hotels and resorts is that these products sometimes involve a significant amount of design work. In contrast to BRM's other products which have logos and design that are standardized by license agreement, the hotel products fall into two categories. First, there are some well-established hotels and resorts that have a global logo and for which the design effort is negligible. The customer's logo or design is well specified and easy to work with in the production of the bathrobes, towels or other products. Second, there are some hotels and resorts that are not a part of a large chain, which may not have a well-designed logo for their towels and bathrobes. These customers require a significant amount of extra work in helping the customer develop a design that is workable for the desired products. The extra work can be as much as 18-26 hours per order, but is more often less than 10 hours. The bathrobes require more design time, roughly 2-16 hours per order, while the towels usually require 1-6 hours per order, when the additional design work is necessary. From recent months' results, it appears that the new products will become a significant part of BRM's overall business, especially the customers from smaller hotels and resorts that need design help. In view of the success of the new products, BRM is thinking of putting in place a product development team, a permanent activity within the firm, which would search out new product ideas and develop new products on an on-going basis.

REQUIRED:

1. What is BRM's strategy now that it has developed the new products and become a global competitor? Has the strategy changed?

2. How should BRM adapt to the new competitive environment?

10-3 Nebraska Toaster Company: Target Costing Case

Through market research and competitor analysis Nebraska Toaster Company has found a market for toaster oven new product that is not currently being produced by competitors. This new toaster can toast bagels or regular toast bread or grill sausages. It will be targeted for a consumer group of young family households. The customer requirements and important features to the consumer have been identified and the Nebraska Toaster Company will focus on these for the toaster oven design. The criteria are:

Toasts properly
Size
Speed of toasting
Toaster capacity
Appearance
Easy to clean

Nebraska Toaster Company wants to competitively match the price toaster oven to basic toasters; the competitive market price is $20.00. Nebraska Toaster Company wants to earn a profit of 20 % of sales price. Relevant cost information for the company follows in Table 1. Most of the life cycle activities are done inside the firm, but shipping is outsourced.

Table 1 Life Cycle and Value Chain Analysis

Value Chain	***Inside***			***Outside***			***Total***		
Life Cycle	**Target**	**Current**	**Gap**	**Target**	**Current**	**Gap**	**Target**	**Current**	**Gap**
R&D	$ 4.00 (25%)	$ 4.20	$ 0.20				$ 4.00 (25%)	$ 4.20	$0.20
Manufacturing	9.00 (56%)	12.00	3.00				9.00 (56%)	12.00	3.00
Selling	1.60 (10%)	1.80	0.20				1.60 (10%)	1.80	0.20
Shipping				$ 0.90 (6%)	$ 1.00	$ 0.10	0.90 (6%)	1.00	0.10
General Adm.	0.50 (3%)	0.70	0.20				0.50 (3%)	0.70	0.20
Total	**$ 15.10 (94%)**	**$ 18.70**	**$ 3.60**	**$ 0.90 (6%)**	**$ 1.00**	**$ 0.10**	**$16.00**	**$19.70**	**$3.70**

The toaster company through value engineering and continuous improvement plans to determine a way to reach the target cost by looking at the products life cycle and its value chain activities to determine where to reduce costs.

Step 1-- Product Functional Cost analysis

Nebraska Toaster Company plans to implement functional analysis to target areas of cost reduction. Here the company breakdowns the current $12.00 manufacturing costs (from Table 1 "Manufacturing" row and "Total Current" column) for the toaster oven by the components' estimated costs and functions performed. The result is in Table 2.

Table 2 Product Functional Cost Analysis

Component	Function	Current Cost	% of Cost
Heating Unit	Toast bagels or grill sausages	$2.40	20
Display Light	Indicates the process of toasting or grilling	1.60	13
Lever	Lowers bagels or sausages into toaster & initiates toasting or grilling	0.60	5
Spring Coil	Pops up bagels or sausages when toasted or grilled	0.60	5
Temperature Control Timer	Controls degree of toasting or grilling	0.60	5
Body Design	Holds bagels or sausages	5.10	43
Crumb and Grease Catcher	Catches crumbs and greases & is removable for cleaning	1.10	9
TOTAL		$12.00	100%

The Nebraska Toaster Company plans to rank the features of the new bagel toaster according to customer preferences and requirements, in Step 2.

Step 2 -- Customer Requirement Analysis

Nebraska Toaster Company selected a customer focus group to rank the six most important characteristics or requirements as shown in Table 3.

Table 3 Customer Requirement Analysis

Customer Requirements	Customer Ranking	Relative Ranking	
	Ranking is from 1-5, 5 the most important	Raw Score	%
Toasts and grills properly	5	5	28
Size	3	3	17
Speed of toasting or grilling	3	3	17
Toaster oven capacity	2	2	11
Appearance	1	1	5
Easy to clean	4	4	22
TOTAL		**18**	**100**

The customers rank the criteria -- toast or grill properly, cleaning, and size -- as the most important relative to the other customer characteristics or requirements. The next process compares the customer requirement features to the component functions.

Step 3 -- Quality Function Development Analysis

Nebraska Toaster Company engineers assessed the new toaster oven product's functional performance as shown in Table 4.

Table 4 Quality Functional Performance Assessment

Components or Functions	Heating Unit	Display Light	Lever	Spring Coil	Temp. Control & Timer	Body Design	Crumb Catcher	
Customer Requirements								**Total**
Toasts properly	50 %		20 %	20%	10%			100%
Size	50 %					50 %		100%
Speed of toasting	70 %				10 %	20 %		100%
Toaster capacity	30 %		5 %			60 %	5 %	100%
Appearance		20 %				80 %		100%
Easy to clean	50 %					45 %	5 %	100%

Required:

1. Calculate the target cost for the toaster
2. Using the information above, develop a ranking of product functions that gives the company the importance and value of each component relative to the features that create value to the customer.

10-4. Mercedes-Benz All Activity Vehicle (AAV)[3]

During the recession beginning in the early 1990s, Mercedes-Benz (MB) struggled with product development, cost efficiency, material purchasing and problems in adapting to changing markets. In 1993, these problems caused the worst sales slump in decades, and the luxury carmaker lost money for the first time in its history. Since then, MB has streamlined the core business, reduced parts and system complexity, and established simultaneous engineering programs with suppliers.

In their search for additional market share, new segments, and new niches, MB started developing a range of new products. New product introductions included the C-class in 1993, the E-class in 1995, the new sportster SLK in 1996, and the A-class and M-class All Activity Vehicle (AAV) in 1997. Perhaps the largest and most radical of MB's new projects was the AAV. In April 1993, MB announced it would build its first passenger vehicle-manufacturing facility in the United States. The decision emphasized the company's globalization strategy and desire to move closer to its customers and markets.

Mercedes-Benz United States International used function groups with representatives from every area of the company (marketing, development, engineering, purchasing, production, and controlling) to design the vehicle and production systems. A modular construction process was used to produce the AAV. First-tier suppliers provided systems, rather than individual parts or components, for production of approximately 65,000 vehicles annually.

THE AAV PROJECT PHASES

The AAV has moved from concept to production in a relatively short period of time. The first phase, the concept phase, was initiated in 1992. The concept phase resulted in a feasibility study that was approved by the board. Following board approval, the project realization phase began in 1993, with production commencing in 1997. Key elements of the various phases are described below.

CONCEPT PHASE, 1992-1993

Team members compared the existing production line with various market segments to discover opportunities for new vehicle introductions. The analysis revealed opportunities in the rapidly expanding sports utility vehicle market that was dominated by Jeep, Ford, and GM. Market research was conducted to estimate potential worldwide sales opportunities for a high-end AAV with the characteristics of a Mercedes-Benz. A rough cost estimate was developed that included materials, labor, overhead, and one-time development and project costs. Projected cash flows were analyzed over a 10-year period using net present value (NPV) analysis to acquire project approval from the board of directors. The sensitivity of the NPV was analyzed by calculating "what-if" scenarios involving risks and opportunities. For example, risk factors included monetary exchange rate fluctuations, different sales levels due to consumer substitution of the AAV for another MB product, and product and manufacturing cost that differed from projections.

Based on the economic feasibility study of the concept phase, the board approved the project and initiated a search for potential manufacturing locations. Sites located in Germany, other European countries, and the United States were evaluated. Consistent with the company's globalization strategy, the decisive factor that brought the plant to the United States was the desire to be close to the major market for sports utility vehicles.

---

[3] Prepared by Thomas L. Albright, © Institute of Management Accountants, 2000. Used with permission.

PROJECT REALIZATION PHASE, 1993-1996

Regular customer clinics were held to view the prototype and to explain the new vehicle concept. These clinics produced important information about how the proposed vehicle would be received by potential customers and the press. Customers were asked to rank the importance of various characteristics including safety, comfort, economy, and styling. Engineers organized in function groups designed systems to deliver these essential characteristics. However, MB would not lower its internal standards for components, even if initial customer expectations might be lower than the MB standard. For example, many automotive experts believed the superior handling of MB products resulted from manufacturing the best automobile chassis in the world. Thus, each class within the MB line met strict standards for handling, even though these standards might exceed customer expectations for some classes. MB did not use target costing to produce the lowest-price vehicle in an automotive class. The company's strategic objective was to deliver products that were slightly more expensive than competitive models. However, the additional cost would have to translate into greater perceived value on the part of the customer.

Throughout the project realization phase, the vehicle (and vehicle target cost) remained alive because of changing dynamics. For example, the market moved toward the luxury end of the spectrum while the AAV was under development. In addition, crash test results were incorporated into the evolving AAV design. For these reasons, MB found it beneficial to place the design and testing team members in close physical proximity to other functions within the project to promote fast communication and decision making. Sometimes new technical features, such as side air bags, were developed by MB. The decision to include the new feature on all MB lines was made at the corporate level because experience had shown that customers' reactions to a vehicle class can affect the entire brand.

PRODUCTION PHASE, 1997

The project was monitored by annual updates of the NPV analysis. In addition, a three-year plan (including income statements) was prepared annually and reported to the headquarters in Germany. Monthly departmental meetings were held to discuss actual cost performance compared with standards developed during the cost estimation process. Thus, the accounting system served as a control mechanism to ensure that actual production costs would conform to target (or standard) costs.

TARGET COSTING AND THE AAV

The process of achieving target cost for the AAV began with an estimate of the existing cost for each function group. Next, components of each function group were identified, with their associated costs. Cost reduction targets were set by comparing the estimated existing cost with the target cost for each function group. These function groups included the following: doors, sidewall and roof, electrical system, bumpers, powertrain, seats, heating system, cockpit, and front end. Next, cost reduction targets were established for each component. As part of the competitive benchmark process, MB bought and tore down competitors' vehicles to help understand their costs and manufacturing processes.

The AAV manufacturing process relied on high value-added systems suppliers. For example, the entire cockpit was purchased as a unit from a systems supplier. Thus, systems suppliers were part of the development process from the beginning of the project. MB expected suppliers to meet established cost targets. To enhance function group effectiveness, suppliers were brought into the discussion at an early stage in the process. Decisions had to be made quickly in the early stages of development.

The target costing process was led by cost planners who were engineers, not accountants. Because the cost planners were engineers with manufacturing and design experience, they could make reasonable estimates of costs that suppliers would incur in providing various systems. Also, MB owned much of the tooling, such as dies to form sheet metal, used by suppliers to produce components. Tooling costs are a substantial part of the one-time costs in the project phase.

INDEX DEVELOPMENT TO SUPPORT TARGET COSTING ACTIVITIES I[4]

During the concept development phase, MB team members used various indexes to help them determine critical performance, design, and cost relationships for the AAV. To construct the indexes, various forms of information were gathered from customers, suppliers, and their own design team. Though the actual number of categories used by MB was much greater, Table 1 illustrates the calculations used to quantify customer responses to the AAV concept. For example, values shown in the importance column resulted from asking a sample of potential customers whether they consider each category extremely important when considering the purchase of a new MB product. Respondents could respond affirmatively to all categories that applied.

Table 1. Relative Importance Ranking by Category

Category	Importance	Relative Percentage
Safety	32	41%
Comfort	25	32
Economy	15	18
Styling	7	9
Total	79	100

To gain a better understanding of the various sources of costs, function groups were identified together with target cost estimates. (MB also organizes teams called function groups whose role is to develop specifications and cost projections.) As shown in Table 2, the relative target cost percentage of each function group was computed.

Table 2. Target Cost and Percentage by Function Group

Function Group	Target Cost	Percentage of Total
Chasis	$x,xxx	20%
Transmission	$x,xxx	25
Air conditioner	$x,xxx	5
Electrical System	$x,xxx	7
Other function groups	$x,xxx	43
Total	$xx,xxx	100%

[4] All numbers have been altered for proprietary reasons; however, the tables illustrate the actual process used in the development of the AAV.

Table 3 summarizes how each function group contributes to the consumer requirements identified in Table 1. For example, safety was identified by potential customers as an important characteristic of the AAV; some function groups contributed more to the safety category than others. MB engineers determined chassis quality was an important element of safety (50% of the total function group contribution).

Table 3. Function Group Contribution to Customer Requirements

Function Group/Category	Safety	Comfort	Economy	Styling
Chassis	50%	30%	10%	10%
Transmission	20	20	30	
Air conditioner		20		5
Electrical system	5		20	
Other systems	25	30	40	85
Total	100%	100%	100%	100%

Table 4 combines the category weighting percentages from Table 1 with the function group contribution from Table 3. The result is an importance index that measures the relative importance of each function group across all categories. For example, potential customers weighted the categories of safety, comfort, economy, and styling as .41, .32, .18, and .09, respectively. The rows in Table 4 represent the contribution of each function group to the various categories. The importance index for the chassis is calculated by multiplying each row value by its corresponding category value, and summing the results ((.50 x .41) + (.30 x .32) + (.10 x .18) + (.10 x .09) = .33.

Table 4. Importance Index of Various Function Groups

Function Group/ Category	Safety .41	Comfort .32	Economy .18	Styling .09	Importance Index
Chassis	.50	.30	.10	.10	.33
Transmission	.20	.20			.20
Air conditioner		.20	.05	.05	.07
Electrical system	.05				.06
Other systems	.25	.40	.85	.85	.35
Total	1.00	1.00	1.00	1.00	

As shown in Table 5, the target cost index is calculated by dividing the importance index by the target cost percentage by function group. Managers at MB used indexes such as these during the concept design phase to understand the relationship of the importance of a function group to the target cost of a function group. Indexes less than one may indicate a cost in excess of the perceived value of the function group. Thus, opportunities for cost reduction, consistent with customer demands, may be identified and managed during the early stages of product development. Choices made during the project realization phase were largely irreversible during the production phase because approximately 80% of the production cost of the AAV was for materials and systems provided by external suppliers.

The AAV project used a streamlined management structure to facilitate efficient and rapid development. The streamlined MB organization produced an entirely new vehicle from concept to production in four years. Using the target costing process as a key management element, MB manufactured the first production AAV in 1997.

Table 5. Target Cost Index

Function Group/Index	(A) Importance Index	(B) % of Target Cost	(C) A/B Target Cost Index
Chassis	.33	.20	1.65
Transmission	.20	.25	.80
Air conditioner	.07	.05	1.40
Electrical Systems	.06	.07	.86
Other systems	.35	.43	.81
Total		1.00	

Questions for Discussion:

1. What is the competitive environment faced by MB?
2. How has MB reacted to the changing world market for luxury automobiles?
3. Using Cooper's cost, quality, and functionality chart, discuss the factors on which MB competes with other automobile producers such as Jeep, Ford, and GM.[5]
4. How does the AAV project link with MB strategy in terms of market coverage?
5. Explain the process of developing a component importance index. How can such an index guide managers in making cost reduction decisions?
6. How does MB approach cost reduction to achieve target costs?
7. How do suppliers factor into the target costing process? Why are they so critically important to the success of the MB AAV?
8. What role does the accounting department play in the target costing process?

---

[5] Robin Cooper, When Lean Enterprises Collide, Boston: Harvard Business School Press, 1995

Readings

TARGET COSTING AT ITT AUTOMOTIVE

By George Schmelze, CPA; Rolf Geir; and Thomas E. Buttross, CMA

Intense competition and pressure from customers to reduce prices has forced many companies to reduce their costs to survive. These companies have found that most costs are committed once production begins, and, therefore, the costs must be reduced earlier in the product life cycle, particularly while the product is in the planning and design stages. Target costing is a proven, effective method of reducing production costs throughout the product life cycle, without reducing quality or functionality and without increasing the time it takes to design and develop a product. At ITT Automotive, the brakes area has been using target costing for three to four years, and it provides an excellent model that other areas of the company are beginning to emulate.

Target costing is a proactive, strategic cost management philosophy that is price-driven, customer focused, design-centered, and cross-functional.[1] Unlike traditional cost control systems, which do not control costs until production has commenced, the target costing philosophy requires that aggressive cost management occur in the product planning stage, the product design stage, and the production stage. By designing lower costs into the product, companies realize the best sources of cost savings—before the product reaches the production stage. These cost savings cannot be realized, however, with traditional costing systems, such as standard costing systems and activity-based costing systems.[2]

Target costing transcends the functional areas of a company. For target costing to be successful, integration is needed in the form of cross-functional teams comprising engineering, product design, production, purchasing, sales, finance, cost accounting, cost targeting, and, in many cases, customers and suppliers. Upper-level management support is crucial to the success of target costing because resources need to be allocated to the target costing area, and the cross-functional teams must be empowered to make many critical decisions.

Target costing differs from traditional "cost-plus" costing. Rather than the selling price being a function of estimated costs, the target cost is a function of the selling price and a desired profit. Furthermore, with target costing, the target cost is determined before the product is designed. The target costing equation is as follows:

Target Price – Target Profit = Target Cost

Various factors are considered when computing the future selling price of the proposed product including functionality of the product, projected sales volumes, and quality. For example, management strategy may call for a price that maintains or increases market share.

Due to intense competition, many companies have little flexibility when setting a price. When market conditions are extremely competitive, the price may be driven by the market. In other cases, the target cost of the downstream company is the target price of the upstream company. Where selling price and profit margin are fixed by competitive pressures and management policies, respectively, reducing the firm's production costs may be the only source of increased earnings.

Once the target cost is computed, it must be assigned to final assembly, subassemblies, and components before design can begin. After the product is designed, estimated costs of production are compared with target costs. If the estimated costs are higher than the target costs, value engineering is employed to help the company achieve its target. Value engineering is a process in which the cross-functional team attempts to reduce costs during the design and preproduction stages without compromising quality and functionality by determining the optimal processes, materials, and machinery needed for production.

Estimated costs are compared with the targets throughout the product life cycle. Once the product reaches production, however, cost maintenance (as opposed to cost reduction) generally becomes the objective.

TARGET COSTING AT ITT AUTOMOTIVE

To illustrate the process of target costing, let's look at the target costing practices at ITT Automotive. ITT Automotive, one of the world's largest suppliers of auto parts, produced sales of $4.8 billion in 1994, which represented an increase of more than 34% compared to 1993. In 1995, sales were approximately $5.7 billion. Products produced include brake systems and components, wiper handling systems and components, fluid handling systems and components, structural systems and components, electric motors, switches, and lamps. More than 35,000 employees work for the company, with the vast majority of these employees located in the United States and Germany.

The brakes area has used target costing extensively for the last few years because of an extremely competitive environment. For example, the price of anti-lock brake systems, which currently sell for about $200, is expected to drop to $100 by the year 2000. Furthermore, the functionality of the product is expected to increase.

ESTABLISHING THE TARGET PRICE AND TARGET MARGIN

At ITT Automotive, price is generally set externally, either by competitive pressure or by the customer's target costing system. For example, the price that Mercedes-Benz offers ITT Automotive for an anti-lock brake system (ABS) is Mercedes-Benz's target cost.

The first step in the process occurs when ITT Automotive receives an invitation to bid from the customer. Due to the competitive nature of this industry, ITT Automotive cannot use "cost-plus" pricing when setting the price. The price that the company generally will quote is a price that already has been set by market conditions. An analysis then is performed to determine if the product fits ITT Automotive's strategic goals and if the volume can be produced. Financial information including internal rate of return (IRR) and return on investment (ROI) also are calculated to ensure that ITT Automotive can earn a proper return. If productivity increases (reductions in price) are expected by the customer, the analysis must include an explanation concerning how the productivity increases will be achieved.

To determine whether the price is feasible, a permanent cost targeting group made up of employees with backgrounds in engineering, cost accounting, and sales receives the quote. Keeping in mind that the product being quoted will not be produced for several years, the ITT Automotive cost targeting group makes a determination concerning whether enough value engineering can be accomplished before the product is produced in order to meet the quoted price. Other factors considered by the cost targeting team when determining the feasibility of a price include previous quotes issued, economic factors such as anticipated inflation and interest rates, competitor pricing, and cost structure.

Because ITT Automotive does not produce automobiles, it does not have information concerning prices (and costs) of competitors' component parts. Information from a tear-down analysis of a competitor's product, however, may provide ITT Automotive with information that is useful in determining a competitor's costs and, by adding a reasonable margin, the competitor's price. Tear-down analysis, sometimes referred to as reverse engineering, is an analytical process in which a company will examine in detail a competitor's product. During tear-down analysis, a competitor's product is torn apart by engineers, component by component. An indication of the competitor's design, estimated cost structure, quality, functionality, and possible processes used to build the product are garnered from this process. From this analysis, ITT Automotive may be able to improve designs or processes in order to reduce cost without losing functionality (or to increase functionality and quality without increasing costs). The information garnered from this study is recorded on a standardized document that compares each competitor's product with ITT Automotive's product. This information is useful for price setting because the tear-down analysis provides information concerning the estimated cost structure of the competitor.

Price setting is an iterative process. The cost targeting team will try to find ways to reduce costs in order to accept a bid without comprising ITT Automotive's expected return. For example, the cost targeting team may consult with the design engineers who may suggest that some new process or technology will be available when the produce is produced that will reduce the cost of the product.

ASSIGNING THE TARGET COST.

The target cost is the target price minus the target margin. Finding the target cost is a relatively straightforward calculation; the difficulty for most companies is reaching the target cost in order to meet the company's profit objectives. The target cost should include all costs related to the new product. At ITT Automotive, target costs include direct materials, direct labor, tooling costs, depreciation, promotion, service, and working capital.

Once the target cost has been computed, specific targets are assigned first to final assemblies, then to subassemblies, and then finally to individual components. This work is performed by individuals in the permanent cost targeting group. Although the setting of the targets is a cross-functional procedure, the ITT Automotive team believes that it is critical for someone who is independent to first set the targets. Once the targets are set initially in cost targeting, feedback is given to the cost targeting area from various members of the cross-functional team, including purchasing and production, concerning targets that are considered unreasonable. This step allows the cross-functional team to be involved in the target-setting process without bogging down the process.

Individual targets are set for each component that is purchased, along with targets for burden and labor. The target costs are tracked throughout the product's life cycle, beginning with the design of the product, continuing when tooling is released, and not concluding until the product is discontinued.

In many situations, the price that ITT Automotive will receive for the product will become lower each year. Thus, the target costs will have to be lower each year to provide the company with the same return from year to year. Eventually the margin will become too small, and new products will have to be developed. Figure 1 shows a typical target costing situation, where cost targets are lower each year fueled by productivity increases. The targets are met by using cross-functional teams, setting early cost targets, engaging in value engineering (including tear-down analysis of competitor products and concurrent engineering and production), and forming partnerships with suppliers.

Then these targets are compared with quotes (or estimated costs for items such as depreciation). If the targets are not met, costs are reduced through value engineering and value analysis.

FIGURE 1
A MOVING TARGET

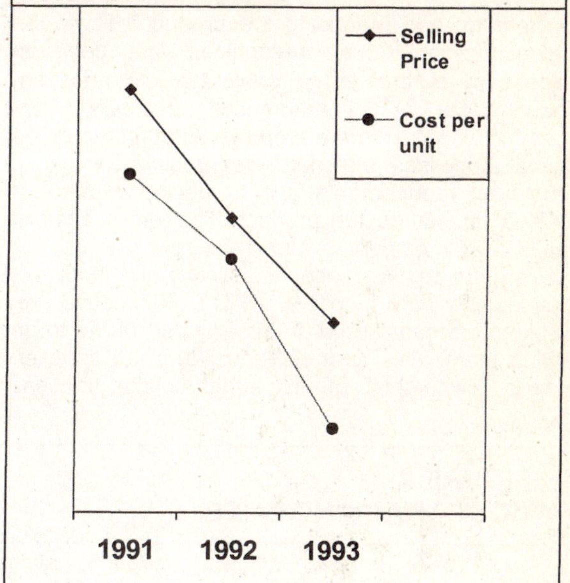

SOME TARGET COSTING TOOLS USED AT ITT AUTOMOTIVE

Achieving the target cost requires companies to take a disciplined approach toward value improvement. Value improvement occurs when functionality and quality are held constant while costs are reduced or when quality and functionality are increased while price is held constant,[3] At ITT Automotive, achieving the target cost is accomplished through several techniques including the use of cross-functional teams, setting early cost targets, value engineering, and forming partnerships with suppliers.

The target costing process, however, does not end in the early stages of the product life cycle. Once the product reaches production, cost maintenance is practiced through profit improvement planning and value analysis. These techniques help individuals in all of the functional areas take ownership for meeting cost targets throughout the product's life cycle.

One byproduct of the use of cross functional teams is increased understanding of processes and product design by members of the cross-functional team. Members of the cross-functional team at ITT Automotive must have knowledge of processes and design to contribute in a meaningful way to the target costing process. For example, purchasing personnel must have a working knowledge of how the product is designed to make optimal decisions concerning the purchase of components and parts. Similarly, the cost targeting personnel must have a basic understanding of the prices of component parts and subassemblies in order to make decisions concerning the allocation of target costs.

Value engineering is another important component of target costing at ITT Automotive. The objective of value engineering is to reduce costs without reducing functionality or quality without increasing costs before the product reaches the production line. During value engineering, the cross-functional team will try to determine optimal processes, materials, and equipment for designing, engineering, and producing the product.[4] The value engineering philosophy recognizes that decisions made early in the design process affect price and product costs. At ITT Automotive, members of the cross-functional team are empowered to find the most optimal processes, materials used, tooling and capital investment requirements and to decide whether to make or outsource the product. Tear-down analysis also is performed during value engineering.

Target costing should result in improved relationships with suppliers. At ITT Automotive, key suppliers are considered an integral part of the target costing team. This arrangement allows the suppliers to take "ownership" of the target costing process. These suppliers should be consulted early in the product life cycle, and they should play a significant role in product design and development.

Occasionally, a supplier may have a difficult time in meeting the target cost. In cases where the supplier is having this type of problem, ITT Automotive will ask for a detailed analysis of the supplier's cost to help the supplier reduce costs. This analysis is extremely detailed and provides the starting point for ITT Automotive to suggest some "value analysis" that will help the supplier reduce its costs.

Cost tracking sheets are used in the cost targeting area to keep track of the "targets" and to compare the targets with actual costs. At ITT Automotive, these sheets are used to assign the target cost from the final product to final assemblies, subassemblies, and components. Each tracking sheet becomes more

FIGURE 2
COST TRACKING SHEETS

ABS System

Description	Design Stage Target	Design Stage Quote	Tool Stage Target	Tool Stage Quote	Production Stage Target	Production Stage Quote
Control Unit	a	a + 1	a	a + 5	a	a – 1
Motor etc.	x	x	x	x	x	x
Production Cost	x	x	x	x	x	x
Other	x	x	x	x	x	x
Total Cost	x	x	x	x	x	X

Control Unit-Final Assembly

Description	Design Stage Target	Design Stage Quote	Tool Stage Target	Tool Stage Quote	Production Stage Target	Production Stage Quote
Bracket	X	X	X	X	X	x
ECU	X	x	x	x	x	x
Piston Assembly	b	b + 2	b	b + 1	b	b – .1

Piston Assembly-Subassembly

Description	Design Stage Target	Design Stage Quote	Tool Stage Target	Tool Stage Quote	Production Stage Target	Production Stage Quote
O-ring	x	x	x	x	x	x
Valve	x	x	x	x	x	x
Spring	x	x	x	x	x	x

Cost tracking sheets are prepared for the final product, final assemblies, and sub-assemblies, the latter includes tracking of individual components specific until, finally, the individual components are tracked.

The tracking sheets track the cost of the product throughout the product life cycle: at the design stage (DS), when the tooling is in place (TS), and finally, when the product reaches production (PS). Setting early targets helps ITT Automotive investigate and try to remedy problem situations. For example, if the Quote of a certain supplier is higher than the target, the cross-functional team may decide to visit the supplier to determine why there is a difference between the target and the quote. Figure 2 shows a hypothetical example of this process. Investment in capital equipment, which can be quite substantial, also is tracked through the use of cost tracking sheets.

ITT Automotive periodically conducts meetings with the cross-functional team to hold them responsible for the targets that were set and to develop, through brainstorming, ways to further reduce costs. At these "profit improvement planning" meetings, a "checklist" of problems are discussed among the cross-functional team. Before the meeting, each member of the team is handed a document detailing each of the problem areas, the person(s) responsible for eliminating the problem, comments on why the problem is occurring, and a suggested completion date for solving the problem. During the meeting, the person responsible for the area where the problem is occurring will discuss the steps that are being taken to solve the problem and receive suggestions from members of the cross-functional team.

Value analysis at ITT Automotive is used on products that are not yielding an adequate return. The results of value analysis may not be as great as the results from value engineering because value analysis is performed during the production stage—after ITT Automotive is locked into a good portion of its costs. The results from value analysis, however, can be dramatic.

Readers interested in more information about target costing can look forward to the research monograph, *Target Costing and Value Engineering* by Robin Cooper and Regine Slagmulder, to be published by the IMA Foundation for Applied Research, Inc., in early 1997. It is the first in a series of five books by Cooper on Japanese cost management practices. CAM-1 (Consortium for Advanced Manufacturing-International) recently issued *Target Costing: The New Frontier in Strategic Cost Management*, which provides practical insights on how to use target costing for profit planning and cost management. It can be ordered (C1/$50) by calling (800) 638-4427, ext. 278, or faxing (201) 573-9507.

TARGET COSTING MARKET SHARE

ITT Automotive uses target costing to maintain its profitability and increase its market share during these extremely competitive times in the automotive industry. Although the process is difficult at times, and costly resources are needed to have an effective target costing system, companies such as ITT Automotive have found the investment critical to meeting their corporate objectives successfully.

Target costing basically is a bottom-up, team-oriented philosophy. It is a very structured method of setting and achieving goals. For target costing to be successful, setting up cross-functional teams is not enough. Most important, there must be senior management support for the process. Senior management must allocate the necessary resources to the project and must empower the cross-functional teams to make critical decisions. Other requirements include setting early cost targets, performing competitive analysis and value engineering, forming partnerships with suppliers, and applying pressure to everyone in the value chain to reduce costs.

George Schmelzle, CPA, is an assistant professor of accountancy at the University of Detroit, Mercy. He was a faculty intern at ITT Automotive in the summer of 1995. He is a member of the Detroit Chapter of the IMA, through which this article was submitted. He can be reached at (312) 993-3327.

Rolf Geier heads the target costing/value analysis team in the brakes department at ITT Automotive. Additional credits are given to Gerd Klostermann. He is head of the target costing/value analysis team in Europe with worldwide responsibilities.

Thomas E. Buttross, CMA, is an assistant professor of accountancy at Indiana University, Kokomo. He is a member of the Detroit Chapter of IMA. He can be reached at (317) 455-9471.

INTEGRATING ACTIVITY-BASED COSTING AND THE THEORY Of CONSTRAINTS

By Robin Cooper and Regine Slagmulder

The profitability maps created by an activity-based costing system are powerful strategic tools designed to help firms become more profitable. But they are based on "general-purpose" costs designed to focus managerial attention, not to directly support decisions. For example, while an ABC system might indicate that a particular product is highly profitable and therefore a candidate for more aggressive selling, it cannot confirm that selling more of that product will indeed lead to higher profits. To make an informed decision, a company must undertake a special study to convert the ABC resource usage analysis into a resource supply one. These special studies are not failures of the ABC approach but are outcomes of a cascading cost benefit trade-off. Sometimes, these special studies are one-time events designed to answer a specific question (such as, "Should I sell more of this product?"), while other times, they are ongoing analyses designed to fine-tune the ability of the firm to generate profits.

The conversion from resource usage to resource supply is particularly important when the proposed change in resource usage predicted by the ABC system is not mirrored by an equivalent change in resource supply The underlying cause of this difference is the way that contracts for the acquisition of resources are structured. If the contract for a resource is on an "as-needed" basis, then resource supply and usage will be equal and the profitability map will be decision relevant. But if the contract is written on an "in-case" basis, then resource supply and usage are not necessarily equal. Here, resource supply will remain unchanged until a capacity limit established by the contract is reached. Then resource supply will change, not by the same amount as usage but by a contractually stipulated amount. Consequently, the ABC profitability maps lose their decision relevance, and special studies are required to understand the implications of decisions that involve these resources.

There are two ways in which capacity limits can be managed. Either management accepts that a capacity limit exists and the objective is to try to maximize the revenue (and hence profit) that can be generated given the constraint, or management decides to change the level of resource supply and hence the capacity limit. When managers accept a capacity limit, they must be sensitive to bottlenecks and undertake a special study to optimize around them.

A bottleneck occurs when the demand for a resource, in a given time period, outstrips the firm's ability to deliver it. A pure ABC system is unable to acknowledge bottlenecks because it assumes that resource demand and usage always match. Consequently, a product that consumes a large quantity of the bottleneck resource is not penalized compared to a product that consumes only a small amount of that resource. This limitation of the ABC approach leads to poor decisions if the ABC profitability maps are used to manage the firm's short-term product mix when bottlenecks are present. In particular, decisions based upon an ABC analysis will not keep the bottleneck resources optimally loaded and hence will not lead to maximum profits.

To accommodate bottlenecks, the best solution is to use the theory of constraints (TOC) to identify the optimal short-term mix of products that can be manufactured. The superiority of TOC over ABC for resolving the short-term implications of bottlenecks can be demonstrated using a simple numerical example. Assume that the firm has to choose among manufacturing three products: A, B, and C. The three products consume four different resources: material, labor, machining (the current bottleneck resource), and inspection. The cost of the supplied capacity for labor is $50, for machining $20, and for inspection $50. All three products have the same selling price, but product A has the lowest ABC costs (see Table 1). Consequently, ABC favors the manufacture of product A because it has the highest reported profits.

TOC takes a different approach; it splits resources into two categories. The first category incorporates all resources that are purchased on an "as needed" basis. These are the resources that vary directly with the changes in the level of production. The other category of resources is acquired on an "in-case" basis. The costs of these resources will be incurred irrespective of the level of usage. Under TOC, the costs of these "in-case" resources are grouped into the category "operating expenses" and treated as fixed costs. For the purpose of the TOC analysis relating to product mix they are essentially ignored. Thus, TOC can be viewed as an extreme form of contribution analysis.

The objective under TOC is to maximize "throughput" defined as revenues minus the cost of the "as needed" resources. In the illustrative example, the only cost that is subtracted is material. Consequently, product A has the highest unit throughput and, on the surface, is the favored product under both TOC and ABC (see Table 2). Product A, however, consumes twice as much of the bottleneck resource "machining" as products B and C. Therefore, in a given time frame, the firm can manufacture two units of product B or C for every unit of product A. Despite the fact that product A has the higher unit throughput, product C generates the highest overall throughput and hence profits (see Table 3). Thus, the correct decision is to manufacture product C, not product A. Thus, the appropriate metric for such short-term decisions is not ABC profits but the throughput per unit of the constrained (or bottleneck) resource.

Initially, there is no apparent correspondence between the ABC and TOC reported profits. Under TOC, the reported profits include a charge for all of the unused nonbottleneck resources, so product C reports the highest profits. In contrast, under ABC only the consumed resources are included, and the initial ABC profitability report indicates that manufacturing and selling two units of product B generates almost double the profit compared to manufacturing and selling a single unit of product A or two units of product C (see Table 4-ABC Profit). The ABC profits will match those reported by the TOC once the unused labor and inspection costs are taken into account (see Table 4-Net Profit).

TOC outperforms ABC when bottlenecks are present because it can better match currently available resources to outputs and thus enables higher revenues and hence profits to be generated. The drawback to the TOC approach comes from ignoring operating expenses that can be managed over the long term. To illustrate this point we revisit the example. The ABC system indicates that product C is approximately half as profitable as products A and B (see Table 1), raising the question: Should product C be discontinued? A special study indicates that the inspection resource is dedicated to the production of product C. Therefore, if product C is discontinued, the inspection costs of $50 can be avoided and the overall profits of the firm will increase. A TOC analysis between products A and B now indicates that the best solution is to manufacture two units of product B, generating an overall profit of $60 (see Table 5), which is higher than the original TOC profit of $14.

The important point is that TOC and ABC are complementary, not competing, cost management techniques. They can coexist and be used together to identify the best short-term and long-term product mixes. TOC assumes that the existing infrastructure is a given and sets out to optimize throughput and hence short-term profits. As such, it is a tactical cost management technique. Alternatively, ABC assumes that the supply of most resources can be managed over the long-term; it sets out to identify the product mix that will lead to the highest long-term profits. As such, it is a strategic cost management technique. Thus, TOC can be viewed as a formal on-going special study that is used to render the ABC profitability maps more effective for a particular class of decisions -- those associated with short-term optimization of the use of capacity.

Table 1		Products		
	A	B	C	Supplied Capacity
Revenue	$70	$70	$70	
Material	2	5	3	N/A
Labor	6	20	17	50
Machining	20	10	10	20
Inspection	0	0	20	50
Total Cost	**28**	**35**	**50**	
ABC Profit	**$42**	**$35**	**$20**	

Table 2		Products	
	A	B	C
Revenue	$70	$70	$70
Material	2	5	3
Throughput	**$68**	**$65**	**$67**

Table 3		Products		
	A	B	C	Supplied Capacity
Revenue	$70	$140	$140	
Material	2	10	6	N/A
Throughput	**68**	**130**	**134**	
Labor	50	50	50	50
Machining	20	20	20	20
Inspection	50	50	50	50
Operating Expenses	120	120	120	
Net Profit	**$ (52)**	**$10**	**$14**	

Table 4		Products	
	A	B	C
Revenue	**$70**	**$140**	**$140**
Material	2	10	6
Labor	6	40	34
Machining	20	20	20
Inspection	0	0	40
Total Cost	**28**	**70**	**100**
ABC Profit	**42**	**70**	**40**
Unused Capacity	94	60	26
Net Profit	**$(52)**	**$10**	**$14**

Table 5		Products
	A	B
Revenue	**$70**	**$140**
Material	4	10
Throughput	**$66**	**$130**
Operating Expenses	$70	$70
Net Profit	**$(4)**	**$60**

1. *Target Costing—The New Frontier in Strategic Cost Management,* The Consortium for Advanced Manufacturing-International (CAM-1), Bedford, Tex., 1995.
2. Activity-based costing can provide valuable input for the target costing product design stage. Product designers can use cost tables that include actual cost data from the ABC system as well as pro forma amounts for processes not currently used by the company. See Takeo Yoshikawa, John Innes, and Falconer Mitchell, "Cost Tables: A Foundation of Japanese Cost Management," *Journal of Cost Management*, Fall 1990, Vol. 4, No. 3, pp. 30-36.
3. The personal computer is a good example of the latter. Although the price of computers has remained constant the past few years, functionality has increased dramatically.
4. *Implementing Target Costing—Management Accounting Guideline #28*, a joint research project of the Society of Management Accountants of Canada, the Institute of Management Accountants, and the Consortium for Advanced Manufacturing-International, 1995.

Chapter 11
Process Costing

Cases

11-1 The Rossford Plant (Two Production Processes with the Traditional Volume-Based Costing System)
11-2 The United L/N Plant (Scraps and Defects)

Readings

"How Boeing Tracks Costs, A to Z"

This articles explains the change in Boeing's costing approach, from one based on job -costing to a process costing approach.

Discussion Questions:

1. Explain what Boeing means by process accounting.
2. What are the advantages of the process accounting approach at Boeing?
3. How does the new process accounting approach affect each business unit's incentives and tools to control costs?

Cases

11-1. The Rossford Plant

Having heard Robert Kaplan speak on some of the shortcomings of current cost accounting systems, I decided to undertake a review of the cost accounting system at our Rossford Plant. I was particularly concerned whether the overhead costs were being allocated to products according to the resource demands of the products. Costing our products accurately has become more important for strategic purposes because of pressures to unbundle sets of original equipment windows for the automakers.

Mark MacGuidwin, Corporate Controller
Libbey-Owens-Ford Co.

BACKGROUND

Libbey-Owens-Ford Co. (L-O-F), one of the companies in the Pilkington Group, has been a major producer of glass in the United States since the turn of the century. Its Rossford Plant produces about 12 million "lites" of tempered glass per year. (A lite is a unit such as a rear window, which is called a "back lite," or a side window, which is called a "side lite.") The plant makes front door windows, quarter windows, back windows, and sunroofs. About 96 percent of the lites produced are sold to original equipment (OE) automotive customers; the remaining 4 percent are shipped to replacement depots for later sale to replacement glass wholesalers. Lite sizes range from .73 square feet for certain quarter windows to about 13 square feet for the back lite of a Camaro/Firebird. The average size is approximately four square feet.

The Rossford Plant is comprised of two production processes: float and fabrication ("fab"). The float process produces raw float glass, the raw material for automotive windows. Blocks of float glass are transferred to the fab facility, where lites are cut to size, edged, shaped, and strengthened. The final product is then inspected, packed, and shipped.

Parts of the Rossford Plant date to the founding of the company. Unlike other L-O-F plants, which were designed around the automated Pilkington float-tank process with computer controlled cutting and finishing operations, the Rossford Plant was designed for the older process of polishing plate glass to final products. Pilkington float-tanks were installed in the plant during the 1970s, and the cutting processes were substantially automated during the 1980s. However, the finishing processes have not yet been automated to the extent as at the other plants.

Mark MacGuidwin, Corporate Controller of L-O-F, and Ed Lackner, Rossford's Plant Controller, became concerned during 1987 about the cost allocation process at Rossford for several reasons. First, the process had not been critically evaluated since the automation of the cutting processes. Second, the overhead cost structure at Rossford differed dramatically from that of other L-O-F plants. A larger pool of indirect costs was allocated to equipment centers. Third, they had collected evidence that the cost alloca-tion process at Rossford was not accurately assigning costs to units of product. And fourth, changes in the company's competitive environment were raising strategic issues that demanded accurate product cost information for pricing, product mix, and production scheduling purposes.

RELATIONSHIP OF SIZE TO PROFIT

In his investigation, MacGuidwin discovered what he believed were two key observations made by the Vice Presidents of Engineering and Manufacturing. Historically in the automotive glass business, original equipment customers have purchased a complete set of windows for a car model from a single glass manufacturer. From the glass manufacturer's perspective it was therefore necessary that the markup on cost for the entire set, or bundle, of glass units be adequate for profitability. Despite the buying habits of these OE customers, firms in the industry quoted selling prices for individual units of glass within each set. As easy benchmarks, the selling prices were customarily set in proportion to the size in square feet of the units, with smaller lites priced lower than larger lites.

However, the cost of producing automotive glass is not related proportionately to the size of the unit produced. The production process involves two principal fabricating operations: cutting the unit from a larger block of glass, and then bending it to the necessary shape and strengthening it in a tempering furnace. Neither the cost of cutting nor the cost of tempering is proportional to the size of the unit produced. Only a limited number of units can be fed into either a cutting machine or a tempering furnace regardless of the size of the units, with little or no difference in feed rates or resource consumption related to size.

The joint effect of these two observations is an understanding in the glass industry of the average relationship between unit size and unit profit that is depicted in Figure 1. Margin percentages for passenger car lites are somewhat higher than the industry average.

Recent changes in the competitive structure of the OE automotive glass industry have led to the possibility of "unbundling" sets of windows. Major customers are considering not only allowing different manufacturers to supply units for the same car model (for example, windshields from one and rear windows from another) but also setting target prices based on the manufacturing costs of the units, a process already begun by General Motors. Under these circumstances, the costs reported by the accounting system for individual units of glass have strategic implications that were not relevant in the past.

CURRENT PRODUCT COSTING PROCESS

Figure 2 shows the cost center groupings for the production process. The float and fabricating operations report to the same plant manager and have a common support staff. Raw glass is transferred from float to fab at standard variable plus standard fixed cost. (Profits are measured only at the point of sale of the finished product to the customer.) Direct labor and overhead costs are assigned to units of final product as follows:

(1) Direct labor costs are assigned to equipment centers (lines of machines in PC&E and furnaces in Tempering) based on standard crew sizes. Thus, a labor cost per equipment hour is developed for each of the several machines and furnaces based on crew sizes and standard wage and fringe benefit rates.

(2) Overhead costs, both variable and fixed, that are directly traceable to a specific equipment center are pooled to develop a rate per equipment hour for that center.

(3) A standard feed rate is established for each lite for each applicable cutting machine and furnace, and costs are applied to product based on costs per equipment hour/units fed per hour. (Feed rates to different tempering furnaces differ substantially.)

(4) General (indirect) plant overhead costs are allocated in two steps:

(i) 20 percent of the total is allocated to the float process and 80 percent to fabricating, then

(ii) the 80 percent allocated to fabricating is assigned to units of product at a flat rate per square foot (approximately $1.00 per square foot in 1987, adjusted for differing yield rates).

The costs classified as general plant overhead amount to 30 percent of the total indirect costs of the plant. General plant includes approximately 100 salaried employees involved in plant management, engineering, accounting, material control, pollution control, quality control, maintenance management, research and development, production management, and human resources. It also includes depreciation of equipment and buildings not assigned to operating departments, property taxes and insurance, general plant maintenance, and post retirement costs.

MacGuidwin decided to limit his initial analysis to the automotive glass fabricating facility at the Rossford Plant. He and Lackner were confident that the process of assigning costs to units of raw float glass was sufficiently accurate. They also believed that the direct costs of labor and overhead associated with the PC&E and Tempering Furnace equipment centers were being properly attached to units of product based on the units' standard feed rates per hour. The rates had been set with downtime assumptions intended to cover mechanical and electrical problems, stockouts, and part changeovers.

"On the whole, Ed Lackner and I felt pretty good about what we were discovering," commented MacGuidwin. "Over two-thirds of the costs of the plant were being assigned to units of product based on metered usage of our two constraining resources, machine time in the PC&E center and furnace time in the Tempering center."

"On the other hand," Lackner pointed out, "we had a potential problem with our general plant costs. For years we had been assigning them to units produced based on square footage. We knew that this allocation base didn't capture activities that were driving the overhead costs, but we didn't know whether the allocation process was substantially distorting the final product costs. Until recently it didn't matter how these costs were allocated because unit price/cost differentials did not enter into any strategic decisions."

ALTERNATIVE ALLOCATION METHOD

The allocation of general plant overhead costs between float and fab seemed reasonable to the two Controllers. They analyzed a number of factors that could have been driving the allocation, including the number of hourly employees, the space occupied, and the variable costs incurred. They also interviewed managers concerning where time was spent by employees in the overhead base. All indicators pointed to the appropriateness of assigning 20 percent of the general plant costs to float and 80 percent to fab.

"The principal outcome of our analysis was to propose and implement on a test basis an alternative method for re-allocating the 80 percent allocated to fab," explained MacGuidwin. "Under the old method we allocated a flat rate per square foot produced. This might be reasonable if each square foot of glass costs the same to make in the PC&E and Tempering departments. However, we knew from our production engineers and from our own tracking of direct costs in those cost centers that this was just not the case."

To test an alternative allocation method, MacGuidwin and Lackner chose four parts with the following characteristics:

(1) a small, high volume, low profit margin part (Truck Vent);
(2) a small, high volume, moderate profit margin part (Passenger Car Rear Quarter Window);
(3) a large, high volume, moderate profit margin part (Passenger Car Front Door); and
(4) a large, moderate volume, high profit margin part (Passenger Car Back Lite, Heated).

As indicated in the following table, the direct costs of fabricating these parts differ substantially:

Part	Square Feet Per Unit	Cost Per Cutting	Square Foot Furnace
Truck Vent	.77	$2.870	$1.676
Passenger Car Rear Quarter	.73	1.494	3.312
Passenger Car Front Door	5.03	.340	.634
Passenger Car Back Lite	7.07	.206	.682

The input measure selected as the basis for allocating general plant overhead costs to units of product was the most scarce (bottleneck) resource in the facility—time spent in the tempering furnaces. The production plan indicated a furnace capacity of 48,500 hours per year. Dividing the portion of the costs assigned to fab by the furnace capacity resulted in a rate of $503 per furnace hour.

Using the feed rates of the individual pieces, MacGuidwin was able to compute a new standard cost for each of the four products. Figure 3 shows the standard cost per square foot, the cost per lite, and the gross margin percentage of each product under both the old and new methods of allocating general plant overhead. The Corporate Controller was pleased with the results:

"Although the results shown for the four products are not as dramatic as I've seen for some manufacturers, they do indicate a need to rethink and reanalyze our cost allocation system. Basically, the new method of allocating general plant overhead represents more closely what the Engineering and Manufacturing Vice Presidents were telling me about cost incurrence. The old system allocated a large pool of indirect costs equally to output, whereas the new system makes some attempt to associate those costs with the resource demands placed on our productive capacity by individual products. The old method clearly distorted our product costs. The new method should work better as long as we produce at plant capacity."

REQUIRED:

1. What is the cost object before the change in the product costing system? After the change? Why did MacGuidwin and Lackner change the focus of the system?
2. What are the characteristics of a good product costing system?
3. How do the process control and product costing functions of Rossford's cost accounting system interact? What conversion costs are treated as direct product costs in the system?
4. In your opinion, is the new allocation method for general plant costs better than the old method? Why or why not?

FIGURE 1

Unit Size/Profit Relationship

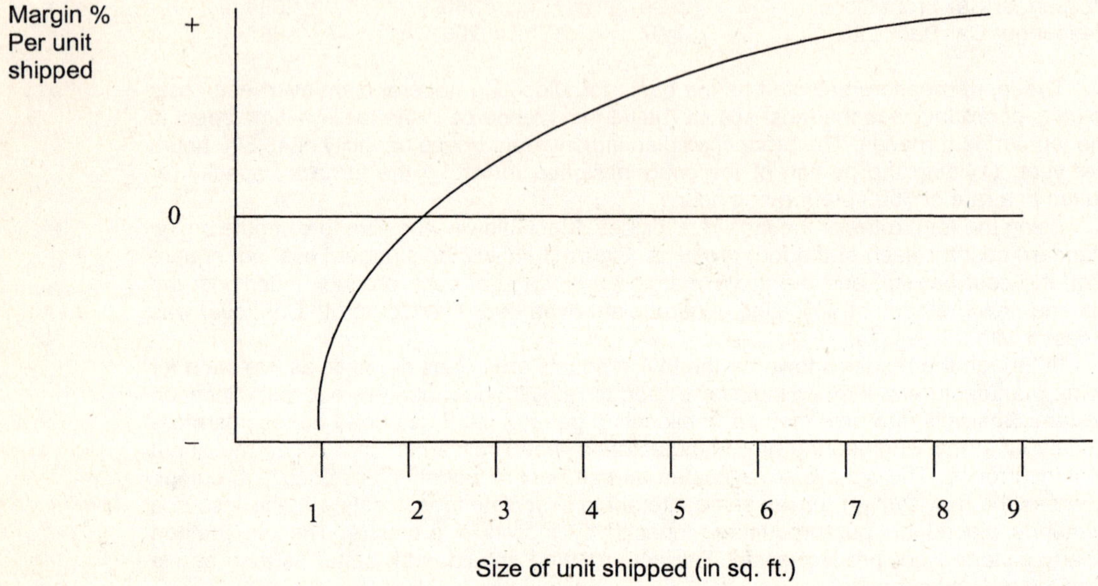

FIGURE 2

Production Cost Centers

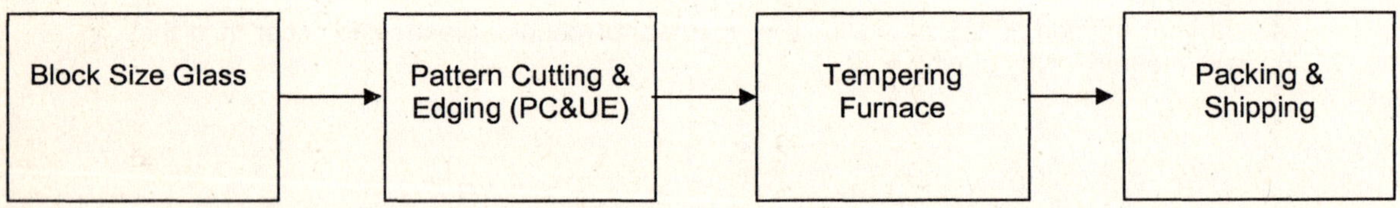

Figure 3
Unit Data Under Old and New Allocation Methods

	Truck Vent				Passenger Car Front Door			
	Old		New		Old		New	
	Amount	Percent	Amount	Percent	Amount	Percent	Amount	Percent
Cutting	$2.870	47	$2.870	42	$0.340	12	$ 0.340	14
Furnace	1.676	27	1.676	24	0.634	23	0.634	25
General Plant	1.020	17	1.740	25	1.036	38	0.800	32
All Other Costs	0.566	9	0.566	8	0.716	26	0.716	29
Std. Cost Per Sq. Ft.	$6.132	100	$6.852	100	2.726	100	$2.490	100
Sq. Ft. Per Lite	0.770		0.770		5.030		5.030	
Cost Per Life	$4.722		$5.276		$13.712		$12.525	
Selling Price	$2.820		$2.820		$16.820		$16.820	
Gross Margin (Percent)	(67)		(87)		18		26	

	Passenger Car Rear Quarter				Passenger Car Back Lite			
	Old		New		Old		New	
	Amount	Percent	Amount	Percent	Amount	Percent	Amount	Percent
Cutting	$1.494	21	$1.494	16	$0.206	5	$ 0.206	6
Furnace	3.312	47	3.312	36	0.682	18	0.682	20
General Plant	1.022	14	3.020	33	1.064	28	0.674	20
All Other Costs	1.266	18	1.266	14	1.810	48	1.810	54
Std. Cost Per Sq. Ft.	$7.094	100	$9.092	100	$3.762	100	$3.372	100
Sq. Ft. Per Lite	0.730		0.730		7.070		7.070	
Cost Per Life	$5.179		$6.637		$26.597		$23.840	
Selling Price	$6.680		$6.680		$56.120		$56.120	
Gross Margin (Percent)	22		1		53		58	

11-2. The United L/N Plant

We never imagined that we'd ever be looking at the type of costing issues at our United L/N Plant that have now become apparent. The plant design was engineered from the beginning as a state-of-the-art production process that would avoid most of the traditional problems. Now we're in the process of taking a second look.

Ken Marvin
Director, Planning and Control
OE Business Unit
Libbey-Owens-Ford Co.

BACKGROUND

Libbey-Owens-Ford Co. (L-O-F), one of the companies in the Pilkington Group, has been a major producer of glass in the United States since the turn of the century. Its newest plant, United L/N, began producing glass products in November 1987. Located in Kentucky, United L/N is a joint venture between L-O-F and a Japanese company, Nippon Sheet Glass.

Unlike the Rossford Plant, which produces the raw float glass used in its fabrication process, United L/N is a fabrication plant only. The organization of the plant reflects the just-in-time, pull through philosophy. The production process is fully automated, requiring no human intervention from beginning to end. Very high quality and minimal scrap were expected to be the norm.

L-O-F treats the Rossford Plant as a standard cost center, but United L/N is organized as a strategic business unit (SBU). SBUs are evaluated on profit as well as cost control and other goals. The company charges United L/N Rossford's standard manufacturing cost for raw glass transferred between the two plants, whereas transfer prices between SBUs are usually negotiated by their managements.

FABRICATION PROCESS AND PLANT DESIGN

The steps in the fabrication process are essentially the same as at other L-O-F facilities. First, the raw glass goes through pattern cutting where it is trimmed to the basic shape of the lite (window) it will become. Second, the cut pattern is edged. Third, the edged pattern goes through a furnace where it is formed (bent to shape) and tempered. Fourth, the final product is inspected, packed, and shipped.

The principal difference between United L/N's process and the fabrication process of traditional plants lies in the organization of these discrete steps. At the Rossford Plant, for example, pattern cutting and edging, tempering, and packing and shipping are treated as individual cost centers and are physically separated. Each department creates a work-in-process inventory, which is periodically moved to the next stage in the process. The next stage in most cases is located in a different section of the plant. Also, all processes at Rossford require human participation.

By contrast, United L/N's fabrication process is entirely in-line and automated. Raw glass from Rossford plant and other plants arrives packed on special racks that are designed for United L/N's automated loading process. (The racks are also designed to protect the raw glass from damage between the shipping plant and the receiving area.) The glass has been inspected at the shipping plant to determine that each piece meets the specifications of the fabrication process.

A forklift operator loads racks of glass at the beginning of one of United L/N's two production lines. From that point on, the entire process is operated through a numerical control computer system. Human intervention occurs only during planned downtime periods when the line undergoes preventive maintenance, when a problem stops the line's progress, and when finished pieces are inspected prior to packing. Glass is continuously pulled through the process, so that ideally there should be no idle work-in-process inventory.

A small team of operators monitors the process, performs regular preventive maintenance, changes the computer settings for different lites, and makes unscheduled repairs as needed.

PRODUCT COSTING SYSTEM

The product costing system at United L/N is very straightforward compared to those of less automated L-O-F plants. Overhead costs associated with handling, storing, protecting, and accounting for work-in-process inventories are dramatically lower. The major components of cost include short-term fixed operating costs, labor costs of the operating teams, and the transfer prices of raw glass from other plants.

Because the entire process is automated and in-line, the feed rate is constant across all sub-processes for each individual lite being fabricated. The costing system consequently was designed as one large pool, which is assigned to units based on standard input prices and standard feed rates. The system allows for standard levels of downtime and anticipated yields. Products are not charged for either planned downtime or planned scrap, which were expected to be minimal due to the care with which the plant was designed, engineered, and monitored.

PRODUCTION AND COSTING PROBLEMS

"It wasn't long before we began experiencing problems with our yields," commented Ken Marvin, Planning and Control Director of L-O-F's Original Equipment Business Unit. "At first we thought that the problems would be confined to adjusting and learning about the automated process. We thought that as we gained experience with it we could solve our difficulties without introducing more complicated costing mechanisms."

One of the first difficulties encountered was keeping the furnaces on the two lines working efficiently. Each one was designed to work perfectly when a certain number of glass pieces were being fired, a certain number were on the threshold entering the furnace, and a certain number were leaving it.

"In our traditional plants we stockpile pieces in front of the furnaces so that we can keep them filled to their optimal levels when forming and tempering," Marvin explained. "However, the United L/N lines were designed with no accumulators in front of the furnaces to keep them running efficiently at all times. For any number of reasons there might be gaps in the lines as they enter the furnaces. Partly because of these gaps and the resulting imperfect furnace operations, we have had unacceptably high scrap variances. Of course, scrap decreases the plant's yield."

"From the United L/N point of view the problem with scrap is caused by imperfections in the raw glass rather than by problems with the process. The plant's management therefore believes that the scrap variance should be charged to the shipping plants (including Rossford plant.) Shipping plant managers, on the other hand, believe that the charge-back, even if appropriate (which remains an issue), is much too high. United L/N's costing system costs every piece as if it goes through the entire process rather than dropping out at, for example, pattern cutting or edging stages."

Another factor contributing to furnace inefficiency and ineffectiveness is that a line sometimes goes down unexpectedly because of a problem in pattern cutting or edging. The plant then incurs the opportunity costs associated both with having an empty tempering furnace and with having to reset the furnace after it has been empty during periods of time when it was programmed to be full.

"We have been tracking all sorts of variances trying to get some insights into the effects on costs of the kinks in the process," continued Marvin. "We calculate a combined materials usage and spending variance, a downtime variance, a throughput variance, and a scrap (yield) variance. However, all of them are valued on the basis of costs of the entire production process rather than on the value added to the stages of production where problems occur. Now we're reevaluating the design of our costing system at United L/N, especially in light of the ongoing negotiations with Rossford plant and other shipping plants."

REQUIRED:

1. As a member of the Rossford Plant negotiating team, what would be your position regarding the proper treatment of the United L/N scrap variance? As a member of the United L/N team?
2. How could United L/N's management determine the specific causes of defects (for example, bad glass or defective cutting, edging, or tempering operations) in units that are scrapped at the plant? What are the implications for the product costing system?
3. What could be done to solve the problems with furnace inefficiency and ineffectiveness that Ken Marvin discussed? What are the probable effects of your suggestion(s)?

Readings

How Boeing Tracks Costs, A to Z

When Boeing's internal customers clamored for better cost information, the company decided to empower its business units by giving them more responsibility for their own costs.

By Robert J. Bowlby

A few years ago, two of Boeing's internal customers, engineering and operations, told the finance department they weren't getting the cost information they needed to manage airplane design and production. They lacked relevant economic information on which to base their decisions.

When we heard that, we knew we had to do something to remedy the situation. Boeing's cost-accounting system worked for tax and financial accounting and could be used to determine product cost and profitability at an airplane model level. But we realized that at an operating level, we were giving our engineering and operations organizations budgets for only a few cost elements.

Further, the cost information we provided individual managers didn't align with their responsibilities or areas they could control or influence. Engineering and operations couldn't use the cost information they routinely received to perform reliable economic design trade studies or to make economically sound investment decisions. They had to generate such information almost exclusively by special analysis.

At Boeing, we've committed ourselves to continuously improving our processes so we can stay ahead of the competition and maintain or increase our long-term market share. We are rethinking and reshaping our corporate strategies, the cornerstone of which is "Customer In," a concept that means we continually seek input from our internal and external customers through internal feedback, customer-satisfaction surveys and market research.

With this type of strategy, finance must be a partner in all aspects of a business, from marketing and product design to production and customer support. One of finance's most important jobs is to help create a systematic framework of financial and nonfinancial information and measures that contribute to making the decisions that ensure the enterprise's success.

Therefore, to improve the cost-management process, Boeing finance, operations and engineering decided to team together to study and rethink our managers' real information needs with respect to unit costs. The team spent some time identifying and reviewing "best practices" by studying industry, academia and our own internal practices. We came up with several key concepts aimed at improving the relevancy of our cost-management information.

FRONT-END ALIGNMENT

First, we decided to align our accounting practices to support the way we manage the enterprise. This includes being flexible and responsive enough so that we can change or redirect the system to enhance continuous process improvement, even in the middle of an accounting period.

Also, we realized we had to routinely provide the financial data that management needs to improve our processes and ultimately our products. We agreed that this data, which includes the costs of such items as materials, labor and energy, should represent the sum of all the resources actually used to build the part or assembly and that the area building that part or assembly must assume the responsibility for generating and tracking the data. From these key concepts, along with others like activity-based analysis, Boeing finance has been progressing toward implementing a modified process cost-accounting system.

Using process accounting means significantly changing cost-management practices and cost-assignment techniques. Part of the problem is that our current system was designed when our primary business was producing military aircraft. Our production methods, the makeup of our costs and the information we need about them have changed a lot since then.

Over time, our traditional job-cost system and cost-accounting practices have caused more and more costs that we'd traditionally categorized as overhead to be unloaded onto an ever-smaller direct-labor base. This evolved to the point where between 70 percent to 80 percent of the costs assigned to the final cost objectives of a manufacturing or engineering line organization were allocations from common overhead pools. Building and equipment maintenance, depreciation costs and the costs of industrial-engineering support activities and other support functions were lumped together in general overhead pools.

In today's factory, it's not uncommon to find that depreciation, technology, energy and nondirect labor expenses are often individually more significant than direct-touch or shop labor. The 20 percent to 30 percent of our costs that were mostly direct-touch labor assigned to the final cost objectives were the only cost elements the manufacturing or engineering line organizations had responsibility for and could directly link to the products they make. This meant that any process-improvement or cost-reduction initiative made by the line organization that didn't involve direct-labor savings wasn't directly reflected, or maybe not reflected at all, in the costs allocated to it. In many cases, the line organization couldn't be sure if total company costs would decrease or increase as a result of its actions.

To better manage the other 70 percent to 80 percent of the costs, traditional cost accounting and cost management separately identified significant chunks of the overhead cost and managed them individually. But, identifying separate cost elements, such as depreciation computing and nondirect labor, and trying to budget and control each one separately, didn't show the ways in which these cost elements interacted with one another.

These old accounting practices meant the overhead the manufacturing or engineering line organization did receive was based on the direct-labor dollars it incurred. Because technology-related costs were buried in overhead, this approach tended to move the dollars from areas with higher technology costs into units with the larger direct-labor elements. What we needed were ways to better align more of our costs directly to what we really do—designing and assembling airplanes and manufacturing parts and assemblies for them.

THAT BILL HAS YOUR NAME ON IT

Aligning costs to operating decisions is an important component of the new management and operating philosophy we're striving to implement. The changes we're going through are substantial. We are moving from a functional enterprise to one organized around product processes, and from a company that allocates its resources by organization to one that aligns them to product processes. And we are replacing part/resource management with product-focused process management.

This new philosophy will allow us to match resources to small, focused product groups. These small business units will then contain one or more product-focused process units. Costs incurred at a broader level in the company will not become the responsibility of the product- or service-producing unit. Rather, these broader-level costs will be the responsibility of the general-purpose processes, such as the sales and marketing organization or the central tax staff. These groups will be accountable from the costs they are adding to the final product shipped to our customers.

By way of comparison, think about a typical activity-based costing model, which you could use to develop the cost drivers for overhead and manufacturing activities. The overhead drivers include the square footage, the headcount, direct-labor hours, and the number of products. Manufacturing's drivers are the unit volume, the number of shifts and the weighted unit volume. With an ABC model, you would use these drivers to link the overhead activities to the manufacturing processes and the manufacturing processes to products.

With process accounting, we trace the overhead costs to product-related manufacturing processes based on the business unit's responsibility for and ability to control and influence the costs that result from operating that process. This is important for several reasons. Under traditional accounting, a business unit can spend less money and thus help the company meet its overall cost-reduction targets. But it's the direct, measurable, cause-and-effect link back to the business unit's products that was missing. Reducing a few direct heads was about the only action the business-unit manager could take to actually see the business unit's costs, or rather the 20 percent to 30 percent of business-unit costs, go down.

Our new process-accounting approach has changed that situation dramatically. Today, the organization can exercise significant influence and control over the costs it incurs. In fact, the basic ground rule for assigning costs is the organization must be able to take some action on that cost element and see a predictable change in the overall costs being charged to it.

The costs the business unit is accountable for and can control now include those for detail and supplier parts, computing, depreciation, support labor and di-

A FRACTION OF THE COSTS

Boeing's new cost-accounting system allows individual business units to portray their planned unit costs in today's environment and how they might compare to the unit costs upper management wants to achieve. The business units calculate their costs with the help of numerator and denominator charts like the ones below. The total dollar cost divided by good parts out equals the cost for good part shipped. Typical elements included under total costs are shown in the numerator chart. The denominator chart shows how we calculate our costs for good parts shipped.

In this example, the expected production, from the denominator table, is 13,439 units of output. The cost to product 13,439 units is estimated at $58.517 million (numerator table). Dividing 13,439 units into $58.517 million yields an expected average unit cost of $4,354.

Boeing's Cost Numerator...

Cost Element	Product Plan Costs (in $ thousands)
Touch Labor	12,150
Support Labor	9,223
Raw Materials	15,113
Equipment Depreciation	2,990
Equipment Maintenance	2,357
Tooling Depreciation	1,983
Tooling Maintenance	1,317
Distributed Material	503
Shop Supplies	915
Computing	6,662
Facilities Cost	3,552
Miscellaneous	1,752
Total	**$58,517**

...and Output Denominator

Part Number	Quantity	Product Weighting Factor	Units of Output
A	158	2.10	332
B	405	3.30	1,337
C	288	13.60	3,917
D	528	5.30	2,798
E	332	13.20	4,382
F	673	1.00	673
	2,384		13,439

rect labor, and other nonlabor costs. The business manager has a much broader sphere of influence in which to exercise control and make improvements within the business unit.

But tracing this bigger bucket of costs to the business units is only part of the solution. The business units now need some tools with which they can manage their costs. Once they identify the resources they consume, they must analyze them and learn to recognize their process and resource cost drivers and the relationship among them by continually asking why a certain item or process costs what it does. Business units need to understand their cost drivers to increase product quality, cut costs, improve customer response time and so on. Our business units will use their unit cost targets and ad-hoc analysis techniques for the data they will track internally (see box on this page).

As you can see from the example shown in the box, our basic approach is to compare and weight the individual parts produced in a product process, based on the differences between the parts or part families. We calculate the relative differences in the resources required to produce the different parts. Then we multiply the result—the product weighting factor for each part or product—by the expected production quantity for each part. The result is the business unit's expected production expressed in equivalent output units.

IT'S ALL RELATIVE

The normal procedure for determining these factors is to first identity the typical or base part or part family. Often that turns out to be the part that is the simplest. We give the base part a value of 1, 10 or 100, depending on the scale we want to use.

Then we review the other parts we produce, compare their features' relative value to the base part and determine their values. Take airplane skin panels, for example. We might assign a simple panel a value of one. A panel with a window could have a value of five, while a panel with an unusual shape could be a nine, and so on. The method also allows us to calculate the relative value of adding to or modifying various features.

Determining the relative value is probably the most complicated part of the whole process, but it's an essential aspect of process accounting. It's important to understand what's driving out current production costs, as well as the relative value of the parts being produced and the impact of process improvements and future production plans.

Individual business units can now project their costs for expected future levels of production. The production-producing business units will now be able to better understand how they fit into the total company production and cost picture.

With this knowledge, Boeing can relate many aspects of the total business to one another in a manner that allows us to take actions at all levels of the company—actions with predictable results and a common focus. For example, we can now begin to trace the hidden costs of capacity to individual business units, and this brings up some different, interesting questions. What is the unit's excess capacity? What's the cost of holding inventory? Who's accountable for excess capacity and why?

Also, process accounting supports other concepts in our continuous process-improvement strategy, including total accountability, responsibility and control: flexibility; and total cost tied to customer value. With our process-accounting tools in hand, we can begin to answer the next round of questions we're asking ourselves in our continuing quest for quality.

Chapter 12
Cost Allocation: Service Departments and Joint Product Costs

Cases

12-1 Southwestern Bell Telephone (Revenue Allocation)
12-2 Brookwood Medical Center (Cost Allocation)

Readings

"Managing Shared Services with ABM"

This article outlines the benefits of using shared services (i.e., finance and accounting services) in large companies such as Ford Motor Company, Sun Microsystems and Marriott. There is also a discussion of how activity-based management (ref: chapter 4) is used to manage the costs of these shared services.

Discussion Question:

How do concepts for cost management of shared services differ from the concepts and methods presented in Chapter 12? Who are the customers referred to in the article? What do you think is the best way to manage the costs of shared services such as finance and accounting?

Cases

12-1. Southwestern Bell Telephone

In the fall of 1989, the Texas Division of Southwestern Bell Telephone Company (SWBT) was facing considerable earnings uncertainty. Nine months had passed since the Texas Public Utilities Commission (PUC) had initiated an inquiry into SWBT's earnings in Texas. The Company was trying to negotiate a settlement but was having difficulty reaching an agreement with the commission staff and other interested parties. One group was proposing a decrease in SWBT revenues that would result in a 76% reduction in the company's Texas revenues and adversely affect Southwestern Bell Corporation's stock price.

At the same time that the PUC was investigating alleged overearnings related to SWBT's Texas intrastate operations, company officers in Texas were trying to meet budgeted net income objectives. These targets were necessary to keep earnings growing at a conservative yet steady rate. With actual data already available for much of the year, it was apparent that the overall target for 1989 might not be met. One of the main causes of this probable shortfall was the decrease SWBT was experiencing in revenues from long distance telephone calls. This decrease was due largely to increased payments in the form of settlements to other local exchange telephone companies in Texas. SWBT's management was searching for alternatives to the settlement process that would allow the company to retain its fair share of long distance revenues without financially ruining smaller telephone companies operating in the state.

INDUSTRY BACKGROUND

In January 1984, SWBT and six other regional telephone companies were divested from American Telephone and Telegraph Company (AT&T). In addition to retaining ownership of Western Electric (manufacturing), Bell Labs (research and development), and AT&T Information Systems, AT&T was allowed to retain ownership of interstate long distance services and a portion of intrastate long distance. Under the provisions of the Justice Department's Modified Final Judgment decree, each state was divided into Local Access Transport Areas (LATAs). Texas was divided into seventeen LATAs in addition to the standard metropolitan statistical area of San Angelo, which belongs solely to General Telephone (GTE).

Long distance calling between LATAs (interLATA) may be provided only by interexchange carriers (IXCs) such as AT&T, MCI, and Sprint. Local exchange carriers (LECs) such as SWBT and GTE provide basic telephone service and long distance calling within each LATA (intraLATA). In Texas, there are 59 LECs. SWBT is by far the largest, serving approximately 6.6 million telephone lines.

Because IXCs access their customers through LEC facilities, LECs charge IXCs for using their local networks. Theoretically, these per-minute-of-use charges are based on LEC costs. However, state commissions often inflate the rates to subsidize basic telephone rates, thus keeping them priced below cost.

INTERSTATE INTRALATA LONG DISTANCE

When a customer of an LEC makes an intrastate intraLATA long distance (toll) call, completion of the call often requires the use of another LEC's facilities. For example, a call from Dallas to Denton is an intraLATA toll call that originates in a Southwestern Bell area (Dallas) but terminates in a GTE area (Denton). The originator of the call is billed by Southwestern Bell, which must reimburse GTE for costs incurred in assisting in the call. In Texas, this reimbursement is currently handled through a toll revenue pooling agreement among the LECs.

The pooling of intraLATA toll revenues is administered by the Texas Exchange Carrier Association (TECA). Each LEC reports monthly to the TECA administrator not only its billed toll revenues but also its expenses and investment incurred in providing toll service. TECA combines the revenue, expense, and investment information for all 59 LECs and calculates a rate of return equal to billed revenues less expenses (including taxes) divided by investment. Each LEC is allowed to recover its expenses plus the pool rate of return on its investment.

In 1987 the pool rate of return was approximately 19%. Although SWBT billed $555.3 million in toll revenues, it was allowed to retain only the total of its expenses ($285.4 million) and return ($147.9 million). The $122 million difference between what SWBT billed and what it was allowed to keep was paid to the pool administrator for disbursement to those companies whose costs exceeded their billed revenues.

CONCERNS WITH THE POOLING PROCESS

Southwestern Bell's managers have several concerns with the current pooling process. One of their major concerns is that few incentives exist for companies to control costs. IntraLATA toll service is a much larger portion of the total operations of many of the smaller LECs than of SWBT. Consequently, each dollar of additional cost incurred by the smaller companies results in approximately one dollar of additional settlements. On the other hand, Southwestern Bell's retained toll revenues (after settlement with other LECs) decrease by approximately $1 million for each one percent reduction in its costs. This situation is not conducive to the efficient provision of telephone service and therefore is not in the best interest of the public.

The company's managers also are concerned about the manner in which total expenses and investment related to intraLATA toll service are calculated. Each company's accountants computes these amounts using procedures developed by the Federal Communications Commission (FCC). The very complex procedures, referred to in the industry as "separations," allocate monthly journalized expense and investment amounts to various categories of telephone service based on factors developed from studies of call traffic patterns and studies showing how telephone plant resources are utilized. The separations process was developed to provide a means of dividing expenses and investment amounts between state and interstate jurisdictions to facilitate rate setting by regulatory agencies. It never was intended to represent an accurate allocation system.

The first step in separations is to divide expense and investment amounts into traffic-sensitive and non-traffic-sensitive (NTS) categories. Traffic-sensitive expenses are primarily variable and are relatively easy to trace to specific categories of service. NTS expenses are primarily fixed. These amounts (over half the total SWBT reports to the pool) are incurred to provide and service connections between customers' premises and company's central offices. The same investment is required whether a customer makes no calls, a few calls, or hundreds of calls, and also whether those calls are intrastate or interstate.

NTS amounts are separated into three categories: interstate, intrastate toll, and intrastate local. In 1982, the FCC froze at approximately 20% the portion of Southwestern Bell's NTS expenses and investment allocated to intrastate toll operations. Thus, the initial separation of NTS amounts does not represent the current usage of the telephone network's resources. However, the interLATA toll and intraLATA toll components of the 20% factor are determined monthly based on relative actual usage. Therefore, if interLATA toll usage is increasing at a faster rate than intraLATA toll usage, less will be allocated to the intraLATA toll category. IntraLATA toll expenses and related investment could be increasing, but due to the separations process fewer dollars would be assigned to the category and thus recoverable through the pooling process. SWBT's intraLATA toll NTS factor is approximately 8%, whereas the factors of several smaller telephone companies are in the 30% to 50% range.

A third concern of Southwestern Bell managers is that revenues from non-joint-provided toll calls are included in the pooling process. For example, consider that the largest intraLATA toll market in Texas is between Dallas and Ft. Worth. Most toll calls between the two cities use only SWBT facilities, but through the pooling process revenues from the calls are shared with the state's other LECs. Company officials believe both revenues and costs of single-company toll calls should be excluded from the pool, but currently there is no means to isolate those amounts.

A final concern relates to the telecommunications industry goal of providing adequate telephone service to all U. S. citizens at reasonable rates. All telephone companies as well as the entire nation have benefited from the subsidies that higher cost companies have received from lower-cost companies. If local telephone service, especially in rural areas, were priced to cover its costs, the number of residences with service would be substantially lower. The concern at Southwestern Bell is that subsidization of high-cost companies has exceeded its historical intent; publications of the Texas PUC show that many high-cost LECs are earning well over their authorized rates of return.

After reviewing the situation, Southwestern Bell's senior managers realized they had their work cut out for them. They know that the course of action they recommended would have to effectively address both the concerns of SWBT and the financial needs of the other companies.

REQUIRED:

1. Assuming toll revenue sharing will continue to be administered by the TECA, what is the most important modification that could be made to the pooling procedures to produce a more equitable distribution of revenues from the perspective of Southwestern Bell?
2. Should SWBT officials negotiate changes in the subsidization procedures directly with the other Texas LECs or take their concerns to the state Public Utilities Commission and seek mandated changes?
3. What strategy would you recommend to Southwestern Bell managers? How would your recommendation address the four concerns expressed in the case?

(IMA adapted)

12-2. Brookwood Medical Center[1]

"In 1990, a major insurer asked us to bid on performing all of their open-heart surgeries in the Southeast United States. We prepared a bid by pulling charges on all (not just Medicare) patients we had treated in the four diagnostic related groups (DRGs) and applying the hospital-wide cost-to-charge ratio. We did not get the bid and had *no idea* whether to be disappointed or relieved. From talks with third-party payers and major employers, we believed that by the mid-1990s we would be bidding for portions of business, like open-heart surgeries, on a regular basis. We realized that we needed a much better understanding of costs at the DRG and individual patient levels if we're to be able to compete effectively."

—Carolyn Johnson, Vice President of finance

INTRODUCTION

By the end of the 1980s, cost management had become one of the most important issues faced by Brookwood Medical Center (BMC) administrators. BMC faced pressure from managed care providers such as health maintenance organizations (HMOs) and preferred provider organizations (PPOs) to keep medical costs low while continuing to provide high-quality health care services. For the first time, BMC was asked to bid on specific health care services for members of managed care insurance plans. To provide bids that were competitive yet profitable, hospital administrators needed detailed cost information about specific health care procedures. In addition, Medicare and other insurance providers moved to fixed fee reimbursement schedules, paying a defined fixed rate depending on a patient's diagnostic related group (DRG) and severity level. The use of fixed payment rates provided incentives for BMC to identify costs associated with providing health care to specific patients in each DRG. Health care providers realized that reductions in the average length of stay (ALOS) as a result of shorter inpatient hospital stays and increased outpatient services could decrease costs without decreasing the quality of care.

THE NEW COST SYSTEM

As more payers moved to a fixed fee form of reimbursement, BMC administrators determined the existing cost system was not providing sufficiently accurate or detailed cost information. The old methodology provided aggregated cost data by department; but no reliable method existed to trace costs to individual patients or diagnostic groups. The new health care environment required hospitals to compete for managed care contracts and to make strategic decisions based on a solid understanding of costs.

Jan Kelly, Director of cost accounting, identified the following issues to support the need for a new cost management system:

- *Unexplained variation in practice patterns.* Physicians largely drove the health care delivery process through treatment protocols and medical orders that determined patient charges and length of stay. A new cost system could help identify costs associated with specific physician practice patterns.
- *Concern with costs and more appropriate care.* BMC recognized the opportunity to reduce tests and procedures for patients (e.g., ordering a component test rather than a whole profile on blood work). Some inpatient testing and care could be effectively done on an outpatient basis due to advances in medications and

[1] Prepared by Thomas L. Albright and Robin Cooper, © Institute of Management Accountants, 1998. Used with permission.

other technology. Many diagnostic tests and longer inpatient stays may not result in better patient outcomes.

- *Questions regarding effectiveness.* Questions concerning the effectiveness of care, especially when evaluating new technology or treatments, were becoming increasingly commonplace. Thus, BMC required more sophisticated cost management tools.
- *Beliefs regarding cost vs. value of care.* Balancing the quality of care with the costs of providing care was a fundamental concern for BMC. For example, if a new surgical procedure allows early discharge or little scarring but costs 10 times more than an old procedure, is it necessary for the hospital to offer the new procedure and incur additional costs? Executives had to identify a strategy for new technology and the existing methodology, management began to explore alternatives to the old cost accounting methodology. They required a cost system that would provide a product-line focus, i.e., open heart surgery, diabetes care, rehabilitation, or respiratory therapy, and that would permit segmentation of the patient population. Details of Mason's oncological study were reviewed, and the results reinforced the belief that costs calculated on a facility-wide basis were not helpful for making decisions that were DRG-specific.

In March 1991, BMC executives hired an Atlanta-based CPA firm to work with Kelly to gain an understanding of departmental operating costs and to build cost standards. They backloaded cost data for 20 months and identified two types of costs, direct and indirect. Meetings were held twice a week with key hospital administrators and clinicians to determine activities that caused costs.

BMC used a computerized information system known as Transition I (TSI) to assist with standard costing, financial modeling, and forecasting. The software allowed cost managers at BMC to identify activities, link activities to costs, and categorize costs based on predetermined or specific allocation bases. The system also generated simultaneous algebraic equations used to allocate indirect costs to revenue-generating departments. TSI allowed the creation of a database with cost and demographic information that could be sorted by both traditional and nontraditional demographic elements. Detailed information allowed BMC to obtain more accurate measurements of costs to provide care and to monitor and improve the quality of care provided to patients. For example, the patient number, length of stay, total charges, direct costs, and indirect costs for all appendectomy patients treated during a specific time period were summarized by the TSI system (see Table 1).

DIRECT COSTS

Direct costs could be traced to a patient or procedure and included resources consumed in providing testing services, supplies, pharmaceuticals, and nursing care. Costs for patient testing and procedures (including X-ray, laboratory services, operating room costs, labor and delivery room costs) were associated with each patient, using the internally calculated direct cost for each test or procedure. Major supplies and pharmaceuticals were individually assigned to the patient based on the actual cost of the supply or drug.

Nursing care costs were driven to the patient level through daily patient classification and room rate charges. These charges were based on the nursing skill level required to care for patients in each specialty area, as well as the average acuity levels in each specialty area. Nursing staff skill levels were divided into three classifications as follows: registered nurse (RN), licensed practical nurse (LPN), and aide. Examples of specialty areas were obstetrics, surgical, psychiatric, and cardiovascular. BMC divided six acuity levels according to the level of clinical attention required by the patient. For example, a direct cost of $123 per day was incurred in the Nursing-MED/SURG department acuity level 1 (see Table 2).

The cost system produced departmental reports identifying the daily rate by acuity level and the underlying assumptions of the allocation routine (see Table 3). Because the number of minutes required to attend patients varied across acuity levels, the estimated (budgeted) volume of patient days was adjusted for daily service levels, expressed in minutes. The department's budgeted cost was allocated to each acuity level as a percentage of total budgeted minutes. Finally, a daily rate for each acuity level was calculated by dividing the allocated costs by the budgeted volume of days within each acuity level.

INDIRECT COSTS

Indirect costs such as depreciation, administrative, and general were allocated to revenue-producing activities using simultaneous algebraic equations. The calculations were performed by BMC's computerized accounting system using allocation percentages based on the amount of services provided to other departments. The system allocated costs among several departments with reciprocal service relationships. For example, assume an organization has two support departments, housekeeping, information systems (IS), and two revenue-producing departments, operating room (OR) and emergency room (ER). The IS department manager estimated the housekeeping department consumed 10% of the IS department's activities, while the ER and OR required 40% and 50%, respectively. Thus, the IS department's direct costs of $100,000 were allocated to housekeeping, OR, and ER consistent with the resources demanded (see Table 4). Next, the housekeeping department's direct ($60,000) and allocated ($10,000) costs of $70,000 were allocated to IS, OR, and ER using 30%, 40%, and 30%, respectively. Though the IS department had allocated all costs total $100,000 in the first step, the housekeeping department transferred costs ($21,000) back into the department that had to be reallocated in the second iteration. Iterations continued until the costs remaining in the support departments were too small to be significant. Thus, after multiple iterations, all support department costs were transferred to the OR and ER (see Table 4).

The cost system used by BMC simultaneously allocated costs associated with all indirect activities to revenue-producing activities based on cost drivers identified by BMC. For example, the education department allocated its costs to various departments including pain management, diabetic services, and emergency room using the percentage of paid hours within each department as the allocation base. Though the process required multiple iterations (see Table 4), the cost management system produced reports after each allocation iteration (see Table 5). When the allocation procedure had completed the final iteration, all costs for support-related departments were contained in the accounts of revenue-producing departments. Thus, education costs were included in the emergency room indirect cost per hour of $142 (see Table 2).

As the health care environment changed, new information demands were placed on the cost reporting system. The Mason study (discussed in the BMC Introduction) added length of stay as well as direct costs within DRG categories to the cost-to-charge ratio. According to Kelly, "TSI represented a significant step toward understanding and managing the costs of delivering health care services at BMC."

REQUIRED:

1. Why didn't the cost data make any sense?
2. What motivated the managers to build a new cost system?
3. How does the TSI system attach costs to a patient or procedure? What are the major design issues?
4. How is the daily rate determined for the Nursing Med/Surg department acuity level 1?
5. How does the reciprocal method allocate indirect costs to revenue producing departments?
6. Given your understanding of the manner in which TSI allocates costs to patients, would you classify Brookwood's cost system as activity based?

Table 1 Brookwood Medical Center: Appendectomy Patient Listing

Patient Number	Length of Stay	Total Charges	Direct Cost Variable	Direct Cost Fixed	Indirect Cost	Total Cost
1	3	$8,486	751	164	1,187	2,102
2	4	18,394	2,960	566	3,106	6,631
3	2	7,297	926	245	1,280	2,451
4	2	12,350	2,069	258	1,556	3,884
5	2	5,854	765	210	1,152	2,126
6	3	14,574	1,966	395	2,160	4,522
7	2	14,289	2,440	332	1,577	4,349
8	1	5,772	856	102	661	1,619
9	2	11,589	1,404	325	1,553	3,282
10	2	8,398	1,192	365	2,045	3,601
11	2	8,771	1,033	225	901	2,159
12	3	14,920	2,626	295	2,546	5,466
13	3	10,320	1,751	487	2,644	4,882
14	3	8,871	1,097	178	1,460	2,735
15	1	9,103	1,998	221	1,647	3,865
16	2	8,365	1,563	168	1,050	2,781
17	5	13,355	2,195	687	3,237	6,119
18	2	11,235	2,414	258	2,195	4,867
19	1	8,976	1,170	201	1,067	2,438
20	5	18,033	3,123	563	3,457	7,143
21	4	11,756	1,739	229	1,279	3,247
22	1	8,068	1,698	210	1,350	3,258
23	1	8,133	1,669	247	1,257	3,174
24	1	7,396	1,232	160	825	2,217
25	1	6,926	911	147	637	1,695
26	1	7,558	1,268	188	1,141	2,598
27	5	20,140	3,151	468	3,419	7,037
28	2	6,211	718	167	843	1,728
29	2	8,740	1,324	189	1,212	2,724
30	1	6,931	779	140	736	1,656
31	1	8,493	1,345	152	1,013	2,510
32	1	6,580	1,041	153	863	2,056
33	2	8,646	1,328	195	1,200	2,723
34	2	11,319	1,214	247	1,424	2,885
35	1	7,435	1,042	161	817	2,020
36	2	11,765	1,564	267	1,647	3,478
37	1	9,822	1,443	165	1,143	2,752
38	2	10,354	1,929	184	1,669	3,782
39	3	9,117	1,117	126	1,309	2,552
40	1	11,097	1,623	348	1,847	3,818
41	1	9,030	900	141	859	1,901
42	1	7,659	1,558	112	1,045	2,716
43	2	9,943	1,619	174	1,217	3,010
44	2	11,238	1,177	202	1,273	2,651
Total	91	$443,309	67,688	11,017	66,506	145,210

Source: sample of appendectomy patients from TSI data.

Table 2. DRG 470 - Appendectomy Utilization Report

Department Description	*Product Description*	*Direct Cost*	*Indirect Cost*	*Quantity*	*Total Cost*
NURSING - MED/SURG	Acuity level 1 -- daily rate	$123.00	$190.00	1	$313.00
	Acuity level 2 -- daily rate	140.00	229.00	2	738.00
OPERATING ROOM	Major surgery -- 1 hour	174.00	170.00	1	344.00
OPERATING ROOM SUPPLIES	Sutures	17.00	7.00	5	120.00
	Basic surgical pack	17.00	6.00	1	23.00
	Additional OR supplies*	118.00	50.00	1	168.00
RECOVERY	Recovery level II -- 1/4 hours	24.00	11.00	3	105.00
CENTRAL STORES	Central store supplies*	25.50	58.00	1	83.50
LABORATORY SERVICES	Blood profile, potassium, renal profile	29.50	11.00	2	81.00
CARDIOLOGY / EKG	EKG 3 channel w/o physician in	13.00	12.00	1	25.00
PHARMACY	Pharmaceuticals*	163.50	133.00	1	296.50
RESPIRATORY THERAPY	Incentive spirometer	4.00	3.00	5	35.00
	New start spirometer & oxygen	6.00	4.00	1	10.00
EMERGENCY ROOM	ER visit level II -- intensive	80.00	142.00	1	222.00
DIETARY	Daily hospital service	24.00	18.00	3	126.00
LAUNDRY / LINEN	Daily hospital service	9.00	6.00	3	45.00
					2,735.00

* Detail of specific items charged collapsed into one line item.

Table 3. Brookwood Medical Center, Department 6103, Nursing MED/SURG

Budget $95,759

Description	Budgeted Volume in Days	Minutes Daily Service	Budgeted Minutes	Percent Allocation	Allocation	Daily Rate
Acuity level 1	18	346	?	?	?	?
Acuity level 2	264	394	?	?	?	?
Acuity level 3	199	464	92,336	0.343	$32,864	$165
Acuity level 4	25	547	13,675	0.051	4,867	195
Observation	165	40	6,600	0.025	2,349	14
Observation	133	30	3,990	0.015	1,420	11
All others	211	200	42,200	0.157	15,020	71
Total			269,045	1.000	95,759	

Table 4. Calculations for Reciprocal Service Department Allocation

	Service Departments		Revenue Departments	
	IS	**Housekeeping**	**OR**	**ER**
Beginning balance	100,000	60,000	0	0
IS allocation (100,000)	10,000[1]	50,000[2]	40,000[3]	
Balance after allocation	*0*	*70,000*	*50,000*	*40,000*
Housekeeping allocation	21,000[4]	(70,000)	28,000[5]	21,000[6]
Balance after allocation	*21,000*	*0*	*78,000*	*61,000*
2nd IS allocation	(21,000)	2,100	10,500	8,400
Balance after allocation	*0*	*2,100*	*88,500*	*69,400*
2nd housekeeping allocation	630	(2,100)	840	630
Balance after allocation	*630*	*0*	*89,340*	*70,030*
3rd IS allocation	(630)	63	315	252
Balance after allocation	*0*	*63*	*89,655*	*70,282*
3rd housekeeping allocation	19	(63)	25	19
Balance after allocation	*19*	*0*	*89,680*	*70,301*
Transfer minimal balances	(19)	0	10	9
Ending balance	0	0	89,690	70,310

[1] $100,000 * 10%

[2] $100,000 * 50%

[3] $100,000 * 40%

[4] $70,000 * 30%

[5] $70,000 * 40%

[6] $70,000 * 30%

Table 5. Brookwood Medical Center, Education Allocation to Emergency Room

Allocation base: paid hours
Budget -- $500,000

Department	Paid Hours	Percentage of paid hours by department	Amount allocated
Pain Management	2,083	?	?
Diabetic Services	8,993	?	?
Emergency Room	124,212	?	?
Monitoring Services	40,634	?	?
Quality Assurance	21,314	?	?
Dietary	167,411	?	?
Collections	13,650	0.279320	$1,396.60
Outpatient Registration	19,776	0.404677	$2,023.39
All others	4,488,783	91.854210	$459,271.05
Total	4,886,856	100.00%	$500,000.00

Readings

MANAGING SHARED SERVICES WITH ABM

By Ann Triplett and Jon Scheumann

Shared service operations combine the efficiency and leverage of centralization (standardization, economies of scale, and a single base for improvement) with the superior customer service usually associated with decentralization.

Companies try to achieve this balance by drawing together activities performed similarly in various locations across the business (often focusing on transaction processes), standardizing on a common process design that emphasizes high quality and customer responsiveness, and putting in place measurement tools to monitor performance and guide improvement efforts.

Companies choose shared services for various reasons, but lower costs are a primary benefit, as are improvements in productivity and customer service. In addition, some companies see shared services as a platform for growing their business without growing administrative costs at the same rate.

Ford has been operating a shared services center (SSC) for finance in Europe since the early 1980s, and DuPont, Digital Equipment, and General Electric established shared services organizations in the United States in the late 1980s. A second wave of companies, including Hewlett-Packard, Dow Chemical, Dun & Bradstreet, IBM, and Allied Signal, followed that lead in the early 1990s, and today many of the top 500 companies in the United States have implemented some form of shared services.

Regardless of the services they provide—Payroll, Payables, Receivables, Fixed Asset Accounting, etc.—all SSCs are faced with the same three cost-related questions:

- What causes costs in our operation, and how can we manage them?
- How do we determine how much to charge each customer for the services we provide?
- How do our costs compare to those of others, in particular the costs of outsourcers who can provide the same services?

SSC managers are discovering that activity-based management (ABM) can be used to create a framework that provides the cost information required to answer these questions. Gunn Partners found that 16% of the service centers in its 1999 Global Shared Services Research project have completed their ABM implementation. But even more interesting is that 30% of the companies are in the process of implementing ABM, and an additional 21% expect to implement within the next three years. This means that by the end of 2002 nearly 70% of the research companies will have implemented ABM. These results clearly show the expected use of ABM as an important management tool.

HOW DO WE MANAGE SSC COSTS?

Critical to the success of any shared service center is a thorough understanding of costs and the ability to impact those costs. After all, most SSCs were founded on the premise of saving money for the corporation. Cost management is key—possibly more so than for any other part of the business. SSC managers must understand what activities are performed and how each activity contributes to total cost. They need to understand the drivers of cost—especially the drivers that are completely under their control. For example, an internal driver might be the number of internal approval levels required for a particular transaction.

A methodology to identify and evaluate the potential of improvement opportunities, on an ongoing basis, also should be in place. In operating shared service centers, managers strive to continually reduce the cost for existing services and to free resources for providing other services that customers may want.

This information has to be developed and maintained with minimum complexity and cost.

In recent years, many companies have learned that an activity-based model of operations provides all of the information required to effectively understand and manage costs. Through use of this ABM model on an ongoing basis, they manage the business and answer the first question, "What causes costs in our operation, and how can we manage them?"

The success of an SSC depends on cost management, but the ability to understand how customer requirements, actions, and demands for various types of services drive costs also is critical. It's absolutely necessary for managers to identify which activities are required to provide specific services and understand the external drivers of SSC cost—that is, those factors controlled by customers. The percentage of errors in customer-provided information is an example of an external driver. From this cost information, service prices can be developed, and a center should be able to develop and maintain the information with minimum complexity and cost.

If you need to explain cost information to customers, what language do you use? Answer: The activity-based model of operations can be used and expanded with the information required to determine the cost of providing each service. This process, known as service level costing, involves identifying the activities and costs associated with providing services, using that information to support discussions with customers, and then providing the level of service for which each customer is willing to pay. Customers can relate to this language when you discuss costs in terms of how they are caused by activities.

It's also possible, with additional detail, to establish differential pricing, that is, to charge customers different prices for the same service. These prices can be determined by identifying the specific impact that each customer has on cost, based on behavior as measured by cost drivers. A model to support differential pricing takes more time to develop and is larger and more complex to maintain, but some SSCs feel that it's worth the effort.

For many SSCs, service level costing supports the actual charge-out of appropriate costs to customers based on the types of services they receive. For SSCs whose cost is absorbed at a corporate level, the information is equally valuable and can be used to justify and explain decisions made about the services that will be provided. Approximately 60% of corporations who have implemented shared services charge out shared service costs, according to Gunn Partners research.

Furthermore, the research has shown that charging customers a differential rate based on ease or complexity of the transaction hasn't led to a position of cost or productivity leadership. While charging differential rates in an attempt to influence behaviors is emotionally appealing to the SSC leadership, this isn't yet a leading practice according to the data.

Ideally, a shared service center should regularly compare its cost of providing a service to the cost at which others can provide the service. But this isn't always easily accomplished. In some cases, a center can compare service costs with others in a group benchmarking study. For some services it may be possible to obtain information about how much an outsourcing provider would charge.

Here, again, the activity-based model of operations can provide the required information. The center's cost per output of a service is often the piece of information required to benchmark. It's also important to know whether this cost has increased or decreased over time, and a well-maintained model will facilitate this comparison.

One of the challenges is to ensure a valid comparison; the model provides detailed information about which activities are required to provide any given service. Activity costs can be combined in varying ways, if necessary, to arrive at an "apples to apples" comparison for benchmarking.

HOW DO YOU DEVELOP AN ACTIVITY BASED FRAMEWORK?

Companies go through three phases in the development of an activity-based framework to support a shared service center:

- Initial model building effort,
- Customer education and service-level review process, and
- Ongoing maintenance and use of the activity-based framework.

Typically, an ABM modeling software package is used to ensure that the SSC model can be easily sustained over time.

INITIAL MODEL BUILDING

The steps in this phase, illustrated in Figure 1, are those traditionally required to build an activity-based model. Actual implementation of this phase should begin with a much more detailed work plan.

These steps encompass all of the effort required to gather activity and cost information, define the relationships among activities, costs, and services provided, then build the information and relationships into a model. The amount of time it takes to do this will vary according to a number of factors including, but not limited to, resource commitment, size, and scope of center to be modeled, project leadership, and prior experience with ABM.

CUSTOMER EDUCATION AND SERVICE LEVEL REVIEWS

Once the model has been built, the center can begin to use the information to communicate with customers. Typically, the first step in this process is for the center to develop a proposed Service Level Agreement (SLA) for each customer. This document consists of information about which services are being provided, the activity-based cost of each service, and historical information about past service levels. The proposed SLA is the starting point for discussions with your clients.

The client reviews should begin with an introduction to the basic concepts of ABM. Accordingly, initial customer education is critical to the successful, ongoing use of an ABM framework. The rest of the session is spent reviewing the services provided, the level of service provided in the past, the basis for costing, and the actual cost of each service.

The detailed information about the activities required to provide each service should be available but used only if the additional detail is necessary. As each service is reviewed, determine whether or not that service will be provided in the future and, if so, at what level. Remember that the types of services, as described above, will impact these reviews. Some of the services are required for all customers, and others are provided based on customer needs and requirements.

Based on the results from each customer negotiating session, the center can prepare a final SLA for signature. Details about how required information will be gathered and reported over time should be included (for example, number of occurrences). The center should also cover agreements about how billing will be accomplished, whether review is allowed periodically, and so on.

ONGOING MAINTENANCE AND USE

A completed and signed SLA doesn't signify the end of the process, but rather the beginning of an ongoing mutually beneficial relationship between a service center and customer. The three key elements of the ongoing process are:

- Continuous improvement efforts,
- SLA maintenance, and
- Benchmarking.

All of these are linked through the ongoing maintenance of the original ABM model, as illustrated in Figure 2.

Continuous improvement efforts, especially with customer participation, can result in lower costs of services to be incorporated in each ensuing SLA. Information about service cost and customer requirements can support benchmarking efforts. Comparisons can be internal, as in customer to customer, or external comparison can be made to the cost of other service centers or outsourcing service providers. Benchmarking results, in turn, can provide ideas and goals for continuous improvement efforts.

Our work with many clients has demonstrated that a service center goes through three phases during its creation: *installation* (the "birth" of a center), *start-up* (the period of bringing a new center under control), and *steady state* (the ongoing movement into a mode of continuous improvement). It's in the last of these phases that the benefits of ABM can be realized. In earlier phases, activities aren't necessarily well defined, and processes aren't stable. The priorities of a center, then, should be more basic. Each center's situation is unique, and some may move through the phases more quickly than others. A general rule of thumb for when to consider implementing ABM is the second to fourth year of a center's existence.

And you can achieve impressive results by using an activity-based framework to manage a shared service center. First, it supports a new way of management. The activity-based cost model provides a more effective means of managing service center operations than can traditional cost statements and cost accounting analyses.

Service level costing results in more satisfied customers because they understand and have impacted exactly what services they will receive for their payments.

An improved understanding of costs and drivers by both service center providers and customers can result in a lower total cost to the corporation as a whole. Finally, this effort can provide an improved ability to assess outsourcing, or even insourcing, opportunities. A thorough understanding of processes, activities, and costs results in the information required to make cost-effective and correct decisions.

As a point of reference, the Gunn Partners research data show that the leaders in cost and productivity are more likely to be using ABM as a management tool than their peers. But these leaders almost certainly would tell you it isn't a simple exercise and isn't a "project" to be done once and forgotten. The adoption of an activity-based framework for an SSC requires an ongoing commitment. Your rewards, though, will be great!

FIGURE 1

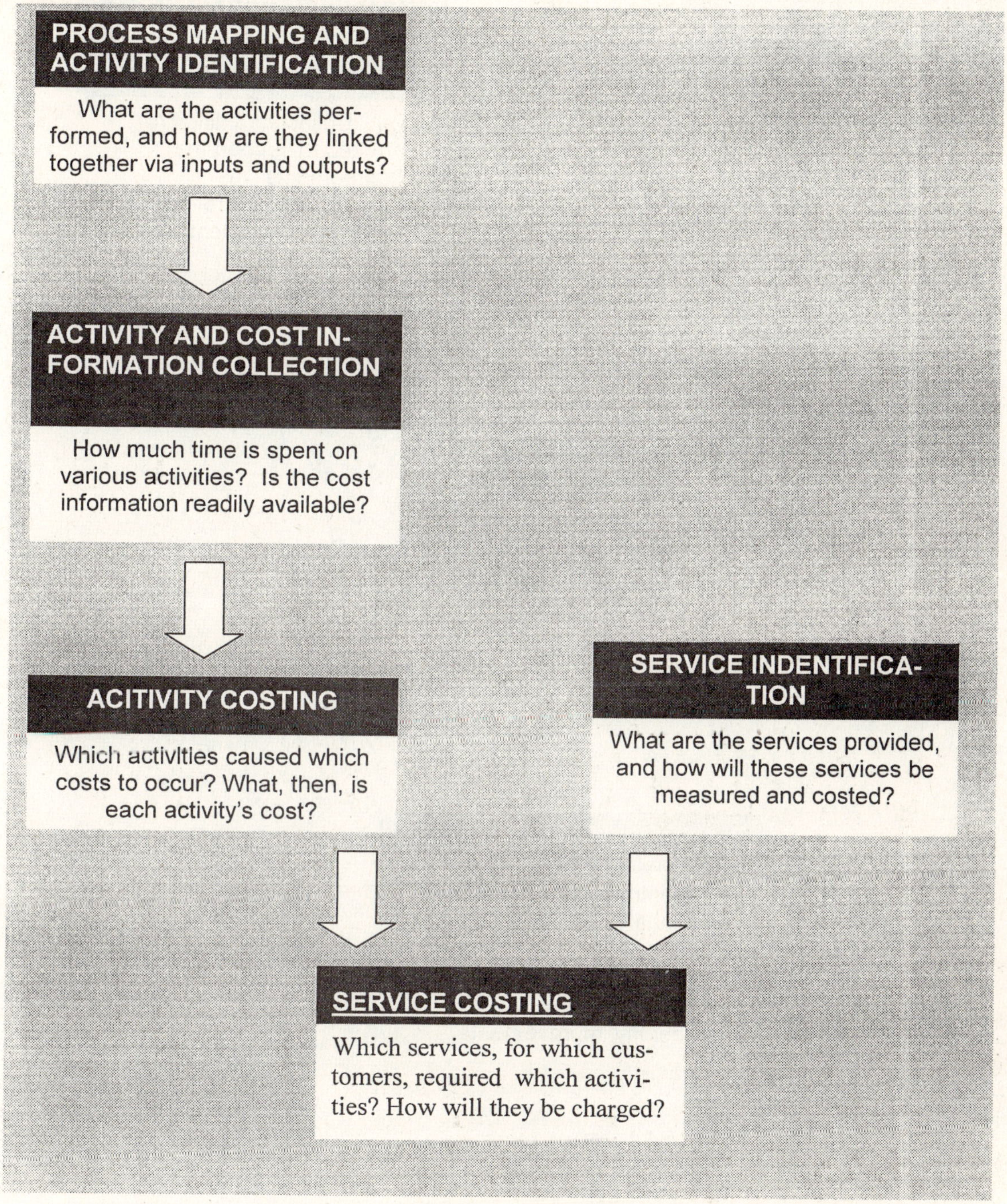
PROCESS MAPPING AND ACTIVITY IDENTIFICATION
What are the activities performed, and how are they linked together via inputs and outputs?
ACTIVITY AND COST INFORMATION COLLECTION
How much time is spent on various activities? Is the cost information readily available?
ACITIVITY COSTING
Which activities caused which costs to occur? What, then, is each activity's cost?
SERVICE INDENTIFICATION
What are the services provided, and how will these services be measured and costed?
SERVICE COSTING
Which services, for which customers, required which activities? How will they be charged?

FIGURE 2

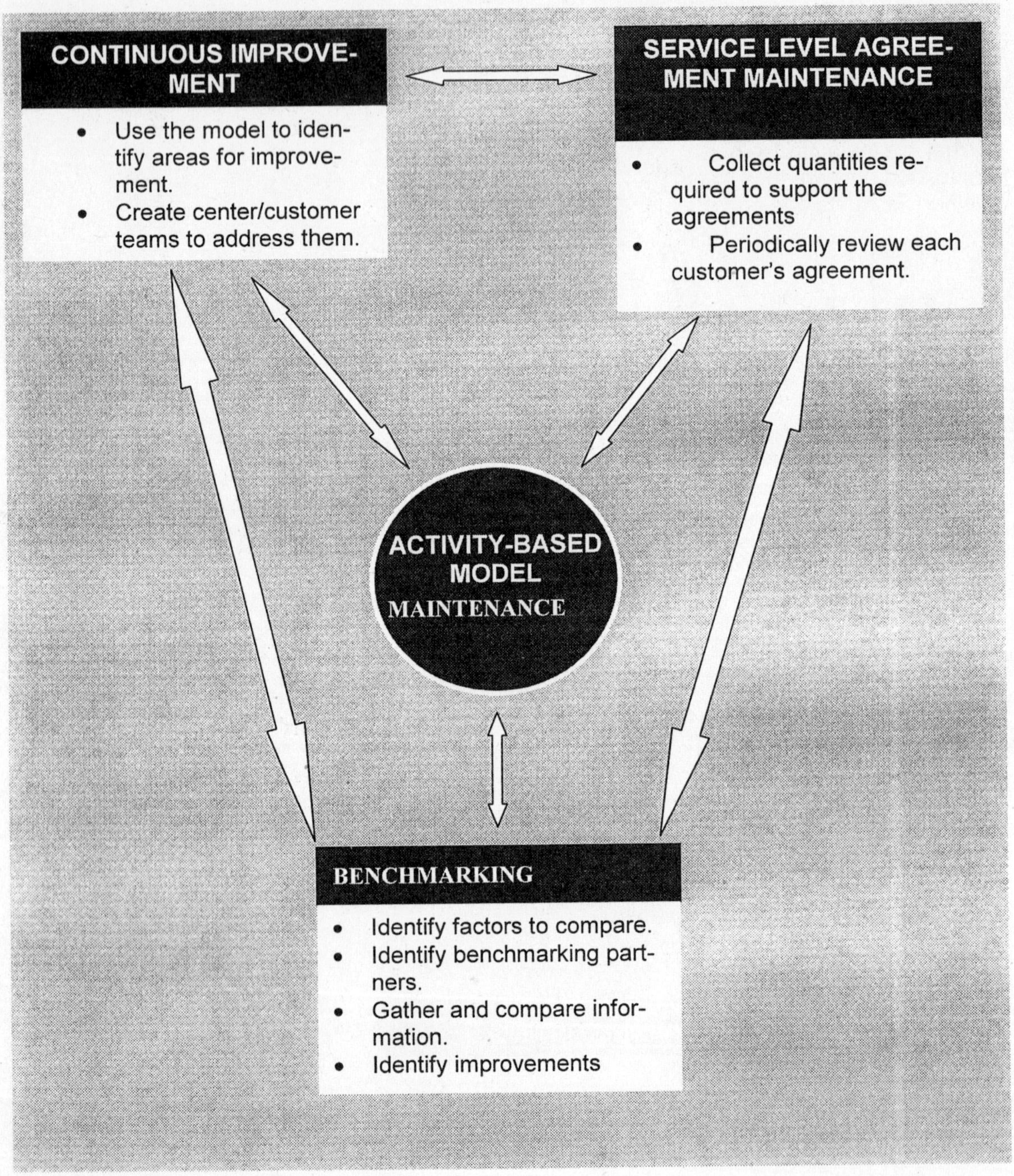
CONTINUOUS IMPROVEMENT
Use the model to identify areas for improvement.
Create center/customer teams to address them.
SERVICE LEVEL AGREEMENT MAINTENANCE
Collect quantities required to support the agreements
Periodically review each customer's agreement.
ACTIVITY-BASED MODEL
MAINTENANCE
BENCHMARKING
Identify factors to compare.
Identify benchmarking partners.
Gather and compare information.
Identify improvements

Chapter 13
The Flexible Budget and Standard Costing: Direct Materials and Direct Labor

Cases

13-1 Hoof and Fin Restaurants

Readings

"Standard Costing Is Alive And Well At Parker Brass"

The Brass Products Division of the Parker Hannifin Corporation is a world-class manufacturer of tube and brass fittings, valves, hose, and hose fittings. Despite the introduction of popular new costing systems, the Brass Product Division operates a well-functioning standard costing system.

Discussion Questions:

1. What features in the firm's standard costing that make it a success?
2. In addition to variances seen in the textbook Parker Brass created several new variances. Describe these variances. Why are these variance added at Parker Brass?

"Redesigning Cost Systems: Is Standard Costing Obsolete?"

The article shows some new ways to analyze standard cost data, going beyond the traditional emphasis on production costs variances that focus on price and efficiency. Variances for product quality are developed and explained, as well as sales variances based on sales orders received and orders actually shipped. There is also a discussion of how to incorporate activity-based costing, and continuous standard improvement, including benchmarking and target costing.

The main premise of the article is that standard cost systems are the most common cost systems in use, and while there are a number of limitations to these systems, a careful and creative effort can transform them into more useful cost systems.

Discussion Questions:

1. What are the main criticisms of traditional standard cost systems?
2. What is meant by "push through" production? Is it preferred to "pull through" production, and why?
3. What are the best ways to make standard cost systems more dynamic?
4. Considering the suggestions make in this article, in contrast to the chapter presentation of standard costing, which ideas make the most sense to you and why?

Cases

13-1 Hoof and Fin Restaurants

David Green is considering his operating report for the most recent year. David is a restaurant manager for one of the 20 restaurants owned and operated by Hoof and Fin, Inc. The first Hoof and Fin restaurant was opened in Austin Texas almost 40 years ago, but has since grown to a 20-location chain throughout the major cities in Texas. The owner, Roger Nisbett, owns most of the stock in the company, which went public 16 years ago to finance the growth of the company. David has been working for Hoof and Fin for 6 years, first as an assistant manager, and currently as the manager for the restaurant located in Waco, Texas. This year is his first year as a manager.

The principal attraction for the restaurant, and the basis for its success, is that diners can select from either a steak menu or a seafood menu, and in each case the prices are very low relative to most restaurants in the area. The menu and restaurant décor is designed to appeal to budget-conscious diners, such as college students. Each of the 20 restaurants is successful, though some more so than others.

Each manager is evaluated on his or her performance relative to a budget set at the beginning of the year. The budget is set by Marv Gregson, chief financial officer for the company, who looks at trends for each of the locations and sets a budget for each location based on past sales and desired future sales and earnings goals for the company. Each manager participates in the budget setting process to a degree, though each manager is quite aware that Marv will have the last say in the determination of the final budget. Each manager is told that a significant bonus is in order for managers whose profit exceeds the budget, and the amount of the bonus will be determined from the amount of the difference from budget. In prior years, managers who have exceeded their budgets by more than 10% have gotten a bonus equal to 20% of the improvement over budget. For some managers this has been a significant monetary reward. For those who do not meet the budget, there is no bonus, but constructive counseling about what can be done to improve performance in the coming year.

David is an ambitious and hard working manager, who has applied himself to the job and has looked for different ways to attract customers and to reduce costs. For example, he has noticed the trend for more customers to prefer the seafood menu, and he has added more selections to that portion of the menu. While the number of steak dinners has fallen slightly, the sales of seafood dinners has increased substantially as a result. Moreover, because of the increased interest in seafood, and because of the increased quality and variety of his seafood offerings, he has been able to increase the average price of his seafood dinners.

Now that the results are in for2004, it is time for the annual review and bonus determination with Mr. Gregson.

REQUIRED:

You are to play the role of David Green, and develop an analysis and a one-half page memo to Mr. Gregson which explains your performance for the year ended December 31, 2004.

Hoof and Fin Restaurant
Operating Statement
Year Ended Dec. 31, 2004

	Actual	**Budget**
Gross Sales	$1,811,160	$1,664,000
Net Sales	1,587,560	1,612,000
Less Variable Expenses		
Food	724,350	676,000
Labor	484,688	500,000
Operating Expenses	74,550	83,200
Total Variable Expenses	1,283,588	1,259,200
Net contribution	303,973	352,800
Other Expenses		
Advertising	83,450	83,200
Misc.	3,200	2,000
Depreciation	33,000	33,000
Insurance	7,960	8,800
Taxes	9,220	6,500
Interest	49,000	49,000
Management	84,000	84,000
Total Other Expenses	269,830	266,500
Profit	$34,143	$86,300
Other Data:		
Average no. of customers/wk	4,300	4,000
Steak dinners %	40%	50%
Seafood dinners %	60%	50%
Average price for dinner (before discount)		
Steak dinner	$9.00	$9.00
Seafood dinner	$7.50	$7.00
Average discount (both dinners)	$1.00	$0.25
Number of employees	25	25
Hours worked, all employees	2,350	2,500
Wage rate for employees	$8.25	$8.00

Notes about the Operating Statement:

1. Food, labor and operating expenses are considered variable costs, under the control of the restaurant manager.
2. Food costs, the largest element of total costs, are budgeted at $3.50 per meal for steak dinners and $3.00 for seafood dinners. All food items are purchased centrally and delivered to each restaurant daily. Due to David's diligence, he was able to save $.08 per meal by substituting food items of equal value for those of higher cost. As a result, David was able to achieve food usage (at standard prices) of $3.42 and $2.92 for steak and seafood dinners, respectively.
3. Each restaurant manager had control over the hiring, firing and wage rates for their employees, and for the number of hours worked.
4. Operating expenses included maintenance, supplies, bags and boxes for take-aways, and miscellaneous other expenses. These were controllable by each restaurant.
5. Advertising expenses were controlled at the home office and allocated to the 20 restaurants based on a % of actual sales at each location. The budget was based on 5% of gross sales.
6. Miscellaneous expenses were a category for a variety of home office expenses, which were allocated to each restaurant on an equal share basis.
7. Depreciation expense was determined for each store based on a straight-line depreciation of that restaurant's building and equipment costs.
8. Insurance, taxes, licenses, interest, and other corporate costs were allocated to each restaurant based on the net book value of the building and equipment at each restaurant.
9. Management costs consisted of the base salary of the restaurant manager and assistant manager, plus and allocated portion of home office management costs, including legal, accounting, and other corporate management costs.

Readings

STANDARD COSTING IS ALIVE AND WELL AT PARKER BRASS

By David Johnsen and Parvez Sopariwala, Ph.D.

Many people have condemned standard costing, saying it is irrelevant to the current just-in-time based, fast-paced business environment. Yet surveys consistently show that most industrial companies in the United States and abroad[1] still use it. Apparently, these companies have successfully adapted their standard costing systems to their particular business environments. In addition, many academics have contributed ideas on how the standard costing system could be and has been made more responsive to the needs of companies operating in this new economy.[2]

The Brass Products Division at Parker Hannifin Corporation (hereafter, Parker Brass), a world-class manufacturer of tube and brass fittings, valves, hose and hose fittings, is one of the standard costing success stories. It operates a well-functioning standard costing system of which we will show you some highlights.

WHAT'S SPECIAL ABOUT THE STANDARD COSTING SYSTEM AT PARKER BRASS?

Parker Brass uses its standard costing system and variance analyses as important business tools to target problem areas so it can develop solutions for continuous improvement. Here are some examples of these standard costing-related tools:

- **Disaggregated product line information.** Parker Brass has been divided into Focus Business Units (FBUs) along product lines. Earnings statements are developed for each FBU, and variances are shown as a percentage of sales. If production variances exceed 5% of sales, the FBU managers are required to provide an explanation for the variances and to put together a plan of action to correct the detected problems. To help the process, a plant accountant has been assigned to each FBU. As a result of these steps, each unit is able to take a much more proactive approach to variance analysis.
- **Timely product cost information.** In the past, variances were reported only at month-end, but often a particular job already would have been off the shop floor for three or more weeks. Hence, when management questioned the variances, it was too late to review the job. Now exception reports are generated the day after a job is closed (in other words, the day after the last part has been manufactured). Any jobs with variances greater than $1,000 are displayed on this report. These reports are distributed to the managers, planners or schedulers, and plant accountants, which permits people to ask questions while the job is still fresh in everyone's mind.
- **Timely corrective action.** Because each job is costed (in other words, transferred out of Work-in-Process and into Finished Goods) 10 days after the job has closed, there is adequate time for necessary corrective action. For example, investigating a large material quantity variance might reveal that certain defective finished parts were not included in the final tally of finished parts. Such timely information would allow management to decide whether to rework these parts or to increase the size of the next job. This kind of corrective action was not possible when variances were provided at the end of each month.
- **An effective control system.** Summary reports are run weekly, beginning the second week of each month, to show each variance in total dollars as well as each variance by product line and each batch within the product line. In addition, at the end of each month, the database is updated with all variance-related information. As a result, FBU managers can review variances by part number, by job, or by high dollar volume.
- **Employee training and empowerment.** Meetings are held with the hourly employees to explain variances and earnings statements for their FBU, thereby creating a more positive atmosphere in which the FBU team can work. These meetings help employees understand that management decisions are based on the numbers discussed and that if erroneous data are put into the system, then erroneous decisions may be made. For example, a machine may not be running efficiently. An operator may clock off of the job so that his or her efficiency does not look bad. Because the machine's efficiency is not adversely impacted, no

FIGURE 1

PANEL A: THE FACTS

Standard production in 1 hour (units)	50
Standard batch quantity (units)	2,000
Standard hours needed for 2,000 units	40
Standard time needed for 1 setup (hours)	4
Standard labor rate per hour	$10
Actual quantity produced (units)	1,200
Actual setup hours for 1 setup	4
Actual productive labor hours to make 1,200 units	24
Actual labor cost for 28 hours at $10 per hour	$280

PANEL B: WORKINGS

	Setups	Production	Total
Standard time per unit:			
Standard setup time (hours)	4		
Standard production time (hours)		40	
Standard batch size (units)	2,000	2,000	
Hence, standard time per unit (hours)	0.002	0.020	0.022
Standard time charged for 1,200 units:			
Standard time per unit (hours)	0.002	0.020	0.022
# of units actually produced	1,200	1,200	1,200
Standard time charged (hours)	2.40	24.00	26.40

PANEL C: SOLUTION

If SRQV is determined, the journal entry would be:		
Work in process [(26.40)($10)]	$264	
SRQV [(4.00 - 2.40)($10)]	$16	
Accrued payroll		$280
If SRQV is not determined, the journal entry would be:		
Work in process [(26.40)($10)]	$264	
LEV [{28.00 - (1 .200)(0.022)}{$10}]	$16	
Accrued payroll		$280

maintenance is done to that machine, and the inefficiency continues. In addition, because the operator is not charging his/her cost to a job, the cost is being included in indirect labor, and manufacturing costs increase. If the operator had reported the hours correctly, management would have questioned the problem, and the machine would have been fixed or replaced based on how severe the problems were.

WHAT NEW VARIANCES HAS PARKER BRASS DESIGNED?

In addition to the aforementioned innovations that Parker Brass has made to adapt its standard costing system to its particular business environment, the company has created the following new variances:

- The standard run quantity variance to explain situations where the size of a lot is less than the optimal batch quantity.
- The material substitution variance to evaluate the feasibility of alternative raw materials.
- The method variance to assess situations where different machines can be used for the same job.

THE STANDARD RUN QUANTITY VARIANCE

The standard run quantity variance (SRQV) represents the amount of setup cost that was not recovered because the batch size was smaller than the earlier determined optimal batch size. Because setup costs are included in the standard labor hours for a standard batch quantity is likely to create an unfavorable labor efficiency variance (LEV). Unless,

FIGURE 2

PANEL A: THE FACTS

Standard price per pound of material Ml	$10
Standard price per pound of material M2	$11
Standard material quantity (Ml & M2) to make 100 units (lbs.)	2
Actual quantity produced (units)	2,000
Actual pounds of M2 purchased and used	43

PANEL B: WORKINGS

Standard quantity to produce 2,000 units:	
Standard material quantity to make 100 units (lbs.)	2
Actual quantity produced (units)	2.000
Hence, standard quantity to produce 2,000 units	40

PANEL C: SOLUTION

If MSV is determined, the journal entry would be:		
Work in process [(40.00)($10)]	$400	
MEV [(43.00 - 40.00)($11)]	$33	
MSV [(40.00)($11 - $10)]	$40	
Material—M2 [(43.00)($11)1		$473

If MSV is not determined, the journal entry might be:		
Work in process [(40.00)($11)]	$440	
MEV [(43.00 - 40.00)($11)]	$33	
Material—M2 [(43.00)($11)]		$473

however, the impact of actual production inefficiencies is separated from setup-related inefficiencies, the LEV reflects the combined impact of these two causes of inefficiencies and is not really useful for taking the necessary corrective action.

See Figure 1 for an illustration of this issue. Panel A shows that standard batch quantity is 2,000 units, the standard production during one hour is 50 units, and, hence, 40 standard hours are needed to produce 2,000 units. In addition, it takes four standard and actual hours to set up one batch. Panel B reveals that standard hours for setup and production labor are 0.002 and 0.020 per unit, respectively, for a total of 0.022 per unit. In addition, because actual quantity produced is 1,200 units, the total standard hours chargeable to these 1,200 units is 26.40 [(0.002 + 0.020)(1,200)].

Finally, Panel C shows the recommended journal entry whereby an SRQV is created. This SRQV represents the unrecovered setup costs because 1,200 units were manufactured instead of the standard batch quantity of 2,000 units. Thus, because the company expected to spend $40 [(4 hours)($10 per hour)] on each setup, the setup cost relating to the 800 (2,000 - 1,200) units not produced, or $16 U, is considered an unfavorable SRQV or the cost of producing small lots. On the other hand, using traditional standard costing, this amount of $16 U would most likely have been categorized as an LEV. Yet there really is no LEV,[3] and the variance of $16 U attributed to labor efficiency is merely the unabsorbed portion of the setup cost attributable to the 800 units that were not produced.

The advantages of extracting the standard run quantity variance are many. First, the SRQV ordinarily would be included in the LEV and could provide a misleading impression of labor's efficiency. Second, because just-in-time practices recommend smaller lots and minimal finished goods inventory the SRQV is essentially the cost of adopting JIT Third, to the extent that setup cost and the cost of carrying inventory are competing undesirables, a determination of the cost of small lots could be used in the trade-off analysis against the cost of holding and carrying inventories. Finally, to the extent that this variance can be separated for each customer, it would reveal how much of a loss was suffered by allowing that customer to purchase in small lots. Such information could be used in future bids. If a customer's schedule required a smaller lot, then that customer's job cost could be enhanced appropriately.

THE MATERIAL SUBSTITUTION VARIANCE

The material substitution variance (MSV) assumes perfect or near perfect substitutability of raw materials and measures the loss or gain in material costs when a different raw material is substituted for the material designated in the job sheet. Substitutions may be made for many reasons. For example, the designated material may not be available or may not be available in small-enough quantities, or the company may want to use up material it purchased for a product that it has since discontinued.

The usefulness of MSV is discussed in Figure 2. Panel A shows that both materials, M1 and M2, can be used to manufacture a product, and it is assumed that two pounds is the standard input per unit for both materials. Material M1 is the material designated in the job sheet, but material M2 can be substituted for M1. The standard cost of M2 ($11 per lb.) is higher than that for M1 ($10 per lb.), and M2 is used because M1 is currently not available and a valued customer needs a rush job.[4] Panel B reveals that the standard quantity needed to manufacture 2,000 units is 40 lbs.

For the purposes of this illustration, we assume that material price variance (MPV) is detected when material is purchased (in other words, the material account is maintained at standard cost). Hence, Panel C reveals the recommended journal entry whereby MSV is created. The MSV represents the benefit obtained by substituting a more expensive material (M2) for the less expensive material (M1) and hence represents the loss through substitution. The MSV is $40 U because (1) 40 lbs. is the standard quantity of M1 and M2 needed to manufacture 2,000 units, and (2) M2 costs $1 more per lb. than M1. In addition, the material efficiency variance (MEV) is $33 U because 43 lbs. instead of the standard quantity of 40 lbs. were used to manufacture 2,000 units.

In contrast, the traditional standard costing system might ignore the substitution, and the job might be charged with the standard cost of using 40 lbs. of M2. In that scenario, the job would cost $40 more and could have an impact on customer profitability analysis even though the customer did not request the substitution.

Now Parker Brass is evaluating an extension that would be to relax the simplifying assumption that both materials require the same standard input. See Figure 3. It adopts the facts from Figure 2 except that 1.9 lbs. of material M2 are required for 100 units instead of 2 lbs. for both materials in Figure 2. In this situation, we have two MSVs, one for the price impact called "MSV-Price" and the other for the efficiency impact, called "MSV-Efficiency."

Panel C shows the recommended journal entry whereby two MSV variances are created. First, MSV-Price is unfavorable because M2, a more expensive material, is being substituted for M1. As a result, MSV-Price is $40 U as material M2 costs $1 more per lb. than material M1. On the other hand, as you might expect, the MSV-Efficiency is favorable because only 1.9 lbs. of M2 are required to make 100 units as compared to 2 lbs. required for M1. Thus, MSV-Effieiency is $22 F because each batch of 100 units requires 38 lbs. of M2 against 40 lbs. of M1. The net result of the MSV variances is $18 U [(38 lbs.)($11)- (40 lbs.)($10)], suggesting that, barring any other complications, the substitution of M2 for M1 is not likely to be profitable under existing circumstances.

Finally, the MEV using material M2 is $55 U, reflecting the fact that 43 lbs. of material M2 actually were used whereas only 38 lbs. of material M2 should have been used. This variance could have been
caused because M2 was a new material and required initial learning and other nonrecurring costs. In such a case, the standard quantity of 38 lbs. for 2,000 units may not need to be changed. On the other hand, the MEV variance may have been caused because of the inherent difficulty in working with material M2. In such a case, the standard of 38 lbs. for 2,000 units may need to be amended. In contrast, as was shown in Panel C of Figure 2, the journal entry that is likely to be made using traditional standard costing would completely ignore the impact of material substitution and would likely inflate the cost of this particular job. The advantages of extracting the MSV are as follows. First, determining MSV lets the company assign the MSV cost to a customer whose rush job may have required using a more expensive material like M2. On the other hand, the MSV could be written off if the substitution were made to benefit the company. Also, creating an MSV and breaking it up into its price and efficiency components allows the company to evaluate whether the substitution of M2 for M1 is a profitable one. While all these calculations can also be performed off the accounting system, creating the MSV makes the process a part of the system so a history of such evaluations is available for future reference.

METHOD VARIANCE

A method variance occurs when more than one machine can be used to manufacture a product.[5] For example, a plant may have newer machines that it normally would expect to use to manufacture a product, so its standards would be based on such new machines. Yet the same plant may also keep, as backups, older and less efficient machines that also could manufacture the same product but would require more inputs in the form of machine and/or labor hours. For this example, we assume that labor hours and machine hours have a 1:1 relationship.[6] As

FIGURE 3
PANEL A: THE FACTS

Standard price per pound of material M1	$10
Standard price per pound of material M2	$11
Standard material quantity of M1 to make 100 units (lbs.)	2
Standard material quantity of M2 to make 100 units (lbs.)	1.9
Actual quantity produced (units)	2,000
Actual pounds of M2 used	43

PANEL B: WORKINGS

	Material M1	Material M2
Standard quantity to produce 2,000 units:		
Standard material quantity for 100 units (lbs.)	2	1.9
Actual quantity produced (units)	2,000	2,000
Hence, standard quantity to produce 2.000 units	40	38

PANEL C: SOLUTION

If MSV is determined, the journal entry would be:		
Work in process [(40.00)($10)]	$400	
MEV [(43.00 - 38.00)($11)]	$ 55	
MSV-Price [(40.00)($11 - $10)]	$ 40	
MSV-Efficiency [(40.00 - 38.00)($11)]		$ 22
Material—M2 [(43.00)($11)		$473

If MSV is not determined, the journal entry might be:		
Work in process [(38.00)($11)]	$418	
MEV [(43.00 - 38.00)($11)]	$55	
Material—M2 [(43.00)($11)]		$473

a result, the method variance becomes pertinent because the traditional LEV from operating the older machines could potentially include the following two impacts. First, an older machine may need additional labor hours to perform the same task, and the additional hours would be reflected in the LEV. Second, the LEV would include the workers' efficiency or lack thereof on the older machine.

We evaluate the usefulness of the method variance in Figure 4. Panel A shows that both machines, A and B, can be used to manufacture a product. Machine A is the more efficient machine and the one used for setting the standard time. Machine B is the backup. Panel B shows that the standard machine hours needed to produce 1,800 units are 30 on machine A and 36 on machine B, which can be compared to the 35 hours actually used to manufacture 1,800 units on machine B.

Panel C of Figure 4 reveals the recommended journal entry whereby a method variance is created. This method variance represents the loss incurred by substituting the backup machine B for machine A. Because machine B's standard of 36 labor hours is greater than machine A's standard of 30 hours, there is an unfavorable method variance of $120. On the other hand, because machine B took 35 hours to manufacture 1,800 units instead of its standard of 36 machine hours, there is a favorable LEV of $20. As you can see, while there was a loss incurred by using machine B instead of machine A, the actual usage of machine B was efficient. In contrast, assuming the traditional costing system recognizes that machine B was used, it is likely to charge the job $720 [(36 hours)($20 per hour)] instead of the $600 [(30 hours)($20 per hour)] that would have been charged if machine A had been used.

Here are the advantages of extracting the method variance. First, the impact of the method variance ordinarily would be included in the LEV and would provide a misleading impression of labor's productivity. Second, the method variance could be used to isolate the additional cost that was incurred during the year by operating machine M2. This could permit a trade-off between purchasing a new machine

FIGURE 4

PANEL A: THE FACTS

Machine A: standard time needed for one unit (minutes)	1.0
Machine B: standard time needed for one unit (minutes)	1.2
Labor rate per hour	$20
Actual quantity produced (units)	1,800
Actual labor hours used to make 1,800 units using machine B	35
Actual labor cost	$700

PANEL B: WORKINGS

	Machine A	Machine B
Standard hours needed for 1.800 units on:		
Standard time needed for one unit (minutes)	1.0	1.2
Actual quantity produced (units)	1,800	1,800
Hence, the standard hours needed	30	36

PANEL C: SOLUTION

If method variance is determined, the journal entry would be:

Work in process [(30.00)($20)]	$600	
Method variance [(36.00 - 30.00)($20)]	$120	
LEV [(36.00 - 35.00)($20)]		$ 20
Accrued Payroll		$700

If method variance is not determined, the journal entry might be:

Work in process [(36.00)($20)]	$720	
LEV [(36.00 - 35.00)($20)]		$ 20
Accrued Payroll		$700

and continuing to maintain the older machine, especially if tight delivery schedules are not the norm. Finally, the product cost would still be based on the standards for the more efficient new machine, and the job would not be charged a higher cost merely because a less efficient machine was used. That means a job that was completed on the older machine would not be penalized.[7]

RELEVANT, NOT IRRELEVANT

As you can see from the Parker Brass examples, standard costing has not become irrelevant in the new rapid-paced business environment. Parker Brass not only has managed to modify its standard costing system to achieve disaggregated and timely cost information for timely corrective action, but it has also designed additional variances to determine how setup time relating to small batches should be absorbed, whether an alternative raw material is economically feasible, and how a product's cost might reflect the use of alternate production facilities.

David Johnsen is cost accounting supervisor of the Brass Products Division at Parker Hannifin Corporation in Otsego, Mich. You can reach him at (616) 694-9411.

Parvez Sopariwala, Ph.D., is a professor in the Accounting and Taxation Department at Grand Valley State University in Allendale, Mich. You can reach him at (616) 895-2176 or sobariwp@gvsu.edu.

1 Studies reporting on the widespread use of standard costing in the U.S., the U.K., Ireland, Japan, and Sweden are summarized by Horngren, Foster, and Datar on page 225 of the 9th edition of their cost accounting text published by Prentice-Hall in 1997.

2 C. Cheatham, "Updating Standard Cost Systems," *Journal of Accountancy,* December 1990, pp. 57-60; C. Cheatham, "Reporting the Effects of Excess Inventories," *Journal of Accountancy,* November 1989, pp. 131-140; C. Cheatham and L.R. Cheatham, "Redesigning Cost Systems: Is Standard Costing Obsolete," *Accounting Horizons,* December 1996, pp. 23-31; H. Harrell, "Materials Variance Analysis and JIT: A New Approach," *Management Accounting,* May 1992, pp. 33-38.

3 The standard production hours needed for 1,200 units were 24 [(1,200)(0.020)], whereas the actual labor hours used have been intentionally set at 24. In addition, the standard and actual labor hours for one setup have been intentionally set at four.

4 An alternative scenario could have the cost per pound of M2 ($9 per lb.) being lower than that for M1 ($10 per lb.) because M2 is used to manufacture other products as well and the company obtains quantity discounts for large purchases of M2.

5 To a limited extent, the rationale behind the method variance is similar to that for the material substitution variance (MSV) discussed earlier.

6 That is, the machine does not work independent of the worker. Hence, the labor hours spent on the machine are the same as the number of hours the machine was operated.

7 A similar reasoning is applied in situations wherein the routing for the manufacture of a product is amended during the year, possibly because the customer wants an additional processing step. In such a case, the resulting process variance could be charged to the customer.

Redesigning Cost Systems: Is Standard Costing Obsolete?

By Carole B. Cheatham and Leo B. Cheatham, Professors at Northeast Louisana University.

SYNOPSIS: Since the early 1980s standard cost systems (SCSs) have been under attack as not providing the information needed for advanced manufacturers. In spite of its critics, SCSs are still the system of choice in some 86 percent of U.S. manufacturing firms.

This paper discusses the criticisms of SCSs that (1) the variances are obsolete, (2) there is not provision for continuous improvement, and (3) use of the variances for responsibility accounting result in internal conflict rather than cooperation. Updates for SCSs in the form of redesigned variances, suggestions for dynamic standards, and refocused responsibility and reporting systems are presented.

The compatibility of SCSs and its main competitor as a cost system, activity-based costing (ABC), is examined. The authors discuss when it is appropriate to use ABC or SCS or some combination of the two.

Since Eli Goldratt's (1983) charge that cost accounting is the number one enemy of productivity in the early 1980s, traditional cost systems have been under attack. Although Goldratt subsequently softened his stand to say that *cost* rather than accounting was the culprit (Jayson 1987), others were quick to jump on the bandwagon to condemn the cost systems in use. New systems were proposed of which the most popular was activity-based costing (ABC).

In spite of all the criticism, a 1988 survey shows 86 percent of U.S. manufacturers using standard cost systems (Cornick et al. 1988). A survey by Schiff (1993) indicates that 36 percent of companies use activity-based costing, but only 25 percent of those use it to replace their traditional cost system. It would seem that only about 9 percent (25 percent of the 36 percent) of companies are using ABC as their main system while the vast majority use a standard cost system (SCS).

This is not to say that traditional SCSs could not benefit from being updated. However, accountants in industry (as well as academia) seem unaware that a redesigned SCS can provide the information they need, and that updating their present system is an easier process than adopting a new system. The SCS is one vehicle of articulation among managerial, financial and operations accounting, and it is a *control* system while the candidates for its replacement typically are only cost *accumulation* systems.

In this article the major criticisms of SCSs are examined along with ways that the weaknesses can be remedied or ameliorated. The criticisms relate to the use of specific variances, the lack of provision for continuous improvement, and the fact that administration of the system results in internal competition rather than cooperation. The appropriate use of ABC systems in conjunction with SCSs is also discussed.

UPDATING THE VARIANCES IN AN SCS

Concerning the variables analyzed in an SCS, most criticisms center on the overemphasis on price and efficiency to the exclusion of quality. Other criticisms center on the use of the volume variance to measure utilization of capacity while ignoring overproduction and unnecessary buildups of inventory. In making such charges, critics fail to realize variance analysis is not "locked-in" to a particular set of variables. Standards are only benchmarks of what performance should be. The particular variables used can be changed as the need arises.

The following discussion focuses on concerns of the new manufacturing environment—raw material ordering and inventory levels, quality, production levels, finished goods inventory levels and completion of sales orders.

VARIANCES PERTAINING TO RAW MATERIALS

The set of variances in Fig. 1 centers on the function of raw material ordering and inventory levels (Harrell 1992). The Raw Material Ordering Variance gives information about the effectiveness of suppliers. It contrasts the raw materials ordered with the raw materials delivered (purchased). Any variation may be considered unfavorable because the goal is to have orders delivered as placed. Too much delivered will result in unnecessary buildups of raw material stocks. Too little delivered is unfavorable because production delays may result.

The Price Variance in Fig. 1 is the traditional price variance computed on materials purchased. This variance has been criticized on the grounds that over-emphasis on price leads purchasing managers to

FIGURE 1
VARIANCES RELATING TO MATERIAL PURCHASING

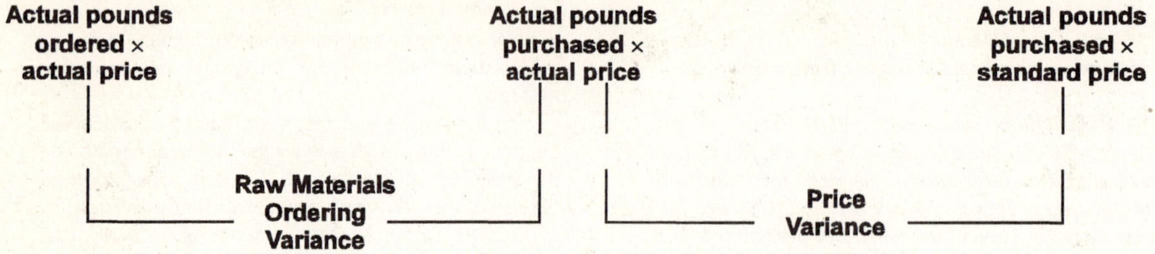

ignore quality. However, price is a legitimate concern that should not be overlooked. This system also uses a Quality Variance (presented in a following section). If low quality materials are purchased in order to gain a low price, this will result in an unfavorable Quality Variance.

VARIANCES PERTAINING TO MATERIAL INVENTORIES AND EFFICIENT USE

The set of variances in Fig. 2 focuses on raw material inventory levels and quantity or efficiency of material use.

The Raw Materials Inventory Variance (Harrell 1992) shows either more material purchased than used (an inventory buildup) or more material used than purchased (an inventory decrease). With the JIT philosophy, purchasing more than used causes an unfavorable variance, while decreasing previous buildups causes a favorable variance.

The Efficiency Variance in Fig. 2 is based on the difference between the actual pounds of material used and the standard amount for *total* production. The traditional Efficiency or Quantity Variance is the difference between the actual pounds of material used and the standard amount for *good* production. The traditional variance is actually as combination of quality and efficiency factors. As can be seen in the next section, quality is better treated in a separate variance.

VARIANCES PERTAINING TO PRODUCTION LEVELS AND QUALITY

The next set of variances (Fig. 3) turns from input analysis to output analysis and relates to production levels and quality. All cost factors are included in the "standard cost per unit" including labor and overhead.

The Quality Variance is the standard cost of units produced that did not meet specifications (the difference between total units produced and good units produced). In traditional variance analysis, this variance is buried in the efficiency variances of the various inputs.

Ignoring labor and overhead, suppose a company used two pounds of material per finished unit at a standard cost of $1.00 per pound. Further assume they used 4,900 pounds in the production of 2,500 total units, of which 100 were defective. Traditional variance analysis would show an unfavorable Efficiency Variance of $100 computed on the difference between the standard cost of the 4,800 pounds that should have been used to produce the 2,400 good units and the 4,900 pounds actually used.

A better breakdown of the traditional variance shows a favorable Efficiency Variance of $100 and an unfavorable Quality Variance of $200. The Production Department did use only 4,800 pounds to produce 2,500 units that should have taken 5,000 pounds. The fact that some of these units were defective should appear as a Quality Variance, as it does in this analysis. The Quality Variance is $200 unfavorable representing $2.00 per unit invested in 100 defective units.

This analysis also yields a Production Variance based on the difference between the standard cost of good units produced and the scheduled amount of production. The goal in advanced manufacturing environments is to produce exactly what is needed for sales orders (scheduled production). A variance from scheduled production either way is unfavorable because too much production results in unnecessary buildups of inventory while too little results in sales orders not filled. As is the case with the Raw Material Inventory variance, the critical factor is the cost of the capital invested in excess inventories. It is desirable to highlight this cost in responsibility reports by applying a cost of capital figure. to the excess (Cheatham 1989).

For simplicity's sake, the above illustrations of input analysis pertain to materials. Labor and volume-related variable overhead can be analyzed in a similar manner. Since there is no difference between labor purchased and labor used in production, the labor input variances would include the traditional Rate Variance and the updated Efficiency Variance.

Other than showing a budget variance for the various elements of fixed overhead, there is no point in further analysis in terms of a Volume Variance. The updated Production Variance serves the same purpose in a far better fashion.

FIGURE 2
VARIANCES RELATED TO MATERIAL USAGE

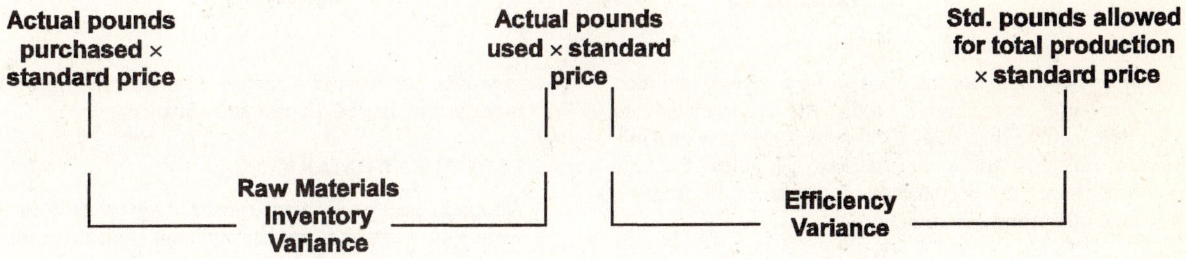

FIGURE 3
VARIANCES RELATED TO QUALITY AND PRODUCTION LEVELS

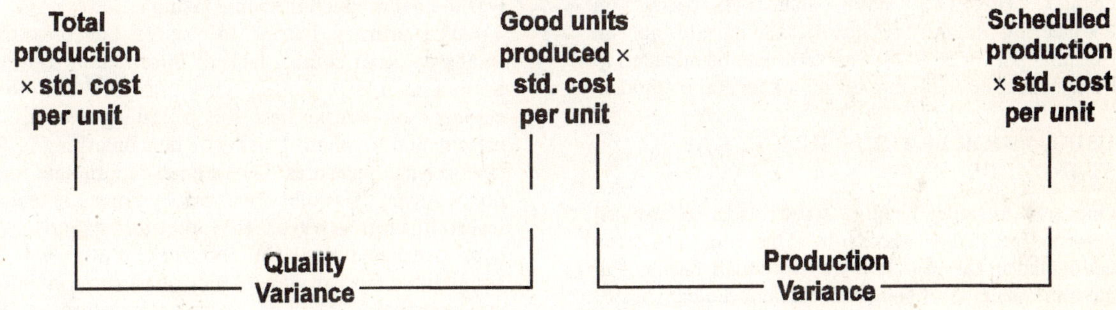

VARIANCES PERTAINING TO SALES ANALYSIS

There are various ways to analyze sales. One method is to use price, mix and volume variances. A further analysis is to break down the volume variance into market size and market share variances. The analysis in Fig. 4 is presented because it articulates well with the output analysis for production.

The sales variances indicate customer service as well as the cost of lost sales. The variances use budgeted contribution margin as a measure of opportunity cost. The Finished Goods Variance indicates the opportunity cost associated with orders completed but not shipped. A delay in shipment causes a loss because of subsequent delay in receiving payment. The Sales Order Variance represents the opportunity cost associated with sales orders that could not be filled during the time period for whatever reason—lack of capacity, scheduling problems, etc.

The above discussion presents a variety of variances that are not used in a traditional standard cost system. The variances can be used for control purposes alone or can be integrated into the financial accounting records (Cheatham and Cheatham 1993).

FIGURE 4
VARIANCES RELATED TO SALES

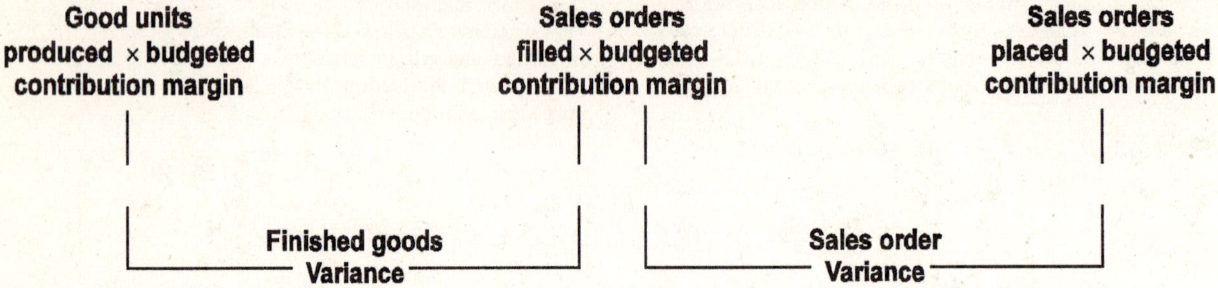

The system is not intended to be a generic solution for any company's needs. It is intended to demonstrate that, with a little creativity, it is possible to redesign SCSs to measure variables that are important to a particular company in today's manufacturing environment.

UPDATING THE SCS FOR CONTINUOUS IMPROVEMENT

In a manufacturing environment in which continuous improvement is a goal of most companies, the charge has been made that SCSs do not encourage positive change. However, static standards based on engineering studies or historical data are not an essential part of an SCS. Standards can be adjusted to be dynamic, or changing, by any of several methods.

USING PRIOR PERIODS' RESULTS AS STANDARDS

One way to have dynamic standards is to use last period's results as standards. This idea has been advocated in the past as a way for small business to have the benefits of standards without the expense of engineering studies (Lawler and Livingstone 1986; Cheatham 1987). The objection can be made that last period's results may not make very good standards if last period was unrepresentative for whatever reason. If this is the case, last period's results can be modified.

Another variation on using past performances as standards is the use of a base period. Comparisons can be made with the base period and all subsequent periods, if desired. Boer (1991, 40) describes a system of using a base year as a "pseudo flexible budget" from which unit costs are developed. He comments that the system "encourages continuous improvement and never implies that a level of performance is adequate. Instead, it encourages managers to improve continuously."

Still another variation on using prior periods' results as standards is the use of best performance-to-date (BP). BP is a rigorous standard for self-improvement because it motivates workers as well as managers to exceed all past performance.

USING BENCHMARKING

Although past performance costs may be used in a variety of ways to formulate dynamic standards, any such system has an inward focus. Benchmarking looks outside the firm to the performance of industry leaders or competitors. Benchmarking typically is applied to performance measures rather than standard costs. However, using the performance of industry leaders as a standard provides motivation to become world-class in much the same fashion.

The primary barrier to use of benchmarking standards is, of course, lack of information. Edward S. Finein (1990), former vice president and chief engineer of Xerox, lists the following sources of information when using benchmarking for performance measures: (1) external reports and trade publications; (2) professional associations; (3) market research and surveys; (4) industry experts; (5) consultants' studies; (6) company visits; and (7) competitive labs. In the absence of hard information, an approach may be taken to estimate the performance of industry leaders. Trying to meet the supposed standards of industry leaders (or other competitors) can have results that are useful as long as the company is striving toward beneficial goals.

USING MOVING COSTS REDUCTIONS

Still another way to have dynamic standards is through use of predetermined cost reductions. Horngren et al. (1994) describe a system of what they call a "continuous improvement standard cost" or a "moving cost reduction standard cost." This system reduces the standard cost by a predetermined percentage each time period, such as a one percent reduction in standard cost per month computed by setting the new standard at 99 percent of the previous month's standard.

The question that their system raises is how to determine the amount of the cost reduction. One possibility is the use of cost improvement curves. Cost improvement curves are a new variation of the old learning curve idea. Learning curves were based on reduction of direct labor costs due to learning by the workers. With a large percentage of product conversion being brought about by automated equipment rather than laborers, potential cost reductions relate to the experience factor for the organization as a whole which may be measured by cost improvement curves.

Pattison and Teplitz (1989) calculate the new rate of learning for an organization that replaces labor with automated equipment as:

$$Rate_{new} = Rate_{old} + (1 - Rate_{old}) * L * R$$

where $Rate_{old}$ is the rate of learning for the old system, L is the proportion of learning attributed solely to direct labor stated as a percentage, and R is the proportion of direct labor being replaced. The formula actually reduces the learning rate applicable to labor only, the assumption being that workers can learn but not machinery. An updated version of the formula is needed which encompasses factors such as managers', supervisors' and engineers' experience.

The Japanese stress the formula 2V=2/3C, or if volume is doubled, the cost should be two-thirds of what it was originally. This formula equates to a 67 percent learning curve which represents a high degree of learning. However, their attitude is that learning does not just happen—it should be made to happen.

USING TARGET COSTS

Another idea borrowed from the Japanese is the use of target costs based on the market. Target costs are used in Japan primarily for new products that are still in the design stage. The idea is to set a cost that is low enough to permit a selling price that is viable on the market. The price is the starting point for calculating costs, and the various costs are backed out from the price. Typically, the target cost is very low. Hiromoto (1988) describes the use of target costs at the Daihatsu Motor Company. First, a product development order is issued. Then an "allowable cost" per car is calculated by taking the difference between the target selling price and the profit margin. Then each department calculates an "accumulated cost" based on the standard cost achievable with current technology. Finally, a target cost is set somewhere between the allowable and accumulated cost. All this takes place before the product is designed. The design stage typically takes three years. When the product is finally in production, the target cost is gradually tightened on a monthly basis. Later the actual cost of the previous period is used to drive costs down further.

Market-based target costs have a strong appeal on a basis for standard costs because they focus on the customer rather than on internal engineering capabilities. However, using target costs is easiest with new products because as much as 90 percent of product costs are set in the design stage (Berliner and Brimson 1988). The way a product is designed determines the way it has to be manufactured and sets the stage for further cost reductions.

Standard costs do not have to be static. Dynamic standards can be formulated using a variety of methods including past performance, industry leader's performance, or target costs based on predetermined reductions or the market. Market-based target costs have the most intuitive appeal because the focus is on the future and on the customer. However, they may work better for new products rather than for established products.

UPDATING MANAGEMENT RESPONSIBILITY AND REPORTING

Besides revamping the SCS to better reflect today's concerns in terms of variables to be measured and continuous improvement, there needs to be improved reporting of variances. Old reporting systems tended to foster internal competition and arguments about whose department was to blame for unfavorable variances. There needs to be an attitude of cooperation among workers, managers and departments.

Revised lines of responsibility used with new plant layouts are improving some of the competitive attitudes that once prevailed in manufacturing organizations. Plants that used to feature "push through" production with large masses of raw materials and semifinished product moving from one process to another are changing to work cells or similar arrangements. The work cell arrangement features equipment that can process a product from start to finish. Workers in the work cell typically can operate all or several types of machinery. This leaner "pull through" approach allows a sales order to be rapidly processed within the work cell which decreases cycle time and holds work in process and finished goods inventories to a minimum.

The work cell arrangement allows a team of workers to be responsible for the entire product and reduces the likelihood that defects will be passed along to the next department. Along with the work cell arrangement many companies are decentralizing functions such as engineering and making these personnel responsible for a particular work area or product line. With the decentralization, there is more focused responsibility. Decentralization and a team approach to production eliminates many conflicts that once existed.

FIGURE 5
WORK CELL A
VARIANCE TRADE-OFF REPORT FOR MONTH OF JULY 19X6

Raw Materials:

	Price	**Quantity**	**Total**
Material X	100 F	200 U	100 U
Material Y	50 F	100 U	50 U
Material Z	200 F	150 F	350 F
Total	350 F	150 U	200 F

Labor:

	Rate	**Efficiency**	**Total**
Type A	400 F	200 F	600 F
Type B	550 U	250 F	300 U
Total	150 U	450 F	300 F

Traceable Overhead Variances:

	Spending	**Efficiency**	**Total**
Power	150 F	50 U	100 F
Supplies	100 U	10 U	110 U
Other	50 F	10 F	60 F
Total	100 F	50 U	50 F

Quality Variance on Dept. A Contribution to Product Cost 100 Defective Units @ $7.00	700 U
Total	150 U

In addition to the new attitudes about responsibility, there needs to be improved reporting. The variances outlined in this paper can be reported in two types of management reports. The report illustrated in Fig. 5 shows the trade-offs between price, efficiency and quality. This type of report can be done on a plant level or department level as well as a work cell level. The price variance for work cells or departments should be computed on material used rather than purchased because this gives a better picture of the trade-offs involved. Upper-level management reports should probably show both types of price variances if there are significant differences between purchases and use.

The report illustrated in Fig. 6 shows the effects of variances related to inventories. Raw material excesses at cost, related to both current and past purchases, are listed along with the related cost of capital. In this case it is assumed the excess was held the entire month and the cost of capital was one percent. Work in Process excesses are measured in terms of the Production Variance. This variance measures the difference between scheduled and actual production. Presumably if there were excesses from the previous month, there was an adjustment made in the scheduled production. Cost of capital figures show the effect of holding these excess inventories.

In the case of Finished Goods, the crucial factor is the opportunity cost of sales orders not filled measured by the lost contribution margins. Therefore, if orders are completed but not shipped or there is an inability to fill a sales order because of lack of capacity, this is indicated by the Finished Goods Variance or the Sales Order Variance. The illustration assumes a favorable Finished Goods Variance because more sales orders were filled than units produced, indicating a decrease in previous finished goods stock.

Although a reporting system such as that illustrated in figures 5 and 6 may not eliminate all conflicts, it is certainly helpful to recognize that trade-offs occur. It is also beneficial for upper-level managers to see the cost of excesses or deficiencies in inventories measured in terms of lost contribution margins and cost of capital.

FIGURE 6
PROFITABLE MANUFACTURING COMPANY
EXCESS INVENTORY REPORT FOR MONTH OF JULY 19X6

	Cost	Cost of Capital
Raw Materials		
Excess from previous month	$5,000	$ 50
Current inventory variance	3,000 F	($ 30)
Total	$2,000	$ 20
Work in Process		
Cell A Production variance	$4,000 U	$ 40
Cell B Production variance	$1,000 U	$ 10
Total	$5,000 U	$ 50
Total Excess and Cost of Capital	$7,000 U	$ 70
Finished Goods:		
		Contribution
Finished goods variance	$ 5,000 F	$(1,500)
Sales order variance	8,000 U	2,400
Total	$ 3,000 U	$ 900
Total Cost of Capital and Lost Contribution Margins		$ 970

STANDARD COST SYSTEMS AND ABC

A final consideration in updating SCSs is how an SCS relates to ABC. Although ABC potentially has broader uses, it primarily has been used for manufacturing overhead.

When a company has a significant amount of indirect product cost, ABC results in better product costing because ABC is superior for allocating these costs among products. This permits company managers to more knowledgeably price products. However, ABC is a cost *accumulation* system rather than a cost *control* system. When used with process value analysis (PVA) or activity based management (ABM), ABC can have a cost *management* feature, but there is no day-to-day monitoring system to assure that costs are within certain parameters.

Most companies can benefit from some combination of ABC and an SCS. One possibility is use of ABC for indirect costs and an updated SCS for direct costs. Another possibility is use of an SCS for financial records and ABC for analysis of indirect costs outside the main record-keeping system. A combination of the two systems retains the advantages of the superior control features of an SCS with the benefits of better overhead analysis from ABC.

CONCLUSION

SCSs are not really the dinosaurs of cost systems, but they may benefit from a little evolution. Updated variances along with dynamic standards will vastly improve the usefulness of most SCSs. ABC can coexist with an SCS and bring some order to the general area of indirect costs. Improvements in the reporting of variances can allow managers to assess trade-offs and inventory stocks and their impact on profits.

REFERENCES

Berliner, C., and J. Brimson, eds. 1988. Cost Management for Today's Advanced Manufacturing: The CAM-I Conceptual Design. Boston: Harvard Business School Press.

Boer, G.B. 1991. Making accounting a value-added activity. Management Accounting 73 (August): 36–41.

Cheatham, C. 1987. Profit and productivity analysis revisited. Journal of Accountancy 164 (July): 123–130.

_______. 1989. Reporting the effects of excess inventories. Journal of Accountancy 168 (November): 131–140.

_______, and L. Cheatham. 1993. Updating Standard Cost Systems. Westport, CT: Quorum Books.

Cornick, M., W. Cooper, and S. Wilson. 1988. How do companies analyze overhead? Management Accounting 69 (June): 41–43.

Finein, E.S. 1990. Benchmarking for superior quality and performance. Performance Measurement for Manufacturers Seminar, Institutes for International Research (October).

Goldratt, E.M. 1983. Cost accounting is enemy number one of productivity. International Conference Proceedings, American Production and Inventory Control Society (October).

Harrell, H. 1992. Materials variance analysis and JIT: A new approach. Management Accounting 73 (May): 33–38.

Hiromoto, T. 1988. Another hidden edge—Japanese management accounting. Harvard Business Review 69 (July-August): 22–26.

Horngren, C. et al. 1994. Cost Accounting: A Managerial Approach. 8th ed. Englewood Cliffs, NJ: Prentice Hall: 246.

Jayson, S. 1987. Goldratt & Fox: Revolutionizing the factory floor. Management Accounting 68 (May): 18–22.

Lawler, W., and J. Livingstone. 1986. Profit and productivity analysis for small business. Journal of Accountancy 163 (December): 190–196.

Noreen, E. 1991. Conditions under which activity-based cost systems provide relevant costs. Journal of Management Accounting Research 3 (Fall): 159–168.

Pattison, D., and C. Teplitz 1989. Are learning curves still relevant? Management Accounting 71 (February): 37–40.

Schiff, J. 1993. ABC on the rise. Cost Management Update Issue No. 24 (February). In Cost Accounting: A Managerial Emphasis, 1991, cited by C. Horngren, G. Foster, and S. Datar, 161. Englewood. Cliffs, NJ; Prentice Hall, Inc.

Chapter 14
Standard Costing: Factory Overhead

Cases

14-1 Berkshire Toy Company
14-2 The Mesa Corporation

Readings

"Using Enhanced Cost Models in Variance Analysis for Better Control and Decision Making"

This article points out that oversimplifications of fixed and variable costs can result in the standard costing system not being used or, if used, can lead to bad decisions. For variance reporting to be useful, financial managers need to develop cost models that reflect how costs actually behave.

Discussion Questions:

1. Describe the implications on operating decisions of analyzing a semi-variable cost as either a variable or fixed cost.
2. Describe the implications on operating decisions of analyzing a step-fixed cost as either a variable or fixed cost.
3. Describe the implications on operating decisions of analyzing an operation with mixed costs as either a variable or fixed cost.

"Variance Analysis Refines Overhead Cost Control"

This article attempts to analyze the full costs of selected medical procedures using examples from a healthcare organization. A key feature of the analysis is how the overhead variances are handled, and in particular how to develop an understanding of the volume variance and how it affects profitability. Standard costs are determined for a hypothetical "Procedure 101" and there is an illustration of how variances can be obtained and interpreted, given example actual results for the procedure over a year's time. The analysis shows the effect of volume changes on overhead recovery and on profit contribution.

Discussion Questions:

1. What is the key driver of profitability based on the analysis in this article?
2. Explain how the two variances are developed and interpreted in Exhibit 3.
3. Consider the example in Exhibit 4. Why are expenses improperly matched and the reported income overstated?

"Overhead Control Implications of Activity Costing"

This articles shows limitations of the traditional treatment of standard cost overhead variances. Using a problem from a CMA exam the authors solved the problem both in a traditional format and again using activity-based cost drivers. Regression is used to identify the cost drivers, and a revised solution is derived.

Discussion Questions:

1. What are the limitations of standard cost overhead analysis?
2. How does the activity approach improve upon the standard cost analysis of overhead?

"Better Information Through The Marriage Of ABC And Traditional Standard Costing Techniques"

This article introduce a set of improved standard costing techniques that provide additional relevant information for decision making within the contemporary manufacturing environment that is not provided by traditional standard overhead cost analyses.

Discussion Questions:

1. Why traditional standard costing and variance analyses have severe limitations when used to analyze overhead costs, but less so when used to analyze direct materials and variable direct labor costs?
2. How can the marriage of ABC and traditional standard costing techniques improve usefulness of information?

Cases

14-1 Berkshire Toy Company[1]

Janet McKinley is employed by the Quality Products Corporation, a publicly traded conglomerate. The corporation manufactures and sells many different kinds of products, including luggage, music synthesizers, breakfast cereals, peanut butter, and children's toys. McKinley is Vice President in charge of the Berkshire Toy Company, a division of Quality Products.

It is late July 2002 and McKinley has just received the preliminary income statement for her division for the year ended June 30, 2002 (see Table 1). The master (static) budget and master budget variances for the same period are included for comparison purposes. McKinley looks at the bottom line, a loss approaching a million dollars, then picks up the phone to call you. You are an accountant in the controller's office at the headquarters of Quality Products Corporation. You worked with McKinley when her company was acquired by Quality Products, and now she has called you for advice.

"I know the bottom line looks pretty bad," she says. "But we made great strides this year. Sales are higher than ever. Customers love our product and respect our quality. There must be a way to make this business work and turn a profit, too. The budget variances should provide some insights. Could you do an analysis of the budget variances?"

BACKGROUND

The Berkshire Toy Company was founded by Franklin Berkshire, Janet McKinley's father, in 1974. Berkshire was an industrial artist who enjoyed making stuffed animals in his spare time. His first creation, a teddy bear that he presented to Janet on her seventh birthday, occupies a place of honor at Berkshire Toy Company's headquarters. In 1974, Frank Berkshire acquired an old pneumatic pump that had been used to fill life-jackets for the Navy during World War II. He modified the machine to mass produce stuffed animals, and the Berkshire Toy Company was born.

The company started small at first, but grew quickly as Berkshire's reputation for quality spread. By 1986, annual sales exceeded a million dollars for the first time. Janet McKinley had learned the business from the bottom up. She had started out with the company in the mailroom as a part-time summer employee. As a college student, she had spent summers and Christmas vacations working on the production floor, in the sales department, and finally in the accounting department. She was named Assistant to the President in 1988 after receiving her M.B.A..

In 1991, at her urging, the company launched an initial public offering (IPO) of common stock and became publicly traded on the NASDAQ. Janet McKinley became CEO of the company on July 1, 1993 when her father retired. On March 17, 1995, Berkshire Toys was acquired by the Quality Products Corporation in a friendly exchange of common stock valued at $23.2 million.[2] The terms of the acquisition included an agreement to employ McKinley for no fewer than five years at an annual salary of $120,000.

The Berkshire Toy Company produces the Berkshire Bear, a fifteen-inch teddy bear enjoyed by children and adult toy collectors around the world. The company touts the handcrafted features of the bear and advertises its product as the only teddy bear made in America. The bears are fully jointed, constructed of washable acrylic pile fabric, and stuffed with a polyester fiber filling. The toys are dressed in various accessories, such as bow ties, sports

---

Source: Dean Crawford and Eleanor G. Henry. Budgeting and Performance Evaluation at the Berkshire Toy Company, *Issues in Accounting Education,* 15 (2) May, 2000, pp. 283-309.

[1] This case is based on field research at an existing toy company. The essential facts relating to production and sales have been retained. However, all names, dates, actual events, and identifying details have been concealed to protect the privacy and identity of the company. Thus, if any names used in this case are those of actual firms or individuals, then it is purely coincidental.

[2] In a friendly acquisition, the terms of the exchange are negotiated by the acquiring company and the incumbent management of the target (acquired) firm. This method of merging two companies is quite different from a "hostile takeover," which is initiated by the acquiring company over the objections of the target's incumbent management.

jerseys, or character and occupational costumes. Thus, the product can be personalized for numerous occasions. The Berkshire Bear is sold with an unconditional lifetime guarantee. In communicating with customers, the company refers to its repair center as the "bear hospital." A damaged bear may be returned by the customer and repaired (or replaced, at the company's discretion) free of charge.

TABLE 1

Berkshire Toy Company
A Division of Quality Products Corporation

Preliminary Statement of Divisional Operating Income
for the Year Ended June 30, 2002

	Actual	Master (Static) Budget	MasterBudget Variance	
Units sold	325,556	280,000	45,556	F
Retail and catalog (174,965 units)	$8,573,285	$11,662,000	$3,088,715	U
Internet (105,429 units)	4,428,018	0	4,428,018	F
Wholesale (45,162 units)	1,445,184	1,344,000	101,184	F
Total revenue	14,446,487	13,006,000	1,440,487	F
Variable production costs:				
Direct materials				
Acrylic pile fabric	256,422	233,324	23,098	U
10-mm acrylic eyes	125,637	106,400	19,237	U
45-mm plastic joints	246,002	196,000	50,002	U
Polyester fiber filling	450,856	365,400	85,456	U
Woven label	16,422	14,000	2,422	U
Designer Box	69,488	67,200	2,288	U
Accessories	66,013	33,600	32,413	U
Total direct materials	1,230,840	1,015,924	214,916	U
Direct labor	3,668,305	2,688,000	980,305	U
Variable overhead	1,725,665	1,046,304	679,361	U
Total variable production costs	6,624,810	4,750,228	1,874,582	U
Variable selling expenses	1,859,594	1,218,280	641,314	U
Total variable expenses	8,484,404	5,968,508	2,515,896	U
Contribution margin	5,962,083	7,037,492	1,075,409	U
Fixed costs:				
Manufacturing overhead	658,897	661,920	3,023	F
Selling expenses	5,023,192	4,463,000	560,192	U
Administrative expenses	1,123,739	1,124,000	261	F
Total fixed costs	6,805,828	6,248,920	556,908	U
Operating income[a]	$(843,745)	$788,572	$1,632,317	U

[a] The actual operating income reported in Table 1 is a preliminary figure that has not been adjusted for fiscal 1998 bonuses, if any.

The Berkshire Toy Company's 241 employees are organized into three departments: purchasing, production, and marketing. The purchasing department consists of David Hall, the purchasing manager, and a staff of ten. The department is responsible for acquiring and maintaining the supply of production materials. Bill Wilford manages 174 employees in the production department, where the manufacture and assembly of the product takes place. The marketing department is headed by Rita Smith. She is responsible for all aspects of marketing and she supervises the nine sales clerks and 42 sales representatives that make up Berkshire's sales force. The remaining three employees are McKinley, her secretary, and her secretary's assistant.

PRODUCTION

Production begins with a large press that cuts the acrylic pile fabric into the required pattern pieces. The press-cutter machine applies 23,000 pounds per square inch of pressure to a tray of pattern stainless steel dies[3] that are stamped into the fabric. The bolts[4] of fabric are rolled out and layered on the cutting table. The fabric is measured at this time for length and width and inspected for fabric flaws, tears, and soiled areas. Fabric flaws create waste. Shortages in length or width may require a different cutting set-up and increase fabric waste. Additional cutting set-ups increase production time. The press-cutter machine cuts 14 layered bolts at a time, enough for 588 units. The machine produces a clean, crisp, cut edge that will not fray or ravel.

The fabric is also inspected for trueness of color. The Berkshire Bear is advertised as a honey bear. Thus, fabric dye lots are important for matching shades of brown. The toy animal is available also in off-white and dark brown. Off-color fabric must be scrapped or returned to the supplier. Because the toy is designed to be washable, the fabric must be colorfast. Berkshire obtains the most economical price for specified colors by timing its fabric orders with the production runs of its suppliers. Rush orders almost always increase substantially the price of the required fabric.

In the next stage of production, operators of industrial sewing machines construct the six parts of the finished unit: two arms, two legs, the head, and the torso. Each piece is sewn inside-out and then turned right-side-out for assembly. Sewing is the most labor-intensive phase of the production process. Any additional sewing steps, such as appliques[5] or monograms, require additional production time.

In the next step, two optical-grade, acrylic eyes are attached to the head with plastic rivets. If the rivet posts are too short, the eyes may fall off later. If the rivet posts are too long, the eyes will stand out from the head, giving a nonstandard appearance. Eye color is also somewhat important. Acrylic eyes are purchased from vendors in "dark brown," but the exact shade may vary from supplier to supplier. Defects are not discovered until the eyes are used in production. At that point, defective eyes are discarded and replaced with ones that meet specifications.

After the cut pieces have been sewn together and eyes attached, the company's unique pneumatic stuffing machine[6] is used to blow the polyester fiber filling into the unassembled parts. Except for two replacements of the electric motor and a new power cord, this is the same machine that Franklin Berkshire acquired from Navy surplus in 1974. Bags of filling are loaded into the machine hopper and mechanically fluffed to the proper loft.[7] An operator places the empty arm, leg, body, or head over a stationary nozzle and uses a foot pedal to control the flow of filling. The machine operator judges whether the part has been filled correctly. Too little filling affects the firmness of the bear; too much filling is unnecessary and expensive. Inferior grade fiber filling is less expensive but can cause clumping and clogging in the hopper. When this happens, production is interrupted and the operator must unclog the vacuum hose and reset the machine.

Next, the arms, legs, and head are attached to the torso using three-part, snap-on, hard plastic disc joints. The disc joints allow the head and limbs to rotate and eliminate the need for sewn attachment. The plastic joints are designed to be foolproof in production and dependable for the life of the product. However, the joints cannot be removed without destroying them. Occasionally, after initial joint insertion, the parts do not fit together properly and they must be removed and replaced.

At the end of the construction process, a woven satin label that states "Made in America by the Berkshire Toy Company" is attached to the back of each bear. More polyester filling is stuffed into the torso and the back seam is hand-stitched, using essentially the same "shoelace" procedure practiced by surgeons. Each seam is brushed by hand to give the bear a seamless look.

---

[3] Dies are heavy-duty, three-dimensional patterns used to cut the fabric into parts for the bear. Dies function in a manner similar to cookie cutters.

[4] Fabric is shipped from the manufacturer wrapped around a cylindrical core or "bolt." A standard bolt of fabric is ten yards long and 72 inches wide.

[5] Appliques are descriptive or ornamental features made from contrasting materials that are applied to the outside surface of the bear. The alligator emblem used by Izod on sweaters and polo shirts is a common example of an applique. Another example is an identifying patch applied to pockets of uniforms bearing the employer's name and logo.

[6] Berkshire Toy Company adapted technology used by the Navy. The stuffing machine is not patented.

[7] Fiber filling is a loose material. Two pounds of bagged filling occupy approximately one cubic foot of space. The filling is loaded manually into a metal bin or "hopper." Rotating sets of fork-like tines separate the strands of filling and increase the volume by incorporating air. The proper mixture of air and filling is the "loft."

The production process is a continuous source of airborne polyester and acrylic fibers that must be controlled, both to protect the health and safety of the employees and to safeguard the production equipment. The company has taken several steps to control the fibers. First, an air filtration system works constantly to remove dust and fibers from the factory. Second, production employees wear dust masks while they are working with fabric or filling. Finally, regular cleaning and maintenance of the sewing, cutting, and stuffing machines is performed to prevent the fibers from building up.

Maintenance is especially important for the sewing machines. Machine oil and static electricity attract pile fabric lint. Lint buildup can cause lines of stitches that are uneven and seams that do not hold. The Berkshire Bear workmanship is guaranteed for life. Burst seams require rework during the production phase and during the lifetime of the product.

All production employees are paid a regular wage for a 40-hour work week. They receive their regular wage plus an overtime premium of one-half the regular wage rate for overtime. The cost of fringe benefits and employer taxes, such as social security, health insurance, and vacation time, adds 20.55 percent to the cost of labor. The employees' regular wages are charged to direct labor. The overtime premium and the fringe benefits are carried as variable overhead costs.

MARKETING

Marketing of the product takes place at the retail level via catalogue sales and in the company's retail store adjacent to the factory. Retail Internet sales are a new addition to the overall marketing effort. The company also sells wholesale to department stores, toy boutiques, and other specialty retailers. The product can be delivered by two-to-five-day ground service, next-day air, or holiday express. The customer pays the insurance and delivery charges. Berkshire promises same or next-day shipment. Most orders are shipped the same day as received.

When the company receives a customer's order, an employee takes a bear of the requested color and dresses it according to the customer's wishes. Then the bear is packaged with a protective air bag and complimentary piece of chocolate candy, and shipped in a designer box. The designer box contributes to the product image. It is reminiscent of the packaging used for a famous-name cologne and intended to lend an air of status and exclusivity to the product. The box is also important to toy collectors who expect to pay or receive a price premium in the secondary market for items that are in "mint-in-box" condition. Producing the box is a custom job involving a box manufacturer and a printing company. The unit cost of the box decreases with the size of the order that the company places with the manufacturer. Rush orders are more costly than normal orders. In July 1997, the purchasing manager placed an order for enough boxes to cover budgeted sales in the coming year.

Berkshire's policy on sales commissions has remained stable over the past several years. Commissions of 3 percent are paid on retail store sales and sales to wholesale buyers. No commissions are paid on catalog sales. The company-owned retail outlets have proved unprofitable, so all of them, except for the factory store, have been closed in previous years.

THE ACCOUNTING PROBLEM

"I think I know what some of the problems are, but I would like a detailed analysis that provides confirmation from our accounting data," McKinley continues.

"Did inventory change much?" you ask.

"It's pretty negligible. Our peak selling time is from Christmas to Mothers Day, so we don't have much on hand at the June 30 year-end. We started last year with almost nothing and it was all we could do to keep up with demand, so we ended up with almost nothing as well." You jot down a note to ignore changes in raw materials and finished goods inventories and to assume that production volume equals sales volume.

"Didn't you put a new incentive compensation plan in place this year?"

"As a matter of fact, we did. Perhaps it was a factor in what happened this year."

The new incentive compensation plan was adopted effective July 1, 1997. Under this plan, each of the three department heads is rewarded based on the performance of his or her responsibility center. Performance is measured against the company's master budget and its standard cost system. The plan was the result of several meetings with McKinley and her managers who argued and bargained for a plan that rewarded the managers fairly for individual contributions and achievements. McKinley's plan was intended to promote participation and teamwork and the managers accepted the new program enthusiastically. The plan provides for the following:

- David Hall, the purchasing manager, will receive a bonus equal to 20 percent of the net materials price variance, assuming the net variance is favorable. Otherwise, the bonus is zero.

- Rita Smith, the marketing manager, will receive a bonus equal to 10 percent of the excess, if any, of actual net revenues (revenues minus both variable and fixed selling expenses) over master budget net revenues.
- Bill Wilford, the production manager, will receive a bonus equal to 3 percent of the net of several variances: the efficiency (usage or quantity) variances for materials, labor, and variable overhead; the labor rate variance; and the variable and fixed overhead spending variances. Wilford receives no bonus if his net variance is unfavorable.

INTERNET SALES PROGRAM

"It seems that the incentive plan produced results," continues McKinley. "Smith had a terrific year this year. Unit sales were more than 16 percent above budget (Table 1). She says one of the principal factors was the new Internet sales policy she instituted and the advertising campaign to support it. We've never had that kind of year in sales before."

The Berkshire Toy Company began selling over the Internet in November 1997. At the same time, the company launched a nationwide radio advertising campaign. All radio advertisements are tagged with a reference to the web site that, in turn, provides visual support for the radio advertising and an opportunity for customers to order online. As an additional incentive to attract Internet customers, Rita Smith proposed that Berkshire offer a substantial discount to customers who ordered over the Internet. Because the discounted Internet price ($42.00) was still greater than the price that Berkshire was charging its wholesale customers ($32.00), McKinley approved the price change.

To boost its Internet sales, the company held special holiday sales. The Christmas and Valentine's Day sales featured the Berkshire Bear in special seasonal costumes. Both events were immediate successes not only with Internet customers, but also with retail and wholesale customers who paid the customary prices. The greatest success was the Mother's Day campaign. For this event, the web site displayed an image of "Mama's Boy," a bear sporting sunglasses, jeans and T-shirt, and an appliqued tattoo on its upper arm that said "Mom."

The 15-inch bears produced by the Berkshire Toy Company are identical except for their color and their accessories. Although the bears may be purchased with differing accessories, the unit cost of the accessories per bear has been relatively stable over time. The average historical cost of accessories has been a very small part of the total cost of the bear, and the standard cost of accessories is computed as an average. The price differences in the product reflect the company's discounting practices and not differences in accessories.

The master (static) budget for the year ended June 30, 1998 was prepared before the Internet program and price change were adopted. It called for the sale of 280,000 units, allocated as follows:

Retail and mail order	238,000 units	x	$49.00	=	$11,662,000
Wholesale	42,000 units	x	$32.00	=	1,344,000
Total	280,000				$13,006,000

The expected distribution of 85 percent retail and 15 percent wholesale was based on the company's experience in prior years. Thus, the budgeted average selling price was $46.45. Actual sales for the year were as follows:

Retail and catalog	174,965 units	x	$49.00	=	$8,573,285
Internet	105,429 units		$42.00	=	4,428,018
Wholesale	45,162 units	x	$32.00	=	1,445,184
Total	325,556 units				$14,446,487

MATERIALS AND PRODUCTION

"Hall had a few triumphs of his own this year," said McKinley. "He managed to get some substantial price discounts on acrylic pile fabric, plastic joints, and polyester fiberfilling. Price discounts of 7 to 10 percent on our three main inputs add up to some real savings." Berkshire Toy Company's schedule of standard manufacturing costs is reproduced in Table 2. The schedule of actual manufacturing costs for the year ended June 30, 2002 is in Table 3.

"So," McKinley continues, "at least on the surface, it looks like marketing and purchasing had a good year, but production is another story. Bill Wilford was not part of the original Berkshire team. Headquarters sent him here from Hercules (the luggage division) to learn the ropes after Jack Johnson left. Jack joined a competitor last July."

"During Bill's first week on the job, we had a freak thunderstorm and the storm drain backed up, ruining a large amount of fiber filling. The loss was uninsured. Since then, I have gotten plenty of feedback from Bill who has been struggling to keep up with production. He has complained about the substandard direct materials, deviations from standard production plans, and the amount of overtime required to meet sales demand. The plant has been operating at near to maximum capacity of 350,000 units. His people are tired. Some of them quit and had to be replaced at higher-than-standard wage rates. Bill also said that extra maintenance was required on the machinery and that, even so, they've experienced frequent breakdowns. He's been vehement about stock-outs of some of the imported accessories. At one point, sales commitments made it necessary to schedule overtime to copy some of the bear outfits and make them in-house. But he tries to be fair and responsible. He admitted that he was the person who moved some of the plastic parts to an empty box marked 'refuse' that was hauled away later by the trash collectors. This is a small place and I hear almost everything that goes on."

"By the way," McKinley winds up, "did you get the information I faxed you?"

"Let's see," you reply. "I have the 2001-02 income statement (prior to bonus calculations), the breakdown of budgeted and actual revenues, and schedules of standard and actual direct production costs. I do need some more detailed information about manufacturing overhead and selling costs. After that, I'll get back to you as soon as I can." McKinley agrees to send you details of actual overhead expenditures for the last five years and actual selling expenses for 2001 and 2002. These are shown in Tables 4 and 5.

REQUIRED

1. a. Using the information in the case and Tables 1-5, prepare a flexible budget[8] for the Berkshire Toy Company for the year ended June 30, 2002. Analyze the company's total master (static) budget variance for the year. Compare the flexible and master (static) budgets and prepare a schedule showing the sales volume variance. Compare the actual results and the flexible budget, and prepare a schedule showing the flexible budget variance. Subdivide the flexible budget variances into the appropriate price (rate or spending) and efficiency (usage or quantity) variances for materials, labor, and variable overhead.
   b. Compute the bonuses earned in fiscal 1998, if any, by David Hall of the purchasing department, Rita Smith of the marketing department, and Bill Wilford of the production department.
2. a. You will be assisting in the investigation of certain variances. Using the information provided, formulate some likely explanations for the observed variances.
   b. Comment on the advantages and disadvantages of the incentive compensation plan as it applies to department heads. What is the appropriate role of the budget in performance evaluation? What modifications to the incentive plan would you recommend? Why?
3. (Optional) Suppose that Berkshire Toy Company adopts a balanced scorecard (BSC) to measure its performance. What performance dimensions are typically included in a BSC? What specific performance measures (indicators) might be included in the scorecard? For useful background information on BSCs, see Chapter 2 of Cost Management, 3rd edition, by Blocher, Chen, Cokins, and Lin, McGraw-Hill/Irwin, 2005.

---

[8] For the sales revenue categories shown in Table 1, prepare a flexible budget based on actual units sold multiplied by the master (static) budget prices. For Internet sales, use a "revised" budget price of $42. To analyze sales volume effects, also prepare a second flexible budget for the sales revenue categories based on the total of 325,556 units sold, multiplied by the budgeted mix (85 percent for retail, 0 percent for Internet, and 15 percent for wholesale). Multiply these quantities by the respective budgeted sales prices. The difference between the two flexible budget amounts is generally termed a "sales mix variance," which quantifies the effect on income that results because the actual mix of distribution channels deviates from the budgeted mix. A comparison between the master (static) budget and the flexible budget prepared on the basis of the budgeted mix is the "sales volume variance." This variance measures the effect on operating income of selling more or fewer units than planned. The net of the sales mix variance and the sales volume variance equals the "sales activity variance."

TABLE 2
Berkshire Toy Company
A Division of Quality Products Corporation

Schedule of Standard Costs: Fifteen-Inch Berkshire Bear

Normal Capacity: 280,000 units	Quantity Allowed Per Unit	Input Price	Standard Cost Per Unit
Direct materials			
Acrylic pile fabric[a]	0.02381 bolts	$35.00/bolt	0.8333
10-mm acrylic eyes	2 eyes	$0.19/eye	0.3800
45-mm plastic joints	5 joints	$0.14/joint	0.7000
Polyester fiber filling	0.90 lbs.	$1.45/lb.	1.3050
Woven label	1 label	$0.05/each	0.0500
Designer box	1 box	$0.24/each	0.2400
Accessories[b]	various		0.1200
Total direct materials			3.6283
Direct labor			
Sewing	0.50 hours		
Stuffing and cutting[c]	0.30 hours		
Assembly	0.30 hours		
Dressing and packaging	0.10 hours		
Total direct labor	1.20 hours	$8.00/hour	9.6000
Variable manufacturing overhead[d]	1.20 DLH	$3.1140/DLH	3.7368
			16.9651
Fixed manufacturing overhead	1.20 DLH	$1.9700/DLH	2.364
			$19.3291

[a] One bolt of fabric is 10 yards long by 72 inches wide. Fabric for 42 finished units can be cut from one bolt.

[b] The cost of accessories varies from 7 cents per unit for a bow tie to 45 cents per unit for fisherman's gear. The standard of 12 cents per unit reflects the historical assortment of accessories chosen by customers.

[c] Less than 0.01 hour per unit is spent cutting the fabric. Therefore, hours spent in the cutting operation are not separately recorded. They are included with hours spent operating the pneumatic stuffing machine because both operations are usually performed by the same employees.

[d] Variable and fixed overhead are allocated to production on the basis of standard direct labor hours allowed. Standard amounts are computed at normal capacity of 280,000 units. Maximum practical capacity is 350,000 units of production attainable in consideration of planned maintenance and scheduled down time for holidays. Normal capacity is the long-run average productive output that smoothes out seasonal, cyclical, and other variations in customer demand.

TABLE 3
Berkshire Toy Company
A Division of Quality Products Corporation

Schedule of Actual Manufacturing Costs for the Year Ended June 30, 2002

	Quantity Used	Input Price	Total Cost	
Direct materials				
Acrylic pile fabric	7,910 bolts	$32.4174/bolt	$256,422	
10-mm acrylic eyes	661,248 eyes	$0.1900/eye	125,637	
45-mm plastic joints	1,937,023 joints	$0.1270/joint	246,002	
Polyester fiber filling	344,165 lbs.	$1.3100/lb.	450,856	
Woven label	328,447 labels	$0.0500 each	16,422	
Designer box	315,854 boxes	$0.2200 each	69,488	
Accessories		various	66,013	a
Total direct materials			1,230,840	
Direct labor				
Sewing	189,211 hours			
Stuffing and cutting	104,117 hours			
Assembly	121,054 hours			
Dressing and packaging	34,615 hours			
Total direct labor	448,997 hours	$8.1700/hour	3,668,305	
Overtime premium	103,787 hours	$4.0850/hour	423,970	
Other variable manufacturing overhead			1,301,695	b
Fixed manufacturing overhead			658,897	
			$7,283,707	

a The actual input price for accessories is derived by dividing the actual cost of $66,013 by units sold (325,556), yielding an average accessories cost of $0.20277 per bear.
b The actual input price for variable overhead is obtained by dividing the total variable overhead ($1,301,695 + $423,970) by actual direct labor hours worked, yielding a price or rate of $3.843377 per direct labor hour.

TABLE 4

Berkshire Toy Company
A Division of Quality Products Corporation

Schedule of Actual Manufacturing Overhead Expenditures for the Years Ended June 30, 1998 through 2002

	2002	2001	2000	1999	1998
Units produced	325,556	271,971	252,114	227,546	201,763
Variable overhead:					
Payroll taxes and fringes	$840,963	$524,846	$467,967	$413,937	$356,150
Overtime premiums	423,970	24,665	2,136	1,874	1,965
Cleaning supplies	4,993	6,842	6,119	5,485	4,996
Maintenance labor	415,224	256,883	232,798	244,037	216,142
Maintenance supplies	27,373	15,944	12,851	15,917	14,323
Miscellaneous	13,142	11,244	9,921	8,906	7,794
Total	$1,725,665	$840,424	$731,792	$690,156	$601,370
Fixed overhead:					
Utilities	$121,417	$119,786	$117,243	$116,554	$113,229
Depreciation-machinery	28,500	28,500	28,500	28,500	28,500
Depreciation-building	88,750	88,750	88,750	88,750	88,750
Insurance	62,976	61,716	57,211	55,544	54,988
Property taxes	70,101	70,101	68,243	68,243	66,114
Supervisory salaries	287,153	274,538	275,198	269,018	254,469
Total	$658,897	$643,391	$635,145	$626,609	$606,050

TABLE 5

Berkshire Toy Company
A Division of Quality Products Corporation

Schedule of Actual Selling Expenses for the Years Ended June 30, 2002 and 2001

	2002	2001
Units sold:	325,556	271,971
Variable expenses:		
Packing and shipping	$1,580,089	$1,015,913
Commissions	129,080	216,116
Catalogs, brochures, and samples	150,425	65,658
Total	$1,859,594	$1,297,687
Fixed expenses:		
Salaries	$2,734,868	$2,345,121
Advertising and promotion	2,288,324	2,086,021
Total	$5,023,192	$4,431,142

14-2 THE MESA CORPORATION

The Mesa Corporation, a medium sized manufacturing firm, uses injection molding machines to produce a variety of custom-ordered products for the airline and automotive industries. Recent recessionary pressures in the economy have negatively affected both the airline and the automotive industries. The major airline and auto firms are "squeezing" their suppliers, including Mesa. Consequently, there is a lot of pressure to control costs.

Adrian Bates is the production superintendent for Mesa (see the partial organization chart for Mesa in Figure 1). Her job includes aiding managers in solving production problems, in using management accounting information, and in using techniques to control production costs.

One of Ms. Bates' subordinates, Chris Kenyon, manages the Molding Department of Mesa Corporation. Mr. Kenyon has asked Ms. Bates' opinion about some perceived problems in his department and a potential solution which he is considering. Based on his rudimentary knowledge of cost control and some feedback data from recent production reports, Mr. Kenyon thinks that one of the standards in his department may be outdated. As a proposed solution, he is considering revising the standard usage of plastic which is used as a benchmark to signal an out-of-control machine.

The Molding Department has twelve identical molding machines (Machines A through L) which produces subassemblies for various products. When a machine is properly adjusted, it uses an average of 100 pounds of plastic (with a standard deviation of 3 pounds) to produce a subassembly. When a machine is not properly adjusted, it uses an average of 110 pounds of plastic (with a standard deviation of 5 pounds) to produce a subassembly. Since it is quite costly to adjust the machines, adjustments are made only when variances indicate that a machine might be out-of-control.

Mr. Kenyon's responsibilities include determining which variances should be investigated and whether the existing standard is correct or should be revised. The primary criterion underlying his decisions is to minimize the department's production costs per subassembly and to meet quality expectations. Figure 2 illustrates the situation in Mr. Kenyon's department. The bell-shaped curve on the left represents the distribution of the material usage per unit of output when a machine is in-control. The mean of this distribution, $C_i = 100$, is used as the performance standard. The bell-shaped curve on the right is the distribution of material usage when a machine is out-of-control. The mean of this distribution, C_O, is 110. Since performance is typically subject to a multitude of random factors, actual material usage may be lower (a favorable variance) or higher (an unfavorable variance) than C_i or C_O.

Table I illustrates the two basic types of decision errors which increase the cost of producing the subassemblies. The rows of the table indicate the two alternative actions which Chris may take, while the columns indicate the two alternative states of nature which can occur. A Type I error results in the cost of an unnecessary investigation when a machine is actually in-control and does not need adjustment. A Type II error results in the cost of continuing to use too much plastic by not adjusting a machine which is actually out-of-control. Type I errors are caused by large random unfavorable variances from the in-control distribution. Type II errors are caused by large random favorable variances from the out-of-control distribution.

Recently, Mr. Kenyon received the variance report (shown in Table 2) for the twelve machines in his department. The observations from these twelve machines also are shown in Figure 2. The report shows usage variances, from the standard quantity of 100 pounds, ranging from a favorable 8 pounds to an unfavorable 17 pounds. Because Mr. Kenyon did not want to incur excessive and unnecessary investigation costs, he decided to have the firm's mechanic inspect and adjust only those machines with unfavorable variances two or more standard deviations from the standard (machines G, H, I, J, K, and Q. From his investigations the mechanic found machines G and H to be in-control while machines L J, K, and L were out-of-control (see Table 3).

Mr. Kenyon feels that knowing the means of both the in-control distribution and the out-of-control distribution is necessary to making sound investigation decisions. Based upon the mechanic's findings, Mr. Kenyon was considering revising the standard quantity allowed for production of the subassemblies from 100 to 108 (the amount used by machine H) pounds of plastic per unit; this is the standard which would have prevented the Type I errors resulting in the unnecessary investigation costs associated with machines G and H. He also was considering revising the expected mean usage of an out-of-control machine from 110 to 113 pounds of plastic per unit (the average usage of the four out-of-control machines).

Source: Capettini, Robert, C. W. Chow, and J. E. Williamson. 1992. Instructional cases: the proper use of feedback information. *Issues in Accounting Education*. 7, 1 (Spring). 48-56.

Adrian Bates is concerned that Chris might be wasting resources by doing unnecessary investigations. However, Ms. Bates also is concerned that if Chris does not do enough investigations, the resultant lower quality may cause the product to be rejected by the airline and automotive firms. This may lead to expensive rework or loss of profitable contracts with these industries.

QUESTIONS

Suppose that you are Adrian Bates who has been asked to evaluate Chris Kenyon.

1. Has Chris Kenyon performed his job well?
2. Which of the twelve machines would you have investigated (i.e., which cost variances do you think were caused by a machine NOT being in proper adjustment)? Why?
3. Why were the means of the two distributions (when a machine is properly adjusted and when a machine is not properly adjusted), based on the variances selected for investigation, higher than what Chris Kenyon thought they were?
4. Re-estimate the means of the two distributions. Is the mean plastic usage of 100 pounds when a machine is in proper adjustment still an appropriate standard or is 108 or some other number a better standard? Is the existing mean plastic usage of 110 pounds when a machine is not in proper adjustment still an appropriate estimate of the mean of that distribution or is 113 or some other number a better estimate?
5. What methods can you suggest to improve Chris Kenyon's ability to update, in the future, the means of the two distributions?
6. Do you agree with Chris is raising the standard to 108 pounds? Why? How often should a standard be reviewed for revisions?

FIGURE I
Mesa Corporation Organization Chart

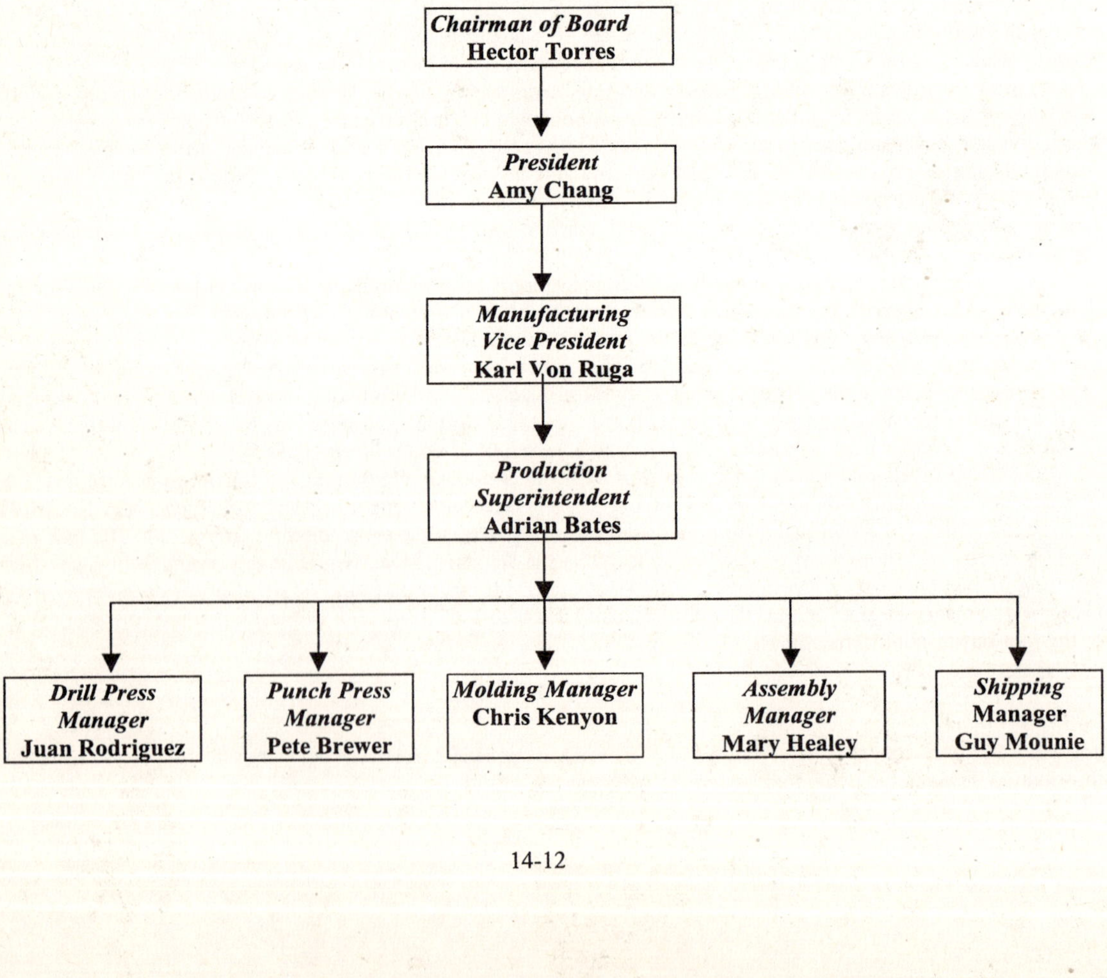

FIGURE 2
Distribution of In-Control and Out-of-Control Costs with the Twelve Machines

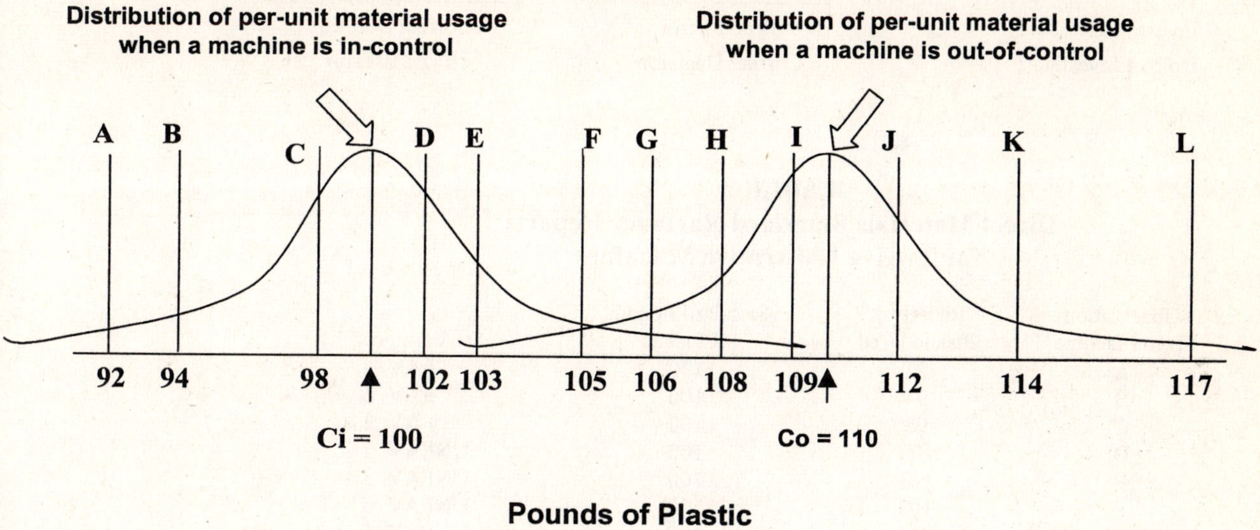

TABLE 1
Decision Table for Variance Investigation Decision

	Machine Is In-Control	Machine Is Out-of-Control
Investigate	Type I Error	Correct Decision
Do Not Investigate	Correct Decision	Type II Error

TABLE 2
Direct Materials Standard Variance Reports for Twelve Illustrative Machines

Observation from Machine	Pounds of Plastic Used	Standard Pounds of Plastic	Variance
A	92	100	FAV 8
B	94	100	FAV 6
C	98	100	FAV 2
D	102	100	UNFAV 2
E	103	100	UNFAV 3
F	105	100	UNFAV 5
G	106	100	UNFAV 6
H	108	100	UNFAV 8
I	109	100	UNFAV 9
J	112	100	UNFAV 12
K	114	100	UNFAV 14
L	117	100	UNFAV 17

TABLE 3
Mechanic's Report of the Physical Inspection of Six Machines

	In-Control Machines Lbs. Used		Out-of-control Machines Lbs. Used
G	106	I	109
H	108	J	112
		K	114
		L	117
Total Useage	214	Total Usage	214
Average Usage	107	Average Usage	113

Readings

USING ENHANCED COST MODELS IN VARIANCE ANALYSIS FOR BETTER CONTROL AND DECISION MAKING

By Kennard T. Wing, CMA

The budget and the analysis of variance between budget and actual are two of the most fundamental financial management tools. Yet in many organizations, these tools are "paper tigers" that can encourage or foster a lack of budget discipline. Managers who are called to account for their numbers in these organizations attack the budget variance report rather than going after the problems in their units. Their criticism might go something like this: "That report doesn't take into account the fact that once we pass 100,000 units per month, our preventive maintenance expenses go up. It only looks like we spent too much this month. Following recommended PM schedules is a key to successful financial performance long term." It sounds plausible. The result is that the managers are "off the hook" for their whole variance because no one knows how much of the budget variance for the month the increased maintenance activity should or actually does account for.

The reality is that the typical variance report is not particularly helpful even if managers want to use it to identify meaningful exceptions, which leads to a comment such as: "I can't tell which of those line item variances are just noise in the accounting system and which ones are something I should he doing something about."

Worse still, bad decisions can result when managers do not understand the limitations of the reports. For example, someone might offer: "The report says labor is a variable cost. Volume's down, so people ought to be laid off."

Here's the basic problem. Variance analysis is based on overly simplistic cost models in which every cost has to he treated as either fixed or variable. In the real world, however, many costs do not behave according to those idealized models, which means that managers can always legitimately point to shortcomings in the variance analysis. The reports either do not help them identify cost issues, or managers can use the limitations to reduce their own financial accountability.

Let's take a simple example. XYZ Organization has a cost that is semi-variable. That is, the cost is fixed up to a certain level of volume and variable beyond that point. Suppose the cost is treated as fixed in the variance reporting system. When volume is high and the unit is over budget, the manager can indicate that the variance is from the increased volume (not controllable), the report is no good, and the cost is what it ought to be. Now suppose the cost is treated as variable. When volume is low and the unit is over budget, the manager can say that the variance is due to decreased volume (not controllable), the report is no good, and the cost is what it should be. It does not take too many of these experiences before the budget variance report carries little weight in the organization.

Does every cost need to be treated as fixed or variable? No. We have merely relied on what we were taught in Management Accounting 101 or on whatever capabilities were built into the reporting software we happened to have available. The time has come for financial managers to develop:

- models of cost reflecting how costs actually behave, and
- variance reporting using enhanced cost models.

Calculating a Volume Variance with Semi-Variable Costs in Excel

Let BVOL be the address of the cell containing budgeted volume.

AVOL be the address of the cell containing actual volume.

BKPT be the address of the cell containing the breakpoint between fixed and variable.

ICU be the address of the cell containing the budgeted (or standard) incremental cost per unit for volumes above the breakpoint.

Then the volume variance is equal to the expression:
= (If(BVOL>BKPT, BVOL, BKPT)
– If(AVOL>BKPT, AVOL, BKPT))
* ICU.

A sample is shown at right. The 50 units above breakpoint should have cost $55 each, implying semi-variable costs should have been $2,750 higher than budgeted. This is our volume variance.

	BUDGET	ACTUAL	VARIANCE
Unit Volume	2,000	2,100	(100)
Total Step-Fixed Costs	$70,000	$78,000	$(8,000)
Budgeted Incremental Unit Cost	$55		
Breakpoint	2,050		
Volume Variance			$(2,750)
Controllable Variance			$(5,250)

I'll explain how to handle variance calculations for semi-variable costs, for step-fixed costs, and for several situations where a shifting mix affects cost behavior. Developing other, more sophisticated cost models and variance reporting is an important direction for the management accounting and financial management profession that will lead to improved control and decision making.

CALCULATING VOLUME VARIANCE WITH SEMI-VARIABLE COSTS

Let's examine how to calculate volume variance with semi-variable costs. Semi-variable costs are fixed below a certain level of volume, called the breakpoint, and are variable above that level. As an example, consider the emergency department of a hospital with which I worked. The largest cost in the department was nursing labor. Because emergency departments must be ready to handle large increases in volume instantaneously, nurses are not sent home or reassigned when volume is low. The department is staffed at a level that is consistent with a wide range of volumes. Still, there is some level of patient volume at which staff must be added. Flexing up above the department's core staffing level in either small or large increments can be handled by overtime, on-call staff and staff pulled from other units. These characteristics suggested that the semi-variable cost model would be appropriate for nursing labor in this department.

The question was: How much of the budget variance was due to uncontrollable changes in patient volume, and how much was attributable to factors the manager was supposed to control? To provide an answer, we need to decompose the budget variance into a volume variance and a controllable variance.

Because semi-variable costs act like fixed costs over part of the range of volume and like variable costs over the rest of the range of volume, the volume variance associated with semi-variable costs behaves similarly.

- In the fixed cost range, the volume variance is zero.
- In the variable cost range, the volume variance is the same as for a variable cost.

In total, there are four eases financial managers need to be concerned about, depending on how budgeted and actual volume compare to the breakpoint at which semi-variable costs change from fixed to variable:

Calculating a Volume Variance with Step-Fixed Costs

Step-fixed costs are readily handled in Excel using the HLOOKUP function. Let VOL be the address of the cell containing unit volume for which a corresponding step-fixed cost is required. Let ARRAY be the range reference for a two-row section of the spreadsheet, the first row containing the list of unit volumes at which costs step up and the second row containing the amounts to which step-fixed costs are supposed to increase at those points. Then the expression =HLOOKUP(VOL, ARRAY, 2) will return the standard step-fixed cost corresponding to the unit volume at VOL. If AVOL is the address of the cell containing actual volume and BVOL is the address of the cell containing budgeted volume, then the volume variance is equal to the expression: =HLOOKUP(BVOL, ARRAY, 2) – HLOOKUP(AVOL, ARRAY, 2).

A sample is shown below. The additional 50 units above budget should not have led to any increase in cost, so the volume variance is zero.

STEP-FIXED COST FUNCTION				
Volume	o	1,000	2,000	3,000
Cost at that Volume	$5,000	$10,000	$15,000	$20,000

	BUDGET	ACTUAL	VARIANCE
Unit Volume	1,900	1,950	(50)
Total Step-Fixed Costs	$10,000	$15,000	$(5,000)
Volume Variance			$ —
Controllable Variance			$(5,000)

Case 1. Budgeted and actual volume are less than breakpoint. In this case, the department was budgeted to operate and actually operated in the fixed cost range. The volume variance is zero.

Case 2. Budgeted volume is less than breakpoint, and actual volume is greater than breakpoint. Cost is fixed between budgeted volume and the breakpoint. This means that the volume variance for this portion of the difference between budgeted and actual volume is zero. Between the breakpoint and actual volume, semi-variable costs act just like variable costs. Therefore, the volume variance for this portion is calculated the same as for a variable cost.

Case 3. Budgeted volume is greater than breakpoint, and actual volume is less than breakpoint. Between budgeted volume and the breakpoint, semi-variable costs behave just like variable costs. The result is that the volume variance for this portion of the difference between budgeted and actual volume is calculated the same way as a traditional volume variance. Cost is fixed between the breakpoint and actual volume, which means that the volume variance for this portion of the difference between budgeted and actual volume is zero.

Case 4. Budgeted and actual volume are greater than breakpoint. In this case, the department was budgeted to operate, and actually did operate, in the variable cost range. Therefore, the volume variance is the same as for a variable cost.

See the sidebar "Calculating a Volume Variance with Semi-Variable Costs in Excel" to learn how to use an Excel spreadsheet for this calculation.

CALCULATING VOLUME VARIANCE WITH STEP-FIXED COSTS

In the step-fixed cost model, costs are fixed tip to a certain level of volume. Then the costs suddenly jump to a higher level of cost that is fixed over a range of volumes until another point is reached at which costs jump suddenly to a higher level, and so on. To calculate the volume variance, we need to know at what points costs jump up and to what levels they jump. The volume variance is merely what the cost is sup-posed to be at budgeted volume minus what the cost is supposed to be at actual volume.

See the sidebar above on "Calculating a Volume Variance with Step-Fixed Costs" for some calculations.

CALCULATING VOLUME VARIANCE FOR COST CENTER WITH MIXED COSTS

Most cost centers contain several kinds of costs, some of which are best modeled as:

- Variable;
- Fixed;
- Semi-variable; and
- Step-fixed.

The volume variance for the entire cost center is simply the sum of the volume variances for each of these four types. Obviously the volume variance associated with fixed costs is zero.

When different semi-variable costs have different breakpoints, variances may need to be calculated by line item and then totaled. If there are different step-fixed costs with different step-up points and amounts, it might be easier to calculate variances by line item and then sum as opposed to creating the aggregate step-fixed cost function required to treat them together.

CALCULATING A MIX VARIANCE

Let's examine the calculation of a mix variance using the same hospital I mentioned before. In that hospital, the radiology department performed a significant variety of procedures that required quite different quantities of labor, materials, and equipment. The mix of procedures was not under the control of the department manager. The idea was to separate the budget variances attributable to procedure volume and procedure mix from those considered under the managers control.

Mix variances have been calculated in other situations. For example, sales mix variances have been used to calculate the effect on a firm's profitability of changes in the mix of products it sold. These variances are not relevant here because revenues are generally not available for individual procedures in hospital billing. Materials mix variances have also been applied in manufacturing to calculate the effect of using a mix of raw materials different from that specified in the standard. This is also unlike the hospital case, where a mix variance can exist even when every procedure is performed in accordance with standards. In any case. the mix variance developed is analogous to those two. Note that all costs in the radiology department were classified as either fixed or variable.

The total variable cost variance was decomposed into volume variance, mix variance, and unit variable cost variance. See sidebar; "Calculating a Mix Variance."

Calculating a Mix Variance

Let each row of the spreadsheet represent data for a different procedure. We'll need columns for actual volume for each procedure, budgeted volumes for each procedure, and budgeted unit variable cost for each procedure. To calculate the mix index, create a column in which each cell is the product of that procedure's actual volume and budgeted variable unit cost. Use the sum function to calculate the sum of all the values in the column you just created. The result is the mix index.

To calculate the flexible budget, create a column in which each cell is the product of that procedure's budgeted volume and budgeted variable unit cost Use the sum function to calculate the sum of all the values in the column you just created. Multiply that sum by total actual volume and divide by total budgeted volume. The result is the flexible budget.

The volume variance is total budgeted variable costs minus the flexible budget The mix variance is the flexible budget minus the mix index. The unit variable cost variance is the mix index minus actual variable costs.

A sample is shown below.

PROCEDURE	ACTUAL VOLUME	BUDGETED VOLUME	BUDGETED VARIABLE UNIT COST	MIX INDEX	BUDGETED VARIABLE COSTS	FLEXIBLE BUDGET
A	200	150	$100	$20,000	$15,000	
B	1,800	2,000	$35	$63,000	$70,000	
C	2,700	3,000	$25	$67,500	$75,000	
Total	4,700	5,150		$150,500	$160,000	$146,01

	BUDGET	ACTUAL	VARIANCE
Volume	5,150	4,700	450
Variable Costs	$160,00	$155,000	$5,000

Volume Variance	$13,981
Mix Variance	$(4,481)
Unit Cost Variance	$(4,500)

Calculating a Mix Variance with Semi-Variable Costs

Let each row of the spreadsheet represent data for a particular visit type. We'll need columns for actual volume for each visit type, budgeted volume for each visit type, and budgeted incremental cost per visit above the breakpoint for each visit type. Let SV be the address of the cell containing budgeted semi-variable costs below the breakpoint and BKPT be the address of the cell containing breakpoint volume.

First, calculate the mix index. Create a column in which each cell is the product of that visit type's actual volume and budgeted incremental variable unit cost Use the sum function to calculate the total of the column you just created. Call the cell address of that total M. Call the cell address for total actual volume SUMA and the cell address for total budgeted volume SUMB. Then the following Excel expression is equivalent to the mix index: = If (SUMA>BKPT, ((SUMA - BKPT)/SUMA)*M + SV, SV).

Next calculate the flexible budget. Create a column in which each cell is the product of that visit type's budgeted volume and budgeted incremental variable unit cost. Use the sum function to calculate the total of the column you just created. Divide that total by SUMB. Call the cell address of the result F. Then the following Excel expression is equivalent to the flexible budget:
= If (SUMA>BKPT, (SUMA – BKPT)*F + SV, SV).

The volume variance is budgeted semi-variable costs minus the flexible budget. The mix variance is the flexible budget minus the mix index. The unit cost variance is the mix index minus actual semi-variable costs.

An example is shown below.

VISIT TYPE	ACTUAL VOLUME	BUDGETED VOLUME	BUDGETED INCREMENTAL VARIABLE UNIT COST	MIX INDEX	BUDGETED VARIABLE COSTS	FLEXIBLE BUDGET
A	200	50	$100	$20,000	$5,000	
B	1,900	1,925	$35	$66,500	$67,375	
C	2,950	2,975	$25	$73,750	$74,375	
Total	5,050	4,950	$30	$160.250	$146,750	$151,482
				$151,587		

Breakpoint Volume		5,000
Cost at Breakpoint		$150,000

	BUDGET	ACTUAL	VARIANCE
Volume	4,950	5,050	—100
Step Fixed Costs	$150,00	$155,000	$(5,000)

Volume Variance	$(1,482)
Mix Variance	$(104)
Unit Cost Variance	$(3,413)

Creating "what-if" budgets. The basic approach to calculating these variances is to create a pair of "what- if" budgets. Budgeted variable costs are based on budgeted unit volume, budgeted procedure mix, and budgeted unit cost for each procedure. Actual variable costs are based on actual volumes, actual procedure mix and actual but unknown unit costs for each procedure.

The first "what-if" budget is based on budgeted procedure mix, budgeted unit cost per procedure. and actual volume. It is comparable to the flexible budget of traditional variance analysis. Because it uses the same values as total budgeted variable cost for procedure mix and unit costs, differing onlv in using actual instead of budgeted volume, the difference between budgeted variable cost and the flexible budget is the volume variance—how much variable costs should have differed from budget if the uncontrollable change in volume were the only change from budget that occurred.

The second "what-if" budget is called the mix index. It is based on actual procedure mix and actual volume but budgeted unit costs by procedure. As it differs from the flexible budget only in using actual mix rather than budgeted mix, the flexible budget minus the mix index is the impact of the shift in mix—how much costs should have differed from budget if only the mix had differed from budget.

The mix index differs from actual variable costs only in using budgeted unit costs instead of actual unit costs, so the mix index minus actual variable cost is the impact of departures from budgeted unit cost that usually are held to be controllable by the manager. The first time this mix variance was implemented, a problem developed in which the variances for individual months failed to sum to the variance as calculated on the year-to-date numbers. I investigated the problem to see under what conditions this would be the case. I concluded that as long as the budgeted mix was the same each month, the monthly variances would sum to the variance of the year-to-date. If the budgeted mix changes from month to month, then the monthly variances generally will not sum to the variance of the year- to-date. In that case, variances should he calculated from the individual months and then summed to create variances for aggregate time periods Although I have not investigated this, I suspect that analogous limitations would affect the sales mix and materials mix variances others have developed.

CALCULATING A MIX VARIANCE WITH SEMI-VARIABLE COSTS

The hospital's emergency department also had a mix issue. That department dealt with even-thing from sore throats to cardiac arrests, and it classified all cases into 16 visit types. You would expect some costs to be higher if the visit mix shifted toward more serious cases, even if overall visit volume was flat. The severity of cases was beyond the department manager's control. Unfortunately the mix variance developed above could not he applied directly to the emergency department because it assumed all costs could he classified as either fixed or variable. Thus, what the hospital needed was to extend the mix variance to cases including semi-variable costs.

For an example, see the sidebar on "Calculating a Mix Variance with Semi-Variable Costs." The method is similar to the mix variance created above. We need to calculate two "what-if" budgets that will allow a comparison of numbers that differ in only one respect. As before, the flexible budget is based on actual volume, budgeted mix, and budgeted unit cost. The mix index is based on actual volume actual mix, and budgeted unit cost. Volume variance is budgeted semi-satiable costs minus the flexible budget. Mix variance is the flexible budget minus the mix index. The unit cost variance is the mix index minus actual semi-variable costs.

The situation is more complicated because semi-variable costs force us to deal with multiple cases. Fortunately the calculations for volume variance with a mix are identical to the case with no mix. Two cases are presented as a result of the mix variance, although the first is trivial. When actual volume is less than or equal to the breakpoint, the mix variance is zero. The calculation is as shown in the sidebar when actual volume exceeds the breakpoint.

It may seem counterintuitive that there is no mix variance when actual volume is less than the breakpoint but budgeted volume is greater than the breakpoint. Here is the explanation: Mix is irrelevant below the breakpoint. For actual volume below the breakpoint, any mix should generate the fixed portion of cost. Therefore, the variance is due solely to the fact that volume is below breakpoint and has nothing to do with possible variations in mix.

The unit cost variance also presents us with two cases, depending on whether actual volume is above breakpoint. See the sidebar for calculations. Given the difficulties with the original mix variance, it seemed appropriate to investigate whether these variances calculated on a monthly basis would sum to the variance on the year-to-date numbers. The answer generally is no. If some periods are above breakpoint but others are below it, the variance calculation on the year-to-date numbers will be erroneous.

When there is a mix variance with semi-variable costs, variances should not be calculated on data for aggregate periods. Rather, variances for the shortest reporting period ought to be aggregated in order to report variances for longer periods.

CALCULATING MIX VARIANCES WITH STEP-FIXED COSTS

Under the standard step-fixed cost model, it is assumed that each unit of output makes a uniform demand on the step-fixed resource. Obviously there is no mix variance under that assumption. A mix variance is possible only when different kinds of output make different demands on a resource.

For example, different diagnostic procedures might require different amounts of hours on a leased machine. Each machine is available for a fixed number of hours but may be augmented by additional leased machines. The method for calculating a mix variance for a step-fixed cost of this sort is shown in the sidebar titled, "Calculating Mix Variances with Step-Fixed Costs."

As before, a flexible budget is created based on actual volume, budgeted mix, and the budgeted step-fixed-cost function. Also created is a mix index based on actual volume, actual mix, and the budgeted step-fixed-cost function. The volume variance is budgeted step-fixed costs minus the flexible budget. The mix variance is the flexible budget minus the mix index.

There is an additional wrinkle for this type of cost. Actual step-fixed costs could differ from the mix index for either of the following reasons:

Calculating Mix Variances with Step-Fixed Costs

Let each row of the spreadsheet represent data for a particular procedure type. We'll need columns for actual volume for each procedure type, budgeted volume for each procedure type, and budgeted or standard unit consumption by each procedure type of the step-fixed resource. Let AC be the address of the cell containing actual consumption of the step-fixed resource. Let ARRAY be the range reference for a two-row section of the spreadsheet the first row containing the level of resource consumption at which costs step up, and the second row containing the amounts to which step-fixed costs are supposed to increase at those points.

First calculate the mix index. Create a column in the spreadsheet in which each cell is the product of that procedure's actual volume and budgeted hours per procedure. Use the sum function to calculate the total of the column you just created. Call the cell address of that total M. Then the mix index is calculated by the following Excel expression: =HLOOKLUP(M, ARRAY, 2).

Next calculate the flexible budget. Create a column in which each cell is the product of that procedure's budgeted volume and budgeted hours per procedure. Use the sum function to total the column you just created. Call the cell address of that total BC. Call the cell address of total actual volume SUMA and of total budgeted volume SUMB. Then the flexible budget is calculated by the following Excel expression: =HLOOKUP(SUMA*BC/SUMB, ARRAY, 2).

Now calculate the consumption index. It is simply the expression =HLOOKUP(AC, ARRAY, 2).

The volume variance is budgeted step-fixed costs minus the flexible budget. The mix variance is the flexible budget minus the mix index. The unit consumption variance is the mix index minus the consumption index. The price variance is the consumption index minus actual step-fixed costs.

An example is shown below.

STEP-FIXED COST FUNCTION				
Hours per Month	0	240	480	720
Cost at that Volume	$5,000	$10,000	$15,000	$20,000

PROCEDURE	ACTUAL VOLUME	BUDGETED VOLUME	HOURS PER PROCEDURE	MIX INDEX	FLEXIBLE BUDGET	CONSUMPTION INDEX
A	50	15	1.0	50	15	
B	275	200	0.5	138	100	
C	320	300	0.2	64	60	
Total	645	515		252	175	
				$10,000	$5,000	
Total Hours Used	270					$10,000

	BUDGET	ACTUAL	VARIANCE
Volume	515	645	-130
Step-Fixed Costs	$5,00	$12,000	$(7,000)
Volume Variance			$ —
Mix Variance			$(5,000)
Unit Consumption Variance			$ —
Price Variance			$(2,000)

- Too much of the step-fixed resource was used for the amount of volume, or
- The proper amount was used, but the price was too high.

To separate out these two causes, calculate another "what-if" budget called the consumption index, which is based on actual consumption of the step-fixed resource and the budgeted step-fixed-cost function. The cost of using more of the step-fixed resource than budget or standard would be the mix index less the consumption index. Because these two "what-if" budgets differ only in that the mix index is based on the use of budgeted or standard amounts of the resource per unit of output, while the consumption index is based on the actual amount of the resource used per unit of output, the difference between them isolates the effect of consuming more of the step-fixed resource per unit of output than called for in the budget or standard. Call this the unit consumption variance.

The other element can be called the price variance. It is calculated by taking the consumption index minus actual step-fixed costs. As both are based on actual use of the step-fixed resource, they differ only in how much cost that use generates. Thus, this expression isolates the variance due to the price of the resource.

Again, we investigated whether variances in step-fixed costs can be calculated on data from aggregate time periods or if variances for aggregate time periods must be calculated by summing variances from the shortest reporting periods. Consider this: Thc cost associated with leasing a single machine month after month is likely to be much different from the cost of leasing multiple machines for a single month. Here is the impact of this difference: When calculating variances where there are both a mix variance and step-fixed costs, it is a mistake to calculate variances directly on data for aggregate time periods. Variances should be calculated on the shortest reporting period and summed to get variances for aggregate time periods.

CALCULATING VARIANCES FOR DEPARTMENTS WITH MIXED COSTS

I limited my analysis to semi-variable costs or step-fixed costs. In reality departments have a mix of costs. As long as all costs in a department are classified as one kind or another, the department's total budget variance will be equal to the sum of the variances of each different kind of cost. In some cases, multiple costs can be lumped together when their cost behavior is similar. When different semi-variable costs have different breakpoints, separate variance analyses will have to be run for different costs. For step-fixed costs, it is probably both easier and more useful to aggregate line-item variances than to create the aggregate cost function needed to calculate variances on aggregated costs. Obviously, the effort and cost involved in developing these analyses must be weighed against the materiality of the costs and the likely benefit of the better information.

APPLYING THE METHODS

I have shown how to decompose budget variances for several cost models more sophisticated than the traditional cases of fixed and variable costs. While the methods I reported grew out of work in the healthcare field, they have wider applicability in other industries.

Calling a cost semi-variable instead of fixed may seem like a small matter. Such is not the case. A large healthcare system, for example, decided to classify all costs as variable. When volume dropped, it laid off more than 1,000 people, and the workload of most of them had no direct relation to patient volume. The result was that morale of the survivors plummeted, and within a year the system was scrambling to replace not only those it had let go, but many others who had quit.

The point is, the accounting systems we design and implement really do affect management decisions in significant ways. A system built on a bad model of the business will either not be used or, if used, will lead to bad decisions. The assumed behavior of a cost— whether fixed, variable, semi-variable, step-fixed, or something else—is a basic assumption affecting any kind of planning, financial analysis, or control. The stakes today are high. We can no longer afford the over-simplification of fixed and variable. Significant costs must be modeled more accurately in order for management accounting systems to better support executive deliberation and decision making. The extensions of variance analysis developed here are merely a first step along that road.

Kennard T Wing, CMA, is a project director at the OMG Center for Collaborative Learning in Philadelphia, Pa., where he heads the practice that helps nonprofit and public sector organizations build their capacity for financial and performance management. Yon can reach him at Ken@omgcenter.org or (215) 732-2200.

Variance Analysis Refines Overhead Cost Control

BY JEAN C. COOPER, PhD, CPA, AND JAMES D. SUVER, FHFMA, DBA

Many healthcare organizations may not fully realize the benefits of standard cost accounting techniques because they fail to routinely report volume variances in their internal reports. If overhead allocation is routinely reported on internal reports, managers can determine whether billing remains current or lost charges occur. Healthcare organizations' use of standard costing techniques can lead to more realistic performance measurements and information system improvements that alert management to losses from unrecovered overhead in time for corrective action.

Because of current cost reduction pressures from healthcare payers, healthcare decision makers need better cost information for performance measurement, pricing decisions, and management of activities. Like other service organizations, many healthcare facilities have adapted cost accounting systems and techniques developed for the manufacturing sector—such as standard costing and variance analysis—to generate necessary information. But healthcare managers may not realize all potential benefits from variance analysis.

Because of high fixed and indirect costs, estimated at 80 to 85 percent of total costs in most healthcare organizations, overhead control is challenging to healthcare managers.[9] Standard cost systems, such as overhead volume variance, can aid overhead cost control because they are based on predetermined measures of resource consumption. These measures help managers control operations and evaluate performance by giving them standards with which to compare actual results.[10]

PRICING DECISIONS

For effective management of pricing and budgeting decisions, full costs per unit must be determined in advance of providing a service. Determining a service's variable cost component is fairly straightforward because facilities use variable costs directly in the pricing process and can estimate them accordingly.

Most healthcare providers, however, have relatively few true variable costs—costs that vary directly with changes in volume of input or output. Although only fee-for-service and material-related costs such as food and inpatient supplies meet this definition, many healthcare providers treat nursing or other clinical labor costs as variable costs. But unless staff members are paid fee-for-service, their labor is not a true variable cost.

Since most caregivers are salaried, their pay does not change automatically with patient volume. Only their time allocation between patient and nonpatient activities will change as patient volume changes. To change total costs, administrators must decide to increase or decrease staff.

As a result, fixed costs present a more challenging pricing problem. A healthcare organization must estimate the total amount of fixed cost and the volume used as an allocation base. Because most organizations provide several products or services, using a common surrogate, such as labor hours, can be problematic. For example, when the amount of nursing time for a specific diagnosis related group (DRG) already is being recorded, it may be expedient to use nursing hours to allocate direct and indirect overhead costs. If more nursing hours are used than planned, more overhead would be allocated even if total overhead costs were not increased. This apparent change in overhead costs must be recognized in pricing and control decisions.

Estimated per-unit costs are unique, however, to the specific level of estimated fixed costs and the specific volume of estimated output. Whether fixed costs are direct fixed costs in a department or indirect fixed costs of general administration, both must be recovered through pricing.

Exh. 1 presents standard costs for a healthcare procedure. The per-unit costs ($127) and desired profit margin (10 percent or $12.70) could be used to evaluate offers discounted from the full charge of $164.35. Standard costs also can provide useful planning data for budgeting and control purposes.

---

[9] Overhead costs in this article are defined as all general and administrative expenses. General expenses include indirect patient care costs and all direct patient care costs which are fixed in nature, such as equipment and personnel or salaries.

[10] Adapted from Fundamentals of Management Accounting by Anthony, Weber and Reece, 4th ed. (Richard D. Irwin, 1985), Problem 9-32, pp. 346–347.

EXHIBIT 1 STANDARDS FOR ABDOMINAL SCAN PROCEDURE 101

Variable costs	
Labor (1/2 hour at $12.00)	$ 6.00
Materials (7 scans at $3.00 per scan)	21.00
Fixed costs	
Overhead A (direct and indirect)	100.00
Total cost per procedure	$127.00
Profit margin B (10% of total cost)	12.70
Charge for procedure 101 before deductions	$139.70
Deductions from revenue C	$24.65
Charge to be established	$164.35
Estimated number of procedures to be completed	50,000
a. The per-unit overhead costs are determined in the following manner:	
Estimated total overhead costs	$5,000,000
Estimated number of labor hours for next accounting period (50,000 procedures x 0.5 hours)	25,000
Overhead rate per labor hour ($5,000,000/25,000 labor hours)	$200
Overhead rate for procedure 101 per labor hour (0.5 x $200)	$100

b. The profit margin in this organization is determined by a 10% markup on full cost.

Note: The flexible budget equation for procedure 101 would be:

Total costs=$5,000,000 + ($27.00 × quantity of procedures)

c. Deductions from revenue for uncompensated care are estimated at 15% of charges.

A hospital department could develop an income statement to estimate the next month's profit for a certain procedure, assuming a forecast of 50,000 procedures. This income data also would determine the department's budget:

Gross revenues (50,000 × $164.35)	=	$8,217,500
Allowances for uncompensated care (50,000 × $24.65)	=	1,232,500
Net revenues (50,000 × $139.70)	=	6,985,000
Expenses: Standard cost of services (50,000 × $127.00)	=	6,350,000
Projected profit margin (10% of total cost)	=	$ 635,000

Projected profit of Procedure 101 for the next accounting period would be $635,000, assuming that:

50,000 procedures will be completed during the month and capacity in the department is sufficient to accomplish this level without additional costs (such as overtime) being incurred;

- All 50,000 procedures will be billed at the stated charge of $164.35 and allowances will equal 15 percent of charges;
- All cost figures (such as salary costs) occur as planned; and
- The organization achieves all productivity measures (0.5 labor hours per test).

If any assumption is incorrect, a variance from planned profit will occur. Administrators then must determine whether variance was controllable and by whom.

PERFORMANCE MEASUREMENT

If the results for Procedure 101 were achieved as shown in Exh. 2, the 49,000 procedures actually performed would be expected to provide $622,300 in profits ($12.70×49,000). The actual profit ($522,300), however, is $100,000 less than the expected profit ($622,300) and $112,700 less than the projected profit in the original budget ($635,000).

To evaluate the actual results for Procedure 101, a variance analysis report (Exh. 3) could be constructed from the data in Exh. 1 and 2 to explain the difference in profits. A profit of $12,70 is lost on each of the 1,000 procedures not completed. In addition, the $5,000,000 in overhead is not fully allocated to the 49,000 procedures actually billed. Because the overhead rate of $100 assumes that 50,000 procedures will be performed ($5,000,000 / 50,000), completing only 49,000 procedures results in an under-recovery of $100,000 ($100 × 1000) in overhead never billed to clients.

EXHIBIT 2 ACTUAL RESULTS FOR PROCEDURE 101

Standards:		
Procedures planned	50,000	
Planned profit (50,000 × $12.70)	$635,000	
Standard charge per procedure		$164.35
Standard costs per procedure		127.00
Standard profit per procedure		12.70
Standard discount from charges		24.65
Actuals:		
Procedures completed	49,000	
Gross revenues (49,000 × $164.35)		$8,053,150
Discounts (49,000 × $24.65)		1,207,850
Net revenues (49,000 × $139.70)		6,845,300
Actual labor and material costs (49,000 × $27.00)		1,323,000
Actual overhead		5,000,000
Actual profit		$ 522,300
Variance between planned and actual profit for		
Expected profit (49,000 × $12.70)	$522,300	
Actual profit	522,300	
Variance	$100,000 under-recovery	

Failure to achieve the planned volume used in developing the overhead allocation for pricing always will result in an under-recovery of overhead costs. Each examination *not* completed results in a loss of $100 in fixed overhead recovery in addition to the loss of $12.70 in profit margin.

Because the planned and actual overhead totals were the same ($5,000,000), no overhead variance would show on the income statement. The charge for a procedure was established using the planned volume ($5,000,000 / 50,000 or $100), but the actual rate for 49,000 procedures would be $5,000,000 / 49,000 or $102. The difference results in an under-recovery of overhead. Unless a manager is aware of potential under-recovery of overhead, corrective action such as an increase in charges or a reduction in actual overhead expenses will not be taken in time to alleviate the shortfall in profit.

In this example, timely identification of the volume decrease of 1,000 could have led to a recovery of the $100,000 loss through overhead cost reductions or price increases. Managers can always estimate the amount of overhead that will be over- or under-recovered by multiplying the planned overhead rate by the forecasted difference between the planned volume used to establish the rate and the actual volume estimated to be billed.

Effective performance evaluation requires differentiation of costs controllable by managers from those heavily influenced by external events. Most healthcare administrators and managers are not able to control volume of services or even prices set under prospective reimbursement agreements. Physicians admit patients and order services. Only when lost volume is due to capacity constraints can management be held responsible. Assigning responsibility and planning dollar implications *before* a contract is signed are the keys to successful contracting. Penalty clauses for not achieving volume and incentives for overachieving need to be negotiated with managed care organizations.

One way to prevent under-recovery of overhead is to stipulate contractually that HMOs will pay the fixed costs per day for each patient day not delivered and only the variable costs per day for each patient day in excess of the agreed on volume. Because variable costs per patient day are lower than fixed costs per patient day, HMOs have an economic incentive to deliver more than the negotiated total, limited, of course, by the provider's current capacity.

Focusing on the bottom line without fully understanding why variances occur can lead to dysfunctional decision making. A flexible budget, as shown in Exh. 3, separates the profit expected under the planned volume from the profit variance caused by under-recovery of fixed overhead. Due to their high fixed costs, healthcare providers are particularly vulnerable to overhead under recovery.

MANAGEMENT CONTROL

Some managers eliminate overhead volume variances by treating overhead as a period expense and not allocating it to individual outputs as done above. Because direct expensing of overhead eliminates the potential for volume variances, it also eliminates two powerful management tools: identifying impacts of fixed overhead on per unit prices, and monitoring recovery of overhead expenses to determine if and when fixed expenses should be reduced.

EXHIBIT 3 VARIANCE ANALYSIS FOR PROCEDURE 101

	Projected budget (50,000 procedures)	(49,000 procedures)	Variances
Gross revenue	$8,217,500	$8,053,150	$164,350 Unfavorable
Discount	1,232,500	1,207,850	24,650 Favorable
Net Revenues	6,985,000	6,845,300	139,700 Unfavorable
Costs[A]	6,350,000	6,323,000	27,000 Favorable
Profit	$ 635,000	$ 522,300	$112,700 Unfavorable
Volume variance[B]		$ 100,000 Unfavorable	=$100,000 Unfavorable
Profit margin variance[C]			=$ 12,700 Unfavorable
Net variance			$112,700 Unfavorable

A. Based on flexible budget costs of $5,000,000 fixed costs + $27 variable costs per procedure.

B. 50,000 procedures were used to determine $100 overhead rate. 1,000 shortfall in procedures × $100 overhead rate per procedure = $100,000 of fixed overhead costs not recovered through billing process.

C. Profit margin lost due to reduced volume. 1,000 reduction in procedures × $12.70 profit per procedure = $12,700 reduction in profit.

A standard cost system that allocates fixed cost on a per unit basis provides information on the amount of fixed costs over- or under-recovered with volume changes. By monitoring changes between actual and planned (standard) volume, managers can make necessary changes in budgeted fixed costs as required. Volume shortfalls are also critical to other management decisions such as cashflow planning, hiring, and strategic planning. Effective management control requires understanding how volume changes help achieve planned levels of performance and profits.

HIDDEN INVENTORY

Many healthcare organizations do not report work in process or finished goods inventories in their financial statements, implicitly assuming that all services provided by various cost centers have been entered in the billing system for accounting purposes. However, anecdotal evidence indicates that most clinical departments do not carry interim in-process charges, such as estimating inpatient charges for patients not yet discharged, on year-end financial statements.

The quantity of services provided by various cost centers can differ from the quantity reported in revenue accounts and recognized in accounting statements because of the normal time lag required to complete billing. For example, services (such as radiology, laboratory, and surgical procedures) provided to hospital inpatients usually are not billed until the entire procedure is finished.

Also, work completed at the end of a day typically is not forwarded to the accounting system immediately because patient care has highest priority, while billing comes later. (Time lag does not exist for expense accounts, which usually are recorded promptly.) Lost charges tend to increase when output and billing are not monitored.

Many overhead expenses are incurred as functions of time passing rather than patient volume. For example, most salaried employees insist on being paid without waiting for patient or client billing to be completed or cash received. If revenues and costs are to be monitored by departments, and if a matching of revenues and expenses is to occur, some type of cost system must be implemented to measure output that is in process or completed but not billed.

In manufacturing, unbilled activities are captured in work-in-process and finished goods inventories. As noted above, most healthcare providers do not maintain this type of formal inventory account. As a result, a "hidden inventory" of unbilled output can exist, distorting financial statements and information for management decisions.

For example, Exh. 4 presents data for a healthcare organization providing routine physical examinations including EKG and blood tests. Three hundred and ten examinations are billed on the income statement for the current period:

Revenues		
(310 exams × $80)		$24,800
Expenses: standard cost of service billed		
310 × $52.00	$16,120	
Volume variance	800	
Administrative expenses	$2,000	18,920
Net profit		$ 5,880

EXHIBIT 4 STANDARDS FOR ROUTINE PHYSICAL EXAM

Standard charge per exam[A]	$ 80.00
Standard costs for the laboratories:	
Supplies per exam	$ 8.00
Labor per exam	6.00
Variable laboratory overhead	18.00
Fixed laboratory overhead per month[B]	10,000.00
Fixed general administrative expenses per month[C]	2,000.00
Planned volume of exams per month	500
Standard unit cost per exam:	
Supplies	$ 8.00
Labor	6.00
Variable overhead	18.00
Total variable cost per exam	32.00
Lab overhead costs [D]	20.00
Standard full cost per exam	$ 52.00
Standard profit per exam: $80–$52=$28	

A. All patients pay charges for this exam. There are no uncompensated care accounts.
B. Fixed laboratory overhead is considered a product cost and allocated to individual products for control purposes.
C. Fixed administrative costs are treated as a period cost and not allocated to individual exams.
D. The per unit fixed overhead cost is determined in the following manner. $10,000 lab overhead cost divided by the 500 exams estimated to be completed for the month = $20 lab overhead per exam.

The 460 examinations completed in the reporting period are used in calculating the volume variance for the department. The shortfall of 40 exams (500 planned - 460 actual) times the overhead rate of $20 equals the $800 volume variance reported.

Management is concerned because the profit at 310 exams should be $2,880 as determined below:

Revenues 310 × $80		$24,800
Expenses		
Variable 310 × $32.00	$9,920	
Fixed	$12,000	
Total expenses		21,920
Expected profit		$ 2,800

The $800 unfavorable volume variance explains why the reported profit ($5,800) is $3,000 greater than planned ($2,800).

While only 310 examinations were billed, the reported volume variance indicates that 460 were completed. Accordingly, 150 examinations (460 - 310) were *completed by the laboratory but not yet billed.*

Whether the paper work is still in the laboratory or has been lost (intentionally or unintentionally), revenues and expenses are improperly matched and reported income is overstated.

Performance evaluation is difficult to assess if only the bottom line is stressed and actual output measures are not available. A reconciliation can be determined in the following manner:

Expected net profit	$2,880
Actual reported profit	5,880
Unbilled overhead (150 exams × $20 fixed overhead)	$3,000
Actual net profit	$2,880

The difference between examinations completed and examinations billed (460 - 310 = 150) times laboratory overhead costs per examination ($20) equals the $3,000 profit overstatement. If only 310 examinations had been completed, the volume variance would have been $3,800 instead of $800 and profit would have been as planned. Most managers like to report a higher level of productivity for their performance evaluation. Unless performance reports are matched with financial reports, unbilled charges will not be known.

In-process inventories exist in healthcare organizations whenever completed services are not billed. Standard cost accounting allows administrators to monitor both production and billing. Reporting unbilled services on internal financial statements or management reports draws attention to potential problems. Accounts similar to work-in-process and finished goods inventories for external reporting can be used to properly match revenues and expenses and provide more appropriate data for cost management and performance evaluation.

OVERHEAD CONTROL IMPLICATIONS OF ACTIVITY COSTING

By Robert E. Malcom

Management accountants' "overhead control" analysis has historically been a contradiction in terms. We have understood for some time that traditional overhead analysis gave us no really useful control information. Recent research on cost drivers for activity based product cost determination has given us a new perspective on overhead control.[1] In addition to overhead pools being too aggregated and allocation of overhead being based on a single, probably irrelevant base, variance formulas are also being misapplied. As a result, accounting performance reports may signal that no deeper investigation is needed when one is warranted or indicate that consumption is a problem when price changes are to blame, etc.

The objective of this article is to assist in changing accounting practice, management education, and the professional examinations away from traditional overhead analysis and toward cost driver based flexible budgets. At best, any time being spent on the usual meaningless reports is a waste and should be avoided. Additionally, the credibility of other accounting reports may suffer by being tarred with the same brush. At worst, any managers relying on current reports may be misled into costly, incorrect decisions.

THE PROBLEM

Garrison's *Managerial Accounting,* a leading text in the field, contains the following typical treatment. "The variable portion of manufacturing overhead can be analyzed and controlled using the same basic variance formulas that are used in analyzing direct materials and direct labor."[2] As is common, the results are labeled Spending Variance and Efficiency Variance. Garrison then notes, "Most firms consider the overhead spending variance to be highly useful..., feeling that the information it yields is sufficient for overhead cost control."[3] Garrison does warn, as do most other authors, that *"...efficiency variance* is a misnomer" as efficiencies are "...not in the use of overhead *but rather in the use of the base itself."*[4] The efficiency variance simply tells the overhead effect of the difference between planned labor use and actual labor use. In a similar vein, Horngren and Foster say, "The spending variance is really a composite of price and other factors....For this reason, most practitioners used the term 'spending' variance rather than merely 'price variance.'"[5] As will be demonstrated later with a case problem, faith in the spending variance to provide useful information can be very misplaced. If it can be demonstrated that the traditional spending variance is potentially misleading, and if we can agree that the efficiency variance is really just a reconciling item between absorbed overhead and budgeted overhead, why do we put ourselves through these analyses?

INDUSTRIAL PRACTICE

The traditional overhead analysis method—calculation of spending and efficiency variances—is a common procedure of major American manufacturers. Surveys of overhead accounting practices of *Fortune 500 Industrial Companies* from about a decade ago found that virtually all firms using standard costing computed summary overhead variances. It was also found that the number of firms using both spending and efficiency variances exceeded those using just a spending variance.[6]

---

[1] See, for example, R. Cooper and R. Kaplan, "How Cost Accounting Distorts Product Costs," *Management Accounting* (April 1988), pp. 20-27 or J. Shank, "Strategic Cost Management: New Wine or Just New Bottles?" *Journal of Management Accounting Research* (Fall 1989), pp. 47-65.

[2] R. Garrison, *Managerial Accounting: Concepts for Planing, Control, Decision Making,* 6th ed. (Homewood, IL: Richard D. Irwin, Inc., 1991), p. 371. The views quoted from Garrison are deemed representative of many managerial and cost accounting texts, especially those oriented toward undergraduate majors.

[3] Ibid., p. 416.

[4] lbid., p. 417.

[5] C. Horngren, and G. Foster, *Cost Accounting:A Managerial Emphasis,* 7th ed. (Englewood Cliffs, NJ: Prentice-Hall, Inc., 1991), p. 255.

[6] See J. Chiu and Y. Lee, "A Survey of Current Practice in Overhead Accounting and Analysis," contained in *Proceedings of the Western Regional Meeting, Amen-can Accounting Association* (San Diego, CA: San Diego State University, 1980), p. 240; or, J. Chiu and J. Talbott, Factory Overhead Analysis," *Managerial Planning* (July/August 1978), pp. 36-39.

In a broader based survey reported in 1990 at the American Accounting Association annual meeting, Emore and Ness reported, "cost information...has not progressed very far over the past few years, [....despite...] considerable literary attention.... ...[M]ost companies are still using the same labor-focused costing systems that have characterized U.S. industry since the early 1900s.... Even though direct labor accounts for less than 10 percent of production costs for the majority of firms responding, alternative bases for attaching indirect manufacturing costs to products (e.g., machine hours, material value, cycle time, etc.) were being used by fewer than 25 percent of the companies....The majority of firms do not break down overhead into its major component cost elements. Sixty-five percent....maintain five or fewer manufacturing cost elements in their product cost buildups [including materials and labor].... [M]any companies placed greater weight on the computational accuracy of their cost systems than their conceptual integrity."[7]

PROFESSIONAL EXAMINATIONS

As would be expected, standard costing problems have been an important part of the Certified Management Accountant examination since its inception. Problems with an emphasis on overhead spending and efficiency variances have continued through 1990 (the latest available at the time of writing).[8] Such problems occur less often on the Certified Public Accountant examinations, but at least two occurred through the 1980s[9]. Such findings should be expected based on usage in practice.

EDUCATION

Emphasis on overhead variances in the classroom is more difficult to detect. Norvin et al. recently synthesized surveys regarding the cost/managerial accounting curriculum. In all four of the synthesized surveys from the 1980s, standard costing/variance analysis was included in the top ten of the most important topics to be covered. [10]

Textbooks being published in the 90s continue to accommodate this preference. In an ad hoc sampling of numerous basic cost/managerial texts oriented toward the undergraduate accounting major, all incorporated the spending and efficiency overhead variances with their standard costing presentations. It is interesting however that Usry and Hammer, another widely used text (in addition to Garrison and Horngren and Foster cited above), has additionally an especially rich development of flexible budget detail articulated into its presentation of standard costing processes."

Most interestingly, a survey in final stages by Bayou reveals that less than two percent of AAA academics teaching cost and/or managerial accounting object to these variances. Bayou's survey was focused toward obtaining terminology preferences. The study produced 600 responses, a rather remarkable 40 percent response rate. He found that 23.5 percent preferred "Price Variance," 74.8 percent preferred "Spending Variance," and a mere 1.6 percent objected to the calculation of variable overhead variances (including a few with strong comments).[12]

A CASE DEMONSTRATION

The deficiencies involved in current overhead control techniques are difficult to convey in abstract terms. A case demonstration is therefore provided. As noted earlier, equivalent CMA examination problems on overhead variances have continued through 1990.

However, a June 1983 CMA problem is unusually rich in detail and was selected for demonstration analysis here.[13] (This problem also appears in Horngren and Foster with the CMA recommended solution.[14]) Relevant data are given in Exhibit 1.

The requirements of the problem include the calculation of variable overhead spending and efficiency variances. Two components make up variable overhead, indirect labor and supplies, but as is typical, only a summary analysis is required. Indeed, in most professional examination and text problems, only the summary data are provided. The published solution is given in Exhibit 2, although in a format to emphasize the generic price and quantity variance formulas and to extend the analysis to the two components.

---

[7]J. Emore, and J. Ness, "Advanced Cost Management: The Slow Pace of Change," *Collected Abstracts of the American Accounting Association's Annual Meeting* (Sarasota, FL: American Accounting Association, 1990—full papers are available from the presenters), pp. 4, 6, 9, 11, and 14. [Ness is a Cost Management Group partner with Price Waterhouse in St. Louis, which has also published overlapping material from this survey.]

[8]See, for example, the following CMA examinations: December 1990, Part 3, Question 1; December 1989, Part 4, Question 1; and December 1988, Part 4, Questions 17 and 18.

[9]For examples from the CPA examinations, see: November 1987 (Theory Number 1, Question 42 and Practice II, Question 4) and May 1984 (Practice II, Problem Number 5).

[10]A. Norvin, M. Pearson, and S. Senge, "Improving the Curriculum for Aspiring Management Accountants: The Practitioner's Point of View," *Journal of Accounting Education* (Fall 1990), pp. 210-211.

GENERIC EQUIVALENCES

As shown in Exhibit 2, the spending variance calculation is generically equivalent to the price variance for materials and labor. A difference in prices (standard and actual overhead rates in this case) is multiplied by an implicit "actual" base quantity. Here the analogy to labor and material price variance begins to break down, because the assumed actual is a very arbitrary base. As is common in most traditional systems, the arbitrary base here is direct labor. The actual overhead exceeds the calculated standard overhead and the calculation suggests an unfavorable variable overhead spending variance of $150.

The efficiency variance is calculated as the difference between the actual and expected bases (labor hours in the problem) multiplied by the standard rate. Again, the calculation follows the form for quantity variance for direct materials and labor. Actual direct labor hours are less than standard direct labor hours, and so a favorable overhead variance results. The calculated efficiency variance is $8,850 and the combined spending and efficiency variance for variable overhead is $8,700 favorable.

What are the implications of the above analysis? At best there is a signal to management that direct labor; the base, was efficiently used. If that is a fact, that knowledge would be more directly available to management from the direct labor variance analysis. Another message is that since spending is close to budget, activity is probably close to plan and that managers might be criticized lightly because the direction is unfavorable. At worst, managers might incorrectly be commended highly because their overhead usage is reported to be highly favorable. The latter two results might or might not be the case, but it will be demonstrated that the report in Exhibit 2 is not the relevant basis for making this determination.

RESPECIFICATION OF VARIABLES

To know whether overhead is being controlled, in general a more disaggregated report should be used. The data given in the CMA examination are not sufficient for this purpose, so additional data (consistent with given totals) are provided by the author in Exhibit 3. The new data show prices and quantities for each of the overhead components. For simplicity, supplies are assumed to be barrels of lubricants.

[11]M. Usry, and L. Hammer, *Cost Accounting: Planning and Control,* 10th ed. (Cincinnati, OH: South-Western Publishing Co., 1991), pp. 562-592.
[12]M. Bayou, Technical Terminology of Management Accounting," research in progress, University of Michigan, Dearborn. Data were provided by personal communication with the author, March 1991.
[13]December 1983 CMA examination, Part 4, Section B, Question 7.
[14]C. Horngren, and G. Foster, op. cit., p. 279.

Exhibit 1
NORTON PRODUCTS' MAY DATA

Variable Overhead	Standard Cost per Unit	Standard per Direct Labor Hour	Planned Costs for May	Actual Costs for May	Standard Costs for May
Indirect Labor	$1.25	$.25	$ 75,000	$ 75,000	$ 82,500
Supplies	1.70	.34	102,000	111,000	112,200
Total	$2.95		$177,000	$186,000	$194,700
Other Activity			**Planned Data**	**Actual Data**	
Output Units			60,000	66,000	
Direct Labor Hours per Output Unit			x 5.000	x 4.772	
Total Direct Labor Hours			300,000	315,000	

Source: Given or derivable from June 1983 Certificate in Management Accounting Examination, Part 4, Section B, Question 7.

Exhibit 2
PUBLISHED SOLUTION PLUS EXTENDED DETAIL

	Total		Indirect Labor		Supplies	
Spending (or Price) Variance:						
Actual Rate ($ Actual / 315,000 DLH)	$ .590476		$ .238095		$ .352381	
Standard Rate (Given)	– .590000		– .250000		– .340000	
Rate Difference (direction may vary)	.000476	U	.0011905	F	.012381	U
Actual Direct Labor Hours	x 315,000		x 315,000		X 315,000	
Spending Variance	$ 150	U	$ 3,750	F	$ 3,900	U
Efficiency (or Quantity) Variance:						
Actual Base (Direct Labor Hours)	315,000		315,000		315,000	
Standard Base (5 DLH x 66,000#)	– 330,000		– 330,000		– 330,000	
Quantity Difference (always same way, here F)	15,000	F	15,000	F	15,000	F
Standard Rate (Given)	x $ .590000		x $ .250000		x $ .340000	
Favorable Efficiency Variances	$ 8,850	F	$ 3,750	F	$ 5,100	F
Total Variance	$ 8,700	F	$ 7,500	F	$ 1,200	F

Source: Institute of Certified Management Accountants, *Questions and Unofficial Answers for June 1983 CMA Examination* (Montdair, NJ: National Association of Accountants, 1983), p. 62. [Data have been rearranged by the author to emphasize the generic price and quantity aspects of the computations; Spending Variance may be viewed as a flexible budget based on actual direct labor.]

In Exhibit 4 the same generic formulas are used for indirect labor and supplies per se as were used for aggregated overhead in Exhibit 2. Labels have been changed to price and quantity variances as now the calculations truly provide these results, i.e., they are not mixed results (except for the generally inconsequential joint portion).

COMPARISON OF ALTERNATIVES

Where before there was a large favorable overhead quantity variance reported, there are now large unfavorable quantity signals. Where before there was a modest unfavorable spending signal, highly favorable price variances are now indicated.

The problem highlighted by this analysis warrants further management attention. The problem is not masked by the offsets of similar favorable and unfavorable variances as was the case in the development of Exhibit 2. A review of Exhibit 4 suggests that the traditional approach to analyzing overhead variances, as exemplified in Exhibit 2, is based on totally false premises.

In this model, actual overhead activity is much different than called for by the original plan. For indirect labor, the indication is that a lower quality or lesser-trained workforce was used, as the hourly rate paid was 20 percent less than standard ($10 versus $12.50). At the same time, much more time had to be spent to accomplish the task. Assuming a review shows that the task was appropriately accomplished, the tradeoff was well worthwhile, with a total favorable indirect labor variance of $7,500. Management should therefore be commended for this action. The variance directions and proportions are the same for supplies as for indirect labor. However, *Exhibit 2 indicates the opposite signal!*

The problems with the traditional approach are several: first, the summary spending variance is too much of an aggregation to provide any useful information for managers. But more importantly, the direct labor hours base for calculating usage (and spending) is at best a gross activity indicator; at worst it is simply irrelevant.

Exhibit 3

ADDITIONAL DATA FOR ILLUSTRATION

	Indirect Labor	Supplies	Totals
Unit of Measure for Inputs	Hours (hr.)	Barrels (bbl.)	
Actual Input Units	7,500 hr.	1,000 bbl.	
Actual Cost per Input Unit	x $ 10 /hr.	x $ 111/bbl.	
Total Actual Cost (given)	$ 75,000	$111,000	$186,000
Standard Input Units	6,600 hr.	990 bbl.	
Standard Cost per Input Unit	x $ 12.50 /hr.	x $113.333 /bbl.	
Total Standard Cost (given)	$ 82,500	$112,200	$194,700
Total Variance (Total Actual less Standard Cost)	$ 7,500 F	$ 1,200 F	$ 8,700 F

Source: Data assumed by author to be consistent with Exhibit 1; details are needed for a complete solution.

HOMOGENEITY PROBLEM

As noted earlier, a simplifying assumption was made in the case of supplies by deeming the category to be all lubricants of the same type. A common characteristic of overhead is that it is a mixture of many different items, so there is often no applicable price or quantity per se. That is, supplies may be pounds of cleaning agents, gallons of solvents, boxes of computer ribbons, etc.

The price and quantity aspects of analysis are not totally intractable even then. Prices may be sampled for representative items as is done for the Consumer Price Index. Then quantities may be inferred as the remainder; albeit an abstract measure. This could become complex and the cost of developing that data must be weighed against the benefit obtained.

The crucial point is still that the traditional computations for overhead spending and efficiency variances yield meaningless outcomes. Appropriate signals from the traditional variances appear only by coincidence. There is a cost to produce that largely irrelevant, perhaps coincidentally correct data. Why not allocate that effort to the development of more useful information?

THE SOLUTION

An increasingly practical alternative to the traditional analysis is to use flexible budgets based on appropriate cost drivers for major components of overhead, as is illustrated in Exhibit 5. In this report the large component variances could then well be the basis for further analyses, just as was done earlier in Exhibit 4.

For a number of reasons it is time for us to redirect our standard cost practices and our standard cost teaching. First, overhead itself is a relatively larger cost. American manufacturing cost structures have changed over the years from labor being more than overhead to overhead being more than three times labor (and this is only on the average).[15] Second, the statistical tools necessary to implement the above are much more widely understood by managerial accountants than just a few years ago. Third, and perhaps most importantly, widespread computer processing has made it economical to do both the statistical analyses and maintain more detailed cost data bases. Variable budgeting has been around for a long time, although at best it has been practiced and taught as an adjunct to the traditional standard cost system. I suggest that it is time for us to switch the order of things and give most attention to the development of variable budgeting systems—because they have the most potential as control tools—and that we relegate the traditional standard cost overhead analysis to an appendix. That clerical analysis may tell us something about the relationship between our estimated product costs and the actual costs of our production, but it gives us very little information that might be useful for the management of our production activities.

[15]J. Miller, and T. Vollmann, The Hidden Factory," *Harvard Business Review* (September-October 1985), Exhibit I, p. 143.

Exhibit 4

SOLUTION PER DETAIL DATA, VOLUME DRIVEN STANDARDS

	Indirect Labor		Supplies		Totals	
Price (Spending) Variance						
Actual Price of Input	$ 10.000	/hr.	$111.000	/bbl.		
Standard Price of Input	–12.500	/hr.	–113.333	/bbl.		
Price Difference (Favorable)	$ 2.500	/hr.	$ 2.333	/bbl.		
Actual Quantity of Input	x 7,500	hr.	x 1,000	bbl.		
Favorable Price Variance	$ 18,750	F	$ 2,333	F	$21,083	F
Quantity (Efficiency) Variance						
Actual Quantity of Input	7,500	hr.	1,000	bbl.		
Standard Quantity of Input	–6,600	hr.	–990	bbl.		
Quantity Difference (Unfavorable)	900	/hr.	10	bbl.		
Standard Price of Input	x $12.500	/hr.	x $113.333	/bbl.		
Unfavorable Quantity Variance	$11,250	U	$1,133	U	$12,383	U
Total Variance	$7,500	F	$1,200	F	$ 8,700	F

Source: Data from Exhibits 1 and 3.

COST DRIVER IDENTIFICATION

Presaging Johnson and Kaplan by many years, B. Goetz wrote in 1949, "Traditional cost data tend to be irrelevant and mischievous" and he proposed that "...the systems should be discontinued to save the clerical costs of operating them." Goetz argued that each overhead account "...should be homogeneous with respect to every significant dimension of managerial problems of planning and control. Some of the major dimensions along which burden may vary are number of units of output, number of orders, number of operations, capacity of plant, number of catalogue items offered, and span of anticipation [life cycle].... These recommendations would tend vastly to increase the number of primary burden accounts...."[16] Such dimensions of variability are today being referred to as cost drivers, i.e., the activity that drives costs.

The identification of cost drivers was an important part of J. Dean's pioneering cost study work of 1936. Indeed, using regression analysis, Dean identified product variety (recently rediscovered) as an important element which influenced cost levels.[17] His nonelectronic computations must have been laborious and a National Association of Accountants research study of 1949-50 implied that the least squares method was little used by industry.[18]

[16]See B. Goetz, *Management Planning and Control: A Managerial Approach to Industrial Accounting,* 1st ed. (New York: McGraw-Hill Book Co., 1949), pp. 162-163, and T. Johnson and R. Kaplan, *Relevance Lost: The Rise and Fall of Management Accounting* (Boston: Harvard Business School Press, 1987).

[17]J. Dean, "The Statistical Determination of Costs with Special Reference to Marginal Costs" in *The Studies of Business Administration,* 7:1 (Chicago: School of Business, University of Chicago, 1936), p. 103 (may possibly be found as a supplement to *Journal of Business);* Dean was not the first to apply the least squares method to the analysis of business costs and he cites an application by R. Livingston, "Control of Operating Expenses," *Mechanical Engineering* (LIV, 1926), p. 18. A Compilation of Dean's cost studies can be found in his *Statistical Cost Estimation* (Bloomington: Indiana University Press, 1976).

[18]National Association of Accountants, *Research Reports 16-18,* "The Analysis of Cost-Volume-Profit Relationships" (New York: National Association of Accountants, 1949-50), p. 16.

REGRESSION UNDERSTANDING

For accounting students the least squares method was included as a brief appendix by both R. Anthony and C. Horngren in the respective first editions of their managerial accounting texts of 1956 and 1962. Horngren then commented that the method was "cumbersome... [and] not so often used."[19] He did not expand this material until his third edition in 1972. Such coverage is now standard, although often the emphasis is merely on cost separation rather than cost driver selection.

In the meantime, Touche had distributed to academics a case based on practice which focused on using regression analysis to select between product units and pounds as the best cost driver for controlling indirect labor in a shipping department.[20] These foresights notwithstanding, there is very little evidence in practice or academe of an integrated treatment of regression analysis in a flexible budgeting cost control system.

AN ILLUSTRATION

In Exhibit 5 it is assumed that machine hours has been found by regression analysis to be the appropriate cost driver for the supplies (here lubricants). Also it is assumed that while all models of the product have the same direct labor hour standard, the more complex models require many more machine hours than the basic high volume model.

Thus, since Exhibit 5 implies a shift in mix from complex to basic models, less lubricants should be needed than otherwise and the previous positive variance has here been transformed into a large negative variance. The analysis method of Exhibit 4 still applies, but now the standard quantity is 900 rather than 990 barrels. This might indicate that a time-based maintenance schedule should be changed to a use-based schedule for optimum cost control.

Too often, the valuable notion of flexible budgeting has been wasted because we have failed to look diligently for the cost driver. For a useful example, consider forklift operator costs. In general, as output rises, so will direct labor and forklift labor. All appear to be associated. Where the flexible budget is based on direct labor, the resultant spending variance can send a seriously misleading signal. If direct labor usage is inefficient, there is no reason at all to expect more forklift labor, but this is the traditional accounting result. Indeed, if direct labor is inefficient, material may have been used more carefully and less fork lift labor should be needed.

The most likely cost driver for forklift labor is number of pallets moved, with pallet density a secondary consideration. Material usage might be a surrogate for number of pallets. Output volume would not usually be the appropriate driver either, as it would be common for material usage to be above or below expectations due to raw material quality or specification changes or machine malfunctions, etc. The most probable cause for forklift use must be found if the variable budget is to send the correct variance signals.

STICKINESS OF COSTS

Not only has there been a long run trend for overhead to grow as a proportion of total operating costs, but many of these new costs tend to be somewhat nonvariable in character i.e., lumpy and not strictly proportional to changes in activity. A common example is materials ordering and handling costs. As production grows, additional employees are added to handle the additional load; but, if production decreases, these personnel are not immediately laid off. Thus these lumpy costs stick even if activity declines and such costs have therefore sometimes been labeled "sticky costs."

Sticky costs have sometimes been found to be driven by product variety rather than units of output. Exhibit 5 assumes that in addition to the basic high volume product, two dozen other models have been offered and every model requires roughly $3,000 per month in labor support costs for materials purchasing and handling. For May, twenty models were produced, which should have required only $60,000 in indirect labor. Since $75,000 was actually spent, there is an unfavorable variance now of $15,000.

R. Beyer devoted considerable attention to the problem of such sticky costs in his 1963 book on profitability accounting. He labeled these items "long-range variable costs," seemingly another oxymoron. Beyer's solution was to create two budget figures. The longer-run figure was the responsibility of top management and the shorter-run figure was the responsibility of operational management. He termed the former the "management decision variance" and noted that layoffs from "this 'hard-line' approach... [would]...ultimately result in the most economical operation."[21]

---

[19]See R. Anthony, *Management Accounting: Text and Casts* (Homewood, IL: R. D. Irwin, 1956), pp. 316-19, and C. Horngren, *Cost Accounting: A Managerial Emphasis* (Englewood Cliffs, NJ: Prentice-Hall, 1962), pp. 215-16.

[20]Touche, Ross, Bailey & Smart (now Deloitte & Touche), "Ralston Electric Company," miscellaneous paper, c.1966.

Exhibit 5

NORTON PRODUCTS' ACTIVITY BASED FLEXIBLE BUDGET FOR MAY
VARIABLE AND STICKY COSTS

Overhead Item (Activity Base)	(1) Budget Cost Per Activity Unit	(2) Activity Units	(3) Flexible Budget	(4) Actual Cost	(5) Variance
Variable Cost:					
Supplies (Machine Hours)	$17 per Machine Hour	6,000 Machine Hours	$102,000	$111,000	$ 9,000 U
Sticky Cost:					
Indirect Labor (Number of Models)	$3,000 per Model	20 Models	$ 60,000	$ 75,000	$15,000 U
Totals			$162,000	$186,000	$24,000 U
	(assumed)	(assumed)	(1) x (2)	Exhibit 1	(3) — (4)

*Implicit Standard supply use is $102,000 + $113.333 = 900 barrels and standard indirect labor hours are $60,000 + $12.50 = 4,800 hours.

If it is assumed for the Norton Products' case that top management had approved for May operations the $75,000 indirect labor planning budget of Exhibit 1 per longer-run expectations, then top management would be responsible for the difference between the planned $75,000 amount (6,000 hours at $12.50) and the activity based $60,000 budget (4,800 hours) of Exhibit 5, or for 1,200 hours. The rationale for the strategic-operational split is that skilled indirect labor cannot be turned off and on as is usual for materials, but must be maintained with at least an intermediate-run outlook. The staffing level is primarily a higher management level decision.

Operational management is then responsible for using approved staffing levels as efficiently as possible. Since they were authorized $75,000 and spent $75,000, they have a zero total variance for indirect labor, albeit in a different manner than anticipated ($18,750 U for quantity and $18,750 F for price). Other inputs could be acquired in a similar manner, e.g., take or pay contracts; these would be amenable to the same treatment. Control is a shared responsibility, of course, and various management levels must work together for optimum operations.

Since sticky, lumpy costs may not be strictly variable with activity, the most viable procedure for their determination is likely by an observant "walking around" manager or accountant and/or an engineering study. It is not possible to generalize this process; each company will have to make that determination based on its own cost and production character.

SUMMARY

Accounting for overhead control is an area ripe for improvement. With overhead costs rising as a proportion of manufacturing activity, with better educated business persons, and with computational power readily available to maintain data on a more disaggregated basis and to perform statistical analyses, better reporting is now likely to be cost beneficial and may make the difference between profitable or unprofitable operations.

[21]R. Beyer, *Profitability Accounting for Planning and Control* (New York: Ronald Press Company, 1963), pp. 156-57. Beyer also described in the same book a cost driver index, called the Control Factor Unit, for measuring departmental workloads; see pp. 144-45. Beyer was then managing partner of Touche, Ross, Bailey & Smart.

Exhibit 6

SOLUTION PER DETAIL DATA, ACTIVITY DRIVEN STANDARDS

	Indirect Labor		Supplies		Totals	
Standard Quantity of Input (Exhibit 5)	4,800	hr.	900 bbl			
Longrun Approved Quantity of Input (Exhibits 1 and 3)	– 6,000	hr.				
Difference	1,200	hr.				
Standard Price of Input (Exhibit 3)	x $12.50	hr.				
Strategic Quantity Variance	$15,000	U				
Longrun Approved Quantity of Input	6,000	hr.				
Actual Quantity of Input (Exhibit 3)	– 7,500	hr.	– 1,000	bbl.		
Difference	1,500	hr.	100	bbl.		
Standard Price of Input	x $ 12.50	/hr.	$113.333	/bbl.		
Operational Quantity Variance	$18,750	U	$ 11,333	U		
Total Quantity Variance	$33,750	U	$11,333	U	$45,083	U
Price Variance (Exhibit 4)	18,750	F	2,333	F	21,083	F
Total Variance (Exhibit 5)	$15,000	U	$ 9,000	U	$24,000	U

Source: Exhibits 1, 3, 4, and 5; adapted from R. Beyer (see text).

As demonstrated, at best the continuance of the traditional standard cost approach to overhead analysis in the CMA and CPA examinations, in textbooks and classrooms, and in accounting reports of manufacturers, is a waste of time. It should be abandoned. The traditional labor based, flexible budget approach is almost as dangerous. At worst, the traditional approaches may be counter-productive, resulting in dysfunctional decisions and in a loss of credibility for other accounting reports.

The groundwork for better overhead control through activity based flexible budgets has been in development over the last half-century. Indeed, the professional literature abounds with success stories of leading edge companies in implementing advanced cost techniques. Many of these advances have more to do with production changes, as with materials requirements planning systems, than they do with underlying cost system changes, however.[22]

Mainstream accountants still have quite a long way to go. "Despite major conceptual and technological developments, little of the new thought in the field of cost management has found its way into practical application..."[23] For homogeneous data, regression and other analyses should be used to identify the underlying cost drivers. For less homogeneous data, sampling may be used to establish the underlying causes for differences from cost expectations. Sticky and strictly variable costs should be identified and controlled, respectively, by strategic and tactical techniques. Whenever activity based costing is appropriate for product cost determination, the same drivers should be equally relevant for cost control applications. It is time to set aside our primary occupation with traditional overhead variance analysis and focus our attention on cost-driver based variable budget systems. It is time for us to put our effort where there is more promise of return.

[22] J. Emore, and J. Ness, op. cit., p. 8.
[23] Ibid.

Better Information Through The Marriage Of ABC And Traditional Standard Costing Techniques

By WIlliam W. Stammerjohan ,C P A

Traditional standard costing and variance analyses have been subject to a great deal of criticism within academic circles, although they are used in industry. The purpose of this article is to introduce a set of improved standard costing techniques that provide additional relevant information for decision making within the contemporary manufacturing environment that is not provided by traditional standard overhead cost analysis.

Standard costing has been criticized for being inflexible, motivating excess production, and failing to provide meaningful information on a timely basis. Although many academics see standard costing as an outdated technique designed for smokestack industries, a marriage of activity-based costing (ABC) and traditional standard costing techniques can provide relevant information within the contemporary, overhead-intensive manufacturing environment.

Few would argue that traditional standard costing and variance analyses fail to provide relevant information on costs that truly change with the number of units produced, such as direct materials and variable direct labor cost. Traditional standard costing and variance analyses, however, have severe limitations when used to analyze overhead costs. Given the increasing importance of overhead cost and the fact that the limitations of traditional standard costing arise primarily in the calculations and interpretations of the overhead variances, this discussion will be restricted to the analysis of overhead.

The most detailed overhead information provided by traditional standard costing techniques, as outlined in popular cost accounting texts, can be summarized as follows:

Variable Overhead Efficiency Variance—The variable overhead efficiency variance is calculated as the difference between the actual usage and the allowed usage of the assigned cost driver, given actual output levels, multiplied by a standard rate per cost driver unit. Unfavorable variances arise when more units of the cost driver are used than would be expected, given actual output level.

Variable Overhead Spending Variance—The variable overhead spending variance is calculated as the difference between the actual cost and the expected cost of variable overhead, given the actual usage of an assigned cost driver, such as production hours, labor hours, or labor dollars. Unfavorable variances arise when overhead spending exceeds expectations after controlling for the actual cost driver level.

Production Volume Variance—The production volume variance is the difference between applied fixed overhead and budgeted fixed overhead. This variance arises when actual output volume differs from the expected output volume. Unfavorable variances arise when actual output volume is less than budgeted output volume.

Fixed Overhead Spending Variance—The fixed overhead spending variance is the difference between actual fixed overhead and budgeted fixed overhead. Unfavorable variances arise when actual fixed overhead cost is greater than budgeted fixed overhead cost.[1]

ABC MOLDING COMPANY

The ABC Molding Company is an example of both the limitations of traditional standard overhead variance information and the improvements that can be gained by incorporating ABC techniques into the calculations.

For the purposes of simplicity and clarity, consider a single injection molding machine and a single operator. The machine and operator are capable of producing 125 parts per hour, or 1,000 parts per eight-hour shift, when operating at full capacity. Although theoretical production over 20 eight-hour shifts should yield 20,000 parts per month, the expected production for the test month was 18,000 parts—after allowing the operator to perform two setups expected to require eight hours each.

There are three components of overhead costs: the cost of the operator, the cost of indirect materials (cleaning solvent), and the cost of utilities (electricity). The operator sets up the machine to produce various parts and then monitors the machine during production runs. Cleaning solvent is used as part of each setup, and electricity is consumed primarily during production runs.

The actual production in the test month was 16,000 parts. The operator performed four setups and

Table 1

ABC Molding Company Budgeted Information for Test Month

Operator:	(20 shifts @ 8 hours per shift @ \$20 per hour)	\$ 3,200
Cleaning Solvent:	(2 setups @ 6 gallons per setup @ \$48 per gallon)	576
Electricity:	(100 kilowatts hours per production hour @ \$0.06 per kilowatt hour = \$6 per production hour) (144 production hours @ \$6 per production hour)	864

ABC Molding Company Actual Information for Test Month

Operator:	(170 hours @ \$21 per hour)	\$ 3,570
Cleaning Solvent:	(16 gallons @ \$60 per gallon)	960
Electricity:	(16,800 kilowatts hours @ \$0.07 per kilowatt hour)	1,176

Table 2: Variances Based on Traditional Standard Variable Overhead Cost Analysis
(Flexible budget amounts are based on the actual production level: 16,000 parts.)

	Actual Cost	Traditional Spending Variance	Expected VMOH@ Actual Cost Driver Level[a]	Traditional EfficiencyVariance	Flexible Budget[b]
Operator Cost Production Hours	\$2,520	\$120 U	\$2,400	\$160 F	\$2,560
Operator Cost Setup Hours	\$1,050	\$ 50 U	\$1,000	\$716 U	\$ 284
Solvent	\$ 960	\$192 U	\$ 768	\$256 U	\$ 512
Electricity	\$1,176	\$456 U	\$ 720	\$ 48 F	\$ 768

Notes: VMOH—Variable Manufacturing Overhead

[a]Expected VMOH @ Actual Cost Driver Level Calculations:
120 production hours @ \$20 per hour = \$2,400
50 setup hours @ \$20 per hour = \$1,000
16 gallons @ \$48 per gallon = \$768
120 production hours @ 100 kilowatts hours per production hour @ \$0.06 per kilowatt hour = \$720

[b]Flexible Budget Calculations:
16,000 parts @ 125 parts per production hour @ \$20 per hour = \$2,560
16,000 parts @ 1 setup per 9,000 parts @ 8 hours per setup @ \$20 per hour = \$284
16,000 parts @ 1 setup per 9,000 parts @ 6 gallons per setup @ \$48 per gallon = \$512
16,000 parts @ 125 parts per production hour @ 100 kilowatts hours per production hour @ \$0.06 per kilowatt hour = \$768

worked a total of 160 regular hours and 10 overtime hours. The operator monitored the machine for 120 production hours and spent the remaining 50 hours performing the four setups. See Table 1 for comparisons.

THE LIMITATIONS OF TRADITIONAL STANDARD OVERHEAD COSTING VARIANCE ANALYSIS

If all three overhead items were treated as unit-level variable costs, traditional standard overhead cost variance analysis would allow 128 production hours (16,000 parts / 125 parts per production hour) and 14.2 setup hours (16,000 parts @ one setup for each 9,000 parts = 1.78 setups @ eight hours per setup).

The variances based on traditional standard variable overhead analysis are presented in Table 2. The flexible budget amounts are presented in the far right-hand column. The actual costs are presented in the far left-hand column. The expected overhead costs based on the actual cost driver levels are presented in the middle column. In this example, assume that the information system is capable of tracking the number of setup hours and production hours separately. If this were not the case, the resulting information would be even more distorted than what is presented because the operator cost efficiencies, including both setups and production, would be combined in a single number.

Table 3: Variances Based on Traditional Standard Fixed Overhead Cost Analysis
(Applied fixed overhead amounts are based on the actual production level: 16,000 parts.)

	Actual Cost	Traditional Spending Variance	Budgeted FMOH[a]	Production VolumeVariance	Applied FMOH[b]
Operator Cost					
Setup Hours	$1,050	$730 U	$320	$36 U	$284
Solvent	$960	$384 U	$576	$64 U	$512

Notes: FMOH—Fixed Manufacturing Overhead

[a]Budgeted FMOH Calculations:
2 setups @ 8 hours per setup @ $20 per hour = $320
2 setups @ 6 gallons per setup @ $48 per gallon = $576

[b]Applied FMOH Calculations:
16,000 parts @ $0.0178 per part ($320/18,000 expected output) = $284
16,000 parts @ $0.0320 per part ($576/18,000 expected output) = $512

These results illustrate how treating batch-level costs (setup costs) as unit-level variable costs can distort and conceal information within the traditional efficiency variances. While the favorable efficiency variances correctly reflect the efficiencies obtained by producing 16,000 parts in eight fewer hours than expected (120 hours versus 128 hours), the efficiency variances associated with the two batch-level costs are highly distorted. The $768 unfavorable operator efficiency variance results from performing 2.22 extra setups (four setups versus the allowed 1.78 setups, given actual production) and from using more hours than expected to perform the four setups (50 hours versus 32 hours, four setups @ eight hours per setup). The $256 unfavorable efficiency variance associated with the solvent results from performing the 2.22 extra setups, and it hides the fact that each setup was performed with less solvent than expected (16 gallons versus 24 gallons, four setups @ six gallons per setup). These efficiency variances conceal the true efficiencies/inefficiencies. Treating batch-level costs as unit-level costs results in an unrealistic expectation of partial setups, and it unrealistically treats extra setups, which may have had legitimate business motivation, as inefficiencies. The unfavorable solvent efficiency variance and unfavorable solvent spending variance conceal the fact that solvent cost per setup was actually less than expected. These limitations may prevent management from investigating an important factor: whether the more expensive solvent ($60 per gallon versus $48 per gallon) led to the $48 per setup savings because less solvent was needed to perform each setup than had been expected (four gallons per setup versus six gallons per setup).

The second source of concealed information resulting from the traditional variances presented in Table 2 lies within the spending variance associated with electricity cost. Although this cost is a true unit-level variable cost, the $456 unfavorable electricity spending variance conceals the fact that this variance is caused by two separate factors. It arises from an increase in the price of electricity ($0.07 per kilowatt hour versus $0.06 per kilowatt hour) and by the fact that the machine consumed 4,800 more kilowatt hours than would be expected, given the hours of operation (16,800 kilowatt hours versus 12,000 kilowatt hours, 120 hours @ 100 kilowatt hours per production hour). Failing to separate these two factors may preclude management from addressing a problem that could be corrected easily (the electrical efficiency of the molding machine) because it is hidden behind a problem that may be outside management control (utility prices).

A separate set of limitations that arises when batch-level costs (operator setup cost and solvent setup cost) are treated as fixed-overhead cost is presented in Table 3. The amount of each fixed overhead item that would be applied to production based on actual output level is presented in the far right-hand column. The actual overhead costs are presented in the far left-hand column, and the fixed-overhead budget amounts are presented in the middle column.

Both unfavorable production volume variances arise from producing 2,000 fewer parts than expected. The limitations arise from combining the results of legitimate business decisions (number of setups), true efficiency information (number of hours and gallons per setup), and price information (cost per operator hour and cost per gallon) into the traditional spending variances. While treating these as fixed costs no longer results in an unrealistic expectation of partial setups, the resulting spending variances do not produce useful information for decision making because several, possibly opposing, factors are reported as a single number. The $730 unfavorable spending variance associated with the

Table 4: Variances Based on ABC Standard Overhead Cost Analysis—Unit-Level Overhead Cost

(Flexible budget amounts are based on the actual production level: 16,000 parts.)

	Actual Cost	ABC Spending Variance	Expected Overhead @ Actual SCD Level[a]	Second-Level Cost Driver Efficiency Variance	Expected Overhead @ Actual BCD Level[b]	Basic Cost Driver Efficiency Variance	Flexible Budget[c]
Operator Cost							
Production Hours	$2,520	$120 U	NA	NA	$2,400	$160 F	$2,560
Electricity	$1,176	$168 U	$1,008	$288 U	$720	$48 F	$768

Notes: BCD—Basic Cost Driver—The basic cost drivers are the level of basic input allowed given the actual output level. An example of a basic cost driver level is production hours.

SDC—Second-Level Cost Driver—The second-level cost drivers are the second level of input, given the basic cost driver level. An example of a second-level cost driver is the amount of electricity consumed by each production hour.

[a]**Expected Overhead @ Actual SDC Level Calculations:** 16,800 kilowatt hours @ $0.06 per kilowatt hour = $1,008

[b]**Expected Overhead @ Actual BCD Level Calculations:**

120 production hours @ $20 per hour = $2,400

120 production hours @ 100 kilowatt hours per production hour @ $0.06 per kilowatt hour = $720

[c]**Flexible Budget Calculations:**

16,000 parts @ 125 parts per production hour @ $20 per hour = $2,560

16,000 parts @ 125 parts per production hour @ 100 kilowatt hours per production hour @ $0.06 per kilowatt hour = $768

cost of the operator performing setups arises from performing two extra setups, using excess hours to perform each setup (50 hours versus 32 hours, four setups @ eight hours per setup), and operator costs that are one dollar per hour above expectations ($21 per hour versus $20). The $384 unfavorable spending variance associated with the solvent cost arises from performing two extra setups, using less solvent than expected (16 gallons versus 24 gallons, four setups @ six gallons per setup), and from paying more than expected for each gallon of solvent ($60 per gallon versus $48 per gallon).

ABC STANDARD OVERHEAD ANALYSIS

The variances produced by combining ABC and traditional standard costing techniques are presented in Tables 4 and 5. The analysis of the two unit-level variable costs are presented in Table 4, and the analysis of the two batch-level costs are presented in Table 5. These results illustrate the ability of these more refined variances to overcome the limitations we have discussed and demonstrate the ability of these variances to produce valuable information for decision making.

The analysis of the operator cost associated with production demonstrates that limitations of the traditional techniques do not extend to the unit-level variable cost that is driven by a single, basic cost driver (production hours). Both the traditional and ABC analysis result in a $160 favorable efficiency variance due to spending fewer hours on production than expected and a $120 unfavorable spending variance because the operator cost exceeded expectations by one dollar per hour.

In contrast, the other unit variable cost—electricity—demonstrates the advantage of the more refined analysis when a single variable overhead costs driven by both a basic cost driver (production hours) and a second-level cost driver (hourly electrical consumption). By monitoring the number of production hours and the consumption of electricity, this analysis separates the cost reduction gained by producing 16,000 parts in fewer hours than expected ($48 favorable basic cost driver efficiency variance) from the cost resulting from consuming more electricity than expected for 120 production hours ($288 unfavorable second-level cost driver efficiency variance) and from the cost of paying more for each kilowatt hour than expected ($168 ABC unfavorable spending variance). These variances provide information that allows management to concentrate their efforts on factors that could improve company performance. They can explore the reasons behind the basic cost driver efficiency, such as why the operator was able to produce more than 125 units per production hour during the test month, and determine if these efficiencies could be repeated in subsequent months and/or carried over to other

Table 5: Variances Based on ABC Standard Overhead Cost Analysis— Batch-Level Overhead Cost

(Flexible budget amounts are based on the actual production level: 16,000 parts and 4 setups.)

	Actual Cost	ABC Spending Variance	Expected Overhead @ Actual BCD Level[a]	Basic Cost Driver Efficiency Variance	Batch-Level Flexible Budget[b]	Batch Size Variance	Unit-Level Flexible Budget[c]
Operator Cost							
Setup Hours	$1,050	$50 U	$1,000	$360 U	$640	$356 F	$284
Solvent	$960	$192 U	$768	$384 F	$1,152	$640 F	$512

Notes: BCD—Basic Cost Driver—The basic cost drivers are the level of basic input allowed given the actual output level. An example of a basic cost driver level is production hours.

[a]Expected Overhead @ Actual BCD Level Calculations:
50 hours @ $20 per hour = $1,000
16 gallons @ $48 per gallon = $768
[b]Batch-Level Flexible Budget Calculations:
4 setups @ 8 hours per setup @ $20 per hour = $640
4 setups @ 6 gallons per setup @ $48 per gallon = $1,152
[c]Unit-Level Flexible Budget Calculations:
16,000 parts @ 1 setup per 9,000 parts @ 8 hours per set up @ $20 per hour = $284
16,000 parts @ 1 setup per 9,000 parts @ 6 gallons per setup @ $48 per gallon = $512

operators and shifts. They could also determine the reason for the inefficiency of the second-level cost driver, electrical consumption, and determine if this could be corrected.

Analysis of the two batch-level costs presented in Table 5 reveals the importance of calculating variances based on flexible budgets based on the number of parts produced and on the number of batches produced. The batch size variances ($356 unfavorable and $640 unfavorable) highlight the fact that the setup cost per part increases when parts are produced in smaller batches (4,000 parts per batch versus an expected 9,000 parts per batch). These variances could result from inefficiencies (inefficient scheduling) or from legitimate business considerations (meeting specific customer demands). Having these separate dollar amounts allows management to either address the inefficiency or calculate the true cost of meeting customer demands.

True efficiency variances result from calculating a basic cost driver variance as the differences between the number of hours consumed by the four setups versus the number of hours expected to perform four setups, and between the number of gallons of solvent consumed by the four setups versus the number of gallons expected to be consumed by four setups. The $360 unfavorable operator cost variance arises because 18 more hours than expected were used to perform the four setups (50 hours versus 32 hours, four setups @ eight hours per setup). The $384 favorable second-level solvent cost efficiency variance arises because eight fewer gallons of solvent than expected were used to perform the four setups (16 gallons versus 24 gallons, four setups @ six gallons per setup). This analysis also results in spending variances that are strictly related to prices. It reveals a potential savings to the company if management can determine that the more expensive solvent was responsible for the decreased consumption. Although the actual cost per gallon of solvent was higher than expected, the solvent cost was $48 per setup less than expected ($240 per setup versus $288 per setup, four gallons @ $60 per gallon versus six gallons @ $48 per gallon).

SYSTEM BUILDING BLOCKS

The simple examples described in this article lay the groundwork for marrying ABC and traditional standard-costing techniques to produce more useful information for managing contemporary manufacturing processes. The examples demonstrate that as manufacturing becomes more overhead intensive, the information limitations of variances produced by traditional analysis become more severe, and, therefore, the techniques described become more valuable.

This marriage of techniques does not represent the ultimate sophistication in overhead analysis, but it does represent the basic building blocks of a system capable of producing more relevant, more sophisticated information. One obvious extension would be to calculate both basic and second-level cost drivers for batch-level overhead costs. A second extension could include situations where efficiency variances based on a third-level cost driver might be applicable. And a third extension could include flexible budgets based on the number of products produced to provide relevant information on product level costs.

Finally, to take full advantage of these techniques, it will be necessary for companies to continually update the standard quantities and the standard prices of inputs. The standard production hours, standard setup hours, and standard prices for labor, indirect materials, and utilities must be reviewed constantly because of continual improvement, learning curves, and business environment changes. Variances contain relevant information only when the standards are reasonable and current. Similar to other activity-based costing (ABC) and activity-based management (ABM) analyses, the information produced by these techniques should help management focus on potential areas for significant cost reduction. After truly understanding the full cost of performing setups, the company may not only focus on correcting the current inefficiency but may be motivated to find ways to reduce the number of setups or the cost of each setup.

Like many other management accounting techniques, these refined variances require information. While traditional standard overhead costing variances could be generated with information on the number of parts produced, the number of hours worked, the operator cost, the indirect materials cost, and the utility cost, these techniques require additional information. While tracking additional information—such as monitoring utility consumption for each machine—may require improvements to existing information systems, we may find, in many cases, that this type of information is already being captured by contemporary, sophisticated information systems.

The true benefits of the techniques described are that, like traditional standard costing techniques, they have the potential to effectively and efficiently provide useful information for decision making. Once these techniques are put in place, they can provide low-cost monitoring and a low-cost means of identifying potential profit-increasing improvements. □

[1] Charles T. Horngren, George Foster, and Srikant M. Datar, *Cost Accounting: A Managerial Focus*, Tenth Edition, Prentice Hall, Upper Saddle River, N.J., 2000, pp. 253-276.

Chapter 15
Productivity, Marketing Effectiveness and Strategic Productivity Analysis

Cases

15-1 Dallas Consulting Group

Readings

"Profit Variance Analysis: A Strategic Focus"

This article uses a fictitious case to demonstrate how variance analysis can be tied explicitly to the strategies of the firm. It expands the Shank and Churchill framework (explained in the article) for variance analysis to include explicitly the strategy and the competitive position of the firm in the analysis and interpretation of results.

Discussion questions:

1. Why is it inadequate and may even be misleading to rely only on the analysis reported in Table 3?
2. Does a favorable variance imply favorable performance?
3. Table 4 shows a rather elaborate and detailed analysis of variances of operating results. The analysis provides us information on the effect of variations of relevant operating factors on the operating result. The analysis includes relevant and important operating factors such as total market size, market share of the firm, sales mix, selling price, and costs. The analysis considers almost all, if not all, the factors that are of interest and important to management. Why is the analysis incomplete?

"Examining the Relationships in Productivity Accounting"

Change in profit of a firm or business unit can be analyzed in terms of a change in productivity and a change in price recovery. Change in product quantities and change in resource quantity drive the change in productivity. Change in product prices and change in resource prices drive the change in price recovery. These relationships can be displayed to provide an instant visual analysis of the causes of profit change. Such visualization can provide a robust method for analyzing strategy and stakeholder relationships.

Discussion questions:

1. What is productivity accounting?
2. How can productivity accounting guide the overall strategy of the firm?
3. Give an example showing that a traditional business performance indicator may give conflicting signals on a firm's performance.
4. What are the elements in using productivity accounting to evaluate changes in profits?
5. What grid diagrams are needed in order to have an overall picture of the business's performance?

Cases

15-1 Dallas Consulting Group

"I just don't understand why you're worried about analyzing our profit variance," said Dave Lundberg to his partner, Adam Dixon. Both Lundberg and Dixon were partners in the Dallas Consulting Group (DCG). "Look, we made $800,000 more profit than we expected in 2001 (see Exhibit 1). That's great as far as I am concerned." Continued Lundberg. Adam Dixon agreed to come up with data that would help sort out the causes of DCG's $800,000 profit variance.

DCG is a professional services partnership of three established consultants who specialize in helping firms in cost reduction through time-motion studies, streamling production by optimizing physical layout, and re-engineering operations. For each project DCG consultants spent the bulk of the total project time studying customers' operations.

The three partners each received fixed salaries that represented the largest portion of operating expenses. All three used his or her home office for DCG business. DCG itself had only a post office box. All other DCG employees were also paid fixed salaries. No other significant operating costs were incurred by the partnership.

Revenues consisted solely of professional fees charged to customers for the two different types of services DCG offered. Charges were based on the number of hours actually worked on the job.

Following the conversation with Lundberg, Dixon gathered the data summarized in Exhibit 2. He took the data with him to Lundberg's office and said, "I think I can identify several reasons for our increased profits. First of all, we raised the price for re-engineering studies to $70 per hour. Also, if you remember, we originally estimated that the 10 consulting firms in the Dallas area would probably average about 15,000 hours of work each in 2001, so the total industry volume in Dallas would be 150,000 hours. However, a check with all of the local consulting firms indicates that the actual total co0nsulting market must have been around 112,000 hours."

"This is indeed interesting, Adam," replied Lundberg. "This new data leads me to believe that there are several causes for our increased profits, some of which may have been negative. . . . . Do you think you could quantify the effects of these factors in terms of dollars?"

EXHIBIT 1: 2005 BUDGET AND ACTUAL RESULT

	Budget	Actual	Variance
Revenues	$12,600	$13,400	$ 800
Expenses: Salaries	9,200	9,200	
Income	**$ 3,400**	**$ 4,200**	**$ 800**

EXHIBIT 2: DETAIL OF REVENUE CALCULATIONS

	Hours	Rate	Amount
Budget:			
Re-engineering	6,000	$ .60	$ 360,000
Streamlining production	9,000	1.00	900,000
	15,000		$1,260,000
Actual:			
Re-engineering	2,000	$ .70	$ 140,000
Streamlining production	12,000	1.00	1,200,000
	14,000		$1,340,000

REQUIRED:
Use your knowledge of profit variance analysis to quantify the performance of DCG for 2005 and explain the significance of each variance to Mr. Lundberg.

Readings

PROFIT VARIANCE ANALYSIS: A STRATEGIC FOCUS

By Vijay Govindarajan and John K. Shank

ABSTRACT: This paper uses a disguised case to compare and contrast three different frame works in analyzing profit variances—two that are in common usage today and one that is not but, in our view, should be. The purpose of the paper is to demonstrate how variance analysis needs to be tied explicitly to the strategic context of the firm and its business units.

Profit variance analysis is the process of summarizing what happened to profits during the period to highlight the salient managerial issues. Variance analysis is the formal step leading to determining what corrective actions are called for by management. Thus it is a key link in the management control process. We believe this element is underutilized in many companies because of the lack of a meaningful analytical framework. It is handled by accountants in a way that is too technical. This paper proposes a different profit variance framework as a "new idea" in management control.

Historically, variance analysis involved a simple methodology where actual results were compared with the budget on a line-by-line basis. We call this Phase I thinking. Phase II thinking was provided by Shank and Churchill [1977] who proposed a management-oriented approach to variance analysis. Their approach was based on the dual ideas of profit impact as a unifying theme and a multilevel analysis in which complexity was added gradually, one level at a time. We believe that the Shank and Churchill approach needs to be modified in important ways to take explicit account of strategic issues. Our framework, which we call Phase III thinking, argues that variance analysis becomes most meaningful when it is tied explicitly to strategic analysis.

John K. Shank is Noble Professor of Managerial Control and Vijay Govindarajan is Associate Professor of Accounting, both at the Amos Tuck School of Business Administration, Dartmouth College.

The authors wish to acknowledge helpful discussions with Ray Stephens.

This paper presents a short disguised case, United Instruments, Inc., to illustrate the three phases or generations of thinking about profit variance analysis. We believe it also demonstrates the superiority of integrating strategic planning and overall financial performance evaluation, which is the essence of Phase III thinking. The purpose of this paper is to emphasize how variance analysis can be, and should be, redirected to consider the strategic issues that have, during the past 15 years, become so widely accepted as a conceptual framework for decision making.[1]

UNITED INSTRUMENTS, INC.: AN INSTRUCTIONAL CASE[2]

Steve Park, president and principal stockholder of United Instruments, Inc., sat at his desk reflecting on the 1987 results (T-1). For the second year in succession, the company had exceeded the profit budget. Steve Park was obviously very happy with the 1987 results. All the same, he wanted to get a better feel for the relative contributions of the R&D, manufacturing, and marketing departments in this overall success. With this in mind, he called his assistant, a recent graduate of a well-known business school, into his office.

---

[1] During the past 15 years, several books (e.g., Andews [1971], Henderson [1979], and Porter [1980]) as well as articles (e.g., Buzzell et al. [1975] and Govindarajan and Gupta [1985]) have been published in the field of strategic management. In addition, two new journals (*Strategic Management Journal* and *Journal of Business Strategy*) have been introduced in the strategy area during the past ten years. Also, traditional management journals such as *Administrative Science Quarterly, Academy of Management Journal,* and *Academy of Management Review* have, during the past decade, started to publish regularly articles on strategy formulation and implementation.

[2] This case is motivated by a similar case titled "Kinkead Equipment Ltd.," which appears in Shank [1982].

TABLE 1
UNITED INSTRUMENTS, INC.

	Budget (1,000s)		Actual (1,000s)	
Sales		$16,872		$17,061
Cost of goods sold		9,668		9,865
Gross margin		$ 7,204		$ 7,196
Less: Other operating expenses				
Marketing	$1,856		$1,440	
R&D	1,480		932	
Administration	1,340	4,676	1,674	4,046
Profit before taxes		$ 2,528		$ 3,150

"Amy," he began, "as you can see from our recent financial results, we have exceeded our profit targets by $622,000. Can you prepare an analysis showing how much R&D, manufacturing, and marketing contributed to this overall favorable profit variance?"

Amy Shultz, with all the fervor of a recent convert to professional management, set to her task immediately. She collected the data in T-2 and was wondering what her next step should be.

United Instruments' products can be grouped into two main lines of business: electric meters (EM) and electronic instruments (EI). Both EM and EI are industrial measuring instruments and perform similar functions. However, these products differ in their manufacturing technology and their end-use characteristics. EM is based on mechanical and electrical technology, whereas EI is based on microchip technology. EM and EI are substitute products in the same sense that a mechanical watch and a digital watch are substitutes.

United Instruments uses a variable costing system for internal reporting purposes.

PHASE I THINKING: THE "ANNUAL REPORT APPROACH" TO VARIANCE ANALYSIS

A straightforward, simple-minded explanation of the difference between actual profit ($3,150) and the budgeted profit ($2,528) might proceed according to T-3. Incidently, this type of variance analysis is what one usually sees in published annual reports (where the comparison is typically between last year and this year). If we limit ourselves to this type of analysis, we will draw the following conclusions about United's performance:

1. Good sales performance (slightly above plan).
2. Good manufacturing cost control (margins as per plan).
3. Good control over marketing and R&D costs (costs down as percentage of sales).
4. Administration overspent a bit (slightly up as percentage of sales).
5. Overall Evaluation: Nothing of major significance; profit performance above plan.

How accurately does this summary reflect the actual performance of United? One objective of this paper is to demonstrate that the analysis is misleading. The plan for 1987 has embedded in it certain expectations about the state of the total industry and about United's market share, its selling prices, and its cost structure. Results from variance computations are more "actionable" if changes in actual results for 1987 are analyzed against each of these expectations. The Phase I analysis simply does not break down the overall favorable variance of $622,000 according to the key underlying causal factors.

PHASE II THINKING: A MANAGEMENT-ORIENTED APPROACH TO VARIANCE ANALYSIS

The analytical framework proposed by Shank and Churchill [1977] to conduct variance analysis incorporates the following key ideas:

1. Identify the key causal factors that affects profit.
2. Break down the overall profit variance by these key causal factors.
3. Focus always on the *profit* impact of variation in each causal factor.

TABLE 2
ADDITIONAL INFORMATION

	Electric Meters (EM)	Electronic Instruments (EI)
Selling prices per unit		
Average standard price	$40.00	$180.00
Average actual prices, 1987	30.00	206.00
Variable product costs per unit		
Average standard manufacturing cost	$20.00	$50.00
Average actual manufacturing cost	21.00	54.00
Volume information		
Units produced and sold–actual	141,770	62,172
Units produced and sold–planned	124,800	66,000
Total industry sales, 1987–actual	$44 million	$76 million
Total industry variable product costs, 1987–actual	$16 million	$32 million
United's share of the market (percent of physical units)		
Planned	10%	15%
Actual	16%	9%
	Planned	**Actual**
Firm-wide fixed expenses (1,000s)		
Fixed manufacturing expenses	$3,872	$3,530
Fixed marketing expenses	1,856	1,440
Fixed administrative expenses	1,340	1,674
Fixed R&D expenses (exclusively for electronic instruments)	1,480	932

4. Try to calculate the specific, separable impact of each causal factor by varying only that factor while holding all other factors constant ("spinning only one dial at a time").
5. Add complexity sequentially, one layer at a time, beginning at a very basic "common sense" level ("peel the onion").
6. Stop the process when the added complexity at a newly created level is not justified by added useful insights into the causal factors underlying the overall profit variance.

T-4 and 5 contain the explanation for the overall favorable profit variance of $622,000 using the above approach. In the interest of brevity, most of the calculational details are suppressed (detailed calculations are available from the authors).

What can we say about the performance of United if we now consider the variance analysis summarized in T-5? The following insights can be offered organized by functional area:

Marketing

Comments:

Market Share (SOM) increase benefited the firm	$1,443 F
But, unfortunately, sales mix was managed toward the lower margin product	921 U
Control over marketing expenditure benefited the firm (especially in the face of an increase in SOM)	416 F
Net effect	$938 F
Uncontrollables: Unfortunately, the overall market declined and cost the firm	$680 U

Overall evaluation: Very good performance

Manufacturing

Comments:

Manufacturing cost control cost the firm $ 48 U

Overall evaluation: Satisfactory performance

R&D

Comments:

Savings in R& D budget $ 548 F

Overall evaluation: Good performance

Administration

Comments:

Administration budget overspent $ 334 U

Overall evaluation: Poor performance

TABLE 3
THE "ANNUAL REPORT APPROACH" TO VARIANCE ANALYSIS

	Budget (1,000s)				Actual (1,000s)			
Sales			$16,872	(100%)			$17,061	(100%)
Cost of goods sold			9,668	(58%)			9,865	(58%)
Gross margin			$ 7,204	(42%)			$ 7,196	(42%)
Less: Other expenses								
Marketing	$1,856	(11%)			$1,440	(8%)		
R&D	1,480	(9%)			932	(6%)		
Administration	1,340	(8%)	4,676	(28%)	1,674	(10%)	4,046	(24%)
Profit before tax			$ 2,528	(14%)			$ 3,150	(18%)

Thus, the overall evaluation of the general manager under Phase II thinking would probably be "good," though specific areas (such as manufacturing cost control or administrative cost control) need attention. The above summary is quite different—and clearly superior —to the one presented under Phase I thinking. But, can we do better? We believe that Shank and Churchill's framework needs to be modified in important ways to accommodate the following ideas.

Sales volume, share of market, and sales mix variances are calculated on the presumption that United is essentially competing in one industry (i.e., it is a single product firm with two different varieties of the product). That is to say, the target customers for EM and EI are the same and that they view the two products as substitutable. Is United a single product firm with two product offerings, or does the firm compete in two different markets? In other words, does United have a single strategy for EM and EI or does the firm have two different strategies for the two businesses? As we argue later, EM and EI have very different industry characteristics and compete in very different markets, thereby, requiring quite different strategies. It is, therefore, more useful to calculate market size and market share variances separately for EM and EI. Just introducing the concept of a *sales mix* variance implies that the average standard profit contribution across EM and EI together is meaningful.

For an ice cream manufacturer, for example, it is probably reasonable to assume that the firm operates in a single industry with multiple product offerings, all targeted at the same customer group. It would, therefore, be meaningful to calculate a sales mix variance because vanilla ice cream and strawberry ice cream, for instance, are substitutable and more sales of one implies less sales of the other for the firm (for an elaboration on these ideas, refer to the Midwest Ice Cream Company case [Shank, 1982, pp. 157–173]). On the other hand, for a firm such as General Electric, it is much less clear whether a sales mix variance across jet engines, steam turbines, and light bulbs really makes any sense. This is more nearly the case for United because one unit of EM (which sells for $30) is not really fully substitutable for one unit of EI (which sells for $206).

An important issue in the history of many industries is to determine when product differentiation has progressed sufficiently that what *was* a single business with two varieties *is now* two businesses. Some examples include the growth of the electronic cash register for NCR, the growth of the digital watch for Bulova, or the growth of the industrial robot for General Electric.

Following Phase II thinking, performance evaluation did not relate the variances to the differing strategic contexts facing EM and EI.

PHASE III THINKING: VARIANCE ANALYSIS USING A STRATEGIC FRAMEWORK

We argue that performance evaluation, which is a critical component of the management control process, needs to be tailored to the strategy being followed by a firm or its business units. We offer the following set of arguments in support of our position: (1) different strategies imply different tasks and require different behaviors for effective performance [Andrews, 1971; Gupta and Govindarajan, 1984a; and Govindarajan, 1986a]; (2) different control systems induce different behaviors [Govindarajan, 1986b; Gupta and Govindarajan, 1984b]; (3) thus, superior performance can best be achieved by tailoring control systems to the requirements of particular strategies [Govindarajan, 1988; Gupta and Govindarajan, 1986].[3]

[3] Several studies have shown that when an individual's rewards are tied to performance along certain dimensions, his or her behavior would be guided by the desire to optimize performance with respect to those dimensions. Refer to Govindarajan and Gupta [1985] for a review of these studies.

TABLE 4
VARIANCE CALCULATIONS USING SHANK AND CHURCHILL'S MANAGEMENT-ORIENTED FRAMEWORK

Key Causal Factors:						
Total Market	Expected	Actual	Actual	Actual	Actual	Actual
Market share	Expected	Expected	Actual	Actual	Actual	Actual
Sales mix	Expected	Expected	Expected	Actual	Actual	Actual
Selling price	Expected	Expected	Expected	Expected	Actual	Actual
Costs	Expected	Expected	Expected	Expected	Expected	Actual
Profit Calculation:						
Sales	$16,872	$15,836	$18,034	$16,862	$17,060	$17,060
Variable costs	5,769	5,440	6,195	5,944	5,944	6,334
Contribution	$11,076	$10,396	$11,839	$10,918	$11,116	$10,726
Fixed costs	8,548	8,548	8,548	8,548	8,548	7,576
Profit	$ 2,528	$ 1,848	$ 3,291	$ 2,370	$ 2,568	$ 3,150

Variance Analysis:

Level 1

Level 2

Level 3

Level 4

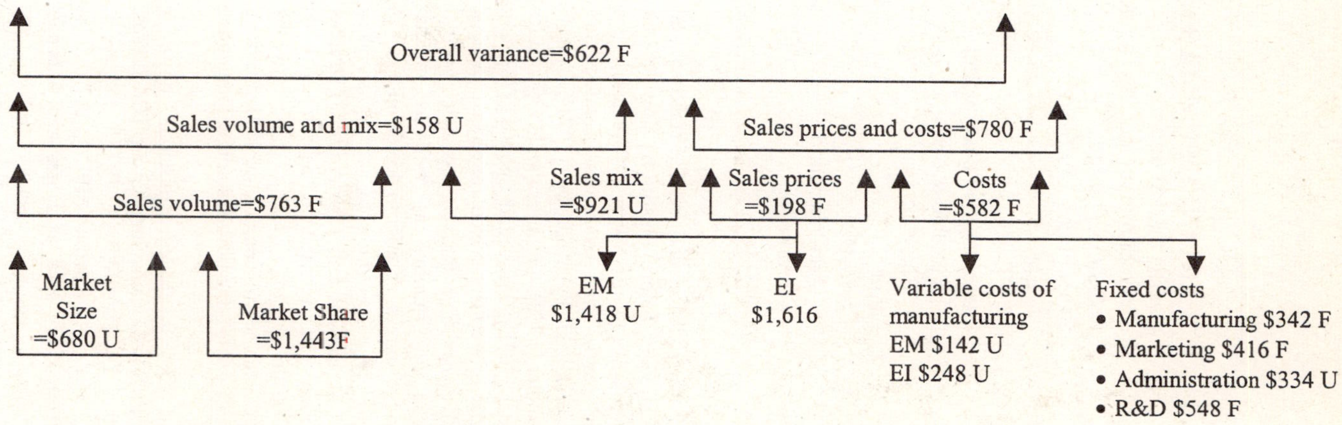

Note: F indicates a favorable variance and U indicates an unfavorable variance.

TABLE 5 VARIANCE SUMMARY FOR THE PHASE II APPROACH		
Overall market decline		$ 680 U
Share of market increase		1,443 F
Sales mix change		921 U
Sales prices improved		198 F
EM	$1,418 U	
EI	$1,616 F	
Manufacturing cost control		48 U
Variable costs	$390 U	
Fixed costs	$342 F	
Other		
R&D		548 F
Administration		334 U
Marketing		416 F
Total		$ 622 F

We will first define and briefly elaborate the concept of strategy before illustrating how to link strategic considerations with variances for management control and evaluation. Strategy has been conceptualized by Andrews [1971], Ansoff [1965], Chandler [1962], Govindarajan [1989], Hofer and Schendel [1978], Miles and Snow [1978], and others as the process by which managers, using a three- to five-year time horizon, evaluate external environmental opportunities as well as internal strengths and resources in order to decide on *goals* as well as *a set of action plans* to accomplish these goals. Thus, a business unit's (or a firm's) strategy depends upon two interrelated aspects: (1) its strategic mission or goals, and (2) the way the business unit chooses to compete in its industry to accomplish its goals—the business unit's competitive strategy.

Turning first to strategic mission, consulting firms such as Boston Consulting Group [Henderson, 1979], Arthur D. Little[Wright, 1975], and A. T. Kearney [Hofer and Davoust, 1977], as well as academic researchers such as Hofer and Schendel [1978], Buzzell and Wiersema [1981], and Govindarajan and Shank [1986], have proposed the following three strategic missions that a business unit can adopt:

BUILD:

This mission implies a goal of increased market share, even at the expense of short-term earnings and cash flow. A business unit following this mission is expected to be a net user of cash in that the cash throw-off from its current operations would usually be insufficient to meet its capital investment needs. Business units with "low market share" in "high growth industries" typically pursue a "build" mission (e.g., Apple Computer's MacIntosh business, Monsanto's Bioechnology business).

HOLD:

This strategic mission is geared to the protection of the business unit's market share and competitive position. The cash outflows for a business unit following this mission would usually be more or less equal to cash inflows. Businesses with "high market share" in "high growth industries" typically pursue a "hold" mission (e.g., IBM in mainframe computers).

HARVEST:

This mission implies a goal of maximizing short-term earnings and cash flow, even at the expense of market share. A business unit following such a mission would be a net supplier of cash. Businesses with "high market share" in "low growth industries" typically pursue a "harvest" mission (e.g., American Brands in tobacco products).

In terms of competitive strategy, Porter [1980] has proposed the following two generic ways in which businesses can develop sustainable competitive advantage:

TABLE 6 STRATEGIC CONTEXTS OF THE TWO BUSINESSES

	Electric Meters (EM)	Electronic Instruments (EI)
Overall market (units):		
Plan	1,248,000	440,000
Actual	886,080	690,800
	Declining Market (29% Decrease)	Growth Market (57% Increase)
United's share:		
Plan	10%	15%
Actual	16%	9%
United's prices:		
Plan	$40	$180
Actual	30	206
	We apparntly cut price to build	We apparently raised price to ration
United's margin:		
Plan	$20	$130
Actual	9	152
Industry prices:		
Actual	$50	$110
	We are well below "market."	We are well above "market."
Industry costs:		
Actual	$18	$46
Procuct/market characteristics:	Mature	Evolving
	Lower technology	Higher technology
	Declining market	Growth market
	Lower margins	Higher margins
	Low unit price	High unit price
	Industry prices holding up	Industry prices falling rapidly
United's apparent strategic mission	"Build"	"Skim" or "Harvest"
United's apparent competitive strategy	The low price implies we are trying for low cost position	The high price implies we are trying for a differentiation position.
A more plausible strategy	"Harvest"	"Build"
Key success factors (arising from the plausible strategy)	Hold sales prices vis-à-vis competition.	Competitively price to gain SOM.
	Do not focus on maintaining and improving SOM.	Product R&D top create differentiation
	Aggressive cost control	Lower cost through
	Process R&D to reduce unit costs.	experience curve effects

LOW COST:

The primary focus of this strategy is to achieve low cost relative to competitors. Cost leadership can be achieved through approaches such as economies of scale in production, learning curve effects, tight cost control, and cost minimization in areas such as R&D, service, sales force, or advertising. Examples of firms following this strategy include: Texas Instruments in consumer electronics, Emerson Electric in electric motors, Chevrolet in automobiles, Briggs and Stratton in gasoline engines, Black and Decker in machine tools, and Commodore in business machines.

DIFFERENTIATION:

The primary focus of this strategy is to differentiate the product offering of the business unit, creating something that is perceived by customers as being unique. Approaches to a product differentiation include brand loyalty (Coca-Cola in soft drinks), superior customer service (IBM in computers), dealer network (Caterpillar Tractors in construction equipment), product design and product features (Hewlett-Packard in electronics), and/or product technology (Coleman in camping equipment).

TABLE 7 VARIANCE CALCULATIONS USING A STRATEGIC FRAMEWORK

Key Casual Factors:					
Total market	Expected	Actual	Actual	Actual	Actual
Market share	Expected	Expected	Actual	Actual	Actual
Selling price	Expected	Expected	Expected	Actual	Actual
Variable costs	Expected	Expected	Expected	Expected	Actual
Electric Meters (EM)					
Sales	$ 4,992	$ 3,544	$ 5,671	$ 4,253	$ 4,253
Variable costs	2,496	1,772	2,835	2,835	2,977
Contribution	$ 2,496	$ 1,772	$ 2,836	$ 1,418	$ 1,276

Market sizee =$724 U; Market share =$1,064 F; Sales price =$1,418 U; Manufacturing Cost =$142 U

Electronic Instruments (EI)					
Sales	$11,880	$18,652	$11,191	$12,807	$12,807
Variable costs	3,300	5,181	3,109	3,109	3,357
Contribution	$ 8,580	$13,471	$ 8,082	$ 9,698	$ 9,450

Market size =$4,891 F; Market share =$5,389 U; Sales price =$1,616 F; Manufacturing Cost =$248 U

Firmwide Fixed Costs (by responsibility centers)

	Budget	Actual	Variance
Manufacturing	$3,872	$3,530	$342 F
Marketing	1,856	1,440	416 F
Administration	1,340	1,674	334 U
R&D	1,480	932	548 F

The above framework allows us to consider explicitly the strategic positioning of the two product groups: electric meters and electronic instruments. Though they both are industrial measuring instruments, they face very different competitive conditions that very probably call for different strategies. T-6 summarizes the differing environments and the resulting strategic issues.

How well did electric meters and electronics instruments perform, given their stratetic contexts? The relevant variance calculations are given in Tables 7 and 8. These calculations differ from Phase II analysis (given in T-4) in one important respect. T-4 treated EM and EI as two varieties of one product, competing as substitutes, with a single strategy. Thus, a sales mix variance was comptued. Tables 7 and 8 treat EM and EI as different products with dissimilar strategies. Therefore, no attempt is made to calculate a sales mix variance. The basic idea is that even though a sales mix variance can always be calculated, the concept is meaningful only when a single business framework is applicable. For the same reason, Tables 7 and 8 report the market size and market share variances for EM and EI separately, and T-4 reported these two variances for the instruments business as a whole. Obviously, a high degree of subjectivity is involved in deciding whether United is in one business or two. The fact that the judgment is to a large extent subjective does not negate its importance. T-9 summarizes the managerial performance evaluation that would result if we were to evaluate EM and EI against their plausible strategies, using the variances reported in T-7 and 8.

TABLE 8 VARIANCE SUMMARY FOR THE PHASE III APPROACH	
Electric Meters	
Market size	$ 724 U
Market share	1.064 F
Sales price	1.418 U
Variable manufacturing cost	142 U
Electronic Instruments	
Market size	4.891 F
Market share	5.389 U
Sales price	1.616 F
Variable manufacturing cost	248 U
R&D	548 F
Firmwide Fixed Costs	
Manufacturing	342 F
Marketing	416 F
Administration	334 U
TOTAL	$ 622 F

The overall performance of United would probably be judged as "unsatisfactory." The firm has not taken appropriate decisions in its functional areas (marketing, manufacturing, R&D, and administration) either for its harvest business (EM) or for its build business (EI). The summary in T-9 indicates a dramatically different picture of United's performance than the one presented under Phase II thinking. This is to be expected because Phase II thinking did not tie variance analysis to strategic objectives. Neither Phase I nor Phasc II analysis explicitly focused on ways to improve performance en route to accomplishing strategic goals. This would then imply that management compensation and rewards ought not to be tied to performance assessment undertaken using Phase I or Phase II frameworks.

CONCLUSIONS

Variance analysis represents a key link in the management control process. It involves two steps. First, one needs to break down the overall profit variance by key causal factors. Second, one needs to put the pieces back together most meaningfully with a view to evaluating managerial performance. Putting the bits and pieces together most meaningfully is just as crucial as computing the pieces. This is a managerial function, not a computational one.

Phase I, Phase II, and Phase III thinking yield different implications for this first step. That is, the detailed variance calculations do differ across the three approaches. Their implications differ even more for the second step. The computational aspects identify the variance as either favorable or unfavorable. However, a favorable variance does not necessarily imply favorable performance; similarly, an unfavorable variance does not necessarily imply unfavorable performance. We argue that the link between a favorable or unfavorable variance, on the one hand, and favorable or unfavorable performance, on the other, depends upon the strategic context of the business under evaluation.

No doubt, judgments about managerial performance can be dramatically different under Phase I, Phase II, and Phase III thinking (as the United Instruments case illustrates). In our view, moving toward Phase III thinking (i.e., analyzing profit variances in terms of the strategic issues involved) represents progress in adapting cost analysis to the rise of strategic analysis as a major element in business thinking [Shank and Govindarajan, 1988a, 1988b, and 1988c].

TABLE 9
PERFORMANCE EVALUATION SUMMARY FOR PHASE III APPROACH

	Electric Meters "Harvest" vs. "Build"	Electronic Instruments "Build" vs. "Skim"
Marketing		
Comments	If we held prices and share, decline in this mature business would have cost us $ 724 U But, we were further hurt by price cuts made in order to build our SOM (our prices was $30 vs. the industry price of $50). $1,418 U 1,064 F Net effect $1,078 U This is a market that declined 29 percent. Why are we sacrificing margins to build market position in this mature, declining lower margin business? We underspent the marketing budget. $ 416 F But why are we cutting back here in the face of our major marketing problems?	We raised prices to maintain margins and to ration our scarce capacity (our price was $206 vs. The industry price of $110). In the process, we lost significant SOM which cost us (netted against $1,616 F from sales prices). $3,773 U This is a booming market that grew 57 percent during this period. Then why did we decide to improve margins at the expense of SOM in this fast growing, higher margin business? Fortunately, growth in the total market improved our profit picture. $4,891 F We underspent the marketing budget. $416 F But why are we cutting back here in the face of our major marketing problems?
Overall evaluation	Poor performance	Poor performance
Manufacturing		
Comments	Manufacturing cost control was lousy and cost the firm $142 U If we are trying to be a cost leader, where are the benefits of our cumulative experience or our scale economies? (industry unit costs of $18 vs. our costs of $21)	Variable Manufacturing costs showed an unfavorable variance of $248 U (industry costs of $46 vs. our costs of $54). Does the higher manufacturing cost result in a product perceived as better? Apparently not based on market share data.
Overall evaluation	Poor performance	Poor performance
R&D	Not applicable	
Comments		Why are we not spending sufficient dollars in product R&D? Could this explain our decline in SOM?
Overall evaluation		Poor performance
Administration		
Comments	Inadequate control over overhead costs, given the need to become the low cost producer ($334 U).	Administration budget overspent. $334 U How does this relate to cost control?
Overall evaluation	Poor performance	Not satisfactory

REFERENCES

Andrews, K.R., *The Concept of Corporate Strategy* (Homewood, IL: Dow-Jones Irwin, 1971).

Ansoff, H.I., *Corporate Strategy* (New York: McGraw-Hill, 1965).

Buzzell, R.D., B.T. Gale, and R.G.M. Sultan, "Market Share—A Key to Profitability," *Harvard Business Review* (January-February 1975), pp. 97–106. _______, and F.D. Wiersema, "Modelling Changes in Market Share: A Cross-Sectional Analysis," *Strategic Management Journal* (January-March 1981), pp. 27–42.

Chandler, A.D., *Strategy and Structure* (Cambridge, MA: The MIT Press, 1962).

Govindarajan, V., "Implementing Competitive Strategies at the Business Unit Level: Implications of Matching Managers to Strategies," *Strategic Management Journal* (May-June 1989), pp. 251–269.

_______, "Decentralization, Strategy, and Effectiveness of Strategic Business Units in Multi-Business Organizations," *Academy of Management Review* (October 1986a), pp. 844–856.

_______, "Impact of Participation in the Budgetary Process on Managerial Attitudes and Performance: Universalistic and Contingency Perspectives," *Decision Sciences* (1986b), pp. 496–516.

_______, "A Contingency Approach to Strategy Implementation at the Business Unit Level: Integrating Management Systems with Strategy," *Academy of Management Journal* (September 1988).

_______, and A.K. Gupta, "Linking Control Systems to Business Unit Strategy: Impact on Performance," *Accounting, Organizations and Society* (1985), pp. 51–66.

_______, and J.K. Shank, "Cash Sufficiency: The Missing Link in Strategic Planning," *The Journal of Business Strategy* (Summer 1986), pp. 88–95.

Gupta, A.K., and V. Govindarajan, "Business Unit Strategy, Managerial Characteristics, and Business Unit Effectiveness at Strategy Implementation," *Academy of Management Journal* (March 1984a), pp. 25–41.

_______, and _______, "Build, Hold, Harvest: Converting Strategic Intentions into Reality," *Journal of Business Strategy* (Winter 1984b), pp. 34–47.

_______, and _______, "Resource Sharing Among SBUs: Strategic Antecedents and Administrative Implications," *Academy of Management Journal* (December 1986), pp. 695–714.

Henderson, B.D., *Henderson on Corporate Strategy* (Cambridge, MA: Abt Books, 1979).

Hofer, C.W., and M.J. Davoust, *Successful Strategic Management* (Chicago, IL: A.T. Kearney, 1977).

_______, and D.E. Schendel, *Strategy Formulation: Analytical Concepts* (St. Paul, MN: West Publishing, 1978).

"Midwest Ice Cream Company," in J.K. Shank, Ed., *Contemporary Management Accounting: A Casebook* (Englewood Cliffs, NJ: Prentice-Hall, 1982), pp. 157–173.

Miles, R.E., and C.C. Snow, *Organizational Strategy, Structure and Process* (New York: McGraw Hill, 1978).

Porter, M.E., *Competitive Strategy: Techniques for Analyzing Industries and Competitors* (New York: The Free Press, 1980).

Shank, J.K., *Contemporary Management Accounting: A Casebook* (Englewood Cliffs, NJ: Prentice-Hall, 1982).

_______, and N.C. Churchill, "Variance Analysis: A Management-Oriented Approach," *The Accounting Review* (October 1977), pp. 950–957.

_______, and V. Govindarajan, "Making Strategy Explicit in Cost Analysis: A Case Study, " *Sloan Management Review* (Spring 1988a), pp. 19–29.

_______, and _______, "Transaction-Based Costing for the Complex Product Line: A Field Study," *Journal of Cost Management* (Summer 1988b), pp. 31–38.

_______, and _______, "Strategic Cost Analysis—Differentiating Cost Analysis and Control According to the Strategy Being Followed," *Journal of Cost Management* (Fall 1988c).

Wright, R.V.L., *A System for Managing Diversity* (Cambridge, MA: Arthur D. Little, Inc., 1975).

EXAMINING THE RELATIONSHIPS IN PRODUCTIVITY ACCOUNTING

By Anthony J. Hayzen, Ph.D., and James M. Reeve, CPA, Ph.D.

Productivity measures an organization's ability to convert labor, capital, and material inputs into valued goods and services. This, of course, is not a new concept. The challenge is to turn the concept into useful measures management can use. Peter Drucker put the case for productivity measurement as follows: "Without productivity goals a business has no direction, and without productivity measurement a business has no control." The purpose of productivity measurement, therefore, is control. Linking changes in productivity to resource allocation facilitates control. Therefore, we believe a useful productivity measure will link productivity changes to resources and hence to profitability.

We will demonstrate this link through an analytical technique we term "productivity accounting."[1] This approach measures the change in total resource productivity (that is, the changes in labor productivity. in materials productivity, capital productivity, and energy productivity) and the effects of these changes, taken together or individually, on the corresponding change in business profitability.

With this approach, a business can:

- **monitor** historical productivity performance and measure how much, in dollars or percent return on investment (ROL), profits were affected by productivity growth or decline;
- **evaluate** business profit plans (budgets) to determine whether the productivity changes implied are overly ambitious, reasonable, or not sufficiently ambitious; and
- **measure** the extent to which productivity performance is strengthening or weakening its overall competitive position relative to its competitors.

SOURCES OF PROFIT CHANGE

Productivity accounting seeks to link the change in profit to its underlying causes. Thus, we want to provide a dynamic assessment of the profit-generating ability of a company by focusing on change in profit rather than static profit levels. The drivers of profit *changes* will provide much greater directional insight than will descriptions of profit *levels*.

With the same basic accounting information used to calculate revenues and costs, we can gain more insight into the precise drivers of profit. We know that change in product prices and change in product quantities drive the change in revenue. Likewise, change in resource prices and change in resource quantities drive the change in the cost of producing the products. All of this information is available in traditional accounting systems. Thus, the change in profit can be described as the sum of two elements: the change in productivity and change in price recovery.

$$\text{Change in Profit} = \text{Change in Productivity} + \text{Change in Price Recovery}$$

In the equation above, productivity can be expressed in the following familiar way:

$$\text{Productivity} = \frac{\text{Product Quanity (Output Quantity)}}{\text{Resource Quantity (Input Quantity)}}$$

Productivity is a measure of process execution, or the ability to efficiently turn inputs into outputs. A company with superior process execution has very little waste or process leakage. Often this is the only way to successfully compete in hypercompetitive markets, such as consumer electronics.

Similarly, price recovery has the following relationship:

$$\text{Price Recovery} = \frac{\text{Product Price (Output Price)}}{\text{Resource Price (Input Price)}}$$

Price recovery is a measure of structural position, or the degree to which a firm is able to capture value it creates through pricing power. For example, a firm that has erected barriers to entry or captured markets through patent protection may be able to enjoy pricing power that would yield attractive price recovery. Examples of attractive price recovery can be found in firms in the aircraft repair and overhaul parts business, where barriers to entry due to customer-specific design and process knowledge make it difficult for new entrants to compete in the after-market parts sector.

Some firms can compete on the basis of structural position (Microsoft or Coca-Cola), others on process execution (Nucor or Lincoln Electric), and a few others on both (Intel).

Table 1: CONVENTIONAL PRODUCTIVITY MEASUREMENT

	1998			1999		
	Value	Quantity	Price	Value	Quantity	Price
Sales	$99	11 units	$9	$110	11 units	$10
Rent	$52	26 sq. yards	$2	$78	26 sq. yards	$ 3
1. Profit	**$47**			**$32**		
2. Sates per sq. yard		**$99/26 sq. yards = 3.8**			**$110/26 sq. yards = 4.2**	
3. Productivity						
Quantity per sq.		**11 units /26 sq. yards = 0.42**			**11 units /26 sq. yards = 0.42**	

Firms without structural position and only average process execution will find it difficult to create and then capture value. More powerful supply chain participants will likely capture any value created. Examples abound in the automotive OEM parts business.

Productivity accounting decomposes these two sources of economic competitiveness—process execution and structural position—to guide the overall strategy of the firm.

TRADITIONAL MEASURES VS. PRODUCTIVITY ACCOUNTING

Traditional business performance indicators, such as sales per square yard, which is used in the retail industry; have the advantage of simplicity and familiarity Their main disadvantage, however, is that they can give conflicting signals because they do not isolate productivity from price recovery effects.

To illustrate this we will use the example of a simple retail business shown in Table 1. This business had revenue of $99 in 1998 from the sale of 11 items priced at $9 each. The revenue increased to $110 in 1999, generated from the sale of 11 items at $10 each. The rent paid for the store was $52 in 1998, which increased to $78 in 1999 for the same floor area of 26 square yards.

The first performance measure in Table 1 compares the profit of the business for the two years. Profitability decreased from $47 in 1998 to $32 in 1999.

The second approach uses the traditional ratio of sales per square yard. This method indicates that the performance of the business improved because the sales per square yard increased from $3.80 to $4.20.

The third method in Table 1 measures the performance of this business using productivity, As the table shows, productivity, and thus performance, has remained constant at 0.42 items per square yard.

We therefore have three conflicting measures of the business's performance. The second approach gives a conflicting signal as it uses revenue in the numerator, which contains both a quantity and a price effect.

The first and third methods (profit and productivity, respectively) give the correct signals. Profits have declined while productivity has remained constant. What would cause this? We must complete the picture by taking into consideration the effect the prices are having on the business. The productivity accounting method takes this into consideration and links both the effect of quantity changes (that is, productivity) and the price changes (that is, price recovery) to the change in profit, thus giving a complete picture of the performance of the business.

We can see from Table 1 what is happening in this business: Product prices have increased by 11% ($9 in 1998 to $10 in 1999) while the rent has increased by 50% ($2 per square yard in 1998 to $3 per square yard in 1999). Thus the decline in profit was due entirely to an inability to recover input price changes and had nothing to do with productivity, which remained constant.

NINE-BOX DIAGRAM

Profit, by itself, provides little managerial guidance. Rather, the manager needs information that identifies the causes for *change* in profit. Using the productivity accounting approach, one can take the *change in productivity* and the *change in price recovery* and relate them to the *change in profit.* If we now analyze the change in product quantities and change in resource quantities we get the change in productivity. If, in addition, we analyze the change in product prices and change in resource prices we get the change in price recovery. Price indexes may be used in situations where it is difficult to access detailed price and quantity information.

Together the measures give the manager a comprehensive analysis of how the changes in product quantity and resource quantity as well as the change in product price and resource price, are

Table2: QUANTITY AND PRICE INFORMATION FOR TWO PERIODS

	January 2000 (Reference Period)			February 2000 (Review Period)		
	Value	Quantity	Price	Value	Quantity	Price
Products						
Shirts	$150.00	10	$15.00	$216.00	12	$18.00
Cost Resources						
Linen (sq. yards)	$ 40.00	10	$4.00	$ 48.00	10	$ 4.80
Labor (staff-hours)	$ 48.00	6	$8.00	$ 60.00	5	$12.00
Total Cost Resources	$ 88.00			$108.00		
Capital Resources						
Machinery	$1,000.00	1	$1,000.00	$1,000.00	1	$1,000.00
% ROI	6.20			10.80		

affecting the profitability of the business. Figure 1 shows a "nine-box diagram" summarizing these concepts.

The middle column of the figure explains the change in profit in the conventional way. But changes in revenues and costs include both price and quantity effects. Therefore, the change in profit also can be explained by the middle row, which explains the change in profitability as a function of the change in productivity and change in price recovery. The change in productivity, in turn, is explained by the change in output quantities over input quantities (the left-hand column). The change in price recovery is explained by the change in product prices over the change in resource (input) prices (the right-hand column).

Figure 1: NINE-BOX DIAGRAM

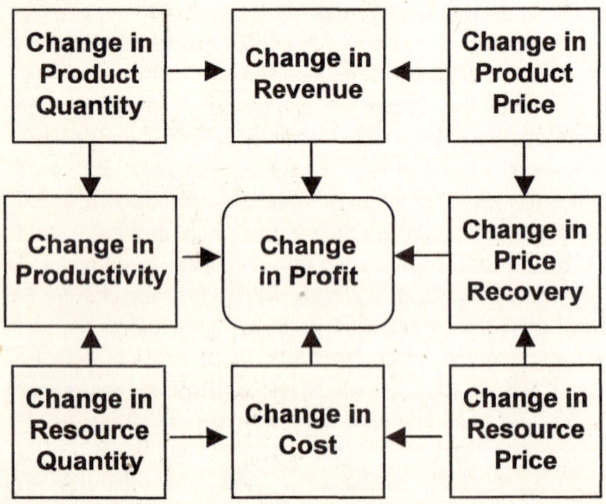

AN EXAMPLE ILLUSTRATING PRODUCTIVITY AND PRICE RECOVERY COMPONENTS

Evaluating changes in profit using productivity accounting requires measures of productivity change and price recovery change over periods of time.

To illustrate changes in productivity and price recovery, we will use a simplified example of a business that manufactures shirts as the only product, using linen and labor as the cost resources and machinery as the capital resource. We ignore for the sake of simplicity buttons, cotton, thread, labels, wrapping, premises, and so on, which are also used to produce the shirts.

In our example we compare the performance of February 2000, the review period, with the performance of January 2000, the reference period, to arrive at the change in productivity and change in price recovery The data are shown in Table 2.

Using the basic definition of productivity and the data shown in Table 2, we can measure the change in productivity for each resource contributing to the business operation. Viewed in this context, labor productivity—by far the most commonly quoted productivity statistic—is but one of many aspects of a total resource productivity analysis. For example, the change in linen "productivity" can be measured as the change in the output/input ratio between shirts and square yards of linen across the two periods. The productivity of linen in January was 10 shirts/10 square yards, or 1.0, while it improved to 12 shirts/10 square yards, or 1.2, in February. The productivity change for linen shown in Table 3 is 20%, or (1.2 - 1.0)/1.0. A similar calculation can be performed for productivity change in labor [44% =(2.4 -1.67)/1.67]. Likewise, the productivity change in machinery must be 20% because the same number of machines produced 20% more output (see Table 3 for a summary of these results).

Table 3: CHANGES IN PRODUCTIVITY AND PRICE RECOVERY

	Profit Variance	Productivity % Change	Productivity Variance	Price Recovery % Change	Price Recovery Variance
	A+B		A		B
Cost Resources					
Linen (sq. yards)	$ 9.60	20.00%	$ 9.60	0.00%	$ 0.00
Labor (staff-hours)	$ 9.10	44.00%	$26.40	(20.00%)	($17.30
Total Cost Resources	$18.70	(*) 33.33%	$36.00	(*) 9.09%	($17.30
Capital Resources					
Machinery	$27.30	20.00%	$12.40	20.0%	$14.90
Total Resources	**$46.00**	**(*) 28.47%**	**$48.40**	**(*) (1.100%)**	**($ 2.40)**

Similarly, there is also a unique price recovery relationship for each resource contributing to a business operation (that is, cost per unit of input). For example, the price recovery for labor can be measured as the change in the output/input ratio for shirt and labor prices across the two periods. The price recovery of labor in January was $15/$8, or 1.875, while it deteriorated to $18/$12, or 1.5, in February The price recovery change for labor shown in Table 3 is -20%, or (1.50- 1.875)/1.875. There was no change in the linen price recovery ($15/$4 = $18/$4.80*)*.

The price recovery for the machine is calculated in the same way. The machine's value remained constant while output prices increased from $15 to $18, thus leading to a positive price recovery of 20% [($18/$1,000) - ($15/$1,000)]/($15/$1,000). This approach intuitively accounts for the opportunity cost of the machine. For example, if the machine's value increased by a hundredfold while the output prices remained steady a strong argument could be made for selling the machine instead of using it. Our approach shows the impact of consuming this opportunity cost.

PRODUCTIVITY ACCOUNTING CONTRIBUTIONS

The percentage changes in productivity and price recovery are in themselves informative to management but do not show the contribution these changes have on profit change, impacts that are far more important to management. The process for converting percentage changes to variances is rather complex as one must eliminate price recovery effects in the productivity variance and productivity effects in the price recovery variance in order to achieve separation of the two effects.

To convert the percentage change in productivity into a dollar measure we take the new resource quantity (five staff—hours of labor) and multiply it by the new price ($12 per hour) and then by the percent change in productivity (44%), that is, 5 x $12 x 44% = $26.40. We have used the new price to show the current effect of the change in productivity. We determine the price recovery variance for labor by first establishing the resource input at assumed constant productivity. For labor, given that output increased by *20%,* the assumed labor (at constant productivity) would also increase by 20%, or from 6 hours to 7.2 hours. Thus, we determine the variance by multiplying the new price by 7.2 hours and then by the percent change in price recovery (-20%), that is, $12 x 7.2 hours x -20% = $17.30. Essentially this calculation holds the productivity effect constant in order to isolate the price effect. The linen variances are calculated in the same way.

For the capital resources (assets) there is an additional step to convert the asset values into a "cost of capital." The asset value must be multiplied by a return on investment (ROI). The ROI could be the ROI achieved in the reference period (January 2000), the ROI in the review period (February 2000), or some other target ROI. In our example we have used the ROI in the reference period (6.2%) and applied it to both the reference and review period assets. For example, the productivity variance for the machinery is 1 x $1,000 x 20% x 6.2% = $12.40. Software developed by one of the authors can be used to facilitate these calculations.[2]

For an illustration of the importance of measuring both productivity and price recovers notice in Table 3 that the financial benefit of the increase in labor productivity was $26.40 but that the unfavorable effect of price recovery of -$17.30 eroded this benefit. Therefore, the overall effect of labor on profit only amounted to a benefit of $9.10 ($26.40 - $17.30).

This simple example clearly illustrates the importance of measuring not only productivity but also price recovery so that the analyst can evaluate the effect of quantity and price changes on the profit of the business. The productivity accounting method of measuring productivity and price recovery shows that you can unambiguously evaluate each and every resource to find its productivity and price recovery impacts (that is, both change in index number and dollar effect) on the products produced. Next we will impacts (that is, both change in index number and dollar effect) on the products produced. Next we will illustrate how this combined information can be displayed graphically for easier interpretation.

GRAPHICAL INTERPRETATION

In order to easily interpret a productivity accounting analysis for a business, the results should be presented in a visual form that is quick and easy to interpret. We will illustrate a grid format to visually represent the analysis. The "nine-box diagram" illustrated previously represents a large number of interactions, each having different implications for a business. A grid diagram helps to refine this information.

THE PROFIT GRID

The Profit Grid shown in Figure *2* is used to explain profit change in terms of a change in productivity and a change in price recovery. The productivity variance is plotted vertically and the price recovery variance is plotted horizontally. As the variances can be either positive or negative numbers, the grid is segmented into four quadrants with the origin in the center of the grid. The diagonal line connects all points where the productivity variance is offset by an exactly opposite price recovery variance. That is, there is no change in profit along this line. The segments above the diagonal (Segments 1, *2,* and 3) signify an increase in profit while the segments below the diagonal (Segments 4, 5, and 6) signify a decrease in profit.

For example, assume that the business increased its profit by $20. This profit change arose from a $10 improvement in productivity and a $10 improvement in price recovery. Moving from the origin +10 in the vertical and horizontal directions places us in Segment *2.* Segment 2 performance indicates the best of both worlds—the organization is improving productivity and price recovery. But excessive price recovery may create an opportunity for competitors to undercut the business's product prices and thereby reduce market share and profit.

Now assume that the $20 change in profit arose from a $25 productivity improvement, but the business lost $5 from price underrecovery. This is an example of a Segment 1 scenario. In Segment 1 the organization has strong competitive advantages from superior process execution while deterring competitors with price underrecovery (that is, the business has only partially recovered its resource price change through its product price change).

Continuing the example, assume that the $20 change in profit arose from a $10 decline in productivity, but there is a $30 price overrecovery. This places us in Segment 3. Profit in Segment 3 may

Figure 2: THE PROFIT GRID

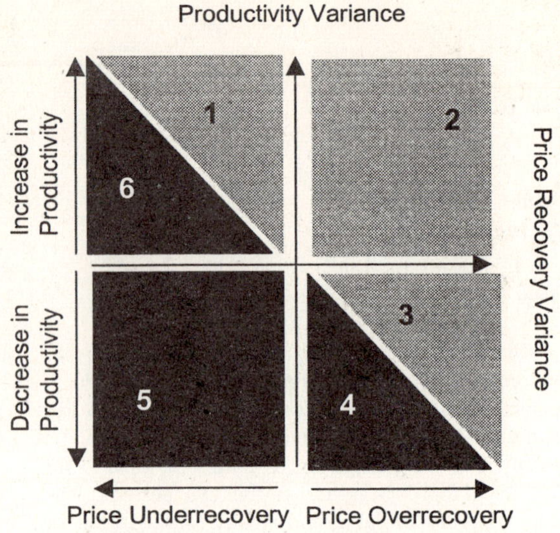

be very temporary. It occurs primarily from very aggressive pricing relative to resource inputs. An organization will sustain such pricing power only in the face of sustainable competitive position. Without such position, competitors surely will be attracted to the business and erode the margin opportunities, leaving the firm to compete on weak process execution.

In each of these examples the same $20 change in profit had very different strategic interpretations. The favorable change in profit alone (that is, the difference between revenue and cost) does not give the insight necessary to evaluate business performance and competitive position in the marketplace.

SUMMARY OF GRIDS

In order to have an overall picture of the business's performance, one needs to evaluate not only the Profit Grid but also the Quantity, Price, and Productivity Grids. Evaluation will clearly show the source of change in profit, productivity and price recovers, which are essential for understanding business performance. All four grids are shown in Figure 3.

The business appears in Segment 1 of the Profit Grid, indicating that the increase in profit arose from an increase in productivity which, however, was reduced by a price underrecovery. This places the business in a strong competitive position as competitors will require an even greater improvement in productivity to counter the price underrecovery. This segment is the classic position of the market leader in a hypercompetitive market.

Figure 3: FOUR-GRID FRAMEWORK

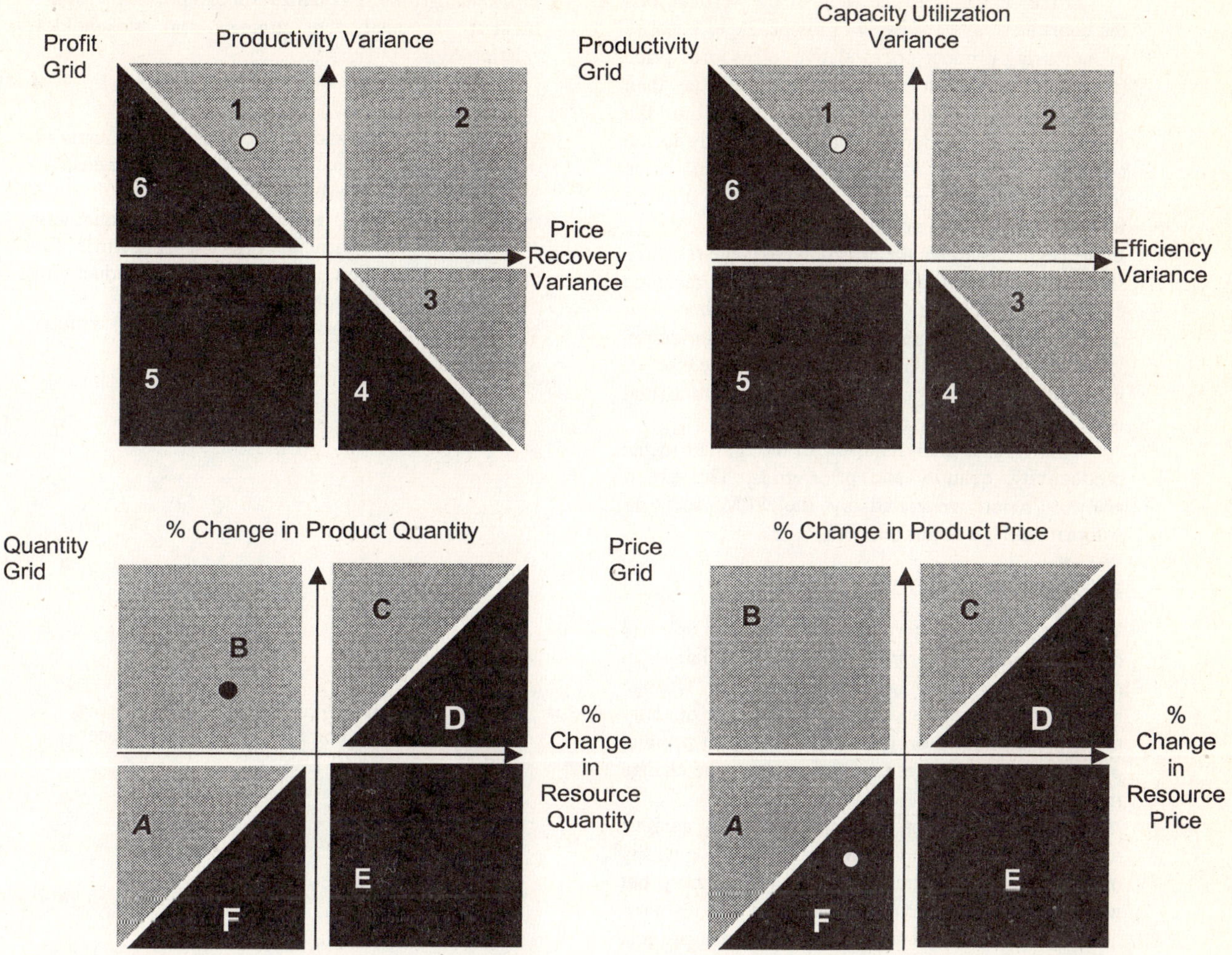

The Productivity Grid (Segment 1) shows that the increase in productivity arose from a large gain in capacity utilization, which was eroded by a decline in efficiency. In the short term, if the business improves its efficiency it will be able to increase productivity and thereby profits. The increase in utilization probably was due to increasing market penetration from the business's price leadership position.

We have introduced the concepts of efficiency and capacity utilization here for completeness. These concepts are used to distinguish between fixed and variable resources. Typically cost resources are regarded as variable and capital resources as fixed. In practice these resources fall somewhere between fixed and completely variable.

The Quantity Grid (Segment B) indicates that the business increased its production while discharging resources. In other words, it increased production and reduced resource use, clearly giving an increase in productivity.

The source of the price underrecovery, which placed the business in Segment 1 of the profit grid, is seen on the Price Grid. The decline of product prices exceeded the decline of resource prices, placing the business in Segment F.

Using this framework, it is clear that a business can generate profit growth through productivity growth or price overrecovery. The course that a business chooses, however, has important implications for its long-term competitive position.

STAKEHOLDER ANALYSIS

A simple value chain will link a company from the supplier to the customer. The impact of productivity and price recovery on suppliers and customers also can be evaluated using the grids, as the profit grid in Figure 4 shows.

In the segments to the right of the vertical axis the consumer pays a subsidy to the producer because of increasing product price relative to resource price (that is, product price is increasing faster than resource price). In the segments to the left of the vertical axis the producer is paying a subsidy to the consumer because of decreasing product price relative to resource price (that is, resource price is increasing faster than product price).

In the segments above the horizontal axis the resource supplier is harmed because of decreasing resource content per unit of product (that is, improved productivity). In the segments below the horizontal axis the resource supplier is favored because of increasing resource content per unit of product (that is, declining productivity).

This type of analysis also can be applied to the productivity, quantity and price grids. The expert analysis report generated by the FPM software automatically gives this analysis.

THE COMPLETE PICTURE

We have seen that a corporation or business unit can *analyze change in profit* in terms of a change in productivity and a change in price recovery. Change in product quantities and change in resource quantity drive the change in productivity. Change in product prices and change in resource prices drive the change in price recovery.

A corporation or business unit can achieve *productivity improvement* when product quantity increases at a faster rate than resource quantity but will experience *productivity decline* if resource quantity increases at a faster rate than product quantity. If all other factors are held constant, productivity improvement will translate directly into profit improvement.

When product price increases at a faster rate than resource price, the result is *price overrecovery.* If all other factors are held constant, price overrecovery will translate directly into increased profits in the short term. *Price underrecovery* occurs when resource price increases at a faster rate than product price. If all other factors are held constant, price underrecovery translates directly into a decrease in profits in the short term.

Instead of the conventional profit analysis represented by the middle column of the "nine-box diagram," many corporations and business units now analyze profit changes as a result of changes in productivity and price recovery, as represented by the middle row

These relationships then can be displayed to provide an instant visual analysis of the causes of profit change. Such visualization can provide a robust method for analyzing strategy and stakeholder relationships.

[1] As descrjbed by

[1] A.J. Hayzen, "Financial Productivity Management— An Overview;" WITS Industrial Engineering Conference, February 1988.

[2] B.J. van Loggerenberg, "Productivity Decoding of Financial Signals: A Primer for Management on Deterministic Productivity Accounting." PMA Monograph, 1988.

[2] Financial Productivity Management (FPM) software.

Chapter 16
Total Quality Management

Cases
16-1 Precision Systems, Inc.

Readings
"GE Takes Six Sigma Beyond the Bottom Line"
Reports on the success of GE Medical Systems Inc.'s Six Sigma effort. The article describes the training programs for employees in statistical process control and services and information offered by the Web site of the company to support the quality improvement efforts of more than 300,000 employees world-wide.

Discussion Questions:
1. What is a Six Sigma approach?
2. Describe the processes that GE used to implement its Six Sigma program.
3. What are black belts? What roles do black belts play in GE's Six Sigma program?

Cases

16-1 Precision Systems, Inc.

Suresh S. Kalagnanam, University of Saskatchewan, Ella Mae Matsumura, University of Wisconsin-Madison

Precision Systems, Inc. (PSD) has been in business for more than 25 years and has generally reported a positive net income. The company manufactures and sells high-technology instruments (systems). Each product line at PSI has only a handful of standard products, but configuration changes and add-ons can be accommodated as long as they are not radically different from the standard systems.

Faced with rising competition and increasing customer demand for quality, PSI adopted total quality management (TQM) in 1989. Many employees received training, and several quality initiatives were launched. Like most businesses, PSI concentrated on improvements in the manufacturing function and achieved significant improvements. However, little was done in other departments.

In early 1992, PSI decided to extend TQM to its order entry department, which handles the critical functions of preparing quotes for potential customers and processing orders. Order processing is the first process in the chain of operations after the order is received from a customer. High-quality output from the order entry department improves quality later in the process and allows PSI to deliver higher-quality systems both faster and cheaper, thus meeting the goals of timely delivery and lower cost.

As a first step, PSI commissioned a cost of quality (COQ) study in its order entry department. The study had two objectives:

- To develop a system for identifying order entry errors,
- To determine how much an order entry error costs.

PSI'S ORDER ENTRY DEPARTMENT

PSI's domestic order entry department is responsible for preparing quotations for potential customers and taking actual sales orders. PSI's sales representatives forward requests for quotations to the order entry department, though actual orders for systems are received directly from customers. Orders for parts are also received directly from customers. Service-related orders (for parts or repairs), however, are generally placed by service representatives. When PSI undertook the COQ study, the order entry department consisted of nine employees and two supervisors, who reported to the order entry manager. Three of the nine employees dealt exclusively with taking parts orders, while the other six were responsible for system orders. Before August 1992, the other six were split equally into two groups: One was responsible for preparing quotations, and the other was responsible for taking orders.

The final outputs of the order entry department are the quote and the order acknowledgment or "green sheet." The manufacturing department and the stockroom use the green sheet for further processing of the order.

The order entry department's major suppliers are: (1) sales or service representatives; (2) the final customers who provide them with the basic information to process further; and (3) technical information and marketing departments, which provide configuration guides, price masters, and similar documents (some in printed form and others on-line) as supplementary information. Sometimes there are discrepancies in the information available to order entry staff and sales representatives with respect to price, part number, or configuration. These discrepancies often cause communication gaps between the order entry staff, sales representatives, and manufacturing.

An order entry staff member provided the following example of lack of communication between a sales representative and manufacturing with respect to one order.

> If the sales reps have spoken to the customer and determined that our standard configuration is not what they require, they may leave a part off the order. [In one such instance] I got a call from manufacturing saying when this system is configured like this, it must have this part added.... It is basically a no charge part and so I added it (change order #1) and called the sales rep and said to him, "Manufacturing told me to add it." The sales rep. called back and said, "No [the customer] doesn't need that part, they are going to be using another option ... so they don't need this." Then I did another change order (#2) to take it off because the sales rep said they don't need it. Then manufacturing called me back and said "We really need [to add that part] (change order #3). If the sales rep. does not want it then we will have to do an engineering special and it is going to be another 45 days lead time...." So, the sales rep and manufacturing not having direct communication required me to do three change orders on that order; two of them were probably unnecessary.

A typical sequence of events might begin with a sales representative meeting with a customer to discuss the type of system desired. The sales representative then fills out a paper form and faxes it or phones it in to an order entry employee, who might make several subsequent phone calls to the sales representative, the potential customer, or the manufacturing department to prepare the quote properly. These phone calls deal with such questions as exchangeability of parts, part numbers, current prices for parts, or allowable sales discounts. Order entry staff then keys in the configuration of the desired system, including part numbers, and informs the sales representative of the quoted price. Each quote is assigned a quotation number. To smooth production, manufacturing often produces systems with standard configurations in anticipation of obtaining orders from recent quotes for systems. The systems usually involve adding on special features to the standard configuration. Production in advance of orders sometimes results in duplication in manufacturing, however, because customers often fail to put their quotation numbers on their orders. When order entry receives an order, the information on the order is reentered into the computer to produce an order acknowledgment. When the order acknowledgment is sent to the invoicing department, the information is reviewed again to generate an invoice to send to the customer.

Many departments in PSI use information directly from the order entry department *(these are the internal customers of order entry).* The users include manufacturing, service (repair), stockroom, invoicing, and sales administration. The sales administration department prepares commission payments and tracks sales performance. The shipping, customer support (technical support), and collections departments (also internal customers) indirectly use order entry information. After a system is shipped, related paperwork is sent to customer support to maintain a service-installed database in anticipation of technical support questions that may arise. Customer support is also responsible for installations of systems. A good order acknowledgment (i.e., one with no errors of any kind) can greatly reduce errors downstream within the process and prevent later non-value-added costs.

COST OF QUALITY

Quality costs arise because poor quality may—or does—exist. For PSI's order entry department, poor quality or nonconforming "products" refer to poor information for further processing of an order or quotation (see Exhibit 1-1 for examples). Costs of poor quality here pertain to the time spent by the order entry staff and concerned employees in other departments (providers of information, such as sales or technical information) to rectify the errors.

CLASS I FAILURES

Class I failure costs are incurred when nonconforming products (incorrect quotes or orders) are identified as nonconforming before they leave the order entry department. The incorrect quotes or orders may be identified by order entry staff or supervisors during inspection of the document. An important cause of Class I failures is lack of communication. Sample data collected from the order entry staff show that they encountered more than 10 different types of problems during order processing (see Exhibit 1-1 for examples). Analysis of the sample data suggests that, on average, it takes 2.3 hours (including waiting time) to rectify errors on quotes and 2.7 working days for corrections on orders. In determining costs, the COQ study accounted only for the time it actually takes to solve the problem (i.e., excluding waiting time). Waiting time was excluded because employees use this time to perform other activities or work on other

Exhibit 1-1. Examples of Failures

1. Incomplete information on purchase order.
2. Transposition of prices on purchase order.
3. More than one part number on order acknowledgment when only one is required.
4. Incorrect business unit code (used for tracking product line profitability) on the order acknowledgment.
5. Freight terms missing on the purchase order.
6. Incorrect part number on order acknowledgment.
7. Incorrect shipping or billing address on the order acknowledgment.
8. Credit approval missing (all new customers have a credit approval before an order is processed).
9. Missing part number on order acknowledgment.
10. Customer number terminated on the computer's database (an order cannot be processed if customer number is missing).
11. Incorrect sales tax calculation on the order acknowledgment.
12. Part number mismatch on purchase order.

orders. The total Class I failure costs, which include only salary and fringe benefits for the time it takes to correct errors, amount to more than 4% of order entry's annual budget for salaries and fringe benefits (see Exhibit 1-2).

Exhibit 1-2. Estimated Annual Failure Costs (as a percentage of order entry's annual salary and fringe benefits budget)

	Order Entry	Other Department	Total Costs
Class I Failure Costs			
Quotations	1.1%	0.4%	1.5%
Orders	0.9%	1.7%	2.6%
Total Class I Failure	2.0%	2.1%	4.1%
Class II Failure Costs			
Order acknowledgments	2.6%	4.4%	7.0%
Change orders	2.6%	—	2.6%
Final customers	0.02%	0.1%	0.1%
Return authorizations	1.9%	—	1.9%
Total Class II Failure	7.12%	4.5%	11.6%
Total Failure Costs	9.1%	6.6%	15.7%

CLASS II FAILURES

Class II failure costs are incurred when nonconforming materials are transferred out of the order entry department. For PSI's order entry department, "nonconforming" refers to an incorrect order acknowledgment as specified by its users within PSI. The impact of order entry errors on final *(external)* customers is low because order acknowledgments are inspected in several departments, so most errors are corrected before the invoice (which contains some information available on the order acknowledgment) is sent to the final customer. Corrections of the order entry errors does not guarantee that the customer receives a good quality system, but order entry's initial errors do not then affect the final customer. Mistakes that affect the final customer can be made by employees in other departments (e.g., manufacturing or shipping).

Sample data collected from PSI's users of order entry department information show that more than 20 types of errors can be found on the order acknowledgment (see Exhibit 1-1 for examples). The cost of correcting these errors (salary and fringe benefits of order entry person and a concerned person from another PSI department) accounts for approximately 7% of order entry's annual budget for salaries and fringe benefits (see Exhibit 1-2).

In addition to the time spent on correcting the errors, the order entry staff must prepare a change order for several of the Class II failures. Moreover, a change order is required for several other reasons not necessarily controllable by order entry. Examples include: (1) changes in ship-to or bill-to address by customers or sales representatives, (2) canceled orders, and (3) changes in invoicing instructions. Regardless of the reason for a change order, the order entry department incurs some cost. The sample data suggest that for every 100 new orders, order entry prepares 71 change orders; this activity accounts for 2.6% of order entry's annual budget for salaries and fringe benefits (see Exhibit 1-2).

Although order entry's errors do not significantly affect final customers, customers who find errors on their invoices often use the errors as an excuse to delay payments. Correcting these errors involves the joint efforts of the order entry, collections, and invoicing departments; these costs account for about 0.12% of order entry's annual budget (see Exhibit 1-2).

The order entry staff also spends considerable time handling return authorizations when final customers send their shipment back to PSI. Interestingly, more than 17% of the goods are returned because of defective shipments, and more than 49% fall into the following two categories: (1) ordered in error and (2) 30-day return rights. An in-depth analysis of the latter categories suggests that a majority of these returns can be traced to sales or service errors. The order entry department incurs costs to process these return authorizations, which account for more than 1.9% of the annual budget (see Exhibit 1-2). The total Class I and Class II failure costs account for 15.7% of the order entry department's annual budget for salaries and fringe benefits. Although PSI users of order entry information were aware that problems in their departments were sometimes caused by errors in order entry, they provided little feedback to order entry about the existence or impact of the errors.

CHANGES IN PSI'S ORDER ENTRY DEPARTMENT

In October 1992, preliminary results of the study were presented to three key persons who had initiated the study: the order entry manager, the vice president of manufacturing, and the vice president of service and quality. In March 1993, the final results were presented to PSI's executive council, the top decision-making body. Between October 1992 and March 1993, PSI began working toward obtaining the International Organization for Standardization's ISO 9002 registration for order entry and manufacturing practices, which it received in June 1993.

The effort to obtain the ISO 9002 registration suggests that PSI gave considerable importance to order entry and invested significant effort toward improving the order entry process. Nevertheless, as stated by the order entry manager, the changes would not have been so vigorously pursued if cost information had not been presented. COQ information functioned as a catalyst to accelerate the improvement effort. In actually making changes to the process, however, information pertaining to the different types of errors was more useful than the cost information.

REQUIRED QUESTIONS

1. Describe the role that assigning costs to order entry errors played in quality improvement efforts at Precision Systems, Inc.
2. Prepare a diagram illustrating the flow of activities between the order entry department and its suppliers, internal customers (those within PSI), and external customers (those external to PSI).
3. Classify the failure items in Exhibit 1-1 into internal failure (identified as defective before delivery to internal or external customers) and external failure (nonconforming "products" delivered to internal or external customers) with respect to the order entry department. For each external failure item, identify which of order entry's internal customers (i.e., other departments within PSI that use information from the order acknowledgment) will be affected.
4. For the order entry process, how would you identify internal failures and external failures? Who would be involved in documenting these failures and their associated costs? Which individuals or departments should be involved in making improvements to the order entry process?
5. What costs, in addition to salary and fringe benefits, would you include in computing the cost of correcting errors?
6. Provide examples of incremental and breakthrough improvements that could be made in the order entry process. In particular, identify prevention activities that can be undertaken to reduce the number of errors. Describe how you would prioritize your suggestions for improvement.
7. What nonfinancial quality indicators might be useful for the order entry department? How frequently should data be collected or information be reported? Can you make statements about the usefulness of cost-of-quality information in comparison to nonfinancial indicators of quality?

Readings

GE TAKES SIX SIGMA BEYOND THE BOTTOM LINE

By GREGORY T. LUCIER AND SRIDHAR SESHADRI

Imagine working for a company where every employee is required to go through two weeks of intensive training in statistical process control. Then at the end of this training, participants are required to demonstrate proficiency by completing two projects that directly improve either company or customer performance.

On top of that, the company's website provides 24/7 access to the tools and methodology required to support the quality improvement efforts of more than 300,000 employees world-wide. The site is constantly and consistently measuring and quantifying thousands upon thousands of active projects.

Has your satellite TV system somehow mingled the contents of the business channel with a late-night science fiction film? No. You're experiencing GE's Six Sigma quality program, one that has netted the corporation such amazing results that now GE's customers are clamoring for help.

GETTING STARTED

Roll back to 1981, when Jack Welch first took the helm at GE and began to transform (or reshape) the company from a $25 billion bureaucratic quagmire into a well-run and highly respected $100 billion giant. Welch understood the "command and control" management approach had run its course and spent the next 20 years resolutely pursuing other options, borrowing best practices, and implementing winning strategies.

Through the remainder of the '80s, GE employed corporate-wide streamlining to get the fat out of its organization while maintaining the muscle. In 1989, as the tumult began to settle, Welch realized the need to empower employees and give them a greater level of participation in the decision-making process. Despite a decade of change, the level of hierarchy and top-down communication had remained an impediment. To solve this, Welch launched an initiative known as Work-Out™, which is designed to facilitate focused decision making, resolve issues, and improve processes. A Work-Out session is generally led by those closest to a process or issue, with the goal toward finding workable solutions and developing action plans. Work-Out can be used to eliminate unnecessary steps and streamline tasks or to remove barriers between different departments or reporting levels. Built into this process are mechanisms for ensuring management buy-in and follow-through.

Some Work-Out session examples are:

- Improving back-office processing with new financial systems,
- Improving internal paperwork flow, and
- Streamlining approval processes.

By the mid-'90s it was time to shake things up again, this time with a focus on quality. Not because GE wasn't performing well, but because feedback from employees convinced the CEO that, despite top- and bottom-line growth, quality wasn't where it should be.

Welch decided Six Sigma was the way to go. He had learned about Six Sigma from Larry Bossidy, a former GE executive who left to take the helm at Allied Signal, a company then implementing the program. Bossidy introduced Welch to Mikel Harry of the Six Sigma Academy and to this breakthrough strategy for statistical process control. Jack Welch had always maintained that GE must look outside itself to identify and adopt best practices wherever they could be found. So in the spring of 1995, Welch asked Bossidy to share his unique Six Sigma philosophy with GE's executive council.

They were impressed. Welch set targets out past five years and proclaimed Six Sigma the largest, most significant initiative ever undertaken at GE. Since that proclamation, Six Sigma has been implemented aggressively and has become deeply ingrained in the corporation's culture. The company has deployed the methodology more extensively than any other to date, and maintaining its vitality continues to be a top priority. Throughout GE, there's a commonly echoed phrase...Six Sigma is "The Way We Work." Acquiring and using Six Sigma skills is considered a

Figure 1: GE's Results from Six Sigma

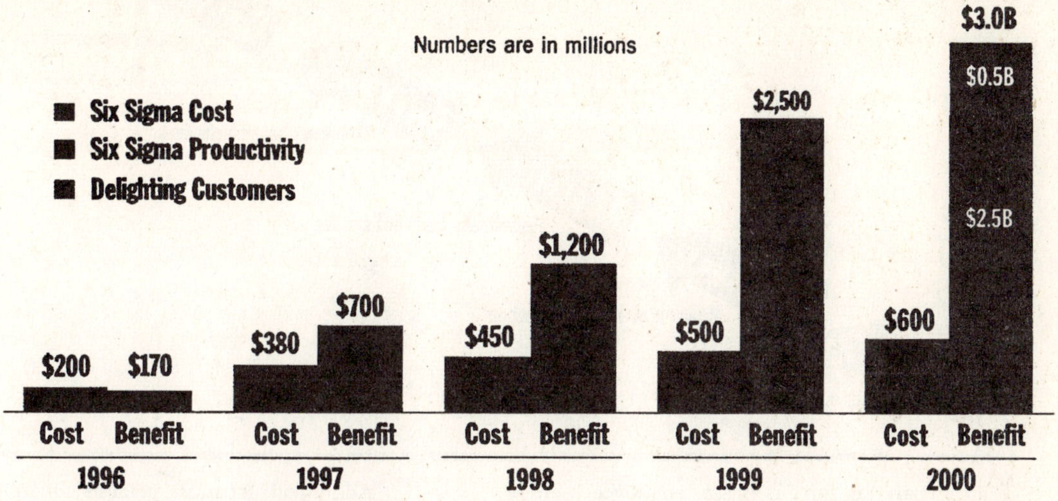

core competency for leadership roles, and each year new "stretch" goals and projects are established.

In terms of bottom-line impact, payback, ROI, benefit—whatever you want to call it—GE has achieved it. During the first five years of the program, the company increased annual productivity gains by over 266% and improved operating margins from 14.4% to 18.4% (see Figure 1). The bottom line was enhanced tremendously, and stock-holders were rewarded handsomely and consistently.

Six Sigma wasn't invented by GE (Motorola initiated a version of Six Sigma in the late 1980s). But the results the corporation has achieved from its implementation have attracted attention from several fronts, especially a large segment of the international business community and GE's customers. In response, GE decided to offer customers high-level instruction in Six Sigma. For example, last year our group, GE Medical Systems, began taking Six Sigma to healthcare customers. That first effort resulted in over $94 million in benefits after touching only a fraction of the market. And as recognition grows, so will the numbers.

A CLOSER LOOK AT THE SIX SIGMA APPROACH

The name Six Sigma is derived from a statistical heritage and focus on measuring product or process defects. Sigma is the Greek letter assigned to represent standard deviation. Achieving a Six Sigma level of quality equates to nearly error-free performance—where a given process produces only 3.4 defects out of a million opportunities.

Here are some perspectives on levels of Sigma:

SIGMA	Defects Per Million Opportunities
2	308,537
3	66,807
4	6,210
5	233
6	3.4

Most organizations would probably rate their current quality at between Three and Four Sigma. When Jack Welch challenged GE to become a Six Sigma organization in four years, he was in effect calling for a reduction in defect levels of 84% per year. At stake was an estimated $8-$10 billion in costs consumed by lower levels of quality.

While the measure of quality is the cornerstone of the Six Sigma approach, it's the methodology and tools driving process change that translate to the difference between a simple quality campaign slogan and a rigorous management philosophy based on science. At the heart of the Six Sigma approach is a method summarized by the acronym DMAIC (see Figure 2).

Define. The GE process starts here. Teams work to clearly define problems related to the business or critical to customer satisfaction. CTQ (Critical to Quality) factors essential for customer satisfaction are correlated with the overall business process at issue. Project charters are established, required resources are identified, and leadership approvals are obtained to maximize project outcomes.

Figure 2: D M A I C

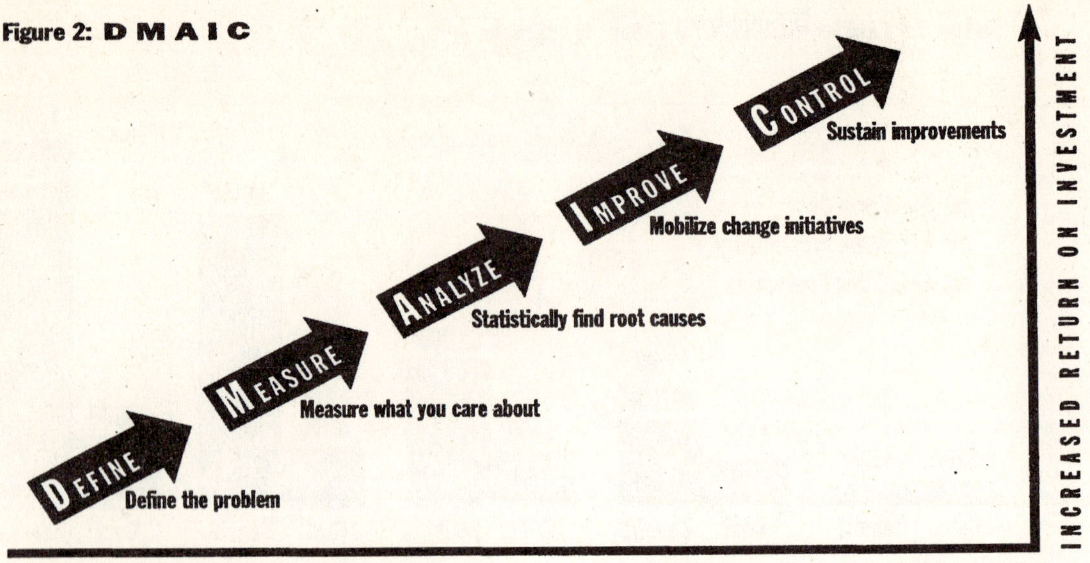

In preparation for this phase, employee training includes a review of process mapping techniques and orientation to online tools available to support teams.

Measure. The next stage is to establish base-level measures of defects inherent in the existing process. Customer expectations are defined to determine "out of specification" conditions. Training for this phase consists of basic probability and statistics, statistical analysis software, and measurement analysis.

While this heavy bombardment of statistics causes many participants to run for cover, GE makes it easier for employees to learn. It partners experienced Six Sigma practitioners with employees going through the training for the first time, which helps beginners overcome the challenge of mastering the concepts. And the use of automated tools minimizes the time required for complex calculations.

Analyze. In this phase, teams explore underlying reasons for defects. They use statistical analysis to examine potential variables affecting the outcome and seek to identify the most significant root causes. Then they develop a prioritized list of factors influencing the desired outcome.

Tools used for this phase include multivariate analysis, test for normality, ANOVA, correlation, and regression. Again, these tools aren't for those who have difficulty balancing a checkbook, but most participants succeed with help from their mentors.

Improve. During this phase, teams seek the optimal solution and develop and test a plan of action for implementing and confirming the solution. The process is modified and the outcome measured to determine whether the revised method produces results within customer expectations.

Additional statistical methods covering design of experiments and multiple linear regression are reviewed with trainees to support the final analysis of the problem and to test the proposed solutions.

Control. To ensure changes stick, ongoing measures are implemented to keep the problem from recurring. Control charting techniques are used as the basis for developing the ongoing measures.

The concept of control—taking concrete steps to make sure improvements don't unravel over time—has been missing from other process improvement initiatives. It's this phase of Six Sigma that leads to long-term payoffs—both in quality and monetary terms.

IMPLEMENTING THE PROGRAM

Training for GE employees takes about 10 classroom days spread over four sessions and 90 calendar days. Action teams are created in each class to attack an existing business problem. As each aspect of Six Sigma is taught, the team immediately applies the concepts to the chosen problem.

There's a progression of competency levels beginning with Green Belts—and all employees from clerical staff up are required to reach this level of proficiency. Green Belts must complete the required training and two projects to achieve certification. They must also complete one additional project and eight hours of post-certification training each year. While Green Belts are trained in Six Sigma, they hold non-Six Sigma positions within the company. New employees are expected to obtain Green Belt certification within the first year of employment.

Taking Six Sigma to Customers

Once we had proof that the system really works, we decided to take Six Sigma beyond internal projects. Our group, GE Medical Systems, is offering its expertise to customers to enhance value and provide additional benefits.

The healthcare industry continues to experience monumental changes and tough challenges. Lower reimbursement, competition, and consolidation have transformed organizations from a 1980s' model—targeting quality at all costs—to today's approach where quality and efficiency must be the driving forces in the delivery of care.

In the 1990s, the industry saw a bevy of quality and reengineering consultants attempt to remedy the situation, but such efforts at cost cutting were quickly cancelled by the need to rehire personnel. Old operational habits also died hard for a lack of sustainable change management that should have included—among other elements—skills transfer.

The healthcare industry has quickly responded to the promise of Six Sigma. As of December 2000, GE Medical Systems reported 1,149 active Six Sigma projects for customers. GE even created a service unit expressly dedicated to providing Six Sigma management tools and processes to healthcare organizations requesting more extensive assistance in improving performance.

Is it working? Yes. Commonwealth Health Corporation, a 478-bed medical center in Kentucky, began its journey to implement a Six Sigma improvement culture over three years ago. Results have been overwhelming as the medical center reports a reinvigorated and transformed management culture. Within a mere 18 months, errors in one ordering process were reduced over 90%, overall operating expenses had been reduced by $800,000, and employee survey results had improved by 20%. These results were from a single division within the organization. Now the medical center has realized improvements in excess of $1.5 million and is expanding the program to other areas.

One of the main reasons the program is working is because customers determine project scope, acquire on-site training and tools, and verify the benefits they have received. During last year alone, 466 customer projects were completed that resulted in $91.2 million in customer benefits. Because it relies on rigorous statistical methods and puts control mechanisms in place, Six Sigma actually connects the dots among quality, cost, process, people, and accountability.

Some customers are using GE'S Six Sigma program to achieve even higher measures of success. As part of their Star Initiative, a system-wide performance improvement effort, Virtua Health of Marlton, N.J., saw the Six Sigma program as an opportunity to vault their system to the next level of clinical quality, patient satisfaction, and financial performance. Walter Ettinger, M.D., executive vice president at Virtua, credits the partnership with GE and the use of the Six Sigma program as helping to make vital changes in the organization. "The Six Sigma program has provided everyone in the organization with a common language and toolbox for achieving our objectives. The methodology is sound, and we have begun to get buy-in from our medical staff, who are very results oriented and turned off by initiatives du jour. Our goal is to use Six Sigma to create an outstanding experience for our patients, which is the first priority of our Trustees."

All other "Belts" are 100% Six Sigma assignments and are selected from the top performers in our talent pipeline:

- Black Belts act as technical and cultural change agents for quality. They are leaders of small teams implementing/executing the Six Sigma methodology in business-related projects, and they coach Green Belts on their projects. Today there are more than 4,500 Black Belts within GE.
- Master Black Belts teach, mentor, and develop Six Sigma tools and are full-time teachers of the Six Sigma process. Today there are over 800 Master Black Belts within GE.
- Champions back and promote the Six Sigma initiative and work with executives to help drive initiatives into daily operations and business metrics.

The mentoring structure behind Six Sigma training and the full-time dedication of the Black Belts and Master Black Belts have provided the momentum necessary to complete thousands of projects at GE.

THE PAYBACK

To evaluate the payback of the significant commitment during the initial five-year implementation, we can look at individual projects and the cumulative results of thousands of projects.

One division recently reduced its annual expense for teleconferencing by $1.5 million encompassing a total of 19 million minutes. Another team cut

Variations on a Theme

There are a couple of variations to the DMAIC process we mentioned. One involves the opportunity-to create a Six Sigma process where there are existing processes in place. In this case, participants use a variation of DMAIC called Design for Six Sigma (DFSS).

Here's an example of an actual DFSS project that author Sridhar Seshadri completed in working to-ward his Green Belt certification. In this project, one of GE'S businesses developed and implemented an entire business plan to provide professional services ranging from project management, systems integration, and consulting services regarding installation of complex medical imaging systems.

Prior to this project, GE. typically installed such equipment with value-added services almost being an afterthought. The DFSS team—operating under the notion that the "whole solution" included hardware, software, and professional services—went through a formal DEFINE and MEASURE phase where customer requirements and analyses of the market were rigorously scrutinized.

The team then developed a business plan using a statistical modeling tool called Crystal Ball. The "stakeholders," including business leaders and other participants essential to making the project work, reviewed the business plan. Finally, the process was test-run at a few customer sites, then formalized and implemented.

So how is this different from a traditional rollout of a new project? First, DFSS applies a level of rigor not consistently seen in traditional business plans— consistent being the key word. Second, since Six Sigma is "institutionalized," everyone involved immediately understood the details of the project and could provide meaningful feedback and advice. Third, with project tracking the team was able to review similar projects across all of GE and learn from them. This set of services first implemented in the fall of 1999 is now routinely offered in over 90% of customer projects.

customer order processing time in half. As a rule of thumb, GE managers expect that each project will save between $50,000 and $150,000.

When talking about the payback associated with Six Sigma, think about popcorn. One kernel popping by itself (or one project completed) won't make much of a difference. But if you keep the heat on and thousands of kernels pop, you've multiplied the results exponentially. GE has kept the heat on now for five years, and the results are in. The following is a summary of some key performance measures at GE.

	SIX SIGMA BEGINS: 1995	FIVE YEARS LATER 2000
Annual Productivity Gain	1.5%	4.0%
Operating Margin	14.4%	18.4%
Inventory Turns	5.8%	9.2%

By internal calculations, the benefits of Six Sigma exceeded $2 billion in 2000. Certainly a four-to-one pay-back in quality and the associated savings resulting from reduced cycle times and defects would interest many considering similar options for their organizations.

The lesson we learned at GE is that there is definitely a payback. Complete dedication to the program and enterprise-wide implementation is attainable and rewarding in terms of quality, productivity, and the bottom line.

Greg Lucier is president and CEO of GE Medical Systems Information Technologies. With more than 15 years of technology management experience, he joined GE in 1995 as a manager of business development and later that year was named president and general manager of GE Transportation Systems, GE-Harris Railway Electronics. In 1999 he became vice president and general manager of global services at GE Medical Systems. He was promoted to his current position in August 2000. You can reach Greg at Greg.Lucier@med.ge.com.

Sridhar Seshadri is vice president and general manager of Healthcare Solutions with GE Medical Information Systems Information Technologies. He has held this position since July 2000. Before joining GE Medical Systems in 1998 as business manager, IT Services, he served as lead engineer, imaging systems, with the University of Pennsylvania's Radiology Department and launched the Medical Informatics Group, responsible for developing Picture Archiving and Communication Systems. You can reach Sridhar at Sridhar.Seshadri@med.ge.com.

Both authors hold Green Belts.

Chapter 17
Management Control and Strategic Performance Measurement

Cases

17-1 Industrial Chemicals Company (Control of Research and Development)
17-2 Full Versus Variable Costing and Ethical Issues
17-3 Strategic Performance Measurement
17-4 Strategic Performance Measurement: Employee Benefits
17-5 Contribution Income Statement

Readings

"Transforming the Balanced Scorecard from Performance Measurement to Strategic Management: Part 1"

This article explains the emerging role of the balanced scorecard—a change from a focus only on performance evaluation to a concern also for strategic management. Through the use of strategy maps, the authors show how the balanced scorecard can be used to inform the development of the firm's strategy and improve shareholder value. This is accomplished through the linking of the scorecard perspectives: from the learning and growth perspective to the internal perspective, then to the customer perspective, and finally to the financial perspective and shareholder value.

Discussion questions:

1. Give an example of a nonprofit or governmental organization that uses the balanced scorecard and explain how it links the scorecard to its overall strategy.
2. What is a Key Performance Indicator (KPI) scorecard and how does it differ from a balanced scorecard?
3. How can the balanced scorecard be used to supplement conventional financial reporting?
4. Explain the strategy map and how it is used.

Cases

17-1. Industrial Chemicals Company

In 19X5, events which were thought about and planned for the past several years in the Industrial Chemicals Company (ICC) culminated in the most significant change in the company's 80-plus year history. A major corporate restructuring was announced including the purchase of a large U.S. based pharmaceutical company, for $2.8 billion. ICC is a large multinational manufacturer of industrial chemicals. The parent company is located in Amsterdam, and manufacturing plants and customers are located worldwide.

In February of 19X6, the Chairman of the Board and Chief Executive Officer told a reporter of a major financial magazine: "We felt that if we were to build a strong technology base of biology and biotechnology that would simultaneously serve agriculture, animal nutrition, and health care, we could build a unique powerhouse backing it up in a way that companies in these individual businesses couldn't do; and we've built it." The changes initiated were thus not merely pruning and trimming, but changing the very direction of the company by getting out of commodity chemicals and into more innovative areas.

The magazine article made a key observation in its February 10, issue:

A major problem looms: Can ICC support the level of research needed to make a major impact in biotechnology? Earnings for the first three quarters of 19X5 dropped and the company expects to show a loss for the fourth quarter, even before write-offs on closed chemical plants.

The chairman of the board was well aware of this major concern. In fact, as 19X5 drew to a close, he commissioned a special subgroup of the Executive Management Committee (the EMC is the senior management group dealing with major strategic and operational issues) to review the company's overall R&D spending, its affordability and priorities, and bring back recommendations to the EMC in time for inclusion in the 19X6 budgeting process.

RESEARCH AND DEVELOPMENT

From a total corporate perspective, the R&D effort falls into three classifications:

Class I—Maintain existing businesses—

This effort is associated with managing existing business assets, maintaining competitiveness of products in existing businesses, and supplying technical service.

Class II—Expand existing businesses—

R&D associated with expanding existing business assets, expanding markets of existing products, or substantially lowering costs of existing processes.

Class III—Create new businesses—

R&D associated with creating new business assets.

Organizationally, each of the operating units administers its own R&D efforts which cut across all three categories above. In very simple terms, the operating unit is relatively self-sufficient across all three categories where technology *already exists*. They "purchase" some support services from the corporate R&D group as described later. In terms of performance assessment for incentive compensation, the operating unit R&D groups are tied to the "bottom-line" results achieved by the respective units.

CORPORATE R&D

The corporate R&D group, in addition to providing support services to the operating unit's R&D efforts, is primarily responsible for required *new technology* in creating new businesses. At the point in time in the product invention time line when new-technology-based products reach a level of commercial viability, these programs are "handed-off" to an operating unit R&D group for eventual movement to commercialization. In the past several years, this corporate R&D group has been successful in "inventing" and "handing off" commercial leads despite some operating unit reluctance to fund the research costs. In these instances, funding sometimes remained with corporate R&D after the "hand-off."

A more detailed description of the corporate R&D group follows. The corporate research and development group is headed by a senior vice president reporting to the Chairman of the Board and CEO. The central research laboratory group consists of an information center (20 percent of its costs are charged to operating units on a fee for service basis), an MIS facility, bioprocess development and cell culture groups (which are essentially involved in devising production processes for biotechnology-based products),

SUMMARY OF CORPORATE RESEARCH AND DEVELOPMENT

Research Laboratory Group
- Information Center
- MIS Facility
- Bioprocess Development and Cell Culture
- Physical Sciences Center
- Analytical Chemistry Group
- Chemistry Group

Biological Sciences Group

Patent Group

a physical sciences center (a central analytical chemistry group providing very specialized and highly skilled support to many users across the company—65 percent of this group's costs are charged out directly on a fee-for-service basis), a group called controlled delivery which develops vehicles for the transfer of pharmaceutical and animal science products into the living systems within which they must act, and a chemistry group providing very specialized skills in both conventional and biotechnology process chemistry (about 25 percent of this group's costs are charged directly on a fee-for-service basis). In addition to the direct fee-for-service chargeouts described above, a portion of the costs of this central laboratory group (primarily the bioprocess development and cell culture groups) is assigned to the biological sciences segment. The remaining costs, along with overall corporate R&D administrative costs, are allocated as a part of corporate charges.

The biological sciences group has been the major focal point for new technology in the pharmaceutical and animal sciences area. It supports plant sciences for the agricultural unit as well. The costs for the biological sciences group are reported as being for new direction basic research. Also controlled within corporate R&D and reported in this segment are costs of key university relationships supporting basic and applied biomedical, crop chemicals, and animal sciences research efforts.

The patent group has always been decentralized with a patent counsel and staff assigned to each operating unit reporting on a "dotted line" basis to the operating unit and administratively to the general patent counsel. Thus, about 80 percent of patent cost is already directly borne by operating units with the remainder allocated as part of corporate charges.

REQUIRED:

As the controller reflected on the information obtained and the important issues being addressed by the EMC subcommittee, the following questions surfaced in his mind. Develop a response for each question.

1. What is the role of R&D in the firm's overall strategy?

2. Would operating unit control of our key R&D growth programs enhance or mitigate our chances of meeting our goals? That is, should R&D be organized as cost SBUs within each of the operating units? What amount and type of R&D, if any at all, should be done at the corporate level?

3. I know there'll be pressure to level off our R&D spending across the company, including corporate R&D. We've got to make sure we get more for our money in terms of prioritizing those efforts to go after the most promising commercial opportunities if we're going to achieve our goals in biotechnology! How can we be sure we're prioritizing these efforts toward increased commercial success? That is, how do we evaluate the effectiveness of both the R&D cost SBUs in the operating units and corporate-level R&D?

4. How does the fact that ICC operates in several different countries affect the decisions the controller is facing?

(IMA adapted)

17-2. Full Versus Variable Costing and Ethical Issues

HeadGear, Inc is a small manufacturer of headphones for use in commercial and personal applications. The HeadGear headphones are known for their outstanding sound quality and light weight, which makes them highly desirable especially in the commercial market for telemarketing firms and similar communication applications, despite the relatively high price. Although demand has grown steadily, profits have grown much more slowly, and John Hurley, the CEO, suspects productivity is falling, and costs are rising out of hand. John is concerned that the decline in profit growth will affect the stock price of the company and inhibit the firm's efforts to raise new investment capital, which will be needed to continue the firm's growth. While the firm is now operating at 68% of available production capacity, John thinks the market growth will soon exceed available capacity.

To improve profitability, John has decided to bring in a new COO with the objective of improving profitability very quickly. The new COO understands that profits must be improved within the coming 10-18 months. A bonus of 10% of profit improvement is promised the new COO if this goal is achieved. The following is the income statement for HeadGear for 2002, from the most recent annual report. Product costs for HeadGear include $25 per unit variable manufacturing costs and $1,920,000 per year fixed manufacturing overhead. Budgeted production was 120,000 units in 2002. Selling and administrative costs include a variable portion of $15 per unit and a fixed portion of $2,400,0000 per year. The same units costs and production level are also applicable for 2001.

HeadGear Inc. Income Statement for the Period Ended 12/31/2002		
Sales (125,000 @$75)		$ 9,375,000
Cost of Sales:		
Beginning Inv: 5,000 @ $41	$ 205,000	
Cost of Production: 120,000 @ $41	4,920,000	
Goods Available: 130,000	$5,125,000	
Less Ending Inv: 0 @ $41	-0-	$5,125,000
Gross Margin		$4,250,000
Selling and Administrative		
Variable Costs: 125,000 @ $15	$ 1,875,000	
Fixed Costs	2,400,000	$4,275,000
Net loss		$ <25,000>

The new COO is convinced that the problem is the need to aggressively market the product, and that the apparent decline in productivity is really due to underutilization of capacity. The COO increases fixed manufacturing costs to $2,100,000 and variable selling costs to $16 per unit and fixed selling costs to $2,750,000 to help achieve this goal. Budgeted sales and production for 2003 are set at 175,000 units.

Actual production was 175,000 as planned but sales for 2003 turned out to be only 140,000 units, short of the target. The new COO claims that profits have increased considerably, and is looking forward to the promised bonus.

REQUIRED:

1. Calculate the absorption cost net income for 2003, assuming the new selling costs, and that manufacturing costs remain the same as 2002.
2. Calculate the variable cost net income for 2003 and explain why it is different from the absorption cost net income.
3. Is the new COO due a bonus? Comment on the effectiveness of Hurley's plan to improve profits by hiring the new COO and promising the bonus.
4. Identify and explain any important ethical issues you see in this case.

17-3. Strategic Performance Measurement

Johnson Supply Company is a large retailer of office supplies. It is organized into six regional divisions, five within the United States, and one international division. The firm is growing steadily, with the greatest growth in the international division. Johnson evaluates each division as a profit SBU. Revenues and direct costs of the divisions are traced to each division using a centralized accounting system. The various support departments, including human resources, information technology, accounting, and marketing, are treated as cost SBUs and the costs are allocated to the divisions on the basis of sales revenues. The international division has cash, receivables, payables, and other investments in foreign currencies. As a result, this division experiences occasional significant losses and gains due to fluctuations in the value of foreign currencies. Based on the idea that these effects are uncontrollable, the effects of currency changes on the international division is retained in a single home-office account and is not traced to the division. Similarly, taxes paid by this division to other countries is pooled in a home office account and is not traced to it.

Because of rapidly increasing costs in the information technology (IT) department, Johnson's top management is considering changing this department to a profit SBU. IT would set prices for its services, and the user divisions could choose to purchase these services from IT or from a vendor outside the firm. The manager of IT is upset at the idea, and has told top management that this move would eventually create chaotic and ineffective information services within the firm.

REQUIRED:

1. Should Johnson's six divisions be treated as profit SBUs or some other type of strategic performance measurement system? Explain.
2. Comment on the firm's decision not to trace currency gains and losses and foreign tax expense to the international division.
3. Comment on the firm's consideration of changing the IT department from a cost SBU to a profit SBU. What are the likely effects on the firm and on the IT department?

17-4. Strategic Performance Measurement: Employee Benefits

In its thirteen year of operations, Mount Drake Software is reviewing the methods it has used to evaluate its profit SBUs. Mount Drake has six product divisions, each of which is a profit SBU, and each markets specialized software products to specific customer groups. For example, one unit markets software systems to dental practices, and another provides software for real estate management firms. A critical factor in Mount Drake's success is the commitment and competence of its systems development and programming staff. While there is a relatively high turnover for these employees, Mount Drake has managed to retain the very best and to attract the very best. In recent months, as their business has grown, and as the software industry generally has grown significantly, it has become more and more difficult for Mount Drake to attract and to retain the best staff. Mount Drake is looking for ways to become more competitive in attracting and retaining these employees. One idea is to increase employee benefits by adding training opportunities, additional paid vacation, stock investment programs, and improved health insurance. The cost of some of these additional benefits could be traced directly to the divisions, while the cost of other benefits (such as improved group health coverage and company-wide training programs) could not be directly traced to the divisions.

REQUIRED:

How should Mount Drake handle employee benefits within its current performance measurement system? Should Mount Drake change the performance measurement system, and if so, how should it be changed?

17-5. Contribution Income Statement

Cathy's Classic Clothes is a retail organization that sells to professional women in the Northeast. The firm leases space for stores in upscale shopping centers, and the organizational structure consists of regions, districts, and stores. Each region consists of two or more districts; each district consists of three or more stores. Each store, district, and region has been established as a profit center. At all levels, the company uses a management by objective (MBO) system and a responsibility accounting system that focuses on information and knowledge rather than blame and control. Each year, managers, in consultation with their supervisors, establish goals which are not solely financial, and these goals are integrated into the budget. Actual performance is measured each month.

The Northeast Region consists of Districts A and B. District A consists of three stores, 1, 2, and 3 with District B consisting of three stores, 4, 5, and 6. District A's performance has not been up to expectations in the past. For the month of May, the district manager has set performance goals with the managers of Stores 1 and 2 who will receive bonuses if certain performance measures are exceeded. The manager of Store 3 decided not to participate in the bonus scheme. Since the district manager is unsure what type of bonus will encourage better performance, the manager of Store 1 will receive a bonus based on sales in excess of budgeted sales of $570,000 while the manager of Store 2 will receive a bonus based on net income in excess of budgeted net income. The company's net income goal for each store is 12 percent of sales. The budgeted sales for Store 2 are $530,000.

Other pertinent data for the month of May 2004 are given below.

- At Store 1, sales are 40 percent of District A sales while sales at Store 2 are 35 percent of District A sales. The cost of goods sold at both Stores 1 and 2 is 42 percent of sales.
- Variable selling expenses (sales commissions) are 6 percent of sales for all stores, districts, and regions.
- Variable administrative expenses are 2.5 percent of sales for all stores, districts, and regions.
- Maintenance cost includes janitorial and repair services and is a direct cost for each store. The store manager has complete control over this outlay; however, this cost should not be below one percent of sales.
- Advertising is considered a direct cost for each store and is completely under the control of the store manager. Store 1 spent two-thirds of District A's total outlay for advertising which was ten times more than Store 2 spent on advertising.
- The rental expenses at Store 1 are 40 percent of District A's total while Store 2 incurs 30 percent of District A's total.
- District expenses are allocated to the stores based on sales.

REQUIRED:

1. Complete the May 2004 performance report for District A and Stores 1 and 2.
2. Discuss the impact of the responsibility accounting system and bonus structure on the manager's behavior and the effect of this behavior on the financial results for Store 1 and Store 2.

Readings

TRANSFORMING THE BALANCED SCORECARD FROM PERFORMANCE MEASUREMENT TO STRATEGIC MANAGEMENT: PART I

Robed S. Kaplan and David P. Norton
Robert S. Kaplan is a Professor at Harvard University and David P. Norton is founder and president of the Balanced Scorecard Collaborative in Lincoln, Massachusetts.[1]

Several years ago we introduced the Balanced Scorecard (Kaplan and Norton 1992). We began with the premise that an exclusive reliance on financial measures in a management system is insufficient. Financial measures are lag indicators that report on the outcomes from past actions. Exclusive reliance on financial indicators could promote behavior that sacrifices long-term value creation for short-term performance (Porter 1992; AICPA 1994). The Balanced Scorecard approach retains measures of financial performance—the lagging outcome indicators—but supplements these with measures on the drivers, the lead indicators, of future financial performance.

THE BALANCED SCORECARD EMERGES

The limitations of managing solely with financial measures, however, have been known for decades.[2] What is different now? Why has the Balanced Scorecard concept been so widely adopted by manufacturing and service companies, nonprofit organizations, and government entities around the world since its introduction in 1992?

First, previous systems that incorporated nonfinancial measurements used *ad hoc* collections of such measures, more like checklists of measures for managers to keep track of and improve than a comprehensive system of linked measurements. The Balanced Scorecard emphasizes the linkage of measurement to strategy (Kaplan and Norton 1993) and the cause-and-effect linkages that describe the hypotheses of the strategy (Kaplan and Norton 1996b). The tighter connection between the measurement system and strategy elevates the role for nonfinancial measures from an operational checklist to a comprehensive system for strategy implementation (Kaplan and Norton 1996a).

Second, the Balanced Scorecard reflects the changing nature of technology and competitive advantage in the latter decades of the 20th century. In the industrial-age competition of the 19th and much of the 20th centuries, companies achieved competitive advantage from their investment in and management of tangible assets such as inventory, property, plant, and equipment (Chandler 1990). In an economy dominated by tangible assets, financial measurements were adequate to record investments on companies' balance sheets. Income statements could also capture the expenses associated with the use of these tangible assets to produce revenues and profits. But by the end of the 20th century, intangible assets became the major source for competitive advantage. In 1982, tangible book values represented 62 percent of industrial organizations' market values; ten years later, the ratio had plummeted to 38 percent (Blair 1995). By the end of the 20th century, the book value of tangible assets accounted for less than 20 percent of companies' market values (Webber 2000, quoting research by Baruch Lev).

Clearly, strategies for creating value shifted from managing tangible assets to knowledge-based strategies that create and deploy an organization's intangible assets. These include customer relationships, innovative products and services, high-quality and responsive operating processes, skills and knowledge of the workforce, the information technology that sup-

---

[1] This article is adapted from R. S. Kaplan and D. P. Norton (2001a, 2000). © 2001 American Accounting Association, *Accounting Horizons*, Vol. 15 No.1, March 2001, pp. 87-104

[2] For example, General Electric attempted a system of nonfinancial measurements in the 1950s (Greenwood 1974), and the French developed the Tableaux de Bord decades ago (Lebas 1994; Epstein and Manzoni1998).

ports the work force and links the firm to its customers and suppliers, and the organizational climate that encourages innovation, problem-solving, and improvement. But companies were unable to adequately measure their intangible assets (Johnson and Kaplan 1987, 201-202). Anecdotal data from management publications indicated that many companies could not implement their new strategies in this environment (Kiechel 1982; Charan and Colvin 1999). They could not manage what they could not describe or measure.

INTANGIBLE ASSETS: VALUATION VS. VALUE CREATION

Some call for accountants to make an organization's intangible assets more visible to managers and investors by placing them on a company's balance sheet. But several factors prevent valid valuation of intangible assets on balance sheets.

First, the value from intangible assets is indirect. Assets such as knowledge and technology seldom have a direct impact on revenue and profit. Improvements in intangible assets affect financial outcomes through chains of cause-and-effect relationships involving two or three intermediate stages (Huselid 1995; Becker and Huselid 1998). For example, consider the linkages in the service management profit chain (Heskett et al.1994):

- investments in employee training lead to improvements in service quality
- better service quality leads to higher customer satisfaction
- higher customer satisfaction leads to increased customer loyalty
- increased customer loyalty generates increased revenues and margins

Financial outcomes are separated causally and temporally from improving employees' capabilities. The complex linkages make it difficult, if not impossible, to place a financial value on an asset such as workforce capabilities or employee morale, much less to measure period-to-period changes in that financial value.

Second, the value from intangible assets depends on organizational context and strategy. This value cannot be separated from the organizational processes that transform intangibles into customer and financial outcomes. The balance sheet is a linear, additive model. It records each class of asset separately and calculates the total by adding up each asset's recorded value. The value created from investing in individual intangible assets, however, is neither linear nor additive.

Senior investment bankers in a firm such as Goldman Sachs are immensely valuable because of their knowledge about complex financial products and their capabilities for managing relationships and developing trust with sophisticated customers. People with the same knowledge, experience, and capabilities, however, are nearly worthless to a financial services company such as etrade.com that emphasizes operational efficiency, low cost, and technology-based trading. The value of an intangible asset depends critically on the context—the organization, the strategy, and other complementary assets—in which the intangible asset is deployed.

Intangible assets seldom have value by themselves.[3] Generally, they must be bundled with other intangible and tangible assets to create value. For example, a new growth-oriented sales strategy could require new knowledge about customers, new training for sales employees, new databases, new information systems, a new organization structure, and a new incentive compensation program. Investing in just one of these capabilities, or in all of them but one, could cause the new sales strategy to fail. The value does not reside in any individual intangible asset. It arises from creating the entire set of assets along with a strategy that links them together. The value-creation process is multiplicative, not additive.

THE BALANCED SCORECARD SUPPLEMENTS CONVENTIONAL FINANCIAL REPORTING

Companies' balance sheets report separately on tangible assets, such as raw material, land, and equipment, based on their historic cost—the traditional financial accounting method. This was adequate for industrial-age companies, which succeeded by combining and transforming their tangible resources into products whose value exceeded their acquisition and production costs. Financial accounting conventions relating to depreciation and cost of goods sold enabled an income statement to measure how much value was created beyond the costs incurred to acquire and transform tangible assets into finished products and services.

Some argue that companies should follow the same cost-based convention for their intangible assets—capitalize and subsequently amortize the expenditures on training employees, conducting research and development, purchasing and developing databases, and advertising that creates brand awareness. But such costs are poor approximations of the realizable value created by investing in these intangible assets. Intangible assets can create value for or-

[3] Brand names, which can be sold, are an exception.

ganizations, but that does not imply that they have separable market values. Many internal and linked organizational processes, such as design, delivery, and service, are required to transform the potential value of intangible assets into products and services that have tangible value.

We introduced the Balanced Scorecard to provide a new framework for describing value-creating strategies that link intangible and tangible assets. The scorecard does not attempt to "value" an organization's intangible assets, but it does measure these assets in units other than currency. The Balanced Scorecard describes how intangible assets get mobilized and combined with intangible and tangible assets to create differentiating customer-value propositions and superior financial outcomes.

STRATEGY MAPS

Since introducing the Balanced Scorecard in 1992, we have helped over 200 executive teams design their scorecard programs. Initially we started with a clean sheet of paper, asking, "what is the strategy," and allowed the strategy and the Balanced Scorecard to emerge from interviews and discussions with the senior executives. The scorecard provided a framework for organizing strategic objectives into the four perspectives displayed in Figure 1:

1. *Financial*—the strategy for growth, profitability, and risk viewed from the perspective of the shareholder.
2. *Customer*—the strategy for creating value and differentiation from the perspective of the customer.
3. *Internal Business Processes*—the strategic priorities for various business processes that create customer and shareholder satisfaction.
4. *Learning and Growth*—the priorities to create a climate that supports organizational change, innovation, and growth.

From this initial base of experience, we subsequently developed a general framework for describing and implementing strategy that we believe can be as useful as the traditional framework of income statement, balance sheet, and statement of cash flows for financial planning and reporting. The new framework, which we call a "Strategy Map," is a logical and comprehensive architecture for describing strategy, as illustrated in Figure 2. A strategy map specifies the critical elements and their linkages for an organization's strategy.

- Objectives for growth and productivity to enhance shareholder value.
- Market and account share, acquisition, and retention of targeted customers where profitable growth will occur.
- Value propositions that would lead customers to do more higher-margin business with the company.
- Innovation and excellence in products, services, and processes that deliver the value proposition to targeted customer segments, promote operational improvements, and meet community expectations and regulatory requirements.
- Investments required in people and systems to generate and sustain growth.

By translating their strategy into the logical architecture of a strategy map and Balanced Scorecard, organizations create a common and understandable point of reference for all organizational units and employees.

Organizations build strategy maps from the top down, starting with the destination and then charting the routes that lead there. Corporate executives first review their mission statement, why their company exists, and core values, what their company believes in. From that information, they develop their strategic vision, what their company wants to become. This vision creates a clear picture of the company's overall goal, which could be to become a top-quartile performer. The strategy identifies the path intended to reach that destination.

FINANCIAL PERSPECTIVE

The typical destination for profit-seeking enterprises is a significant increase in shareholder value (we will discuss the modifications for nonprofit and government organizations later in the paper). Companies increase economic value through two basic approaches—revenue *growth* and *productivity*.[4] A revenue growth strategy generally has two components: build the franchise with revenue from new markets, new products, and new customers; and increase sales to existing customers by deepening relationships with them, including cross-selling multiple products and services, and offering complete solutions. A productivity strategy also generally has two components: improve the cost structure by lowering direct and indirect expenses; and utilize assets more efficiently by

[4] Shareholder value can also be increased through managing the right-hand side of the balance sheet, such as by repurchasing shares and choosing the low-cost mix among debt and equity instruments to lower the cost of capital. In this paper, we focus only on improved management of the organization's assets (tangible and intangible).

FIGURE 1

The Balanced Scorecard Defines a Strategy's Cause-and-Effect Relationships

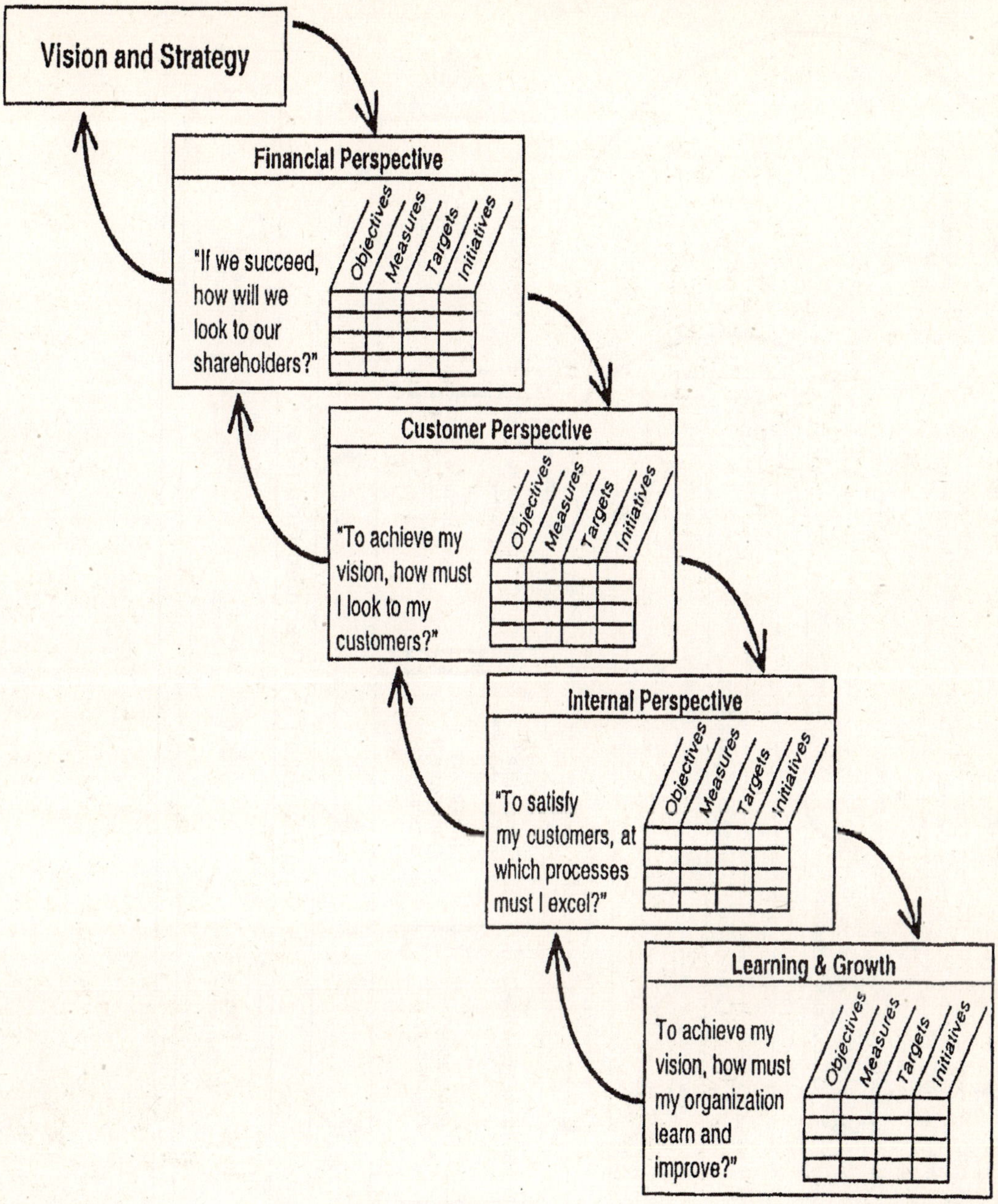

FIGURE 2
The Balanced Scorecard Strategy Map

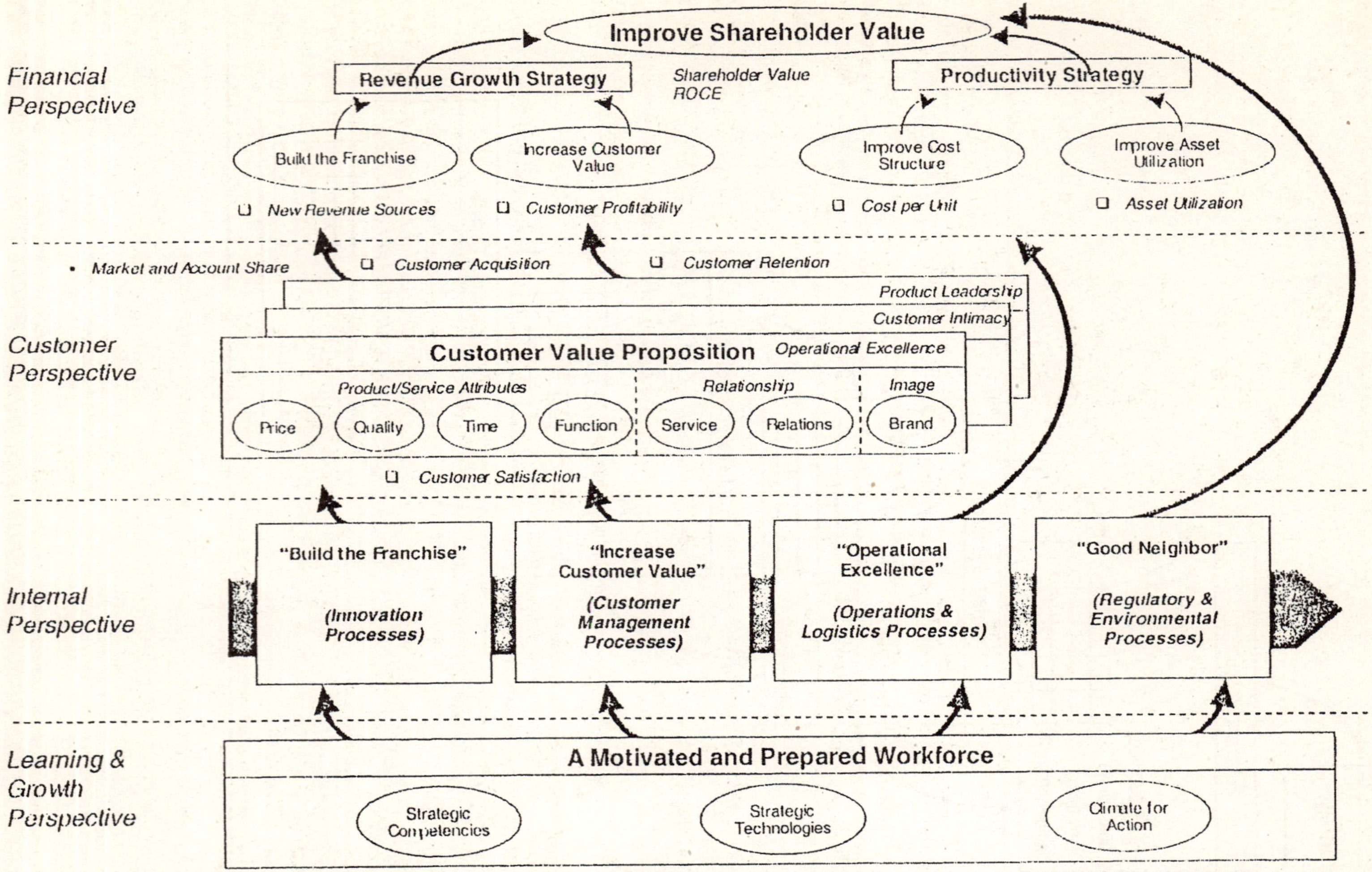

reducing the working and fixed capital needed to support a given level of business.

CUSTOMER PERSPECTIVE

The core of any business strategy is the *customer-value proposition,* which describes the unique mix of product, price, service, relationship, and image that a company offers. It defines how the organization differentiates itself from competitors to attract, retain, and deepen relationships with targeted customers. The value proposition is crucial because it helps an organization connect its internal processes to improved outcomes with its customers.

Companies differentiate their value proposition by selecting among *operational excellence* (for example, McDonalds and Dell Computer), *customer intimacy* (Home Depot and IBM in the 1960s and 1970s), and *product leadership* (Intel and Sony) (Treacy and Wiersema 1997, 31-45). Sustainable strategies are based on excelling at one of the three while maintaining threshold standards with the other two. After identifying its value proposition, a company knows which classes and types of customers to target.

Specifically, companies that pursue a strategy of operational excellence need to excel at competitive pricing, product quality, product selection, lead time, and on-time delivery. For customer intimacy, an organization must stress the quality of its relationships with customers, including exceptional service, and the completeness and suitability of the solutions it offers individual customers. Companies that pursue a product-leadership strategy must concentrate on the functionality, features, and performance of their products and services.

The customer perspective also identifies the intended outcomes from delivering a differentiated value proposition. These would include market share in targeted customer segments, account share with targeted customers, acquisition and retention of customers in the targeted segments, and customer profitability.[5]

INTERNAL PROCESS PERSPECTIVE

Once an organization has a clear picture of its customer and financial perspectives, it can determine the means by which it will achieve the differentiated value proposition for customers and the productivity improvements for the financial objectives. The internal business perspective captures these critical organizational activities, which fall into four high-level processes:

1. *Build the franchise* by spurring innovation to develop new products and services and to penetrate new markets and customer segments.
2. *Increase customer value* by expanding and deepening relationships with existing customers.
3. *Achieve operational excellence* by improving supply-chain management, internal processes, asset utilization, resource-capacity management, and other processes.
4. *Become a good corporate citizen* by establishing effective relationships with external stakeholders.

Many companies that espouse a strategy calling for innovation or for developing value-adding customer relationships mistakenly choose to measure their internal business processes by focusing only on the cost and quality of their operations. These companies have a complete disconnect between their strategy and how they measure it. Not surprisingly, organizations encounter great difficulty implementing growth strategies when their primary internal measurements emphasize process improvements, not innovation or enhanced customer relationships.

The financial benefits from improvements to the different business processes typically occur in stages. Cost savings from increases in *operational efficiencies* and process improvements deliver short-term benefits. Revenue growth from enhancing *customer relationships* accrues in the intermediate term. Increased *innovation* generally produces long-term revenue and margin improvements. Thus, a complete strategy should generate returns from all three high-level internal processes.

LEARNING AND GROWTH PERSPECTIVE

The final region of a strategy map is the learning and growth perspective, which is the foundation of any strategy. In the learning and growth perspective, managers define the employee capabilities and skills, technology, and corporate climate needed to support a strategy. These objectives enable a company to align its human resources and information technology with the strategic requirements from its critical internal business processes, differentiated value proposition, and customer relationships. After addressing the learning and growth perspective, companies have a complete strategy map with linkages across the four major perspectives.

Strategy maps, beyond providing a common framework for describing and building strategies, also are powerful diagnostic tools, capable of detecting flaws in organizations' Balanced Scorecards. For ex-

[5] Measurement of customer profitability (Kaplan and Cooper 1998, 181-201) provides one of the connections between the Balanced Scorecard and activity-based costing.

ample, Figure 3 shows the strategy map for the Revenue Growth theme of Mobil North America Marketing & Refining. When senior management compared the scorecards being used by its business units to this template, it found one unit with no objective or measure for dealers, an omission immediately obvious from looking at its strategy map. Had this unit discovered how to bypass dealers and sell gasoline directly to end-use consumers? Were dealer relationships no longer strategic for this unit? The business unit shown in the lower right corner of Figure 3 did not mention quality on its scorecard. Again, had this unit already achieved six sigma quality levels so quality was no longer a strategic priority? Mobil's executive team used its divisional strategy map to identify and remedy gaps in the strategies being implemented at lower levels of the organization.

STAKEHOLDER AND KEY PERFORMANCE INDICATOR SCORECARDS

Many organizations claim to have a Balanced Scorecard because they use a mixture of financial and nonfinancial measures. Such measurement systems are certainly more "balanced" than ones that use financial measures alone. Yet, the assumptions and philosophies underlying these scorecards are quite different from those underlying the strategy scorecards and maps described above. We observe two other scorecard types frequently used in practice: the *stakeholder scorecard* and the *key performance indicator scorecard.*

STAKEHOLDER SCORECARDS

The *stakeholder scorecard* identifies the major constituents of the organization—shareholders, customers. and employees—and frequently other constituents such as suppliers and the community. The scorecard defines the organization's goals for these different constituents, or stakeholders, and develops an appropriate scorecard of measures and targets for them (Atkinson and Waterhouse 1997). For example, Sears built its initial scorecard around three themes:

- "a compelling place to shop"
- "a compelling place to work"
- "a compelling place to invest"

Citicorp used a similar structure for its initial scorecard—"a good place to work, to bank, and to invest." AT&T developed an elaborate internal measurement system based on financial value-added, customer value-added, and people value-added.

All these companies built their measurements around their three dominant constituents—customers, shareholders, and employees—emphasizing satisfaction measures for customers and employees, to ensure that these constituents felt well served by the company. In this sense, they were apparently *balanced.* Comparing these scorecards to the strategy map template in Figure 2 we can easily detect what is missing from such scorecards: no objectives or measures for *how* these balanced goals are to be achieved. A vision describes a desired outcome; a strategy, however, must describe *how* the outcome will be achieved, how employees, customers, and shareholders will be satisfied. Thus, a stakeholder scorecard is not adequate to describe the strategy of an organization and, therefore, is not an adequate foundation on which to build a management system.

Missing from the stakeholder card are the drivers to achieve the goals. Such drivers include an explicit value proposition such as innovation that generates new products and services or enhanced customer management processes, the deployment of technology, and the specific skills and competencies of employees required to implement the strategy. In a well-constructed *strategy scorecard,* the value proposition in the customer perspective, all the processes in the internal perspective, and the learning and growth perspective components of the scorecard define the "how" that is as fundamental to strategy as the outcomes that the strategy is expected to achieve.

Stakeholder scorecards are often a first step on the road to a strategy scorecard. But as organizations begin to work with stakeholder cards, they inevitably confront the question of "how." This leads to the next level of strategic thinking and scorecard design. Both Sears and Citicorp quickly moved beyond their stakeholder scorecards, developing an insightful set of internal process objectives to complete the description of their strategy and, ultimately, achieving a strategy Balanced Scorecard. The stakeholder scorecard can also be useful in organizations that do not have internal synergies across business units. Since each business has a different set of internal drivers, this "corporate" scorecard need only focus on the desired outcomes for the corporation's constituencies, including the community and suppliers. Each business unit then defines how it will achieve those goals with its business unit strategy scorecard and strategy map.

KEY PERFORMANCE INDICATOR SCORECARDS

Key Performance Indicator (KPI) scorecards are also common. The total quality management approach and variants such as the Malcolm Baldrige and European Foundation for Quality Management (EFQM) awards generate many measures to monitor internal processes. When migrating to a "Balanced Scorecard,"

FIGURE 3

Mobil Uses Reverse Engineering of a Strategy Map as a Strategy Diagnostic

The Template (Strategy Map: Partial)

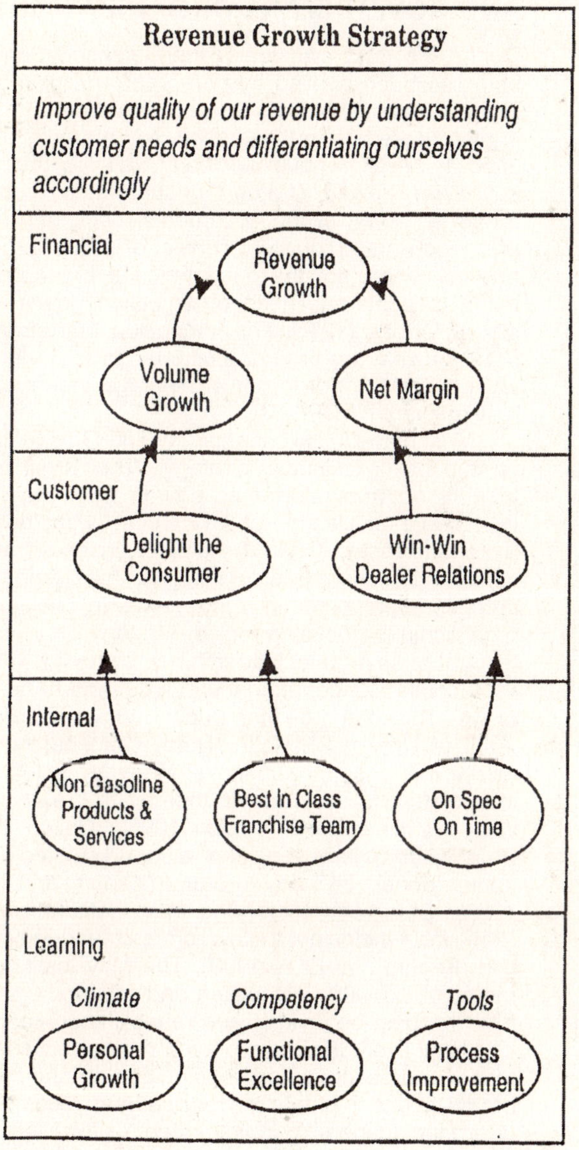

SBU A: "Did we eliminate the dealer?"

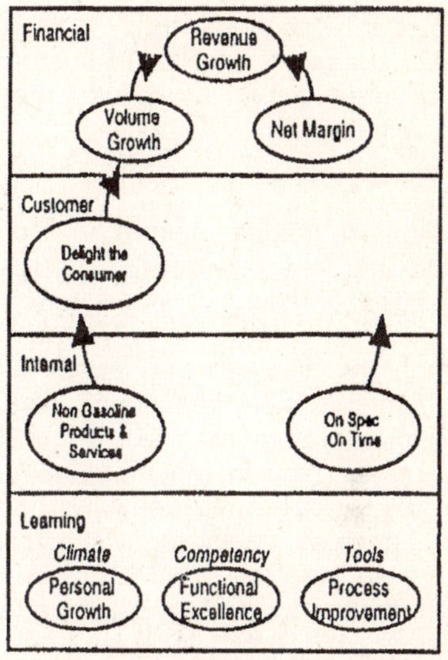

SBU B: "Have we achieved perfection?"

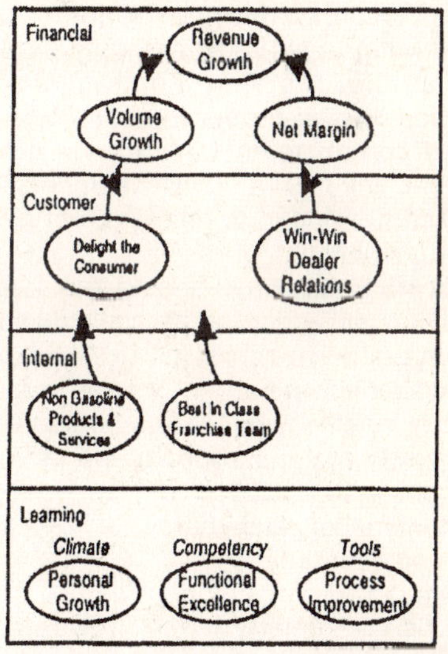

organizations often build on the base already established by classifying their existing measurements into the four BSC categories. KPI scorecards also emerge when the organization's information technology group, which likes to put the company database at the heart of any change program, triggers the scorecard design. Consulting organizations that sell and install large systems, especially so-called executive information systems, also offer KPI scorecards.

As a simple example of a KPI scorecard, a financial service organization articulated the 4Ps for its "balanced scorecard:"

1. Profits
2. Portfolio (size of loan volume)
3. Process (percent processes ISO certified)
4. People (meeting diversity goals in hiring)

Although this scorecard is more balanced than one using financial measures alone, comparing the 4P measures to a strategy map like that in Figure 2 reveals the major gaps in the measurement set. The company has no customer measures and only a single internal-process measure, which focuses on an initiative not an outcome. This KPI scorecard has no role for information technology (strange for a financial service organization), no linkages from the internal measure (ISO process certification) to a customer-value proposition or to a customer outcome, and no linkage from the learning and growth measure (diverse work force) to improving an internal process, a customer outcome, or a financial outcome.

KPI scorecards are most helpful for departments and teams when a strategic program already exists at a higher level. In this way, the diverse indicators enable individuals and teams to define what they must do well to contribute to higher level goals. Unless, however, the link to strategy is clearly established, the KPI scorecard will lead to local but not global or strategic improvements.

Balanced Scorecards should not just be collections of financial and nonfinancial measures, organized into three to five perspectives. The best Balanced Scorecards reflect the strategy of the organization. A good test is whether you can understand the strategy by looking only at the scorecard and its strategy map. Many organizations fail this test, especially those that create stakeholder scorecards or key performance indicator scorecards.

Strategy scorecards along with their graphical representations on strategy maps provide a logical and comprehensive way to describe strategy. They communicate clearly the organization's desired outcomes and its hypotheses about how these outcomes can be achieved. For example, *if* we improve on-time delivery, *then* customer satisfaction will improve; *if* customer satisfaction improves, *then* customers will purchase more. The scorecards enable all organizational units and employees to understand the strategy and identify how they can contribute by becoming aligned to the strategy.

APPLYING THE BSC TO NONPROFITS AND GOVERNMENT ORGANIZATIONS

During the past five years, the Balanced Scorecard has also been applied by non-profit and government organizations (NPGOs). One of the barriers to applying the scorecard to these sectors is the considerable difficulty NPGOs have in clearly defining their strategy. We reviewed "strategy" documents of more than 50 pages. Most of the documents, once the mission and vision are articulated, consist of lists of programs and initiatives, not the outcomes the organization is trying to achieve. These organizations must understand Porter's (1996, 77) admonition that strategy is not only what the organization intends to do, but also what it decides *not* to do, a message that is particularly relevant for NPGOs.

Most of the initial scorecards of NPGOs feature an operational excellence strategy. The organizations take their current mission as a given and try to do their work more efficiently—at lower cost, with fewer defects, and faster. Often the project builds off of a recently introduced quality initiative that emphasizes process improvements. It is unusual to find nonprofit organizations focusing on a strategy that can be thought of as product leadership or customer intimacy. As a consequence, their scorecards tend to be closer to the KPI scorecards than true strategy scorecards.

The City of Charlotte, North Carolina, however, followed a customer-based strategy by selecting an interrelated set of strategic themes to create distinct value for its citizens (Kaplan 199S). United Way of Southeastern New England also articulated a customer (donor) intimacy strategy (Kaplan and Kaplan 1996). Other nonprofits—the May Institute and New Profit Inc.—selected a clear product-leadership position (Kaplan and Elias 1999). The May Institute uses partnerships with universities and researchers to deliver the best behavioral and rehabilitation care delivery. New Profit Inc. introduces a new selection, monitoring, and governing process unique among nonprofit organizations. Montefiore Hospital uses a combination of product leadership in its centers of excellence, and excellent customer relationships—through its new patient-oriented care centers—to build market share in its local area (Kaplan 2001). These examples demonstrate that NPGOs can be strategic and build competitive advantage in ways other than pure operational excellence. But it takes vision and leadership to move from continuous improvement of existing processes to thinking strategically about which processes and activities are most important for fulfilling the organization's mission.

MODIFYING THE ARCHITECTURE OF THE BALANCED SCORECARD

Most NPGOs had difficulty with the original architecture of the Balanced Scorecard that placed the financial perspective at the top of the hierarchy. Given that achieving financial success is not the primary objective for most of these organizations, many rearrange the scorecard to place customers or constituents at the top of the hierarchy.

In a private-sector transaction, the customer plays two distinct roles—paying for the service and receiving the service—that are so complementary most people don't even think about them separately. But in a nonprofit organization, donors provide the financial resources—they pay for the service—while another group, the constituents, receives the service. Who is the customer—the one paying or the one receiving? Rather than have to make such a Solomonic decision, organizations place both the donor perspective and the recipient perspective, in parallel, at the top of their Balanced Scorecards. They develop objectives for both donors and recipients, and then identify the internal processes that deliver desired value propositions for both groups of "customers."

In fact, nonprofit and government agencies should consider placing an over-arching objective at the top of their scorecard that represents their long-term objective such as a reduction in poverty or illiteracy, or improvements in the environment. Then the objectives within the scorecard can be oriented toward improving such a high-level objective. High-level financial measures provide private sector companies with an accountability measure to their owners, the shareholders. For a nonprofit or government agency, however, the financial measures are not the relevant indicators of whether the agency is delivering on its mission. The agency's mission should be featured and measured at the highest level of its scorecard. Placing an over-arching objective on the BSC for a nonprofit or government agency communicates clearly the long-term mission of the organization as portrayed in Figure 4.

Even the financial and customer objectives, however, may need to be re-examined for governmental organizations. Take the case of regulatory and enforcement agencies that monitor and punish violations of environmental, safety, and health regulations. These agencies, which detect transgressions, and fine or arrest those who violate the laws and regulations, cannot look to their "immediate customers" for satisfaction and loyalty measures. Clearly not the true "customers" for such organizations are the citizens at large who benefit from effective but not harsh or idiosyncratic enforcement of laws and regulations. Figure 5 shows a modified framework in which a government agency has three high-level perspectives:

1. *Cost Incurred:* This perspective emphasizes the importance of operational efficiency. The measured cost should include both the expenses of the agency and the social cost it imposes on citizens and other organizations through its operations. For example, an environmental agency imposes remediation costs on private-sector organizations. These are part of the costs of having the agency carry out its mission. The agency should minimize the direct and social costs required to achieve the benefits called for by its mission.
2. *Value Created:* This perspective identifies the benefits being created by the agency to citizens and is the most problematic and difficult to measure. It is usually difficult to financially quantify the benefits from improved education, reduced pollution, better health, less congestion, and safer neighborhoods. But the balanced scorecard still enables organizations to identify the outputs, if not the outcomes, from its activities, and to measure these outputs. Surrogates for value created could include percentage of students acquiring specific skills and knowledge; density of pollutants in water, air, or land; improved morbidity and mortality in targeted populations; crime rates and perception of public safety; and transportation times. In general, public-sector organizations may find they use more output than outcome measures. The citizens and their representatives—elected officials and legislators—will eventually make the judgments about the benefits from these outputs vs. their costs.
3. *Legitimizing Support:* An important "customer" for any government agency will be its "donor," the organization—typically the legislature—that provides the funding for the agency. In order to assure continued funding for its activities, the agency must strive to meet the objectives of its funding source—the legislature and, ultimately, citizens and taxpayers.

FIGURE 4

Adapting the Balanced Scorecard Framework to Nonprofit Organizations

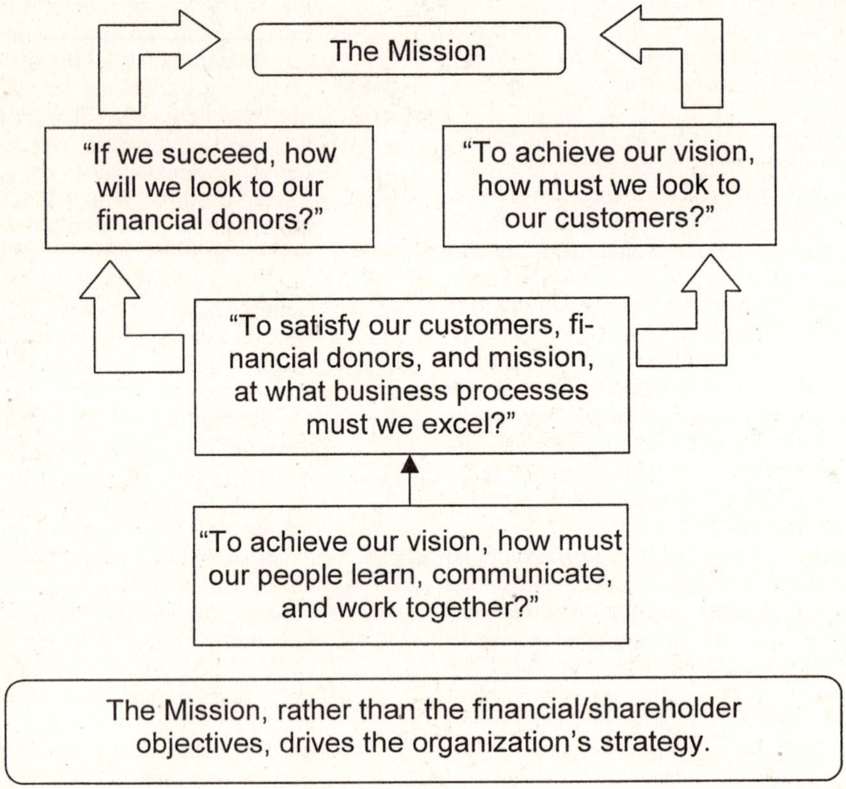

FIGURE 5
The Financial/Customer Objectives for Public Sector Agencies May Require Three Different Perspectives

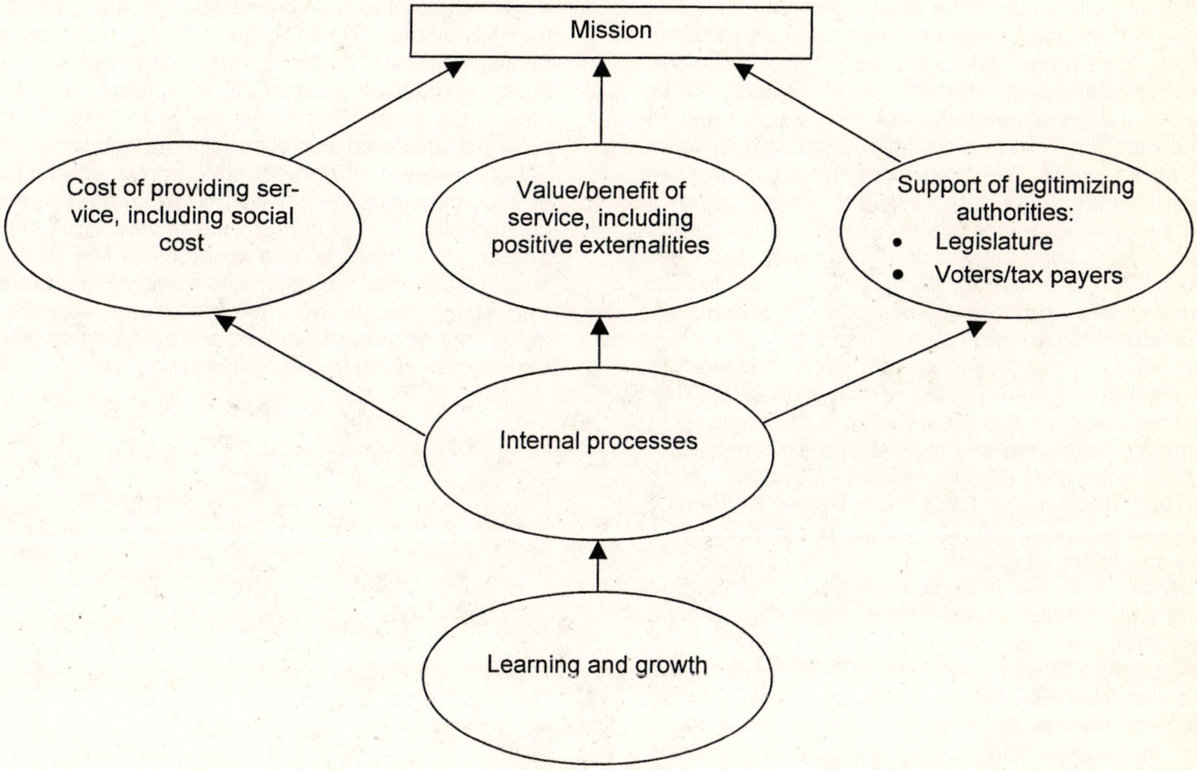

Professor Dutch Leonard, Kennedy School of Government, Harvard University, collaborated to develop this diagram.

After defining these three high-level perspectives, a public-sector agency can identify its objectives for internal processes, learning, and growth that enable objectives in the three high-level perspectives to be achieved.

BEYOND MEASUREMENT TO MANAGEMENT

Originally, we thought the Balanced Scorecard was about performance measurement (Kaplan and Norton 1992). Once organizations developed their basic system for measuring strategy, however, we quickly learned that *measurement* has consequences far beyond reporting on the past. Measurement creates focus for the future. The measures chosen by managers communicate important messages to all organizational units and employees. To take full advantage of this power, companies soon integrated their new measures into a *management system.* Thus the Balanced Scorecard concept evolved from a performance measurement system to become the organizing framework, the operating system, for a new strategic management system (Kaplan and Norton 1996c, Part II). The academic literature, rooted in the original performance measurement aspects of the scorecard, focuses on the BSC as a measurement system Ittner et al. 1997; Ittner and Larcker 1998; Banker et al. 2000; Lipe and Salterio 2000) but has yet to examine its role as a management system.

Using this new strategic management system, we observed several organizations achieving performance breakthroughs within two to three years of implementation (Kaplan and Norton 2001a, 4-6, 17-22). The magnitude of the results achieved by the early adopters reveals the power of the Balanced Scorecard management system to focus the entire organization on strategy. The speed with which the new strategies deliver results indicates that the companies' successes are not due to a major new product or service launch, major new capital investments, or even the development of new intangible or "intellectual" assets. The companies, of course, develop new products and services, and invest in both hard, tangible assets, as well as softer, intangible assets. But they cannot benefit much in two years from such investments. To achieve their breakthrough performance, the companies capitalize on capabilities and assets—both tangible and intangible—that already exist within their organizations.[6] The companies' new strategies and the Balanced Scorecard unleash the capabilities and assets previously hidden (or frozen) within the old organization. In effect, the Balanced Scorecard provides the "recipe" that enables ingredients already existing in the organization to be combined for long-term value creation.

Part II of our commentary on the Balanced Scorecard (Kaplan and Norton 2001b) will describe how organizations use Balanced Scorecards and strategy maps to accomplish comprehensive and integrated transformations. These organizations redefine their relationships with customers, reengineer fundamental business processes, reskill the work force, and deploy new technology infrastructures. A new culture emerges, centered not on traditional functional silos, but on the team effort required to implement the strategy. By clearly defining the strategy, communicating it consistently, and linking it to the drivers of change, a performance-based culture emerges to link everyone and every unit to the unique features of the strategy. The simple act of describing strategy via strategy maps and scorecards makes a major contribution to the success of the transformation program.

---

[6] These observations indicate why attempts to value individual intangible assets almost surely is a quixotic search. The companies achieved breakthrough performance with essentially the same people, services, and technology that previously delivered dismal performance. The value creation came not from any individual asset—tangible or intangible. It came from the coherent combination and alignment of existing organizational resources.

REFERENCES

American Institute of Certified Public Accountants (AICPA), Special Committee on Financial Reporting. 1994. *Improving Business Reporting—A Customer Focus: Meeting the Information Needs of Investors and Creditors.* New York, NY: AICPA.

Atkinson, A. A., and J. H. Waterhouse. 1997. A stakeholder approach to strategic performance measurement. *Sloan Management Review* (Spring).

Banker, R., G. Potter, and D. Srinivasan. 2000. An empirical investigation of an incentive plan that includes nonfinancial performance measures. *The Accounting Review* (January): 65-92.

Becker, B., and M. Huselid. 1998. High performance work systems and firm performance: A synthesis of research and managerial implications. In *Research in Personnel and Human Resources Management,* 53-101. Greenwich, CT: JAI Press.

Blair, M. B. 1995. *Ownership and Control: Rethinking Corporate Governance for the Twenty-First Century.* Washington, D.C.: Brookings Institution.

Chandler, A. D. 1990. *Scale and Scope: The Dynamics of Industrial Capitalism.* Cambridge, MA: Harvard University Press.

Charan, R., and G. Colvin. 1999. Why CEOs fail. *Fortune* (June 21).

Epstein, M., and J. F. Manzoni. 1998. Implementing corporate strategy: From Tableaux de Bord to Balanced Scorecards. *European Management Journal* (April).

Greenwood, R. G. 1974. *Managerial Decentralization: A Study of the General Electric Philosophy.* Lexington, MA: D. C. Heath.

Heskett, J., T. Jones, G. Loveman, E. Sasser, and L. Schlesinger. 1994. Putting the service profit chain to work. *Harvard Business Review* (March-April): 164-174.

Huselid, M. A. 1995. The impact of human resource management practices on turnover, productivity, and corporate financial performance. *Academy of Management Journal:* 635-672.

Ittner, C., D. Larcker, and M. Meyer. 1997. Performance, compensation, and the Balanced Scorecard. Working paper, University of Pennsylvania.

_____, D. Larcker, and M. Rajan. 1997. The choice of performance measures in annual bonus contracts. *The Accounting Review* (April): 23 1-255.

_____, and D. Larcker. 1998. Innovations in performance measurement: Trends and research implications. *Journal of Management Accounting Research:* 205-238.

Johnson, H. T., and R. S. Kaplan. 1987. *Relevance Lost: The Rise and Fall of Management Accounting.* Boston, MA: Harvard Business School Press.

Kaplan, R. S., and D. P. Norton. 1992. The Balanced Scorecard: Measures that drive performance. *Harvard Business Review* (January-February): 71-79.

_____, and _____. 1993. Putting the Balanced Scorecard to work. *Harvard Business Review* (September-October): 134-147.

_____, and E. L. Kaplan. 1996. United Way of Southeastern New England. Harvard Business School Case 197-036. Boston, MA.

_____, and D. P. Norton.].996a. Using the Balanced Scorecard as a strategic management system. *Harvard Business Review* (January-February): 75-85.

_____, and _____. 1996b. Linking the Balanced Scorecard to strategy. *California Management Review* (Fall): 53-79.

_____, and _____. 1996c. *The Balanced Scorecard: Translating Strategy Into Action.* Boston, MA: Harvard Business School Publishing.

_____, 1998. City of Charlotte (A). Harvard Business School Case 199-036. Boston, MA.

_____, and R. Cooper. 1998. *Cost and Effect: Using Integrated Cost Systems to Drive Profitability and Performance.* Boston, MA: Harvard Business School Press.

_____, and J. Elias. 1999. New Profit, Inc.: Governing the nonprofit enterprise. Harvard Business School Case 100-052. Boston, MA.

_____. 2001. Montefiore Medical Center. Harvard Business School Case 101-067. Boston, MA.

_____, and D. P. Norton. 2000. Having trouble with your strategy? Then map it. *Harvard Business Review* (September-October): 167-176.

and . 2001a. *The Strategy-Focused Organization: How Balanced Scorecard companies Thrive in the New Business Environment.* Boston, MA: Harvard Business School Press.

_____, and . 200 lb. Transforming the Balanced Scorecard from performance measurement to strategic management. Part II. *Accounting Horizons.* (forthcoming).

Kiechel, W. 1982. Corporate strategists under fire. *Fortune* (December 27): 38.

Lebas, M. 1994. Managerial accounting in France: Overview of past tradition and current practice. *European Accounting Review* 3 (3): 471-487.

Lipe, M., and S. Salterio. 2000. The Balanced Scorecard: Judgmental effects of common and unique performance measures. *The Accounting Review* (July): 283-298.

Porter, M. E. 1992. Capital disadvantage: America's failing capital investment system. *Harvard Business Review* (September-October).

_____. 1996. What is strategy? *Harvard Business Review* (November-December).

Treacy, F., and M. Wierserma. 1997. *The Wisdom of Market Leaders.* New York, NY: Perseus Books.

Webber, A. M. 2000. New math for a new economy. *Fast Company* (January-February).

Chapter 18
Strategic Investment Units and Transfer Pricing

Cases

18-1 Investment SBUs; Strategy; International Issues
18-2 Transfer Pricing; Strategy
18-3 Transfer Pricing (Foreign Sales Corporations); Use of the Web

Readings

"Does ROI Apply to Robotic Factories?"

This article provides a useful summary of the limitations of ROI performance evaluation of investment SBUs. Three criteria for appropriate ROI measures are proposed: (1) the ROI measure must include long-term performance, (2) the ROI measure must consider cash flows, and (3) the ROI measure must consider the time value of money. Also, the authors argue that the ROI measure should be consistent with the phases of the project life:

- First: acquisition of the new investment
- Second: use of the new investment
- Third: disposition of the investment

Four methods are developed and illustrated for a hypothetical investment in robotics. The four methods are: (1) annual book ROI, (2) average ROI (over the project's life), (3) discounted book ROI, and (4) discounted cash flow ROI. The authors explain how the different methods are to be used at the different phases of the project's life.

Discussion Questions:

1. Which ROI method(s) should be used at each of the phases of the project's life?
2. What is the profitability index and how is it used?
3. What are the limitations of ROI, and how does the authors' proposed approach deal with these limitations?

Note: This article makes extensive use of the concept of the time value of money, and thus can also be used in Chapter 11: Capital Budgeting.

"Transfer Pricing with ABC"

This article explains how Teva Pharmaceutical Industries Ltd adopted transfer pricing and ABC to enhance profits, to improve coordination between operations and marketing, and to reduce the proliferation of new product lines and small volume orders. The article explains why a marginal cost (based on materials cost only) approach and other traditional approaches to transfer pricing did not work for Teva. Teva introduced ABC costing in its plants, and used this cost information for transfer pricing. The article explains how the ABC based transfer pricing system incorporated batch level costs, product based costs, and plant based costs.

Discussion questions:

1. Why did Teva introduce transfer pricing?
2. What were the goals of the transfer pricing system? How did top management, division managers, and financial staff differ about these goals?
3. Why did traditional approaches for transfer pricing not work at Teva, and why did the ABC approach work instead?
4. How did the ABC transfer pricing system incorporate batch level costs? product level costs? plant level costs?
5. What are some of the benefits of the ABC transfer pricing system at Teva?

Cases

18-1. Investment SBUs; Strategy; International Issues

In 2000, the Polymer Products Company was a multinational company engaged in the manufacture of a widely diverse line of products including chemical and agricultural products, man-made fibers, electronic materials, health care, process controls, fabricated products, and oil and gas. Sales in 2000 were $6.7 billion with the following breakdown as to operating units and major markets:

Operating Unit	Percent	Major Markets	Percent
Agricultural products	18	Agriculture	20
Biological sciences	3	Construction and home furnishings	19
Fibers & intermediates	18		
Industrial chemicals	14	Capital equipment	13
Polymer products	28	Pharmaceuticals & personal products	13
Electronic materials & fabricated products	8	Motor vehicles	9
Baker controls	8	Apparel	7
Oil & gas	3	Chemicals and hydrocarbons	7
		Other markets	12

For the past five years the firm has been restructuring its core businesses (industrial chemicals, fibers and intermediates, and polymer products) by withdrawing from those product lines that do not fit with the firm's long-term strategy or which are not expected to produce adequate long-term results.

Polymer's management has carefully examined each of the various business units and is prepared to fully support those that have the potential to compete successfully in selected markets. Businesses which cannot produce returns that exceed the company's cost of capital have been, or will be, disposed of or shut down.

As 2001 ended, the company realigned its financial reporting of operating unit segments to more closely align it with the restructuring and to better reflect the company's operations. These new operating unit segments are:

- Agricultural products
- Crop chemicals
- Animal sciences
- Chemicals
- Electronic materials
- Baker controls
- Pharmaceuticals
- Sweeteners
- Oil and gas (this business was sold during the 4th Quarter of 19X5.)

Fibers and intermediates, industrial chemicals, polymer products, and a portion of fabricated products have been combined to form a new segment—chemicals. Two new segments, pharmaceuticals and sweeteners, include the acquired operations of a pharmaceutical company. The electronics business, previously part of fabricated products, has been transferred to and combined with Baker controls, serving similar process control equipment markets. The former biological sciences segment has been eliminated and their animal nutrition products are now part of animal sciences. The health care division was merged with the acquired company and is included in the pharmaceuticals segment.

COMPANY PERFORMANCE MEASUREMENT PHILOSOPHY

Up until the start of the decade, Polymer focused on a performance income measure of an operating unit's performance; assigning only the directly controllable elements of sales, cost of goods sold, marketing, administrative, technical expenses, inventory, and receivables to the operating units for internal reporting purposes. Non-directly controllable elements, such as corporate staff support groups, interest expense/interest income and foreign currency gains and losses were pooled corporately and various formulae were used to assign these corporate charges to operating units for determining a pro-forma net income, return on investment, and cash flow. Such overall indicators of performance were thus only directionally representative at the operating unit level.

As some of the company's core businesses matured and declined, an awareness began to emerge of the need to shift business strategies thus requiring tougher decisions as to divestment/investment/acquisition activities. Top management recognized the need for more accurate measurement and understanding of worldwide operating unit results.

For example, currency gains and losses were treated as a component of corporate charges. Thus, if a U.S. produced product were sold to a French customer on 180-day terms, the selling business unit reflected the full sales value at the then current exchange rate; leaving the company exposed to devaluation of the French franc. If devaluation occurred, performance of the operating unit was not affected but the company results were.

As another example, all operating units applied an average worldwide tax rate to compute a pro-forma net income, return on capital, and cash flow. When an operating unit had a choice to source the same product from Belgium or the U.K., a dilemma was created. Although costs were nominally higher in the U.K., lowering a unit's performance income, the company was in a non-tax position there which drastically improved real net income. However, by reporting results using an average worldwide tax rate, all product sourcing from the U.K. appeared disadvantageous. Also, the company was not taking advantage of an entity's tax loss carry-forward situation in various pricing and sourcing decisions.

Top management wanted a reporting and performance measurement system which brought operating unit managements' attention to ***all*** the financial impacts of a business decision. To accomplish this, it was decided that as many of the income statement and balance sheet items as was practicable would be identified with each operating unit and charged out accordingly. Each operating unit would then be measured by the achievement against goals established for return on investment and cash flow as defined below.

cash flow = net income + depreciation and obsolescence – capital expenditures +/- (change in receivables, inventories, payables, net capitalized interest, deferred taxes, other assets, and other liabilities)

$$\text{return on investment} = \frac{\text{net income} + \text{after tax interest expense}}{\text{investment}}$$

(Where investment is defined as net long-lived investment, working capital, and deferred taxes)

The incentive compensation system employed for upper management positions is essentially based upon the relative success in achieving annual budgets established for the above measures. The total corporate annual incentive award is determined somewhat rigidly, based upon where earnings fall within a budget range determined at the beginning of each year. The award is apportioned to cascade down the organization. Thus a similar quantitative assessment of results is made to reward or penalize managers for their ultimate contribution to results. The incentive awards are then presented 2/3 in cash and 1/3 in restricted stock which is accessible only after 3 years and only if stock prices meet certain appreciation tests. This latter feature was recently employed to add a long-term dimension to the program in addition to near-term annual income/cash flow results.

Prior to the new reporting and measurement scheme (called asset management) the amount of corporately pooled costs allocated as a corporate charge was over 3 percent of worldwide sales. After the asset management program was instituted, along with selected decentralization of certain corporate staff groups, these corporately pooled costs were less than 2 percent of worldwide sales.

REQUIRED:

1. What type of performance measurement system did Polymer Products use prior to the recent change?
2. What type of performance measurement system is Polymer Products using now? Why did Polymer Products move to this new system? How does the change affect the firm's global competitiveness?
3. In the new performance measurement system, should managers be held responsible for foreign currency exchange gains and losses and income taxes.

(IMA adapted)

18-2. Transfer Pricing; Strategy

Robert Products Inc. consists of three decentralized divisions: Bayside Division, Cole Division, and Diamond Division. The president of Robert Products has given the managers of the three divisions authority to decide whether to sell outside the company or among themselves at an internal price determined by the division managers. Market conditions are such that sales made internally or externally will not affect market or transfer prices. Intermediate markets will always be available for Bayside, Cole, and Diamond to purchase their manufacturing needs or sell their product.

The manager of the Cole Division is currently considering the two alternative orders presented below.

- The Diamond Division is in need of 3,000 units of a motor that can be supplied by the Cole Division. To manufacture these motors, Cole would purchase components from the Bayside Division at a price of $600 per unit; Bayside's variable cost for these components is $300 per unit. Cole Division will further process these components at a variable cost of $500 per unit.
- If the Diamond Division cannot obtain the motors from Cole Division, it will purchase the motors from London Company which has offered to supply them to Diamond at a price of $1,500 per unit. London Company would also purchase 3,000 components from Bayside Division at a price of $400 for each of these motors; Bayside's variable cost for these components is $200 per unit.
- The Wales Company wants to place an order with the Cole Division for 3,500 similar motors at a price of $1,250 per unit. Cole would again purchase components from the Bayside Division at a price of $500 per unit; Bayside's variable cost for these components is $250 per unit. Cole Division will further process these components at a variable cost of $400 per unit.

The Cole Division's plant capacity is limited, and the division can accept either the Wales contract or the Diamond order, but not both. The president of Robert Products and the manager of the Cole Division agree that it would not be beneficial in the short or long run to increase capacity.

REQUIRED:

1. Determine whether the Cole Division should sell motors to the Diamond Division at the prevailing market price, or accept the Wales Company contract. Support your answer with appropriate calculations.
2. What strategic factors should Robert Products consider as the Cole and Diamond divisions make their respective decision?

(CMA adapted)

18-3. Transfer Pricing (Foreign Sales Corporations); Use of the Web

The Foreign Sales Corporation Act, enacted by the U.S. Congress in 1971 provides special tax advantages for U.S. based exporters. The foreign subsidiaries of U.S. corporations are allowed to act as agents for the company, so that the parent firm can exempt up to 15% of the export earnings from federal tax. This apparent subsidy has angered some countries in the European Union. To learn more about Foreign Sales Corporations, search the Web and use whatever other research resources available to you. As a start, you might want to look at web site of the United States Mission to the European Union: http://www.useu.be/ISSUES/FSCdossier.html.

REQUIRED:

1. Explain foreign sales corporations and the nature of the benefits to U.S. exporters. Why have countries in the European Union disputed the existence of these corporations.
2. What role do foreign sales corporations play in transfer pricing, and what is the management accountant's responsibility regarding these types of corporations?

Readings

DOES ROI APPLY TO ROBOTIC FACTORIES

By Gerald H. Lander and Mohamed E. Bayou

Return on investment (ROI) has been the most popular method of performance evaluation in most companies for the past 50 to 70 years. Many companies adopted a decentralized management philosophy along with the RO technique. Even though the decentralized structures in large corporations were very complex, the easily understandable ROI ratio offered top management a handy tool for comparing performances of numerous divisions. But ROI has come under increasing criticism, raising the question: Does the growing trend toward automation alter the validity of this criticism? In other words, is the traditional ROI still valid for managerial performance evaluation in the new robotic manufacturing environment?

MAJOR ATTACKS ON ROI

We evaluate various measures of ROI in the context of the three phases of the decision cycle: acquisition, utilization, and disposition of robotic equipment. Then we present an ROI measure that satisfies the other criteria of acceptance.

Several critics have questioned the validity of the ROI method of performance evaluation. Elements targeted by this criticism appear in the ROI model commonly known as the DuPont formula, shown in Table 1. Typically, the variables of earnings, sales, and investments in this formula are all measured annually. Cash flows, time-value of money, and analysis beyond one year are excluded from the ROI measurement. As machinery replaces labor, with the consequent shift to more fixed costs and fewer variable costs, this criticism becomes more cogent. For example, Dearden contends that while ROI is a valid measure of past performance, it is not valid for setting future objectives because the historical costs of assets used in the formula are meaningless in planning future actions.[1]

Another criticism is that ROI creates dysfunctional intercompany goals. For example, an investment project with an ROI higher than the firm's cost of capital may be acceptable, yet the divisional manager may reject it unless it exceeds the currently attained ROI rate. Acceptance would dilute the manager's current ROI level, so many acceptable projects probably never get proposed to top management.

Another dysfunctional type of behavior arises when the investment in the denominator of the ROI formula is evaluated at net book value. Thus, as assets get older, stable earnings augment ROI, which in turn, may lead to management reluctance to replace the old assets with new advanced technology. This criticism of ROI is especially to the point in a robotic factory—robot obsolescence is more significant than obsolescence gnificant than obsolescence in a labor-intensive factory.

Send argues that the use of ROI motivates management to operate near full capacity in order to maximize ROI,[2] Even worse, divisional management may manipulate short-term income, and the asset base to the point of long-term detriment to the earning power of the company.[3] Consider this scenario: An insecure manager would be unlikely to accept projects that generate negative ROI results during the earlier years and large positive ones during later periods. Recognizing this problem, the corporation may be obliged to centralize several strategic discretionary programs such as R&D in order to minimize these ROI manipulations. Such interference by corporate headquarters does not harmonize with the decentralization philosophy.

In spite of these criticisms, ROI still enjoys internal popularity in evaluating managerial performance, for several reasons:

- As a ratio, ROI is simpler to understand than other evaluation methods such as residual income.

- It is a single measure that combines the effects of three critical performance variables—sales, earnings, and investment.
- ROI is popular with financial analysts, investors, creditors, and other external information users, a fact that encourages corporate top management to tie divisional performance to the way the public views the corporation.[4]

So strong are these reasons that ROI gained popularity as attacks on it increased during the '70s.[5] Because the use of ROI as an evaluation method undoubtedly will continue in practice, managers and other business people need to understand the mechanics and limitations of ROI.

CRITERIA FOR AN ACCEPTABLE ROI MEASURE

Given the serious criticisms of ROI and the nature of machine-intensive environments, the following criteria become necessary for an acceptable ROI measure:

- An ROI measure must consider long-term performance. This criterion is particularly relevant to the robotic factory; automation decreases variable labor and variable overhead costs and increases fixed costs over several years.
- An ROI measure must consider cash flows, a corollary of the first criterion. In the long run, cash flows are more relevant than accrual income because most accrued revenues and expenses will be settled in cash. In addition, the use of cash flows instead of accrual income avoids the distortions caused by the latter, namely, discouragement of growth by the use of net book value in ROI computations[6] and the meaningless use of historical costs of assets for planning future actions.[7]
- An ROI measure must consider the time-value of money, a corollary of the first two criteria. Because the ROI measure incorporates cash flows in long-run planning, discounting these flows in the ROI computations becomes natural.

To apply these criteria properly, managers need to understand the role of ROI in the various decision processes for acquisition, utilization, and disposition of robotic assets.

THE DECISION CYCLE FOR ROBOTIC ASSETS

The life cycle of a robotic asset as an investment generally goes through three different phases. First, it is acquired, then used in operations, and finally disposed of by replacement, sale, or discarding. Each phase requires different decisions and information. Furthermore, each phase has a different impact on the goals of the manager making the investment decision and on the goals of the division as an economic entity.

For fairness and accuracy in performance measurement, the three phases have to be analyzed from the manager's viewpoint separately from that of the division. Dearden argues that the current performance evaluation system fail to distinguish between the financial performance of the manager and that of the organizational unit being managed.[8] The distinction is important because the manager's potential for success and failure often differs from the division's. Moreover, the extent of the manager's controllability of revenues and expenses is irrelevant to measuring a division's performance because the division's performance incorporates both controllable and uncontrollable income determinants.

Fig. 1 shows how ROI and capital budgeting techniques generally are applied in practice to the three phases of the decision cycle.

The acquisition phase includes all activities necessary for the purchase, installation, and preparation for use of a new robotic asset. Capital budgeting models such as the net present value, internal rate of return, profitability index, and payback period commonly are applied in practice for this phase (Box 1 in Fig. 1). ROI usually is not applied in the evaluation of the division's performance during this phase (Box IV in Fig. 1).

The utilization phase involves the actual use of the asset in operations, which normally affects the

TABLE 1
THE DUPONT FORMULA

$$ROI = \frac{\text{Earnings}}{\text{Sales}} \times \frac{\text{Sales}}{\text{Investment}} = \frac{\text{Earnings}}{\text{Investment}}$$
$$= \text{Margin} \times \text{Turnover}$$

FIGURE 1
ROI AND CAPITAL BUDGETING MODELS APPLIED TO THE THREE PHASES OF THE DECISION CYCLE

	Acquisition	Utilization	Disposition Replacement
Capital Budgeting	I Applied	II N/A	III Applied
ROI	IV N/A	V Applied	VI Applied

TABLE 2
ROI ANALYSIS IN THE SHORT AND LONG RUN

		Year 1	Year 2	Year 3	Year 4	Year 5
Cost of robot and accessories	(a)	90,000	90,000	90,000	90,000	90,000
Installation	(b)	10,000	10,000	10,000	10,000	10,000
Total (a + b)	(c)	100,000	100,000	100,000	100,000	100,000
Annual Costs:						
Depreciation	(d)	20,000	20,000	20,000	20,000	20,000
Maintenance	(e)	1,000	2,000	3,000	4,000	5,000
Operating & program	(f)	3,000	3,000	3,000	3,000	3,000
Insurance	(g)	3,000	3,000	3,000	3,000	3,000
Total (d + e + f + g)	(h)	27,000	28,000	29,000	30,000	31,000
Annual Benefits:						
Quality effect:						
On sales & rework	(i)	20,000	20,000	20,000	20,000	20,000
Materials savings	(j)	12,000	12,000	12,000	12,000	12,000
Labor savings:						
$10/hour	(k_1)	20,000	20,000	20,000	20,000	20,000
$20/hour	(k_2)	30,000	30,000	30,000	30,000	30,000
$30/hour	(k_3)	40,000	40,000	40,000	40,000	40,000
Overhead savings (30% of labor cost):						
$3/hour	(l_1)	6,000	6,000	6,000	6,000	6,000
$6/hour	(l_2)	9,000	9,000	9,000	9,000	9,000
$9/hour	(l_3)	12,000	12,000	12,000	12,000	12,000
Annual Net Benefits = $(I + j + k_l + l_l) - h = m_l$						
Labor = $10/hour	(m_1)	31,000	30,000	29,000	28,000	27,000
Labor = $20/hour	(m_2)	44,000	43,000	42,000	41,000	40,000
Labor = $30/hour	(m_3)	57,000	56,000	55,000	54,000	53,000

1. Annual Book ROI = $\dfrac{\text{Net Annual Benefits}}{\text{Initial Investment}} = \dfrac{m_i}{c}$

The term "net benefits" indicates the use of accrual income rather than cash flows in the computations.

Annual Book ROI:	Year 1	Year 2	Year 3	Year 4	Year 5
at $10/hour	31%	30%	29%	28%	27%
at $20/hour	44%	43%	42%	41%	40%
at $30/hour	57%	56%	55%	54%	53%

2. Average ROI = $\dfrac{\text{Average Net Benefits Over 5 Years}}{\text{Initial Investment}} = \dfrac{\Sigma m/5}{c}$

This ROI also is known as the accounting rate of return

Average ROI when labor is $10/hour = 29%
Average ROI when labor is $20/hour = 42%
Average ROI when labor is $30/hour = 55%

3. Discounted Book ROI = $\dfrac{\text{Present Value of Net Benefits}}{\text{Initial Investment}}$

(The discount rate, i.e., cost of capital used = 10%)

Discounted ROI when labor is $10/hour = 111%
Discounted ROI when labor is $20/hour = 160%
Discounted ROI when labor is $30/hour = 209%

4. Discounted-Cash-Flow ROI (DCF ROI) = $\dfrac{\text{Present Value of Net Cash Inflows}}{\text{Initial Investment}}$

Because depreciation expense (d) is not a cash item it is added back:

Net Cash Inflows $= m_i + d - c = n_i$ for year 1

$= m_i + d = n_i$ for each of years 2-5

		Year 1	Year 2	Year 3	Year 4	Year 5
$10/hour	(n_1)	(49,000)	50,000	49,000	48,000	47,000
$20/hour	(n_2)	(36,000)	63,000	62,000	61,000	60,000
$30/hour	(n_3)	(23,000)	76,000	75,000	74,000	73,000

The discount rate, i.e., cost of capital used = 10%: DCF ROI:

When labor is $10/hour = 0.86
When labor is $20/hour = 1.36
When labor is $30/hour = 1.85

manager's performance. Hence, ROI is applied frequently (Box V in Fig. 1), and capital budgeting models rarely are applied (Box V in Fig. 1), and capital budgeting models rarely are applied (Box II). This phase has two problems. First, with robotic assets, the manager's controllability decreases because of the large value of the assets, with costs that become sunk as soon as the assets are acquired. In addition, in some companies top management evaluates major investments in robots, reducing the divisional manager's influence over the investment base and decreasing the applicability of ROI as a means to evaluate the manager's performance. Yet these limitations do not affect ROI's usefulness in evaluating the investment center's performance. Second, the apparent inconsistency of applying capital budgeting models for the acquisition phase (Box I) and ROI for the utilization phase (Box V) creates confusion and unfair reporting if only one performance report is issued for evaluation.

The disposition phase is, in effect, an acquisition phase if it leads to replacing the old asset with a new one. Thus, capital budgeting models usually are applied (Box III) but only as a secondary justification. That is, a manager rationally would apply ROI first to determine if the replacement improves the currently attained ROI level (Box VI). If it improves the ROI, the manager models to justify the replacement decision to senior management. On the other hand, if the replacement decision negatively affects the current ROI, the replacement issue may be suppressed and never be made known to superiors even if it is acceptable to the corporation.

SCREENING DIFFERENT ROI MODELS

To avoid these conflicts, a modified ROI model should be used in all of the six boxes of Fig. 1. Table 2 illustrates how to accomplish this consistency. A flexible robotic system with an economic life of five years is considered as a replacement for an older labor-intensive system. Flexible manufacturing systems are the new trend in manufacturing. They integrate machines and systems to produce a particular product or a major component from start to finish. A flexible manufacturing system can take different forms. It can be a series of interlocked electronic machining centers, controlled by a computerized robot, which performs a set of prescribed operations or it can be one machine performing a complex series of mechanical tasks. These systems normally provide several benefits: reduced material handling and work-in-process and increased quality, flexibility, and throughput.[9] The example in Table 2 is designed to capture most of these features. In reality, precisely predicting benefits and costs beyond one year is difficult. Probability distributions can be applied to incorporate these uncertainties, but to simplify the analysis, Table 2 does not include probability assessments.

Table 2 shows four different measures of ROI:

1. The Annual Book ROI. This traditional ROI measure, which involves no discounting or averaging and ignores cash flows and the time-value of money, concentrates on a single year of performance. Notice in Table 2 that the ROI ratio increases as automation replaces labor costs. This measure is simple to understand.
2. The Average ROI. This method also is known as the accounting rate of return. The method improves upon the traditional annual ROI because it considers the entire life of the asset. (A moving average ROI may be employed. For example, when the first year of the planning period expires, the sixth year would be added at the end of the period. Thus, a new average for ROI will be calculated every year, giving the manager a continuous five-year planning horizon.) The average ROI method, however, ignores cash flows and the time-value of money.
3. Discounted-Book ROI. This method considers the time-value of money and the long-run performance. Nevertheless, it includes accrual income (which we call net benefits) rather than

TABLE 3
THE CAPITAL BUDGETING MODEL OF PROFITABILITY INDEX

$$\text{Profitability Index} = \frac{\text{Present Value of Total Cash Inflows}}{\text{Initial Investment}}$$

$$\text{Since Net Cash Inflows} = \text{Total Cash Inflows} - \text{Initial Investment}$$

$$\text{Profitability Index} = \frac{\text{P.V. of Net Cash Inflows} + \text{Initial Investment}}{\text{Initial Investment}}$$

$$= \frac{\text{P.V. of Net Cash Inflows}}{\text{Initial Investment}} + \frac{\text{Initial Investment}}{\text{Initial Investment}}$$

$$= \text{DCF} + 1.00$$

$$\text{Thus...DCF ROI} = \text{Profitability Index} - 1.00$$

cash flows in the computations. Accordingly, depreciation expense on line "d" in Table 2, which is not a cash item, is incorporated into the computation. Can the discounted-book ROI be used to evaluate a manager's performance? A manager's performance should be measured over a period longer than one year, a requirement for applying this method, using budgeted and actual data. Therefore, a good performance results when the actual discounted-book ROI ratio equals at least the budgeted ratio.

4. Discounted-Cash-Flows ROI (DCF ROI). This method satisfies all three criteria for acceptance, and it considers the time-value of cash flows over the life of the robotic asset. The mathematical format of this model is shown in the first line of section 4, Table 2. The DCF ROI measure relates to the capital budgeting model of the profitability index. This index is defined in the literatures of accounting and finance as shown in Table 3.

Table 2 shows DCF ROI ratios of .86, 1.36, and 1.85 when hourly labor wage rates are $10, $20, and $30, respectively. Thus, larger savings in labor costs increase the DCF ROI ratio. Generally, interpretation of DCF ROI ratios parallels that of the profitability index. For instance, if a project has a DCF ROI ratio of zero, it indicates that the project's internal rate of return (IRR) equals the interest rate (or cost of capital) used in the discounting process. Similarly, a positive DCF ROI ratio indicates an IRR greater than the cost of capital, and a negative DCF ROI means an IRR lower than the cost of capital. In general, the larger the DCF ROI ratio, the more profitable the project. Greater cost of capital used in discontinuing the cash flows also lowers the DCF ROI ratio.

The application of this DCF ROI model to the six cells of the decision cycle depicted in Fig. 1 eliminates the inconsistency problems caused by applying capital budgeting and the traditional ROI models to the decision cycle as discussed above. The DCF ROI model satisfies the three acceptance criteria of: (1) the emphasis on long-run performance, (2) cash flows, and (3) time-value of money. Finally, the DCF ROI can be used in conjunction with the traditional ROI. Probability distributions can be incorporated into the analysis to account for uncertainties of future cash flows. These computations can be made easily by using available software packages on present value applications.

---

[1] J. Dearden, "The Case Against ROI," *Harvard Business Review*, May-June 1969, pp. 124-135; his arguments on the subject are still valid today.

[2] A. H. Seed, III, "Cost Accounting in the Age of Robotics," MANAGEMENT ACCOUNTING®, October 1984, pp. 39-41.

[3] L. B. Hoshower and R. P. Crum, "Straightening the Tortuous—and Treacherous—ROI Path," MANAGEMENT ACCOUNTING®, December 1986, pp. 41-44.

[4] J. S. Reece and W. R. Cool, "Measuring Investment Center Performance," *Harvard Business Review*, May-June 1978, pp. 28-176.

[5] Ibid.

[6] J. J. Mauriel and R. N. Anthony, "Misevaluation of Investment Center Performance," *Harvard Business Review*, March-April 1966, pp. 98-105.

[7] J. Dearden, "Measuring Profit Center Managers," *Harvard Business Review*, September-October 1987, pp. 84-88.

[8] Ibid.

[9] R. A. Howell and S. R. Soucy, "The New Manufacturing Environment: Major Trends for Management Accounting," MANAGEMENT ACCOUNTING®, July 1987, pp. 21-27.

TRANSFER PRICING WITH ABC

BY ROBERT S. KAPLAN, DAN WEISS, AND EYAL DESHEH

Here's the story of how a multinational pharmaceutical company solved its transfer pricing problems by using activity-based costing.

In the mid-1980s, Teva Pharmaceutical Industries Ltd. decided to enter the generic drug market. Already a successful worldwide manufacturer of proprietary drugs, the Israel-based company wanted to vie globally in this competitive new market, particularly in the United States. The move has proved lucrative so far, as sales have been increasing at an annual rate of nearly 20%. In 1996, Teva's worldwide sales were $954 million and its after-tax net income, $73 million.

As part of its new strategy, Teva reorganized its pharmaceutical operations into decentralized cost and profit centers consisting of one operations division and three marketing divisions. The operations division is made up of four manufacturing plants in Israel, which are organized as cost centers because plant managers have no control over product mix or pricing. The plants produce to the orders placed by the marketing divisions, and plant managers are responsible for operational efficiency, quality, cost performance, and capacity management.

The marketing divisions are organized into the U.S. market (through Teva's Lemmon subsidiary), the local market (Israel), and the rest of the world. All three have substantially different sales characteristics. The Lemmon USA division handles about 30 products, each sold in large quantities. The Israel division handles 1,200 products in different packages and dosage forms, with many being sold in quite small quantities. The division handling sales to the rest of the world works on the basis of specific orders and tenders [a request from a customer for a price/bid to deliver a specified product or service], some of which are for relatively small quantities. All three divisions order and acquire most of their products from the operations division, although occasionally they turn to local suppliers. The marketing divisions are responsible for decisions about sales, product mix, pricing, and customer relationships.

Until the late 1980s, the marketing divisions were treated as revenue centers and were evaluated by sales, not profit, performance. Manufacturing plants in the operations division were measured by how well they met expense budgets and delivered the right orders on time. The company's cost system emphasized variable costs, principally materials expenses—ingredients and packaging—and direct labor. All other manufacturing costs were considered fixed.

Teva's managers decided to introduce a transfer pricing system, which they hoped would enhance profit consciousness and improve coordination between operations and marketing. They were concerned with excessive proliferation of the product line, acceptance of many low-volume orders, and associated large consumption of production capacity for changeovers. They proposed a transfer pricing system based on marginal costs, defined to be just materials cost. Direct labor would not be included in the transfer price because the company was not expecting to hire or fire employees based on short-term marketing decisions. High costs were associated with laying off workers in Israel, and, more important, pharmaceutical workers were highly skilled. With Teva's rapid growth, managers were reluctant to lay off workers during short-term volume declines because if new employees had to be hired later, they would need up to two years of training before they acquired the skills of the laid-off workers.

But the proposed transfer pricing system generated a storm of controversy. First, some executives observed that the marketing divisions would report extremely high profits because they were being charged for the materials costs only. Second, the operations division would get "credit" only for the expenses of purchased materials. There would be little pressure and motivation to control labor expenses and other so-called fixed expenses or for improving operational efficiency. Third, if Teva's plants were less efficient than outside manufacturers of the pharmaceutical products, the marginal cost transfer price would give the marketing divisions no incentive to shift their source of supply. Finally, the executives concluded that using only a short-run contribution margin approach would not solve the problems caused by treating the marketing divisions as revenue centers. Measuring profits as price less materials cost would continue to allow marketing and sales decisions to be made without regard to their implications for production capacity and long-run costs. An alternative approach had to be found.

WHAT EVERYONE WANTED

Teva senior management wanted a new transfer pricing system that would satisfy several important characteristics:

1. The system should encourage the marketing divisions to make decisions consistent with long-run profit maximization. The transfer price should not encourage actions that improved the profit or cost performance of a division at the expense of Teva's overall profitability.
2. The system should be transparent enough so that managers could distinguish costs relevant for short-run decisions—such as incremental, occasional bids for orders—from long-term decisions—such as acquiring a new product line, deleting product lines, and adding to existing product lines.
3. The transfer prices could be used to support decisions in both marketing and operating divisions, including:

Marketing	Operations
• Product mix	• Inventory levels
• New product introduction	• Batch sizes
• Product deletion	• Process improvements
• Pricing	• Capacity management
	• Outsourcing: make vs. buy

Division managers wanted a transfer pricing system with the following characteristics:

1. The transfer prices would report the financial performance of their divisions fairly.
2. Managers could influence the reported performance of their divisions by making business decisions within their scope of authority. That is, the reported performance should reflect changes in product mix, improved efficiency, investments in new equipment, and organizational changes.
3. The decisions made by managers of marketing divisions would reflect both sales revenue and associated expenses incurred in the operations division.
4. The system must anticipate that division managers would examine, in depth, the method for calculating transfer prices and would take actions that maximized the reported performance of their divisions.

Finally, the financial staff wanted a transfer pricing system such that:

1. The transfer prices and financial reports derived from them would be credible and could be relied upon for decision making at all levels of the organization without excessive arguments and controversy.
2. The transfer pricing system would be clear, easy to explain, and easy to use. Updating transfer prices should be easy, and the components of the transfer price calculation should promote good understanding of the underlying factors driving costs.
3. The system would be used for internal charging of costs from the operations division to the marketing divisions.

Table 1. PAIN RELIEVER 10 TABLETS, 250 mg.

Annual Sales 1996—$2.1 Million

ABC Cost per Package	
Materials use	$1.50
Production costs	2.10
(The traditional production costs per package were only $1.50, 40% difference)	
Total	$3.60
Production Cost Analysis:	
Resources	
Salaries	$0.86
Energy	0.27
Utilities	0.34
Depreciation	0.41
Administrative	0.22
Total	$2.10
Main Activities	
Storage	$0.25
Manufacturing	0.61
Packaging	0.71
Q.A.	0.42
Logistics	0.11
Total	$2.10
Cost Drivers	
Number of materials	$0.55
Batches	0.24
Labor hours	0.71
Machine hours	0.47
Samples	0.13
Total	$2.10

TRADITIONAL TRANSFER PRICE APPROACHES WOULDN'T WORK

Teva's managers considered but rejected several traditional methods for establishing a new transfer pricing system: market price, full cost, marginal cost, and negotiated price. Market price for the transferred product was not feasible because no market existed for Teva's manufactured and packaged pharmaceutical products that had not been distributed or marketed to customers. A full cost calculation including materials, labor, and manufacturing overhead was rejected because the traditional methods for allocating overhead (labor or machine hours) did not capture the actual cost structure in Teva's plants. Also, the accumulation of all factory costs into average overhead rates could encourage local optimization by each division that would lower Teva's overall profit. For example, manufacturing plants would be encouraged to overproduce in order to absorb more factory overhead into inventory, while marketing divisions might be discouraged from bidding aggressively for high-volume orders and encouraged to accept more low-volume custom orders. Also, this system would not reveal the incremental costs associated with short-run decisions or the relative use of capacity by different products and different order sizes.

Using short-run marginal cost, covering only ingredients and packaging materials, was the system proposed initially, which the managers already knew was inadequate for their purposes. And, finally, senior executives believed strongly that negotiated transfer prices would lead to endless arguments among managers in the different divisions, which would consume excessive time on nonproductive discussions.

ACTIVITY-BASED COSTING IS THE ANSWER

In December 1989, Teva's senior management attended a presentation on the fundamentals of activity-based costing and decided to implement ABC in its largest production plant. They wanted to investigate the use of ABC for calculating transfer prices between that plant and the marketing divisions. Teva put together a multidisciplinary project team consisting of managers from the production, finance, and marketing divisions. The team worked for about six months to develop an activity dictionary, drive factory costs to activities, identify cost drivers for each activity, collect data, and calculate ABC based product costs. It took the team several more weeks to analyze the results. Table 1 shows a sample calculation (updated to reflect 1996 data) of the costs to produce 10 tablets of a pain reliever. With this information, managers believed they now had a defensible, quantifiable answer to a question about how much it cost to manufacture a special small batch for a customer.

After seeing how ABC worked at the first plant, in subsequent years the project team rolled out the ABC analysis to the remaining production plants. The ABC models were retrospective, calculating the activity costs, activity cost driver rates, and product costs for the prior year. By the end of 1993, senior managers wanted to use ABC prospectively, to calculate transfer prices for the coming year. In November, Teva built its ABC production cost model for 1994 using data from the first three quarters 1993. But managers objected to calculating costs for 1994 based on 1993 historical data. The numbers would not incorporate the impact of new products, new machines, and expected changes in production processes. Also, the historical data contained volume and spending variances that occurred in 1993 but that were not expected to be representative of production operations in 1994.

The project team took this issue to the company's Financial Control Forum where representatives from the operations and marketing divisions and company headquarters met to discuss costing and financial reporting methodologies. After several meetings, the group decided to use the next year's (1994) forecasted costs—based on budgeted expense data, forecasted volume and mix of sales, and projected process utilization and efficiencies—to calculate the transfer prices.

THE ABC TRANSFER PRICE MODEL STRUCTURE

The structure of the early retrospective ABC models and the current prospective model recognizes the ABC hierarchy of unit, batch, product sustaining, and plant-level costs.[1] Unit-level costs represent all the direct expenses associated with producing individual product units such as tablets, capsules, and ampoules. These expenses principally include the cost of raw materials, packaging materials, and direct wages paid to production workers.

Batch-level costs include the expenses of resources used for each production or packaging batch, mainly the costs of preparation, setup, cleaning, quality control, laboratory testing, and computer and production management. The lot sizes for pharmaceutical production usually are predetermined based on the capacity of containers in the production line,[2] but a second batch process, determined by customer orders, occurs for packaging the tablets or syrup. The costs of a production or a packaging batch can vary among different products and, of course, among different plants. For example, a small customer order can trigger the production of a large batch of tablets or syrup of which only a small portion may be packaged for the particular customer order.[3] Thus, the batch costs assigned to a particular order include two components: a pro-rata share of the batch cost of the production setup and the full batch cost of the packaging setup. The calculation of batch-level costs for several different types of customer orders is shown in Table 2.

Product-specific costs include the expenses incurred in registering the products,[4] making changes to a product's production processes, and designing the package. Plant-level costs represent the cost of maintaining the capacity of production lines including depreciation, cost of safety inspections, and insurance, as well as the general expenses of the plant such as security and landscaping. In many ABC applications, machine appreciation would be included in the unit and batch costs associated with producing products and changing from one product to another. Teva decided to treat equipment depreciation as a plant-level cost so the calculated unit and batch costs could be used to estimate more closely the marginal costs associated with producing one more unit or batch of a product.

USING ABC COSTS FOR TRANSFER PRICING

Teva bases its transfer price system on a prospective ABC calculation. Prices are set for the coming year based on budgeted data. The company calculates standard activity cost driver rates for each activity. During the year these costs get charged to products based on the actual quantity of activities demanded during the year. The use of standard activity cost driver rates enables product costs to be calculated in a predictable manner throughout the year. It also eliminates monthly or quarterly fluctuations in product costs caused by variations in actual spending, resource usage, and activity levels.

Transfer prices are calculated in two different procedures. The first one assigns unit and batch-level costs, and the second assigns product-specific and plant-level costs. The marketing divisions are charged for unit-level costs (principally materials and labor) based on the actual quantities of each individual product they acquire. In addition, they are charged batch-level costs based on the actual number of production and packaging batches of each product they order (see examples in Table 2). Now that Teva has the ability to analyze the costs of different presentations, the trend of having a large number of presentations for each product has slowed. For example, the marketing divisions realized that producing special sample packages of six tablets was very expensive and that it was cheaper to give physicians the regular packages of 20 tablets. In general, the procedure has given marketing managers the flexibility to decide when to accept a small order from a customer or how much of a discount to grant for large orders. Table 3 shows a sample calculation

Table 2. BATCH-LEVEL TRANSFER PRICE

The batch-level transfer price has two components: the production setup and the packaging setup. Consider the production and packaging process for a cough syrup. In the production process, the active ingredients, a syrup simplex, and flavors, are mixed together in a 600 liter container to produce the syrup solution. The cost of setup—labor, cleaning, maintenance, and quality control resources—is $300. The setup cost is assigned proportionally to the entire output.

Subsequently, bottles are filled with the syrup solution and packed into cardboard boxes. The entire packaging process is performed on an automatic filling and packing line. The setup of the line costs $500, which includes the cost of a skilled technician, cleaning, maintenance, and quality control. Packing the same syrup into two different presentations, such as different sized bottles (50 ml and 100 ml), or different packaging materials requires two different setups.

The batch-level transfer price consists of the pro-rata share of the production setup and the full cost of the packaging setup. We illustrate the approach with three numerical examples:

Produce a full batch of 6,000 bottles of 100 ml syrup for a large order from a customer in the local market

[$300/6,000] + [$500/6,000] = $.05 + $.083 = $.133/bottle
mixing packing

Produce a small order of 1,000 bottles of 100 ml syrup, packed in special boxes, for a special tender in South America

[$300/6,000] + [$500/1,000] = $.05 + $.50 = $.55/bottle
mixing packing

Produce a full batch of 12,000 bottles of 50ml syrup for a large order from a customer in the local market

[$300/12,000] + [$500/12,000] = $.025 + $.042 = $.067/bottle
mixing packing

Table 3. MONTHLY DEBIT — MAY 1995

From Plant A to Local Market Division

Product	Quantity Produced	Material (Per Package)	Unit Based Costs (Per Package)	Batch Based Costs (Per Package)	Total Costs † (Per Package)	Total Debit ‡
Pain reliever 20 tablets, 500 mg.	1,000,000	$2.10	$0.22	$0.41	$2.73	$2,730,000
Pain reliever 30 Capsules	1,200,000	1.60	0.20	0.32	2.12	2,544,000
Syrup 200 cc.	200,000	0.81	0.43	0.11	1.35	270,000
•						•
•						•
•						•
Total						$15,100,200

† Total costs = material + unit based costs = batch based costs
‡ Total debit = total costs per package x quantity produced

of the monthly unit and batch-level charges from a plant to a marketing division.

The product-specific and plant-level expenses are charged to marketing divisions annually based on budgeted information (see Table 4). The product-specific costs are easy to assign because each marketing division has specific products for its own markets. No individual product is sold to more than one marketing division. The plant-level (capacity-sustaining) expenses are charged to each marketing division based on the budgeted use of the capacity of the four manufacturing facilities.

Activity cost driver rates are calculated based on the practical capacity of each of the four plants. In this way, the rates reflect the underlying efficiency and productivity of the plants without being influenced by fluctuations in forecasted or actual usage. Analysts estimated the practical capacity by noting the maximum production quantities during past peak periods.

What about unused capacity? Unused capacity arises from two sources: (1) declines in demand for products manufactured on an existing line, and (2) partial usage when a new production line is added because existing production lines cannot produce the additional quantities requested by one of the marketing divisions. To foster a sense of responsibility among marketing managers for the cost of supplying capacity resources, Teva charges the marketing division that experienced the decline in demand a lump-sum assignment (see Table 4) for the cost of maintaining the unused production capacity in an existing line. When a marketing division initiates an increment in production capacity or manufacturing technology, it bears the costs of all the additional resources supplied unless or until the increment begins to be used by one of the other marketing divisions. At that point, each marketing division would be charged based on its percentage of practical capacity used.

The assignment of the plant-level costs (still referred to as "fixed costs" at Teva because of its long history with the marginal costing approach) receives much attention, particularly from the managers of the marketing divisions. They want to verify that these costs do indeed stay "fixed" and don't creep upward each period. By separating the unit and batch-level costs from the product-sustaining and plant-level costs, the marketing managers can monitor closely the costs incurred in the manufacturing plants. In particular, the marketing managers make sure that increases in plant-level costs occur only when one or more of them requests a change in production capacity. The responsibility for the fixed cost increment is then clearly assignable to the requesting division.

The integrated budget process lets marketing managers plan their product mix with knowledge of the cost impact of their decisions. When they propose increases in variety and complexity, they know the added costs they will be charged because of their increased demands on manufacturing facilities. Active discussions occur between marketing and operations personnel about the impact of product mix and batch sizes.

Table 4. ANNUAL DEBIT — 1995

From Plant A to Lemmon Marketing Division (USA)

Product	Annual Budgeted Quantity	Product Based Costs (Per Package)	Plant Based Costs (Per Package)	Total Costs † (Per Package)	Total Debit ‡
Pain reliever 20 tablets, 500 mg.	12,000,000	$0.10	$0.21	$0.31	$3,720,000
Pain reliever 30 Capsules	20,000,000	0.12	0.20	0.32	6,400,000
Syrup 200 cc.	3,500,000	0.14	0.12	0.26	860,000
•					•
•					•
•					•
Cost of used capacity					141,900,000
Cost of unused capacity					1,300,000
Total					$143,200,000

† Total costs = product based costs + plant based costs
‡ Total debit = total cost per package x annual budgeted quantity

Marketing managers now distinguish between products that cover all manufacturing costs versus those that cover only the unit and batch-level expenses but not their annual product-sustaining and plant-level expenses. Because of the assignment of unused capacity expenses to the responsible marketing division, the marketing managers incorporate information about available capacity when they make decisions about pricing, product mix, and product introduction.

One example illustrates the value of assigning product-sustaining and plant-level expenses to individual products in the new transfer pricing system. The initial and subsequent ABC analyses revealed that quite a few of Teva's products were unprofitable; that is, the revenues they earned were below the cost of the unit, batch, and product and plant-sustaining expenses associated with these products. But managers were reluctant to drop these products because many of the expenses assigned to them, including direct labor, would remain for some time even if production of the unprofitable products were to cease.

In the early 1990s, however, Teva's growing sales volume led to shortages in capacity. Teva eventually decided to sell 30 low-volume products to another company. These products were not central to Teva's strategy, yet they consumed a great number of resources and managers' attention. By shifting the product mix away from the unprofitable products, Teva was able to use the freed-up capacity of people, machines, and facilities to handle the production of newly introduced products and the expanded sales of existing profitable products. While the debate about selling off the 30 products lasted three years, the ABC system contributed to the final decision by revealing that the cheapest source of new capacity was the capacity released by reducing the production and sales of currently unprofitable products.

ONGOING BENEFITS FROM ABC TRANSFER PRICING SYSTEM

With Teva's continued growth, requests for investments in new production capacity arise continually. ABC's highlighting of unused capacity often reveals where production can be expanded without spending additional money. A second source is the capacity released by ceasing production of unprofitable products—when feasible without disrupting customer relations. Beyond these two sources, investments in a new production line can be assessed by simulating production costs if the line were to be installed. For example, a new line can reduce batch-level costs because of less need for changeovers on both the existing and the proposed production lines. These cost reductions could provide the justification for the investment decision. In addition, the investment decision for a new production line explicitly incorporates the cost and assignment of responsibility for the unused capacity in the early periods while market demand has not yet built to long-term expected levels. Teva executives say that the discipline of recognizing and assigning unused capacity costs of new production lines provides valuable realism to the demand forecasts provided by the marketing divisions.

The transfer pricing system also motivates cost reduction and production efficiencies in the manufacturing plants. Managers in the different divisions now work together to identify ways to reduce unit and batch-level expenses. Manufacturing, purchasing, and marketing employees conduct common searches for lower-cost, more reliable, and higher-quality suppliers to reduce variable materials costs. Marketing managers compare Teva's production costs with those of alternative suppliers around the world. They share this information with manufacturing managers who learn where process improvements are required and may concur with a decision to outsource products where the external suppliers' costs are lower than Teva could achieve in the foreseeable future. These actions contribute to increasing Teva's long-term profitability.

The activity-based cost information also helps managers determine which manufacturing facility is appropriate for different types of products. For example (see Figure 1), Plant A has a relatively inflexible (high capital-intensive) cost structure with a high percentage of plant-level costs and a low percentage of unit costs. This plant is most appropriate for high-volume production of standard products. Plant B, with a significantly lower percentage of plant-level costs and a relatively high percentage of unit costs, is much more flexible and is appropriate for producing small batch sizes and test runs of newly introduced products. Thus, ABC information also is being used to determine operating strategy.

Figure 1 Structure of Costs in Plants A and B

	Plant A	Plant B
Unit Based Cost	42%	45%
Batch Based Cost	32%	30%
Product Based Cost	20%	23%
Plant Based Cost	6%	2%

THE BEST NEWS: HARMONY IS GROWING

An unexpected benefit of the activity-based transfer price system is the ability to measure profit performance under changing organizational structures. Teva, like many other pharmaceutical companies, undergoes periodic organizational changes. By understanding cost behavior at the activity and product level, financial managers can forecast the potential performance of newly created profit centers and reconstruct what the past profit performance history would have been, assuming that the proposed profit center reorganization had existed for the past several years. The ABC system also enables senior executives to measure profit performance across organizational—cost and profit center—boundaries. For example, Table 5 shows the profitability of a significant product family whose individual products are manufactured in different plants and are sold by more than one marketing division.

Jacob Winter, Teva's vice president of pharmaceutical operations, commented on the benefits derived from the ABC transfer price system:

In our changing environment, it is important for us to be able to understand and forecast our cost behavior. Some products remain in certain stages of production for a long time. These stages require resources of professional production and quality assurance staff even when no direct labor is involved. On the other hand, since the supply of these resources is relatively fixed in the short run, we understand that we can use their capabilities for several small batch runs.

He also recognized that activity-based costs are not the primary information used for short-term operational decision making:

The ABC data provide an indication that must be supported by other information and facts One cannot rely only on costing information when making operational decisions. Our short-term operational decisions focus on current bottlenecks and lead-time considerations. ABC provides guidance and insights about where we should be looking, but it is not the primary data for operational decisions.

Perhaps most important, the introduction of ABC-based transfer prices has led to a dramatic reduction in the conflicts among marketing and manufacturing managers. The managers now have confidence in the production cost economics reported by the transfer price system. Manufacturing managers who "sell" the product and marketing managers who "buy" the product concur with the reasonableness of the calculated transfer prices. Teva's senior executives interpret the sharp reduction in intraorganizational conflicts as one of the most important signs that the use of activity-based transfer prices is succeeding.

Table 5. 10 LEADING PRODUCTS (Segment A): 1995

	$ Million
Sales revenue	50
Marketing expenses	
USA Lemmon division	10
Local market division	9
Other export division	-
Total	19
Manufacturing expenses	
Plant A	11
Plant B	-
Plant C	9
Plant D	-
Total	20
Total expenses	39
Profit	11

[1] R. Cooper, "Cost Classification in Unit-Based and Activity-Based Manufacturing Cost Systems," *Journal of Cost Management,* Fall 1990, pp. 4-14.

[2] Production lot sizes can be expanded, if demand increases to a higher, sustainable level, by making technical changes to the production process and performing a quality control procedure to verify and validate that the product characteristics and quality have not been altered by the larger production batch.

[3] At present, the Teva transfer price system does not charge the customer order for the full cost of setting up the production batch nor for the inventory carrying cost of the unused tablets or syrup. This is a refinement that could be added to the system in future years.

[4] Registration costs include the costs of gaining and maintaining approval from governmental agencies for the right to manufacture each product.

Chapter 19
Management Compensation and Business Valuation

Cases

19-1 Midwest Petro-Chemical Company (Evaluating a Firm)
19-2 Evaluating a Firm
19-3 OutSource, Inc. (Economic Value Added)

Readings

"Using Shareholder Value to Evaluate Strategic Choices"

The basic principle of the article is that performance evaluation based on accounting measures alone is not sufficient. The evaluation of a business unit or of the unit's manager must also consider the business unit's performance in creating shareholder value. Based on ideas from Alfred Rappaport's book, Creating Shareholder Value, the article develops the measures of cash flow and market risk. An illustration for a hypothetical firm is provided.

Discussion Questions

1. Explain the differences between the two measurement methodologies presented in the article.
2. Why is it important for firms and managers to consider shareholder value?
3. What are the key factors in determining shareholder value?

"The Role of Strategy"

This article presents a careful look at the role of local culture in the desirability of different management control systems. Local culture is defined in terms of Hofstede's research paradigm, including the measures: individualism, uncertainty avoidance, power distance, masculinity, and Confucianism. The culture of several major countries (including the U.S., U.K., Japan, Germany, and others) is considered and suggestions are provided for designing the management controls system for foreign SBUs. Companies should include both the firm's strategy and the culture of the foreign country in determining the most effective form of SBU and how it is to be implemented.

Discussion Questions

1. Identify and explain the meaning of each of the cultural factors (or "dimensions") used in Hofstede's research of cultures in various countries.
2. How should each of the cultural factors be used in developing effective SBU control systems?
3. For which countries do you think it would be most difficult to develop an effective management control system, and why?
4. For which countries do you think it would be easiest to develop an effective management control system, and why?

Cases

19-1. Midwest Petro-Chemical Company (Evaluating a Firm)[1]

Midwest Petro-Chemical, an industrial chemical distributor, was formed in 1960 by James Fletcher, a chemical engineer who had spent 10 years with the petrochemical division of a major oil company. His oil company experience which included a variety of technical, sales, and management positions, provided valuable business training. His final oil company position was regional marketing manager. He felt hindered by the slow-moving oil company bureaucracy, so he left a corporate career to begin Midwest Petro-Chemical.

The company began operation in Chicago in a rented warehouse with Fletcher as the only full-time employee. First-year sales totaled $113,000 and the company reported a loss of $6,200. Although first-year sales were less than planned and most of his initial capital was lost, Fletcher remained optimistic. Unable to obtain debt capital, he sought equity investors. He approached his college fraternity brothers and oil company colleagues to invest in the new venture. Six accepted, with each providing between $10,000 and $20,000 of much needed capital.

Sales exceeded $300,000 the second year of operations, but the company still reported a small loss of $4,000. The company reported its first profit of $14,000 in year three. Its first bulk distribution facility, capable of handling truck, rail, and barge transportation, was leased the next year.

Over the next 35 years, the company expanded operations beyond Chicago. New offices and plants were opened in five metropolitan cities: St. Louis, Kansas City, Louisville, Cincinnati, and Memphis. Plants were built in industrial areas on sites ranging from two to four acres. Each facility included a warehouse and tank farm with multiple-size tanks with capacities ranging from 1.5 million gallons (barge shipments) to 10,000 gallons (truck shipments). Chemical manufacturers and oil companies were the major supplier of chemicals. Midwest would purchase in bulk (barge, rail, or truck), blend chemicals as necessary, repackage, and ship product in smaller quantities (less than truckload, tote tanks, 55-gallon drums, and other smaller package sizes) to a variety of users.

CURRENT SITUATION

The company prospered and remains a privately held corporation. Annual sales exceeded $95 million in 1995, and a profit of $2,315 million was reported. Fletcher, now in his late 60s, is still CEO and the largest shareholder, owning 314,260 shares or 41.8% of the total shares outstanding. Three of the original investors (Stan Davis, Tom Williams, and Don Stewart) own another 326,216 shares (43.4%), and the company's pension fund owns 78,000 shares. Ron Allen, the company's chief financial officer, is the pension trustee and votes the shares. The remaining 32,524 shares are owned by 37 current or former employees.

There is not an active market for Midwest's stock. Sales or transfers of the stock occur infrequently between a buyer and seller, and Midwest does not participate in the exchange transaction. The sale price of stock is negotiated at arm's length between the buyer and seller. During 1995, approximately 18,000 shares were exchanged in 27 transactions at prices ranging from $21 to $24 per share.

Fletcher, the three remaining original investors (Davis, Williams, and Stewart) and Midwest's local counsel, Frank Armstrong, compose the Board of Directors. Despite

[1] Prepared byDavid A. Kunz and Keith A. Russell, © Institute of Management Accountants, 1996. Used with permission.

Midwest's consistent growth and profitability, recent Board meetings have resulted in heated discussions concerning three issues.

1. ***Succession plan***. Despite his age, Fletcher remains a more capable leader and has no desire to retire or even plan for retirement. The Board is concerned that no succession plan exists.
2. ***Stock value and liquidity***. Stan Davis (age 72) wants to sell his Midwest stock (126,415 shares) but feels the stock is substantially undervalued at its recent trading range of $21 to $24. Like Fletcher, Davis has started his own business—Western Solvents, Inc., a chemical distribution company on the West Coast. With the aid of an investment banking firm, he recently sold Western Solvents at a price that was 16 times earnings. He has been pressuring Fletcher to purchase his Midwest shares.
3. ***Offer to purchase the company***. Davis's interest in selling has been heightened due to an unsolicited purchase inquiry from Georgia Chemical, a chemical distributor in Atlanta. The inquiry was made via letter to Fletcher asking if there were any interest in selling Midwest. It is Fletcher's position that Midwest is not for sale, and he does not want to talk about the offer.

At the most recent Board meeting, Fletcher stated he was going to send a letter to Georgia Chemical indicating Midwest is not for sale. Davis objected and argued that it is their fiduciary responsibility as directors to consider all serious offers. Fletcher responded by saying, "Georgia Chemical's inquiry didn't even include a price, so how could it be considered an offer to buy?" Fletcher, Davis, and Allen offered their opinions as to what the stock was worth, but all agreed that their value estimates were not based on systematic or quantifiable processes. They also felt the current stock trading range was low. Stewart felt that without an established valuation of the stock, it would be very difficult, if not impossible, to evaluate objectively any offer to buy the firm. Frank Armstrong agreed with Stewart.

Before a response can be given to the Atlanta inquiry, a reasonable price must be determined. Don Stewart suggested an independent study be undertaken to determine the fair market value of Midwest's common stock. Stan Davis agreed and recommended using the investment banking firm of Warner and David, which recently valued his company. Ron Allen had worked with Warner and David with his previous employer and also thought highly of that firm's ability. Allen also commented that one of the hot new services offered by public accounting firms is business valuation. In fact, a partner in Midwest's auditing firm had mentioned this service in a recent meeting.

Despite his many years in business, Fletcher is unfamiliar with the procedures used to value a business. He is unwilling to bring in any outsider at this point. As a compromise, Tom Williams, a retired banker, suggested that Allen perform an in-house valuation by comparing Midwest's performance with industry norms. Analyses of ratios such as profit margin, return on assets, and return on equity were effective profit measures. Benchmarking Midwest's performance with industry data should be an indication of strength or weakness, which relates to value. Williams also mentioned the price-to-earnings ratio and the price-to-book-value ratio as other possible value indicators. He said that as a banker, he began evaluation of all loan requests with a detailed historic performance analysis using ratios. Sources such as Value Line Investment Survey and Robert Morris Associates Annual Statement Studies provide industry data. Allen agreed that financial analysis was beneficial but was skeptical about it yielding a usable value. Another approach Williams suggested was to perform a valuation using the market values of the firm's assets (appraisals were performed on all properties over the last two years for insurance purposes).

Allen thought a valuation process based on projected future cash flows might be a more accurate measure of the firm's value. Fletcher agreed with Allen because he feels the company is poised for considerable future growth. Davis suggested Allen use the sale of Western Solvents as a reference because the businesses were almost identical except for geographic location.

As the Board members began discussing the various proposals and the advantages and disadvantages of each, Frank Armstrong proposed yet another course of action: giving Ron Allen and his staff the assignment to (1) investigate valuation alternatives, (2) perform an in-house valuation, and (3) prepare a report for review at the next Board meeting (one month away). All Board members agreed, and Allen was given the assignment.

THE ASSIGNMENT

The next day, Ron Allen met with Linda Warren, Midwest's controller, to discuss the task. Warren mentioned that her previous employer used yet another valuation method—capitalization of earnings—to determine its worth. Allen said he planned to use all the methods suggested by the board members plus any other appropriate methods.

Together they reviewed each valuation method and prepared a description of each. They also listed information needed for each technique.

1. ***Financial Ratio Analysis***: Allen directed Warren to obtain industry comparative data and suggested starting with Value Line Investment Survey. Other sources of industry comparative data are Robert Morris Associates Annual Statement Studies and Standard and Poor's Industry Surveys.

2. ***Asset-Based or Market Value Method***: Although Tom Williams didn't refer specifically to this valuation method, Ron Allen thought he was describing it when he suggested using "market value of the assets." Linda Warren was to gather the most recent appraisals based on replacement values (see Table 1).

3. ***Market Comparison Method***: This approach suggested by Stan Davis is based on the assumptions that value of a privately held company can be estimated by comparing it to a similar company whose market values are known. As Davis's company recently sold at 16 times earnings, it can be used as the known market value.

4. ***Discounted Cash Flow***: Ron Allen and James Fletcher favor this approach based on expected future cash flows. Linda Warren pointed out that this technique requires forecasting future cash flows. Allen agreed and thought forecasting for five years would be appropriate. In preparing the forecasts, Allen suggested they project revenues to grow at 3.5% per year and forecast operating expenses (including depreciation) as a percentage of sales using an average of actual 1995 and 1994 percentages. As annual depreciation expense has been about $1.4 million the past two years, and no major acquisitions are expected, it was decided to use $800,000 for annual net cash from depreciation (assume $600,000 is reinvestment in existing operations). To keep it simple, Warren suggested forecasting interest expense of $900,000 in 1996 and reducing the amount by $50,000 each subsequent year. She also suggested projecting income tax expense at 30% of income before income taxes. Allen recognized this was an oversimplification, but agreed.

   Warren asked how she should handle working capital changes, dividends, and residual values. Allen commented that because the current relationship between revenues, current assets, and current liabilities was close to optimum, they should assume it is maintained. Dividends per share of $.35 should be projected for 1996 with a $.05 per share increase each year thereafter. Book value should be used for residual values.

The rate of return that investors require on equity capital depends on the riskiness of the cash flow stream. The risk premium on equity frequently is regarded at 3% higher than debt capital. Further, the risk and liquidity premium on private small companies without a liquid market indicated an additional premium in the range of 20%.

5. ***Capitalization of Earnings***: The capitalization of earnings approach embodies the concept that an investor in a going business has in mind a desired or "target" return on capital. Warren thought it would be another good technique but that they should perform two calculations, one based on past earnings and another using projected earnings. Allen agreed. The target return is expressed as a percentage of after-tax earnings to invested capital or equity and is referred to as return on equity (ROE). Warren thought they should use a capitalization rate based on an average ROE for 1995 and 1994. Allen concurred but told her to use beginning-year equity to calculate ROE.

REQUIRED:

Assume the roles of Ron Allen, Midwest Petro-Chemical's chief financial officer, and Linda Warren, controller, and prepare the required report for the Board. The report should address the following:

1. What is Midwest's strategic competitive advantage, and what type of compensation plan is most consistent with this strategy?
2. Analyze company performance using financial ratio analysis and industry norms as a bench mark. What are the strengths and weaknesses of this evaluation process?
3. Why did financial ratio analysis serve as an effective tool for Tom Williams?
4. Discuss each valuation method. What are the strengths and weaknesses of each? What difficulties are encountered when applying each method?
   a. Asset-based or market value
   b. Market comparison
   c. Discounted cash flow
   d. Capitalization of earnings
      1. Historic earnings
      2. Projected earnings
5. Develop values for Midwest Petro-Chemical's stock using the four valuation methods discussed in requirement 4.
6. Based on your previous answers, develop a fair-market value for Midwest's common stock. Support your value.
7. Recommend a negotiating strategy for dealing with the inquiry from the Atlanta company.
8. Once a price is agreed upon by a buyer and seller, sale terms must be structured.
   a. Will the price be paid in cash at closing? As an initial cash payment plus future payments? As stock or some combination of the aforementioned?
   b. Will stock or assets be sold? Will the sale terms affect price? If so, how? Explain your answer.

(IMA adapted)

TABLE 1

	Acquisition Date	Land	Plant Prop.& Equip	Accumulated Depreciation	Net Book Value
Chicago	1963	$ 634	$ 4,415	$ 3,012	$ 2,037
St. Louis	1967	960	4,602	3,118	2,444
Louisville	1970	1,100	5,809	4,019	2,890
Cincinnati	1980	2,600	6,222	3,216	5,606
Memphis	1982	2,466	7,214	3,037	6,643
		$7,760	$28,262	$16,402	$19,620

	Appraisal Date	Land	Plant. Prop. & Equip	Total
Chicago	1994	$2,010	$2,050	$ 4,060
St. Louis	1991	1,580	1,738	3,318
Louisville	1992	1,720	1,612	3,332
Memphis	1989	2,910	3,702	6,612
Cincinnati	1990	2,700	4,313	7,013
				$24,335

		Shares	%
James Retcher	CEO/Director	314,260	41.8
Stan David	Director	126,415	16.8
Tom Williams	Director	105,060	14.0
Don Stewart	Director	94,741	12.6
Pension fund*		78,000	10.4
Other		32,524	4.4
	Total	751,000	100.4

*Shares voted by trustee Ron Allen

Table 1 (Continued)

Balance Sheets (000s).
December 31

	1995	**1994**		1995	1994
Current assets			Current liabilities		
Cash	$ 510	$ 212	Accounts payable	$11,264	$8,944
Receivables	13,925	12,816	Accrued expenses	2,245	1,745
Inventories	9,310	10,463	Total current liabilities.	13,509	10,689
Prepaid expenses	745	413			
Total current assets	$24,490	$23,904	Long-term obligations	10,899	15,600
			Total liabilities	24,408	26,289
Property and equipment at cost			Shareholders'equity		
Land	7,760	7,760	Common stock $1 par value		
Plant, property and equipment	28,262	27,232	2,000,000 shares authorized		
Less accumulated depreciation ...	(16,402)	(14,995)	751,000 shares outstanding	751	751
Total plant and property	19,620	19,997	Paid in capital	2,253	2,253
			Retained in earnings	16,198	14,608
			Total shareholders'equity	19,702	17,612
Total assets	$44,110	$43,901	Total liabilities and equity	$44,110	$43,901

Table 1 (continued)

FINANCIAL STATEMENTS
MIDWEST PETRO-CHEMICAL, INC.
Statement of Income (000s)
For the Years Ending December 31

	1995	1994	1993	1992
Net Sales	$95,652	$92,333	$90,114	$86,414
Costs of Sales and Selling cost				
Cost of sales	77,719	74,882	74,374	70,859
Selling	13,712	13,388	13,049	12,703
Total costs	91,431	88,270	87,423	83,562
Operating income	4,221	4,063	2,691	2,852
Interest expense	914	1,214	1,612	1,728
Income before income	3,307	2,849	1,079	1,124
Income tax expense	992	854	270	259
Net Income	2,315	1,995	809	865
Earnings per share	$3.08	$2.66	$1.08	$1.15
Dividends per share	.30	.25	.22	.20

Statement of Cash Flows (000s)
For the Year Ending December 31, 1995

Operating activities	
Net income	$2,315
Additions (sources of cash)	
Depreciation	1,407
Decrease in inventory	1,153
Increase in accounts payable	2,320
Increase in accrued expense	500
Subtractions	
Increase in accounts receivable	(1,109)
Increase in prepaid assets	(332)
Net Cash provided by operating activities	6,254
Long-term investing activities	
Cash used to acquire fixed assets	(1,030)
Financing activities	
Decrease on long-term debt	(4,701)
Payment of dividends	(225)
Net cash provided by financing activities	(4,926)
Net increase in cash	298
Cash at beginning of year	212
Cash at end of year	$ 510

19-2. Evaluating a Firm

REQUIRED:

Consider the financial data below for the Example Company, and assess the value of the Company. Explain your choice(s) of valuation method(s). All figures are 000s except for share price

Example Company
Selected Financial Data

Account Description	1999	2000	2001	2002	2003	2004
Cash	25,141	25,639	32,977	34,009	49,851	30,943
Accounts Receivable	272,450	312,776	368,267	419,731	477,324	542,751
Prepaids	3,982	4,402	5,037	5,246	5,378	6,648
Inventories	183,722	208,623	222,128	260,492	298,696	399,533
Property & Equipment (net)	47,578	49,931	55,311	61,832	77,173	91,420
Other Assets	18,734	20,738	23,075	26,318	36,248	39,403
Total Assets	551,607	622,109	706,795	807,628	944,670	1,110,698
Accounts Payable	49,831	64,321	70,853	80,861	94,677	78,789
Accrued Expenses	86,087	102,650	113,732	131,899	143,159	164,243
Notes Payable	99,539	118,305	182,132	246,420	237,741	390,034
Long-term Debt	62,622	43,251	35,407	32,301	128,432	126,672
Deferred Taxes Payable	7,551	7,941	8,286	8,518	9,664	11,926
Other Liabilities	5,279	5,521	5,697	5,593	5,252	4,695
Total Liabilities	310,909	341,989	416,107	505,592	618,925	776,359
Capital Stock	73,253	87,851	79,009	71,601	81,238	73,186
Retained Earnings	167,445	192,539	211,679	230,435	244,507	261,153
Total Stockholders Equity	240,698	280,120	290,688	302,036	325,745	334,339
Total Liabilities & Equity	551,607	662,109	706,795	807,628	944,670	1,110,698
Net Sales	982,244	1,095,083	1,214,666	1,259,116	1,378,251	1,648,500
Cost of Goods Sold	669,560	739,459	817,671	843,192	931,237	1,125,261
Depreciation Expense	8,303	8,380	8,972	9,619	10,577	12,004
Interest Expense	11,248	13,146	14,919	18,874	16,562	21,128
Income Tax Expense	26,650	34,000	38,000	32,800	26,500	25,750
Dividends Paid	13,805	17,160	19,280	20,426	20,794	20,807
Net Income	32,563	37,895	41,809	39,577	35,212	37,787
Number of common shares outstanding at year-end	12,817	13,714	13,728	13,684	14,023	13,993
Market price per share	38	43	55	65	43	31

19-3. Economic Value Added; Review of Chapter 18; Strategy[1]

"I've been hearing a lot lately about something called EVA, which stands for Economic Value Added, and I was curious whether it is something we can use at OSI," Keith Martin said as he finished his lunch. Keith is president and CEO of OutSource, Inc. His guest for lunch that day was a computer industry analyst from a local brokerage firm. Keith had invited him to lunch so he could get more information on EVA and its uses.

"Yes," the analyst replied, "I've heard a great deal about EVA. It's a residual income approach in which a firm's net operating profit after taxes—called NOPAT—is reduced by a minimum level of return a firm must earn on the total amount of capital placed at its disposal.

"Have you seen the recent articles on EVA? The after-tax operating profit, NOPAT as you called it, and the amount used for capital don't come directly off the financial statements. You have to analyze the footnotes to determine the adjustments that have to be made to come up with those amounts."

"The article sounds like interesting reading for me, especially at this point," Keith said. "Can you send me a copy?"

"Sure," said the analyst. "But tell me, what is it about EVA that piqued your interest in trying it at OSI?"

"In tracking our industry," Keith replied, "I see the stock prices of some of our key competitors, like Equifax, increasing. Yet, when I compare OSI's recent growth in sales and earnings, our return on equity and earnings per share compare well to those firms, but our stock price doesn't achieve nearly the same rate of increase, and I don't understand why."

The analyst suggested, "Some of those firms might be benefiting from using EVA already, and the market value of their stock probably reflects the results of their efforts. It has been shown that a higher level of correlation exists between EVA and a stock's market value than has been found with the traditional accounting performance measures like ROE or EPS."

"But will EVA work in a small service firm like OSI?"

"I've read about EVA being used at smaller firms," said the analyst. "I'm not an expert on EVA, but I don't see any reason why it wouldn't work at OSI."

"I'd like to find out more about EVA and how we can use it at OSI. For example, we've talked about a new incentive plan-will EVA work in that area? And, if so, will it help us in deciding how we should organize and manage our operations as we expand and grow? What can you do to get more information on these things to me?"

COMPANY INFORMATION

OutSource, Inc. (OSI) is a computer service bureau that provides basic data processing and general business support services to a number of business firms, including several large firms in the immediate local area. Its offices are in a large city in the mid-Atlantic region, and it serves client firms in several Mid-Atlantic States. OSI's revenues have grown rapidly in recent years as businesses have downsized and outsourced many of their basic support services.

---

[1] Prepared by Paul A. Dierks, © Institute of Management Accountants, 1998. Used with permission.

The CorpInfo Data Service (CIDS) classifies OSI as an Information Services firm (SIC 7374). This group is composed, in large part, of smaller, independent entrepreneurs that provide a variety of often disparate services to both corporate and government clients. Market analysts feel a continuously healthy economy translates into strong potential for higher earnings by members of this group. A factor sustaining an extended period of growth is the increased attention of firms to control costs and to outsource their non-core functions, such as personnel placement, payroll, human resources, insurance, and data processing. This trend is expected to continue, probably at an increasing rate. Several firms in this industry have capitalized on their growth and geographic expansion to win lucrative contracts with large clients that previously had been awarded on a market-by-market basis.

Although OSI operates out of its own facilities, which include some computing equipment and furniture, the bulk of its computer processing power is obtained from excess computer capacity in the local area, primarily rented time during third-shift operations at a large local bank. To be successful in the long term, however, OSI management knows it must expand its business considerably, and, to ensure it has full control over its operations, it must set up its own large-scale computing facility in-house. These items are included in OSI's strategic plan.

As OSI's reputation for accurate, reliable, and quick response service has spread, the firm has found new business coming its way in a variety of data processing and support services. The issue has been deciding which services to take on or to stay out of in light of the current limitations on OSI's computing resources and assurance it can continue to provide high-quality service to its customers. Things definitely are looking up for OSI, and industry market analysts recently have begun to look more favorably on its stock.

In 1993, OSI's board decided to pursue additional opportunities in payroll processing and tax filing services, and OSI purchased a medium-sized firm that had an established market providing payroll calculations, processing, and reporting services for several Fortune 500 firms on the East Coast. Now OSI is in the midst of developing a new payroll processing system, called PayNet, to replace the outmoded system that was originally created by the firm it acquired.

Once PayNet is developed, it will give users an integrated payroll solution with a simpler, more familiar graphic user interface. From an administrative perspective, it will allow OSI to reduce its manual data entry hiring, to speed data compilation and analysis, and to simplify administrative tasks and the updating of customer files for adds, moves, and changes. PayNet will serve as the backbone for OSI's service bureau payroll processing operations in the future, but developmental and programming costs have been higher than expected and will delay the roll out of the final version of the new payroll program. Beta testing of the production version of PayNet is being delayed from the second to the third quarter of 1996.

TABLE 1. OUTSOURCE INC.
Balance Sheet
December 31,

	1995	1994
ASSETS		
Current Assets:		
Cash	$144,724	$169,838
Trade and other receivables (net)	217,085	192,645
Inventories	15,829	23,750
Other current assets	61,047	49,239
Total current assets	438,685	435,472
Noncurrent Assets:		
Property, plant, equipment	123,135	109,600
Software and development costs	33,760	14,947
Data processing equipment & furniture	151,357	141,892
Other noncurrent assets	3,650	8,844
	311,902	275,283
Less: Accumulated depreciation	85,108	57,929
Total (net) noncurrent assets	226,884	217,354
Goodwill	88,200	96,600
	$753,769	$749,426
LIABILITIES AND SHAREHOLDERS' EQUITY		
Current liabilities		
Short-term debt & current portion of long-term note	$27,300	$31,438
Accounts payable	67,085	57,483
Deferred income	45,050	32,250
Income taxes payable	19,936	12,100
Employee compensation and benefits accrued	30,155	28,950
Other accrued expenses	28,458	27,553
Other current liabilities	17,192	29,769
Total current liabilities	235,176	219,543
Long-term note, less current portion	98,744	117,155
Deferred income taxes	6,784	4,850
Shareholders' Equity:		
Cumulative Nonconvertible Preferred Stock, $100 par value, authorized 5,000 shares, issued and outstanding 1,000 shares	100,000	100,000
Common stock, $1 par value; 300,000 shares authorized; 219,884 shares issued & outstanding	219,884	219,884
Additional paid-in capital	32,056	32,056
Retained earnings	61,125	55,938
Total shareholders' equity	413,065	407,878
	$753,769	$749,426

OutSource, Inc. - Statement of Income for The Year Ended December 31, 1995

Operating revenue	$2,604,530
Less: Costs of services	1,466,350
Gross profit	1,138,180
Less: Operating expenses	
Selling, general and administrative	902,388
Research and development	89,089
Other expense (income)	59,288
Write-off of goodwill and other tangibles	13,511
Earnings (Loss) before interest and taxes	73,904
Interest income	1,009
Interest expense	12,427
Earnings (Loss) before income taxes	62,486
Income tax provision	21,870
Earnings (Loss)	$40,616

OutSource, Inc. - Statement of Cash Flows for The Year Ended December 31, 1995

Cash Flows from Operating Activities	
Net Earnings (Loss)	$40,616
Depreciation	21,978
Amortization of software & development	5,111
Decrease (Increase) in trade & other receivables	(24,440)
Decrease (Increase) in inventories	7,921
Decrease (Increase)in other current assets	(11,808)
Increase (Decrease) in deferred income	9,602
Increase (Decrease) in accounts payable	12,800
Increase (Decrease) in income taxes payable	7,836
Increase (Decrease) in employee compensation and benefits	1,205
Increase (Decrease) in other accrued expenses	905
Increase (Decrease) in other current liabilities	(12,577)
Increase (Decrease) in deferred income taxes	1,934
Net cash provided by (used for) operating activities	61,083
Cash Flows from Investing Activities	
Expended for capital assets	(36,619)
Goodwill amortized	8,400
Net cash provided by (used for) investing activities	(28,219)
Cash Flows from Financing Activities	
Payment of long-term note	(4,138)
Payment of short-term note	(18,411)
Preferred dividends paid	(11,000)
Common stock dividends paid	(24,429)
Net cash provided by (used for) financing activities	(57,978)
Net Cash Flows Provided (Used)	**(25,114)**
Cash at beginning of year	**$169,838**
Cash at end of year	**$144,724**

ADDITIONAL ACCOUNTING INFORMATION

OSI's financial statements for 1995 appear in Table 1. The following list of information is pertinent to calculating a firm's EVA extracted from the footnotes to OSI's annual report for 1995.

A. Inventories are stated principally at cost (last-in, first-out), which is not in excess of market. Replacement cost would be $2,796 greater than the 1994 inventory balance and $3,613 greater than the 1995 inventory balance.

B. On July 1, 1993, the company acquired CompuPay, a payroll processing and reporting service firm. The acquisition was accounted for as a purchase, and the excess cost over the fair value of net assets acquired was $109,200, which is being amortized on a straight-line basis over 13 years. One-half year of goodwill amortization was recorded in 1993.

C. Research and development costs related to software development are expensed as incurred. Software development costs are capitalized from the point in time when the technological feasibility of a piece of software has been determined until it is ready to be put on line to process customer data. The cost of purchased software, which is ready for service, is capitalized on acquisition. Software development costs and purchased software costs are amortized using the straight-line method over periods ranging from three to seven years. A history of the accounting treatment of software development costs and purchased software costs follow:

	Expensed	Capitalized	Amortized
1993	$166,430	$ 9,585	0
1994	211,852	5,362	$ 4,511
1995	89,089	18,813	5,111
	$467,371	$33,760	$ 9,622

ADDITIONAL FINANCIAL INFORMATION

OSI's common stock is currently trading at $2 per share. A preferred dividend of $11 per share was paid in 1995, and the current price of preferred stock is approximately at its par value. Other information pertaining to OSI's debt and stock follows:

Short-term debt	$ 8,889	8.0%
Long-term debt:		
Current portion	$ 18,411	10.0%
Long-term portion	$ 98,744	10.0%
Total long-term debt	$117,155	

Stock market risk-free rate (90-day T-bills)	=	5.0%
Expected return on the market	=	12.5%
Expected growth rate of dividends	=	8.0%
Income tax rate	=	35.0%

REQUIRED:

1. The management of OutSource, Inc. has asked you to prepare a report explaining EVA (Economic Value Added), how it is calculated, and how it compares to traditional measures of a firm's financial performance. As part of your answer, calculate EVA from OSI's financial report.

2. What are the advantages and disadvantages of using EVA to evaluate OSI's performance on an on-going basis, as well as in assessing the performance of individual managers throughout its organization? How might EVA help OSI attain its strategic goals?
3. OSI management wants to know if EVA can be used as part of an incentive program for its employees, and if so, how it should be implemented.

(IMA, adapted)

USING SHAREHOLDER VALUE TO EVALUATE STRATEGIC CHOICES

Financial metrics is a realistic way for companies to measure value.

By Nick Fera

Creating shareholder wealth or value has become the mantra for most corporate boards, especially in the United States. Yet as recently as the mid-1980s, the idea of "shareholder value" or "shareholder wealth" was not an overwhelmingly accepted principle. But as academics began to teach the principle in business schools around the world, such noted authorities as Professor Alfred Rappaport of Northwestern University's J. L. Kellogg Graduate School of Management, author of *Creating Shareholder Value*,[1] began to apply it to corporate mergers and acquisitions in the 1980s. Shareholder value, or free cash flow analysis, became the measurement standard for the 1980s and into the 1990s. Given today's increased demand for international capital returns, as well as the proliferation of private baby boomer pension funds in the United States, investors have imposed new stringency in their vigil against corporate wealth destruction. Even the brightest stars are not immune to the pressure of pension funds or Wall Street. Witness the pressure that CALPERS (the state of California's teachers' retirement funds) placed on Michael Eisner at Walt Disney Co. despite Eisner's laudable success in increasing Disney's market value from $5 billion to more than $42 billion during his first 10 years in office. During a 10-year period from January 1986 to December 1996, Disney's stock price grew at a cumulative annual growth rate of more than 21%, while the S&P 500 index has returned approximately 15%. Historical performances are not always enough; investors continue to ask for more.

Measuring performance no longer can be left to the traditional accounting department's calculations of earnings per share (EPS) or return on equity (ROE), as these accrual-based accounting measures aren't always useful indicators of future growth or performance. Thus, it is necessary to understand and adopt measurement techniques that will help make decisions while driving increasing profitability. One of the economic measurement techniques that can be used is free cash flow analysis or Shareholder Value Analysis (SVA).

SHAREHOLDER VALUE ANALYSIS

Because managers began to realize that businesses needed a more realistic means of assessing their value than accrual-based accounting standards offered, such respected academics as Professor Rappaport sought to develop sophisticated economic models for strategic evaluations. As a result, shareholder value analysis was conceived. SVA works by explicitly measuring the economic impact of each strategy on the value of a business. Any strategic decision, regardless of whether it involves internal or external investment, should be evaluated. Examples of such strategic decision-making situations include mergers and acquisitions, joint ventures, divestitures, new product development (R&D), and capital expenditures (major plant and equipment investments).

The actual measurement of shareholder value combines three main factors: 1) cash flow, 2) cash as measured over a given period of time (value growth

[1] Alfred Rappaport, *Creating Shareholder Value: The New Standard for Business Performance*, New York: The Free Press, 1986.

duration), and 3) risk, otherwise known as the cost of capital. (See Fig. 1.) With a basic understanding of these three components, you are well on your way to valuing a business or entity. Next, let's discuss the difference between corporate value and shareholder value.

CREATING VALUE

FIGURE 1
FACTORS IN SHARHOLDER VALUE

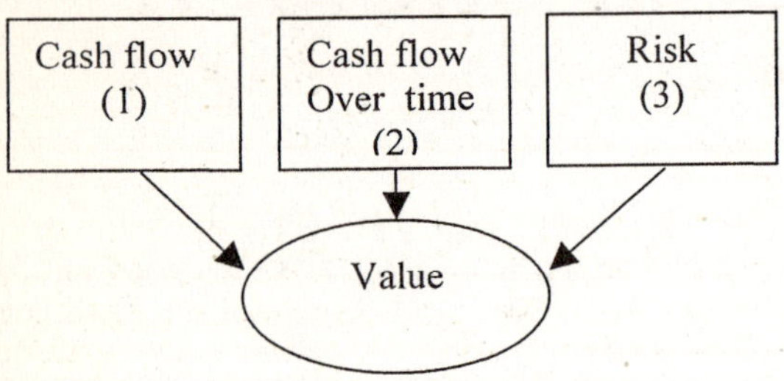

Corporate value is equal to the net present value of all future cash flows to all investor types, including both debt and equity holders. Shareholder value is the corporate value minus all future claims to cash flow (debt) before equity holders are paid. Future claims typically include both short-and long-term debt, capital lease obligations, underfunded pensions, and other claims such as contingent liabilities—lawsuits brought against the company. (See Fig. 2.) Another way to define shareholder value is to say that it is equal to the net funds a company generates that shareholders could receive in the form of a cash distribution, such as a dividend.

Be careful not to confuse this figure with the actual dividend a company pays. A company's dividend policy has little or nothing to do with the actual cash the company generates. Look at the high growth of businesses such as computer software or biotechnology. Few pay dividends because they have strategic opportunities to reinvest cash flows and earn the higher returns investors desire.

Generally, it's easy to determine the market value of future obligations or debt. In most cases, it's the accumulation of several debt instruments. To obtain the market value of these financial instruments, use the yield to maturity to calculate the *market value* of each debt instrument. Avoid adding the face value of each debt or bond issue. The question to ask is, "If this obligation were to be paid in full today, how much would the lender need to retire it?"

FIGURE 2
CORPORATE AND SHAREHOLDER VALUE

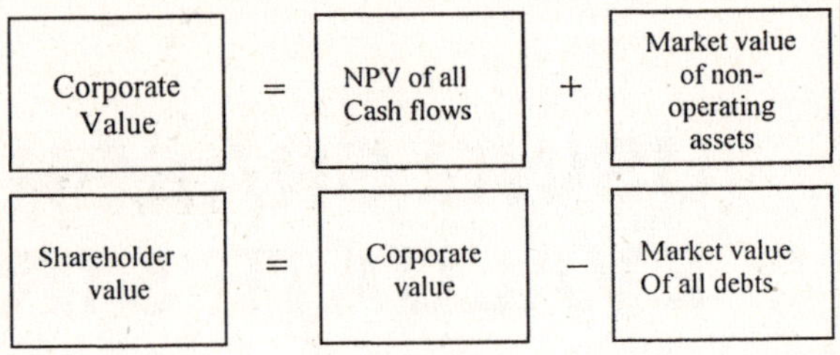

MEASURING CASH FLOW

After determining corporate and shareholder value, the next step is to measure cash flow. The most tangible measurement of cash flow (also referred to as operating cash flow or free cash flow) can be calculated as shown in Table 1.

Notice that the calculation focuses on the relationship between operating cash income and expenses, specifically by using operating cash taxes rather than the provision for income taxes. It accounts for the investments made on the balance sheet. Many companies measure cash flow by looking at net operating profit after taxes (NOPAT), but it tells only part of the story. Investments to grow the business, either by expansion of the plant and facilities or with working capital policies such as extending the receivable period from net 30 to net 60 days, have a significant impact on the capital employed. Remember: Shareholders are looking for returns on their capital invested in business growth, which requires well-planned capital expenditures. Failure to account for the investment makes for a crucial mistake in the evaluation of strategic alternatives.

CALCULATING CASH FLOWS

The calculation of cash flow illustrates a high level of performance in an organization and produces a result that approximates the net cash of a company. In effect, these funds are a potential dividend to shareholders because they reflect optimal use of shareholder monies for ongoing growth. That is why dividend policy and free cash flow are not synonymous. Few companies base their dividend payout on net

TABLE 1
MEASURING CASH FLOW

	Formula	Example	Value Drivers
	Sales	$1,000	Sales growth (Sg)
Less	Operating expenses	–$ 600	Margin (P)
Equals	Pre-tax profit	$ 400	
Less	Cash taxes	–$ 100	Tax rate (T)
Equals	Net operating profit after taxes (NOPAT)	$ 300	
Add	Depreciation expense	$ 75	
Less	Fixed capital investment	–$ 125	Fixed capital investment (F)
Less	Incremental working capital investment	–$ 50	Working capital investment (W)
Equals	Operating cash flow (free cash flow)	$ 250	

cash flow, while others are justified in generating free cash flow, without paying dividends.

To forecast cash flow, most companies require a more detailed formula, as presented in Table 1. In most cases, sales growth tells very little about actual sales activity, so companies use metrics such as price, volume, GNP, and other micro or macroeconomic factors to forecast revenues and costs more realistically. This calculation usually is conducted at a strategic business unit level and then consolidated for corporate purposes. The key is to plan accurately at the appropriate level of business activity (business unit, value chain, or some other distinction).

Sales or market growth estimations can be achieved many different ways. Predicting price and volume, for instance, provides for a more manageable metric that can be evaluated readily and used later for compensation purposes. In other words, sales growth is a "*value driver.*" But what *drives* the value drivers? Herein typically lies the metric operational professionals can get their hands on. Planning and forecasting can become a real *operating activity rather than a boardroom exercise.*

CASH FLOW OVER TIME

Once cash flow has been defined, the next step is to determine the length of the forecast period. The definition of cash flow over time or value growth duration is the length of time expected for a company to invest in opportunities that will yield internal rates of return (IRR) above their weighted average cost of capital (WACC). This premise is the core of value creation—performing above expectations for a sustainable period of time.

Management usually plans for cycles of three to five years. If this is the case and if the cash flows are discounted over a period of time, the valuation probably will be inaccurate as it does not allow for fluctuations in cash flow throughout the requisite growth period. To determine the appropriate length of the forecast period (or the value growth duration), consider several factors.

One is Michael Porter's work on the competitive structure and five forces of industries (see Fig. 3). Porter says that management's responsibility is to map the company and its competition according to several factors. Some areas to consider are distribution channels, established brand names, and research and development. Take the pharmaceutical industry, for instance. It has a relatively long value growth duration because of patented products, proven processes, and research and development investment that raise the barriers of entry.

Also, read Alfred Rappaport's discussion of the use of public information to assess the market's expectation for a company's value growth duration.[2] He suggests gathering forecasting information on a particular company as well as identifying competitors. He also advises managers to employ the researched information and forecast the cash flows, as discussed previously. But rather than changing any value driver assumptions, change only the length of the forecast until the present value of the cash flows less debt equals the market value of your company. Surprisingly, most companies in a given industry tend to fall

[2] Alfred Rappaport, "Stock Market Signals to Managers." Harvard Business Review, November-December 1987, pp. 57-62.

within a certain range; thus, the market is suggesting an implied value growth duration. These "market signals" are helpful for starting an internal analysis and discussion.

RESIDUAL VALUE

Once you have determined the value growth duration, you must address the value of the cash flows beyond the current period. This determination is called the terminal or residual value. Assume that, after the forecast period, new investments (fixed and working capital) will yield returns equal to the cost of capital. In other words, the internal rate of return is equal to the weighted average cost of capital. Therefore, the net present value of cash flows from new or incremental investments beyond the value growth duration will be equal to zero. The only cash flow left to value in the residual period is the preinvestment cash flow, or NOPAT (see Table 1). Note that depreciation is *not* included because it is viewed as a proxy for reinvestment. Given that the cash flows are valued infinitely, the business probably would not continue to generate the same level of cash flow if the plant, equipment, or other physical assets were allowed to deteriorate fully. In fact, some companies recognize a higher level of "maintenance" spending and will adjust the cash flow in the residual period to reflect higher replacement costs.

TERMINAL VALUE

At this point, it is necessary to discuss some assumptions of terminal value. The net present value of the residual cash flows is equal to an infinite stream of cash flow (as measured by NOPAT) discounted back at the WACC. Mathematically, this is NOPAT at the end of the value growth duration divided by the WACC. Once this calculation is complete, it is necessary to discount the value back to the current period. The formula is presented in Table 2 (assuming a five-year value growth duration and 12% WACC).

DEFINING RISK

The last component of determining the value of an entity is deciding on the overall risk. The risk of a company usually is measured with WACC. The approach assumes there is some mixture of debt and equity that is financing the company. The cost of debt is measured as the after-tax cost, that is, the cost accounting for the tax deductibility of interest payments. The marginal cost of debt is not necessarily the average coupon rate on various debt instruments. Instead, it is the rate for which banks will lend the company an incremental dollar.

The cost of equity is somewhat more complex. If companies use the Capital Asset Pricing Model approach developed by economists Sharpe, Lintner, and Treynor in the mid-1960s, the cost of equity has two basic components: a risk-free return required by investors and a premium for investing in equities that are of higher risk. The risk-free rate is the treasury rate on 30-year U.S. government bonds. This standard generally is used because these bonds typically are seen as delivering the most risk-free, long-

FIGURE 3
FORCES DRIVING INDUSTRY COMPETITION

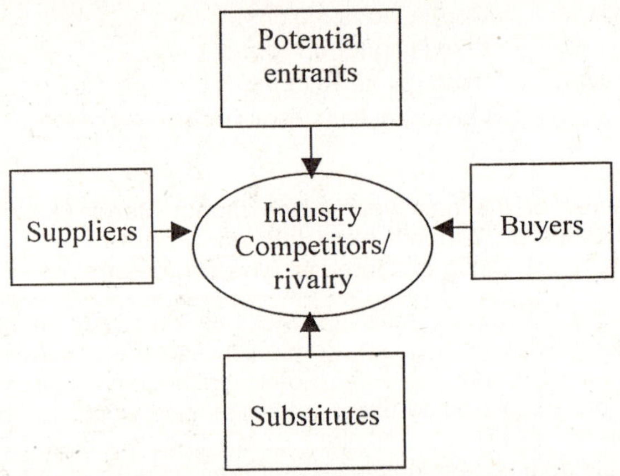

term returns investors can earn. The second component is the premium for investing in something that is of higher risk than the U.S. government. This element is called the market risk premium (MRP itself and a multiplier, called beta, for investments that are more

TABLE 2
SHAREHOLDER VALUE ANALYSIS: AN EXAMPLE

		Forecasted cash flows					Terminal
		Year 1	Year 2	Year 3	Year 4	Year 5	CF (NOPAT)
		$10	$15	$17	$23	$25	$30
NPV CF	$ 61.79	←					↓
NPV RV	$141.86	← Discounted to Current period					$250 (Future value)
	$203.65						

Total NPV CF		$203.65
Add	Marketable securities	$ 25.00
Equals	Corporate value	$228.65
Less	MV debt	$ 15.00
Shareholder Value		$213.65

or less risky than the market portfolio.

MARKET RISK PREMIUM

The market risk premium is calculated and published by sources such as Ibbotson Associates in its annual SBBI (Stocks, Bonds, Bills, and Inflation). Historically, the premium for holding a portfolio of equities, as opposed to investing in a risk-free instrument, is between 6% and 7%, depending on whether you use the arithmetic or geometric average.

Beta is a measure of the relative riskiness of an individual company or portfolio as compared with the market. Thus a beta of 1.0 correlates exactly with market returns. Beta is measured by comparing the returns of an individual security or portfolio with those of the market. Sources of beta estimates include Merrill Lynch, ValueLine, and Alcar.

There is another way to measure the MRP that is consistent with a forecasting approach. This tack uses estimates of the expected return on the market for the next year. Each month Merrill Lynch publishes a 12-month expected return on the market (S&P 500). Using this forecast, you can determine the expected MRP by subtracting the current risk-free rate, as measured by 30-year treasuries, from the current forecast of market returns. As of October 1, 1997, Merrill Lynch's forecast of market returns was 10.9%, while the risk-free rate is currently 6.38%. As a result, the expected market risk premium is 4.52%. Some companies prefer to use the ex-ante approach because it matches the *forecasting* of cash flows with the *forecasting* of expected returns.

Putting all the components of the cost of equity equation together yields the following formula:
Cost of Equity = Risk-free rate + Beta * (Market Risk Premium) or, $K_e = R_f + ß * (MRP)$

Once you have calculated the cost of equity and the cost of debt, you may use the WACC approach to combine both costs (debt and equity). In calculating the WACC, use the market values of debts and equity, not the book values, because the market costs of each source of financing are being measured. The equation is as follows:
WACC (K_c) = % of Debt * [Cost of Debt (K_d)] + % of Equity * [Cost of Equity (K_e)]
Let's look at an example involving a manufacturing company using risk estimation:

A U.S. manufacturing company is publicly traded and has a market capitalization of $550 million. Its outstanding debt totals $250 million at a marginal borrowing rate of 8.5% (assume this is the market value of debt and includes all obligations of the company). The current risk-free rate is 7%, the expected return on the market is 12%, the beta of this company has been published as .90, and its marginal tax rate is 28%. What is the weighted average cost of capital (WACC)?

MRP	=	12 – 7	=	5%
K_e	=	.07 + .9(.05)	=	11.5%
K_d	=	.085 * (1 – 28)	=	6.12% (after tax)
WACC	=	(250/800) * .0612 +		(550/800) * .115 = 9.8%

Measurement Methodologies:

1. Economic Principles
   Shareholder Value Analysis
   (SVA)—also known as Discounted Cash Flow analysis (DCF) or Net Present Value (NPV)
   - Evaluates cash inflows to cash outflows on a risk-adjusted basis
   - Most widely accepted approach to business evaluation

   Economic Value Analysis (EVA)
   - Primarily used as a performance measurement tool to calculate period-by-period performance
   - Helps an organization to focus on value creation or increased cash flow
   - Measuring the change in EVA also may be an effective financial measurement tool

   Cash Flow Return on Investment (CFROI)
   - Derived from market data to determine cash flow growth and the overall discount rate
   - Helps an organization to focus on value creation or increased cash flow
   - Seen as a complex financial measurement device
2. Accounting Principles
   Return on Capital (ROC)
   Return on Invested Capital (ROIC)
   Return on Equity (ROE)
   Earnings per Share (EPS)

FROM THE BOARDROOM TO THE SHOP FLOOR

Once you have established the methodology, take it out of the boardroom (as a planning exercise), and implement it at all levels, including the shop floor (or any manufacturing or operating activity). The importance of moving the analysis out of the boardroom and into regular practice is that managers and shareholders will have the same economic interests. If managers are compensated on accrual-based accounting measures, they may optimize their own interest when there is a conflict between cash flow and accrual accounting. But if you align the interest and performance measurement of all managers to be the same, both are optimized.

Moving the methodology to the shop floor may pose a challenge. Not only is it more difficult to identify key value drivers on the shop floor (such as production yield, waste, inventory management), but there also is an important educational component. Not all managers have been introduced to the concepts and methodologies of financial metrics. Many still are entrenched with the simpler accrual-based accounting measures. Yet once key drivers are identified and their relative impact on value is measured, managers relate to the results.

ONGOING MAINTENANCE AND PERFORMANCE MEASUREMENT

Once the methodology is in place, the final challenge is to put it into practice every year. What adds to the complexity of the implementation is the ability to monitor performance in a timely manner due to the multitude of manual and multiple systems currently in place to do the job. Many companies implement and attempt to monitor their performance with the use of disconnected spreadsheet technology. Beyond all the difficulties of performing rigorous economic analysis in a spreadsheet (with factual integrity and documentation leading the pack), the use of spreadsheets can create pockets of information that are disjointed from the rest of the organization. These pockets of information make it difficult to monitor performance, test new scenarios regularly, and make new, informed decisions on a timely basis.

Fortunately, the recent development of new technologies that interface seemlessly with each other is making it easier to gather data quickly and spend the majority of analytical time on planning, testing, and choosing new strategic alternatives. Thus, the planning process is changing from an annual event generally found on the bookshelf to a regularly used strategic exercise that becomes a living document, enabling companies to manage their business by making value-based strategic choices in our ever-evolving environment.

THE ROLE OF STRATEGY

By Priscilla Q. Clock, CPA, Ph.D, and Kevin Devine, Ph.D.

A primary challenge facing many U.S.-based multinational corporations (MNCs) is the evaluation of foreign strategic business units (SBUs). The way an organization evaluates and measures performance determines the motivation behind the decisions and actions of an SBU's managers. Failure to consider the strategic objectives of an SBU or the cultural identity of its management is an error many MNCs commit when they export the evaluation systems of the parent entity to the foreign SBU. This often results in decisions by the SBU's managers that are incongruent with corporate goals and objectives.

The consideration of cultural differences is particularly important when the management of an international SBU is delegated to host country personnel. All too frequently, multinational corporations mistakenly evaluate their performance using return on investment (ROI) or one of its variants, such as residual income (RI) or economic value added (EVA), regardless of the business unit strategy. This can lead to management control systems that result in suboptimal decision making, conflicting corporate and SBU objectives, and a negative impact on morale. Return-based measures play a role in evaluating performance, but, used improperly, they perpetuate a short-term orientation and may be inconsistent with the cultural preferences that motivate the local manager.

When developing control systems to evaluate the performance of an international SBU—and rewarding its managers—companies should design performance measures that consider the impact of business unit strategies and cultural differences. In this article, we will present competing business unit strategies and suggest variants to the control system to compensate for these differences. We also will discuss cultural dimensions as identified by Geert Hofstede and make a case that the impact of these cultural differences needs to be incorporated into the design and implementation of management control systems for foreign SBUs.[1] Finally, we suggest performance measures to emphasize and implementation issues to consider when designing accounting control systems that integrate strategic and cultural differences.

STRATEGIC OBJECTIVES

There is no one-size-fits-all answer for the effective design of control systems. When an SBU manager's reward system is matched with the SBU's strategy, performance will match corporate strategy, and objectives will be enhanced. Failure to match strategy and reward will adversely affect the manager's motivation and efforts. The strategy for an SBU is dependent on its mission and the consideration of environmental opportunities, internal strengths, and the resources available to accomplish its goals and objectives.[2] Three approaches to control system design that foster goal congruence are: situation specific, universalistic, and contingency.[3] The situation-specific model views each situation as unique, so application of general rules is not possible. Universalists argue that an optimal control system design will be effective in all settings. The contingency approach, which has become the prominent paradigm, is positioned between these two extremes. It suggests that the appropriateness of the control system depends on the business setting (like the situation-specific approach), but generalization (universalistic approach) can be made across similar settings. If the SBU mission or competitive strategy varies across divisions within the organization, the control system must be modified to capture the relevant performance measures and motivate SBU managers accordingly.[4] Strategic mission or business unit strategies are commonly grouped into the following areas: build, hold, harvest, and divest.[5] Competitive strategies include: low cost, differentiation, focus, defender, or prospector.[6]

STRATEGIC MISSION

The mission of an international SBU is related to lifecycle concepts. A build mission implies the goal of increasing market share and typically applies to any SBU with low market share in a high-growth industry. In order to build a competitive advantage, it may be necessary for the manager to sacrifice short-term earnings and/or cash flow. Also, a build strategy implies an increase in production, which results in additional use of the firm's resources. Performance measures that focus mainly on profit or return would be in conflict with the overall mission of the SBU. The manager, therefore, should be evaluated and rewarded primarily on achieving a targeted increase in sales or market share, with profitability measures (with a great deal of slack) a secondary objective.

The hold strategy applies to an SBU with a high market share in a high-growth industry. Though profit oriented accounting performance measures would be appropriate, nonfinancial measures also should be incorporated, such as customer service, maintaining market share, and quality measures.

The goal of a harvest SBU is to maximize short-term cash flows and earnings at the expense of market share (high market share, low-growth industry). These earnings can then supplement other business units that may be in build strategies. To align management decision making with the harvest strategy, the control system should evaluate performance using one of the conventional return measures, such as ROI, RI, or EVA. Measures of cash flow also may be appropriate. Profit and return measures have a much tighter acceptable range and should be adhered to strictly. In a low-market-share, low-growth industry, the SBU's strategy may be to divest through a process of slow withdrawal or outright sale. The appropriate control system at this stage is unique to the particular situation. Presumably, the objective is to maximize cash flows. This strategy represents the end of the life-cycle stages, however, and is a unique situation with a limited ability to generalize. Therefore, we will skip the discussion of control models for the divest strategy.

COMPETITIVE STRATEGIES

An SBU with a low-cost competitive strategy attempts to achieve lower costs relative to competitors. Typical low-cost actions include taking advantage of economies of scale; learning-curve effects; reducing customer service, research and development, advertising, and/or sales force; and maintaining a stable product line. Strict adherence to cost standards through variance analysis and other measures of operating efficiency, such as cycle time and inventory turnover, would be appropriate measures to evaluate and control performance in this competitive environment. Further, A. A. Thompson and A. J. Strickland, III, suggest that significant cost advantages can emerge from an analysis of an entity's internal and external value chain.[7]

Low-cost participants must be careful, however, because the marketplace will still demand a minimum level of product quality and functionality. A differentiation strategy focuses the SBU manager's attention on brand loyalty, customer service, product design, and technology. The goal is to create a product that customers view as unique and exclusive. Product innovation is critical. To create uniqueness, the SBU is likely to have a more diversified set of products or functionally superior products compared to a low-cost competitor, and it must invest in research and product development, technology, marketing, and customer service. Achieving a target ROI does not measure progress effectively within this strategy. While traditional financial performance measures still play a role, nonfinancial performance measures, such as quality, on-time deliveries, customer satisfaction, and number of new products to market, must be emphasized.

An SBU with a focus strategy targets a narrow competitive market within an industry segment. The specific objectives could be either low cost or differentiation. Design of the control system must be tailored to the selected objective. SBUs with a defender strategy engage in limited product/market research, have limited product lines, and have a stable environment. Defenders compete through cost and quality control. This strategy is consistent with the features of the hold and harvest missions. ROI, RI, and EVA may be effective control measures if they are incorporated with variance analysis, operating efficiency measures, and quality variables.

Prospector SBUs, similar to differentiators, compete by focusing on market development, new product development, and searching (prospecting) for market opportunities. These SBUs are often in a build strategic mission. Profit-oriented performance measures would not capture progress toward goals and objectives. The number of new products to market, customer satisfaction, quality, sales from products developed in the last 24 months, and market share would evaluate and control the manager more appropriately.

As we said, there is no single performance measure or control system applicable across different business unit strategies that provides a basis for aligning management decision making with corporate goals. The specific control system must be modified and aligned with the particular strategy of the SBU. The preferences of the SBU manager in the design of the control system, therefore, must not be ignored. For example, the preferences of international SBU managers for autonomy, level of uncertainty, risk, participation, group versus individual rewards, and short- versus long-term rewards may be influenced by their cultural identity. In turn, consideration of cultural differences in the design of a control system can increase its effectiveness.

CULTURAL FACTORS

These days, more and more MNCs use local management talent to operate a foreign subsidiary rather than relying on "imported" expatriates.[8] U.S. MNCs frequently export the home country control system to the host country SBU but fail to consider the impact of cultural factors. Effectiveness of the management control system depends on whether the local manager of the SBU perceives the control system as aligned with the shared values maintained in the host country.[9] Hofstede defined culture as "the collective programming of the mind that distinguishes the members of one category of people from those of another."[10] In perhaps the most extensive and most frequently cited research conducted with respect to cultural differences, Hofstede identified five underlying cultural dimensions—power distance, uncertainty avoidance, individualism versus collectivism, masculinity versus femininity, and Confucian dynamism—and assigned scores on them to more than 50 countries.[11] Table 1 shows the relative scores for some of these countries.

Let's look at these dimensions. **Power distance** indicates the extent a society accepts an unequal distribution of power, and this is one of the most important dimensions to consider when designing a control system. A manager of an SBU in a high power distance culture (Malaysia, Guatemala, Mexico, Singapore, Brazil, Hong Kong) is more likely to accept tight budgetary controls, discretionary bonuses, and subjective performance evaluation. Managers and subordinates in a low power-distance country (Austria, New Zealand, Sweden, U.K., Germany, Canada, U.S.) desire more equity in performance evaluation, less budgetary control, participative budgeting, standardized (perhaps formula-based) rewards, easy access to superiors, and open channels of communication. An autocratic manager in these countries is likely to run into resentment and discontent from subordinates.

Uncertainty avoidance refers to the society's preference for risk-free, unambiguous situations. A culture with a high uncertainty-avoidance score (Greece, Guatemala, Japan, Chile, Argentina, Spain) reflects a preference for control systems that adhere to clearly defined performance measures with unambiguous links to performance evaluation and reward. A low uncertainty-avoidance culture (Singapore, Hong Kong, Sweden, U.K., Malaysia), on the other hand, is more open to less structured control systems where rewards are either discretionary or include a bonus scheme rather than fixed compensation. With a preference for uncertainty avoidance, security in one's position is paramount and rigid, and specific rules that reduce uncertainty are generally accepted. Ambiguity in the control system may be perceived as a continuous threat and result in low morale, high turnover, and increased stress and anxiety.

In Hofstede's research, there appears to be an interaction of power distance and uncertainty avoidance. Though the surveyed countries scatter across all four quadrants, there is a significant grouping of countries in the low power distance, low uncertainty avoidance sector (Sweden, U.K., U.S., Canada) and in the high power distance, high uncertainty avoidance quadrant (Spain, Mexico, Argentina, Chile, Brazil).[12] The countries in the former group prefer participation in the budget process, but they also would accept increased risk in the reward structure. Countries in the latter group represent cultures that accept inequality in the power structure and a lack of participative budgets, but they would demand certain fixed rewards.

Individualism versus collectivism represents the degree that members of a society perceive themselves as individuals rather than as members of a group. Countries with a high score on this dimension (U.S., U.K., Canada, New Zealand, Italy, Sweden) reflect a culture with preferences for individual versus group rewards, independence, and recognition of personal achievement. Tight budgetary controls can be perceived as stifling individual performance. In contrast, a control system with slack budgetary controls and individual rewards imposed on a collectivist culture (Guatemala, Singapore, Hong Kong, Malaysia, Mexico, Greece, Brazil, Chile) would be perceived as contrary to societal norms. Such a system highlights individual differences and promotes competition and interpersonal rivalries, contrary to a preference for group harmony and equality.

Masculinity versus femininity indicates the extent that the "masculine" values of assertiveness, ambition, independence, competitiveness, and male dominance are revered over the "feminine" values of nurturing, interdependence, service motivation, quality of life, and equality between sexes. In Hofstede's research, the higher a country scored on masculinity, the greater the gap between the values of its men and women. In a high-masculinity country (Japan, Austria, Mexico, Germany, U.K.), managers are more accepting of stretch budgets and would prefer a focus on individual achievement with performance evaluated relative to peers. In a high-masculinity country such as Japan, the high Confucianism factor (discussed next) and relatively low individualism score may mitigate the desire for individual recognition. In addition, anecdotal evidence suggests that managers of SBUs in some high-masculinity countries may be open to stretch budgets, but when they fail to deliver they still expect their fixed reward. In low-masculinity countries (Sweden, Chile, Spain, Singapore, Brazil, Canada), a strong emphasis on bottom-line profitability with little concern for members of the organization will be met with resistance and is therefore counterproductive to achieving SBU goals. Quality-of-life values such as a friendly work environment, cooperation, and intrinsic rewards are likely to be motivational factors combined with a preference for group performance evaluation versus individual, incentive-based rewards.

The fifth cultural dimension, **Confucian dynamism,** reflects the relative importance of persistence, perseverance, ordered status, and thrift. These characteristics have been interpreted to refer to differences between Eastern and Western cultures and the extent that a culture pursues long-term orientation and growth. A proactive approach prevails in high-Confucianism countries, resulting in a willingness to sacrifice current success in exchange for future profitability. The SBU manager in a country scoring high on Confucianism (Hong Kong, Japan, Brazil) can be motivated by deferred compensation plans with a focus on growth and less emphasis on current financial performance measures. The manager in a low-scoring culture (New Zealand, Canada, U.K., U.S.) is oriented toward the past and present with a preference for evaluation of the unit's ability to meet short-term financial goals.

The potential exists for conflict in preferences across cultural factors within the same country. In a high uncertainty-avoidance culture, the manager's preference would be for tight budget control with a fixed performance reward. If the country also scores high on individualism, however, a tight budget control would conflict with the manager's preference for independence and performance-based rewards. When factors conflict within a single culture, the control system should target congruence with the dominant cultural dimension as well as align with business strategy.[13]

INTEGRATION OF STRATEGY AND CULTURE

A thorough discussion of each combination of business unit strategies and cultural factors is beyond the scope of this article, but Table 2 does present a summary of both the performance measures to be considered (what) and the manner in which these factors should be determined, budgeted, and rewarded (how) across competing strategies and cultural dimensions.

The performance measures to be considered—the "what"—are factors "a" through "f" in the Table key. The "how" to measure is represented by factors "g" through "z." The columns of Table 2 list business unit/competitive strategies, and the rows list high or low scores on each of the five cultural dimensions. For example, the first two rows present how evaluations and rewards should be determined for managers of SBUs in countries scoring high or low on individualism. If the country scored high, the reward system should permit slack in the process, reward individual effort, and reward the business unit rather than utilizing company based rewards ("h" is slack in budgetary controls; "j" is individual rewards; "l" is business-unit versus companybased rewards). Note that for each row the factors related to how ("g" through "z") are consistent across the respective high or low cultural dimension.

Each cell also integrates the appropriate performance measures (what) to consider across competing business unit strategies or competitive strategies within this cultural dimension. Within each strategy, these factors are also consistent across all cultural dimensions. For example, when the business unit strategy is hold, the suggested performance measures are: maintain market share (b) and quality and/or customer service measures (d). Thus, each cell of Table 2 considers the joint impact of strategy and culture when indicating the most appropriate performance measurements and evaluations.

For an SBU with a harvest strategy in a culture with high scores on individualism, the suggested measurement tools are return metrics, but these measurements should be calculated and evaluated at the business-unit level rather than being incorporated into measures of overall company performance. In addition, the manager would tend to have a strong aversion to tight or strict standards and would more than likely prefer individual versus group rewards. An SBU pursuing a differentiate strategy in a high-masculinity culture should be evaluated using quality and/or customer service measures and number of new products to market. The manager of this SBU will be motivated by extrinsic rewards and individual evaluation relative to peers.

If an SBU in Mexico, which has high scores in power distance and uncertainty avoidance, has a build mission and a differentiate competitive strategy, the performance measures should emphasize market share as well as quality, customer service measures, and the number of new products brought to market. Cultural dimensions suggest that the manager will accept tight budgetary controls with respect to targets but would like some input in setting these targets. In addition, high uncertainty avoidance predicts the manager will prefer frequent fixed rewards with a short-term orientation. High power distance, however, indicates the manager will be open to subjective evaluations and discretionary bonuses. Where cultural dimensions are in conflict like this, the dominant dimension should be given more weight. A control system that provides for evaluation using a strict profit orientation with no input from the manager into the budget process would be frustrating, dysfunctional, in conflict with both strategic and cultural factors, and probably would result in low morale and decision making in conflict with the SBU's strategic objectives.

As these examples suggest, the integration of strategy and culture in the design of control systems can be difficult. The complexity of this task increases when a company considers different approaches to the development and the management of international business units. For example, some MNCs may choose to rely heavily on local managers while others may export management from their home country. When local management is used, there can be significant variation in the degree of experience the local manager has within the parent company. A local manager who has extensive experience with the parent entity and has been indoctrinated in the MNC's home country culture may be less affected by the dominant cultural dimensions in the host country. In each of the examples, the importance of the host country's dominant cultural dimensions may vary. Similarly, the competitive strategies we discussed may not be all-inclusive. Some MNCs may continue to operate SBUs that would otherwise be divested because they provide a source of raw materials or meet the needs of strategically important customers. In such cases, the parent entity should adopt a control system aligned with the purpose of the SBU.

Evaluating the performance of foreign SBUs and their managers is an imposing task for multinational companies. Critical to the design of management control systems is the need to consider both the mission of the SBU and the cultural identities of its management. We have proposed guidelines related to which performance measures are most appropriate for a given business unit or competitive strategy while providing insight into how control system measures should be implemented across different cultures. Consideration of what to measure—as well as how to measure it—will result in the design of control systems that increase goal congruence and reduce conflict between an SBU and its parent entity. Failure to consider the impact of strategy and culture in the design of control systems can result in dissonance, suboptimal decision making, dysfunctional behavior, and managers who lack motivation and suffer from low morale.

Table 1: Relative Scores for Selected Countries on Cultural Dimensions

Country	Individualism	Uncertainty Avoidance	Power Distance	Masculinity	Confucian-ism
Argentina	46	86	49	58	NA
Austria	55	70	11	79	NA
Brazil	38	76	69	49	65
Canada	80	48	39	52	23
Chile	38	86	63	28	NA
Germany	67	65	35	66	31
Great Britain	89	35	35	66	25
Greece	35	112	60	57	NA
Guatemala	6	101	95	37	NA
Hong Kong	25	29	68	57	96
Italy	76	75	50	70	NA
Japan	46	92	54	95	80
Malaysia	26	36	104	50	NA
Mexico	30	82	81	69	NA
New Zealand	79	49	22	58	0
Singapore	20	8	74	48	48
Spain	51	86	57	42	NA
Sweden	71	29	31	5	33
United States	91	46	40	62	29
Range	6-91	8-112	11-104	5-95	0-96
Median	38	68	60	49	2

Table 2: Performance Evaluation Measures and Control Characteristics
Integrating Strategy and Culture

	Business Unit Strategy			Product Line Strategy				
Cultural Dimension	**Build**	**Hold**	**Harvest**	**Low Cost**	**Differentia-tion**	**Focus**	**Defender**	**Prospec-tor**
High indi-vidualism	a,h,j,l	b.d.f.h.j.l	e.f.h.j.l.	e,h,j,l	c,d,h,j,l	a,h,j,l	d,ef,b,j,l	a.c.d.h.j.l
Low indi-vidualism	a,g,i,m	b,d,f,g,i,m	e,f,g,i,m	e,g,i,m	c,d,g,i,m	a,g,i,m	d,e,f,g,i,m	a,c,d,g,i,m
High Power distance	a,g,o	b,d,f,g,o	a,f,g,o	e,g,o	c,d,g,o	a,g,o	d,e,f,g,o	a,c,d,g,o
Low power dis-tance	a,h,n	b,d,f,h,n	e,f,h,n	e,h,n	c,d,h,n	a,h,n	d,e,f,h,n	a,c,d,h,n
High un-certainty avoidance	a,g,n,w,z	b,d,f,n,w,z	e,f,n,w,z	e,n,w,z	c,d,n,w,z	a,n,w,z	d,e,f,n,w,z	a.c.d.n.w.z
Low un-certainty avoidance	a.h.o.v	b,d,f,h,o,v	e,f,h,o,v	e,h,o,v	c,d,h,o,v	a,h,o,v	d,e,f,h,o,v	a,c,d,h,o,v
High mas-culinity	a,k,r,y	b,d,fk,r,y	e,f,k,r,y	e,k,r,y	c,d,k,r,y	a.k.r.y	d.e.f.k.r.y	a.c.d.k.r.y
Low mas-culinity	a,i,q,s	b,d,f,i,q,s	e,f,i,q,s	e,i,q,s	c,d,i,q,s	a,i,q,s	d,e,f,i,q,s	a,c,d,i,q,s
High Con-fucianism	a,v,x,z	b,d,f,v,x,z	e,f,v,x,z	e,v,x,z	c,d,v,x,z,	a,v,x,z	d,e,f,v,x,z	a,c,d,v,x,z
Low Con-fucianism	a,p,t,u	b,d,f,p,t,u	e,f,p,t,u	e,p,t,u	c,d,p,t,u	a,p,t,u	d,e,f,p,t,u	a,c,d,p,t,u

a) focus on market share and/or sales growth
b) maintain market share
c) new products to market
d) quality and/or customer service measures
e) cost management/efficiency measures
f) return-based measures (e.g., ROI, EVA)
g) tight budgetary controls
h) slack in budgetary controls
i) group-based rewards
j) individual-based rewards
k) preference for evaluation relative to others
l) business units vs. company rewards
m) company-based vs. business unit rewards
n) formula-based evaluation/rewards/bonuses
o) subjective evaluation/rewards/bonuses
p) pay for performance/contingent rewards
q) performance-based rewards less motivating
r) desire for incentive based extrinsic rewards
s) intrinsic rewards likely to be valued
t) focus n short-term financial performance
u) past/present orientation
v) future orientation/long planning horizons
w) preference for immediate rewards
x) motivated by deferred compensation
y) acceptance/desire for stretch budgets
z) preference for interactive budget process

---

[1] Geert Hofstede, "Motivation, Leadership, and Organization: Do American Theories Apply Abroad?" Organizational Dynamics, Summer; 1980, pp. 42-63; Geert Hofstede, Cultures Consequences:International Differences in Work-Related Values, Sage Publications,Newbury Park, Calif., 1984; Geert Hofstede and Michael Harris Bond, "The Confucius Connection: From Cultural Roots to Economic Growth," Organizational Dynamics, vol. 16, no. 4,Spring 1988, pp. 5-21.

[2] J. Fisher and V. Govindarajan, "Incentive Compensation Design, Strategic Business Unit Mission, and Competitive Strategy," Journal of Management Accounting Research, vol. 5, Fall 1993, pp.129-144.

[3] J. Fisher, "Contingency-based Research on Management Control Systems: Categorization by Level of Complexity," Journal of Accounting Literature, vol. 14, 1995, pp. 24-53.

[4] The contingency model proposes that, in addition to mission and competitive strategy, other contingent factors include the external environment, technology, firm diversification and size, and the ability to observe effort and output. Modifications to the control system in this article are limited to discussion of the impact of alternative missions or competitive strategies. In order to generalize a contingency model across similar business situations, however, the cultural dimension (discussed later) must also be similar.

[5] B.D. Henderson, Corporate Strategy, Abt Books, Cambridge, Mass., 1978; R.D. Buzzell and F.D. Wiersema, "Modeling Changes in Market Share: A Cross-sectional Analysis," Strategic Management Journal, vol. 2, no. 1, January-March 1981, pp. 27-42. These mission-driven strategies are more recently discussed in numerous strategy and accounting textbooks, including: R.N. Anthony and V. Govindarajan, Management ontrol Systems, 9th Edition, McGraw-Hill/Irwin, Boston, 1998,p. 53-589

[6] M.E. Porter, Competitive Strategy, Free Press, New York, 1980;.E. Miles and C.C. Snow, Organizational Strategy, Structure and Process, McGraw-Hill, New York, 1978. Miles and Snow also consider analyzer- and reactor-type strategies. These strategies are adaptations of defender and prospector and will not be considered. See pages 68-93 for further discussion.

[7] .A. Thompson and A.J. Strickland, III, Strategic Management: Concepts and Cases, 13th Edition, McGraw-Hill/Irwin, Boston, 2003, pp. 151-163.

[8] R.M. Hodgetts and F. Luthans, "U. S. Multinationals' Expatriate Compensation Strategies," Compensation & Benefits Review, January/February 1993, pp. 57-62. R.M. Hodgetts and F. Luthans, "U. S. Multinationals' Compensation Strategies for Local Management: Cross-Cultural Implications," Compensation & Benefits Review, March/April 1993, pp. 42-48.

[9] G.L. Harrison, "Reliance on Accounting Performance Measures in Superior Evaluative Style—The Influence of National Culture and Personality," Accounting, Organizations and Society, vol. 18, May 1993, pp. 319-339; S.J. Kachelmeier and M. Shehata, "Internal Auditing and Voluntary Cooperation in Firms: A Cross-Cultural Experiment," The Accounting Review, vol. 72, no. 3, July 1997, pp. 407-431.

[10] Hofstede, 1988.

[11] In addition to reporting scores for 50 specific countries, Hofstede(1984) grouped 14 countries into three cultural regions: East Africa, West Africa, and Arabic-speaking countries. Several companies that specialize in global consulting and cross-cultural training rely extensively on the research of Geert Hofstede. For example: ITAP International refers to the work of Geert Hofstede as the "gold standard" of cultural profiles. The company uses the Hofstede cultural dimensions extensively in its programs (see www.itapintl.com/ITAPCWfr.htm). ITIM, one of the leading companies worldwide in the field of management and culture, incorporates the findings of the Hofstede research into its consulting and training practices (see www.itim.org/3.html). Also see Grovewell LLC (www.grovewell.com). Hofstede's (1988) study identified the fifth dimension, "Confucianism," after analyzing data from 22 countries, 20 of which were overlapped from the 1980 report.

[12] Hofstede (1980) presents a map of countries that cluster into four quadrants: 1) high power distance, high uncertainty avoidance, 2) high power distance, low uncertainty avoidance, 3) low power distance, high uncertainty avoidance, and 4) low power distance, low uncertainty avoidance.

[13] The country scores on cultural dimensions in the Hofstede studies are relative scores. Scales were chosen in such a way that the distance between the lowest- and highest-scoring country was approximately 100 points.

Chapter 20
Capital Budgeting

Cases

20-1 The Case of the Almost Identical Twins
20-2 ACE Company (A)
20-3 Ace Company (B)
20-4 Component Technologies, Inc.: Adding Flexconnex Capacity
20-5 General Medical Center

Readings

"How Forest Product Companies Analyze Capital Budgets"

This article presents the result of a survey on the uses of capital budgeting techniques by forest product companies. Capital budgeting for this industry has become more challenging and riskier because of increasing competitiveness and government and environmental pressures.

Discussion Questions:

1. The survey result shows that more firms use one or more discounted cash flow methods in evaluating timber-related capital investments. However, more firms use payback period methods to assess plant and equipment purchases. What are reasons for these differences?
2. List changes in the uses of capital budgeting techniques over the years.
3. List some of the methods for adjusting risks in capital investments.
4. What is post-audit? How do forest product companies conduct post-audits?

"How ABC Was Used in Capital Budgeting"

This article presents a case study on the difference that ABC makes on the investment decision of a new project. A business forecast signaled "Go" to an interactive TV project, but the ABC analysis said, "Stop." The article discusses the utilization and limitations of activity-based costing (ABC) in capital budgeting including capacity to predict operating and capital costs, benchmarking model and steps in using ABC in capital investment project.

Discussion Questions:

1. What is the general business case approach to capital budgeting?
2. How does an ABC model approach to capital budgeting differ from the general business case approach?
3. What are the roles of value chain in capital budgeting?
4. List advantages and limitations of ABC approach to capital budgeting.

Cases

20-1 The Case of the Almost Identical Twins[1]

Once upon a time twin boys were born into a typical Ozian family. The boys, named Spender and Saver, were alike in every respect except the one indicated by their names. While they were in high school, both worked at part-time jobs earning the minimum wage of $4.445 per hour for the maximum hours permitted by law, viz., 44 hours per month. There was no income tax in Oz. Spender found many things on which to spend all of his income, while Saver arranged with his parents to add his monthly income to their money market fund which earned 8% per *annum, compounded monthly*.

At the end of four years of high school, each of the boys bought a car costing the amount of Saver's accumulated savings, which he withdrew from his parents' money market account to pay for the car. Spender financed his car on a "no money down," 18% per annum, compounded monthly contract for 48 months. Thus, during four years of university, both boys had cars, both spent the same amounts on other things, but Saver invested each month an amount equal to what Spender was paying on his car, the saving again being at 8% per *annum, compounded monthly*. Both boys financed their expenses while at the university in the same way: partly by working and partly with help from their parents.

When they graduated from the university, the two men continued their identical spending patterns, except that Saver was able to buy a home, using the accumulation of his savings from avoiding car payments in the previous four years as the down payment (20% of the purchase price), financing the remainder on a *10% fixed* rate mortgage, payable monthly over 30 years. Spender rented a similar home, paying (the first year) "net rent" equal to Saver's monthly mortgage payments. Spender's lease also required that he reimburse his landlord for property taxes and insurance on the rental unit-amounts equal to Saver's costs for those items. Thus, Spender continued his pattern of spending all of his income, while Saver paid off his mortgage over 30 years.

Unfortunately for Spender, his "net rent" increased at the rate of 5% per annum, so his housing costs escalated considerably over the 30 years. In the meantime, Saver invested the difference between Spender's escalating "net rent" and his own fixed mortgage payment. Each year he accumulated the monthly saving in his 8% money market fund, then at the end of the year invested in a mortgage bond mutual fund yielding the same rate as he was paying on his own mortgage: 10% perannum, *compounded* monthly. His investments and earnings in that fund continued to compound over the remaining life of his own mortgage.

Upon "burning his mortgage" at the end of 30 years, Saver, now 52 years of age, let his accumulated investment in the mortgage bond mutual fund continue to earn interest for two years but did not add to it. Instead, he departed from his brother's spending pattern by *adding consumption expenditures* equal to what Spender was paying in "net rent." Two years later (age 54) Saver retired to Eve off the income earned on his mortgage bond mutual fund, but kept *the* level of principal unchanged for the rest of his life, leaving it to his heirs. Spender, alas, was in a different position. What does the future hold for him?

---

[1] Adapted from Staubus, George J. 1993. The case of the almost identical twins. *Issues in Accounting Education.* 187-188.

REQUIREMENTS:

1 Specific calculations to be made; please describe any shortcuts or approximations you use:
   a) How much did each lad spend on his car upon graduating from high school?
   b) How much did Saver pay down on his home? What was the total purchase price?
   c) What were Saver's monthly mortgage payments?
      1) Saver invested the difference between his mortgage payments and his brother's rents. What had this investment accumulated to at the mortgage burning date? At age 54? (Note: The calculations involved here may be quite time-consuming; some planning_might pay off.)
      2) What annual income did Saver have from age 54 until his death?
2. Describe the differences between Spender's and Saver's consumption expenditures over the several segments of their lives and the positions of their heirs upon their deaths.
3. Which bits of information given, or assumptions made, do you regard as unrealistic on the basis of your own experience? Roughly speaking (or precisely, if you wish), how would the results be affected by substituting your more realistic calculations?

Note: Abbreviated solution: 1(a) $11,021; 1(b) $18,243, $91,213; 1(c) $640; 1(d) $826,621, $1.000.212; 1(e) $100,017. (2) Spender consumed more in high school; same_for 34 years; Saver consumed more after age 52. Saver left his mortgage bond mutual fund and his home to his heirs. (3) Income tax, home maintenance, interest rates. etc. Nominal dollar accounting is inherently "unrealistic" during inflation.

20-2 ACE Company* (A)

ACE Company is the technology and market leader in the portable electronic games industry. The company is currently enjoying great success with its Model X, which has been on the market for several years. ACE's management believes that because of increased competition from other types of entertainment, the demand for Model X will dry up after three more years. The company has forecast Model X's net cash inflows in the next three years to be $400 million, $300 million, and $200 million, respectively.

NEW PRODUCT DEVELOPMENT

ACE's senior managers are considering the development and introduction of a replacement for Model X, to be called Model Z. According to the engineers, ACE already possesses the technical expertise to develop Model Z. However, the earliest that this product can be introduced into the-market is one year from now, as it will take this long to develop and test the new product, coordinate with suppliers for parts, set up the production process, and arrange for other related logistic activities. The total cost of these development activities is estimated at $550 million.

All of ACE's top managers agree that Model Z's market potential in terms of net cash inflow would be $200 million in year 2, $400 million in year 3, $300 million in year 4, and $100 million in year 5. They also agree that Model Z would maintain ACE's leadership position in the portable electronic games industry.

Management expects that in addition to developing its own customer base, Model Z also would draw some sales away from Model X. The expected amount of this "cannibalization" is $100 million of net cash inflows per year. The following table summarizes ACE's prediction of net cash flows (in millions) for the next five years for Model X by itself and with the introduction of Model Z at the end of year 1 (or, equivalently stated, the beginning of year 2). For simplicity, cash outflows are assumed to occur at the beginning of the year while cash inflows are assumed to occur at year end. Thus, for example, the $550 million development cost in year 1 is assumed to occur at time zero, while the net cash inflow from introducing Model Z at the beginning of year 2 is assumed to occur at the end of that year. Also note that in the table, net cash inflows of $100 million per year are shifted from Model X to Model Z in years 2 and 3.

		Introduce Model Z After One Year				
Year	Model X Only	Model X	+	Model Z	=	Total
0	$ 0	$ 0	+	$ (550)	=	$ (550)
1	$400	$ 400	+	0	=	$ 400
2	$300	$ 200*	+	300*	=	$ 500
3	$200	$ 100*	+	$ 500*	=	$ 600
4	$ 0	$ 0	+	$ 300	=	$ 300
5	$ 0	$ 0	+	$ 100	=	$ 100

* Reflects $100 cannibalization of Model X by Model Z.

EXTENDING THE DEVELOPMENT PERIOD FOR PRODUCT Z

Several members of top management are concerned about Model Z's erosion of Model X sales. They propose that it would be better to spread the development of Model Z over two years and to introduce it at the beginning of year 3 instead of year 2. They suggest that this plan has two major advantages: (1) it would avoid the $100 million erosion in Model X's net cash inflows in year 2; and (2) the engineers have projected that extending the time for the development process will yield substantial savings due to efficiencies in scheduling. They have estimated that the two-year plan would reduce Model Z's total development cost to $300 million. Half of this total would be spent in each of the two years.

The table below summarizes the estimated net cash flows (in millions) for the two-year plan. Compared to the one-year plan, Model X's year 2 net cash inflow is higher by $100 million. This is due to avoiding cannibalization by Model Z in year 2.

---

* Chow, Chee W., Yuhchang Hwang, and Dennis F. Togo, *Issues in Accounting Education* Vol. 10, No. 2, Fall 1995. 389-391.

Year	Model X Only	Model X	+	Model Z	=	Total
		Introduce Model Z After One Year				
0	$ 0	$ 0	+	$ (150)	=	$(150)
1	$400	$ 400	+	$(150)	=	$ 250
2	$300	$ 300	+	0	=	$ 300
3	$200	$ 100*	+	$ 500*	=	$ 600
4	$ 0	$0	+	$ 300	=	$ 300
5	$ 0	$0	+	$ 100	=	$ 100

* Reflects $100 cannibalization of Model X by Model Z.

Proponents of the two-year plan acknowledge that delaying Model Z's introduction by one year would require foregoing its year 2 $300 million net cash inflow. But they emphasize that this sacrifice is more than made up by the additional $100 million cash inflow from Model X in year 2 and the $250 million savings in Model Z development costs.

OTHER CONSIDERATIONS

Supporters of the one-year plan argue that proponents of the two-year plan have overlooked a major factor: that the timing of Model Z's introduction could have an impact on competitors' actions. They maintain that if ACE does not introduce Model Z as quickly as possible, ACE's major competitor would most certainly come in with a comparable product. In response to a query from these managers, ACE's engineers have conducted a study of the competitor's current capabilities, They have reported that due to the competitor's less sophisticated technologies, it will require two years to develop a comparable product for market introduction.

The nature of the industry is such that there is a significant first-mover advantage. Similar products that reach the market at the same time tend to get equal shares of the market. But once a product is introduced, it tends to get so entrenched that comparable products introduced subsequently can gain only inconsequential market shares.

ASSIGNMENT

1) Using net present value computations and ignoring income taxes, analyze the one-year and two-year development alternatives. At this time, ignore the potential introduction of a comparable product by ACE's major competitor. Should either alternative be selected? If so, which would you recommend? ACE's cost of capital is 10 percent.#

2) How would you modify your analysis in part (1) to address the potential introduction of a competing product by ACE's major competitor?

Source: Balakrishnan, Ramji and Utpal Bhattacharya 1997. Ace Company (B): The Option Value of Waiting and Capital Budgeting. *Issues in Accounting Education.* Vol. 12, No. 2 (Fall) 399-402

\# Some instructors may feel that tax considerations also should be part of the case. We have omitted tax effects out of a concern that the computation of tax depreciation and depreciation tax shield effects may overly distract student attention from the strategic aspects of the case. Instructors who think otherwise can readily incorporate tax considerations by augmenting the assignment questions and the numerical aspects of the case analysis.

20-3 Ace Company (B)

Upon receiving the analysis of the data provided in Ace Company (A), the firm's managers wanted to better explore the effect of competition on whether and how to introduce Model Z. Diane Callahan, the Marketing Director, believes that the analysis is incomplete. She argues:

> I believe that accelerating the development of Model Z is the right choice if we will not receive any new data. Accelerated development eliminates the possibility of our competitors introducing a product that will significantly erode our market share. Thus, even though accelerated development results in greater cannibalization of our current product (Model X), it is better than spreading the cost out over two years. However, phased development does give us some flexibility that is not available with accelerated development. In particular, if we phase in developmental costs for Model Z over two years, we only commit $150 toward developmental costs in year 1. At the end of that year, we will have a much better idea of total market demand for Model Z. If the demand turns out to be bad, phased development gives us the option of abandoning Model Z without spending too much money. My department has put together some data on expected market conditions (table 1). From that data, I would guess that we may be better off abandoning Model Z unless the market conditions are good. Such an option is not available with accelerated development because it requires us to spend all of the developmental money of $550 in the first year itself. Ignoring the value of the option on further development could have given us an incomplete understanding of the tradeoffs.

Norm Peterson, Director (Product Development), then commented:

> What Diane says make sense to me. In fact, if we defer the decision to introduce Model Z by a year and wait for new market information, there is a third development choice. In particular, we can do all of the development during year 2, *after* we have made the decision to launch or abort. This choice would cost $400. I did not bring this choice up earlier because the phased development strategy of developing Model Z over two years seems to dominate this delayed development strategy.[1] But, Diane's comments indicate that we should consider this alternative as well. After all, if there is a possibility we will abort Model Z at the end of year 1, why waste $150 in year one under the two-year development time table?

Sam Mask, the CEO, summarized as follows before adjourning the meeting.

> I think we have made substantial progress in understanding the tradeoffs in timing the development of Model Z. I suggest we revisit the issue taking Diane's and Norm's comments into account. For simplicity, let us assume a 40 percent chance that a competitor will emerge and a 50-50 chance that the market will have strong demand for Model Z. Finally, let us retain the simplifying assumptions about the timing of cash flows and do the analysis ignoring tax considerations. Why don't we meet early next week to figure out the best strategy?

ASSIGNMENT QUESTIONS

1. For this question only, assume that competition will never emerge and that Ace will obtain no new information regarding market conditions. Notice that expected cash flows, using the CEO's suggested probability estimates, are identical to those given in case A. Compute the expected cash flow for the delayed development strategy. Determine if this alternative is preferred to accelerated or phased development.
2. For this question only, assume that Ace will obtain no new information regarding market conditions. How does the analysis change if there is a 40 percent chance that competition will emerge?

---

[1] Case B compares this new strategy (delayed development) with the strategies considered in case A. From case A, notice that phased development (i.e., developing Model Z over two years) costs $300. Also, Model Z would only get introduced at the start of year 3 (t = 2) under both the phased and delayed development strategies. Hence, absent information regarding market conditions, delayed development has no incremental benefit but, even with discounting, has a higher cost relative to phased development. Also, notice that delayed development has lower development costs than accelerated development (i.e., develop Model Z in year I itself and introduce at the start of year 2) even though both choices develop Model Z in one year. The lower cost is expected because the firm would have learned from its experience with other projects and changes in technology.

3. Assume that Ace will obtain information regarding realized market conditions at the end of year 1. How does the rank ordering of the development choices change? Why?

COMPUTATIONAL HINTS

1. For all three questions, discount cash flows using a 10 percent rate. Assume that all cash outflows occur at the beginning of the year and all cash inflows occur at the end of the year. It also is helpful to construct a timeline for cash flows. Label the first node (start of year 1) as t = 0, the next node (end of year 1 and start of year 2) as t = 1, etc.

2. To determine whether or not to proceed with Model Z at time t = 1, construct a payoff matrix with 4 cells corresponding to Ace's and the competitor's entry choices. To minimize the potential for errors, look at time t = 1 NPV of cash flows at or after time t = 1. After you determine optimal choices at t = 1, step back to construct a payoff matrix where the rows correspond to Ace's various product development strategies and the columns correspond to the competitor entering and not entering.

TABLE I

Estimated Cash Flows from Model X and Model Z Under Different Scenarios

Panel A: No Development of Model Z

	Market Condition: Good				Market Condition: Bad			
Time (t)	Competitor Enters		Competitor Does Not Enter		Competitor Enters		Competitor Does Not Enter	
	X	Z	X	Z	X	Z	X	Z
0	0		0		0		0	
1	400		400		400		400	
2	300		300		300		300	
3	25		200		175		200	
4	0		0		0		0	
5	0		0		0		0	

Panel B: Accelerated Development of Model Z

	Market Condition: Good				Market Condition: Bad			
Time (t)	Competitor Enters		Competitor Does Not Enter		Competitor Enters		Competitor Does Not Enter	
	X	Z	X	Z	X	Z	X	Z
0	0	-550	0	-550	0	-550	0	-550
1	400	0	400	0	400	0	400	0
2	150	500	150	500	250	100	25	100
3	25	850	25	850	175	150	175	150
4	0	550	0	550	0	50	0	50
5	0	150	0	150	0	50	0	50

Panel C: Phased Development of Model Z

	Market Condition: Good				Market Condition: Bad			
Time (t)	Competitor Enters		Competitor Does Not Enter		Competitor Enters		Competitor Does Not Enter	
	X	Z	X	Z	X	Z	X	Z
0	0	-150	0	-150	0	-150	0	-150
1	400	-150	400	-150	400	-150	400	-150
2	300	0	300	0	300	0	300	0
3	25	425	25	850	175	75	200	150
4	0	275	0	550	0	25	0	50
5	0	100	0	200	0	0	0	0

Panel D: Defer Development Decision on Model Z

	Market Condition: Good				Market Condition: Bad			
Time (t)	Competitor Enters		Competitor Does Not Enter		Competitor Enters		Competitor Does Not Enter	
	X	Z	X	Z	X	Z	X	Z
0	0	0	0	0	0	0	0	0
1	400	-400	400	-400	400	-400	400	-400
2	300	0	300	0	300	0	300	0
3	25	425	200	850	175	75	200	150
4	0	275	0	550	0	25	0	50
5	0	100	0	200	0	0	0	0

1. All cash-flows are assumed to occur at the beginning of the year. Ignore taxes in your analysis. Time t = 0 corresponds to the start of the first calendar year and t = 1 corresponds to the end of year 1 and the start of year 2.
2. There is a 50% chance that market conditions will be good.
3. There is a 40% chance that the competitor will develop a product that competes with Model Z. The competitor's decision, however, is independent of realized market conditions. The competitor only has the choice of developing the product over 2 years and, thus, makes the launch/abort decision at time t = 0 itself.

20-4 Component Technologies, Inc.: Adding FlexConnex Capacity

In 2002, Component Technologies, Inc. (CTI)[1] manufactured components, such as interconnect components, electronic connectors, fiber-optic connectors, flexible interconnects, coaxial cable, cable assemblies, and interconnect systems, used in computers and other electronic equipment. CTI's global marketing strategy produced significant growth; CTI was now one of three major suppliers in its market segments. Major customers included other global companies, such as IBM, HP, Hitachi, and Siemens. These companies, in turn, manufactured and marketed their products worldwide.

FlexConnex, one of CTI's largest selling products, was very profitable (see Exhibit 1). The Santa Clara, California plant that manufactured the FlexConnex component was projected to reach its full capacity of 75 million units in 2003. With sufficient capacity to meet demand, CTI expected its sales of FlexConnex could continue to increase 10 percent per year as applications of computer technology extended into industrial products and consumer products such as automobiles and appliances.

PLANNING MEETING

At a meeting of his staff, Tom Richards, director of manufacturing planning, stated that they needed to plan to bring additional capacity for FlexConnex online in about two years. He suggested that they begin by proposing possible alternatives. The staff quickly identified three promising alternatives:

1. The Santa Clara plant had been designed for future expansion. Additional space was available at the site, and new production capacity could be easily integrated into the existing production processes as long as compatible manufacturing technologies were employed.

2. CTI owned a plant in Waltham, Massachusetts that manufactured a product line that was being phased out. Some existing equipment in the Waltham plant was compatible with the Santa Clara plant's manufacturing technology and could be converted to the production of FlexConnex. Half of the Waltham plant would be available in 2003, and the remainder in 2005.

3. CTI could build a greenfield plant[2] in Ireland, close to its major European customers. To attract such industries, the Irish government would make a site available at low cost. A new technology currently being Beta-tested[3] by an equipment manufacturer could be used to equip this plant.

Tom believed that these three were promising proposals. To ensure CTI could bring additional, profitable, FlexConnex capacity online in two years, Tom felt that they should begin developing plans for these alternatives. Nonetheless, he wanted the staff to keep an open mind to additional alternatives even as they evaluated these three. As the discussion started to wind down, Gracie Stanton, an engineer, said that she had a suggestion.

Gracie: Before we spend our time developing these three alternatives in detail, I'd like to get a rough feel for the potential profitability of each alternative. We shouldn't waste our time developing detailed plans for an alternative if there is no chance it will ever show a positive NPV.

Source: *Issues in Accounting Education*, by Julie H. Hertenstein, May 2000, Vol. 15 Issue 2, p. 257-261

[1] This case is based on decisions faced by an actual company. Component Technologies, Inc., is a disguised name. Other facts have been changed for instructional purposes.

2The term "greenfield plant" is commonly used to refer to a brand new plant built entirely from scratch, as contrasted with the expansion, conversion, refurbishment, or renovation of an existing plant.

[3]A "Beta-test site" refers to equipment being tested using an actual workload at a customer site. Beta-test is often the final testing phase before the equipment is released as commercially available to customers. A customer who consents to be a Beta-test site agrees not only to use equipment that is not fully tested (thus being, in the American vernacular, a "guinea pig"), but also to provide the vendor detailed feedback on operations and problems encountered. In return, the equipment manufacturer often provides incentives such as financial discounts, extra on-site vendor personnel, etc.

Tom: Good point, Gracie. Let's break up into three groups, and do back-of-the-envelope calculations based on what we currently know about each alternative. Gracie, would you head up the Santa Clara group, since you were part of the engineering team for that plant? Edward Lodge, how about Waltham? Ian Townsley, could you and your folks take a look at Ireland? To start, what are the facts and assumptions about each facility?

Gracie: Well, there's enough space at the Santa Clara site to produce an additional 30 million units annually. I expect it would cost about $23 million to expand this plant, and bring its total capacity to 105 million units. Of the $23 million, we would spend $5 million to expand the building, and $18 million for additional equipment compatible with Santa Clara's existing manufacturing process. All $23 million would probably be spent in 2003, and the plant would be ready for production in 2004.

I assume that the selling price per unit will remain at its current level; further, since the same manufacturing technology will continue to be used, the variable manufacturing cost will remain the same as we show on the 2002 Santa Clara Cost Analysis Sheet [Exhibit 1]. Expanding the existing plant would allow some fixed manufacturing costs, like the plant manager's salary, to be shared with the existing facility, so I estimate that the additional fixed manufacturing costs, excluding depreciation, will be $2.1 million annually beginning in 2004. In 2006, these fixed costs will rise to $2.4 million and remain at that level for the foreseeable future.

Edward: Well, the Waltham plant is smaller than the space available in Santa Clara, so I think its capacity will be about 25 million units. It will require renovations to adapt the plant to manufacture FlexConnex, say, about $2 million, and approximately $12 million for equipment. Half of this would be spent in 2003, and half in 2005. Initial production would begin in 2004; half of the 25-million-unit capacity should be available in 2004; two-thirds in 2005; the remainder in 2006.

Since the Waltham plant will use the same technology as Santa Clara, we can assume that the variable manufacturing costs will be the same as Santa Clara's. Selling prices will also be the same. However, since Waltham will be a stand-alone faculty, its fixed manufacturing costs, excluding depreciation, would be somewhat higher: $2.4 million annually beginning in 2004. In 2006, however, fixed costs will increase to $2.6 million annually, where I expect them to remain for the foreseeable future.

Ian: I just visited the Beta-test site for the manufacturing equipment using the new technology that I propose we use for the greenfield plant. There I learned that the economic size for a plant using this technology to manufacture a product such as FlexConnex is about 70 million units, so I propose that we prepare our estimates for Ireland based on a 70-million-unit capacity plant. Of course, this will cost more, since it is much larger than other sites. With the help of the Irish government, an appropriate site can be obtained for about $1 million. A building large enough to produce 70 million units can probably be built for about $10 million, and equipping the facility with the new technology equipment will cost about $50 million. Most of this would be spent in 2003, although as much as 10 percent might be spent before the end of 2002 to acquire and prepare the site. The plant would begin production in 2004; some areas of the plant would not be complete, however, and as much as 20-25 percent of the investment would remain to be spent during 2004.

Although FlexConnex's worldwide selling price will be the same as for the other facilities, the new equipment will lower the variable manufacturing cost to $0.195 per unit. The efficiency of this new plant will help keep fixed manufacturing costs down, as well, but since the facility will be so large, fixed manufacturing costs, excluding depreciation, would be higher than the other two facilities: $2.8 million annually beginning in 2004, rising to $2.9 million annually beginning in 2008.

Tom: These assumptions sound like reasonable first cuts to me. Let's just start with a five-year analysis, 2003 through 2007, using the discount rate of 20 percent, which the corporate finance manual states is the hurdle rate for capital investments. For simplicity, let's assume all cash flows occur at the end of the respective year. Discount everything to today's dollars, that is, as of the end of 2002. And, consistent with corporate policy, we'll do a pretax analysis; we'll ask the corporate finance staff to evaluate the tax implications later.

A few minutes later, the buzzing of the small groups died down, and the tapping on the laptop keyboards had ceased.

Tom: Well, what have you learned from this first glance?

Edward: The Waltham site looks promising.

Ian: Not Ireland.

Gracie: This is odd. The Santa Clara plant is right on the margin, and that surprises me since the existing manufacturing facility is one of CTI's most profitable, and we get further economies of scale by expanding that plant. I wonder if the discount rate we are using is too high. At the "Finance for Manufacturing Engineers" seminar I attended recently, we discussed the problems associated with using a discount rate that was too high. The professor stated that there was a sound theoretical basis for using a discount rate that approximated the company's cost of capital, but many companies "added on" estimates for risk, corporate charges, and other factors that were less well grounded. Based on what I learned in that seminar, I tried to estimate CTI's actual cost of capital; it was about 10 percent. I wonder what would happen if we used 10 percent instead?

Tom: With these laptops and spreadsheet programs, that's easy enough; let's check it out.
A few seconds later . . . .

Gracie: Now, that's better!

Edward: Ours too.

Ian: Well, at least we're moving in the right direction. But it doesn't make sense to me that a facility with lower variable cost per unit, and lower average fixed cost per unit at capacity, shows a negative NPV when the others are positive. We checked our calculations; what's the story? Could it be that Ireland would not even be up to capacity production in five years because the plant is so big?

Gracie: Maybe, but our plants are being penalized, too; after all, even though they reach capacity in the first five years, they will presumably continue to produce FlexConnex. Although there is constant technological change in this industry, there is a reasonable probability that demand for FlexConnex will remain strong for at least 10 years.

Ian: Well, then, let's look at each of the three plants over a ten-year period, using Gracie's 10 percent discount rate.
Later . . . .

Edward: Aha! Waltham continues to improve.

Gracie: However, Santa Clara has you beat now!

Ian: I've got bad news for both of you!

QUESTIONS:

1. Prepare the manufacturing staff's calculations for the three alternatives:
    a. In the first set of calculations, the staff used a discount rate of 20 percent, a five-year time horizon, and ignored taxes and terminal value. What is the relative attractiveness of these three alternatives?
    b. In the second set, they used a 10 percent discount rate. What happens to the NPV of each alternative? What happens to their relative attractiveness? Why?
    c. In the third set, they changed the time horizon to ten years, but kept the 10 percent discount rate. Why does Ian say he has "bad news" for the others?
2. In addition to reducing costs, the new technology proposed for the greenfield plant would increase manufacturing flexibility, which would enable CTI to respond more quickly to customers and to provide them more custom features. Should these factors be considered in the analysis? If so, how would you incorporate them?
3. Should other factors be taken into consideration in choosing the location of the FlexConnex plant? If so, what are they?
4. Should Tom Richards continue to develop more detailed plans for these three alternatives? If not, which should be eliminated? Are there other alternatives that his staff should consider? If so, what are they?

EXHIBIT 1 FlexConnex Cost Analysis Sheet
Santa Clara Plant, 2002

Plant Capacity:	75 million units
Selling Price/Unit:	$0.85
Variable Cost/Unit:	$0.255
Fixed Manufacturing Cost:	$9.5 million annually (includes $2.5 million depreciation)

Estimated Plant Profitability at Capacity:

Revenue	$63,750,000
Variable Cost	<19,125,000>
Fixed Manufacturing Cost	<9,500,000>
Plant Profitability [a]	$35,125,000

[a] Excludes interest expenses and corporate selling, general and administrative expenses.

20-5 General Medical Center

The phone rang in the office of Gwen Allbright, a partner in a consulting firm that specializes in health services management. On the line was Dr. George Westford, Chief of Cardiovascular Medicine at General Medical Center (GMC) and Gwen's next-door neighbor. Dr. Westford explained that he needed Gwen's help in understanding an analysis prepared by Brian Alexander, General Medical Center's Chief Financial Officer, of the pending purchase of new imaging equipment for the evaluation of patients with suspected coronary artery disease (CAD). GMC is evaluating two types of imaging equipment—a Thallium scanner and a Positron Emission Technology (PET) scanner. Dr. Westford explained the situation as follows:

> Based on his cost analysis, Brian Alexander has recommended that the hospital purchase the Thallium scanner rather than the PET scanner. The physicians in the cardiovascular medicine department are very upset by this. They want the hospital to purchase the PET scanner because it incorporates the latest imaging technology. In addition, I am not convinced by Brian's analysis that the Thalhum scanner is really the better choice even from a purely financial perspective.

Dr. Westford asked Gwen to evaluate the analysis prepared by Mr. Alexander and to recommend changes to his analysis if she felt that they were warranted. He agreed to bring the analysis to Gwen's house later that evening.

GENERAL MEDICAL CENTER

General Medical Center is a not-for-profit 500-bed community-based hospital. It is located in a metropolitan area with a population of one million people, which has six major hospital systems that provide cardiovascular services. It is the third "busiest" cardiovascular center in the metropolitan area when judged on the number of cardiac catheterizations performed.

GMC recently has become part of an integrated health care delivery system for its metropolitan area. Now that GMC participates in a capitated payment system, its revenue is much more "fixed" than it was under the former fee-for-services arrangement. Capitated payments are per-patient payments to a health care provider (hospital or physician group) for a defined set of benefits for a defined period of time. In a strictly capitated system, a provider receives a predetermined amount for each beneficiary.[1] The actual costs of caring for a beneficiary may be more or less than this predetermined amount. When the actual costs of care are less than the predetermined payment, the provider keeps the "profit." When actual costs exceed the payment, however, the provider is financially responsible and incurs a "loss."

This is in stark contrast to the former fee-for-services system in which the hospital was reimbursed for each imaging procedure performed and for all follow-up procedures (such as cardiac catheterizations) that were triggered by the imaging results. Under the fee-for-services arrangement, the provider's profit increased as a direct function of the number of imaging and follow-up procedures performed, so long as the fee for each exceeded its cost. In effect, the former system rewarded the misdiagnosis of normal individuals as diseased, because of the revenue impact of additional procedures.

---

[1] While this case assumes strict capitation for all payors, such a system is the exception and not the norm—both in the U.S., generally, and in the particular market served by GMC. A more realistic analysis would recognize that (1) patient care may be reimbursed under various combinations of arrangements—including by capitation, by diagnosis and by fee-for-service or discounted fee-for-service schemes; (2) different payors—which include for-profit and not-for-profit private-sector organizations, government and individual patients—are involved; and (3) the relative amount of reimbursement for Thalhurn and PET may differ across the various payors (in fact, some payors may consider a particular technology "experimental" and provide no reimbursement). Thus, the payor mix is an extremely important consideration in a decision such as that faced by GMC. For pedagogical reasons, however, the case abstracts from this complexity on the revenue dimension in order to focus on the role of costs in this decision setting.

Adapted from Alison Hubbard Ashton, Robert H. Ashton and Laureen A. Maines. 1998. *Issues in Accounting Education.* 13, 4 (November). pp. 985-993. This case is based on a class project prepared by Pamela Jones and John Janes in Duke University's Weekend Executive M.B.A. Program.

Under a capitated system, however, costs that are triggered by misdiagnoses are borne by the hospital. In effect, this payment method merges the insurance function with the provider function in that a portion of the financial risk is borne by the provider. By merging the insurance and provider functions, the capitated payment system encourages the provider to analyze the appropriateness (quality) of care. However, it also provides the short-term financial incentive to reduce costs by undertreating patients. For example, referrals to specialists may be reduced, further testing curtailed, or less costly (but less effective) approaches to treatment prescribed. Future costs of undertreating patients may not be borne by the hospital due to the high mobility level of the working-age patient base.

Dr. Westford and the other physicians in the cardiovascular division realize that in a capitated system the division will be evaluated more on the appropriateness and cost of its care. Since revenues will not increase with the number of procedures performed, they will need to be concerned about performing unnecessary catheterization procedures. The capitation approach strives to lower the cost of care, subject to quality standards, and match the financial risks with the quality of care. Dr. Westford and the other physicians are convinced that the higher accuracy of the PET scanner vis-á-vis the more conventional Thallium scanner will result in more medically appropriate referrals of patients for cardiac catheterization. Dr. Westford is concerned that Mr. Alexander has failed to consider the cost of *inappropriate* referrals in his analysis of the imaging equipment purchase. This is also of concern to the physicians since they typically are directly penalized in their compensation for inappropriate patient referrals.

HEART DISEASE AND CARDIAC IMAGING

Patients undergo diagnostic imaging to provide physicians with information that will be used to verify a diagnosis, order further testing, or prescribe treatment. A patient with suspected heart disease undergoes a tiered diagnostic process to provide a diagnosis in a cost-effective manner. This process can be represented by a type of decision tree that dictates the sequence of diagnostic testing and/or treatment. A simplified version of such a tree appears in exhibit 1.

As the tree demonstrates, the physician uses a combination of clinical judgment and diagnostic testing results to determine which patients will undergo cardiovascular imaging and perhaps further procedures. Once a patient is referred for cardiovascular imaging, the results of that procedure dictate whether the patient will proceed to diagnostic cardiac catheterization. Patients with normal cardiac imaging results have no further evaluation, whereas almost all patients with abnormal imaging results undergo cardiac catheterization. Currently at GMC, this catheterization costs $2,000 and carries a .01 percent mortality rate. The catheterization procedure is used to determine whether the imaging technique has correctly identified the patient as having heart disease. If the imaging technique has correctly identified the patient, the catheterization provides the physician with information that is useful for deciding among medical treatment, coronary angioplasty and coronary artery bypass surgery as the preferred treatment for the disease.

Since the results of the cardiovascular imaging procedure dictate whether the patient will be subjected to cardiac catheterization, it is easy to see why the diagnostic accuracy of the imaging procedure is of paramount importance. An ideal or perfect imaging procedure would correctly differentiate those patients who do and do not have heart disease. A technique that fails to correctly identify patients who actually have heart disease may allow the disease to go undetected for some time, possibly resulting in greater health care risks and costs when the disease later becomes clinically evident. Likewise, a technique that incorrectly diagnoses a healthy patient as having heart disease will result in inappropriate and costly referral for diagnostic cardiac catheterization. The misdiagnosis of a healthy patient as diseased can be a significant factor in the cost analysis of imaging equipment.

GMC is considering two alternative imaging technologies: Thallium and PET. The Thallium scanner has been the standard in cardiovascular medicine for many years. It offers the advantages of lower initial capital outlay, lower annual maintenance costs and a general acceptance by the medical community. The more technologically advanced Positron Emission Technology (PET) scanner was largely restricted to academic medical centers until a few years ago because of its cost. More recently, commercial PET scanners have become available that offer greater clinical accuracy than Thallium scanners. Although the initial costs and maintenance fees of PET have come down in the last few years, they are still substantially higher than those associated with Thallium imaging.

EXHIBIT 1
Decision Tree

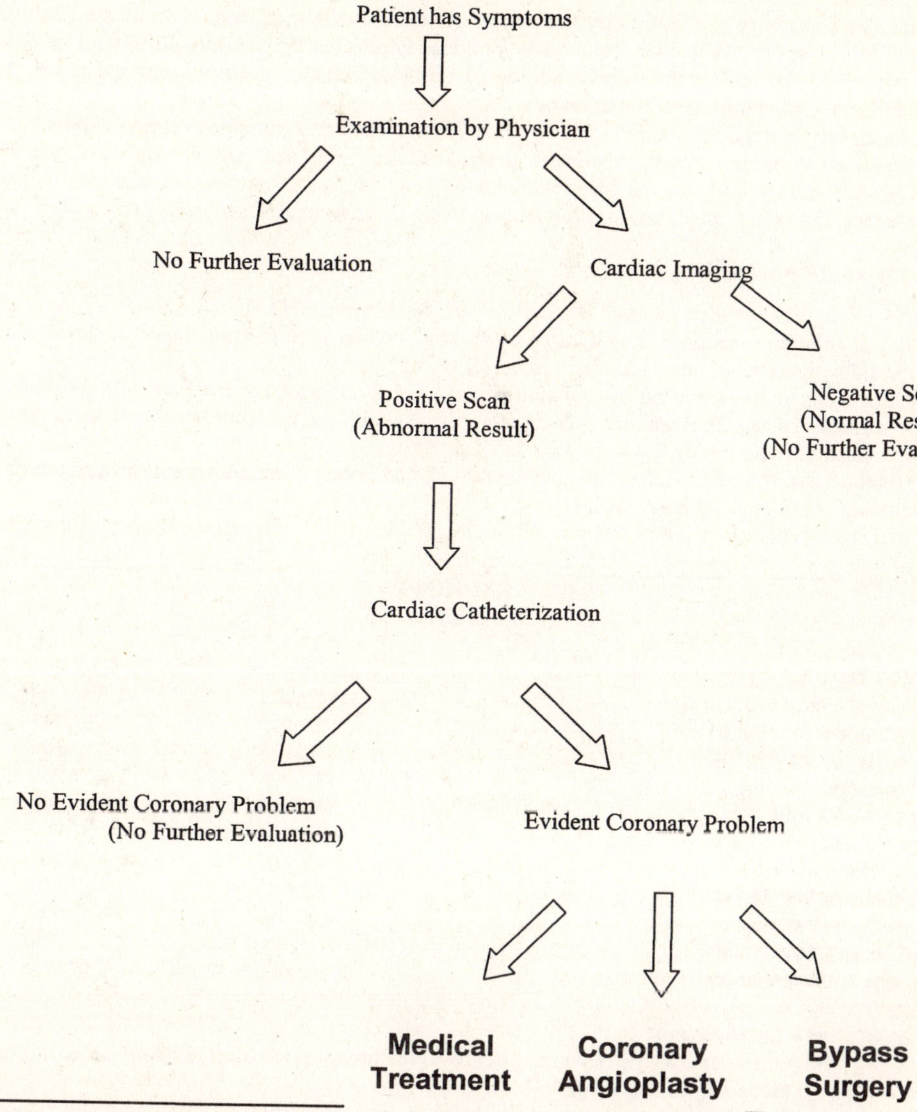

THE CFO'S ANALYSIS

Brian Alexander, the CFO, analyzed this equipment purchase using an equivalent annual cost (EAC) method. Because the Thallium and PET scanners have different useful lives, EAC appeared to be the best way to determine which type of equipment would be more cost effective for the health care system. Essentially, EAC is the amount of an annuity that has the same life and present value as the investment option being considered. EAC can be viewed as the annual rental payment that would cover both the purchase of the equipment and its operating costs, or the annual amount that GMC would pay if it chose to Outsource the scanning procedure. Thus, Mr. Alexander based the cost comparison on the initial outlay costs of both types of imaging equipment and on the annual maintenance, personnel-related and other costs associated with the two equipment types. His cost estimates are listed and explained in exhibit 2.

Mr. Alexander had to make several assumptions in his analysis. These assumptions, described in exhibit 3, relate to the expected number of cardiac scans in a typical year, the expected useful life of the two scanners, the predicted inflation rate for the various costs associated with scanning and the likely base rate of cardiac disease in the hospital's patient population. Two assumptions are particularly important: the "sensitivity" and "specificity" of the alternative imaging techniques.

Understanding sensitivity and specificity is essential for a comprehensive evaluation of the Thallium and PET scanners. Realizing this, Mr. Alexander included as an addendum to his analysis the definitions of sensitivity and specificity, as well as the definitions of four additional terms on which sensitivity and specificity depend. Mr. Alexander's addendum is summarized in exhibit 4.

Mr. Alexander applied the EAC approach using the relevant data and assumptions from exhibits 2, 3 and 4. The results are presented in exhibit 5. Mr. Alexander determined from this analysis that the EAC for the Thallium scanner is $745,818 and the EAC for the PET scanner is $1,148,004. Based on these calculations, he recommended the purchase of the Thallium scanner because it results in lower cost for the health care system.

SUGGESTED ASSIGNMENT QUESTIONS

1) Evaluate the strengths and weaknesses of the analysis prepared by the CFO.
2) Use the information on sensitivity, specificity and disease prevalence in the population to develop a framework for incorporating the costs of misdiagnoses into the CFO's analysis.
3) Quantify the costs of the expected annual number of cardiac catheterizations that will result from both the Thallium scanner and the PET scanner. After taking these additional costs into account, is the purchase of the Thallium scanner still indicated?
4) How should the costs of the False Negative diagnoses (i.e., classifying diseased patients as normal) be handled?
5) What additional considerations are relevant?

EXHIBIT 2
Cost Information

Cost Classification	Thallium Scanner	PET Scanner
Purchase Price of Equipment	$450,000	$1,600,000
Equipment Maintenance (Per Month)	$3,750	$13,333
Medical Supplies (Per Patient)	$100	$100
Nuclear Isotope (Per Month)	$20,000	$27,000
Lease Space (Per Month)	$2,000	$3,000
Utilities (Per Month)	$500	$1,000
Secretary (Per Month)	$1,667	$1,667
Nuclear Technician (Per Month)	$2,500	$2,500
Nursing Personnel (Per Month)	$2,917	$2,917
Employee Benefits (% of Salary)	28%	28%
Cost of Cardiac Catheterization	$2,000	$2,000

Explanation of Cost Classifications:

Purchase Price:	Guaranteed by the manufacturer to be the lowest price offered to any other hospital in the preceding 12-month period.
Equipment Maintenance:	First-year maintenance is included in the purchase price. Continuing maintenance is fixed for the life of the equipment at 10 percent of the purchase price.
Supplies:	These include patient gowns, EKG electrodes and paper, intravenous kits and pharmacological agents.
Isotope:	For the PET technology, a nuclear generator is purchased each month, which supplies the nuclear tracer used in the imaging technique. For the Thallium technology, the nuclear tracer is purchased on a per-dose basis from a nuclear pharmaceutical firm.
Lease Space:	The PET equipment requires 50 percent more space than the Thallium equipment.
Utilities:	The back-up electrical generators and specialized cooling for the sophisticated computer bank results in twice the utility requirements for the PET scanner as for the Thallium scanner.
Personnel:	The two technologies have the same staffing requirements.

EXHIBIT 3
Assumptions

Category	**Thallium Scanner**	**PET Scanner**
Sensitivity	85%	95%
Specificity	65%	95%
Useful Life of Equipment	7 years	10 years
Patient Scan Days Per Month	20	20
Patient Scans Per Day	8	8
CAD Rate in Patients	25%	25%
Hospital Cost of Capital	10%	10%
Inflation Factor for Catheterization Procedure	3.2%	3.2%
inflation Factor for Personnel	3.5%	3.5%
Inflation Factor for Other Costs	2.8%	2.8%
Tax Rate for Hospital	0%	0%

Explanation of Assumptions:

Patient Scan Days Per Month:	Each manufacturer guarantees equipment "up-time" of approximately 92 percent. The scanners will operate Monday through Friday. Thus, approximately 240 scan days are available each year.
Scans Per Day:	This assumes that each scanner will scan the number of patients that currently are referred for imaging. Any potential annual increase in volume is assumed to be offset by the effect of implementing appropriate guidelines for the referral for this type of imaging procedure.
Thallium Specificity:	The medical literature provides a range of values. For a community-based patient population, the best studies indicate a specificity of 55 percent to 65 percent. The value of 65 percent was chosen to provide a best-case analysis.
Thallium Sensitivity:	The medical literature provides a consensus that this value is 85 percent.
PET Specificity:	The medical literature provides a consensus that this value is 95 percent.
PET Sensitivity:	The medical literature provides a consensus that this value is 95 percent.
Prevalence of Heart Disease:	A review of the hospital's experience, along with reports from the medical literature, reveals that the best estimate of this value is 25 percent.
Useful Life of Imaging Equipment:	The manufacturers have provided historical data and engineering projections for these estimates.
Hospital Cost of Capital:	The CFO estimates that the hospital's cost of capital in the new integrated health care system will be approximately 10 percent.
Inflation Factors:	The CFO has used information from similar integrated health care systems in the region for estimates of inflation rates.
Tax Rate for the Hospital:	Since both the hospital and the integrated health care system are not-for-profit, there are no corporate taxes.

EXHIBIT 4
Definitions of Key Terms

True Positive: A test result is positive (abnormal) in a patient with disease. Correct labeling of a diseased patient as having disease.

False Positive: A test result is positive (abnormal) despite the fact that the patient actually does not have disease. Incorrect labeling of a normal patient as having disease.

True Negative: A test result is negative (normal) in a patient who does not have disease. Correct labeling of a normal patient as not having disease.

False Negative: A test result is negative (normal) despite the fact that the patient actually has disease. Incorrect labeling of a diseased patient as not having disease.

Sensitivity: The proportion of diseased patients diagnosed correctly. The ratio of true positives to all patients who have disease (sum of true positives and false negatives above). The ability of a test to correctly identify patients with disease.

Specificity: The proportion of normal patients diagnosed correctly. The ratio of true negatives to all patients without disease (sum of false positives and true negatives above). The ability of a test to correctly identify normal patients.

EXHIBIT 5
The CFO's Analysis

Thallium Scanner Cost Analysis

Year	Initial Cost	Maintenance	Personnel[a]	Other[b]	Total	Present Value
0	$450,000				$450,000	$450,000
1		-0-	$108,810	$462,000	570,810	518,918
2		$45,000	112,619	474,936	632,555	522,772
3		45,000	116,560	488,234	649,794	488,200
4		45,000	120,640	501,905	667,545	455,942
5		45,000	124,862	515,958	685,820	425,840
6		45,000	129,232	530,405	704,637	397,749
7		45,000	133,756	545,256	724,012	371,533
Total						$3,630,954

Equivalent Annual Cost for Thallium Scanner: $745,818 [$3,630,954 / 4.86842 (present value factor for 7-year, 10 percent annuity)].

PET Scanner Cost Analysis

Year	Initial Cost	Maintenance	Personnel[a]	Other[c]	Total	Present Value
0	$1,600,000				$1,600,000	$1,600,000
1		-0-	$108,810	$564,000	672,810	611,646
2		$160,000	112,619	579,792	852,411	704,472
3		160,000	116,560	596,026	872,586	655,587
4		160,000	120,640	612,715	893,355	610,173
5		160,000	124,862	629,871	914,733	567,977
6		160,000	129,232	647,507	936,739	528,765
7		160,000	133,756	665,638	959,394	492,320
8		160,000	138,437	684,275	982,712	458,443
9		160,000	143,282	703,435	1,006,717	426,946
10		160,000	148,297	723,131	1,031,428	397,660
Total						$7,053,989

Equivalent Annual Cost for PET Scanner: $1,148,004 [$7,053,989 / 6.14457 (present Value factor for 10-year, 10 percent annuity)].

[a] [($1,667 + $2,500 + $2,917)1.28] x 12 = $108,810 for year 1, increasing by 3.5% each year.
[b] ($20,000 + $2,000 + $500)12 + $100(1,920) $462,000 for year 1, increasing by 2.8% each year.
[c] ($27,000 + $3,000 + $1,000)12 + $100(1,920) $564,000 for year 1, increasing by 2.8% each year.

Readings

HOW FOREST PRODUCT COMPANIES ANALYZE CAPITAL BUDGETS

BY JACK BAILES, JAMES NIELSEN, AND STEPHEN LAWTON

Twenty years ago we conducted a survey of forest products companies to investigate the nature of the capital budget project evaluation techniques, methods of risk analysis, and post audit procedures. Because the forest products industry has changed so much, it is appropriate to once again look at the issue of capital budgeting practices within the industry.

A survey was sent to the chief financial officers of 87 U.S. forest products companies, consisting of all of the independent firms (i.e., separate divisions of a single parent company were not included) currently participating in the Oregon State University Forest Products Industry Monograph Program.[1] The survey questionnaire was completed by 29 firms, representing a response rate of 33%—slightly lower than the 47% response rate received in the 1977 survey. Sixteen of these firms operated in the wood products side of the industry. There were only two firms operating exclusively in the pulp, paper, and packaging side of the industry, and the remaining 11 firms sold both wood and paper-related products. This industry breakdown of firms was similar to the breakdown of firms responding in 1977.

Although there are still a number of smaller forest products companies operating in the U.S., the largest percentage of firms (over 33%) had annual sales and total asset levels exceeding $500 million. Such a finding was not surprising given the consolidation that has taken place within the industry in the past 20 years.

The companies also were asked to report the dollar amount of their annual capital budgets for both timber-related investments and plant and equipment. These results are shown in Table 1. As was the case in 1977, the annual capital budgets were found to be approximately 10% of total assets.

CAPITAL BUDGETING EVALUATION METHODS

The survey provided description of the four major capital budgeting techniques used most often by financial analysts in order to determine the degree to which sophisticated capital budgeting methodologies were being used. These techniques include accounting rate of return, payback period, internal rate of return, and net present value. The company was asked to identify which of these methods were used in the capital budgeting decision-making process and whether or not they were used as a primary evaluation technique, secondary evaluation technique, or only a project screening technique. This was done separately for timber-related investment decisions and plant and equipment investment decisions. In addition, each company was asked to describe other formal evaluation techniques that they employed as well as other factors they considered relevant to the capital budgeting process.

PRIMARY EVALUATION TECHNIQUES

Several interesting results emerge from the data showing the number and percentage of firms using each of the four methodologies as a primary evaluation technique to judge the acceptability of both timberland and plant and equipment purchases. First, a far greater percentage of firms use one of the discounted cash flow techniques in evaluating timber-related investments (76%) than they do in the case of plant and equipment purchases (55%). These results are conceptually reasonable because the long life of timber-related investments makes the time value of money particularly important. By the same token, fewer companies use pay-back period as a primary evaluation technique when making timber investment (15%) than in the case of plant and equipment purchases (33%). The payback period is most useful as a short-term screening technique; therefore, it should be less useful when looking at timber purchases (Table 2).

The most significant finding, however, is the fact that the discounted cash flow techniques of internal rate of return and net present value are much more widely used today as a primary evaluation technique than they were in 1977 when they were used by only 44% of the forest products companies. Furthermore, in 1977, several of the smaller companies reported that they only used subjective judgment in making capital budgeting decisions. Only one of the smaller companies in the current survey relied solely on subjective judgment.

Table 1. SIZE OF CAPITAL BUDGET

Capital Budget (in millions)	Timber Investments	Other Capital Investments	Total Capital Investments
Less than $5	7 Companies	12 Companies	11 (38%) Companies
$5 to $10	5 Companies	1 Company	2 (7%) Companies
$11 to $50	4 Companies	6 Companies	6 (21%) Companies
Over $50	2 Companies	9 Companies	10 (34%) Companies
Total	**18 Companies**	**28 Companies**	**29 Companies**

Table 2. PRIMARY EVALUATION TECHNIQUES

Capital Budgeting Technique	Timber Investments	Other Capital Investments
Accounting rate of return	3 (9%) Companies	6 (13%) Companies
Payback period	5 (15%) Companies	15 (33%) Companies
Internal rate of return	13 (38%) Companies	15 (33%) Companies
Net present value	13 (38%) Companies	10 (22%) Companies
Total	**34 Companies**	**46 Companies**

Table 3. SECONDARY EVALUATION TECHNIQUES

Capital Budgeting Technique	Timber Investments	Other Capital Investments
Accounting rate of return	5 (23%) Companies	6 (22%) Companies
Payback period	8 (36%) Companies	13 (48%) Companies
Internal rate of return	5 (23%) Companies	3 (11%) Companies
Net present value	4 (18%) Companies	5 (19%) Companies
Total	**22 Companies**	**27 Companies**

Table 4. PROJECT SCREENING TECHNIQUES

Capital Budgeting Technique	Timber Investments	Other Capital Investments
Accounting rate of return	1 (6%) Company	4 (15%) Companies
Payback period	4 (24%) Companies	11 (42%) Companies
Internal rate of return	6 (35%) Companies	8 (31%) Companies
Net present value	6 (35%) Companies	3 (12%) Companies
Total	**17 Companies**	**26 Companies**

SECONDARY EVALUATION TECHNIQUES

The number and percentage of firms using each of the four methodologies as their secondary evaluation technique has not changed much from the 1977 results (Table 3). The payback period is still the dominant secondary technique although it is more widely used for plant and equipment decisions than for timber investments. In addition, the accounting rate of return is used substantially more as a secondary evaluation technique than as a primary evaluation technique for all types of investment decisions.

While arguments can be made that neither the accounting rate of return nor payback methods consider the time value of money and the economic impact that this has on the market value of the firm, both of these methodologies have some redeeming features. Both are intuitive and easy to understand. Both are easy to calculate. In the case of the payback period, the focus is on liquidity, which is clearly an important issue for a capital-intensive firm. Moreover, accounting information is almost always available for the project under consideration and for the firm as a whole. Thus, the calculation of accounting rate of return is a normal by-product of the companies' financial accounting information systems.

PROJECT SCREENING TECHNIQUES

In the 1977 survey we did not ask about the use of any of these four methodologies as screening techniques in the capital budgeting process. These results for 1997 in Table 4 show once again the emphasis forest products firms place on the discounted cash flow methodologies in evaluating timber investments. Seventy percent of the firms find these techniques useful even at the project screening stage. On the other hand, payback is the most commonly used screening technique for investments in plant and equipment.

COMPANY SIZE AND EVALUATION TECHNIQUES

In an analysis of the size of the forest products companies in relationship to the type of evaluation techniques, we see that size is still the dominant factor when it comes to using discounted cash flow analysis in analyzing anything other than timber investments. For timber investments, even the smaller companies favor the discounted cash flow techniques. On the other hand, in plant and equipment decisions, the combined accounting rate of return and payback method responses equaled or exceeded the discounted cash flow responses in all companies whose sales were less than $500 million.

It is also interesting to note that none of the largest forest products firms used either accounting rate of return or payback when evaluating timber purchases, and only two out of the 12 largest firms used accounting rate of return when evaluating plant and equipment. The shares of many of these firms are publicly owned, so it is not surprising that investment decisions tend to be market driven. Because book value and net income do not have much to do with cash flow and market value, accounting rate of return measures do not tell the managers of these publicly owned firms what they really need to know.

OTHER FACTORS RELEVANT TO THE CAPITAL BUDGETING DECISION

When we review the comments that were received from respondents regarding capital budgeting decisions, two conclusions emerged. In the case of timber investments, the most important issue centered on strategic wood supply considerations—namely, current availability, expected acquisition cost, location, age, and class of timber, as well as what was likely to happen to any of these factors in the future. To firms selling wood, pulp, paper, or packaging products, this issue of availability is of prime importance. To remain in business, firms need an ongoing supply of timber. As a result, financial analysis techniques that emphasize the accounting concepts of breakeven analysis and shutdown costs are getting increased attention by forest products firms.

On the plant and equipment side, it was not surprising to learn that one of the most important issues has become the need to comply with the regulatory standards concerning health, safety, and the environment. With more and more of these types of pressures likely in the future and with the dollar cost of failing to satisfy these concerns rising, traditional financial analysis may very well become a secondary criterion used to evaluate investment options. Two companies also mentioned the importance of the custodial role they feel forest products companies have with regard to maintaining the timber resource and the overall welfare of their employees.

RISK ADJUSTMENT METHODOLOGIES

An extended time horizon is implicit in all capital projects. This factor is particularly true in timber acquisition projects and increases the difficulty of accurately forecasting the future costs and returns in these projects. For this reason, risk is an important concern in capital budgeting. Traditionally, there have been three common quantitative methods of adjusting capital projects for risk. The first technique is to raise the cost of capital used as a cutoff rate or used in discounting future cash flows in the net present value methodology. The second technique is to adjust the project life downward. The third approach involves the use of sensitivity analysis where a range of future expectations is considered in the project analysis. In particular, the projected costs can be increased, and/or the projected benefits can be decreased. This approach can determine the extent to which the actual costs and benefits could deviate from the most likely estimate before an acceptable project would become unacceptable.

In 1977 only 44% of the respondent companies reported using one of these three quantitative risk adjustment techniques. Moreover, the majority of the companies used the sensitivity analysis approach. In the 1997 survey, the percentage of companies using formal risk adjustment had risen to 76% (22 of the 29 firms). Only 17% (five firms) reported that they do not adjust for risk at all in evaluating capital budgeting decisions. The remaining 7% (two firms) attempted to consider risk subjectively. These results support the finding noted earlier that forest products companies are becoming more sophisticated in their capital budgeting methodologies.

While sensitivity analysis continues to be the risk adjustment technique of preference for all size categories of firms, and there does not appear to be much difference in the type of risk adjustment technique used in analyzing timber and nontimber investments, some of the larger forest products firms are beginning to use other methods to analyze risk. Some of these techniques include the use of formal probability analysis, in which firms actually attempt to calculate the probability of investments earning a return greater than the cost of capital or earning a positive net present value, and less formal methods such as shortening the payback period and reducing the amount initially invested for projects involving higher risk.

Furthermore, one company reported using a decision tree approach in evaluating plant and equipment purchases. Under this technique, a firm would attempt to lay out several different scenarios, assign probabilities to each scenario, and then calculate expected profitability measures based on either the firm's cash flow or accounting net income. This technique would appear to be particularly relevant in the case of changing regulatory environments or widely fluctuating timber prices noted earlier.

POST AUDIT PROCEDURES

It is generally recommended that companies should conduct a post audit to compare the actual results of a capital project with the original forecasts that were used in determining that the project was acceptable. This procedure not only can serve as an evaluation of project implementation but also as an evaluation of

AN INDUSTRY IN TRANSITION

The forest products industry—an industry composed of firms selling wood, pulp, paper, and packaging products—plays a significant role in the global economy, accounting for nearly 3% of the global Gross Domestic Product. A distinguishing feature of this industry is its degree of capital intensity; the assets of firms operating in this industry consist primarily of timber holdings and substantial plant and equipment.

In recent years, the forest products industry has been transformed by external forces that have exerted pressure for new forestry techniques and an overall structural change within the industry. Inflationary pressures alone have caused the cost of timber and timberland to rise to unprecedented levels. Population and economic growth combined with the increased standard of living in many countries has resulted in an increasing demand for forest products. Heightened government regulation and environmental legislation will continue to increase as society places greater emphasis on nontimber benefits that accrue from forests such as bio-diversity, wildlife habitat, water storage, recreation, and aesthetics.

The forest products industry is responding to these forces by implementing capital and technology intensive strategies throughout its operations from the forest to the marketplace. Many forest products firms are shifting their timber supply from natural forests to plantation forests that utilize costly genetics and breeding technologies in their intensive silvicultural practices. These plantation forests are vertically integrated with capital intensive, eco-efficient production facilities. Those firms that have not been able to meet the above challenges either have had to close down operations or they have been acquired by competitors. The net result has been a significant decline in the number of firms in the industry.

the entire capital budget planning process. Companies can use this information to evaluate the accuracy of their forecasts and whether they have been using the appropriate project analysis techniques. In 1977, two thirds of the forest products companies conducted some form of formal post audit of their capital projects. In the 1997 survey, over three quarters of the respondents report that they do post audits of their capital investment projects.

All 12 of the largest companies in the survey do use post audits for their capital projects as do most of the firms in the \$50-\$100 million and \$101-\$500 million categories. In fact, post audits seem to be the general practice in all but the smallest companies where only one of the respondent firms has a post audit procedure in place.

Comments about post auditing procedures indicate that post audits typically were conducted between six months to one year after projects were fully operational. Second, in most cases, post audits were mandatory on all large projects (i.e., over \$5 million) with the results being reported to the board. Conducting post audits on smaller projects typically was at the discretion of the audit committee, company president, or business unit vice president depending on the size .of the firm involved. Third, most firms conducted post audits on only the first-year results, with one firm reporting that it audited up to five years' results in the case of very large investments.

The most interesting comment received regarding post audits was:

> "We pick a finance person and a manufacturing person from a different plant/mill to act as a team to perform the audit. They are given a copy of the project and all backup information and are given three to four months to complete the audit, while continuing with all their normal job requirements. They prepare the audit report and then give a presentation to our audit committee. Normally, only larger projects are post audited. All other financially justified projects are reviewed in a less formal process. These reports are completed by the responsible plant/mill and routed around for review."

The fact that this firm used individuals from both finance and manufacturing in addition to requiring that they be from a different operating unit increases the likelihood that the post audit results for the major investments would be unbiased.

MORE COMPANIES USE IRR AND NPV

On the basis of the survey, the following conclusions can be made regarding capital budgeting practices in the forest products industry in the last 20 years. First, there has been a significant increase in the use of the more sophisticated and theoretically preferred discounted cash flow methodologies of internal rate of return and net present value for all capital investment decisions. While firm size continues to be the dominant factor when it comes to the use of these methods in evaluating plant and equipment purchases, even smaller firms use them in the case of timber investments. Moreover, a greater percentage of firms are now applying discounted cash flow techniques in the preliminary or project screening stages of their capital budgeting process.

Second, risk analysis has taken on increased importance. A greater percentage of firms are using quantitative techniques, and those that do not at least attempt to consider risk subjectively.

Third, only smaller firms have failed to implement post audit procedures on a consistent basis as a way to both monitor and control their major capital investments. Post audit procedures in medium-sized and large firms not only are becoming more formal in terms of reporting requirements, they are also more extensive in terms of the actual analysis procedures being employed.

Fourth, other procedures such as breakeven analysis, probability analysis, and decision trees are coming into use as relevant capital budgeting methodologies. In addition, noneconomic issues are taking on a greater degree of importance in the decision-making process. The issue most often cited is the changing regulatory climate in the forest products industry especially as it relates to health, safety, and the environment. Each of these areas relates to the company's custodial role concerning both timber resources and employees.

Jack Bailes is a professor of accounting at Oregon State University. He has a Ph.D. degree in business from the University of Washington. Dr. Bailes has authored several previous articles in MANAGEMENT ACCOUTING and has won several awards for articles published in the management accounting field. He is a former president of Salem Area (Ore.) Chapter, through which this article was submitted.

James Nielsen is a professor of banking and finance at Oregon State University with an MBA and a Ph.D. in Business Administration from the University of Colorado. Dr. Nielsen has authored a number of articles in banking and finance journals.

Stephen Lawton was the coordinator for the MacArthur Foundation Sustainable Forestry Working Group with more than 30 researchers that produced a series of business case studies that illustrated the market opportunities and financial viability of sustainable forestry. Mr. Lawton teaches international business in executive programs in the United States, Europe, and Asia. He is also an associate professor of international business at Oregon State University.

---

[1]In 1977, there were a total of 241 companies participating in the Oregon State University Forest Products Monograph Program.

HOW ABC WAS USED IN CAPITAL BUDGETING

By Steve Coburn, CPA; Hugh Grove, CPA; and Tom Cook

How do you estimate cash flows for capital expenditure projects in your company? Many firms use broad strategic approaches for estimating cash flows that are not closely tied to detailed tactical assumptions about future operations. These forecasts may not be very reliable because cash flow projections of new products can have a 30% to 40% margin of error.

A new division of a Fortune 500 company was established to analyze new business opportunities in the electronic (broadband) marketplace of interactive television. The company and data have been disguised here for confidentiality purposes. The initial investment proposal was to develop a "cybermall," similar to the way marketing service organizations bring together sellers and buyers in the traditional television marketplace. At the time, this cybermall proposal was a new idea without any close counterparts in this emerging electronic marketplace.

Senior management of this new division initially had focused upon the marketing strategy of "speed to market" for this cybermall project. Thus, the business case forecast was done at a broad strategic level with few supporting details. A consulting firm provided general forecasts of the electronic market size and market share which it converted into aggregate forecasts of revenue, operating costs, and capital costs. Driven by this "speed-to-market" strategy senior management was willing to commit $50 million to this cybermall project, based upon the business case forecast.

The chief financial officer (CFO) of this new division, however, successfully argued for a tactical translation of the business case's broad strategic view into a detailed analysis of the cybermall's projected business processes and activities. Senior management approved the CFO's proposal because it still had concerns about how the technical development and deployment of the electronic marketplace would impact the cybermall financial forecasts. The CFO's proposal became an activity-based cost (ABC) model (with bench-marking) that created a pro forma process engineering approach for analyzing this business opportunity.

Process analysis typically has been used for reengineering existing—not pro forma—processes.[1] In contrast, this business opportunity related to an emerging industry with new processes. Also, ABC has been advocated for use in annual, not capital, budgeting.[2] Using ABC for capital budgeting analysis of this cybermall project created an example of activity based management (ABM), which has been defined as providing economic information for management decision making.[3]

The ABC model (with benchmarking) forecasted business processes, activities, revenues, operating costs, and capital costs for this cybermall project. This tactical ABC approach generated forecasts that differed significantly from the forecasts of the strategic business case. For example, the ABC model forecasted that an additional $10 million of capital costs would be needed. Also, revenue forecasts were slowed down and startup cost forecasts were increased. Senior management used these ABC results to reverse its initial decision to go ahead with this cybermall project.

Thus, the CFO provided strategic AEM information and became part of the business decision-making process. Senior management also has decided to use this ABC approach for evaluating future business opportunities. Such a strategic role has been advocated as the most important goal for a CFO's mission statement and the future of management accounting.[4]

The ABC analysis provided an understanding of projected business processes and activities that allowed senior management to have more confidence in the detailed tactical ABC forecasts, rather than the initial, broad strategic forecasts. This pro forma ABC approach also is a logical next step for companies currently using ABC and bench-marking to understand existing business processes and activities.

We describe here an overview of the business case and the ABC model approaches; then a description of the ABC approach for analyzing this cybermall project is provided. Finally, the forecasts from both approaches are compared.

BUSINESS CASE VS. ABC MODEL APPROACHES

Figure 1 provides an overview of the business case approach to capital budgeting for this cybermall project. The strategic business case forecasts started with broad market assumptions concerning electronic market size and share provided by a consulting firm. These consultants then converted this market data into general projections of revenues with few supporting details. They also used general cost assumptions to project variable and fixed expenses without any detailed cost analyses.

For example, the budget line items of technology development, video production, and network

Figure 1. BUSINESS CASE MODEL

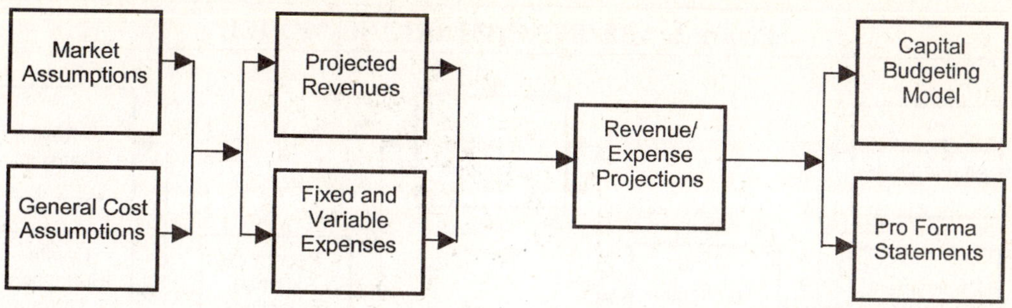

operations were mainly aggregate fixed cost forecasts. The few variable cost forecasts were based upon general revenue projections, such as distribution access as a flat fee per subscriber and order processing as a specified amount per customer. A key capital infrastructure forecast used just one type of client/server technology for all interactive television markets although four different types of client/server technology were being deployed by cable system operators.

The business case provided general revenue and expense projections and pro forma financial statements. Also, the business case provided senior management with capital budgeting information for the decision criteria of net present value (NPV), internal rate of return (IRR), and payback.

Figure 2 provides an overview of the ABC approach to capital budgeting for this cybermall project. The tactical ABC model forecasts were based upon detailed benchmarked data from the cybermall business process analyses provided by the CFO. Using benchmark assumptions, the ABC approach developed a broadband deployment or buildout schedule of the electronic marketplace for potential interactive television subscribers. It also developed a transaction volume schedule for potential cybermall customers. Both schedules were used to help generate the revenue, cost, and capital assumptions and projections of the ABC model.

The ABC model created a broadband network deployment schedule by benchmarking with external parties to obtain detailed data concerning the build-out of the broadband infrastructure for the electronic marketplace. The ten largest cable or multi-system operators (MSOs) were projected to build or deploy broadband infrastructures over five years, starting in 1996, and all other MSOs to deploy over seven years, starting in 1997. This deployment was projected to start in the 50 largest cities or suburbs named as areas of dominant influence (ADI).

Using this deployment schedule as a starting point, the ABC model created a detailed transaction volume schedule by benchmarking shopping participation, purchase frequency, and average spending for this cybermall project. Because no interactive television operators existed for this emerging market, the traditional television marketing operators, Home Shopping Network (HSN) and the QVC system, were used as indirect or "out of market" benchmarks. For example, HSN had about five million active shoppers representing 8.3% of the homes reached, and QVC had four million shoppers representing 8.0% of the homes reached. Also, HSN repeat customers had made purchases between five and seven times a year. Average spending per shopping household for repeat customers was about $300 for HSN and about $500 for QVC.

The tactical ABC model used detailed revenue assumptions and forecasts for this cybermall project, as opposed to the general ones of the strategic business case. The ABC model forecasted slower access to cybermall customers, primarily due to delays in developing and provisioning the broadband network. Accordingly, the revenue forecasts for the early years were lower than in the business case. Concerning the ABC pool costs, the ABC model used a pro forma process engineering approach to construct activity resource consumption profiles and transaction (cost) drivers that were multiplied together to derive the ABC expense projections. A cybermall value chain of workflow or business processes was specified with key activities and cost drivers. This pro forma process engineering approach is described below.

PRO FORMA PROCESS ENGINEERING

A pro forma process engineering approach was used by the ABC model to forecast operating and capital costs for the cybermall project. A cybermall value chain was created with six sequential workflows or business processes as shown in Table 1. First, cybermall seller relationships must be developed to provide the goods and services available for purchase on this interactive television system. Second, the system to operate interactive television applications must be developed. Third, content programs must be purchased or produced. Fourth, the ongoing operations of this interactive television system must be performed, especially the processing of cybermall buyers' orders. Fifth, the marketing of the cybermall

Figure 2. ABC/BENCHMARKING MODEL

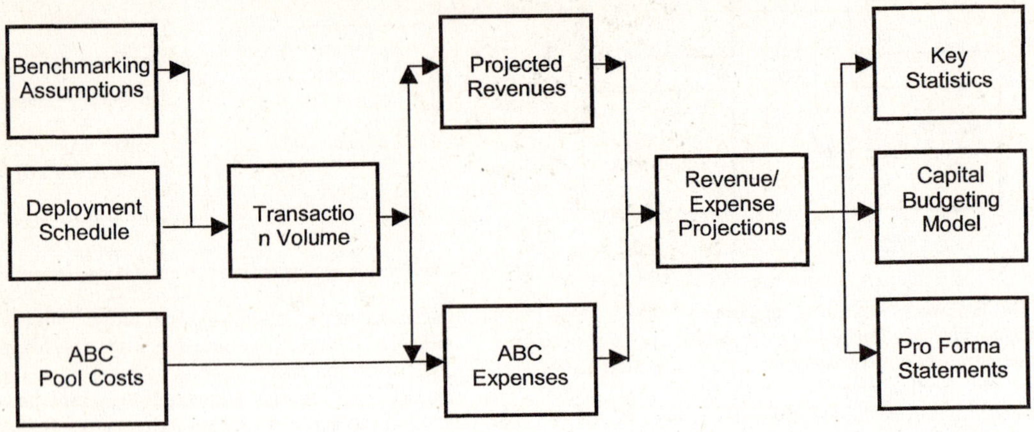

must be done. Sixth, the network distributors and access fees must be managed.

Major activities were identified for each of these six business processes in the cybermall value chain. Resource consumption profiles and cost drivers were identified for the major activities. Cost pool rates were calculated and multiplied by the number of cost drivers needed at various transaction volumes to project the ABC process expenses as summarized in Table 1.

Detailed capital costs also were forecasted for various levels of activities. The $2 million total capital costs in Table 1 represented four initial broadband deployments. Each deployment used a different type of client/server, and each server type was estimated to require $0.5 million in capital costs. Over the initial 10-year period of this cybermall project, 120 network deployments were estimated for total capital costs of $60 million, which was $10 million or 20% higher than the business case estimate of $50 million, as shown in Table 2.

Also, three types of external parties were identified because they were needed to perform critical activities in various business processes for this cybermall project to become operational. First, cybermall sellers were needed to do core programming in the content production process. They also were needed in the operations process for selling, shipping, billing, and collecting the cybermall goods and revenues. Second, software vendors were needed to develop and test network applications, video content programs, and network operations for the cybermall. Third, distributors were needed to develop, operate, and deploy the interactive broadband network where the cybermall will be located.

Seller relationship process. The seller relationship business process for the cybermall has three major activities. First, for the activity of acquiring cybermall sellers, account managers are needed to obtain and maintain sellers of goods and services. One full-time equivalent (FTE) manager and one secretary are projected for 1995, increasing to a cap of seven FTEs by 1997. Second, for the promotion activity, the cybermall will be publicized with an annual budget for promotional mailings to potential sellers and distributors. Third, a general manager is needed for managing seller relationships. One half-time position is needed in 1995, increasing to a cap of two FTEs by 1997.

Application development process. Application development business process for the cybermall has four major activities. First, product concept will be defined and evaluated with product research, product specifications, and simulated operations. Capital costs of $350,000 are needed for simulation equipment, a client/server, workstations, and personal computers. Second, two key types of design application activities are needed. An asset management system will be developed with a simulated startup for this cybermall. Capital costs of $150,000 are needed for video equipment, software, and production workstations. Also, an automated order processing system for cybermall customers will be developed with $100,000 of capital costs.
Third, for the database activity, a database operations center will be developed. Capital costs of $300,000 are needed for the central hardware to coordinate the workstations. Fourth, two key types of technology activities are needed. For the planning activity, three technical employees and $50,000 for test equipment each year are needed to maintain technical core competency and to update technical strategy

Table 1. KEY ACTIVITIES, DRIVERS AND COSTS IN THE CYBERMALL VALUE CHAIN

Business Processes	Major Activities	Cost Drivers	Process Expenses	Capital (000,000)
Seller Relationship	Acquire sellers	No. of sellers	Selling	$0
	Do promotions	No. of direct mailings	Selling	0
	Manage seller relationships	Annual staffing	Selling	0
Application Development	Product concept	No. of product start-ups	Product R&D	$.4
	Design application:	No. of Product Start-ups	Product R&D	
	Asset mgt. system			$.1
	Order process sys.			$.1
	Develop database	No. of product start-ups	Product R&D	
	Technology:			
	Planning	Annual staffing	Product R&D	0
	Deployment	No. of client server types	Product R&D	$.4
Content Production	Brokerage of Program purchases	No. of programs	Content production	0
	Program production	No. of programs	Content production	0
	Post production guidelines	Annual staffing	Content production	0
Operations	Order processing	No. of orders	Operations	$.1
	Customer service	No. of network head-ends	Operations	$.1
	Provision network	No. of fiber loops	Operations	$.5
	Seller interface	Annual staff	Operations	0
Marketing	Buyer acquisition	No. of buyers	Marketing	0
	Advertising	No. of ads	Marketing	0
	Public Relations	Annual staffing	Marketing	0
	Buyer maintenance	Revenue Percent	Marketing	0
Network Distribution	Distributor Relationships	Annual staffing	Distribution	0
	Access Fee	No. of buyers	Distribution	0

Capital Costs in Table 2: 4 types of Deployment * $.5 = $ 2.0

Total Capital Costs in Table 1: 120 Deployments * $.5 = $60.0

continuously. For the deployment activity, this cybermall project will be adapted to four technology types of client/servers and will cost $100,000 for each type of server. Thus, capital costs of $400,000 are needed initially to provision four servers (one for each server type).

Content production process. The content production business process for the cybermall has three major activities. First, for the brokerage of program purchases, rights to use existing programming will be purchased when appropriate for this cybermall. Estimated annual costs are $100,000 in 1995, increasing to a $700,000 cap by 2000. Second, for the program production activity, programs for video content describing the cybermall sellers will be produced in-house or outsourced. It is assumed that the company and the sellers will split these costs equally, which are similar to the brokerage program costs. Third, concerning post-production guidelines, costs to monitor and manage programming and production are estimated as one technical employee in 1995, increasing to cap of four FTEs by 1997.

Operations process. The operations process has four major activities. First, for the order processing activity, there will be two cost structures. Manual processing will be used from 1995 through 1997 until higher cybermall shopper volume is obtained. Thereafter, automated processing will be used with capital costs of $100,000. Second, concerning customer service, employee costs are estimated at one third FTE for each network head-end. Capital costs of $100,000 are estimated for workstations and software.

Third, to provision an interactive (broadband) television network, this cybermall project must be deployed on fiber loops, requiring video server equipment. Each server may feed up to four head-end networks and up to 500,000 interactively passed homes. Capital costs of $500,000 are estimated for the video servers, storage units, and personal computer systems to interface with the fiber loops. Fourth, for cybermall seller interfacing, one manager and three technical employees are needed for the post-production functions of program content and network operations.

Marketing process. The marketing process has four major activities. First, for the buyer acquisition activity, sales persons are needed to obtain cybermall shoppers or buyers. Related selling costs also are included. Such buyer acquisition costs are estimated to decrease over time. Second, advertising primarily via television and radio promotions is necessary. Costs for preparation of such advertisements are budgeted for $200,000 in 1996, increasing up to a $500,000 cap by 1999. Third, public relations activities included marketing management. Personnel are estimated at two FTEs in 1995, four FTEs in 1996, and eight FTEs thereafter. Fourth, concerning buyer maintenance, costs to maintain cybermall shoppers are estimated as a percentage of total revenue.

Network distribution process. The network distribution process has two major activities. First, account managers are needed to manage relationships with the distribution networks used by this cybermall. Personnel are estimated at one half time position in 1995, increasing to a cap of two FTEs by 1998. Second, concerning network access fees from 1995 through 1997, charges are based upon the number of cybermall shoppers making purchases and are paid monthly to the network provider. Thereafter, the charges will be based upon a percentage of total shopping purchases.

In summary, the tactical ABC model engineered pro forma business processes, activities, and cost drivers to calculate detailed revenue and resource consumption patterns, as opposed to the general assumptions of the strategic business case approach. Also, to help senior management make this capital budgeting decision, key operating statistics were compiled by the ABC model. Such statistics were not provided by the business case because it was done without detailed analyses. These statistics were classified by four types of metrics: buyers, sellers, networks, and infrastructure, as shown in Table 3.

If comparisons had been available, the ABC model generally would have provided less optimistic forecasts of operating statistics because its related revenue forecasts were lower and startup cost forecasts higher than the business case. For example, the acquisition cost per buyer would have been higher and the revenue per seller, lower. In the network and infrastructure metrics, the access costs and the cost per minute/content both would have been higher.

If the cost drivers were not already represented in the benchmarked transaction file, they were added to these existing transaction volumes. For example, a new cost driver for the number of client/servers was measured by the interactive television deployment sequence under the cybermall revenue assumptions. From the pro forma engineering analysis, an activity resource consumption profile was established to measure the cost of a client/server. Then, the number and cost of the client/servers were multiplied together to project the ABC expenses at various levels of interactive television deployment. Thus, detailed resource consumption patterns and transaction (cost) drivers were used to generate the ABC expense and capital forecasts, as opposed to general assumptions in the business case forecasts. For example, the application development and design costs were forecasted using the number of product startups as the cost driver. (A fixed cost was used throughout the business case.) For another example, manual order processing initially was assumed due to low customer volume in the startup phase. Subsequently, automated order processing was assumed. (A variable cost per customer was used throughout the business case.) The ABC model forecasted specific network operating costs using the cost drivers of network head-ends and fiber loops. (Aggregate amounts of fixed costs were used in the business case.) The ABC model forecasted capital costs that represented four types of broadband deployments, one for each of the actual types of client/servers being deployed by cable television operators. (Only one client/server type was used in the business case.)

The ABC model calculated key operating statistics and differences between the ABC and the business case dollar projections and NPV, IRR, and payback results. The operating statistics are described in Table 3. The ABC model also generated pro forma financial statements. All this information was provided to help senior management make its final decision on this cybermall project. The ten different categories of the ABC model in Figure 2 were linked together as a series of related Excel spreadsheets to facilitate risk analysis. The final ABC model used six megabytes of random access memory.

COMPARISONS OF FORECASTS

For this cybermall project, 10-year financial forecasts are summarized in Table 2. Panel A has comparisons of key dollar projections for the business case and the ABC model. Panel B has comparisons of key capital budgeting forecasts for the business case and the ABC model. In Table 2, the residual value for this cybermall project represented the net present value of its sales price in year 10. The ABC spreadsheet model calculated both dollar and percent variances between the two approaches as shown in Table 2.

Table 2. COMPARISONS OF ABC VS. BUSINESS CASE
(In millions and 10-year totals)
Panel A: Key Projections:

	Business Case	ABC Model	Variances Increase	(Decrease)
Total revenues	$1,650	$1,480	($170)	(10%)
Total cash operations expenses	$1,000	$ 950	($ 50)	(5%)
Total net income aftertax	$ 250	$ 175	($ 75)	(30%)
Total capital expenditures	$ 50	$ 60	$ 10	20%
Total net cash flow	$ 400	$ 320	($ 80)	(20%)
Panel B: Key Decision Criteria:				
1. Without Residual Value:				
Internal rate of return	43%	33%	(10%)	(23%)
Net present values:				
@20%	$ 60	$ 35	($25)	(42%)
@30%	$ 20	$ 4	($16)	(80%)
@40%	$ 3	($ 8)	($11)	N/A
Discounted payback @20% in yrs.	7	9	2	29%
2. With Residual Value:				
Internal rate of return	61%	50%	(11%)	(18%)
Net present values:				
@20%	$225	$190	($35)	(16%)
@30%	$100	$ 80	($20)	(20%)
@40%	$ 40	$ 25	($15)	(38%)

Key projections of 10-year financial amounts for both approaches were summarized in Panel A of Table 2. For the business case, key dollar projections were (in millions): $1,650 revenues; $1,000 cash operating expenses; $250 net income after taxes; $50 capital expenditures; and $400 net cash flow without residual value. For the ABC model, key dollar projections were (in millions): $1,480 revenues; $950 cash operating expenses; $175 net income after taxes; $60 capital expenditures; and $320 net cash flow without residual value. Concerning the variances, all the business case forecasts were from 5% to 30% higher than the ABC model forecasts, except for capital expenditures, which were 20% ($10 million) lower. Consequently, the ABC dollar projections, especially the 20% reduction in net cash flow, generated lower capital budgeting forecasts than in the business case.

Capital budgeting forecasts for both approaches are summarized in Panel B of Table 2. For the business case, the internal rates of return were 43% without any residual value and 61% with the residual value. The net present values were $60 million, $20 million, and $3 million, using cost-of-capital rates of 20%, 30%, and 40%, respectively, without any residual value. With the residual value, the net present values were much larger at $225 million, $100 million, and $40 million, respectively. The discounted cash flow payback was seven years, using a 20% cost of capital rate.

For the ABC model, the internal rates of return were 33% without any residual value and 50% with the residual value. The net present values were $35 million, $4 million, and negative $8 million, using cost of capital rates of 20%, 30%, and 40%, respectively, without any residual value. With the residual value, the net present values were much larger at $190 million, $80 million, and $25 million, respectively. The discounted cash flow payback was nine years, using a 20% cost-of-capital rate.

The variances for the capital budgeting forecasts showed that the ABC model results were significantly lower than the business case results. The internal rates of return decreased by 23% and 18%, without and with the residual values, respectively The net present values were reduced from 16% to 80%, depending upon which cost of capital rate was used. The discounted cash flow payback was increased by two years or 29%. With higher capital forecasts and lower revenue and cash flow forecasts, the ABC capital budgeting forecasts were less favorable for this cybermall project than the business case forecasts.

From the ABC analysis, the electronic marketplace deployment and resulting market share and revenues were too slow while the startup and investment costs were too big and too early to justify the cybermall project at this time. Also, the operating leverage for profit growth did not become favorable until the mid-life point of this cybermall project, as opposed to an earlier prediction in the business case.

Table 3. KEY OPERATING STATISTICS

Buyers:	Networks:	Infrastructure:	Sellers:
No. of shoppers	Homes passed	Programming shelf life	Items per view hour
Purchases per year	Access cost percent of revenue	Cost per minute/content	Number of sellers
Return percent	ADI coverage percent	Connect time	Revenue per seller
Browse time	Network profitability	Percent automatic fulfillment	Transactions per month
Repeat time	Number of platforms supported	Cost per transaction	Percent ship date target
Acquisition cost per buyer	Number of shopping applications	Transaction response time	Seller renewal rate

ABC PROVIDES TACTICAL APPROACH

The ABC model provided a methodology to analyze future business opportunities concerning new types of products and services in emerging markets. The additional level of detail was the key difference from the business case approach for this cybermall project. The pro forma analysis of the business processes and activities with linkages to revenue and cost structures provided critical information for the final decision on this cybermall project.

This approach appears to be applicable to all types of capital budgeting decisions and should provide a unique opportunity for senior management to understand how business processes and activities impact revenue and cost forecasts. As in this cybermall project, the business case approach typically analyzes the symptoms of changes using various levels of market shares, revenues, and costs, but no clear analyses of the causes or drivers of these changes are provided. By contrast, such causal analyses *are* provided by this ABC approach which attempts to understand how changes in business processes and activities impact market share, revenues, and costs.

The ABC information provided a better understanding of the cybermall business processes and activities. This additional knowledge allowed senior management to have more confidence in its strategic decision making for this project. Senior management agreed that the additional costs spent on the ABC and benchmarking analyses were justified by the benefits of more detailed operating and financial information.

For example, the following key uses of this ABC model were identified for this cybermall project in the emerging electronic marketplace:

- Establishing linkages between technology (the electronic market deployment and distribution of interactive services) and financial forecasts,
- Using indirect or "out of market" benchmarks for revenue and cost forecasts,
- Creating a dynamic model that showed how unitized ABC costs behaved and changed over time in providing interactive services, and
- Specifying operating leverage more precisely with different step-cost functions at different levels of volume.

These key uses also helped clarify marketing strategies for this emerging industry; i.e., broad market coverage versus narrow or niche market development of interactive services.

As shown by the comparisons in Table 2, the tactical ABC model produced less favorable forecasts for the capital budgeting decision criteria than the strategic business case. Thus, senior management decided not to do this project at this time. Because the ABC model also was a working spreadsheet model, sensitivity and "what-if" risk analyses were performed but the final decision was to reject the project. Senior management decided not to be a first or early entrant into this emerging electronic market.

This ABC model provided a detailed tactical methodology to analyze business opportunities in emerging markets, as opposed to the general strategic view of the business case approach. The initial "speed-to-market" strategy in the business case was tempered by the tactical ABC analysis of the cybermall project's feasibility Forecasts of the ABC model created more confidence in making this cybermall decision; therefore, senior management has decided to use this ABC model for analyzing subsequent business opportunities in the electronic marketplace. Thus, by using this ABC and benchmarking methodology to provide strategic information, the CFO became part of the strategic decision-making process in accordance with the key goal for a CFO's mission statement and the future of management accounting.

[1] Refer to M. Hammer and J. Champy, *Reengineering the Corporation,* Harper Business, New York, 1993.

[2] Refer to J. Schmidt, "Is It Time to Replace Traditional Budgeting?", *Journal of Accountancy,* November 1992, pp.103-107.

[3] Refer to R. Kaplan, "In Defense of Activity-Based Cost Management," MANAGEMENT ACCOUNTING®, November 1992, pp. 58-63.

[4] Refer to A. Pipkin, "The 21st Century Controller," MANAGEMENT ACCOUNTING, February 1989, pp. 21-25; and W. Birkett. "Management Accounting and Knowledge Management," MANAGEMENT ACCOUNTING, November 1995, pp. 44-48.